WHAT EVERY
SUPERVISOR
SHOULD KNOW

About the Authors

Lester R. Bittel, Professor of Management Emeritus at James Madison University and a Virginia Eminent Scholar, has had over 30 years' experience in business as an industrial engineer, plant manager, training director, magazine editor, and corporate executive. His credentials include:

- Designer of the *Certificate for Professional Development Program* for the commonwealth of Virginia.
- Codesigner of, and contributor to, the five-volume *Modular Programme for Supervisory Development*, published by the International Labour Office in Geneva.
- Author of the *Complete Guide to Supervisory Training and Development*, published in 1987 by Addison-Wesley.
- Editor of the *Encyclopedia of Professional Management* and coeditor of the *Handbook for Professional Managers*.
- Recipient of the *Wilbur McFeeley Award* (International Management Council) for his "contributions to management education," and the *Frederick W. Taylor Award* (American Society of Mechanical Engineers) for his "contributions to management literature."
- Codirector of the most comprehensive survey of supervisory management practices (1981), reported in *Harvard Business Review* and distributed as a major report by the American Society for Training and Development.

John W. Newstrom, Professor of Human Resources Management, Department of Management Studies in the School of Business and Economics, University of Minnesota at Duluth, has served on the national board of the American Society for Training and Development. He has also been a training consultant to numerous government organizations at the federal, state, and city level as well as to firms in the utilities, paper products, health care, and heavy machinery industries. He is coauthor with Keith Davis of the notable college text *Human Behavior at Work: Organizational Behavior* and author of a number of other books, including *Alternative Work Schedules, The Manager's Book Shelf: A Mosaic of Contemporary Views, A Contingency Approach to Management, Games Trainers Play,* and *More Games Trainers Play.*

Sponsoring Editor: Lawrence H. Wexler
Editing Supervisor: Suzette André
Design and Art Supervisor/Interior Design: Meri Shardin
Production Supervisor: Al Rihner

Illustrator: Marcus Hamilton

Library of Congress Cataloging-in-Publication Data

Bittel, Lester R.
    What every supervisor should know: the complete guide to
supervisory management / Lester R. Bittel, John W. Newstrom.—6th ed.
        p. cm.
    Includes index.
    1. Personnel management.   2. Supervision of employees.
I. Newstrom, John W.   II. Title.
HF5549.B52   1990
658.3′02—dc20   89-33730
    ISBN 0-07-005583-1   CIP

The manuscript for this book was processed electronically.

WHAT EVERY SUPERVISOR SHOULD KNOW:
The Complete Guide to Supervisory Management,
SIXTH EDITION

    2 3 4 5 6 7 8 9 0 DOCDOC   9 6 5 4 3 2 1 0

ISBN 0-07-005583-1

For more information about other McGraw-Hill materials,
call 1-800-2-MCGRAW in the United States. In other
countries, call your nearest McGraw-Hill office.

WHAT EVERY SUPERVISOR SHOULD KNOW

*The Complete Guide
To Supervisory
Management*

SIXTH EDITION

LESTER R. BITTEL

Professor of Management Emeritus
James Madison University

JOHN W. NEWSTROM

Professor of Human Resources Management
Department of Management Studies
University of Minnesota—Duluth

McGRAW-HILL PUBLISHING COMPANY

New York   St. Louis   San Francisco   Auckland   Bogotá
Caracas   Hamburg   Lisbon   London   Madrid   Mexico
Milan   Montreal   New Delhi   Oklahoma City   Paris
San Juan   São Paulo   Singapore   Sydney   Tokyo   Toronto

Contents

Preface

When the first edition of this book appeared, its aim was simply to tell the truth about supervision. Evidence shows that this goal has been reached. This book has been read and consulted by over a half million supervisors and potential supervisors. It has been translated into Dutch, Danish, Portuguese, and Spanish and has been published in an Australian edition and in paperback by the Tata Press in Bombay, India. It is the basic text for supervisory management courses in over 100 two-year colleges. It has been adopted for in-house supervisory training programs by hundreds of industrial companies, commercial firms, and nonprofit institutions. And it has stood the most demanding test of all—the test of practicality and usefulness on the job. Thousands of practicing supervisors have bought, read, and consulted this handbook, which tries to tell them everything they ought to know about their jobs. So, in this sixth edition, let us once again examine the basic premises of *What Every Supervisor Should Know*.

SEVEN COMPELLING OBJECTIVES

The overall approach of this book is guided by seven interlocking objectives:

1. To offer readers practical advice about how to handle real-life, on-the-job situations.
2. To recognize an ever-changing social and work environment.
3. To provide useful insights based upon the job-tested experience of its authors and their associates.
4. To cover all the vital aspects of supervision.
5. To reflect the latest professional concepts of supervisory practice and organizational behavior.
6. To employ the most effective techniques for helping readers enjoy and assimilate the material presented in the text.
7. To maintain a good-humored perspective on what continues to be one of the world's most demanding jobs.

With these objectives as a foundation, *What Every Supervisor Should Know* provides a useful aid to a wide and diverse readership, which includes:

- **Instructors,** who use it as a basic text in preparing their students for the complex world of supervisory management.
- **Students** of first-level management in commerce, industry, and government, who turn to it as a central source of information about the practice of supervision.
- **Supervisors,** who find it to be a complete reference guide of methods for handling people, managing their jobs, and planning their own advancement.
- **Their bosses,** who may gain from it an insight into the problems—human, technical, and personal—supervisors must face daily.
- **Training directors** and other human resources development professionals, who use this text for guiding the training of supervisors in the interpersonal and administrative skills of their jobs.

A COMPREHENSIVE UPDATE

This latest edition of *What Every Supervisor Should Know* reflects an extensive reexamination of every aspect of coverage. It provides readers with the very latest information and the most current points of view from authoritative sources. Throughout, there has been a rigorous updating—of data, language, legal interpretation, situations, and examples.

New or greatly revised materials range from such topical subjects as computer surveillance of employee performance and suggestions for how to counsel an employee who suffers from AIDS, to the everyday problems of employee rights, documentation of disciplinary issues, job competency guidelines for employee training, and ways for improving the quality of employee performance.

The sixth edition contains two new chapters: Chapter 2, which shows supervisors how to cope with their changing environment, and Chapter 17, which provides readers with dozens of ideas for becoming innovative in improving the productivity of a work force.

An entirely new *Personal Development Portfolio* has also been added to this edition. Its four files provide practical guidelines for (1) planning a career, (2) managing job-related time, (3) coping with stress, and (4) moving up in an organization.

Of special assistance to potential and practicing supervisors are the three checklists that appear in the appendixes in Part 9:

- Appendix A, "Checklist for Planning the Day's Work"
- Appendix B, "Supervisory Responsibility Survey"
- Appendix C, "Checklist for Accepting the Assignment of a New Department"

This edition also features extensive coverage of

- Service industries and occupations.
- Government and nonprofit situations.
- Small businesses and entrepreneurial examples.
- Information management and utilization.
- Computer usage and office automation applications.

BOOTSTRAPPING YOUR CAREER

This sixth edition of *What Every Supervisor Should Know* contains a special, 32-page, two-part supplement offering readers (1) expert assistance in preparing a search for a new or better job and (2) point-by-point guidelines for improving performance in 22 key job areas.

The *first part* represents the authors' special "how to do it" advice for job planning, job hunting, and job changing. The *second part* contains 22 *Action Planning Checklists* for reviewing and upgrading the reader's career-advancement potential in the vital performance areas covered in the book's 22 chapters.

UNIQUE LEARNING COMPONENTS

This edition retains the two unique learning methods that differentiate *What Every Supervisor Should Know* from most other texts in its field:

1. **A question-and-answer approach with immediate feedback.** This approach helps to reinforce understanding and to develop application proficiency in a manner similar to that of programmed learning. Additionally, the format enables readers to relate concepts to the problems they face daily at work. It also makes the text a convenient desk or workbench reference.
2. **Practical advice in the form of dos and don'ts.** Although the text is unswervingly based upon accepted theory, the authors do not back away from offering straightforward advice about how to handle difficult situations. Especially in the sticky matters of interpersonal relationships, our intention is to provide supervisors with a starting point for their actions and responses, rather than to leave them with what otherwise might be interpreted as a set of equivocating observations.

Building upon this foundation, a number of other learning aids are now incorporated in this edition. Collectively, they add greatly to the ease of reading and to the effectiveness of instruction. These new, or enhanced, aids include the following:

- **A chapter-opening pictorial**, which illustrates and highlights the five or six major sections in the chapter. These illustrations are numbered so that they relate to the learning objectives and each of the concepts in the chapter.
- **A set of learning objectives**, which alerts readers to what they should know or be able to do as a result of reading the chapter. These objectives are numbered, too, to relate them to the pictorial and the concepts discussed in the chapter.
- **A concept statement**, which previews each numbered section within the chapter.

A set of Review and Application learning aids appear at the end of the text material in each chapter. The Review aids include:

- **Key Concepts to Remember**, which enlarges upon and summarizes each of the numbered concepts presented in the chapter.

- **Supervisory Word Power,** which defines each key word introduced in the chapter.
- **Reading Comprehension,** which consists of 10 questions that probe the reader's understanding of the text material.

The Application aids include:

- **Self-Appraisal,** with a self-scoring guide, which challenges readers to judge how well they have grasped material presented in the chapter.
- **Cases Studies,** three or more for each chapter, each calling for analysis and solution. These cases are numbered sequentially, beginning with Case 1 in Chapter 1 and concluding with Case 72 in the Personal Development Portfolio. Of special note are the cases that appear first in each chapter. These are uniquely structured in the *case-in-point* format—that is, each case presents the reader with five alternate solutions, often called "forced-choice" solutions. The reader is asked to rank the appropriateness of each alternative from first to fifth and to be prepared to defend these choices.

OPTIONAL ANCILLARIES

This textbook is supplemented by a *Study Guide* and an *Instructor's Manual*. The *Instructor's Manual* (available only to qualified instructors) contains a number of useful instructional aids, transparency masters, and additional case studies for class or seminar use. A computerized test bank is also available to adopters of the program.

ACKNOWLEDGMENTS

The authors accept full responsibility for the validity of everything that appears in this text. We are, of course, deeply indebted to hundreds of associates and thousands of practicing supervisors whose thoughts and deeds have contributed directly and indirectly to this work. We could not have built this program without them, and we regret that we cannot name them all. Two individuals, however, deserve special recognition. One is Dr. George Sutcliffe of Central Piedmont Community College, Virginia, who reviewed every word of the manuscript and whose wise counsel is reflected everywhere within. The second person is Gregory R. Fox, Vice Chancellor for Finance and Operations at the University of Minnesota at Duluth, who prepared the *Study Guide*, the *Instructor's Manual*, and the test bank for this edition. Greg's experience as the director of the Duluth Center for Continuing Education adds considerably to the practicality and authority of the ancillary programs.

Lester R. Bittel
John W. Newstrom

Supervisory Management

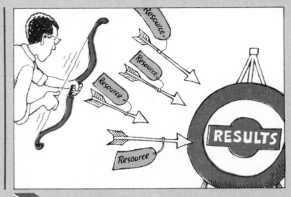

1 Supervisors are an essential part of the management team.

4 Their performance is gauged by results gained from resources.

2 They need a broad range of technical and human competencies.

5 They must develop technical, administrative, and human skills.

3 They provide the linkage between management and employees.

6 Their concerns are balanced between production and people.

CHAPTER 1

The Supervisor's Role in Management

LEARNING OBJECTIVES

After studying this chapter, you should be able to

1. Identify the level of the supervisor's position on a management team.

2. Describe the major competencies that supervisors are expected to bring to their work.

3. Explain the linkage that supervisors provide between management goals and employee performance.

4. Discuss the resources that supervisors must manage and the results that are obtained from them.

5. Describe the different emphases placed upon technical, administrative, and human relations skills at various levels of management.

6. Discuss the need for balancing a concern for output and a concern for the people who perform the work.

CONCEPT   Supervisors are an essential part of the management team that gives an organization purpose and leadership.

What is management? Why is it so important?

Management is a unique occupation. **Management** is described as the process of obtaining, deploying, and utilizing a variety of essential resources in support of an organization's objectives. One of the most important resources of an organization is its employees. Managers devote a large portion of their own efforts to planning, organizing, staffing, activating, and controlling the work of these human resources. One clear distinction between managers and other employees, however, is that managers direct the work of others, rather than performing that work themselves.

Are all managers alike?

No. Managers, and the work they do, differ mainly according to their level in the organization's hierarchy. This difference is illustrated in Figure 1-1. At the top of an organization are its executives. **Executives** are in charge of, and responsible for, a group of other managers. Executives establish broad plans, objectives, and general policies. They motivate, direct, and control the managers who report to them.

Middle managers plan, initiate, and implement programs that are intended to carry out the broader objectives set by executives. Middle managers motivate, direct, and control the supervisors (and any other managers and employees) who report to them.

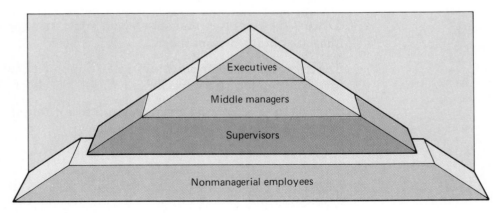

Figure 1-1 Managerial levels.

Supervisors are managers who normally report to middle managers. Supervisors have the responsibility of getting the "hands-on-the-work" employees to carry out the plans and the policies set by executives and middle managers. Supervisors plan, motivate, direct, and control the work of nonmanagerial employees at the operational level of the organization.

What kinds of persons become supervisors?

Just about every kind you can think of. An *average* supervisor, according to statistics describing some 8000 of them, has these characteristics:

Is between 31 and 50 years of age.
Has been with the current employer for 5 to 15 years.
Has been a supervisor less than 5 years.
Was promoted from the ranks.
Is a high school graduate, and has probably attended college; one out of three is a college graduate.

Three out of four supervisors are male; about 10 percent are nonwhite. Half of all supervisors are employed in a white-collar environment. One out of three supervisors once belonged to a trade union. About six out of every ten supervisors have only nonmanagerial employees reporting to them. These are called "first-level supervisors." About four out of ten are "second-level supervisors" and are at the fringes of middle management. They supervise other supervisors as well as nonmanagerial employees.[1]

Why does frontline supervision get so much attention?

Because it represents just about the most important single force in the American economy. Supervisors, as an occupational classification, form a major segment of the overall labor force. In the United States alone, there is a supervisory management force 2 million strong. It holds the power to turn on—or turn off—the productivity of most organizations. These supervisors are the men and women who maintain the crucial interface between the management hierarchy and the vast body of employees who put their hands on, or apply their minds to, the real work of enterprise.

Recognition—and acceptance—of supervisors by top management has helped them to emerge finally as essential and integrated members of the management group and to assume all the responsibilities of full-fledged managers. The way hasn't been easy. Too often it has been painfully slow. Even today there are companies where the supervisor's status is shaky. But on the whole, no single group of men and women has achieved and deserved such stature and attention in so short a time after so long a wait as has supervisory management.

Where did the term *supervisor* come from?

In earlier days the supervisor was the person in charge of a group of towrope pullers or ditchdiggers. That person was literally the "fore man," since he was up forward of the gang. His authority consisted mainly of chanting the "one, two, three, up" which set the pace for the rest of the workers. In Germany the supervisor is still called a *Vorarbeiter* ("fore worker"); in England the term *charge hand* is used. Both terms suggest the lead-person origin.

The term *supervisor* has its roots in Latin, where it means "looks over." It was originally applied to the master of a group of artisans. One hundred years ago it was not uncommon for the master in a New England shop to have almost complete power over the work force. The master could bid on jobs, hire his own crew, work them as hard as he pleased, and make his living out of the difference between his bid price and the labor costs.

Today the supervisor's job combines some of the talents of the "fore man" (or leader) and of the "master" (skilled administrative artisan).

Legally, what makes a supervisor a supervisor?

The federal laws of the United States provide two definitions of a supervisor.

1. The Taft-Hartley Act of 1947 says that a supervisor is

   …any individual having authority, in the interest of the employer, to hire, transfer, suspend, lay off, recall, promote, discharge, assign, reward, or discipline other employees, or responsibility to direct them or to adjust their grievances, or effectively to recommend such action, if in connection with the foregoing the exercise of such authority is not merely of a routine or clerical nature, but requires the use of independent judgment.

   The act specifically prohibits supervisors from joining a union of production and clerical workers, although they may form a union composed exclusively of supervisors.

2. The Fair Labor Standards Act of 1938 (or Minimum Wage Law) set the tone for the above by defining a supervisor as

   …an executive whose primary duty consists of the management of a customarily recognized department or subdivision;
   who customarily and regularly directs the work of two or more employees;

who has the authority to hire or fire other employees or whose suggestions and recommendations as to the hiring or firing and as to the advancement and promotion or any other change in status will be given particular weight; who customarily and regularly exercises discretionary powers; and who does not devote more than 20 percent of his (or her) hours of work to activities which are not closely related to the (managerial) work described above.

The law also stipulates that supervisors be paid a salary (regardless of how many hours they work). This latter provision makes some supervisors unhappy, since it makes them exempt from the provision of the law that calls for overtime pay after a certain number of hours have been worked. Many employers, however, voluntarily compensate for supervisory overtime in one way or another.

The thrust of these two laws is to make supervisors, once and for all, a bona fide part of management.

Are supervisors permitted to do the same work as the people they supervise?

Within the 20 percent stipulation of the Fair Labor Standards Act, there is no law stopping it. Most companies with labor unions, however, often have a contract clause that prohibits the supervisor from performing any work that a union member would ordinarily do (except in clearly defined emergencies, in which the supervisor would do as she or he sees fit).

This is a point on which most managements agree with unions. Few companies want supervisors to do the work their other employees are hired to do. Supervisors are most valuable when they spend 100 percent of their time supervising. It makes little sense for a $500-a-week supervisor, for instance, to do the work of a $300-a-week operator.

2 MANY COMPETENCIES REQUIRED

CONCEPT   Supervisors must bring to their managerial work a broad range of technical and human relations competencies.

How does a person become a supervisor?

Three out of four supervisors are promoted from the ranks of the organization in which they serve. Typically, they are long-service employees. They have greater experience, have held more different jobs in the organization, and have significantly more education than the employees they supervise. Usually, it is apparent that supervisors are chosen from among the best and most experienced employees in the organization.[2]

Other than those supervisors who rise from the ranks, 7 percent are hired directly from a college or technical school. Six percent enter through company-sponsored management training programs, and 13 percent are hired into the position from another company or organization.[3]

What personal characteristics does higher management look for in selecting supervisors?

The job of supervision is so demanding that higher management tends to look for *super*people to fill the role. Most firms, however, do establish a set criteria against which supervisory candidates are judged. Among the most sought-after qualities in a supervisor are these:

- Energy and good health
- Ability to get along with people
- Job know-how and technical competence
- Self-control under pressure
- Dedication and dependability
- Ability to stay on course
- Teachability
- Problem-solving skills
- Leadership potential
- A positive attitude toward management[4]

How can a newly appointed supervisor make the job of crossing over to the managerial ranks a less turbulent one?

A person who is made a supervisor crosses over from one style of thought to another. As an employee, an individual's concerns are with self-satisfaction in terms of pay and the work itself. As a manager, this same person is expected to place the organization's goals above all other job-related concerns. This means that a supervisor worries first about meeting quotas, quality, and cost standards; second about the employees who do the work; and last about himself or herself.

To make the task more difficult, the newly appointed supervisor usually has already made the long climb to the top of the employee ranks. Now the person must cross over to a new field of achievement—management, as shown in Figure 1-2. It will take a while to get a toehold at the supervisory level. For many, however, it will be the beginning of another long climb—this time to the top of the management heap.[5]

The pressures from managers above and from employees below make some new supervisors very uncomfortable.

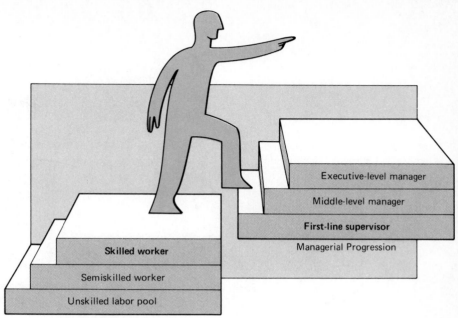

Executive-level manager

Middle-level manager

First-line supervisor

Managerial Progression

Skilled worker

Semiskilled worker

Unskilled labor pool

Employee Progression

Figure 1-2 Crossing over from employee ranks to managerial ranks—from "top of the heap" to "bottom of the heap."

This need not be so, says Professor Keith Davis, one of the most astute observers of organizational relationships. Davis agrees that the supervisor takes pressure from both sides, but he likens the role to a keystone in the organizational arch (Figure 1-3). Says Davis:

> The keystone takes the pressure from both sides and uses this pressure to build a stronger arch. The sides can be held together only by the keystone, which strengthens, not weakens, the arch. The keystone position is the important role of supervisors in organizations.[6]

Experienced supervisors add this advice for the new person:

> Don't throw your weight around. Admit your need for help and seek it from other supervisors and your boss. Make a practice of coming in on time and sticking to your job for the full day; employees despise supervisors who push for productivity but who goof off themselves. Keep yourself physically prepared and mentally alert; the job will be more demanding than you expect. And don't indulge in petty pilfering of supplies or use of shop equipment and time to do personal work; employees may try this themselves but they sure don't respect management people who do.

Working Woman magazine adds this cogent advice for newly appointed supervisors:

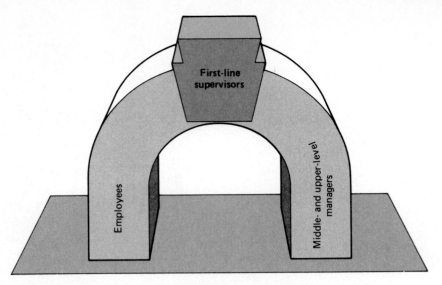

Figure 1-3 Supervisors as the keystone in the organizational arch.

Concentrate on cultivating a look of self-assurance. Appearing overworked or harassed is a liability.[7]

3 LINKING GOALS AND EFFORTS

CONCEPT   Supervisors provide the vital linkage between management goals and meaningful employee effort.

When it comes to job responsibilities, what is expected of supervisors?

Responsibilities encompass four—and occasionally five—broad areas:

Responsibility to management.   Supervisors must, above all, dedicate themselves to the goals, plans, and policies of the organization. These are typically laid down by higher management. It is the primary task of supervisors to serve as a "linking pin" for management to make sure that these are carried out by the employees they supervise. (See Figure 1-4.)

Responsibility to employees.   Employees expect their supervisors to provide direction and training; to protect them from unfair treatment; and to see that the workplace is clean, safe, uncluttered, properly equipped, well lit, and adequately ventilated.

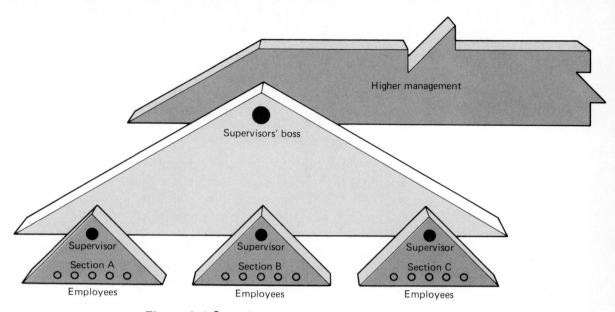

Figure 1-4 Supervisors as link pins who serve to connect employee work groups to the goals of the organization. (Adapted from Rensis Likert, *New Patterns of Management,* McGraw-Hill, New York, 1961, pp. 113–115.)

Responsibility to staff specialists. The relationship between supervision and staff departments is one of mutual support. Staff people are charged with providing supervisors with guidance and help as well as with prescribing procedures to be followed and forms to be completed. Supervisors, in turn, aid the work of the staff departments by making good use of their advice and service and by conforming to their requests.

Responsibility to other supervisors. Teamwork is essential in the supervisory ranks. There is a great deal of departmental interdependence. The goals and activities of one department must harmonize with those of others. This often requires the sacrifice of an immediate target for the greater good of the organization.

Relationships with the union. Labor union and management views are often in conflict, and the supervisor and shop steward are often at loggerheads. It is the supervisor's responsibility, however, to keep these relationships objective, to neither "give away the shop" nor yield responsibility for the welfare of the organization and its employees.

◼4 CONVERTING RESOURCES INTO OUTPUTS

CONCEPT   Supervisory performance is judged by how well supervisors manage their resources and by the results they get from them.

Of all that is expected of supervisors, which tasks loom largest?

Three types of problems seem to persist:

1. **Meeting tight production or operating schedules.**   Take all the fancy talk away, and the supervisor's basic job is still one of "getting out the production." You must see that the goods are finished on schedule, deadlines are met, projects are completed when promised, and quality meets the prescribed standards.
2. **Keeping operating costs in line.**   In simple words, supervisors must do more than getting out the production. They must also attain their operating goals efficiently. More to the point, they must keep their expenses within the allowed or budgeted limits.
3. **Maintaining cooperative attitudes with employees.**   Automation and computers or not, it's the employees who turn the crank. Getting the employees to turn the crank when they should, how they should, and as fast as they should is the ultimate problem for supervisors.

How will supervisory performance be judged by higher management?

It will be judged by two general measures: (1) how well you manage the various resources made available to you to accomplish your assignments and (2) how good the results are that you get from them. (See Figure 1-5.)

Management of Resources   Resources are the things that, in effect, set you up in business as a supervisor. They include:

- **Facilities and equipment.**   Examples are a certain amount of floor space, desks, benches, tools, production machinery, computer terminals, and microfiche readers. Your job is to keep these operating productively and to prevent their abuse.
- **Energy, power, and utilities.**   Among these resources are heat, light, air conditioning, electricity, steam, water, and compressed air. Conservation is the principal measure of effectiveness here.
- **Materials and supplies.**   Included are raw materials, parts, and assemblies used to make a product and operating supplies such as lubricants, stationery, cassette holders, paper clips, and masking tape. Getting the most from every scrap of material and holding waste to the minimum are prime measures here.

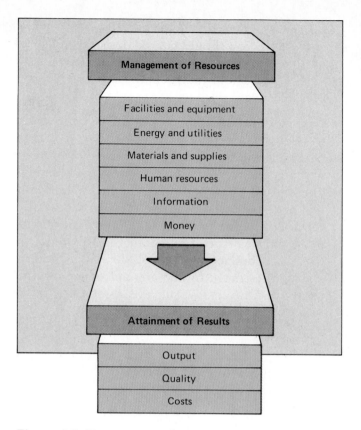

Figure 1-5 Measurement of supervisory performance.

- **Human resources.** This refers to the work force in general and your employees in particular. Since you do little or nothing with your own hands, your biggest job is to see that these people are productively engaged at all times.
- **Information.** Examples are the information made available by staff departments and found in operating manuals, specifications sheets, and blueprints. Your success often depends on how well you can utilize the data and know-how made available to you through these sources.
- **Money.** All the above can be measured by how much they cost, although the actual cash will rarely flow through your hands. Nevertheless, supervisors are expected to be prudent in decisions that affect expenditures and may have to justify these in terms of savings or other benefits.

Attainment of Results It follows that if you manage each of your resources well, you should get the desired results. Whatever your particular area of responsibility and whatever your organization, you can be sure that you will be judged in the long run by how well you meet these three objectives:

- **Output, or production.** Specifically, your department will be expected to turn out a certain amount of work per day, per week, and per month. It will be expected that this will be done on time and that you will meet delivery schedules and project deadlines.
- **Quality and workmanship.** Output volume alone is not enough. You will also be judged by the quality of the work your employees perform, whether it be measured in terms of the number of product defects, service errors, or customer complaints.
- **Costs and budget control.** Your output and quality efforts will always be restricted by the amount of money you can spend to carry them out. Universally, supervisors attest to the difficulty of living up to cost and budget restraints.

What are the main job competencies required of supervisors?

No one knows for sure. There are, however, a number of regularly performed duties, or requirements, of the supervisory job that experts can identify. From these duties, the required competencies can be inferred. For example, one major manufacturing company looks for these seven competencies among its supervisors: technical know-how, administrative skill, ability to develop a plan to meet department goals, ability to deal with the manager to whom you report, communications skills, ability to deal with people inside and outside the operating unit, and ability to deal effectively with people who report to you. Other researchers also identify such success-related qualities as creativity, stress tolerance, initiative, independence, problem analysis, decisiveness, tenacity, flexibility, risk taking, and use of delegation.[8]

The American Telephone and Telegraph Company (AT&T) promotes about 12,000 men and women from the ranks into supervisory positions each year (throughout its system and its now-independent constituent companies). To make the choice of these candidates more reliable and to better prepare them for their new jobs, AT&T spent several years studying the "job content" of its master supervisors (those whose performance is the very best). On the basis of this study, AT&T developed a list of skills that supervisors must acquire if they are to be effective at their work. This list is reproduced in Table 1-1. It is generally regarded as applicable to almost any supervisor. The list may seem formidable, but most of the talents it requires can be acquired by super-

Rank Order	Duties	Percent of Time Spent*	Frequency of Occurrence
	Table 1-1 PRINCIPAL DUTIES OF FIRST-LEVEL SUPERVISORS (Ranked According to Time Required and Frequency of Occurrence)		
1	Controlling the work	17	Every day
2	Problem solving and decision making	13	Every day
3	Planning the work	12	Every day
4	Informal oral communications	12	Every day
5	Communications, general	12	Every day
6	Providing performance feedback to employees	10	Every day
7	Training, coaching, developing subordinates	10	Every day
8	Providing written communications and documentation	7	Every day
9	Creating and maintaining a motivating atmosphere	6	Every day
10	Personal time management	4	Every day
11	Meetings and conferences	4	Twice monthly
12	Self-development activities	2	Weekly
13	Career counseling of subordinates	2	Bimonthly
14	Representing the company to the community	1	Monthly

* Percentages add up to more than 100 because of overlap of duties—that is, *planning* of the work at a *meeting* called for planning purposes.

Source: Adapted from Charles R. Macdonald, *Performance Based Supervisory Development: Adapted from a Major AT&T Study,* Human Resources Development Press, Amherst, Mass., 1982, p. 20.

visors who learn from their experience and take advantage of training and developmental opportunities offered by their employers.[9]

5 SKILLS TO BE DEVELOPED

CONCEPT   Supervisors strengthen their contribution to the management process by developing their technical, administrative, and human relations skills.

Where do supervisors fit in the management process?

They are an essential part of it. Supervisors perform exactly the same functions as all other managers in their organization—up to and including the chief executive. Each specific task, every responsibility, all the various roles that supervisors are called on to perform are carried

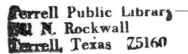

out by the **management process** (Figure 1-6). This process, which is repeated over and over, daily, weekly, and yearly, consists of five broad functions:

- **Planning.** Setting goals and establishing plans and procedures to attain them.
- **Organizing.** Arranging jobs to be done in such a way as to make them more effective.
- **Staffing.** Selecting and placing just the right number of people in the most appropriate jobs.
- **Activating.** Motivating, communicating, and leading.
- **Controlling.** Regulating the process, its costs, and the people who carry it out.

The management process is explained in detail in Chapter 3.

How do supervisory job roles differ from those of other levels of management?

They differ only in degree. Higher-level managers spend more time planning and less time directing, for example. Two people who studied this matter came up with three useful guidelines. They first divided all the

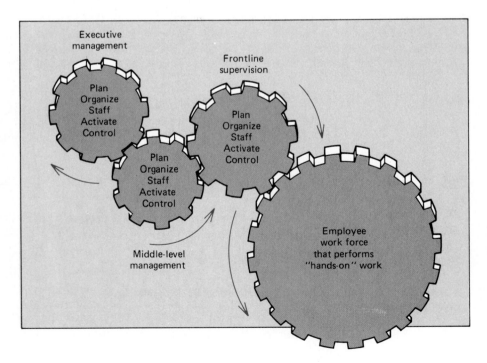

Figure 1-6 The management process: All managers take part in it.

tasks and responsibilities we have listed so far in this text into three kinds of roles. Roles are the parts played by actors on a stage; they are also the real-life parts played by managers and supervisors in an organization. These three roles can be classified as those requiring:

- **Technical skills.** Job know-how; knowledge of the industry and its particular processes, machinery, and problems.
- **Administrative skills.**   Knowledge of the entire organization and how it is coordinated, knowledge of its information and records system, and an ability to plan and control work.
- **Human relations skills.**   Knowledge of human behavior and an ability to work effectively with individuals and groups—peers and superiors as well as subordinates.

The observers then concluded that the role of the supervisor emphasizes technical and human relations skills most and administrative skills least. This emphasis tends to reverse itself with higher-level managers, as illustrated in Figure 1-7.

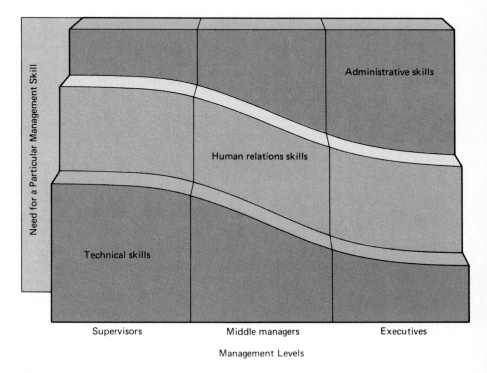

Figure 1-7 How the need for managerial skills varies at different levels of management.

CONCEPT   Effective supervisors balance the application of their skills between the work to be done and a concern for the people who perform this work.

Supervisory balance: What does it mean?

It is a simplification of a very valuable dictum: Pay as much attention to human relations matters as to technical and administrative ones.

In other words, be as *employee-centered* as you are *job- or task-centered* in your interests. Or, said still another way, spend as much time maintaining group cohesiveness, direction, and morale as you do pushing for productivity or task accomplishment.

This view has been borne out by a number of studies. The basis, however, is research carried on by Rensis Likert, the man who saw supervisors as link pins. In a survey of clerical, sales, and manufacturing employees, he found that, on the average, employees who worked for supervisors who were job- or production-centered produced less than employees who worked for employee-centered supervisors.[10]

It would be dangerous to draw the conclusion from Likert's studies that being a nice guy is the answer to employee productivity. It isn't. As in sports, nice guys often finish last. The important conclusion from these studies is that supervisors who focus on job demands to the exclusion of their interest in the welfare and the development of their people don't get the results they are looking for. Conversely, supervisors who bend over backward to make work easy for their employees don't get good results either. It takes a balance between the two approaches, as shown in Figure 1-8.

What's a normal day in the life of a supervisor?

Many supervisors would say that there is no such thing as a normal day. One thing is sure, however: a supervisor's day is full of interruptions. Estimates are that a typical supervisor handles from 50 to 80 problems a day. Accordingly, anything that supervisors can do to bring order to their days is welcome. Appendix A at the back of the book outlines a daily work sequence that can guide supervisors in establishing an orderly structure for their day.

How professional is the work of supervision?

It is getting more professional every day. Two leading management organizations, made up primarily of first-line supervisors, are working

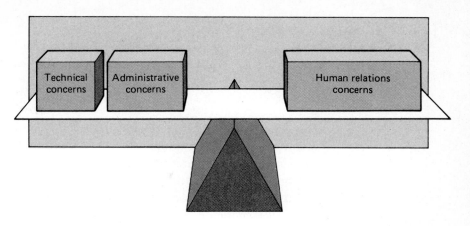

Figure 1-8 How supervisors must balance their task-centered concerns with their employee-centered concerns.

hard to make it that way. The International Management Council (IMC), sponsored originally by the Young Men's Christian Association (YMCA), and the National Management Association (NMA) have pooled their resources to form an independent Institute of Certified Professional Managers (ICPM). The institute, working with a qualified licensing-test consultant, has devised and is administering professional certification tests. Certification is based on a combination of experience and examinations in the following three areas: (1) personal skills, such as skills in communications, government regulation, and time management; (2) administrative skills, such as planning, decision making, staffing, and controlling; and (3) human relations skills.

The addresses of the participating organizations are as follows:

International Management Council
430 So. 20 Street
Omaha, Nebraska 68102

National Management Association
2210 Arbor Boulevard
Dayton, Ohio 45439

Institute of Certified Professional Managers
James Madison University
Harrisonburg, Virginia 22807

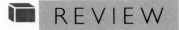 REVIEW

KEY CONCEPTS TO REMEMBER

1. Supervisors are essential, legally franchised members of the management team of an organization. They occupy the vital first level of management that interacts directly with the work force.

2. To be able to learn and perform well in their roles, supervisors must bring to the position a wide range of personal qualities and competencies. Competencies most frequently expected of supervisors include energy and good health, an ability to get along with people, job know-how, self-control under pressure, dedication and dependability, problem-solving skills, leadership potential, and a genuine belief in the contribution that good management can make to the attainment of an organization's goals.

3. Supervisors must respond to the interests of the many constituents present in an organization: the management team, their own employees, staff specialists, other supervisors, and—where present— the labor union. The most critical function that supervisors perform for these constituents is to act as the linkage—or interface—between higher management's goals, plans, and policies and the employees who actually perform the work of an organization.

4. Supervisory effectiveness is judged by two major measures: (a) how well supervisors manage the resources made available to them and (b) the quantity and quality of the results they derive from the use of these resources. Resources include facilities and equipment; energy, power, and utilities; materials and supplies; human resources; information; and money. Results are focused on output attained from resources, its quality, and the containment of costs.

5. As managers, supervisors regularly engage in the management process of planning, organizing, staffing, activating, and controlling. Supervisors improve their effectiveness in this process by developing their technical (or know-how) skills, their administrative (planning, implementing, and innovating) skills, and their human relations (interpersonal) skills. Compared with executives, supervisors rely much more on their technical skills and far less on their administrative skills. While human relations skills are important at all levels of management, they often become a make-or-break factor for supervisors.

6. In carrying out their responsibilities, supervisors must be careful not to be overzealous either in (a) pushing employees too hard for pro-

duction or in (b) being overly protective of these employees. The most effective supervisors strike a balance between a concern for the work to be done and a concern for those people who must do it.

SUPERVISORY WORD POWER

Employee-centered supervision. Management characterized by an emphasis on a genuine concern and respect for employees as human beings and on the maintenance of effective relationships within a work group.

Executive. A highly placed manager who is in charge of, and responsible for, the performance of a group of subordinate managers. Executives establish broad plans, objectives, and general policies.

Job- or task-centered supervision. Management characterized by an emphasis placed on the job or task that employees are expected to perform; a major concern for production or operating results.

Management. The process of obtaining, deploying, and utilizing a variety of essential resources in support of an organization's objectives.

Management process. Five functions uniquely provided for an organization by all managers in a general sequence of planning, organizing, staffing, directing or activating, and controlling.

Manager. An individual who plans, organizes, directs, and controls the work of others in an organization.

Middle manager. A manager who reports to an executive and who directs supervisory personnel toward the attainment of goals and the implementation of plans of an organization.

Nonmanagerial employees. Workers who receive direction from managers, who perform specific, designated tasks, and who are responsible only for their own performance; usually referred to simply as "employees."

Supervisor. A manager who is in charge of, and coordinator of, the activities of a group of employees engaged in related activities within a department, section, or unit of an organization. Supervisors usually report to middle managers. They direct the work procedures, issue oral and written orders and instructions, assign duties to workers, examine work for quality and neatness, maintain harmony among workers, and adjust errors and complaints.

READING COMPREHENSION

1. There is one clear distinction between managers and their employees. What is it?

2. How many levels of management are there in a typical organization? At which level are supervisors found?
3. What characteristics of a supervisory management job are stressed by the two laws that define this position?
4. Why might a company object to the supervisor of a plastic-molding department spending most of her time setting up and operating the molding machines?
5. Energy, good health, and self-control are among the characteristics looked for in a supervisor. Why are these qualities important?
6. Name the four main groups of constituents within an organization with which a supervisor must interact. Describe the nature of a supervisor's responsibilities to each.
7. Which two broad categories of performance are typically used to judge the effectiveness of supervisors at their work?
8. AT&T's master supervisors have ranked fourteen important tasks that supervisors must perform (Table 1-1). Sort these out according to the three categories of supervisory skills: (a) technical, (b) administrative, and (c) human relations.
9. How is supervisory management similar to higher-level management? How is it different?
10. What is meant by the fact that supervisors are advised to achieve "balance" in the application of their skills?

REFERENCES

1. Lester R. Bittel and Jackson E. Ramsey, "The Limited, Traditional World of Supervisors," *Harvard Business Review*, July–August 1982, vol. 60, no. 4, p. 26.
2. Herbert R. Northrup, Ronald M. Cowin, Lawrence G. Vanden Plas, and William E. Fulmer, "The Objective Selection of Supervisors," *Manpower and Human Resources Studies*, no. 8, The Wharton School, Univ. of Pennsylvania, 1978, pp. 58–69.
3. Bittel and Ramsey, op. cit.
4. Lester R. Bittel, *The Complete Guide to Supervisory Training and Development*, Addison-Wesley, Reading, Mass., 1987, chap. 3, "Dimensions of Supervisory Competencies."
5. Carl A. Benson, "New Supervisors: From the Top of the Heap to the Bottom of the Heap," *Personnel Journal*, April 1978, p. 176.
6. Keith Davis, "The Supervisory Role," in M. Gene Newport (ed.), *Supervisory Management: Tools and Techniques*, West, St. Paul, Minn., 1976, p. 5.
7. Jane Ciabattari, "Crossing the Magic Threshold," *Working Woman*, June 1987, p. 94.

8. William C. Byham, "Assessment Center Method," in Lester R. Bittel and Jackson E. Ramsey (eds.), *Handbook for Professional Managers,* McGraw-Hill, New York, 1985, p. 41.

9. Charles R. Macdonald, *Performance Based Supervisory Development: Adapted from a Major AT&T Study,* Human Resources Development Press, Amherst, Mass., 1982, p. 20.

10. Rensis Likert, *New Patterns of Management,* McGraw-Hill, New York, 1961.

SUPPLEMENTARY READINGS

David L. Bain, *The Productivity Prescription: The Manager's Guide to Improving Productivity and Profits*, McGraw-Hill, New York, 1982.

H. Kent Baker and Steven H. Holmberg, "Stepping Up to Supervision: Making the Transition," *Supervisory Management*, September 1981, pp. 10–18.

Lester R. Bittel, *The McGraw-Hill 36-Hour Management Course*, McGraw-Hill, New York, 1988.

Philip Crosby, *The Art of Getting Your Own Sweet Way*, 2d ed., McGraw-Hill, New York, 1983.

Keith Davis, "The Supervisory Role," in M. Gene Newport (ed.), *Supervisory Management: Tools and Techniques*, West, St. Paul, Minn., 1985.

Rosabeth Moss Kanter and Barry A. Stein, *Life in Organizations: Workplaces as People Experience Them*, Basic Books Inc., New York, 1979.

Al Kelley, *How to Make Your Life Easier at Work*, 2d ed., McGraw-Hill, New York, 1988.

John P. Kotter, *The Leadership Factor*, The Free Press, New York, 1988.

Douglas McGregor, *The Human Side of Enterprise*, McGraw-Hill, New York, 1960.

Lynda L. Moore (ed.), *Not as Far as You Think: The Realities of Working Women*, Lexington Books, Lexington, Mass., 1986.

Jon L. Pierce and John R. Newstrom, *The Manager's Bookshelf: A Mosaic of Contemporary Views*, Harper & Row, New York, 1988.

Craig C. Pinder, *Work Motivation*, Scott, Foresman and Company, Glenview, Ill., 1984.

Charles D. Pringle, Daniel F. Jennings, and Justin Longenecker, *Managing Organizations: Functions and Behaviors*, Merrill Publishing Company, Columbus, Ohio, 1988, chap. 2, "Historical Trends in Management Thought and Practice."

F. J. Roethlisberger and William J. Dickson, *Management and the Worker*, Harvard University Press, Cambridge, Mass., 1946.

Leonard A. Schlesinger, *Quality of Work Life and the Supervisors*, Praeger Publishers, New York, 1982.

Malcolm Shaw, *Group Dynamics*, 3d ed., McGraw-Hill, New York, 1980.

Robert A. Sutermeister, *People and Productivity*, 4th ed., McGraw-Hill, New York, 1976.

Frederick W. Taylor, *Scientific Management*, Harper & Row, New York, 1947.

APPLICATION

SELF-APPRAISAL

How ready are you to be a supervisor?

On a separate piece of paper, copy the column headings shown below. Next write the numbers 1 to 20 down the page to correspond to each of the statements that follow. Read each statement carefully. Then place a check mark in the column that most nearly matches your feeling about each statement. After completing this activity, check your answers using the scoring procedure described on page 25.

Column headings:

Agree	Disagree	Neither Agree nor Disagree

1. I like to set my own goals and do things my own way.
2. I have a keen sensitivity to the interests of other people.
3. I see my work as a means only to an end, rather than as a main focus for my life.
4. When I know a job needs to be done well, I will do it myself.
5. I don't want to take the responsibility for someone else's work, good or bad.
6. I consider myself an attentive listener: I don't interrupt.
7. Given a fair chance, most people want to do a good job.
8. I live according to the rule of better late than never.
9. When working with a group of other people on a project, I often find myself prodding them to get the job done.
10. I have a lot to learn about management and supervision.
11. Good employees work safely, obey the rules, and are willing to give a fair day's work.

12. My friends know that I won't criticize them when they come to me with their hard-luck stories.
13. People who break rules should be prepared to pay the penalty.
14. I like to show other people how to do things.
15. The thought of working overtime without extra pay seems extremely unfair.
16. Most of my bosses have been a hindrance rather than a help to me and my co-workers.
17. I consider myself to be a good explainer: I can make things clear to other people.
18. In handling my personal affairs, I rarely fall behind in what I set out to do.
19. When assessing a situation, I find that there is likely to be some good in it as well as the bad and the ugly.
20. When things go wrong, that's a sign that a problem needs to be solved rather than a person blamed.

Scoring Give yourself 1 point for each of the following statements that you *agreed* with: 2, 6, 7, 9, 10, 11, 12, 13, 14, 17, 18, 19, 20. Give yourself 1 point for each of the following statements that you *disagreed* with: 1, 3, 4, 5, 8, 15, 16. There are no points for statements with which you neither agreed nor disagreed.

Interpretation If you scored between 15 and 20 points, you are ready to consider the pursuit of a supervisory position. If you scored between 9 and 14 points, you should try now to gain a fuller understanding of what a supervisory position entails. If you scored less than 9 points, it's probably wise to look to other occupations for a career. Do continue your studies of supervision, however, so that your working life will be made more fruitful from your understanding of the supervisors and managers with whom you will be associated.

CASE STUDIES

CASE I The Ill-at-Ease Supervisor

Betty H. knows order processing for the apparel industry as well as she knows her own parents. In her ten years in the business she has held every sort of job from entry to billing to telephone orders, pricing assistant, and customer service. In recognition of her skills, Betty's employer recently made her the supervisor of the order handling department. Betty was proud of her promotion; she thought it would enable her to bring the highest standards to the whole shop and not just to her own work.

Within three months, however, Betty found herself very uncomfortable in her new position. Betty had always enjoyed the friendly banter with her co-workers; this easy friendship seemed to have been lost since she was made boss. The work schedule was suffering. Often, her employees weren't sure of what they should be doing and lost a lot of time. Betty was certain that meeting the schedule should hold first priority, but she was worried about the paperwork piling up in her office. Nevertheless, she spent a great deal of her time demonstrating to her employees how the work of the various departmental functions could be improved. Inevitably, Betty wound up doing much of the work herself in order to get back on schedule. It all came to a head when Betty's boss expressed his growing dissatisfaction with her work.

If you were Betty, which of the following actions would you consider to be the most effective for you to take? On a separate piece of paper, rank the alternatives on a scale from 1 (most preferable) to 5 (least preferable). You may add another alternative if you wish. In any event, be prepared to justify your ranking.

a. Call your employees together, explain that the schedule is slipping, and ask them to work temporarily harder until the backlog is eliminated.
b. Pick a promising person in the shop and give him or her the job of seeing that everyone knows what work to do.
c. Tell your boss that the schedule cannot be met with the current work force and that you need help to complete your paperwork.
d. Ask to be moved back to your last nonmanagerial assignment, where you can really use your skills best.
e. Let your boss know that you would welcome guidance and training on the managerial aspects of your supervisory job.

Instructions for Cases 2 to 4: The following incidents happened in the lives of three supervisors. How well do you think the supervisor handled each situation? In particular, do you think the supervisor demonstrated supervisory balance? If not, can you suggest some action that might achieve this balance?

CASE 2   The Underproducing Paper Cutter

Tom operates a large paper cutter in a printing plant. He has been having personal problems at home and hasn't been able to concentrate on his work. As a consequence, his output has dropped off, which slows other workers ahead of him who are waiting for the cut paper. His supervisor, who is sympathetic to Tom's problems, says, "I know things have been rough for you lately. Don't worry about your production rate. We can cover for you."

CASE 3   The Eager Loan Clerk

Mary maintains firm discipline in her loan records unit of the bank, and productivity there has been very high. One of her employees is interested in learning more about the entire banking process in order to prepare for advancement in the future. Mary tells him, "I think that's a very good idea, and I'll help you any way I can as long as your output doesn't fall off as a result."

CASE 4   Talk on Your Own Time

Dingo has just been appointed supervisor of the inspection department of a major appliance maker. Dingo's first act is to outlaw all conversation at the inspection stations. He tells his inspectors, "Your jobs are to make certain that every motor installed meets the specifications. Conversation is distracting and is liable to cause costly oversights. If you want to talk, do it on your own time."

1 A supervisor's environment shapes his or her horizons and limits his or her options.

2 Work is characterized by conformity, authority, and structure.

3 Nevertheless, most employees are reasonably happy in their work.

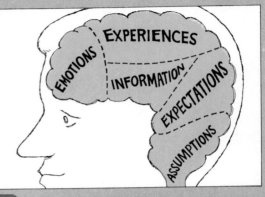

4 Individuals differ greatly in their perception of their jobs.

5 Supervisors can improve the quality of their employees' work.

CHAPTER 2

Coping With Your Unique Environment

LEARNING OBJECTIVES

After studying this chapter, you should be able to

1. Distinguish the differences between a supervisor's work environment and that of higher-level managers.

2. Identify the four characterizing features of work.

3. Discuss the general state of satisfaction that employees have with their jobs.

4. Explain how and why different people have different perceptions of the nature of, and the satisfaction they find in, their work.

5. List a number of ways by which supervisors can improve the quality of work life for their employees.

▣ SEVEN PRESSURES TO COPE WITH

CONCEPT   The unique environment in which supervisors' work shapes their horizons and tends to restrict their options.

In what ways does the supervisors' world differ from that of their superiors?

Higher-level managers tend to be outward-oriented. They are likely to be more influenced by forces and events outside the company or institution than by those within. Supervisors, on the other hand, are more inside-oriented.

A company president or division executive has concerns for such things as what the competition is doing, whether or not the company's creditors can pay their bills, how dependable suppliers are likely to be, and how to keep stockholders satisfied. Higher-level executives are also concerned with general economic conditions, proposed government regulations, and public opinion.

Supervisors are concerned with, and restrained by, a number of more immediate factors. As shown in Figure 2-1, a supervisor's environment is characterized by seven important factors. Some factors were mentioned in the last chapter as "responsibilities." Regardless of terminol-

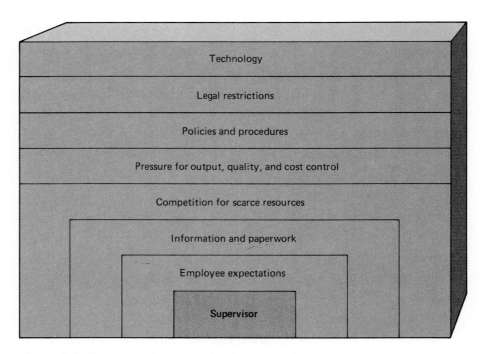

Figure 2-1 Constraints in a supervisor's environment.

ogy, these factors also establish the supervisor's environment. They include:

1. **Technology, existing and changing,** such as the processes and equipment, the know-how, and the way things are done in a particular company, department, or organization.
2. **Legal restrictions,** such as those affecting employee safety, health, and rights to equal opportunity, fair pay, privacy, freedom from discrimination, and representation by a union steward.
3. **Organizational policies and procedures,** to which supervisors, as well as their employees, must conform.
4. **Pressures from above** to meet the organization's goals for output, quality, and cost control.
5. **Competition with other supervisors for scarce resources,** such as equipment, space, skills, and budgets.
6. **A welter of recorded information** that must be generated, processed, maintained, and utilized.
7. **Rising expectations of employees** for considerate treatment, meaningful work, and an opportunity to participate in decisions that affect them.

What about the time factor?

Higher-level executives are, rightfully, more concerned with the future than are supervisors. Executives, and most middle managers, are paid to worry most about what will happen next month or next year. Supervisors, who are on the firing line, have a shorter time horizon. A delay of fifteen minutes in the arrival of operating supplies can loom large in importance when 15 employees are idled by it. Consequently, supervisors keep their eyes on hour-by-hour and day-to-day problems. For most supervisors, a "month from now" is a long look ahead.

Does this mean that supervisors should not look ahead?

Not at all. Supervisors should also keep a weather eye out for changes—external as well as internal—that may affect their future operations. For example, there is hardly an organization whose operational practices won't change in the next ten years due to one of the following changes predicted for the external environment:

- Increasing pace of change in technology, affecting low-tech, as well as high-tech, industries.
- Internationalization of business operations, requiring that a supervisor's operations be competitive with those that are thousands of miles away.

- Changes in the composition of the work force, including more women and immigrants, an increasing number of middle-aged workers, and fewer applicants with the necessary technical skills.
- Greater emphasis on the quality of work life, including flexible work hours and variety in assignments.
- Increasing concern for legal rights of employees as guaranteed by federal legislation.
- Economic uncertainty, requiring organizations to expand, contract, or change structure quickly and efficiently.

As you can see, supervisors are caught up now in a web of uncontrollable circumstances, and they will be even more so in the future.

2 THE WORLD OF WORK

CONCEPT The world of work is characterized by the necessity of employee conformity, the exercise of authority by managers, the subordination of personal interests to organizational goals, and the commanding presence of written records.

What is meant by *work*?

Webster helps here. The dictionary is on target with five related definitions:

- Activity in which one exerts strength or faculties to do or perform.
- Sustained physical or mental effort valued to the extent that it overcomes obstacles and achieves an objective or result.
- Labor, task, or duty that affords one the accustomed means of livelihood.
- Strenuous activity marked by the presence of difficulty and exertion and the absence of pleasure.
- Specific task, duty, function, or assignment, often a part or phase of some larger activity.

Note the key words: physical, mental, effort, exertion, obstacles, difficulty, result, and means of livelihood. Note, too, the implication of work as a part of a larger activity and its age-old association with the absence of pleasure. Modern-day supervisors try to combine work with pleasure for their employees as measured by the degree of personal satisfaction derived from it.

Why do most people work?

For two reasons: first, for the money it brings and for what necessities and pleasures that money will buy; second, for the satisfaction work can bring—either from being with other people or from a sense of personal accomplishment.

Which reward is more important to most workers, money or job satisfaction?

That depends. Most of us want both, of course. But until each of us has a paycheck that is big enough for our own highly personal situation, job satisfaction may take a backseat.

In what ways is work different from many other things people do?

Four factors make work unique:

1. Rules, regulations, and procedures are necessarily designed to demand a degree of conformity in each employee's action and thus to limit free choice. Many people find it hard to channel their efforts into paths that are set by others. Modern supervision tries to keep rules to a minimum and to stress the opportunity for self-control.
2. A chain of authority makes each person more or less beholden to the boss, and the boss in turn to another boss, and so on. In practice this means that most companies are run by relatively few top-level managers. Lower-level managers and employees at the bottom of the organizational pyramid often feel that they have little say in what happens. Employees typically think the only right they have is to complain, not to make constructive suggestions about how to run the business. Supervisors who invite help from employees tend to make the work more appealing to them.
3. Those who hold managerial responsibility are expected to place their own personal interests behind those of the organization. It is no secret that a great many managers do not do so. Instead, they take care of themselves first and the company's resources, especially employees, later. Employees who work for this kind of manager may find their job satisfactions very small. And they may expend their effort in complaints.
4. Much of what happens or is expected to happen is put into written records. Outside of work, most of our activities are loosely defined and rarely put into writing. Written documents—those that record the past and those that set goals for the future—are threatening to many people. There is the fear that no mistake will be forgotten and that every promise will be remembered. Because of so much formal communication, employees often feel more comfortable with supervisors who pass on the word in easy, give-and-take conversation.

These four factors were first identified in the 1890s by a German sociologist named Max Weber, who prescribed them for an "organized system of work directed by hired managers." He called this system *bureaucracy.*

▣ *EMPLOYEE EXPECTATIONS*

CONCEPT   Despite its constraints, the great majority of employees are reasonably satisfied with their work.

How many people are truly happy at their work?

According to a number of authoritative studies, from 80 to 90 percent of all employees are satisfied with their jobs. This doesn't necessarily mean that they are ecstatic about them. The figures also show that blacks (as well as other minorities) and women are not as satisfied as whites and men. Furthermore, factory workers tend to be less satisfied than white-collar workers. And one of the clearest conclusions is that job satisfaction tends to improve with age. Younger people are by far the most dissatisfied with their work.

The trend toward job satisfaction seems to have peaked during the 1970s. Nevertheless, it is still surprisingly high. High enough, it seems, to give supervisors an even break in attempting to move employees toward organizational and departmental goals.

What is it that today's workers expect from their jobs that is often lacking?

Something that challenges their skills and offers fair pay in return for this extra effort. According to Daniel Yankelovich, a noted surveyor of public opinion and director of the nonprofit Public Agenda Foundation, most people can choose to work hard—or to just get by. Only one person in five, reports Yankelovich, says he or she does his or her very best. For one thing, workers assume that an increase in output may not benefit them—only the consumer, stockholders, or management. Down deep, however, most employees will work harder and better, says Yankelovich and other observers, if the work they do makes sense to them and is truly appreciated by their bosses. In fact, eight out of ten Americans say that their jobs are too easy, that they'd prefer a difficult job to an easy one where they merely "put in their time."

Supervisors can minimize both kinds of employee complaints. First, they can make sure that employees have enough to do, especially of the kind of work that capitalizes on their initiative. Second, supervisors can live up to their promises about promotions or relief from boring assignments for those who do go all out to do a good job.

⁴ SATISFACTION AND DISSATISFACTION

CONCEPT Individuals have differing perceptions of their work and seek satisfaction from it in different ways.

What are the chances of developing a 100 percent enthusiastic work force?

Very slim. If the statistics reported earlier can be taken as representative, one or two out of every ten employees are likely to be dissatisfied. Even the best supervisors have to accept that fact.

Why do so many people approach their work with a "show me" or "please me" attitude?

Times are no longer simply "a-changing." For many people, the future has arrived. The Woodstock generation has grown up and the last of the baby boomers have reported for employment. They are better educated than any work force in history, and this induces higher expectations. Applicants and subordinates are aware of their civil rights, too. There's a widespread feeling that "I'm entitled." Some people feel that society owes them a living, and a pleasant one at that. Relatively few believe that hard work, dedication, and perseverance make the best road to success. It's no wonder, then, that so many employees place the burden of their need for job satisfaction on the supervisor. In turn, the supervisor needs all the skills and patience that he or she can muster to motivate today's workers to perform at the levels that society—to say nothing of their employers—expects of them.

What causes employees to perceive similar kinds of work in such different lights?

The way people perceive things—including their jobs or the work they are asked to do—is influenced by five factors:

Past experience with similar work. If the work has been unpleasant with another company or boss, an employee may anticipate that the experience will repeat itself everywhere. The opposite will be true for a person whose experience with this work has been favorable.

Assumptions about the motivation of others. An unhappy person may blame her or his problems on the actions of aggressive co-workers or an unfair boss. For some unfortunate people, this becomes a guideline in dealing with all interpersonal relations. On the other hand, a person who views others as supportive and friendly may perceive every work situation in that light.

Expectations about what will happen. "It's a foregone conclusion," we hear people say. This is based somewhat upon past experience and somewhat upon our beliefs about the motivation of others. Unfortunately, it reflects a rigidity of mind and the unwillingness of some employees to give a new job or a different assignment a fair try.

The reliability of information. Some employees make judgments about their work on the basis of what others tell them. This knowledge may be correct, or it may be unreliable hearsay or bitter prejudice. Supervisors can contend with this problem by providing accurate information upon which employees can then make valid decisions.

The present state of mind. All of us are subject to mood swings. If the boss proposes a new task, for instance, on a day when an employee feels good, the reaction is likely to be more positive than it would be if the idea were proposed on one of those inevitable "bad days."

Is there any cure for boring work?

Yes. Listen to Barbara Garson, author of *All the Livelong Day: The Meaning and Demeaning of Routine Work*. She observes: "People need passionately to do real and serious work: to set a problem for themselves, devise a means whereby the problem can be solved, and then see their realized efforts in a completed task...the need to use judgment, individual skill, or work-educated insight." Garson, a harsh critic of business, points to the solution. Hard and challenging work is real and serious. "Mickey Mouse" jobs are soft and nondemanding. A supervisor can help employees to see the job as a problem to be solved, since that's what a job really is. Supervisors can also show employees what the final results are, even on a short-cycle job such as mounting a relay to an electronic breadboard for a TV set. Employees should know that supervisors do want the use of their judgment, not indifference or carelessness; personal skill, not automatic machine-dependency; and know-how based on work experience.

▣ *QUALITY OF WORK LIFE*

CONCEPT   Supervisors can improve the quality of work life when they facilitate, rather than direct, the work of their employees and encourage feedback from them.

To what extent can supervisors be held responsible for dissatisfied employees?

Only to the extent that employees who ordinarily ought to be satisfied with their work begin to project a general dissatisfaction with it. One observer advises that when a state of "poor satisfaction" occurs, it may also be evidence of "poor management."

What can supervisors do to improve the quality of working life?

There are two views. The first is that improved productivity—greater output from the inputs of labor, materials, money, and machines—continues to be the foundation for a better work life. Higher productivity buys the tools that make work easier and the time for each employee to find the best way of adapting to the task. The second is the conviction on the part of many qualified observers that a greater involvement in decision making at the job level is essential. The early managers believed just the opposite. They divided jobs into the smallest and easiest pieces. Their goal was to create foolproof jobs for "dumb" human beings. The trouble with this view is that the majority of human beings are not dumb at all. They *want* to "work smarter," although not necessarily harder. As a consequence, they will respond to job conditions that make fullest use of their manual and mental skills. They like working in situations that enable each woman and man to make a demonstrably valued contribution to the finished product or service.

To most people, an improved quality of work life simply means that their hours spent at work will not be wasteful ones. They want to feel that, somehow, their lives will be more worthwhile as a result of working than they would be with no job at all.

Is there any sure way to make work more enjoyable?

Given the differences in expectations, the answer must be "no." Some basic approaches, however, will make for greater satisfaction among employees in general.

Offer Employees an Opportunity for "Bottom-Upward" Feedback This is one good way to find out what each person expects from work, even if it cannot always be provided.

View Many Supervisory Functions as Facilitating Rather Than Directing Few people want to be told how and when to do every little thing. Not every worker who is given an inch will take a mile. So try to provide the kinds of information and tools an employee needs to get the job done—the right blueprint or specification, a key bit of know-how. A physical or mental assist, when needed or asked for, encourages employees to enforce their own discipline.

Stay Flexible When and Where You Can   The supervisor whose department rules can't be bent to accommodate a worker's individuality on occasion makes employees feel hopelessly locked in. Keep to a minimum all directives that begin with the words *always* or *never*. Think in terms of *most of the time,* or *on the average,* when you will not permit this or insist on that.

Try to Be a Part of the Total Organization   Know your own superior as well as you can. Find out the company's basic objectives about costs, production, and quality. Understand the real intent of company policy toward employees. If you have this information, you will be in a better position to intercede for your employees. The supervisor who goes to bat for the gang is often the supervisor an employee can face on a rainy Monday morning when there is a temptation to remain in bed.

REVIEW

KEY CONCEPTS TO REMEMBER

1. Supervisors face a different set of restraining factors in their immediate work environment than do higher-level managers. Specifically, a supervisor's horizons and options are greatly influenced by (a) technology, (b) legal restrictions, (c) organizational policies and procedures, (d) pressures for improved output, quality, and cost control, (e) competition with other supervisors for the organization's scarce resources, (f) the need to manage an enormous amount of information (or paperwork), and (g) the rising expectations of employees. Additionally, supervisors need to be more concerned with day-to-day, short-term events than do higher-level managers, who are expected to be prepared much further in advance for important changes in the external environment.
2. Work is a unique activity that is characterized, according to Max Weber, by (a) the necessity of employee conformity to rules, regulations, policies, and procedures, (b) the exercise of authority over others by managers, (c) the subordination of personal interests to the goals of the organization, and (d) the presence of written records for planning and control.
3. The great majority of employees (from 80 to 90 percent) are reasonably satisfied with their jobs. Many good employees, however,

would be better satisfied if their work required more of them and—as a result—was more challenging.

4. Individuals perceive their work differently, and derive satisfaction from it, for different reasons. An employee's perception of the job is affected by past experience, assumptions about the intentions of others that will affect the situation, expectations about what will happen, the reliability of information about the job and its prospects, and the employee's present state of mind.

5. Supervisors can help to improve the quality of work life by maintaining a flexibility that accepts individual differences. Such supervisors also encourage "bottom-upward" feedback. Most importantly, these supervisors facilitate, rather than direct, the work of their employees.

SUPERVISORY WORD POWER

Bureaucracy. An organized system of work directed by professional managers and not, by definition, necessarily enmeshed in red tape.

Facilitating. An approach to management in which a supervisor assists and guides employees in their efforts to perform their jobs rather than emphasizing orders and instructions.

Quality of work life. The idea that work must—in addition to being productive in a material way—be rewarding in a psychological or spiritual way to the person who performs it.

Work. That task, job, or employment in which a person applies mental or physical skills in order to earn a livelihood.

READING COMPREHENSION

1. Who might be more concerned with general economic conditions: a supervisor or a company president? With an employee's request for a less boring assignment? Why?

2. What factors distinguish a supervisor's work environment from that of a higher-level manager? Also, explain the difference in their time horizons.

3. List the four characteristics of a bureaucracy identified by Weber. Which is presumed to be the most threatening to most employees, and why?

4. Contrast the work or job you have done for pay with a task you have done on a voluntary basis. Into which did you put more physical or mental effort?

5. Think of persons you consider to be happy in their work. Describe one such person, the kind of work performed, and the kind of supervision provided.
6. Yankelovich says that only one person out of five does his or her very best on a job. Why don't others do their best too?
7. What's wrong with proposing a new, and difficult, task to an employee when that employee is suffering from an "off day"?
8. Ralph has been asked to perform a particularly nasty job. Surprisingly, he accepts it without hesitation, and he does it well. Ted, when given the same assignment, tries to duck it. When forced to accept it, Ted botches the job. What factors might explain the differing responses to this assignment?
9. Have you ever had a job that was easy but dull? What could you have done to make it more interesting?
10. Explain the difference between a supervisor who facilitates the work and one who directs it.

APPLICATION

SELF-APPRAISAL

How satisfied are you with your present (or previous) job?

Consider the job (large or small, full-time or part-time) that you hold right now. If you do not hold a job now, think of one that you have held recently. On a separate piece of paper, copy the column headings shown below. Next write the numbers 1 to 20 down the page to correspond to each of the statements that follow. Then read each statement. Place a check mark in the column that most nearly matches your feeling about each statement. After completing this activity, check your answers using the scoring procedure that described on page 41.

Column headings:

Agree	Disagree	Neither Agree nor Disagree

1. My pay is fair, if not extravagant.
2. There is little more that I can learn on this job.
3. The people I work with respect my contribution.
4. My boss hardly knows that I'm alive.
5. I frequently find my mind wandering while I'm working.

6. Our department is one of the best in the organization.
7. My job requires that I use many of my skills.
8. Nobody at work has a very professional attitude.
9. The tools I'm given to work with are first-rate.
10. Some days, I just can't force myself to get out of bed.
11. This job may lead to something worthwhile.
12. I put a lot of myself into my work.
13. When my work is criticized, it is done in a tactful manner.
14. I like to tell people what company I work for.
15. I feel that I am kept pretty well informed.
16. My suggestions and complaints are listened to.
17. The output expected of me is unreasonable.
18. Promotions are from within and are made on merit.
19. I believe that what I do is worthwhile.
20. This work isn't really what I've been trained to do.

Scoring Give yourself 1 point for each of the following statements that you *agreed* with: 1, 3, 6, 7, 9, 11, 12, 13, 14, 15, 16, 18, 19. Give yourself 1 point for each of the following statements that you *disagreed* with: 2, 4, 5, 8, 10, 17, 20. There are no points for statements with which you neither agreed nor disagreed.

Interpretation If you scored between 16 and 20 points, you are reasonably satisfied with the job you have (or had). If you scored between 10 and 15 points, either you or your boss hasn't found ways to make your job truly satisfying. Both of you will have to strive to improve the quality of your work life. If you scored less than 10 points, you've got the wrong job or the wrong boss or you have chosen the wrong occupation or the wrong industry.

CASE STUDIES

CASE 5   Mildred and the Mickey Mouse Job

Two employees of the Zebra Hosiery Mills were waiting outside the plant for transportation home on a cold, wet afternoon. Mildred, a 30-year-old loom operator, said, "One more day like this and it's bye-bye Zebra for me."

"What's the problem?" asked Leon, her co-worker.

"This job is boring me to death," said Mildred. "It's a Mickey Mouse all day long. I work my fingers raw racking up those yarn spools. Two hours straight before the break. Then lunch. Then the afternoon break. That's the same routine four times a day. I handle over 800 spools. Toward the end of each period I can hardly wait until I count the two hundredth spool."

"Wow," said Leon. "I never thought of it that way. It just strikes me that it's an easy way to make $60 a day."

"Easy, nothing," said Mildred. "I could show them how to make it easier. All we'd need is some gizmo to let me rack up two spools at a time. But that pumpkin head I work for hasn't listened to a new idea in thirty years."

"That could be," said Leon. "But I'm satisfied as long as the supervisor stays off my back. I just don't like to be hassled."

"If she were to hassle you, you'd know you were something besides a machine," said Mildred. "If there were some place closer to home, I'd walk out on Zebra tomorrow."

"I could get a job nearer to my home," said Leon, "but I'd only make $50 a day. The extra $10 is worth fifteen minutes longer on the bus."

"Not for me," said Mildred. "I've got kids to feed when I get home. I don't want them out on the streets longer than they have to be. I'd take a cut if my job was next door to where I lived."

At this point Leon's bus arrived. "See you tomorrow—if you don't decide to quit," he said as he climbed aboard.

"Fat chance," said Mildred to herself. "What other choices do I really have?"

If you were Mildred's supervisor, which of the following actions would you consider to be the most effective in handling Mildred's dissatisfaction with her job? On a separate piece of paper, rank the alternatives on a scale from 1 (most preferable) to 5 (least preferable). You may add another alternative if you wish. In any event, be prepared to justify your ranking.

a. Demonstrate to Mildred that she is well paid for the work she does compared with the rates for other work in the mill.
b. Ask what Mildred would do to make her job more interesting. Then try to incorporate her suggestions.
c. Change the job so that Mildred would rotate assignments with a co-worker doing related work in the same department.
d. Ignore Mildred's complaints, since your attention may lead her to expect more than you can deliver.
e. Suggest that, if Mildred is so unhappy, she look for another job elsewhere.

Instructions for Cases 6 and 7: For each of the following situations, choose the course of action you think is most suitable. Circle the action you like best, and explain the reasons for your choice.

CASE 6 Hot Job, High Turnover

After Eileen H. was graduated from high school in June, she spent most of the summer hanging around the public swimming pool during the day and with the gang in the shopping mall parking lot at night. By fall, however, her parents insisted that she find a job. The best she could get was a second-shift job as a lay-up operator at the local fiberglass boat factory. The work was difficult and disagreeable. The plant was hot, and the fumes from the plastic solvents were irritating. The pay was just above the minimum wage standard. The only thing really good about the job was her supervisor, Ray J. He was regarded by the boat plant workers as a "good guy." Ray was troubled, however, by the number of young people like Eileen who stayed on the job only a month or two before quitting.

To reduce the chance of Eileen's leaving, Ray J. should:

a. Make the work easier for Eileen.
b. Ask her for ideas about how to make the work more pleasant.
c. Emphasize the value her job adds to the final product.
d. Try to get her a 15-cent-an-hour raise.

CASE 7 The Reluctant Repairperson

"Chico may know his gearboxes," said Alpha, a maintenance mechanic in the Travelnow Mobile Home Factory, "but I sure wish he'd stay off my back. I admit that I make mistakes, but it is not because I'm not trying to learn."

Chico, the supervisor, had different ideas about the trouble with Alpha. In his opinion, Alpha spent too much time talking instead of working. When Alpha was sent to repair a machine in a remote corner of the plant, you could be sure that the job would take twice as long as it would if he were under Chico's watchful eye in the maintenance shop.

Today Alpha was called to unscramble a faulty gearbox on one of the big presses that shape the mobile-home roofs. He was struggling as hard as he could but not making much headway. The press operators were standing around idle, waiting for the job to be finished. After a while, the press supervisor impatiently called Chico on the phone. "Will you get someone working on this press who knows what he is doing?" asked the press supervisor. In order to establish better working relationships with his crew, Chico should:

a. Call Alpha off the job and put another mechanic on it.
b. Go out to the press himself and give Alpha a hand.
c. Let Alpha finish the job alone, regardless of how long it takes.
d. Send out another mechanic to show Alpha how to make the repair.

1 Supervisors apply proven principles to the management process.

2 The management process requires five kinds of managerial work.

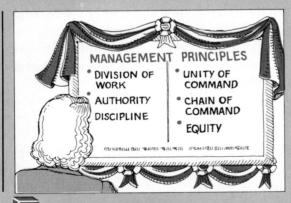

3 Management principles provide guidelines for supervisory action.

4 Three approaches to management practice have evolved.

5 Supervisory action is dependent upon situational awareness.

CHAPTER 3

Supervision and the Management Process

LEARNING OBJECTIVES

After studying this chapter, you should be able to

1. Identify the three most useful sources of generally accepted managerial expertise.

2. List the five functions of the management process and discuss how they involve a supervisor.

3. Given any of Fayol's management principles, explain its application.

4. Name the three approaches to management practice and discuss the particular suitability of each.

5. Explain the value of contingency management in handling situations that occur in an organizational system.

1 A BODY OF KNOWLEDGE FROM WHICH TO DRAW

CONCEPT   Supervisors become active in the management process by applying established management principles and practices to operating problems.

What does it really take for a supervisor to become a manager?

Thinking and acting like one. Management is characterized by a professional—or disciplined—approach to the work environment. Individuals who move into supervision begin to think in a systematic way. They approach their work positively, rather than passively. They accept the responsibility of making things happen for the better in an organization. They shift their roles from those that entail following orders to roles that require solving problems and making decisions. They become increasingly aware of their involvement in a complex system of organizational activities. And they act accordingly.

Where can this be learned?

Newly appointed supervisors are not left alone without guidance. Fortunately, they have a vast background of management evolution to draw upon. First of all, supervisors can begin their new assignments by immersing themselves in the five responsibilities outlined for them in the management process. They can look next for guidance to a set of 11 basic management principles. Then they can select an approach from any of three "schools" (or theories) of management practice. Over a period of time, supervisors finally acquire a sense of the many factors at play in their spheres of influence. And from this sensitivity, they develop an invaluable flexibility. This enables them to do the right things at the right times, on the basis of the peculiarities of each situation they face.

2 THE MANAGEMENT PROCESS

CONCEPT   The management process differentiates the work of managers from that of all others in an organization.

Why is there so much emphasis placed upon the management process?

There are two reasons. First, the process serves to differentiate the work of managers from the work of nonmanagers. Second, the management process provides an underpinning for the practice of management and its various approaches.

The five functions of the management process were shown in Figure 1-6 of Chapter 1 in order to illustrate the interdependence of all levels of managers within an organization. The five functions are shown again here in Figure 3-1. This time the figure illustrates the orderly sequence in which the functions are performed.

Why is it called a process?

It is called a process because it moves progressively from one stage to another in a fairly consistent sequence. In a production shop, for example, a supervisor first plans the daily schedule, then organizes the resources by assigning people to their workstations, then activates the process by giving orders and instructions, and, finally, controls, or checks up on, results. In a typical office a similar management process takes place as supervisors plan the workday, organize the work and the clerical force, activate by communicating and motivating, and control by seeing that paperwork procedures are followed properly.

This process is carried on over and over again, day by day, month by month, and year by year. For this reason many people refer to it as the *management cycle*.

How do the five management functions involve a supervisor?

These five functions are carried out, to a greater or lesser degree, by supervisors, by middle managers, and by top executives. From a supervisor's standpoint, each function has a particular significance:

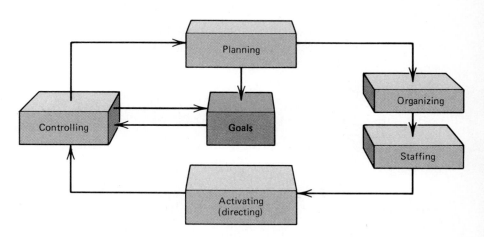

Figure 3-1 Functions in the management process.

Planning. This is the function of setting goals and objectives and converting them into specific plans. For a supervisor, the outcomes of planning will include operating schedules, quality specifications, expense budgets, timetables, and deadlines. The planning process also establishes policies, standard operating procedures, regulations, and rules.

Organizing. In performing this function, a supervisor lines up all available resources. This includes departmental tools, equipment, and materials and—especially—the work force. It is at this stage that the organizational structure of a department is designed and its work divided up into jobs.

Staffing. This is the function whereby supervisors figuratively put flesh on the organizational structure. Supervisors first figure out exactly how many employees a department will need to carry out its work. They then interview, select, and train those people who appear to be most suitable to fill the open jobs.

Activating. This function gets the blood flowing in an organization. Supervisors energize the vital human resources of their department by providing motivation, communication, and leadership.

Controlling. Once departmental plans are set in motion, supervisors must periodically keep score on how well the plans are working out. To do so, supervisors measure results, compare them with what was expected, judge how important the differences may be, and then take whatever action is needed to bring results into line. Controlling is closely linked to planning (as Figure 3-1 shows), since control actions are guided by the goals established during the planning process.

In theory, supervisors perform the five functions of the management process in the order listed above. In practice, however, supervisors perform all the management functions in one way or another each time corrective action is in order. They may find themselves shortcutting the management process sequence or turning back on it, inasmuch as each problem situation is unique and calls for its own solution.

This process must have an objective, mustn't it?

Yes, of course. The purpose of the management process is to convert the resources available to a supervisor's department into a useful end result. Said another way, a supervisor is in charge of seeing that inputs are transformed into outputs in his or her department, as illustrated in Figure 3-2. This end result, or output, is either a product or a service.

A *product* might be a pair of shoes, a loaf of bread, a bicycle, or steel strings for a guitar. Your product may be partially complete, so that it

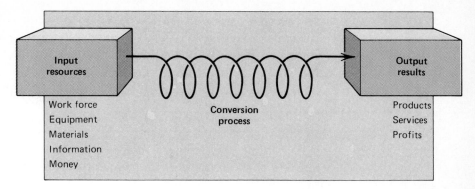

Figure 3-2 Supervisors, and other managers, are responsible for converting an organization's resources into useful results.

becomes the material resource for the next department in your factory. Or it may become the raw material for use in another manufacturing plant. Or it may be ready, like a pair of shoes, to be sold directly to a consumer without further work performed on it.

A *service* may be the provision of accounting information for a production department, the inspection of a product as it is being made, or the creation of a schedule for others to follow. A service may be provided directly for a consumer, as in supplying an insurance policy or handling cash and checks for a bank customer. It may be maintaining machinery in a plant or washing windows in a shopping center.

Whether the end point is a product or a service, the management process is expected to make sure that the result is at least as valuable as the combined cost of the initial resources and the expense of operating the process. In a business enterprise a *profit* is made when the end result can be sold at a price that is higher than the cost of providing it. If the reverse is true, the business assumes a *loss*.

3 MANAGEMENT PRINCIPLES

CONCEPT   Management principles provide basic guidelines for supervisory decisions and actions.

How do management principles relate to the management process?

They stem from the same source—Henri Fayol, an especially effective chief executive of a French mining company. Fayol was the first person to conceive of management as a separate "process of administration," consisting of several distinct functions and based upon certain "principles." Fayol's writings (in 1916) led to the generally accepted notion of the management process. His management principles (stated in those writings) are acknowledged as universally applicable guidelines for carrying out the management process.

Exactly what are the principles of management?

They consist of a number of practical guidelines, held by many authorities to contain the "essence of management." Here, arbitrarily numbered, are those principles that appear to have the greatest value for today's supervisors:

1. Work should be divided so that each person will perform a specialized portion. In making a sailboat, for instance, one person will lay up the hull, another caulk, and another make sails. In running an office, one person will enter orders, another type letters, and another file correspondence. Fayol called these ideas *division of work* and specialization.

2. Managers must have the right (authority) to give orders and instructions, but they must also accept responsibility for whether or not the work is done right. A supervisor needs the right to ask a work crew to load a freight car, for example, but if the car is loaded improperly, the supervisor must accept the blame.

3. Managers are responsible for extracting *discipline* and building morale among members of their work force, but they must also be true to their word in return. Said another way, if you want loyalty and cooperation from employees, you must be loyal and cooperative in return.

4. An individual should have only one boss. Fayol called this *unity of command*. Experience bears this out: if an employee reports to more than one superior, confusion and conflict result.

5. Every organization should have only one master plan, one set of overriding goals. Such *unity of direction* is lost if the purchasing department, for example, slows down the production department's output by buying materials from a less costly but undependable supplier when the company's overall commitment is to ship orders on time.

6. Similar to the principle of unity of direction is Fayol's insistence that all individuals, especially managers, must place their interests second to those of the total organization. If persons in authority went their own way, Fayol reasoned, all others in the organization would suffer as a result.

7. Pay and rewards (remuneration) should reflect each person's efforts and, more important, each person's contribution to the orga-

nization's goal. It was a novel idea in Fayol's time that each employee should be paid according to individual worth rather than at the whim of a manager who might be inclined to play favorites.

8. Orders and instructions should flow down a *chain of command* from the higher manager to the lower one. Fayol also said that formal communications and complaints should move upward in the same channel. In practice, however, it has proved to be a good idea to permit and encourage the exchange of work information sideways between departments (or commands) as well. The real trouble seems to occur when a manager bypasses a supervisor with instructions to an employee or when an employee goes over a supervisor's head to register a complaint.

9. Materials should be in their proper place. Fayol extolled the virtue of all kinds of order; he believed that routine procedures minimized effort and waste.

10. Employees should be treated equally and fairly. Fayol called this *equity*. It invites dissatisfaction and conflict among employees, for example, when a supervisor gives one employee a break while picking on another.

11. Managers should encourage initiative among employees. Fayol advised: "It is essential to encourage this capacity to the full....The manager must be able to sacrifice some personal vanity in order to grant this sort of satisfaction to subordinates. Other things being equal, a manager able to permit the exercise of *initiative* on the part of subordinates is infinitely superior to one who cannot do so."

4 *MANAGEMENT APPROACHES (OR SCHOOLS)*

CONCEPT   Three approaches to management practice have evolved, each with its particular suitability.

To what extent can supervisors develop their own approaches to handling their operational situations?

They have a great deal of leeway. Three managerial approaches, however, have evolved over the past century. These approaches to management practice are sometimes called "schools" or theories. Each has its special usefulness.

1. **Systematic management approach.**   This is known by other names, too, such as scientific, classic, traditional, process, functional, or rational. All names imply a systematic approach that relies on mea-

surement and analysis of the various tasks and activities that take place at work.

2. **Human relations approach.**   This is also known as the behavioral school, because it is based on the thought that a manager who understands human behavior well enough is able to get employees to willingly cooperate with, and produce toward, company goals.

3. **Quantitative approach.**   This approach emphasizes the use of numbers and relies on the sciences of mathematics and statistics. It is also known as the management sciences or systems theory of management.

Some authorities add still another concept: the *systems approach.* This is an outgrowth of the quantitative approach, and it makes much of the fact that all the elements and resources of an organization are parts of an interlocking system. Thus a manager cannot take action regarding one element without that action's having an effect upon one or more other elements in the organization.

Many latter-day students of management take the systems approach one step further. They insist that each organizational situation be studied carefully and approached as a uniquely different problem. Sometimes, they say, the scientific or systematic approach will be best. Other times, the human relations approach will get the best results. Still other times the quantitative approach should be chosen. As a consequence, this view has been labeled the *situational,* or *contingency, approach,* in that what a manager should do depends (is contingent) upon the particular situation at hand.

A summary of the management approaches is presented in Table 3-1.

When does the systematic management approach work best?

A systematic approach is almost always a good way to attack any problem. It requires that you gather facts first. What has really happened to the agitator tank? When did it happen? Who was operating it? Were reasonable production rates set for its operation? How close has actual output been to what was expected?

It emphasizes the value of accurate measurements. How much? How big? How long? How many?

It presumes that most activities are best performed according to a set path. Are the procedures carefully spelled out? Were they followed?

The problem with the systematic approach is that it too often expects that organizations will operate perfectly or that people will function like machines. Its founder, Frederick W. Taylor, was an engineer who hoped that human beings could be motivated by wage incentives to imitate machines. Later advocates of scientific management were also

Table 3-1 DIFFERENT APPROACHES TO MANAGEMENT PRACTICES

Approach	Emphasizes Productivity as a Result of the Following	Impact on Supervision
Systematic Management Also known as scientific, classic, traditional, rational, process, or functional management	Systematic process, management principles, measurement and standards, and firm direction and control	Greater reliance on established company policies and procedures and on prescribed relationships in formal work groups
Human Relations Management Also known as behavioral or organizational behavior management	Individual or group motivation stimulated by management's concern for people and their relationships	Greater reliance on participatory techniques and upon individuals and groups to solve operational problems
Quantitative Management Also known as management sciences or systems theory of management	Use of advanced mathematical and statistical methods as well as theories about how information and other resources interact in an organization system	Greater reliance on staff-directed and/or automatic programs to prescribe operating procedures and to signal for control actions
Contingency Management Also known as situational management	Belief that supervisors and other managers must choose one or more of the three basic approaches to fit the conditions that prevail in a particular situation	Greater need for sensitivity to the demands of different situations along with the skills and flexibility to apply different management approaches selectively

engineers—Henry L. Gantt, who conceived the production control chart, and Frank B. Gilbreth, who perfected the art of motion study of workers. Other proponents were mainly business people. Harrington Emerson, one notable contributor, believed that efficiency would result from better organizational arrangements and elimination of waste—human as well as material.

At what times should human relations management be used?

There is rarely a time when it shouldn't be considered. The stickiest problems in business or elsewhere involve human beings. Supervisors need to know all they can about why people act the way they do. Exaggerated human conflict can be very wasteful. Use of what we know about the psychology and the sociology of human behavior can minimize this conflict. A large platoon of authorities, beginning with Elton Mayo and extending to Burleigh Gardner, has demonstrated the controlling influence that human relations can have in any organization. Mayo, in his famous experiment at the Hawthorne Works of the Western Electric Company in the 1930s, indisputably demonstrated that the performance of workers is more nearly related to psychological and social factors than to the physical makeup of the workplace. In 1945 Gardner wrote a basic text summarizing many research studies. Optimism for this approach was highest in the 1950s, when it was thought that a cookbook of methods could be given to supervisors. The idea was that if you follow the right directions and prescriptions, people will act the way you want them to. Alas, the real world never came up to this promise.

Recent investigations by such authorities as Herbert Simon and Chris Argyris strongly suggest that supervisors should use great caution in applying human relations theory. Their watchwords would appear to be *go slowly*. Clear up technical problems first. Let people try to solve their own problems. Don't oversimplify management tasks. They are all complex because so many factors—materials, machinery, instructions, time pressures, conflicting objectives, hidden relationships—can influence the outcome of a supervisor's actions.

Where will the quantitative approach be most effective?

Where people problems are fewest and process factors are greatest. The quantitative method is a numbers approach. It helps in setting up production and maintenance schedules, in controlling quality statistically, in mapping out shipping routes, and in setting work loads for bank tellers and airline ticket clerks. Quantitative methods have been applied successfully to just about any operational problem where employees' interests and motivations are not controlling factors. Without any doubt, management sciences techniques should be in every supervisor's tool kit. More often than not, of course, supervisors will need the help of industrial engineers, statisticians, or systems analysts to put these techniques to work. On the other hand, these specialists will need a supervisor's keen eye to spot potential applications.

What's all the talk about the Japanese management approach?

It has to do mainly with the Japanese practice in which managers seek a consensus of agreement from the employees and other managers in their organization before moving ahead in a new direction. This leads to mutual goal setting at lower, as well as higher, levels. Once a consensus is reached, employees feel committed to goals and plans. As a consequence, they tend to work together with greater unity and initiative and to require fewer controls and less supervision. The underlying concept, of course, is similar to that of the participation (sharing of responsibilities and goal setting) urged by advocates of the human relations approach to management.

5 SYSTEMS AND SITUATIONS

CONCEPT   Supervisors develop system and situational awareness in adapting theory to practice.

Systematic? System? Both have been mentioned as important. What is the distinction between them?

To be systematic is to be methodical and orderly. As Fayol observed, supervisors must be systematic in carrying out their responsibilities.

A system, however, is an interrelated set of elements functioning as a whole. Each element (or part) is dependent upon others in the system: a change in one part will affect the functioning of the other parts. The human body is an example of a system; so is a clock or an automobile engine.

An organization (a private company, nonprofit institution, or public agency) functions as a system. Within a system there may be many smaller systems that interact among themselves and with the larger system. In a company that makes women's sportswear, for example, the design, fabricating, shipping, and sales departments (1) may each function as individual systems, although (2) they influence—and are influenced by—each other. A supervisor, therefore, not only must manage his or her departmental system but also must see that the department interacts productively with the other departments within the company system.

A contingency approach was mentioned earlier. What is its significance for supervision?

It adds realism—and safety—to the supervisor's job. The contingency approach (sometimes called the situational or operational approach) implies that a supervisor must be ready to employ one or all three of the management approaches. What is used depends on—is contingent on—the particulars in the operation or situation. If you are starting a new project or revising an old one, the scientific, or systematic, approach makes sense. If you are enmeshed in a situation (such as a radical change in procedures) where people's reactions are unusually sensitive, a concern for human relations should prevail. If your employees are looking for a solution to a difficult or recurring operational or process problem, the quantitative approach might get first call. Rarely, however, can you rely entirely on a single approach. Instead, there should be a balance in the application of management approaches. In general, choose the approach that fits your personality and talents best, but do not rely on it exclusively. Always, or almost always, double-check your results to see if you should apply a second or a third approach to the problem. Above all, try to keep Fayol's management principles in mind.

REVIEW

KEY CONCEPTS TO REMEMBER

1. Supervisors are expected to act in a disciplined, or professional, way. They act rationally and think positively. Their manner is characterized by problem solving rather than fault finding. They draw from a vast body of accumulated knowledge concerning the management process, Fayol's management principles, and three basic approaches to management practice—systematic management, human relations management, and quantitative management.
2. Managerial work is different from nonmanagerial work in that managers, including supervisors, devote most of their time and energy to planning, organizing, staffing, activating, and controlling. These functions require that supervisors become problem solvers and decision makers.
3. Fayol's management principles provide guidelines for handling most management situations. They are general in nature, however, and subject to interpretation and judgment in their application. Among the most important principles are division of work, managerial right to authority, unity of command, unity of direction, subordination of interest to the organization, chain of command, and equity.
4. Effective managers apply any or all of the three approaches to management practice that have evolved over the last century. These are systematic (traditional, scientific, or classic) management, human relations (behavioral) management, and quantitative (management sciences or systems) management.
5. Most problems that face supervisors are complex and are influenced by many factors that are present in an organizational system. Thus

the management approach selected or emphasized should depend upon an analysis of each particular situation. This concept of matching the management approach to the situation is called contingency (or situational) management.

SUPERVISORY WORD POWER

Chain of command. The formal channels in an organization that distribute authority from top to bottom.

Contingency management. The selection and use of the management approach (or combination of approaches) that is most appropriate for a particular problem or situation.

Division of work. The principle that performance is more efficient when a large job is broken down into smaller, specialized jobs.

Human relations management. A management approach that seeks to stimulate cooperation on the basis of an understanding of, and genuine concern for, employees as individuals and as members of a work group.

Management principles. A set of guidelines established by Henri Fayol for carrying out the management process.

Management process. The major managerial functions of planning, organizing, staffing, activating, and controlling carried out by all managers in a repetitive sequence or cycle.

Quantitative management. A management sciences (or systems) approach to management that emphasizes the use of advanced mathematics and statistics and the application of information and systems theory.

System. An interrelated set of elements functioning as a whole.

Systematic management. The traditional approach to management that emphasizes the functions performed in the management process as well as systematic measurement and analysis of the various tasks and activities of the workplace.

Unity of direction. The principle that there should be a single set of goals and objectives that unifies the activities of everyone in an organization.

Unity of command. The principle that each individual should report to only one boss.

READING COMPREHENSION

1. Supervisors are advised to have a disciplined approach to their managerial responsibilities. What does that mean?

2. Name three basic sources that help to guide supervisors in their roles as managers.
3. Give a specific example of an activity that might be included in each of the five functions of the management process.
4. What is the purpose, or objective, of the management process?
5. Why did Henri Fayol advise that an organization should have unity of direction?
6. In light of modern experience, should communications be rigidly confined to an up-and-down direction of the chain of command?
7. Why can't a supervisor rely exclusively on the systematic management approach?
8. Name some applications for which the quantitative approach has been found successful. What do these applications have in common?
9. Explain why the human body, an auto engine, and a football team can be described as systems?
10. What is the basic message of the contingency view of management?

▥ APPLICATION

SELF-APPRAISAL

What's your management IQ?

Each of the following items is identified with either the systematic, human relations, or quantitative approach (or school) of management. Your assignment is to match the item to the management approach, or school, with which it is identified. On a separate piece of paper, copy the column headings shown below. Next write the numbers 1 to 20 down the page to correspond to each of the items that follow. Read each item carefully. Then place a check mark in the column that denotes the management approach with which each item is identified. After completing this activity, check your answers using the scoring procedure described on page 59.

Column headings:

	Management Approach	
Systematic	Human Relations	Quantitative

1. Also known as scientific management.

2. Also known as management sciences.
3. Greater reliance on participatory techniques.
4. Emphasis on work measurement.
5. Firm direction and control.
6. Also known as behavioral management.
7. Greater reliance on staff specialists.
8. Key contributors: Taylor, Gilbreth, Gantt.
9. Useful in balancing work loads.
10. Motivation with wage incentives.
11. The Hawthorne experiment.
12. Psychological and sociological methods.
13. Selection of transportation routes.
14. Key contributors: Mayo, Gardner, Argyris.
15. Statistical quality control.
16. Reliance on systems theory.
17. Emphasis on management principles.
18. Concern for group motivation and relationships.
19. Also known as traditional management.
20. Caution advised in applying human relations theory.

Scoring Give yourself 1 point for each correct answer. Items 1, 4, 5, 8, 10, 17, and 19 are identified with the systematic approach. Items 3, 6, 11, 12, 14, 18, and 20 characterize the human relations approach. Items 2, 7, 9, 13, 15, and 16 are associated with the quantitative approach.

Interpretation If you scored between 16 and 20 points, you have a *high* management IQ. That is, you distinguish very well between the three approaches to management practice. If you scored between 10 and 15 points, you have a *mediocre* management IQ. Review pages 51 to 55 and Table 3-1 to find your errors. If you scored less than 10 points, you have a *poor* management IQ. Reread and carefully study pages 51 to 55 and Table 3-1.

CASE STUDIES

CASE 8   The Automated Insurance Office

George's trouble began when the work of his recording clerks was switched from a paperwork system to an automated one. George was supervisor of the fire-damage claims department of the Alpha Insurance Company. For years, his recording clerks had been judged as very efficient in "moving paper" through the department. Nevertheless, a companywide change in data processing had radically altered the jobs of the recording clerks. Instead of typing and collating multileafed forms in several operations, the clerks now accomplished the same thing by making one simple entry at computer terminals. Or at least that was the way it was supposed to happen.

In fact, the recording clerks seemed to have developed an uncanny knack for uncovering every flaw in the system. As a consequence, records would be unaccountably "lost" in the computer network. Or they would be "unintentionally" merged with others. Or the printers would inexplicably malfunction.

Of course, all this put George on the spot with his superiors. "Why is it," asked George's boss, "that the automated records system is working well in every other department of the company, but not in yours?" George did not have a ready answer, but he vowed to find out—and to correct the situation as soon as possible.

If you were George, which of the following actions would you consider to be the most effective in correcting this situation? On a separate piece of paper, rank the alternatives on a scale from 1 (most preferable) to 5 (least preferable). You may add another alternative if you wish. In any event, be prepared to justify your ranking.

a. Meet with the records clerks to find out from them the specific nature of their difficulty with the new system and to elicit their suggestions on what can be done to resolve the problems.
b. Ask the company's computer programmer to redesign the data processing system for the claims office so that it is foolproof.
c. Monitor the recording operation yourself to demonstrate to the records clerks that their output is falling far short of what is possible under the new system.
d. Meet with the records clerks to emphasize that the automated system is working very well elsewhere and that the fault must lie with their work rather than the programming.
e. Ask the company's computer programmer to meet with the records clerks to demonstrate the proper operation of the automated system.

CASE 9   Eight Little Dandies

The actions taken by supervisors and others in the situations described below either follow or violate a number of the management principles set down by Henri Fayol. Your assignment is to select from the list of Fayol's principles below the ones that most nearly match the behavior in the situations described. On a separate piece of paper, write the numbers 1 to 8 down the page to correspond to each of the situations to be evaluated. If the principle set down by Fayol has been followed, write the appropriate letter after the situation's number on your list. If the principle *has not been* followed, write the appropriate letter after the situation's number on your list.

Situations to Be Evaluated

1. The RPQ Company has a primary objective of making and selling goods of only the highest quality. John B. tells his crew that, in his department, it is output that counts most.
2. Tom T. knows his plant superintendent personally, for they both live in the same housing development. When Tom has a problem, he often bypasses his own superior to get an answer directly from the plant superintendent.
3. At the Vroom Muffler factory, Lyle L. has carefully assigned duties and responsibilities to each of his section chiefs. However, he withholds from them the authority needed to get other employees to listen to their instructions.
4. In laying out work for her hospital food service crew, Norma N. tries to have each employee perform a special kind of work.
5. Shippers at Kiwi Kola Bottling get instructions about delivery schedules from the plant manager and instructions about which customers to service first from the sales manager.
6. Zelda B., data processing supervisor for an insurance company, encourages her keypunch and word processing operators to develop improved methods for handling their work.
7. At the Okay Machine Shop, Matt, the maintenance supervisor, gives many of the choice assignments to a mechanic he plays poker with. Another mechanic, with whom Matt has had quarrels, gets more than her share of the dirty work.

Management Principles

a. Equity
b. Chain of command
c. Initiative
d. Authority and responsibility
e. Unity of command
f. Unity of direction
g. Division of work

PART

2

Planning and Control

1 Supervisory planning sets goals and provides road maps.

2 Goals shape targets for supervisory plans and actions.

3 Planning should be systematic; plans should be flexible.

4 Scheduling brings planning down to the shop floor.

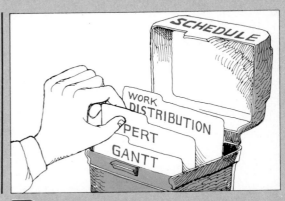

5 There are many techniques for planning and scheduling.

6 Policies provide guidelines for the entire organization.

4

Making Plans and Carrying Out Policy

LEARNING OBJECTIVES

After studying this chapter, you should be able to

1. Differentiate among the various terms associated with the planning process.

2. Create a representative set of objectives for a department supervisor.

3. Explain the planning process and the differences between long- and short-range plans and between standing and single-use plans.

4. Discuss various guidelines for developing efficient departmental schedules.

5. Identify and explain the applications of the Gantt chart, the PERT chart, and the work distribution chart.

6. Discuss a supervisor's responsibilities for interpreting and implementing a company's policies.

◨ ROAD MAPS OF AN ORGANIZATION

CONCEPT   Planning sets the goals and provides the road map for almost all a supervisor's actions.

Don't most organizations have planning specialists? Why should this chore be added to a supervisor's work load?

Most large organizations *do* employ planning and scheduling specialists. These specialists, however, prepare the master, or overall plans. In almost all instances, supervisors must custom-fit the master plan to their own units. It will also be supervisors, rather than specialists, who make the day-to-day assignments and adjustments that are needed to make a master plan effective.

Unless supervisors accept their share of this managerial responsibility, they will waste (1) time—because of avoidable delays; (2) materials and supplies—because of unwarranted haste, spoilage, or unnecessary accumulation of inventories; (3) machinery—because of operation below its optimum capacity; (4) space—because of overcrowding and poor coordination of incoming supplies and outgoing production; and (5) human resources—because of underutilization or improper assignments.

How far ahead should supervisors plan their work?

Long-range planning should be handled largely by those in higher levels of management. Your target is necessarily much closer at hand. American Management Association studies show that supervisors spend 38 percent of their thinking time on problems that come up the same day, 40 percent on those one week ahead, 15 percent on those one month ahead, 5 percent on those three to six months ahead, and 2 percent on those one year ahead.

Check your own habits. If you feel you're too busy to worry about anything but today, chances are you spend most of your time fighting fires that can be avoided by planning a week to a month ahead of time.

Typically, a supervisor is responsible for short-range (or tactical) plans and higher executives for long-range (or strategic) plans. In military language, tactical plans are those concerned with a particular engagement or skirmish or battle; strategic plans are those on which the major battle or entire war is based.

Plans, planning, policies, goals: What is the difference?

If ever there was an area of management where the terms were mixed up, this is it. *Plans* are what come out of the *planning* process. Plans, or programs, are what you intend to do in the future. Before you can develop plans, however, you must set targets. These targets are called *goals, standards,* or *objectives.* After you have set these goals (that is the simplest term to use), you establish general guidelines for reaching them. These guidelines are called *policies.* Policies are, in effect, master plans that have been derived from organizational objectives. Only after policies have been set should the specific, operational plans be formulated. Operational plans will include (1) **schedules,** which dictate what must be done as well as establish starting and finishing times, and (2) **procedures,** which prescribe the exact methods to be used and sequence to be followed in carrying out a plan.

Finally, you may choose to lay down some **rules** and **regulations.** These will establish the limits (or controls) within which employees are free to do the job their own way.

Take this example. You are thinking ahead—planning—about what your department will do during the annual spring cleaning. You make a list of things that you want to accomplish: filing cabinets cleared of all obsolete material, shelving cleaned and rearranged, tools repaired and in tip-top shape. These are your goals. Next you establish some sort of policy. For example, cleaning will be done during normal working hours without overtime; discarding obsolete papers will conform to legal requirements; repairing tools may be done by your own maintenance department or by an outside machine shop. Then you lay out your own operational plan—schedule and/or procedures—of how the housekeeping will be done, when, and by whom. Finally, you set down some firm rules or regulations for your work crew: Only file clerks will make judgments about what paperwork will be discarded; before tools are sent outside for repair, employees must check with you; employees who clean shelving must wear protective gloves. Figure 4-1 illustrates common relationships among these terms.

▣ GOAL SETTING

CONCEPT A supervisor's goals shape the targets toward which all of his or her plans and actions should be directed.

Why must goals come before plans?

Because plans are the means to an end; goals are ends. Logically, then, you must first decide where it is you want to go and what it is that you want your unit to accomplish. These are, of course, your goals or objectives. You should set them carefully and systematically. This can be done by following these seven steps:

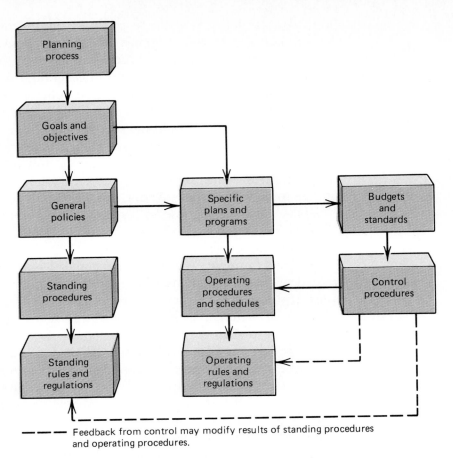

Figure 4-1 Relationships among the various outputs of the planning process.

1. **Consider the goals of the entire organization, not just those of your department.** Think about the needs and wishes of customers—those the company serves as well as those "customers" your department serves internally.
2. **Estimate the strengths and weaknesses of your department.** Ask how they will help or hinder you in trying to meet company goals and in trying to serve external and internal customers.
3. **Don't jump to conclusions at this early stage.** Instead, keep your mind alert to new opportunities—such as ways to improve quality or reduce costs. Don't restrict your thinking to what your goals were last year or how you met them. If you can forecast what may happen to change conditions next year, this will help focus your attention on goals that will be more meaningful in the months to come.

---

4. **Consult with those who will have to help you carry out your plans and with those who can offer you their support along the way.** Employees who are involved in setting goals are more likely to be committed to success in reaching the goals. Staff departments that are consulted in advance may direct your attention to potential pitfalls or to goals that will get the full measure of their support.

5. **Pick a reasonable set of goals.** These should meet two standards. They should (a) contribute to the organization's goals and (b) be attainable by your department, given its strengths and its weaknesses.

6. **Arrange your department's goals in a hierarchy of objectives.** That is, place the most important ones at the top of your list and the least important at the bottom.

7. **Watch out for limitations.** Think about restrictions that may be imposed on you by your company or by the need to coordinate with or serve other departments. Your department cannot operate in a vacuum. It must base its plans on such realistic planning premises.

What kinds of goals are supervisors usually concerned with?

Typically, the goals you set for yourself—or that are set for you, at least partially, as part of a company's overall objectives—are targets to be aimed at in the near future. They pin down your department's output, quality of workmanship, and allowable expenditures. Often, they also include goals in such employee-related areas as departmental attendance, labor turnover, and safety, as shown in Table 4-1. These goals may be stated in terms of tomorrow, next week or next month, or as far ahead as a year. More often than not, the goals are quantitative (expressed as numbers or dollars) rather than merely qualitative (described with such words as *improve, maintain, good,* or *better*).

In many companies and organizations, the manner in which you and your department attain your goals becomes the determining factor in what kind of raise you'll get or how good a job you can be groomed for. This is one big reason why it is so important to lay out a detailed set of plans for meeting your goals.

How can goals be made more compelling?

By making sure that they aren't confused with activity for activity's sake. Professor George Odiorne, author of a dozen books on the setting of objectives, warns that goals should be something to strive for, not just something to do. A few meaningful goals are better than a long "laundry list" to make sure that you look good when reckoning time

Table 4-1	TYPICAL PERFORMANCE GOALS FOR A FIRST-LINE SUPERVISOR	
Area of Measurement	Last Year's Record	Next Year's Goals
1. Ratio of jobs completed on schedule to total jobs worked	85% average, 92% highest, 65% lowest in June	90% average, minimum acceptable 75%
2. Percentage of job costs held within 3% of standard costs	91% average, 95% highest, 75% lowest in June	90% average, bring up low figure to 87% or better
3. Rejects and rework	Less than 1% rejects; rework averages 7%	Keep rejects to less than 1%, but cut rework to 3%
4. Labor stability	Two quits, one discharge	No quits of employees with over three years service
5. Absences, latenesses	5% absences, 7% latenesses	5% absences, 2% latenesses
6. Overtime	Only on jobs okayed by sales department	Only on jobs okayed by sales department
7. Accidents	No lost-time accidents; 37 calls to dispensary for minor ailments	No lost-time accidents; reduce number of dispensary visits to 30 or less

comes around. Accordingly, Odiorne suggests the following key guidelines for making your objectives more effective. A goal should be:

A statement of output. For example, when you are stating a goal, it's all right to say "100 orders will be handled each day," but it is not all right to say, "We will improve productivity." The former is an output; the latter is a hoped-for result of this particular output.

Explicit. That is, goals should be clearly stated in terms, or numbers, that make the output measurable.

Time-oriented. The targeted output must always be related to a time period, such as "10 tons per day," "50 shipments by the end of the month," or "5 percent reduction of absenteeism for the year."

▣ THE PLANNING PROCESS

CONCEPT The planning process should be systematic, yet it should allow for flexibility.

Once goals have been set, how does the planning process proceed?

In six steps. Effective plans flow from clearly stated goals, as illustrated in Table 4-1. These plans, however, depend upon your following a systematic planning process, just as you did when setting goals.

1. **Develop a master plan.**   This should focus on your main objective. If, for example, the company's goal is to have higher-quality products or services, the master plan for your department should give this top priority.
2. **Draw up supporting plans.**   This requires that you think about how each activity in your department can contribute to your master plan. Machinists may need more explicit blueprints. Assemblers may need brighter workplace lighting. Clerks may need a different order-entry procedure.
3. **Put numbers and dates on everything you can.**   Plans work best when employees know how much or how many are required of them. Since plans are for the future—tomorrow, next week, or next month—times and dates are essential.
4. **Pin down assignments.**   Plans are for people. Responsibility for carrying out each part of a plan or procedure should be assigned to a particular individual.
5. **Explain the plan to all concerned.**   Plans should be shared. Their rationales should be explained and their goals justified. Employees who know *why* are more likely to cooperate.
6. **Review your plans regularly.**   Circumstances and restrictions change. Your plans should be examined periodically to see whether they should be changed too.

How flexible must a supervisor's plans be?

They should be stated firmly and clearly so that everyone concerned can understand them. They should not be so rigid, however, that they prevent your making changes to accommodate unexpected circumstances. A good plan should be flexible enough to anticipate—and allow for—an alternate course of action. Suppose, for example, you planned to start a new order or project on Monday, but the necessary materials are not on hand. Your plans should permit postponement of that project and insertion of a productive alternate without delay.

In what way are plans or programs usually classified?

They are usually classified according to their duration and purpose.

Long-range plans are typically set by higher management and are expected to be in operation from one to five years.

Short-range plans are those that supervisors are most concerned with. These are usually based on operations of one year or less. At the department level, short-range plans may be in effect for a day, a week, a month, or a quarter.

Standing plans include just about any activity that goes on without much change from year to year. Standing plans cover general employment practices, health and safety matters, purchasing procedures, routine discipline, and the like.

Single-use plans are used only once before they must be revised. Departmental budgets and operating schedules are examples. They will be good only for a week or a month before new ones are issued.

Generally speaking, then, supervisors will follow short-range, single-use plans for day-to-day operations. But supervisors will also be guided by many standing plans that implement routine, relatively unchanging goals and policies.

What is a good way to double-check your plans and projects?

Try using the five-point planning chart illustrated in Table 4-2.

- **What** spells out objectives in terms of specifications for output, quality, and costs.

Table 4-2	FIVE-POINT PLANNING CHECK CHART	
What	Objectives	Specifications
		Cost/price limits
Where	Locale	Delivery point
When	Time elapsed	Starting date
		Completion date
How	Tactics	Methods Procedure Sequence
	Strategy	
Who	Responsibility	Authority Control Assignment

- *Where* sets the location for the assignment (its workplace) and the place where the product or service must be delivered: the adjoining department, the shipping dock, the home office.
- *When* records your time estimates for the work to be performed and, most important, pins down starting and finishing times and dates.
- *How* verifies short- and long-range methods, procedures, and job sequences.
- *Who* designates the individual responsible for the assignment and specifies that person's authority and extent of control over the resources needed: tools, machinery, additional labor, materials.

How do controls relate to plans?

Controls are like limit switches that keep plans in line. When a plan is moving directly toward its goal, the track is kept clear. The supervisor need apply no control. But when a plan strays from its target, the supervisor must take corrective action to bring it back in line. When planning a department's goals, a supervisor must also plan its control limits, which provide the feedback needed to trigger corrective actions.

4 SCHEDULING GUIDELINES

CONCEPTS   Scheduling brings the planning process right down to the shop floor.

Should you schedule your department to operate at 100 percent capacity?

No. This is a poor practice because it leaves no cushion for emergencies. It's best to call on your past experience and plan only for short periods at 100 percent. No department can run for very long without some unforeseen emergency arising. These emergencies may be only unexpected absences or special rush orders. But you must leave room for them.

What happens if you underschedule your staff?

Exactly what you would expect: employees find a way to stretch the job to fill the time. One way to minimize this is to have a backlog of second-priority jobs on tap for assignment. If regular orders are slow coming in, you can catch up with some of the work that often needs to be done but is not allowed for in the master schedule. These assignments might include cleaning out files in an office, sorting and discarding obsolete inventory in the stockroom, or undertaking any kind of general cleanup.

It should go without saying that if this condition persists, some employees must be transferred or laid off.

Can you expect as much from employees when they work overtime, or should you make an allowance for it in the schedule?

You should probably expect a 5 to 10 percent drop in productivity. Authorities differ on this one, probably because there has been very little definitive research on the subject. Stress and fatigue inevitably take their toll. The more extended the overtime, the greater the drop in output—and probably in the quality of work produced. Our own impression is that a 10 percent figure is reliable for scheduling purposes.

What should supervisors do when they are pressured for faster deliveries or tighter deadlines?

Resist the desire to promise what you can't deliver. Hopes and expectations have no place in planning. Your schedules and promises must be based on fact. Only facts—available equipment and its condition, people and their reliability, material supply and its delivery—can be used as a successful base for planning.

A firm, dependable promise will satisfy most superiors. But don't yield to the temptation to be overcautious. Don't allow for more time than you think the situation actually warrants.

Don't say, for instance, "We can't possibly deliver these parts before the 16th," and then finish the job on the 11th. Others in your plant depend on the accuracy of your forecasts. If everyone allowed too much leeway, that would eat up time and money just as overscheduling might.

Give the best sure date you can figure on. Otherwise, you'll lose friends and respect among your associates and your superiors.

▣ 5 METHODS AND TECHNIQUES

CONCEPTS Supervisors may draw from a wide range of established planning and scheduling techniques.

What is a Gantt chart? How does a supervisor use it?

During World War I Henry Laurence Gantt, an industrial engineer, developed the first production control chart. Its form seems obvious today, since most organizations now use one or another version of it to plan and chart output performance. Its essentials are displayed in Figure 4-2.

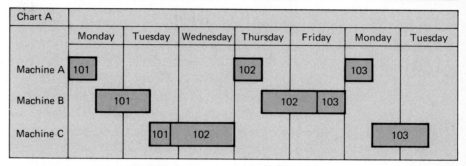

Log of orders for Charts A and B															
Order number	101			102			103			104			105		
Operation sequence	1	2	3	1	2	3	1	2	3	1	2	3	1	2	3
Machine number	A	B	C	C	A	B	B	A	C	A	C	B	B	C	A
Machine time (h)	4	8	2	10	4	6	6	4	8	4	10	12	4	2	6

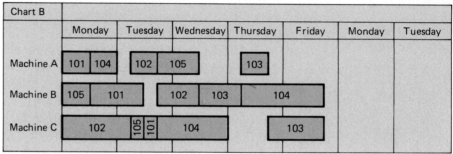

Note: Each day represents 8 hours.

Figure 4-2 Development of a Gantt chart from a series of production orders. Log of orders shows prescribed operation sequence for each job. Chart A shows orders lined up in sequence as they were received. Chart B shows orders rearranged (overlapped) for maximum loading at each machine, with the prescribed sequence of operations for each job maintained. Note the increased utilization of available machine times afforded by the Gantt-chart scheduling.

To understand the unique value of the Gantt chart, put yourself in the place of a supervisor who has just been handed five production orders, stamped serially from 101 to 105. These orders indicate what machines the work must be processed on, the sequence that must be followed, and the estimated number of hours it will take each machine to complete its work.

These orders contain essentially the same kind of information found on a route sheet. The route sheet, however, often includes operations performed in different departments. Thus it is not unusual for the supervisor to collect this information from several route sheets, or the production-control department may issue a number of separate orders to each departmental supervisor.

If the supervisor were to load the machines (they could be benches, workstations, desks, and so on) with the assumption that each order must be finished before another one is begun (straight-line or point-to-point scheduling), the schedule would be something like Chart A in Figure 4-2. The flow of work would be orderly, but the equipment would be extremely underutilized. Worse still, many orders would be delayed. To correct these deficiencies, Gantt overlapped orders and disregarded the sequence in which they were accepted, while still rigidly adhering to the operation sequence each order specifies. Chart B in Figure 4-2 shows how the supervisor can juggle orders, starting order 105 on machine B and order 102 on machine C and at the same time beginning order 101 on machine A. By rearranging and overlapping the jobs, the supervisor can have all five orders finished by Friday afternoon. Furthermore, the supervisor has greatly increased the overall machine utilization. Machine A is now scheduled to be in operation 18 of the first 24 hours of the week (through Wednesday). It works 4 hours on 101 and 4 hours on 104, is idle for 2 hours, then works 4 hours on 102 and 6 hours on 105, and is idle again until the close of the shift on Wednesday. Machine B utilizes 22 hours during the same period: 4 hours on 105, 8 hours on 101, idle for 2 hours, 6 hours on 102, and 4 hours on 103. Machine C utilizes all 24 hours: 10 hours on 102, 2 hours on 105, 2 hours on 101, and 10 hours on 104. This predicts utilization rates of 75 percent, 92 percent, and 100 percent. Whereas the supervisor might not be able to juggle the work so efficiently all week long, it indicates what judicious overlapping of jobs can accomplish.

How does the PERT chart relate to the Gantt chart?

It borrows the ideas of juggling a number of different but related tasks of varying time requirements from the Gantt chart. PERT ties these to the critical events as they should occur and demonstrates graphically how these are all tied together. Finally, PERT enables the planners to identify the bottlenecks in a complex schedule, plan, or program.

What do the initials P-E-R-T stand for? Where is PERT used?

They stand for "program evaluation and review technique." In plainer English, *PERT* is a technique for planning any project that involves a number of different tasks that must be coordinated. It is a graphic technique that enables the planner to see the progressive relationships among many jobs; PERT is also known as the critical-path method (CPM), arrow diagraming, and many other variations.

The technique dramatizes the value of conceiving of doing two or more things simultaneously. It may take 12 minutes to get a haircut, 5 minutes for a shoeshine, and 10 minutes to browse through the newspaper. You could take 27 minutes to do all three—in sequence, one after the other—or you could do all three in 12 minutes by doing them simultaneously, or (as planners say) in parallel.

The PERT method is most useful for scheduling one-of-a-kind projects. It is used to plan and schedule construction projects such as roads, bridges, and dams. It is used to plan the building of very large engines, airplanes, and ships; PERT is helpful, too, in scheduling a number of jobs that must be done in a short period of time. For example, a plant closes for two weeks in the summer and tries to get everything cleaned and repaired during that period. It is also useful for starting a new program in a government agency or for introducing a new product to the market.

What makes PERT so different from ordinary scheduling methods?

The program evaluation and review technique helps a scheduler to plan ahead, to look for critical jobs that will tie up a whole program unless they are begun and completed before they create bottlenecks. For example, it may be logical to wait until a machine foundation pit has been dug and the concrete has been poured before constructing the supporting ironwork for the machine. (See Figure 4-3.) But if steel is in short supply and the ironwork job will take four weeks to fabricate, then perhaps it's wiser to begin this part of the job before digging the pit. And if there are several other jobs that can't be begun until the ironwork is in place, you can see how critical it is to anticipate the ironwork job and ensure its completion in time; PERT charting helps you to identify these critical jobs ahead of time.

What is the basis for scheduling and assigning office and clerical work?

Office scheduling should be based on the same considerations given to production scheduling: (1) the number of tasks to be done, (2) the time it will take to do each task, (3) the number and qualifications of employees available to do the work, and (4) the capacity and availability of proper machines and equipment, when machinery plays a part. A good way to put this all together is to use a work distribution chart, which provides a rule-of-thumb guide to indicate how much work the department can handle with its present staff.

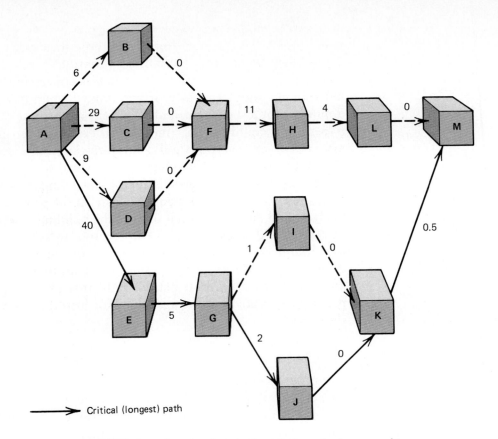

Critical (longest) path

Figure 4-3 PERT chart for planning the installation of a large machine.

Table 4-3 shows how repetitive, routine work in an office might be balanced among eight employees by means of a work distribution chart. (Machine capacity and availability are not considered to be factors in this example.) Note that this supervisor has tried to group together activities of roughly the same skills level into the job assignments for each person. For example, Apgar handles all the mail and part of the copying—fairly simple work. Bond and Crisi handle filing and the balance of the copying—slightly more difficult work. Dalt and Eigo have secretarial jobs, whereas Finch's job is mainly stenography. Grey is a keypunch operator who also handles the check-writing machine, and Hruska is a posting clerk.

6 POLICIES

CONCEPT   Policies provide the guidelines that help keep an entire organization working toward the same goals in the same way.

Table 4-3 WORK DISTRIBUTION CHART FOR OFFICE PLANNING AND SCHEDULING

Weekly Tasks or Activities	Total Hours per Week	Weekly Time Distribution in Hours per Employee							
		Apgar	Bond	Crisi	Dalt	Eigo	Finch	Grey	Hruska
Mail in	15	15							
Mail out	15	15							
Dictation	20				10	10			
Transcription	30				10	10	10		
Typing	80			10	20	20	30		
Copying	30	10	10	10					
Filing in	25		20	5					
Filing out	15		10	5					
Keypunching	30							30	
Check writing	10							10	
Posting	50			10					40
Total hours	320	40	40	40	40	40	40	40	40

What is meant by "company" policy?

Company—or organization—policies are broad guidelines for action. At their best, these guides are a reflection of a company's objectives and a statement of its basic principles for doing business. In a major way, they represent a public commitment to employees, suppliers, customers, and the community. In a very practical way, however, they are intended as a guide for supervisors and managers for getting their jobs done. Many policies at the operational level give supervisors the opportunity to use their own best judgment in implementing them. Other policies are reinforced by firm rules and procedures that greatly restrict supervisory discretion.

Does policy apply only at high levels?

Policy is generally set by managers high up in the company organization. But policy can be no more than a collection of high-sounding words unless the supervisor translates them into action on the firing line.

Take an example of a disciplinary policy. Here's how it might sound as it works its way down from the front office to first-line action by the supervisor:

Company president: "Our policy is to exercise fair and reasonable controls to regulate the conduct of our employees."

Manufacturing vice president: "The policy on attendance in this plant is that habitual absenteeism will be penalized."

Plant superintendent: "Here are the rules governing absences. It's up to you supervisors to keep an eye on unexcused absences and to suspend any employee absent or late more than three times in three months."

Supervisor: "Sorry, I'm going to have to lay you off for three days. You know the rules. You put me in a bad spot when you take time off on your own without warning or getting approval."

Note that no real action takes place until the supervisor puts the words of the policy into effect.

Is policy always in writing?

Far from it. Many rigid policies have never been put down in black and white. And many firm policies have never been heard from an executive's lips. But employees and supervisors alike recognize that matters affected by such policies must be handled in a certain manner and usually do so.

The existence of so much unwritten policy has led many authorities to the conclusion that all policy is better put into writing so that it may be explained, discussed, and understood. Nevertheless, there are many companies that don't subscribe to this way of thinking, and their policies remain implied rather than spelled out.

Should a supervisor change policy?

No. That's a very dangerous thing to do. Policies are set to guide action. It's a supervisor's responsibility to act within policy limits.

Supervisors can influence a policy change, however, by making their thoughts and observations known to the boss, the personnel department, and the top management. After all, supervisors are in the best position to feel out employees' reactions to policy—favorable or otherwise. You do your boss and your company a service when you accurately report employees' reactions. And that's the time to offer your suggestions for improving or modifying the policy.

How responsible will employees hold you for company policy?

If you have done a good job of convincing employees that you fully represent the management of their company, your actions and company policy will be one and the same thing in their eyes. Naturally, you will sometimes have to carry out policy that you don't fully agree with— policy that may be unpopular with you or with your employees. Resist the temptation to apologize for your actions or to criticize the policy to employees. When you do, you weaken your position.

If you have to reprimand an employee, don't say, "I'd like to give you a break, but that's company policy." Or when sparking a cleanup campaign, don't say, "The manager wants you to get your area in order." Handle such matters positively. Give the policy your own personal touch, but don't sell the company down the river or you're likely to be caught in the current yourself.

How can you prevent your policy interpretations from backfiring?

Try to protect your actions in policy matters by asking yourself these questions before making decisions:

- Is policy involved here? What is the procedure? What is the rule?
- Am I sure of the facts? Do I know all the circumstances?
- How did I handle a similar matter in the past?
- Who can give me advice on this problem? Should I ask for it?
- Would my boss want to talk this over with me first?
- Does this problem involve the union? If so, should I see the union steward or should I check with our labor relations people first?

REVIEW

KEY CONCEPTS TO REMEMBER

1. Planning is the process of systematically working out ahead of time what you and your work unit will do in the future. Good planning reduces needless waste of a department's resources. It is planning that establishes an organization's goals and standards and the policies that guide their attainment. From these goals and policies, plans emerge in the form of procedures and schedules. Organizational policies, which are general in nature, are made increasingly specific as

they move down the line as rules and regulations. Supervisory planning is mainly concerned with short-term objectives spanning a few days, a week, a month, or—at most—a year.

2. Goals are usually arranged in a hierarchy. The goals of a supervisor's work unit should support those of the overall organization. The unit's goals should be clearly stated and be attainable, given the limitations of the unit's resources.

3. The planning process flows from the planning of objectives into the development of plans for implementing them. Plans must be supported by details, such as times and dates as well as the anticipated assignment of equipment, facilities, and people. Plans may be long-range (more than one year) or short-range (anything less than one year). There are standing plans, which cover procedures that remain in effect over a long period of time, and there are single-use plans, which cover operating schedules and budgets.

4. When developing schedules for their own units, supervisors should not press their resources too far; neither should they underschedule them. The use of overtime to complete schedules is usually a costly practice, not only in labor premiums but also in reduced productivity.

5. Supervisors should master a variety of planning and scheduling techniques for handling different scheduling problems: (a) the Gantt chart for mixed production runs; (b) PERT, or CPM, for one-of-a-kind projects; and (c) the work distribution chart for standing assignments, especially those in office situations.

6. Decisions and actions in every enterprise are guided by a body of operating principles, called policies, that either have been set down in writing or have evolved informally (like common law) as a result of decisions and actions that management has taken under similar circumstances in the past. Supervisors are expected to act within the limits of these guidelines. In the eyes of employees, then, supervisors are inseparably identified with the policies of the employing organization, since it is at that level that these principles are translated into specific actions.

SUPERVISORY WORD POWER

Gantt chart. A chart that enables a planner to schedule jobs in the most productive sequence and also provides a visual means for observing and controlling work progress.

Objectives. Also referred to as goals and standards, the targets—both short-term and long-range—toward which an organization strives.

The long-range objectives, in particular, are supported by policy guidelines for managerial actions and decisions.

PERT chart. A graphic technique for planning a project in which a great number of tasks must be coordinated. This chart (1) shows the relationship between tasks and (2) identifies the critical bottlenecks that may delay progress toward the project's completion.

Policies. Broad guidelines, philosophy, or principles which management establishes in support of its organizational goals and which it must follow in seeking those goals.

Procedures. Methods, prescribed by management, for the proper and consistent forms, sequences, and channels to be followed by individuals and by units of the organization.

Regulations. Special rules, orders, and controls set forth by management restricting the conduct of units and/or individuals within an organization.

Schedules. Detailed assignments that dictate how facilities, equipment, and/or individuals are to be used, according to times and dates, in the accomplishment of an organization's objectives.

Work distribution chart. A device for visualizing how the tasks and activities of a department—and the times needed to accomplish these tasks—are distributed among its workers so that equitable work loads may be planned and assigned.

READING COMPREHENSION

1. How are plans, goals, and policies related?
2. Why must the establishing of goals precede the developing of plans?
3. How can you judge whether or not a set of objectives for a supervisor's department is reasonable?
4. Identify each of the following as either a standing plan or a single-use plan: a department's monthly budget, a fire-drill procedure, this week's production schedule, the methods prescribed for filling out a purchase order.
5. How are plans and controls related?
6. Why is it not considered good practice to schedule operations at 100 percent of capacity?
7. In what ways is a Gantt chart like a calendar? In what ways is it different from a calendar?
8. In what ways is a PERT chart similar to a Gantt chart? What is the principal difference between the two?

9. When would it be wise for a supervisor to check with the boss before carrying out a particular policy?

10. One company's policy manual states, "It is our intention to listen with an open mind to employee complaints." What supplementary information might a supervisor need to interpret that policy more clearly?

APPLICATION

SELF-APPRAISAL

How high can you score in this planning game?

Each of the examples in the numbered list is related to one of the planning terms and techniques presented in the lettered list. Your assignment is to match the correct term or technique with each of the numbered definitions, descriptions, and clues. On a separate piece of paper, write the numbers 1 to 10 down the page to correspond to each of the definitions, descriptions, and clues. After each number on your list, write the letter of the appropriate term or technique. After completing this activity, check your answers by using the scoring procedure described below.

Definitions, Descriptions, and Clues

1. "No one without a hard hat will be allowed in the construction area."
2. "With this cobwebby-looking chart, we'll be able to spot the bottlenecks in this project before they occur."
3. "Until further notice, the assembly department will inspect all parts at Stages 1, 3, and 5 of the assembly process."
4. "All unsatisfactory purchases will be cheerfully refunded."
5. "Preparation of the Majax advertisement should begin next Wednesday in the design department and be turned over to the copy department by Friday."

Terms and Techniques

a. Gantt chart
b. Objective
c. PERT chart
d. Policy
e. Procedure
f. Schedule
g. Long-range plan
h. Standing plan
i. Rule
j. Work distribution chart

6. "This year, we aim to have zero lost-time absences."
7. "The work will be regularly split up so that Mary and Tom work exclusively on word processing, Joe works half-time on mail sorting and half-time on posting, and Rona works full-time on computer operations."
8. "This thing looks like a calendar, and it will be used for keeping track of our progress against the production schedule."
9. "By improving our productivity by 2 percent a year for the next five years, we hope to be able to undersell our overseas competitors."
10. "This is the format and sequence to be followed when entering customer orders in the logbook."

Scoring   Give yourself 1 point for each correct match. The answers are 1–i, 2–c, 3–h, 4–d, 5–f, 6–b, 7–j, 8–a, 9–g, 10–e.

Interpretation   If you scored 10 points, you've acquired a first-rate grasp of the basic elements used in the planning process. If you scored either 8 or 9 points, you should set your learning goals a little higher. If you scored less than 8 points, you should restudy the chapter and try again.

CASE STUDIES

CASE 10   The New Secondhand Car

When Marsha was appointed head teller at the Riverstone Bank, she received an orientation from the bank's vice president for human resources. As he explained the guidelines for employee relations, the vice president told Marsha: "The bank's policy regarding time off from work is a reasonable one: If employees have personal emergencies to take care of, it is permissible to excuse them, provided that they clock out and do not receive pay for that time. However, we do not approve of time off for pleasurable things like skiing or fishing. Nor should you grant time off for trivial personal matters, such as going to the hairdresser's."

Three weeks later, Marsha was confronted by a request from

Tomas, one of her tellers. Tomas asked Marsha if he could report to work late the next morning. He needed to do so, he said, because he had just bought a new secondhand car and wanted to register it at the motor vehicle agency. There was always a long line of applicants at the lunch hour or after work in the afternoon. "Sure you can," said Marsha. "But come to work as soon as you have attended to your business."

The following morning, while Marsha was planning the day's assignment schedule for her tellers, Don Riggins, supervisor of the bank's posting department, stopped by Marsha's desk. "You certainly have put me in a bad light with my crew. A couple of my posting clerks got wind of the fact that you let Tomas off today to register his new car. I've never accepted an excuse like that. I tell my people that as long as it's urgent, I'll let them go. But I'm not about to rearrange work schedules just to suit one employee's convenience."

If you were Marsha, which one of the following alternatives would you consider to be most effective in handling similar situations in the future? On a separate sheet of paper, rank the alternatives on a scale from 1 (most preferable) to 5 (least preferable). You may add another alternative if you wish. In any event, be prepared to justify your ranking.

a. Never grant any time off except for an extreme emergency, like an accident to an employee's child.
b. Continue to make judgments as you did with Tomas, whose request you considered reasonable and within the policy guidelines.
c. Refer all requests to the human resources department; the people there are the experts on policy.
d. Ask the human resources vice president for greater clarification of the policy, with specific examples of what should, and should not, be approved.
e. Check with Don and other more experienced supervisors to get their advice about what you should do.

CASE 11 Cora's Goals

The order-entry department of a large wholesale distributor owes part of its success to the careful planning done by its supervisors. The department's new computer system has caused some problems, but things generally have been running smoothly. Cora, the supervisor, is now establishing objectives for the coming year, and she wants to set reasonable, but measurable, goals for some important indicators of her department's operations.

The order-entry process consists of (a) accepting mailed or telephoned orders; (b) looking up or verifying the stock number, price, and current availability of each item ordered; (c) looking up the customer number; (d) adding the customer number and requesting a credit check if the customer is new; and (e) entering the customer number, items ordered, and quantities (as well as out-of-stock indicators, if applicable) on a keyboard computer terminal. The computer then automatically prepares packing lists, shipping labels, and invoices and makes appropriate entries in accounting records.

Your assignment is to prepare a list of objectives for Cora and her department. Use Table 4-1 in the text as a model. Supply whatever numbers you think are reasonable and appropriate for the order-entry department. Among the items you should consider are processing time, costs, accuracy, overtime, lateness and absenteeism, employee turnover, and damage to equipment through misuse.

CASE 12 **Spreading the Fertilizer**

It is the first working day of September at the Spreado Fertilizer plant. Its processing operation can produce 20 tons of product a day while working a 5-day week. As of now, the operation has nothing scheduled for September. This morning, however, the sales manager poses this question to the processing supervisor: "We can get an order for 300 tons of fertilizer for a new customer if you can promise that it will be shipped by the end of the third week of September. Can you do it?"

In answering this question, the supervisor must consider these additional facts:

a. The process is due for an overhaul on the second weekend of September.
b. Absenteeism is very high in his department on Friday nights at the beginning of the football season.
c. The supervisor's boss won't permit overtime.
d. Past records show that unscheduled downtime for repairs on processing equipment runs about 10 percent.

Would it be reasonable for the supervisor to tell the sales manager that the new order can be shipped on time? If not, what would be a reasonably sure date? Be prepared to explain your reasoning and to show your calculations.

1 A supervisor controls by acting as judge and problem solver.

2 Effective controls are based upon sound standards.

3 Control requires measurement, comparison, and correction.

4 Controls focus on output, quality, costs, and performance.

5 Supervisors must contend with employee resistance to controls.

CHAPTER 5

Exercising Control Over People and Processes

LEARNING OBJECTIVES

After studying this chapter, you should be able to

1. Understand the dual nature—judgmental as well as problem-solving and decision-making—of the supervisor's role in carrying out the control function.

2. Define and recognize a control standard and explain and evaluate the sources of these standards.

3. Discuss the four steps in the control process and explain the three major types of controls.

4. Identify the six major areas of organizational control that guide supervisory actions and explain the technique of management by exception.

5. Discuss employee resistance to controls, explain some of the ways to reduce it, and explain the relationship of management by objectives to the control process.

A DUAL ROLE

CONCEPT Supervisors act both as judges and problem solvers in an organization's control process.

What is the basic purpose of a supervisor's control function?

To keep things in line and to make sure your plans hit their targets. In the restrictive sense, you use controls to make sure that employees are at work on time, that materials aren't wasted or stolen, and that some persons don't exceed their authority. These controls tend to be the don'ts of an organization, the rules and regulations that set limits of acceptable behavior. In the more constructive sense, controls help to guide you and your department to production goals and quality standards.

How much will control rely on the information system and how much on the supervisor?

That depends. In a large, well-managed organization with tons of surveillance information available, the supervisor may play only a small part in the control system. That's the exception, however. Most supervisors will be an integral part of the control system, and it won't function without their participation, informally as well as formally.

Day-to-day control means that most of the time supervisors should be on their feet—walking around—observing, listening, counting, taking nothing much for granted. In other words, the supervisor's desk is only a part-time workstation. Especially in regard to clerical work, much that goes on is not detailed by a master control system. There are daily and seasonal fluctuations in employee work loads, for example. Only an alert and observant supervisor can provide standards and enforce controls for these conditions.

What are the supervisor's roles in the control process?

Supervisors fulfill two principal functions. In the first role, a supervisor acts somewhat like a judge, watching what happens in the department to see whether or not activities, conditions, and results are occurring as they are supposed to. In the second role, supervisors act as problem solvers and decision makers. They do so in order to find out why something is going (or has gone) wrong and then to decide what to do about it.

In their *judgmental role,* supervisors observe what is happening (or has happened) throughout the conversion process and then compare these observations (or measurements) with the standards of what was supposed to happen. These standards are derived from, or may be exactly the same as, the goals that were set during the planning process. Here are two examples of how the judgmental role is handled: In the first example, a supervisor in a word processing unit of a bank expects that all ten operators will be at their stations within five minutes after the lunch break (a standard he has set for the operators). Now he observes that only eight operators are regularly at their stations when they should be. The supervisor knows that a standard condition is not being met; it is temporarily out of control. In the second example, an assembly supervisor in a video game factory has set a goal of completing 300 assemblies a day. At the end of one day, the production report tells her that only 255 games were assembled. The supervisor knows that her department is 45 assemblies below standard; production is temporarily out of control.

In their *problem-solving and decision-making role,* supervisors must not only find out why conditions or results are below standard but also must correct conditions and bring results up to expectations. Here's how the supervisors might handle the two control problems spotted in the last paragraph: In the first case, the supervisor makes certain that the word processing equipment is in good operating order and that there is plenty of work available for all ten operators. Then he speaks to the latecomers to find out if there are any extenuating circumstances that prevent them from being at their stations immediately following the lunch break. He then outlines the need for promptness to ensure full usage of the equipment and the penalties for being late. Finally, he continues to watch for late arrivals to keep this condition in line with his standard. In the second case, the assembly-line supervisor conducts a similar problem-solving search to find the cause of the missed standard. She might find that the cause arises from a number of conditions: faulty assembly tools, shortages of parts, changed specifications, employee absences, lack of training—or failure of one or more employees to apply themselves to their work. Once the true cause has been identified, the supervisor decides what to do and takes the steps needed to correct the problem and bring the conditions and/or results back under control.

In what way are controls linked to plans?

Controls are directly related to the goals that are set during the planning process. In many instances, controls (or control standards) are actually goals that have been sharpened to make them more detailed and specific. Suppose, for example, that you are the supervisor of the commercial office of a telephone company and your office has been given a goal of handling 2000 service calls for the next month. For a month with 20 working days, that goal can be converted into a control standard of 100 service calls a day. If your office handles 100 calls a day, it has met the target and you need exert no corrective controls. If, however, your office handles fewer than 100 calls a day, it is performing below the control standard. If this persists, your office may not meet the goal planned for that month. You must take some sort of action to improve this performance in order to "bring it into control."

2 CONTROL STANDARDS

CONCEPT   Effective controls are based upon sound standards.

Exactly what is a control standard?

A control standard, usually called simply a *standard,* is a specific performance goal that a product, a service, a machine, an individual, or an organization is expected to meet. It is usually expressed numerically: a weight (14.00 ounces), a rate (200 units an hour), or a flat target (4 rejects). The numbers may be expressed in any units, such as inches, gallons, dollars, or percentages.

Many companies also allow a little leeway from standard, called a *tolerance.* This implies that the performance will be considered to be in control if it falls within specified boundaries. A product, for instance, may be said to meet its 14.00-ounce standard weight if it weighs no less than 13.75 ounces or no more than 14.25 ounces. The control standard would be stated as 14 ounces, ±0.25 ounce. The tolerance is the ±0.25 ounce.

Where do the control standards come from? Who sets them?

A great many standards are set by the organization itself. They may be set by the accounting department for costs or by the industrial engineering or methods department for wage-incentive (or time) standards. They may be issued by the production-control department for schedule quantities or by the quality-control people for inspection specifications. It is typical for control standards in large organizations to be set by staff specialists. In smaller companies supervisors may set standards themselves. But even in large companies the supervisor may have to take an overall, or department, standard and translate it into standards for each employee or operation.

On what information are control standards based?

Standards are based on one, two, or all three of the following sources:

Past performance. Historical records often provide the basis for controls. If your department has been able to process 150 orders with three clerks in the past, this may be accepted as the standard. The weakness of this historical method is that it presumes that processing 150 orders represents good performance. Perhaps 200 would be a better target. This might be especially true if improvements have recently been made in the processing machinery and workplace layouts.

High hopes. In the absence of any other basis, some supervisors ask for the moon. They set unreasonably high standards for their employees to shoot at. Whereas it is a sound practice to set challenging goals, standards should always be attainable by employees who put forth a reasonable effort. Otherwise, workers will become discouraged, or will rebel, and won't try to meet them.

Systematic analysis. The best standards are set by systematically analyzing what a job entails. This way the standard is based on careful observation and measurement, as with time studies. At the very least, standards should be based on a consideration of all the factors that affect attainment of the standard—such as tooling, equipment, training of the operator, absence of distractions, and clear-cut instructions and specifications.

3 | THE CONTROL PROCESS

CONCEPT The control process involves measurement, comparison, and corrective action.

How is the control process carried out?

The control process follows four sequential steps. The first step, setting performance standards, often takes place "off camera." That is, the standards may have been set before the supervisor arrives on the scene. Other times, it is up to the supervisor to set the necessary performance standards for his or her department. Steps 2, 3, and 4 of the control process are illustrated in Figure 5-1. Here are the four process steps in order:

1. **Set performance standards.** Standards of quantity, quality, and time spell out (a) what is expected and (b) how much of a deviation can be tolerated if the person or process fails to come up to the mark. For example, the standard for an airline ticket counter might be that no customer should have to wait in line more than five minutes. The standard could then be modified to say that if only one out of ten

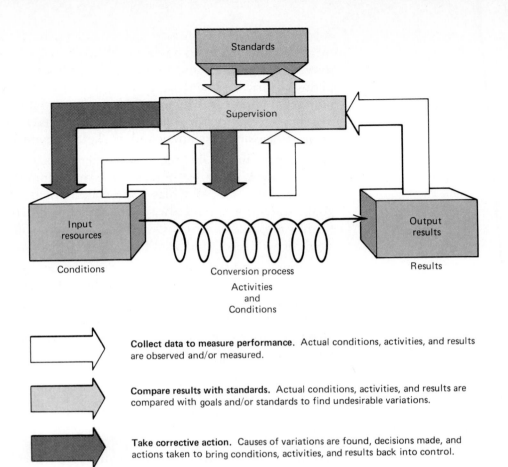

Collect data to measure performance. Actual conditions, activities, and results are observed and/or measured.

Compare results with standards. Actual conditions, activities, and results are compared with goals and/or standards to find undesirable variations.

Take corrective action. Causes of variations are found, decisions made, and actions taken to bring conditions, activities, and results back into control.

Figure 5-1 Steps in the control process, once standards have been set.

customers had to wait more than five minutes, no corrective action need be taken. The standard would be stated as "waiting time of less than five minutes per customer with a tolerance of one out of ten who might have to wait longer." The guideline is that the more specific the standard, the better, especially when it can be stated with numbers as opposed to vague terms such as "good performance" and "minimum waiting time."

2. **Collect data to measure performance.** Accumulation of control data is so routine in most organizations that it is taken for granted. Every time a supervisor or an employee fills out a time card, prepares a production tally, or files a receiving or inspection report, control data is being collected. Whenever a sales ticket is filled out, a sale rung up on a cash register, or a shipping ticket prepared, control data is being recorded—often with a computer-related terminal. Of

course, not all information is collected in written form. Much of what a good supervisor uses for control purposes is gathered by observation—simply watching how well employees are carrying out their work.

3. **Compare results with standards.** From top manager to first-line supervisor, the control system flashes a warning if there is a gap between what was expected (the standard) and what is taking place or has taken place (the result). If the results are within the tolerance limits, the supervisor's attention can be turned elsewhere. But if the process exceeds the tolerance limits—the gap is too big—then action is called for.

4. **Take corrective action.** You must first find the cause of the gap (variance or deviation from standard). Then you must take action to remove or minimize this cause. If travelers are waiting too long in the airline's ticket line, for example, the supervisor may see that there is an unusually high degree of travel because of a holiday. The corrective action is to add another ticket clerk. If, however, the supervisor observes that the clerks are taking extra-long coffee breaks, this practice will have to be stopped as soon as possible.

Where, in the process, are controls applied?

There is always a danger of too much control, somewhat like "oversteering" an automobile. Accordingly, supervisors should look for key places—make-or-break points—in their operations and then focus most of their attention on these areas.

The selective locale of observation points can also provide three distinct types of control opportunities. Refer to Figure 5-1 as you read their explanations.

Preventive controls. These take place at the input stage before the conversion process begins. Materials are inspected. Machinery undergoes inspection and preventive maintenance. The proper kinds of employees are selected for each assignment and trained beforehand. By catching problems before they can affect later operations, preventive controls have the greatest potential for savings.

Concurrent controls. These are controls that take place during the conversion phase of a supervisor's operations. In manufacturing and processing plants, pressures and temperatures are checked and on-line inspections are made as partially converted products flow through the process. In offices and retail shops, supervisors monitor output and quality of employee performance during the workday. Concurrent controls make their biggest contribution by catching and correcting problems before they get out of hand.

Corrective controls. These controls take place at the output-stage after an operation is completed, a product is finished, or a service is delivered. Such "final inspections" occur too late to do much good for what has already happened. Their value is in alerting supervisors to ongoing performance problems to be avoided in the future.

To what extent is control automatic?

Increasingly, operating processes depend upon automatic, or computer-driven, control systems. These try to minimize the human element. We expect "feedback" from a thermostat, for example, to tell the furnace to keep the room warm. In many automobiles, we expect a buzzer to let us know whether or not a seat belt is fastened. Many processes in industry are controlled according to the same principle. A worker feeds a sheet of metal into a press, and the machine takes over. A clerk slips a piece of paper into a copying machine, and the machine automatically reproduces the number of copies the clerk has dialed onto the control mechanism. There will be much more of this in the future.

Computer monitoring of employee performance is the latest in this trend. The computer, by sensing a terminal at which a clerk works—or any mechanism related to an employee's output—automatically counts, times, and records an employee's performance. Such impersonal computer measurement, while viewed as a boon to management, arouses resentment in the minds of many employees. It also raises social issues that are under continuing debate and attack from labor unions.

4 CONTROL TARGETS

CONCEPT   The primary targets of supervisory control are output, quality, time, materials, costs, and employee performance.

What specific kinds of organizational controls are most likely to aid or restrict supervisory actions?

These depend largely on the nature of the organization in which the supervisor works. The following controls, however, are most common:

Output controls. These relate to the demand of almost every organization for some standard of output or production. The quantity of production required is often the basis for all other aspects of control. In other words, a supervisor must first make sure that output quantities measure up. Then the supervisor's attention can turn to controls that specify a certain quality or time, for example.

Quality controls. If, in meeting the production standard, a department skimps on the quality of its work, there can be trouble. Quantity and quality go hand in hand. The inspection function is intended to make sure the final product or service lives up to its quality standards (specifications). As a supplement to routine inspections, many companies practice statistical quality control, a way of predicting quality deviations in advance so that a supervisor can take corrective action before a product is spoiled. (See Chapter 18 for more on quality controls.)

Time controls. Almost every organization must also meet certain deadlines or live within time constraints. A product must be shipped on a certain date. A service must be performed on an agreed-on day. A project must be completed as scheduled. Such time standards point up the fact that it is not enough just to get the job done if it isn't finished on time.

Material controls. These are related to both quality and quantity standards. A company may wish to limit the amount of raw or finished materials it keeps on hand; thus it may exercise inventory controls. Or an apparel firm, for instance, may wish to make sure that the maximum number of skirts is cut out of a bolt of cloth so that a minimum amount of cloth is wasted—a material-yield standard.

Cost controls. The final crunch in exercising controls involves costs. A supervisor may meet the quantity and quality standards, but if in so doing the department has been overstaffed or has been working overtime, it probably won't meet its cost standard.

Employee performance controls. These cover a wide spectrum and are often inseparable from all the above controls. The difference is that employee performance controls focus on individuals or groups of employees, rather than on a department, a machine, or a process. Such controls may be concerned with employee absences, tardiness, and accidents as well as with performance that is directly related to the quantity or quality of the employees' work.

Where do budgetary controls fit into this picture?

You'll have an opportunity to learn about these in greater detail in Chapter 19. For the moment, it is enough to say that many controls and control standards are often incorporated in a single control document—a budget. A budget is typically cost-, or expense-, related, since it is usually prepared by an accounting or financial department. The budget is not limited to cost items, however. It may also include allowable items for quantities of materials to be used and units of product or service to be produced, as well as any other quantifiable activity or condition an organization may wish to control.

Must supervisors spend all their time controlling?

It would appear that way. But by using a simple principle called management by exception, time taken for control activities can be held to a minimum. *Management by exception* is a form of delegation in which the supervisor lets things run as they are as long as they fall within prescribed (control) limits of performance. When they get out of line, the supervisor steps in and takes corrective action.

Figure 5-2 shows how a supervisor can use the management-by-exception principle as a guideline for delegating much of the control work to subordinates.

Take, for example, a broiler chef in a fast-food restaurant. The boss says that the chef should expect to broil between 180 and 200 hamburgers an hour. This is control zone 1. As long as results fall within the prescribed limits, the chef is completely in charge.

If the requests for hamburgers, however, fall below 180 but above 150, the chef keeps the grill hot but puts fewer hamburgers into the ready position; or, if requests build up to 225, the chef moves more hamburgers to the completed stage. This is zone 2. The chef takes this action without first checking with the boss but tells the boss what has been done.

If business falls below 150 but is more than 100 hamburgers an hour, the chef may ask the boss whether the grill can be turned off for a while; or, if the requests build up to 250 an hour, the chef may ask if one of the counter clerks can help. This is zone 3.

If conditions now move to either extreme—hamburger requests drop below 100 or exceed 250, the chef calls this to the supervisor's attention. This is zone 4. The supervisor may in the first instance (below 100) decide to shut down the grill or in the second instance (above 250) decide to start up an auxiliary grill.

5 *HANDLING EMPLOYEE RESISTANCE*

CONCEPT   A supervisor's handling of employee resistance to controls is a critical factor in the entire control process.

The human element in the control process: How important is it?

It is probably the most critical element. Regardless of management's efforts to automate the control system, human activities remain the vi-

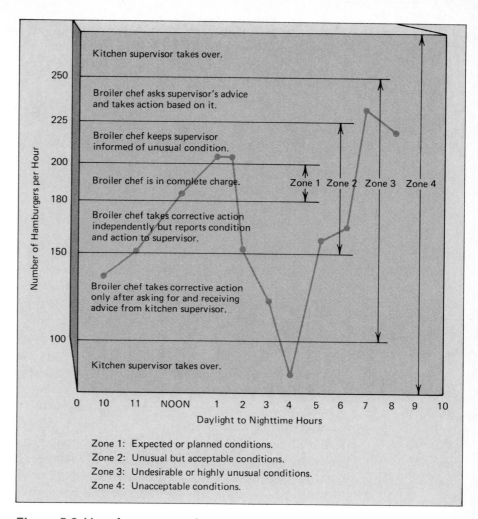

Figure 5-2 Use of management-by-exception chart for controlling the operation of a hamburger grill.

tal factors. Supervisors provide the eyes and ears for the system. They must continually find ways to make sure that employees meet job standards. Especially sensitive is performance relating to (1) attendance, (2) speed and care in feeding or servicing automatic operations, and (3) relationships with other departments and with customers or client organizations.

As noted earlier, organizations are moving toward greater employee participation in decision making. As this occurs, it becomes essential that a supervisor—through observation—determine which employees can work with little supervision (or control) and which ones cannot. This should determine the degree of personal control a supervisor should exert in each particular case. It is a fact of life that many employees will resist control from their supervisors, yet furnish little self-control of their own.

How can you soften employee resistance to controls?

Many people do not like to be "controlled." They don't like to be told what to do, and they feel boxed in when faced with specific standards. Few persons like to be criticized or corrected. Yet criticism or correction is what control often comes down to. When correction means discipline or termination, controls can seem very harsh indeed. For this reason a supervisor should be realistic about controls. Thus controls can have a very negative effect on employees, to say nothing of what they may do to the supervisor.

The negative aspects of controls, however, can be minimized. Supervisors should consider any of the following more positive approaches.

Emphasize the Value of Controls to Employees Standards provide employees with feedback that tells them whether they are doing well or not. Standards minimize the need for the supervisor to interfere and often allow the employee to choose a way of doing the job as long as standards are met. "You do the job, and I will stay out of your hair."

Avoid Arbitrary or Punitive Standards Employees respond better to standards that can be justified by past records that support the standards. "Our records show that 150 a day is a standard that other operators have consistently met." Standards based on analysis, especially time studies, are even more acceptable. "Let's time this job for an hour or two so that we can be sure the standard is reasonable." Compare this with "We'll just have to step up our production rate to 175 units each day."

Be Specific: Use Numbers if Possible Avoid such expressions as "improve quality" and "show us better attendance." Instead, use numbers that set specific targets, such as "fewer than two days' absence in the next six months" or "decrease your scrap percentage from 7 out of 100 to 3 out of 100."

Aim for Improvement Rather Than Punishment Capitalize on instances of missed standards to try to help employees learn how to improve their work. "Your output was below standard again last month. Perhaps you and I ought to start all over again to see what it is that is preventing you from meeting standards. There may be something I haven't shown you about this particular operation."

Make the Penalty for Nonconformance Absolutely Clear   A supervisor must balance rewards with punishment. Most employees respond to positive motivation. Many do not. All employees, however, good and poor alike, want to know what the "or else" is about their jobs. The guiding rule is to hold off punishment if you can, but to make it clear to everyone that standards must be met. Specify in advance what the penalty will be for those who don't meet them.

Avoid Threats That You Can't or Won't Back Up   If an employee is to be disciplined for failing to meet a quota or a standard of workmanship, be specific about the nature and timing of the discipline. "If you don't get your production up to 150 a day by the first of April, I will recommend that you be laid off for good." Don't say, "If you don't shape up soon, your head will be in a noose." If you do make the specific threat, it is good to make certain in advance that the company will help you make it stick.

Be Consistent in the Application of Controls   If you have set standards that apply to the work of several employees, it should go without saying that you will be expected to make everyone measure up to them. If you do feel that exceptions can be made, be prepared to defend that position. In the main, however, standards should be the same for everyone doing the same work. Similarly, rewards and punishment should be the same for all those who meet or fail to meet these standards.

What about encouraging self-control?

Self-control is beautiful for those who can exert it. Douglas McGregor insisted that many people need only to be given the targets for their work—the standards. After that, he said, they wish to be left alone and to be judged on the basis of their results in meeting or not meeting these targets. Many employees will, Douglas McGregor said, provide their own control and do not need a supervisor to threaten them or cajole them into meeting standards.

Our advice is to give an employee the benefit of the doubt. Give a free hand to those who take charge of themselves. Keep the rein on those who soon show that they need, or expect, the control to come from the supervisor.

When do management goals become control standards?

Very often, as shown when the linkage between planning and controlling was explained. More specifically, however, many companies convert their organizational goals into control programs by using a system of management by objectives. *Management by objectives* (MBO) is a planning and control process that provides managers at each organizational control point with a set of goals, or standards, to be attained. The process is usually repeated every six to twelve months. These MBO goals are similar to the supervisory performance goals listed in Table 4-1. It is presumed that if all supervisors reach their goals, the organization will also reach its goals. In companies where MBO is practiced to its full extent, the supervisors' goals literally become the standards of performance that must be met. The assumption is that the supervisors are capable of, and will exert, their own controls in striving to meet these objectives. The MBO system also presumes that the supervisors have been given enough freedom of action to meet these goals with the allocated resources. In essence, MBO is simply a formalization at managerial levels of the principle of self-control. Typically, the goals in MBO are jointly set by the boss and the subordinate, with the subordinate taking the leading role.

REVIEW

KEY CONCEPTS TO REMEMBER

1. The control function is inseparably linked to planning, in that planning goals are converted to control standards. Good control requires that a supervisor keep continual track of progress toward departmental goals so that corrective action can be taken as soon as possible. In exercising control, supervisors (a) apply judgment in determining whether or not deviations from standard are significant and (b) engage in problem solving and decision making when taking corrective action.
2. Good controls are based upon reliable, attainable standards of performance. The best standards are those that are based upon systematic analysis.
3. The control process entails four steps, usually taken in sequence:

(a) setting standards, (b) measuring performance, (c) comparing performance with standards, and (d) taking corrective action. To avoid overcontrolling, supervisors should place controls selectively at key, make-or-break, points in the process. Preventive controls are those exerted before the conversion process begins; concurrent controls take place while operations are under way; and corrective controls occur after the conversion process is completed.

4. The most frequently used organizational controls are targeted at output, quality, time, materials, costs, and employee performance. Since controlling is only one of several functions supervisors must perform, they must take advantage of the exception principle to delegate some of the decisions regarding corrective controls to qualified employees.

5. The human factor in the controlling process is a vital one. While employee resistance to controls is a very natural human reaction, too much of it will disrupt the control system. For this reason, if for no others, controls should be fair, be specific and numerical, motivate rather than coerce, be consistently applied, and encourage the greatest degree of self-control possible.

Management by objectives (MBO) is a method of control that higher management sometimes extends to supervisors to give *them* an opportunity for exercising the greatest degree of self-discipline in controlling their own work.

SUPERVISORY WORD POWER

Budgetary control. A planning and reporting system that incorporates many standards, for operating conditions and results as well as for costs and expenses, into a single control document for a supervisor's unit.

Concurrent controls. Controls applied to conditions to be maintained, and results to be obtained, during the conversion process.

Corrective controls. Controls applied, mainly to results related to products or services produced, after the conversion process has been completed.

Feedback. The process of relaying the measurement of actual performance back to the individual or unit causing the performance so that action can be taken to correct, or narrow, the variance.

Management by exception. A principle of control that enables a supervisor to delegate corrective action to a subordinate as long as the variances in performance are within specified ranges.

Management by objectives (MBO). A planning and control technique in which a supervisor and his or her immediate superior agree on goals to be attained and standards to be maintained.

Preventive controls. Controls applied, primarily to an examination of resources, before the conversion process begins.

Specification. A collection of standardized dimensions and characteristics pertaining to a product, process, or service.

Standard. The measure, criterion, or basis—usually expressed in numbers and/or concrete terms—for judging performance of a product or service, machine, individual, or organizational unit.

Tolerance. The permissible deviation—or variance—from standard.

Variance. The gap, or deviation, between (a) the actual performance, condition, or result and (b) the standard, or expected performance, condition, or result.

READING COMPREHENSION

1. What is the ultimate purpose of the control process?
2. Explain the difference between a supervisor's judgmental role in controlling and his or her problem-solving and decision-making role.
3. How are control standards related to the goals established during the planning process?
4. Of the three chief ways of setting standards, which is the best? Why? What's likely to be wrong with the other two?
5. If a supervisor has been given the standards for her or his department, what three other steps in the control process will she or he still have to deal with?
6. Tammy relies mainly upon checking merchandise just before it is shipped from her department. What kind of control is she relying on? What are the dangers in waiting until then to exercise control?
7. Briefly describe the six areas of organizational control that warrant the most supervisory attention.
8. How are management by exception and control-standard tolerances related?
9. How should supervisors approach the issue of self-control for their employees?
10. What technique, involving self-control or self-discipline, is sometimes made available to supervisors for controlling their own performance?

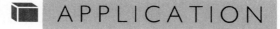

APPLICATION

SELF-APPRAISAL

What kind of "control" rating would you give Steve?

Steve is supervisor of the "pack & ship" department at a mail-order photo-finishing company. A consultant spent a month with Steve observing his attitudes and actions regarding control activities in his department. The consultant's observations are reported below. Your assignment is to indicate, for each observation, your opinion of whether Steve's attitude or action represents a good, bad, or doubtful control practice. On a separate piece of paper, copy the column headings shown below. In the column "Steve and the Control Process," write the numbers 1 to 10 down the page to correspond to each of the control activities observed by the consultant. For each statement, place a check mark in the column that matches your opinion of Steve's attitude or action. After completing this activity, rate Steve as a controller by using the scoring procedure described on page 106. Then compare your judgment with that of the experts.

Column headings:

Steve and the Control Process	Good Practice	Bad Practice	Doubtful Practice

1. Steve has set the department's output standard at 10,000 prints packed a day.
2. He has asked his employees to "be as careful as they can" in stuffing prints into mailing packets "so they won't be damaged."
3. Steve urges employees to "be careful" when operating the package-sealing machine so that they won't get hurt.
4. The addressing operation is a critical one, and Steve places much of his control efforts there.
5. In fact, Steve is so concerned about the addressing operation that he has posted a list of 50 "dos and don'ts" in that area for employees to follow.
6. At the sorting operation, Steve has given the operator a set of guidelines so that she knows when she can proceed if something goes wrong without first checking with him.
7. Steve has also given the sorting operator a standard that he says "ought to be attainable if everything goes smoothly."
8. The majority of the controls in Steve's department are placed at the completion of an operation so that Steve will know that something has gone wrong.

9. Steve's philosophy is to set up enough standards and to issue enough instructions so that "employees will not have any excuse for not keeping their work in line."

10. Steve is very tough with employees whose performance "isn't up to snuff"; they are told that he'll "go all the way to the top to see that they are fired."

Scoring   Give Steve 1 point for each item that you marked as a *good* control practice. Give Steve no points for items that you marked as either *bad* or *doubtful*.

Interpretation   Management experts gave Steve only 3 points. Here's the way they scored it: *good* for items 1, 4, and 6; *bad* or *doubtful* for all other items. If you disagreed with their assessment, can you support your judgment?

CASE STUDIES

CASE 13   **The Overworked Copying Machine**

Bill Blake was the first to admit it. Use of the copying machine at the Regional Water Board, where he was office manager, had gotten out of control. Employees were indiscriminately making copies of everything, not only of official documents but also of personal items. This put Bill's office way over its paper budget. Not unexpectedly, word came down from state headquarters to "get things under control."

Bill's first effort was to post a notice over the copying machine, reminding employees that the machine could be used only for official business. At the end of the month, however, the number of copies run was still as high as ever.

Bill fumed over this development. He called his employees together and read the riot act to them. "The next person I find using that machine to copy personal items will be suspended on the spot," he threatened. Only a day later, Bill saw two employees laughing as they came away from the copier. When he asked to see what they had been copying, they held out a dozen or so sheets of paper. They had been copying a slightly off-color limerick that someone in the office had typed. "Aw, Bill," one said, "we were just having a little fun. After all, what's a few sheets of paper to the government? Why, only last week, we ran off dozens of copies of a report that the State Board later canceled."

"That's not the point," said Bill. "In the future, nothing personal goes on that copying machine. You hear me?"

"We hear you," said the employees.

At the end of the month, however, the situation had not improved.

So Bill decided to take firmer action. He posted a log sheet next to the copier. It instructed employees to record their names and the date, time, number of copies, and purpose each time the machine was used. "Anyone I find cheating on this new system *goes*!" Bill announced.

Two weeks later, Bill checked paper usage and found that the rate of consumption had dropped only a fraction. This month, the regional office would again exceed its budget.

That did it! Bill got the key to the copying machine and locked it. Next, he posted a sign over the machine that read: "From this time forward, anyone who wishes to use the copying machine must fill out a request form and present it to me. The individual will also show me exactly what has been run off when the key is returned."

With this measure, Bill thought he had gained control of the situation. On the other hand, Bill found that he was interrupted several times a day to hand out the key and to check paper usage when the key was returned.

If you were Bill, which of the following actions would you select to attain a more effective form of control? Rank the alternatives on a scale from 1 (most preferable) to 5 (least preferable). You may add another alternative if you wish. In any event, be prepared to justify your ranking.

a. Explain to State Headquarters that it costs more to exert control over copier usage than the extra paper is worth.
b. Post the monthly paper usage next to the machine. Ask one employee to check each day's usage and post the cumulative totals daily. Explain that when the budget total is reached, the machine will be inoperative until the beginning of the next month.
c. Meet with employees to explain the budget and the resulting control problem. Ask for their ideas about control procedures that might work. Try to follow their suggestions.
d. Call your employees together and tell them that the copy machine problem has gotten ridiculous. You have been too soft so far. You are going to unlock the machine and use the original log-sheet method. From now on, however, you will act on your threat to suspend anyone using the machine for personal items.
e. By means of a log sheet, analyze usage during the next month. On the basis of what you find, set up an allotment system for the various legitimate usages really needed for official work. If there is too little paper in the budget, then proceed to ask State Headquarters to increase the paper allowance.

Supervisors are especially concerned with the six areas, or types, of organizational control that are presented in the alphabetic list below. The numbered list contains examples of control activities, standards, and techniques related to these areas. Your assignment is to match the correct organizational control with each of the numbered examples. On a separate piece of paper, write the numbers 1 to 6 down the page to correspond to each of the examples. After each number on your list, write the letter of the appropriate organizational control. (You may decide that some examples illustrate more than one type of organizational control. If so, enter more than one letter for that numbered item, but be prepared to justify your choices.)

Control Activities, Standards, and Techniques

1. Employees at the Abco Warehouse must punch a time card at the beginning and end of each shift.
2. Workers on a construction job are required to report an accident, no matter how minor, on the same day that it occurs.
3. The purchasing manager of the State Health Commission instructs the word processing manager that a new supply of computer paper should be ordered when only five boxes of paper remain in hand.
4. A supervisor gives the capping-machine operator in a soft-drink bottling plant a quota of 5000 bottles a day.
5. The advertising sales manager for a radio station issues a travel allowance of $500 a month to each salesperson.
6. A chef in a fast-food restaurant is told that the hamburgers she makes must weigh at least ¼ pound before cooking.

Areas of Organizational Control

a. Output, or quantity, controls
b. Quality controls
c. Time controls
d. Material controls
e. Cost, or expense, controls
f. Employee performance controls

CASE 15   Checking the Checkout

The store manager for the More-for-Less Food Mart has set up a simple management-by-exception system for checkout counter employees. They are allowed to give cash refunds to customers under the following conditions:

> For soda bottle returns up to $3.
> For merchandise returns up to $5, provided the customer has a sales slip.
> For merchandise returns up to $12, if the clerk first gets the store manager's signature.

All other situations are to be handled by the store manager. The following situations arise one day for a checkout clerk. How should she handle each of them?

a. A little boy comes in with a wagonload of bottles. The clerk totals it up, and the full amount of the refund comes to $4.95.
b. A little girl comes in with six bottles: total refund—$.60.
c. A woman returns $2.75 worth of bottles and wants to return merchandise worth $10, with a sales slip.
d. A man brings in merchandise worth $15, with a sales slip, and merchandise worth $3, without a sales slip, for refund.
e. A woman wishes to return merchandise worth $45. She has a sales slip.

1 Supervisors detect problems by finding gaps in performance.

2 Problems are solved systematically by removing their causes.

3 Decisions are the logical outcome of problem solving.

4 Information helps to solve problems and to make better decisions.

5 Supervisors are vital to a management information system (MIS).

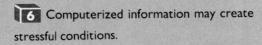

6 Computerized information may create stressful conditions.

CHAPTER 6

Managing Information and Solving Problems

LEARNING OBJECTIVES

After studying this chapter, you should be able to

1. Recognize and define a problem or a potential problem.

2. List the eight steps in problem solving and decision making that lead to the removal of a problem's cause.

3. Discuss the rational and intuitive approaches to decision making and explain cost-benefit analysis, decision trees, and ABC analysis.

4. Describe a management information system and differentiate between data and information.

5. Understand how supervisors can create their own departmental information systems.

6. Discuss the impact of computerized information handling systems upon employees and suggest ways to alleviate the stress associated with systematization.

▣ PROBLEMS: CAUSE AND EFFECT

CONCEPT Problems in organizations occur because of change, and they are revealed by gaps between expected and actual outcomes.

What, specifically, is a problem?

A problem is a puzzle looking for an answer. When problems occur within an organization, a **problem** can be described as a disturbance or unsettled matter that demands a solution if the organization is to function productively. In many instances, the solution requires a decision that is arrived at only after (1) an extensive review of relevant information and (2) application of considerable thought and skill. A supervisor's work is full of such problems. For convenience in analysis, problems can be classified into three groups:

Problems that have already occurred or are occurring now. Examples include merchandise that has spoiled, a valued employee who has quit, costs that are running out of line, and shipments that are not meeting delivery dates. These need immediate solutions to correct what has taken place or is taking place right now.

Identified problems that lie ahead. Examples are how to finish a specific project on time, when to put on a second shift, where to place the new press, and whether or not to tell employees of an impending change in their work. These, too, require immediate solutions to set effective plans and procedures.

Problems that you want to detect and forestall. These lurk in the future. You'd like to take preventive action now so that they will never arise and thus never require solutions.

Problems, and their solutions, are, of course, inseparably related to the management process. Problems arise all along the way. Supervisors must solve them when they plan, organize, staff, direct, and control. Otherwise, problems will stand in the way of the attainment of the department's goals.

What causes a problem?

Change. If everything remained exactly as it should be, problems would not occur. Unfortunately, change, especially unwanted change, is always with us. Changes occur in materials, tools and equipment, employee attitudes, specifications received from customers, the work space itself, and just about anything else you can imagine. The trick to problem solving is often the ability to spot the unwanted and unexpected change that has slipped into an otherwise normal situation.

How can you recognize a problem or a potential problem?

A problem exists when there is a gap (or variance) between what you expect to happen and what actually happens. (See Figure 6-1.) Your budget, for example, calls for 2200 insurance policies to be processed this week; the count at 5 p.m. on Friday shows that you completed only 1975, a gap of 225 policies. Or you expected to hold the total number of employee absences in your department to 300 days this year; the total is 410, a gap of 110 days.

It is almost the same with potential problems. You know what you would like to have occur in the future: a project completed, a perfect safety record, fewer than ten customer complaints. These are your plans. But when you look ahead at your procedures and the potential for mishaps, you feel that your department will fall short of its targets—that there will be gap. In a nutshell, you find problems by spotting a gap (deviation or variance) between actual and expected performance. Note the similarity here to Step 3 in the control process, and note that corrective action (Step 4) is called for at this time (page 95 in Chapter 5).

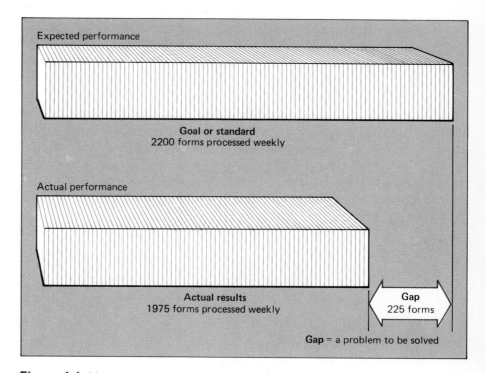

Figure 6-1 How gaps between actual performance and goals or standards help to identify, or "find," problems.

☑ SYSTEMATIC PROBLEM SOLVING

CONCEPT Problems should be approached systematically, with the goal of removing their causes.

How are problems solved?

By removing whatever it is that has caused, or will cause, a gap between the expected (or desired) condition and the actual condition. That's the main idea, at least. Suppose, for example, that your hoped-for safety record of zero accidents is spoiled by three accidents on the punch press machine. You will want to (1) find their cause (bypassing of the safety guard by the operators) and (2) remove it (by designing a foolproof guard).

Finding and removing the cause or causes, however, is usually difficult and requires considerable examination and thought. There will be more discussion about the problem-solving process later.

What is the connection between problem solving and decision making?

The two processes are closely related. (See Figure 6-2.) A decision is always needed in the choice of the problem's solution. In many ways, problem solving *is* decision making. As you will see in a moment, any step along the way of planning, organizing, directing, controlling—and problem solving—that presents a choice of more than one course of action requires also that a decision be made. Take the safety record on the punch press again. A truly complete analysis of the problem might have suggested that the cause could be removed in three different ways: (1) use of an automatic feeding device that would remove the need for a guard, (2) institution of an educational and disciplinary program to

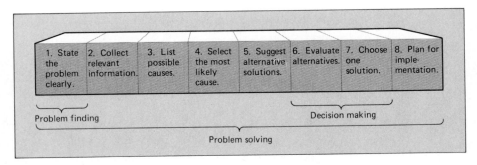

Figure 6-2 The problem-solving process. How problem solving and decision making overlap.

instruct operators about the proper operation of the present guard, or (3) design of a foolproof guarding system. The supervisor, as decision maker, would have to choose among the three alternatives. The first might be judged too costly, the second not completely effective, and the third the best choice because it is relatively inexpensive and foolproof.

Must the approach to problem solving be systematic?

Yes. There are few exceptions to the rule that the best results come from a systematic approach. Here, as illustrated in Figure 6-2, is a fundamental approach to problem solving and decision making:

Step 1: State the problem clearly and specifically. Stay away from a general statement, such as "We have a problem with quality." Instead, narrow it down and put figures on it if you can, as in "Between the first of the month and today, the number of rejects found at final inspection totaled 32, compared with our standard of 15."

Step 2: Collect all information relevant to the problem. Don't go too far afield, but do find data that may shed some light on process changes, materials used, equipment function, design specifications, employee performance, and assignments. Much of the data will not tell you anything except where the source of the problem is not. If your information shows, for example, that there has been no change in the way materials have arrived or machinery has been used, good! You can look elsewhere.

Step 3: List as many possible causes for the problem as you can think of. Remember that a problem is a gap between expected and actual conditions. Something must have occurred to cause that gap. Most particularly, something must have been changed. Is the present operator different from the old one? Was a power source less regular than before? Has there been a change, however slight, in the specifications?

Step 4: Select the cause or causes that seem most likely. Do this through a process of elimination. To test a cause to see if it is a probable one, try seeing (or thinking through) what difference it would make if that factor were returned to its original state. For example, suppose a possible cause of rejects is that compressed air power is now only 75 pounds instead of 90 pounds. Try making the product with the pressure restored to 90 pounds. If it makes no difference, then power irregularity is not a likely cause. Or perhaps you think that the new operator has misunderstood your instructions. Check this out with the operator. See if your instructions are, in fact, being followed exactly. If not, what happens when your instructions are followed? If the rejects stop, then this is a likely cause. If the rejects persist, this is not a likely cause.

Step 5: Suggest as many solutions for removing causes as you can. This is a good time for brainstorming. There is rarely only one way to solve a problem. If the cause of an employee's excessive absenteeism, for instance, is difficulty getting up in the morning, this cause might be removed in a number of ways. You might change the shift, insist that the employee buy an alarm clock, make a wake-up telephone call yourself, or show how failure to get to work is job-threatening. The point is to make your list of alternative solutions as long as possible.

Step 6: Evaluate the pros and cons of each proposed solution. Some solutions will be better than others. But what does better mean? Cheaper? Faster? Surer? More participative? More in line with company policy? To judge which solution is best, you'll have to have a set of criteria like the ones just listed. Evaluation requires that you make judgments based on facts. Consult the information gathered in Step 2. Also consult anyone who can offer specialized opinions about the criteria you have chosen.

Step 7: Choose the solution you think is best. Yes, this—like what you did in Step 6—is the decision phase of problem solving. In effect, you will have weighed all the chances of success against the risks of failure. The strengths of your solution should exceed its weaknesses.

Step 8: Spell out a plan of action to carry out your solution. Decisions require action and follow-up. Pin down exactly what will be done and how, who will do it, where, and when. How much money can be spent? What resources can be used? What is the deadline?

When should you solve problems on your own, and when should you go to others for help?

This depends upon a number of factors. Table 6-1 shows how to look at the whole picture before deciding to handle a problem on your own or to ask another person or a group of employees for their assistance.

▣ *DECISION MAKING: RATIONAL AND INTUITIVE*

CONCEPT Decisions are the logical outcome of problem solving.

How can you recognize the need for a decision?

Whenever there is more than one way of doing things, a decision is needed. Any kind of choice, alternative, or option calls for a decision.

Factors	1. You Decide Alone	2. You Consult With One of Your Employees	3. You Consult With a Group of Your Employees
Whose problem is it?	Yours alone	His or hers	The group's (ours)
Amount of time	Not available	Have some time available	Plenty of time available
Expertise	Fully expert	Expert advice is needed to fill gaps in your own knowledge	Yes, as for No. 2
Technical know-how	Full know-how	Need to fill in gaps in your technical know-how	Yes, as for No. 2
Can others add anything to the decision?	No	Yes	Yes
Will you accept suggestions?	No, not likely	Yes, from someone you respect	Yes, from an effective unit
Will it help others to carry out the project if they are involved in the decision?	No significance; you will carry out the project yourself	Yes, helpful and essential	Yes, necessary and essential
Coordination of effort	Not needed; you will handle it all	Vertical; necessary with your superior or your employees	Horizontal; needed and necessary among your employees
Learning value	No value to anyone else	Value to one employee, potentially	Value to your whole group

Table 6-1 GUIDE FOR SEEKING HELP IN PROBLEM SOLVING

You might ask, "If this is so, why are so many decision opportunities overlooked?" The answer is that managers and supervisors alike get preoccupied with the status quo. In effect they say, "The way we are doing this is the only way." Such supervisors miss the point that there are always alternatives. There is always the choice to do something or not to do it, to speak or to remain silent, to correct or to let well enough alone. All too often a supervisor's decision is made by default. The supervisor does nothing. The tide of events carries the department until a crisis occurs. In reality, however, doing nothing represents a choice. It is a decision not to change, not to plan for improvement, not to anticipate a potential problem.

How systematic must the decision-making process be?

There are good reasons to believe that decision making, unlike problem solving, need not always be systematic—or even logical. System helps up to a point. But when you are dealing with the future, hunches and intuition often pay off.

The systematic, or rational, approach to decision making takes place during Steps 6 and 7 of problem solving: evaluating alternative solutions and selecting the best one on the basis of the facts available. This approach can be made even more rational and more reliable by first setting goals that the decision must enable you to reach. For example, a problem-solving decision about cost cutting must be effective for at least six months and not involve employee separations. Or, if you are developing future plans, the decision may be required to fulfill the requirement of ensuring that production schedules be met without overtime.

This rational step of first setting a goal tends to make the quality of the decision better, even when it is ultimately made by hunch, because you know what your target is or what limitations will be placed on your choice or plans for implementation.

What is meant by mathematical decision making?

Mathematical decision making refers to the use of certain mathematical, statistical, or quantitative techniques to aid the decision maker. These are aids, very valuable ones in many instances, but they are only aids. The techniques do not make decisions. They arrange numerical information in such a way that it can be analyzed mathematically, but the executive, manager, or supervisor must make the final decision on the basis of an interpretation of the results.

How can supervisors make use of decision trees?

A **decision tree** is essentially a graphic portrait of Steps 5 and 6 in the problem-solving process. It shows how each alternative solution forks into various possibilities. Suppose, for example, that a supervisor is faced with a decision about how to treat Edgar, an employee whose attendance has been very poor. One alternative (A_1) is to enforce strict discipline by laying Edgar off for three days. A second alternative (A_2) is

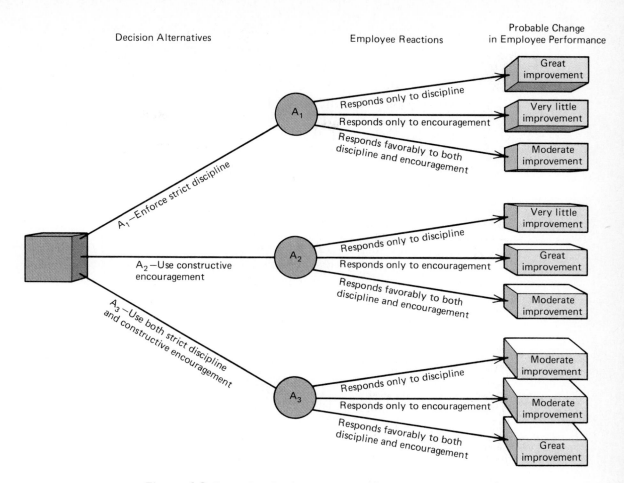

Figure 6-3 Example of a decision tree. Alternative outcomes of various applications of discipline versus constructive encouragement in trying to improve an employee's performance.

to provide constructive encouragement. A third alternative (A_3) is to try a little of both. Figure 6-3 shows how these alternatives work on a decision tree.

The supervisor can presume that there are only three ways Edgar can react. He may respond only to strict discipline, he may respond only to encouragement, or he may respond favorably to both. The probable changes in performance from each kind of response are diagramed, with a range of outcomes from very little improvement to great improvement. Thus, the improvement in Edgar's performance differs according to each decision strategy and to each possibility of how Edgar might respond to it.

Edgar may react three different ways to the A_1 alternative. If he responds to discipline, there may be great improvement; if he responds only to encouragement, then there will be very little improvement. Or, if he responds favorably to both discipline and encouragement, there may be moderate improvement. Similarly, Edgar may react three different ways to alternative A_2 and to alternative A_3. The decision tree helps the supervisor to visualize the various outcomes or possible changes in Edgar's performance. On the basis of this analysis, you may be better able to choose the alternative that has the best chance of being effective.

What is meant by cost-benefit analysis?

It is not unlike the closing steps in problem solving and decision making. This is the phase in which you examine the pros and cons of each proposed solution. Cost-benefit analysis has become a popular technique for evaluating proposals in the public sector. Take, for example, a proposal for a local government to offer a child-care service to its residents. Cost-benefit analysis adds all the costs of implementation and equates them with the value of the services to the community. Typically, the benefits of such nonprofit services are hard to quantify; that is, it is hard to place a dollar value on them. Accordingly, many cost-benefit analyses include quality judgments of benefits as well as dollar estimates.

Cost-benefit analysis is similar to *input-output* analysis, which is an attempt to make sure that the cost and effort expended in carrying out a decision will at least be balanced by its outputs or results. In business, when outputs exceed inputs, the result is a profit. If there is an excess of benefits over costs in nonprofit organizations, the excess is called a surplus.

Are decisions based on intuition as good as those based on logic?

If a decision works out well, it won't make any difference how it was reached. Many decisions based on hunch have proved to be correct. They are harder to defend, however, when they go wrong. More important, any decision is likely to be better if its goals are clearly understood. The logical approach helps to strip away distractions and irrelevancies. Intuition often adds a valuable dimension by calling on some inner sense we don't clearly understand. Many authorities believe the best decisions come from the dual approach—a combination of logic and hunch.

What is a "programmed" decision?

Decisions that are spelled out in advance by a standard procedure or policy are said to be "programmed." That is, a supervisor has only to identify the problem correctly as one that has arisen before. There's no point in solving it a second time. As a consequence, the supervisor simply applies the previous solution or the decision that is dictated by standard procedures and policies. By avoiding the necessity of having to "reinvent the wheel" each time the same problem comes up, a supervisor saves time and energy.

Some problems occur so frequently that you can set up a routine decision for them. You must remember, however, that what worked before may not work again. It can be risky to follow past experience blindly without considering other possible solutions.

What can be done to make your decisions more effective?

Besides starting with a specific goal in mind and laying a foundation of facts and systematic analysis, there are a couple of other kinds of insurance you can turn to.

Pick Your Spots   Try to make decisions only where the potential for payoff is great. You can identify this kind of opportunity by using ABC analysis. (See Figure 6-4.) The ABC concept is based on an established economic fact: A vital few problems or opportunities for action account for the greatest loss or greatest gain. Most problems and oppor-

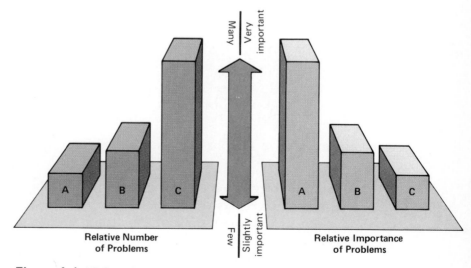

Figure 6-4 ABC analysis.

tunities are basically of little consequence. Economists call this the 20/80 syndrome. It means that 20 percent of your problems will account for 80 percent of your losses or profits. Then, to turn the idea around, 80 percent of your problems will account for only 20 percent of your losses or profits. In ABC analysis the vital few are called "A" items; the inconsequential many, "C" items; and those that fall somewhere in between, "B" items. If you were to take an inventory of items in your stockroom, for example, it is a sure bet that only a relatively few items would account for most of its value. A great many items, however, such as paper clips and erasers, would account for only a small portion of the inventory's total worth. Astute purchasing managers concentrate on the vital few items, not the trivial many. You should apply the same principle to your problems and decisions selection.

Maintain Your Perspective   Statistically, problems fall in what is called a normal distribution, and so do the results of most decisions. We say, "You win some and you lose some." That's really what a normal distribution tells us. If you make ten decisions, one or two will work out fine. One or two are likely to be "bombs." The rest will fall somewhere in between. Knowing this, you should keep the following guidelines in mind when you make decisions:

1. Don't reach too high. Don't set your objectives at the very top; allow some room for mistakes.
2. Don't overcommit or overextend your resources on one problem; you may need them later for an unanticipated problem.
3. Always prepare a fallback position, a way to alter plans and attain at least part of the objective.

▣ INFORMATION AS A RAW MATERIAL

CONCEPT   Information is the substance with which problems are solved and decisions are made.

In seeking information to solve a problem or make a decision, what should be the cutoff point?

Stop looking when the trouble and cost of obtaining the extra information exceeds its value. *The rule is:* The more critical and lasting the effect of a decision, the more you can afford to look for the last scrap of vital information. Don't spend two days hunting for background data on a purchasing decision, for example, if the item plays only an insignificant part in your process and will be used only once or twice.

On the other hand, it might pay to defer a decision to hire a full-time employee until you have made a reference check.

Do guard against using the absence of information as an excuse for procrastination. Some decisions are especially hard to arrive at and unpleasant to carry out. When you are faced with these situations, there is a temptation to put off an answer (yes, answers are decisions—or should be) by asking for more information. Rarely is the questioner fooled by this tactic, and rarely does the additional information add much to the quality of the decision.

The burden of information collection and analysis has now become so enormous, however, that most organizations provide support with some form of management information system.

What, really, is a management information system? Why is it so important?

At its root a **management information system** (MIS) is plain old accounting, but with a much broader base and an electronic twist. An MIS is important because it can provide an informed basis for all management decisions. When the system is a good one, decisions are likely to be good. When the system is skimpy or overdone or misleading, decisions will suffer.

A modern management information system tries to keep track of everything that may help to make a manager's decisions effective. In a manufacturing company, for example, the MIS collects and analyzes information about product development, production, marketing, and finance. In a service company such as a commercial airline, the MIS may encompass other functions, such as aircraft operation, maintenance, scheduling, and customer sales and ticketing.

The ultimate objective of an MIS is to tie together all a company's past and present data into a great big library with instant electronic recall. Managers at all levels draw from this library (called a data bank) any kind of information that aids short-range or long-term decisions. Few organizations reach this ideal. Most management information systems operate in functional pockets with separate systems for each important activity. Production and inventory control may form one system, for example, and payroll accounting another. These functional systems are only loosely tied into the overall company MIS, with little cross-referencing between them. The goal, however, is gradually to link all separate MISs into a fully integrated system.

Should a distinction be made between data and information?

It may seem like hairsplitting, but MIS designers insist there are good reasons to distinguish between them.

Data can be described as merely facts and figures that, until processed, bear little relation to decision making.

Information is data that has been processed for specific use by managers and supervisors in decision making related to planning, organizing, staffing, directing, and controlling.

⬛5 AN MIS OF YOUR OWN

CONCEPT   Supervisors are vital participants in an organization's management information system.

Where do supervisors fit in the MIS computer picture?

Supervisors become involved in computer operations in two basic ways:

1. You may simply be an *end user* of computer output information. If so, make the most of this output. Understand what it means, what you are supposed to derive from it, and what kind of actions you are supposed to take on the basis of it. Is the computer printout you get a yard long, but only six items apply directly to you? Should you make a correction today? Or can you wait until the next report before you get moving?

2. You may be a *prime source* of inputs. If so, find out specifically what information your department is sending to the computer. Which records are selected for keyboarding? Exactly what form should they be in when they leave your department? Are the measures your employees are collecting exactly the same as those required for the computer? For example, are you tallying in inches when the computer needs metric figures? Or are you transmitting daily figures when the computer wants hourly data?

Can supervisors design their own management information systems?

Yes. Even if their parent organizations have an MIS, supervisors can and should develop their own concept of how information needed for decisions is gathered and routed to them. Figure 6-5(*a*) shows a basic management information system. Figure 6-5(*b*) shows how a supervisor can adopt the same principle to explain departmental information needs, sources, and uses. *Primary data* is new information that is collected and analyzed for the specific purpose of running a particular operation. *Secondary data* is any useful information previously collected and published by trade associations, business magazines, the U.S. government, or any other source outside the department.

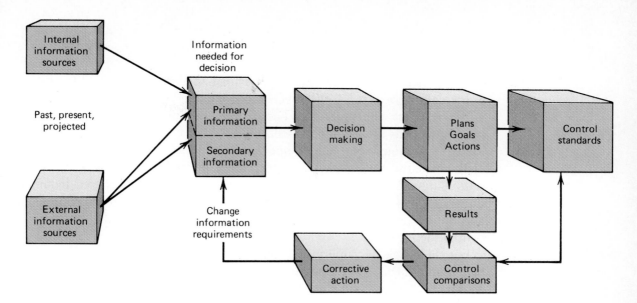

Figure 6-5(a) Basic components of a management information system.

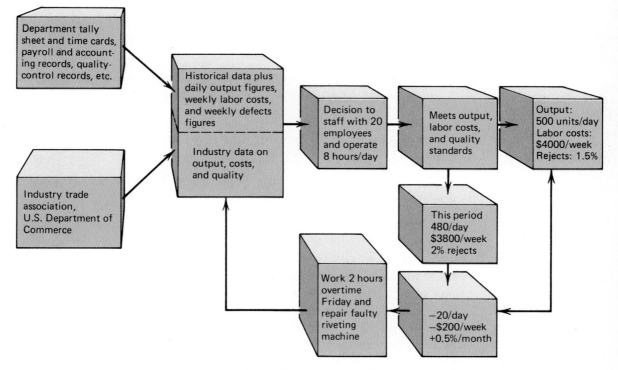

Figure 6-5(b) Assembly supervisor's departmental information system.

Secondary data for your department may simply be the data you can gather from other departments in your own company, agency, or institution.

In Figure 6-5(b) the supervisor set performance standards at 500 units a day, labor costs at $4000 a week, and the average weekly reject rate at 1.5 percent. The supervisor based the decisions for these standards on past records for the department and on what could be learned about industry standards for similar operations.

To make the MIS work, the supervisor requested the following: daily output figures from the shop clerk; weekly labor costs gathered from the time cards, processed by the payroll section, and recorded by the accounting department; and the weekly defects rate from the quality-control department.

For this week the supervisor's daily output has been only 480, or 20 below standard. Labor costs were $3800, or $200 less than budgeted. The weekly reject rate was up to 2 percent, or 0.5 percent over standard. On the basis of these control comparisons, the supervisor decides to take corrective action. The entire staff will work overtime for two hours on Friday to raise output. The supervisor will also place a maintenance request to fix a faulty riveting machine, to which the higher reject rate is attributed.

6 KEEPING THE SYSTEM HUMAN

CONCEPT   Computerized handling of information introduces problems of stress and adjustment to a supervisor's work force.

How does the systematization of information handling, especially with computers, affect people at work?

It has its good aspects and its unfavorable ones. Even these draw conflicting responses. For example:

1. **Systematization reduces job tensions and conflicts by making things more orderly.**   There will always be conflict among people, jobs, and operations. The computer should lessen their intensity, however, because the interfaces will be fixed and predictable. Once an information issue is resolved between the production and the maintenance supervisors, it should be less bothersome, because it will arise in the same manner each time and can be anticipated.

2. **Systematization creates job dissatisfaction because it requires that individuals fit their work into a rigidly prescribed format.**   Those employees who dislike close supervision and control will feel the

same way about any system that makes similar demands. Supervisors must do a better job than in the past of placing people in work that best suits their concept of job satisfaction.

3. **Systematization tends to make work monotonous because it reduces the opportunity to be creative.** If the job is one that is fully dominated by the system, this will be true. People who prefer routine to initiative may like it, however. For many jobs the computer has just the opposite effect. It removes the routine and calls out for creative solutions to the problems it identifies.

4. **Systematization depersonalizes work; people serve the machine more than the machine serves people.** This is unfortunately true at lower levels of employment. At skilled and managerial levels, however, the system takes over much of the tiresome work and allows people to devote a greater portion of their efforts to work that matches their education, experience, and capabilities.

What can be done to make employees more adaptable to the MIS process, electronic data processing, and computers in general?

Electronic data processing (EDP) and other aspects of computer technology are with all of us to stay. Happily, employees coming out of high schools and colleges today are much more familiar with it than are those of previous generations. Nevertheless, there are several positive tacks that supervisors should take.

Try to Reduce Tension by Allowing Employees to Bring Their Irritations Into the Open   Tempers are likely to flare highest when a new system is being debugged. Suppose Mike says, "Nothing matters anymore except getting the data to that electronic monster on time." Don't give Mike this reply: "That's too bad. If you can't keep up with it, maybe you better look for a job somewhere else." Instead, try saying something like this: "I agree that the computer now seems to be dominating our work in the department. Perhaps it won't be that way once we get used to it. After all, look how we adjust ourselves to the exact time for a TV show or a sports event. Let's stick with it and see if we can get the better of this situation."

Acknowledge That It's Only Normal to Be Fearful of What the Computer May Do to Jobs and Job Security   Suppose that Selma says, "When they redesigned the last computer setup, six people in the payroll section were transferred to the sales order department, and not one of them likes it over there. What's going to happen when these MIS analysts finish up with us next month?" Don't dismiss Selma's fear as something silly. Instead, agree that computers and EDP have made changes in the company. And, yes, some of these changes have been hard to accept. But assure Selma that you will do whatever you can do to make certain that higher management is aware of her present contributions. You will also look around to see where and how her talents can best be used if there is a change in her job.

Focus Your Attention on Trying to Make Sure That People Are Assigned to the Work They Do Best and Like Best Abe, Edna, and Malcolm like routine work so that they can socialize to the maximum; assign them to repetitive work that is undemanding mentally. Ella, Dixie, and Vortek have strong creative qualities; assign them to work that requires initiative. All six persons may have to work in a computer-oriented world, but usually enough different kinds of work are available to satisfy individual preferences. People and job matches won't be perfect, of course. But when supervisors show they are willing to make the effort, this act in itself helps to counteract anxieties about computers' depersonalizing the work.

REVIEW

KEY CONCEPTS TO REMEMBER

1. Effective supervisors are able to (a) recognize the existence of a problem or the need for a decision, (b) anticipate potential trouble spots, and (c) identify opportunities for improvement. Problems are caused by changes, or other factors, that disturb normal procedures or conditions. Problems can be recognized by a gap between what is expected (or planned) to happen and what actually occurs.

2. Problems are solved by removing or correcting the cause of the disturbance, which, in turn, closes the gap in performance. Problem solving should always be approached systematically. The process can often be improved by seeking help from those individuals or groups of employees who are best informed and/or more closely involved in the problem and in implementing its solution.

3. Decision making is an inseparable part of the problem-solving process. It is the phase in which solutions, ideas, and new courses of action are examined critically and then chosen on the basis of their chances for success or failure in meeting related objectives. Decision making may be approached mathematically—using a variety of techniques such as the decision tree—or intuitively. It is always more

effective, however, when based upon firm objectives and sound information.

4. Effective problem solving depends upon the quantity and quality of information upon which analysis and judgments are made. Increasingly, formal management information systems (MISs) provide operational information for decision-making purposes in a convenient form for managers and supervisors.

5. Supervisors stand at both ends of the MIS and computer systems. As end users, they receive computer outputs that provide them with operational and cost data. As prime sources of input, supervisors collect and transmit all sorts of sales, production, quality, and cost data to the system. By applying MIS principles, supervisors can also make up their own departmental MIS from time cards, schedules, production tallies, quality specifications, inspection records, and other data related to their unit's operations.

6. Computerized information gathering and monitoring pose a real or imagined threat to many employees. Supervisors should face these problems openly and try to reduce tensions and dissatisfactions by making job assignments as attractive as possible.

SUPERVISORY WORD POWER

Cost-benefit analysis. A technique for weighing the pros and cons of alternative courses of action, especially in nonprofit organizations, in which both the intangible benefits of the action and its costs are assigned dollar values.

Decision making. That part of the problem-solving process that entails evaluation of the alternative solutions and a choice among them of an effective remedial action.

Decision tree. A graphic method of portraying, for comparative purposes, the possible outcomes of each of a number of alternative solutions or remedial actions.

Information. Data—past or present facts, observations, or conclusions collected in numbers and words—that has been selected, arranged, and analyzed (processed) to make it useful for a specific human (managerial) activity.

Management information system (MIS). A system made up of data processing devices, programs, and people, which collects, analyzes, exchanges, and delivers information to the organization in such a way as to help managers make the best possible decisions.

Problem solving. The process wherein the gap that occurs between expected and actual conditions or results is analyzed systematically in order to find and remedy its causes.

Programmed decision.   A decision that is indicated by the solution to a similar, recurring problem or by a procedure or policy that has been established for dealing with such a problem.

READING COMPREHENSION

1. How would you recognize the existence of a problem?
2. What is the primary cause of most problems? What causes a gap to occur?
3. Differentiate between problem solving and decision making.
4. Under what circumstances might it be better for supervisors to seek help in solving a problem rather than handling it all by themselves?
5. If you were asked to decide which of five projects might be chosen for a public health-care program under your supervision, what technique might you use? Why?
6. Supply some examples of how a company's policies, rules, or standard procedures help to "program" a decision for a supervisor.
7. Distinguish between data and information.
8. Which of the following are considered primary data for a supervisor's departmental MIS? Production tallies collected at the end of the day, inventory-status records retrieved from a company's central data file, a count of errors that have occurred in the department during the week, comparative cost data from the U.S. Department of Commerce.
9. Systematization of information handling may have three undesirable effects upon employees. What are they?
10. Besides the obvious value of providing better information on which to make decisions, what particular advantage may a smoothly operating MIS offer to employees. Why?

APPLICATION

SELF-APPRAISAL

How astute a problem solver are you?

The following statements pertain to recognizing and solving problems and to managing information. Your assignment is to determine which statements are true, or represent sound practice, and which are false, or represent unsound practice. On a separate piece of paper, copy the column headings shown below. In the "Statements" column, write the numbers 1 to 15 down the page to correspond to each of the statements. Then place a check mark in the column that most nearly matches your opinion about each statement. After completing this activity, check your answers by using the scoring procedure described below.

Column headings:

Statements	True, or Sound Practice	False, or Unsound Practice Practice

1. When a variance appears between expected and actual performance, you know that you've got a problem.
2. Problems occur spontaneously without any rhyme or reason.
3. There have been lots of changes in your department recently, so you can expect more problems than normal to arise.
4. Problems are solved when gaps are closed.
5. A good statement of a production problem might be, "We're having trouble with our output these days."
6. If you know the cause of a problem, it's a waste of time to consider more than one alternative solution.
7. If Mary is to solve the problem of too many errors among her keyboard operators, she will have to make a decision.
8. A decision tree graphically displays the consequences of alternative solutions.
9. John is a very logical thinker. That is all he'll need to be a good problem solver.
10. When you are selecting the problems that should get most of your attention, ABC analysis will be helpful.
11. The better the information there is about a problem, the better the solution is likely to be.
12. When making a decision in his department, supervisor Brown finds that data is generally more useful than information.
13. Supervisors often find that they are both end users and prime sources of an organization's management information system.
14. The data that Helena, supervisor of rent collections for an apartment complex, posts from monthly rent receipts is secondary data.
15. Since employees are often unduly concerned about computerized data systems, supervisors should assure employees that their jobs will not be affected by the changes.

Scoring Give yourself 1 point for each of the following statements that you checked as *true*, or representing sound practice: 1, 3, 4, 7, 8, 10, 11, 13.

Give yourself 1 point for each of the following statements that you checked as *false*, or representing unsound practice: 2, 5, 6, 9, 12, 14, 15.

Interpretation   If you scored 13 points or more, you're well prepared to handle problems and information effectively. If you scored between 10 and 12 points, you're likely to arrive at some faulty decisions. Review the items you missed. If you scored less than 10 points, you're far too uncertain to be able to handle problems and information effectively. Review the entire chapter.

CASE STUDIES

CASE 16   **The Absent Retail Clerks**

Ramona, who supervises the human resources department of a retail discount store, is listening to complaints from Ted, the store's manager. "You've got to do a better job of screening job applicants, Ramona," says Ted. "Our current crew of retail clerks are absolutely undependable. They are killing us with absences."

"That's not the same impression I have of the situation," says Ramona. "Is this an everyday problem?"

"Well, not every day. Fridays are the worst."

"Then the problem occurs mostly on Fridays?"

"Yes."

"Let's look at the time cards for Fridays," suggests Ramona.

Upon examination of the time cards, this is what Ted and Ramona discovered. Of 30 employees, five were absent on Friday. During the rest of the week, there were never more than two employees absent at any one time.

"Here's something interesting," observes Ramona. "The absences are mostly among the same five people. And they are all assigned to checkout duties."

"That hadn't occurred to me," replies Ted.

"This makes the problem a little clearer," says Ramona. "Perhaps now we can do something to correct it."

If you were Ramona, how would you proceed to solve this problem? Of the five alternatives provided below, which do you think might be the most effective? Rank the alternatives on a scale from 1 (most preferable) to 5 (least preferable). You may add another alternative if you wish. In any event, be prepared to justify your ranking.

a. Introduce a storewide program for reducing absenteeism.

b. Warn the five most absent clerks that a continuation of their absences will lead to dismissal.

c. Since absences are limited to only a few clerks, take no action at this time.

d. Gather more information about the nature of checkout work at the store.

e. Revise the employee interviewing and selection procedure.

CASE 17   The "No Hardship" Problem

Derek Ghandel is the supervisor of a keypunch operation in a data processing section of a federal agency. He has ten operators reporting to him. Last week Derek and other supervisors received a directive from the agency's commissioner. It read: "Effective June 30, due to a reduction in funding, all sections will be expected to reduce their staffs by 10 percent. This should present no hardship since it is forecast that the data processing work load will also be reduced by the same percentage. Please make plans accordingly." Derek looked over his personnel list and selected for transfer or separation the employee who was least productive, Martina M. Derek said to himself, "I see no problem with this as long as I notify Martina of this decision before June 30."

Derek was wrong. Conditions changed that Derek had not foreseen, and he was faced with several problems. What factors can you think of that might affect Derek's decision?

CASE 18   The Careless Inventory Clerk

"Since we installed the computerized inventory system, your work has been sliding downhill," said Dora to Buddy G., an inventory clerk who reported to Dora in her position as warehouse supervisor. "Unless you get your act together, we'll be parting company."

"What's wrong?" asked Buddy.

"It should be clear to you," said Dora. "You have become very careless. The figures you generate on your inventory counts don't match those on the computer. Every month, the computer turns up an armful of errors on your part. I can't run this operation without more dependable information."

Said Buddy: "I don't see why I should be so careful if the computer is going to double-check everything I do. Before it arrived, I could count and calculate faster than anyone else. Now, I'm just an assistant to a machine. I knew that once the company installed the MIS, it wouldn't be long before I'd be one more innocent victim looking for a job."

a. What do you think is the real cause of Buddy's carelessness?
b. How well is Dora handling this problem? Why?
c. Should Dora continue to put Buddy on notice? What are other alternatives she might consider now?

Organizing, Staffing, and Training

1 Organizing arranges jobs into effective work relationships.

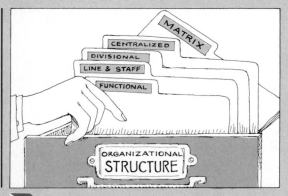

2 Organizational structures follow many traditional patterns.

3 These structures distribute authority (A) and responsibility (R).

4 Delegation of authority (A) and responsibility (R) helps to improve personal effectiveness.

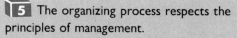

5 The organizing process respects the principles of management.

CHAPTER **7**

Organizing an Effective Department

LEARNING OBJECTIVES

After studying this chapter you should be able to

1. Describe the organizing process and its outcome and differentiate between formal and informal organizations.

2. Identify and differentiate among various organizational structures and formats including functional, line-and-staff, divisional or product, matrix, and centralized and decentralized organizations.

3. Define authority, responsibility, and accountability and explain their relationships.

4. Understand the benefits to be derived from delegation and explain several effective approaches to it.

5. Discuss the relationship of the organizing process to the chain of command and explain the concept of organizational development.

ORGANIZING FOR EFFECTIVENESS

CONCEPT   Organizing arranges jobs and groups of jobs in a department so that employees can perform their work in the most effective way.

What is an organization?

An **organization** is the structure derived from grouping people together so that they can work effectively toward a goal that members of the group want to achieve.

The goals of a business organization are primarily profits for stockholders and salaries and wages for managers, supervisors, and employees. There are other important goals, of course, such as supplying goods and services valued by the general population. While the goals of non-profit and public organizations do not include profit, members of such organizations expect them to provide compensation in addition to delivering valued services to others.

Members of an organization also look to it as a source of personal satisfactions, such as companionship, accomplishment, and prestige.

What is the distinction between organizing and an organization?

Organizing is the process of arranging the pattern of work relationships. An organization is the structure, or framework, that comes out of the organizing process.

Why organize in the first place?

Without an organization, we would have nothing but havoc in the workplace. We take organizations for granted because we have lived so long with them at home, in places of worship, and in the educational system. Little that we do together—anywhere—would be effective, however, if we didn't agree among ourselves on who should do what. We need look no further than team sports to see the extent of organizational structure that prevails. What would professional football be, for instance, without its highly organized structure of tasks for offense, defense, special teams, and special situations (that is, first-down run, third-down pass, goal-line defense, etc.)?

The overriding value of an organization, then, is its ability to make more effective use of human resources. Employees working alone and often at cross-purposes require the coordination and direction that an organization can provide. People working together within a sensible organizational structure have a greater sense of purpose and accomplish more than people whose efforts are allowed to run off in any direction they choose.

Are all organizations formal?

No. In a good many of our activities, even in complex manufacturing plants, some people just naturally take over responsibilities and exercise authority without anyone's ever spelling them out. Chances are that in a group of 15 employees who you might imagine are all at the same level, you'll discover some sort of informal organization. It may be that the person who sweeps the floors actually swings weight in that group. Acting as staff assistant may be the lift-truck driver, who is the informant. The rest of the group may either work hard or stage a slowdown at a nod from a third member of the group, who has authority as surely as if the company president had given it.

So be alert to informal organization—among the employees you supervise, in the supervisory group itself, and in the entire management structure.

How does the organizing process proceed?

Organizing follows planning. The organizational structure must provide the framework for carrying out the plan. Suppose, for example, a supervisor plans to load a boxcar by 5 p.m. The goal will be met if one employee is assigned to remove cartons from the stockroom, another to operate a fork truck, another to stack cartons in the boxcar, and another employee to verify and prepare the inventory and shipping documents.

Essentially, the organizing process moves from the knowledge of a goal or plan into a systematic *division of labor,* or *division of work.* Typically, the process follows these steps:

1. Making a list of all the tasks that must be performed by the organization to accomplish its objectives.
2. Dividing up these tasks into activities that can be performed by one person. Each person will then have a group of activities to perform, called a job. This in turn allows each person to become more proficient at his or her special job.
3. Grouping together related jobs (such as production jobs or accounting jobs) in a logical and efficient manner. This creates specialized departments or sections of the organization.
4. Establishing relationships between the various jobs and groupings of jobs so that all members of an organization will have a clear idea of

their responsibilities and of either their dependence on, or their control over, people in other jobs or groups of jobs.

Which comes first, the organization or the work to be done?

If there were no job to do, there would be no reason for having an organization. So don't make the mistake of being organization-happy and trying to set up an elaborate organization just for the sake of having one. The best organization is a simple one that puts people together so that the job at hand gets done better, more quickly, and more cheaply than any other way.

2 TYPES OF ORGANIZATIONAL STRUCTURES

CONCEPT Organizational structures follow several traditional patterns.

Which is the most basic of all organizational structures?

The **functional organization.** In it, each group of related activities is collected under one functional head. Thus, in Figure 7-1, the meats supervisor may have under her all the meat cutters, trimmers, and packers; the stockroom supervisor all the receivers, inspectors, and pricing clerks; and so forth. The functional approach to organizing yields the simplest structure. It also provides the basic framework from which other types of structures are built. *It is, essentially, a line organization.*

How is a line-and-staff organization formed?

A **line-and-staff organization** adds to the basic features of a functional (or line) organization staff groups that either give advice to, or perform

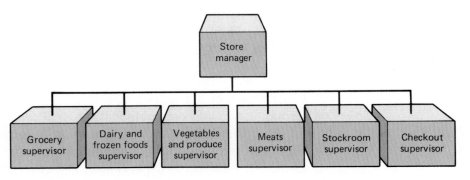

Figure 7-1 Example of a functional organization structure for a supermarket.

services for, the line functions. A line-and-staff organization is illustrated in Figure 7-2.

What is the difference between line and staff groups?

An organization works best when it gets many related jobs done effectively with the minimum of friction. This requires coordination and determination of what to do and who is to do it. Those managers and supervisors whose main job is to see that products and services are produced are usually considered members of the *line* organization. Other management people who help them to decide what to do and how to do it, assist in coordinating the efforts of all, or provide service or special expertise are usually called *staff* people.

In manufacturing plants, line activities are most commonly performed by production departments, sales departments, and, occasionally, pur-

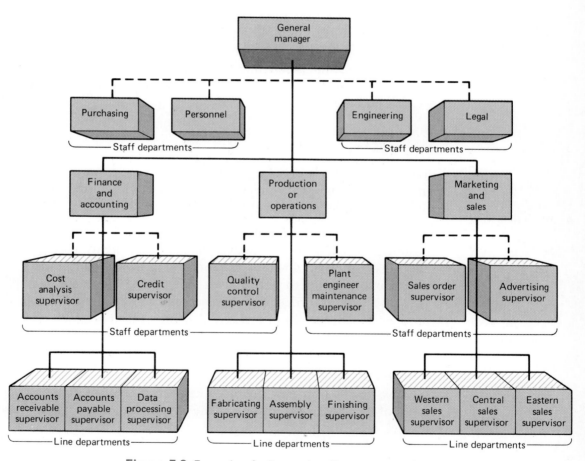

Figure 7-2 Example of a line-and-staff organization for a manufacturing company.

chasing departments. The production supervisor or first-line supervisor is likely to be a member of the line organization.

Departments that help the line departments control quality and maintain adequate records are typically staff departments. Industrial engineering, maintenance, research, MIS, and personnel relations are some examples of typical staff activities.

In service organizations such as banks and insurance firms, the line organization may represent the primary "action" operations (such as deposits, withdrawals, and recordkeeping or premium collections and claim settlements), and the staff organization such support groups as computer departments and actuarial.

In hotels and motels the line may be everything connected with the operation of a geographic unit, and the staff such activities as advertising, accounting, and legal.

In transport companies the line department may be fleet operations; the staff department, equipment repair and maintenance.

In a hospital, medical and nursing may be the line groups, with laboratory, culinary, and housekeeping the staff groups.

It may help you to think of line people as the doers, staff people as the advisers. Each function—line or staff—is important in its own way, even though there has often been rivalry between line and staff people for credit and recognition.

In what other ways may organizations be structured?

The great majority of organizations combine some form of functional segmentation along with a line-and-staff format. This allows for a great many variations. Among the most common are these:

Divisional or product.   All functions needed to make a particular product, for example, are gathered under one highly placed manager. If a firm manufactures tractors for farmers, road graders for construction contractors, and lawn mowers for home use, it might "divisionalize" in order to make and sell each major product in its product line, as shown in Figure 7-3. Note that under each division head this organization is essentially a functional one; as a consequence, labels such as "functional" and "divisional" can be misleading.

Geographic. A firm may divide some of its activities, such as sales, or all of its activities according to the geographic region where these take place.

Customer. A company may also choose to organize some or all of its activities according to the customers it serves, such as farmers, con-

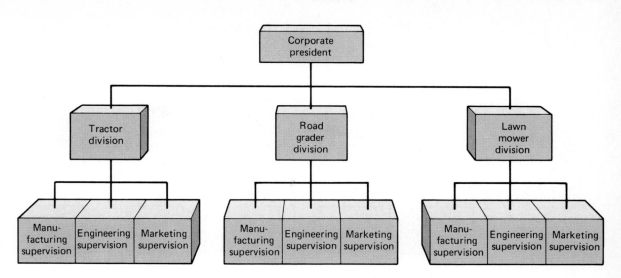

Figure 7-3 Example of a product, or divisional, organization structure for a manufacturing company.

tractors, and homeowners. This kind of organization is closely related to the product organization.

Regardless of organization type, always remember that the purpose of the organizational structure is to make your department's work fit together more closely with the work of other departments.

The matrix organization: What's that all about?

This is a nontraditional format, especially suited for projects, task-force work, or other one-of-a-kind enterprises. It is commonly used in research and development organizations and engineering firms for one-of-a-kind projects or contracts. It allows a project manager to call on the time and skills of personnel—for a limited period of time—with various functional specialties. When the project is completed, the specialized personnel return to their home units to await assignment to another project. Because project managers can exercise their authority horizontally across the basic organization while the specialists receive permanent authority from their functional bosses above them vertically on the chart (Figure 7-4), this form is called a matrix organization. The matrix organization has the drawback of requiring employees to report to more than one superior—a functional supervisor and a project supervisor. There is also some loss of control by both supervisors. Nevertheless, the format has proved to be effective in its chosen applications.

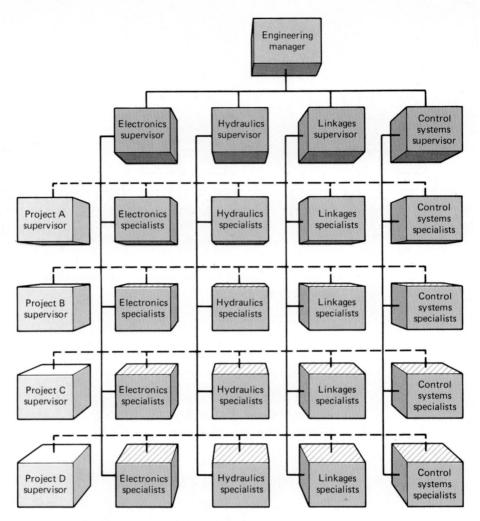

Figure 7-4 Example of a matrix organization structure.

How do you distinguish between a centralized organization and a decentralized one?

A *centralized* organization tends to have many levels of management, to concentrate its facilities in one location, to perform certain functions (such as engineering, labor negotiations, computer operations, and purchasing) from a single source, and to gather together its power and authority at headquarters. A *decentralized* organization tends to have the opposite characteristics, especially when a company is divided into distinctly separate units with varying degrees of independence. These units may be set up along product lines, according to geography, or according to methods of marketing and distribution.

Centralized organizations tend to have more levels of management, to exert tighter controls, and to allow employees less freedom to make their own decisions. Decentralized organizations have fewer levels of management, have looser controls, and allow employees greater freedom in their actions.

How wide can a supervisor's span of control be?

Authorities disagree on this point, but it is a good rule of thumb that no manager or supervisor should have the responsibility for more than six separate activities. The more specialized and complex the activities, the shorter the span of control. The more uniform and less complicated the activities (as with many supervisory responsibilities), the greater the span can be. Sometimes the span of control (or of management) is defined by the number of people rather than by the number of activities. When such is the case, it is not unusual for a supervisor to have a span of 30 or more employees, provided they are engaged in only a few simple, related activities. On the other hand, a middle-level manager might be responsible for the activities managed by the supervisors of six different departments.

What purpose is served by charts of an organization's structure?

They help you understand organizational relationships. Such charts are really pictures of how one job or department fits in with others. Each box, or rectangle, encloses an activity or department. Those boxes on the same horizontal level on the chart tend to have the same degree of authority or power and to have their work closely related. Departments in boxes on the next higher level have greater authority; those at lower levels have less authority. Clusters of boxes that enclose departments performing closely related functions (such as shaping, fabricating, assembly, and finishing in a manufacturing plant) are typically shown at the same level and reporting vertically above to the head manager of that particular function (such as the production manager).

Boxes containing line departments tend to descend from the top of the chart to the bottom (where supervisors' departments typically are) in vertical chains. Boxes that enclose staff departments tend to branch out to either side of the main flow of authority.

Organization charts can be drawn in any way that shows relationships best, even in circles; but for practical purposes most charting is done in the manner just described and illustrated in the figures. One note of caution: Organizational structures and staffing change constantly. Accordingly, organization charts go out of date very quickly.

⒔ AUTHORITY, RESPONSIBILITY, AND ACCOUNTABILITY

CONCEPT   The organizational structure provides the framework for the formal distribution—or delegation—of authority and responsibility.

Are authority and responsibility the same thing?

No. Authority should go hand in hand with responsibility, but the two are no more alike than are the two sides of a coin. Your *responsibilities* are those things you are held accountable for—such as costs, on-time deliveries, and good housekeeping. Responsibilities are also spoken of as your duties—such as checking time cards, investigating accidents, scheduling employees, and keeping production records. *Authority* is the power you need to carry out your responsibilities. A supervisor's authority includes the right to make decisions, to take action to control costs and quality, and to exercise necessary discipline over the employees assigned to help carry out the responsibilities.

It's an axiom that you shouldn't be given a responsibility without enough authority to carry it out. If a supervisor is given responsibility for seeing that quality is up to specifications, that supervisor must also be given authority to stop the production line when the quality falls off or to take any steps necessary to correct the condition.

Where does your organizational authority come from?

Authority, like responsibility, is usually handed down to supervisors from their immediate bosses. The bosses in turn receive their authority and responsibilities from their immediate superiors. And so it goes, on up to the company president, who receives assignments from the board of directors. This process of handing down responsibility and authority is known as delegation.

The biggest chunk of authority and responsibility rests with the company president, who may split this chunk in as few as 3 pieces (to the vice presidents of production, sales, and financing) or as many as 20 (to vice presidents in charge of 20 different products). As the responsibilities and authorities come down the line to you, the pieces get smaller. But they also get much more specific.

Your plant superintendent may have the responsibility of producing goods in sufficient quantities to meet sales requirements, whereas your responsibility may be to see that ten milling machines are operated at optimum capacity so that 200,000 product units are produced each month. Similarly, the plant superintendent's authority may permit the exercise of broad disciplinary measures, whereas yours may be limited to recommending disciplinary action for employees who break rules or whose output is not up to production and quality standards.

Most companies try to make the responsibilities and authorities at each level of management fairly consistent. For instance, a supervisor in Department A should have the same general responsibilities as a supervisor in Department Z. And their authorities would be generally the same even though the specific duties of each might differ widely.

Appendix B in the back of the book provides a checklist that might help you and your boss decide on those duties, policies, and actions for which you should be held responsible.

What other sources can you draw on for your authority?

In addition to your organizational "right" to get things done, you may often need to draw on other, more personal sources. Your employer tries to establish your organizational rights by granting you a title or a rank, by depicting your position on an organization chart, and by providing some visible demonstration of status, such as a desk or an office or some special privilege. Ordinarily, you must reinforce this personal authority—or power—with one of the following:

- Your job knowledge or craftsmanship
- Your personal influence in the organization (whom you know and whom you can get to help you or your team)
- Your personal charm (if you have it)
- Your ability to see that things get done (performance)
- Your persuasive ability (a communication skill)

All these sources are important because employees tend to restrict their acknowledgment of organizational rights over them. They expect their supervisors to show a little more real power than that. When employees come to accept your authority as deserved or earned (*acceptance* theory of authority rather than *institutional*), you will find that your people relationships will improve.

Should a distinction be drawn among authority, responsibility, and accountability?

Yes. Although the distinction may appear to you to be only a technical one, it is not. As your boss, for example, I might be held accountable to higher management for the way in which operating supplies are conserved in my department. But I have the prerogative to delegate this responsibility to you—if I also grant you the authority to take any steps needed to protect these supplies. If you were to misuse these supplies or to lose track of them, I might discipline you for failing to discharge your responsibility in this matter. But I'd still be held accountable to my boss (and would be subject to discipline) for what happened—no matter which one of us was at fault. Similarly, when you delegate a minor responsibility to one of your employees (together with the necessary authority to carry it out), you will still be held accountable to your boss for the way in which this responsibility is fulfilled by your subordinate. In other words, you can delegate responsibility, but you cannot delegate accountability.

How much leeway do supervisors have in taking authoritative action?

You can't draw a hard-and-fast rule to follow. Generally speaking, a company may establish three rough classifications of authority within which supervisors can make decisions:

- **Class 1.** Complete authority. Supervisors can take action without consulting their superiors.
- **Class 2.** Limited authority. Supervisors can take action they deem fit as long as the superior is told about it afterward.
- **Class 3.** No authority. Supervisors can take no action until they check with their superiors.

If many decisions fall into class 3, supervisors will become little more than messengers. To improve this situation, first learn more about your company's policy and then spend time finding out how your bosses would act. If you can convince them that you would handle matters as they might, your bosses are more likely to transfer class 3 decisions into class 2 and, as you prove yourself, from class 2 to class 1.

Note that the existing company policy would still prevail. The big change would be in permitting supervisory discretion. And this would be because you have demonstrated that you are qualified to translate front-office policy into frontline action.

How do staff people exert their influence?

More often than not, staff departments suggest or advise. They may suggest a different, and improved, way of doing something, advise that your department is off target (on quality, for instance), or provide information for your use and guidance.

If supervisors are smart, they will make every use they can of the staff department's knowledge. If you were building a house yourself for the first time and someone offered to give you free the advice of a first-rate carpenter, a top-notch mason, a heating specialist, and an experienced painter, you'd jump at the chance. The same holds true in accepting the advice and guidance available from staff departments and other specialists when you are tackling a management problem.

You should be alert, however, to the fact that in many organizations, staff units are granted functional authority. *Functional authority* entitles a staff department to specify the policies and procedures to be followed in matters within their specialties. For example, supervisors might be told: they cannot hire a new employee unless he or she has been screened by the employment department; nothing can be ordered from outside the company without a completed purchasing requisition; maintenance repairs cannot be made without an approved work order; the production-control department will have final say on the scheduling of customer orders; and so on.

In still other variations, organizational policy may specify that while supervisors have final authority over a functional matter, they may be required either (1) to consult with the functional specialist before taking action or (2) to reach an agreement beforehand on the intended action.

4 DELEGATION FOR LEVERAGE

CONCEPTS Delegation of selected tasks by supervisors can greatly add to their personal effectiveness.

Who can delegate authority and responsibility?

Any member of management, including the supervisor, can usually delegate some responsibility—and authority. Remember, the two must go together.

A supervisor, for instance, who has responsibility for seeing that proper records are kept in the department may delegate that responsibility to a records clerk. But the clerk must also be given the authority to collect time sheets from the operators and to interview them if the data seems inaccurate. The supervisor wouldn't, however, delegate to the records clerk the authority to discipline an employee. Likewise, a supervisor can't delegate the accountability for seeing that accurate records are kept.

When should you delegate some of your work?

Delegate when you find you can't personally keep up with everything you feel you should do. Giving minor time-consuming tasks to others will save your time for bigger things. Let one employee double-check the production report, for example, and send another employee down the line to see who wants to work overtime.

Arrange to have certain jobs taken over when you're absent from your department in an emergency or during vacation. Keep it to routine matters, if you will, and to those requiring a minimum of authority. But do try to get rid of the tasks of filling out routine requisitions and reports, making calculations and entries, checking supplies, and running errands.

How can you do a better job of delegating?

Start by thinking of yourself as primarily a manager. Recognize that no matter how good a person you might be, you'll always have more responsibilities than you can carry out yourself.

The trick of delegating is to concentrate on the most important matters yourself. Keep a close eye, for instance, on the trend of production costs—that's a big item. But let someone else check the temperature of the quenching oil in the heat treater—that's less important.

Trouble begins when you can't distinguish between the big and the little matters. You may feel you can put off checking the production record: it can wait until the day of reckoning at the end of the month. You may think that unless the quenching oil temperature is just right, the heat treater will spoil a $500 die today. But in the long run you'll lose your sanity if you don't see that the small jobs must get done by someone else.

Be ready, too, to give up certain work that you enjoy. A supervisor must learn to let go of those tasks that rightfully belong to a subordinate. Otherwise, larger and more demanding assignments may not get done. And don't worry too much about getting blamed by your boss for delegating to an employee work the boss has given to you. Generally speaking, supervisors should be interested only in seeing that the job is done the right way, not in who carries it out. See Figure 7-5 for an idea of how to decide which jobs should be targeted for delegation.

Should you delegate everything?

Don't go too far. Some things are yours alone. When a duty involves technical knowledge that only you possess, it would be wrong to let someone less able take over. And it's wrong to trust confidential information to others.

What should you tell employees about jobs delegated to them?

Give them a clear statement of what they are to do, how far they can go, and how much checking you intend to do. Let employees know the

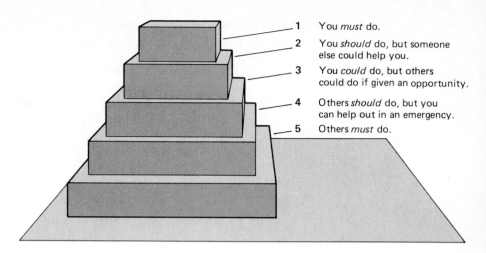

1 You *must* do.

2 You *should* do, but someone else could help you.

3 You *could* do, but others could do if given an opportunity.

4 Others *should* do, but you can help out in an emergency.

5 Others *must* do.

Figure 7-5 Supervisor's task and delegation chart.

relative importance of the job so that they can judge how much attention it should receive. There's no point in letting an employee think that making a tally will lead to a promotion if you consider it just a routine task.

Tell employees why you delegated the job. If it shows you have confidence in them, they will try that much harder. But if they think you're pushing off all the dirty jobs onto them, they may deliberately make mistakes.

Don't mislead employees about authority. You don't want them trying to crack your whip. But do define the scope of the task and see that others in your department know that this new task isn't something an employee assumed without authorization. Let it be known that you gave the assignment and that you'll expect cooperation from the other workers.

Why should employees accept a delegated job?

Employees who accept a delegated job outside their own job responsibilities are really taking the job on speculation. They have a right to know what's in it for them:

- **Employees who take on an extra duty get a chance to learn.** If they have never seen how the individual records in the department are tabulated, here's a chance for them to get a better perception of what's going on.
- **Delegated jobs provide more job satisfaction.** Employees thrive on varied assignments. This is a chance to build interest by letting employees do something out of the ordinary.

- **Delegation is sometimes a reward for other work well done.** If you can truthfully say that you wouldn't trust anyone else with a certain delegated task, this will help build employee pride and a feeling of status.

You may also want to try the concept of "completed staff work." You assign a problem requiring judgment and common sense to a subordinate, and he or she is to provide you with a complete solution according to these specifications:

1. Consulted other personnel who are affected by, or who can contribute to, the problem's analysis.
2. Provided concrete recommendations about how to proceed.
3. Worked out all the details.
4. Avoided overly long and complex explanations.
5. Presented a single, coordinated plan of action in written form.

When can delegating go wrong?

Delegation of personal tasks will invite trouble if you are tempted to engage in any of the following practices:

- Delegating dirty work, trivial work, or boring work that cannot be justified as representing a genuine opportunity for self-development.
- Overloading a subordinate beyond the limits of his or her time or ability.
- Failing to match responsibility with the appropriate authority to obtain the resources needed to complete the job successfully.
- Undercontrolling or overcontrolling the subordinate. You should keep an eye on progress and be ready to help, if requested. Otherwise, try to stand aside and let the subordinate handle the assignment independently.

5 GUIDELINES FOR ORGANIZING

CONCEPT Organizing respects the principles of management while making allowances for flexibility and change.

What is the relationship of the chain of command to the structure of an organization?

The term *chain of command* is a military phrase used to imply that delegation of responsibility and authority and of orders and information in an organization should originate at the top and then proceed toward the bottom from each one-higher management level to the next lower level without skipping any levels or crossing over to another chain of command. The same procedure would be followed regarding information and requests going up the line. Your boss is entitled to first-hand information about your work and its progress.

Is it a bad practice to go out of channels?

It's best to conform to the practice in your company. *Channel* is just a word used to indicate the normal path that information, orders, or requests should travel when following the chain of command. The channel that customer orders travel in going from the sales manager to the production supervisor might be from the sales manager to the production manager, from the production manager to the department superintendent, and from the department superintendent to the supervisor. It would be going out of channels if the sales manager gave the order directly to the supervisor.

The channel used by a supervisor to ask for a raise might be from the supervisor to the department head, from the department head to the production manager, and from the production manager to the manufacturing vice president. The supervisor would be going out of channels if the vice president were asked for a raise before each one of the other managers had been seen in progression.

Since authority and responsibility are delegated through the channels of a chain of command, for the most part it's better to handle your affairs (especially decisions) through them too. It avoids your making changes without letting your boss know what's going on. And it prevents others from feeling that another manager is going over the boss's head.

On the other hand, there are occasions when chain-of-command channels should be circumvented. In emergencies, or when time is essential, it makes sense to get a decision or advice from a higher authority other than your boss if your boss is not readily available.

For purposes of keeping people informed and exchanging information, channels sometimes get in the way. There's really nothing wrong with your discussing matters with people in other departments or on other levels of the company—as long as you don't betray confidences. If you do cross channels, it's a good practice to tell your boss you are doing so, and why. That way, you won't seem to be doing something behind your boss's back. And that is something you should never do.

Are there any organizational no-no's?

Yes, but not very many. Once an organization is set up, practicality ought to prevail. In fact, some odd—and informal—arrangements occasionally work out very well. For example, one leading manufacturing company has operated for years without a visual organization chart. Its maverick president believes that the staff will develop the most effective relationships without one, and apparently it has. Nevertheless, in the design stages, at least, there are a few hazards of organization that ought to be guarded against:

1. **Don't let the chain of command get too long.** Keep the number of responsibility levels at a minimum; otherwise, some information will never trickle all the way to the bottom.
2. **Don't ask one person to report to two bosses.** Anyone caught in this nutcracker knows the dilemma: Which boss's work comes first?
3. **Don't make fuzzy job assignments.** When there is a gray area between two positions, overlap, conflict, and duplication of effort are invited.
4. **Don't be too rigid.** Try to retain flexibility for contingent situations— those problems that inevitably crop up and need handling by nonstandard assignments.

What can be done to help your department's organization adjust to changing conditions?

You can apply some of the techniques of **organizational development** (OD). OD is a participative, rather than a purely management-directed, approach to organizing. It assumes that members of an organization (your employees, for instance) are more aware of conflicts and deficiencies caused by organizational constraints than the boss may be. To institute an informal OD program, a supervisor invites employees, singly at first and later when they are all together, to discuss their job roles and relationships. Specifically, employees are asked to comment on the appropriateness of their duties and responsibilities, the extent of their authority, and the way in which their jobs mesh with or abrade other jobs. Inevitably, this brings into the open problems that can be attributed to the division of labor and the organizational structure. At that point, the supervisor and employees try to solve these problems constructively, rather than criticizing and placing blame on one another. For example:

1. **OD strives to achieve clarity of each person's role in the organization.** Group discussions consider such questions as: "What is Bill's role, and what is my role?" "What is the extent of authority that Mary has when working on urgent, red-rush projects?" "What can we expect from the records department, and how much must we do ourselves?"

2. **OD helps set priorities.** It answers such questions as: "When we have six requests from sales for special handling of orders, which gets our attention first? Who decides this?" "In the event of a conflict between a quality standard and a shipping deadline, who makes this decision?" "When it comes to working on my job or helping out with Pete's job, which comes first?"

3. **OD seeks to settle staffing problems.** It encourages employees to find answers to questions such as these: "Which one of us will get the services of temporary help when it arrives?" "If my job gets to be too much for me during the Christmas rush, what kind of assistance can I expect?" "If there is a slowdown this summer, will Adam continue to work with me, or will he be transferred to another operation?"

REVIEW

KEY CONCEPTS TO REMEMBER

1. The organizing process creates the organizational structure. This structure prescribes the way that different individuals with different skills, and performing different tasks, can combine their efforts effectively into logical groupings (or departments) for the pursuit of common goals. Such structures also encourage order and harmony in the workplace.

2. A variety of organizational structures can be built. The basic structure is the functional organization, which is often modified to incorporate staff, as well as line, departments. Other traditional forms are the divisional (or product), geographic, and customer organizations. The matrix organization is a newer form which is especially suitable to projects and task forces. When a great deal of authority is retained at the top, an organization is said to be centralized; when authority is freely distributed, an organization is said to be decentralized.

3. The formal organizational structure provides the framework—or chain of command—for the formal distribution or delegation of responsibilities and the authority needed to discharge them. A responsibility is a duty or an obligation; authority is the power to carry out that obligation. It is imperative that responsibility and authority be balanced. Rarely is a supervisor's power absolute. There are usually

restrictions placed upon it based upon organizational policies and practices. A supervisor's authority is further affected by the authority often granted to staff specialists. While their main responsibility is to advise or provide service, staff departments may also have functional authority in matters involving their specialties.

4. In addition to the formal delegation of tasks that occurs during the organizing process, there is also an opportunity for supervisors to engage in the informal delegation of tasks to their subordinates. Such delegation, fairly and prudently practiced, adds greatly to the amount of work a supervisor can accomplish.

5. Certain principles prevail in the establishment of effective organizations. Among them are (a) an awareness of the chain of command and a respect for the channels it creates and (b) an adherence to the principle of an employee having only one boss. Organizations are living bodies and subject to change of all kinds. Organizational development (OD) is a participative technique that enables members of an organization to revise the structure of an organization so that it may better cope with change as it occurs.

SUPERVISORY WORD POWER

Accountability. A nonassignable liability for the way in which an organizational obligation held by a supervisor is discharged, either personally or by subordinates.

Authority. The legitimate power to issue orders to other people in an organization and to obtain resources from it.

Delegation. The assignment, or entrustment, to subordinates of organizational responsibilities or obligations along with appropriate organizational authority, power, and rights.

Functional authority. The legitimate authority granted to a staff department to make overriding organizational decisions involving its particular functional specialty.

Functional organization. An organizational structure in which tasks are grouped according to a particular operating function, such as production, sales, information handling, and so on.

Line-and-staff organization. The most common form of organizational structure, in which line managers hold accountability for results that most directly affect profits or institutional goals and staff managers hold accountability for results that most directly affect the processes by which line managers accomplish their goals.

Organization. The structure derived from systematically grouping the tasks to be performed and from prescribing formal relationships that strengthen the ability of people to work more effectively together in pursuing common objectives.

Organizational development (OD). A participative management technique whereby members of an organization review their tasks and roles in order to develop among themselves a more effective organization.

Responsibility. A duty or obligation to perform a prescribed task or service or to attain a specified objective.

READING COMPREHENSION

1. What features distinguish a formal organization from an informal one?
2. Explain the part that the division of work plays in the organizing process.
3. Jill is an assembly supervisor in a plastics novelty company. Her department receives maintenance services on its presses from a plant engineering department. A quality-control department inspects the output of Jill's department and advises her when it is off grade. What common form of organizational structure do these relationships imply? Identify the kinds of departments represented here.
4. Name three traditional kinds of organizational structures besides the functional and line-and-staff organizations.
5. What is a major drawback of the matrix organization?
6. Distinguish between responsibility and authority, and explain how the two are related.
7. Give an example of functional authority.
8. In what way does the concept of accountability place restrictions on the delegation process?
9. What are some of the benefits a subordinate may gain from accepting a delegated task?
10. What is the objective of organizational development? How is that objective accomplished?

APPLICATION

SELF-APPRAISAL

How well organized are you?

The alphabetic list below provides terms and techniques commonly used when supervisors carry out the organizing process. The numbered list contains definitions, descriptions, clues, and examples that relate to these terms and techniques. Your assignment is to match the correct term or technique with each numbered item. On a separate piece of paper, write the numbers 1 to 15 down the page to correspond to each definition, description, clue, and example. After each number on your list, write the letter of the appropriate term or technique. After completing this activity, check your answers by using the scoring procedure described on page 159.

Definitions, Descriptions, Clues, and Examples

1. This is the outcome of the organizing process.
2. Miguel sets his auto repair store up so that two people work on mechanical systems, three on electrical systems, and two on bodywork. What kind of organization has Miguel created?
3. Miguel finds that despite the organization he has established, his repair workers have arranged their own way of handling the various tasks. What kind of organization has evolved among Miguel's employees?
4. When Ann formed her department, she made sure that she retained a great deal of control. How can her department be characterized?
5. This feature of the division of work must always be balanced by an equal amount of authority.

Terms and Techniques

a. Acceptance
b. Accountability
c. Authority
d. Centralized organization
e. Channels
f. Delegation
g. Division of work
h. Functional organization
i. Informal organization
j. Line-and-staff organization
k. An organization
l. Organization chart
m. Organizational development
n. Responsibility
o. Staff department

6. You cannot delegate this.
7. This is the power needed to carry out responsibilities.
8. Some supervisors rely upon this kind of authority more than the institutional kind.
9. This practice of asking subordinates to accept additional assignments outside their normal jobs adds leverage to a supervisor's job.
10. These paths for distribution of responsibility, authority, and communications are created by the chain of command.
11. This occurs when Peter invites all employees in his department to suggest ways in which their work may be better organized to handle changing conditions.
12. Jane's department provides word processing services for the sales department of a major manufacturing company. What kind of department is Jane's likely to be?
13. This term describes the larger organization in which Jane's word processing department and the sales department coexist.
14. The process of organizing greatly involves this practice and is often called by this name.
15. This is the graphic portrayal of organizational groupings and relationships.

Scoring   Give yourself 1 point for each correct match. The answers are 1–k, 2–h, 3–i, 4–d, 5–n, 6–b, 7–c, 8–a, 9–f, 10–e, 11–m, 12–o, 13–j, 14–g, 15–1.

Interpretation   If you scored 12 points or more, there's a good chance that you know how to organize effectively. If you scored between 9 and 11 points, you may not be able to handle an organizing function successfully. You should review the text for the correct answers. If you scored less than 9 points, you should restudy the chapter carefully and try again.

CASE 19   The Back-Posted Overtime

The budgeting department of a large eastern utility company is split into three organizational units. Each is headed by a manager, to whom one or more supervisors report. Grace Ming is the manager of the station-cost accounting department. Only one supervisor reports to her, Tim Coyle. Tim is responsible for timekeeping, job costing, and payroll.

Because of unusually heavy power loads in August, the number of station repair jobs performed on overtime has almost doubled. Accordingly, Tim's staff has had a hard time keeping up to date with job costs. Tim's practice is to wait until time charges are verified against job estimates before he authorizes their transfer to payroll. This causes a great deal of concern among station employees, who feel that payrolls should be kept current with time-worked records.

Last Monday, Grace Ming called Tim into her office and said: "We can't be late again with time charges this week. Will you make certain that we are caught up by Friday?" Tim went back to his desk and thought for a while. Finally, he spoke to the best clerk in the timekeeping section—in fact, the most knowledgeable clerk in the department. "Fred," he said, "I need your help on a touchy problem, right away. Beginning tomorrow, will you lend a hand in the job-cost section? Since I know it so well, I'll take over your timekeeping activity and also make the resolutions of job costs with payroll." Fred agreed to do so.

Now it is Friday, and Tim has found that he hasn't had time to fill in for Fred on timekeeping and still handle the resolutions. The result is that overtime in payroll is still being back-posted. Grace Ming greets this news with dismay and asks, "What's the problem, Tim?" Tim's explanation is that he is being asked to do more than he can handle by himself and that he needs extra help if he is ever to catch up.

If you were Grace Ming, which of the following alternatives would you consider to be the most effective in handling this organizational problem? Rank the alternatives on a scale from 1 (most preferable) to 5 (least preferable). You may add another alternative, if you wish. In any event, be prepared to justify your ranking.

a. Increase the number of employees working in the job-cost section.
b. Appoint a new supervisor, and put that person in charge of the job-cost section.

c. Tell Tim to transfer Fred to the job-cost section and insist that, temporarily at least, Tim delegate responsibility for resolutions to Fred.

d. Advise Tim that he should select and train a backstop for himself in each of his sections.

e. Appoint two new supervisors so that each section has its own supervisor.

CASE 20   The New Quality-Control Department

The Boonetown Forging Company has never had a full-fledged inspection or quality-control department. Up until this year, the various functions have been carried out, irregularly, by the manufacturing and engineering departments. Recently, the company secured a large government contract and was told that it must set up a quality-control department that can ensure proper product quality. Dan Crown, formerly a supervisor in the engineering department, was told that he could head the new department if he could come up with an acceptable organization. Dan got right to work, and after a few days, this is what he had written in his notebook:

The need Make sure that no forged products are shipped that do not meet government standards for size, weight, strength, etc.

Cost Keep number of staff and cost of operating this department to a minimum commensurate with the need for quality assurance.

Tasks to Perform

1. Implement design and engineering of product to conform to specifications.
2. Implement design and engineering of processes and equipment that can manufacture to specifications.
3. Specify, acquire, and maintain proper measuring instruments.
4. Inspect incoming raw materials and parts.
5. Inspect parts in process and assembly.
6. Inspect final products.
7. Inspect tools.
8. Establish and administer statistical control procedures for sampling of materials and for inspection.

Dan has been told that, as the department's manager, he can appoint as many as three supervisors to assist him if he needs them.

Put yourself in Dan Crown's position, and draw up what you think would be an effective organization chart.

a. Divide up the tasks into three logical groupings, or functions.
b. Decide which functions are most likely to be considered "line" for the quality-control department's objectives and which should be "staff."
c. Construct a line-and-staff structure somewhat like that shown in Figure 7-2.
d. Decide which of the functions really requires a supervisor.

CASE 21 Margaret's Delegation Decisions

The Metropolitan Planning Agency was set up to help the governments in a medium-size metropolitan area make plans for guiding future development in their area. The process carried out by the agency includes talking to local officials and members of the public to find out local goals; gathering and analyzing statistical information on population, economic growth, and so forth; as well as writing plans suggesting concrete steps the governments and citizens may take to reach their public goals. The plans may then be adopted by the governments and achieve legal status.

Margaret Walsh is a supervisor for the agency, overseeing nine employees who actually do the planning. Margaret used to be a planner herself, but now her work is entirely supervisory. The following list shows ten activities or duties for which Margaret's department is responsible.

a. Assign sections of overall plan to individual planners.
b. Gather data on which plans will be based.
c. Judge whether plan reports are of acceptable overall quality.
d. Decide what objectives will be included in plans.
e. Establish the number of planner-hours to be allocated to each project.
f. Meet with local officials to get their opinions for inclusion in plans.
g. Write community plans.
h. Work with governing bodies in their legal adoption of plans.
i. Present information about plans to the public.
j. Keep track of whether activities are being carried out within budget.

Mark each activity on the list to show whether Margaret should or should not delegate it. Use one of the following numbered actions to indicate your decision.

1. She must do it.
2. She should do it, but someone else could help her.
3. She could do it, but others could do it if given an opportunity.
4. Others should do it, but she can help out in an emergency.
5. Others must do it.

1 Staffing fills departmental jobs with appropriate workers.

2 The size of the work force must balance a number of factors.

3 Interview questions must be strictly job related.

4 Selection matches personal qualifications with job demands.

5 High absenteeism and turnover are major indicators of ineffective staffing and selection. Effective selection minimizes the potential for absences and turnover.

CHAPTER 8

Staffing With Human Resources

LEARNING OBJECTIVES

After studying this chapter, you should be able to

1. Identify the five steps of the staffing process and explain the extent of a supervisor's participation in each.

2. Know the factors that affect work force size and prepare a forecast of work force requirements.

3. Explain the main features of an employment interview and identify those questions that are most suitable and those that are restricted by equal employment opportunity legislation.

4. Discuss the critical aspects of the selection process and the role of tests, physical examinations, and reference checks.

5. Explain how careful selection can reduce employee turnover and absences and calculate specified turnover and absenteeism measures.

⬛ THE STAFFING PROCESS

CONCEPT   Effective staffing places the right numbers—and kinds—of workers on the right jobs at the right times.

How is organization staffing accomplished?

Through a five-step procedure:

1. **Specifying the kinds of jobs and workers needed to "flesh out" the organization structure.**   This structure was described in Chapter 7.
2. **Forecasting the total number of employees needed to complete a given work schedule.** This is a prime responsibility of supervisors.
3. **Recruiting those candidates to be screened for unfilled job openings.** Candidates may come from either inside or outside your organization. Recruiting is largely the responsibility of the human resources department.
4. **Interviewing job candidates.**   Supervisors participate actively in the interviewing process.
5. **Selecting the most appropriate individuals from among the candidates.** Supervisors play a prime role in the selection decisions.

What phases of work force staffing concern supervisors most?

The supervisor's chief responsibilities for a department's work force management could be summed up by saying the supervisor should have the right worker on the right job at the right time. How can this be done? By making accurate forecasts of the number of workers needed to staff the department, by taking an active interest in the kind of employees the company hires, and by maintaining working conditions that can attract and hold the best employees.

People are an organization's most vital resource. They will make or break your department's performance. People are very costly resources, however. You should select them the way you would a new car and take equally good care of them once they have been hired.

In what ways can you improve your hiring results?

Formalizing the employment procedure and making it systematic help rule out the big mistakes that often occur during haphazard hiring. For instance, every applicant should fill out some sort of form before being given consideration. On such a form the applicant should furnish critical information about work experience and education. A glance at the form will rule out people who don't meet educational or job-experience requirements.

The application form can tell you something more. A work record will reveal the job hopper who has held a dozen jobs in three or four years. This kind of person is usually an employment risk. Periods of prolonged employment are good indicators of stability, even if the indicator doesn't always prove reliable.

Chances are that your responsibility in your company will be limited to cooperating with the people in the employment or personnel department. If you understand what they are trying to do for you, they'll be able to do a better job for you. A prominent personnel executive put it this way: "The personnel department gives the candidate the first interview, checks references, and may conduct mechanical or clerical aptitude tests. The medical department makes certain the applicant is physically fit. But there is no substitute for the supervisory interview. The supervisor has to live and work with the employee. The supervisor should be satisfied that the new person fills the bill."

2 FORECASTING WORK FORCE REQUIREMENTS

CONCEPT Work loads, work schedules, vacations, and anticipated absences determine the size of the work force.

How do you forecast work force requirements?

It's really a matter of looking ahead—and applying simple arithmetic. Time studies and labor standards all make a forecast more accurate, but you can do very well without them.

Step 1. Find out what your department is scheduled to produce for the next week, month, quarter, or as far ahead as you can determine. If you don't know that, the chances are slight that you'll make efficient use of the people who work for you.

Step 2. Calculate how much the work schedule means in terms of total worker-hours. You can do this by getting an estimate from the methods, industrial engineering, accounting, or planning and scheduling department—if one exists in your company. Schedules from these departments are usually based on machine-time and work force estimates.

If worker-hour requirements aren't available elsewhere, you'll have to make your own estimate. Do this either by checking times for previous or similar jobs or by making careful estimates of the time required for each job. Keep your figures in terms of worker-hours or worker-days. But be specific and allow time for setups and teardowns. Try to recall delays associated with each job, and allow time for these.

Where jobs are machine-controlled (that is, the job can't be done any faster than the speed at which the machine runs), base your estimates on (1) how long the machine will take to do each job—allowing for breakdowns and idle time—and (2) how many operator-hours are needed to run the machine.

Step 3. Convert your totals to worker-hours and divide by 8 to see how many worker-days it will take you to complete your schedule for the period you've selected.

Step 4. Divide the total worker-days by the number of working days during the period to find the number of employees you'll need. But don't stop here.

Step 5. Check how many indirect persons—housekeepers, material handlers, setup persons—you'll need to service the required number of employees during this period (unless you included these in Step 2).

Step 6. Add the number of employees (direct labor) to the number of indirect persons to get the total needed.

Step 7. Make allowances for absences. How many days absent each month do employees in your department average? How many worker-days a month do all your employees combined lose? Suppose, for example, it's 5 worker-days a month. That's just the same as saying that you can expect to be short-handed 5 days a month, which may interfere with meeting your schedule. If you add an extra employee to cover absences, you can expect to be overstaffed 15 days a month—which is costly.

Can an example of forecasting work force requirements be shown?

1. Suppose your schedule shows that during July your department must produce 1000 widgets, 250 gadgets, and 60 umphlets.
2. Widgets and gadgets are hand-assembly jobs. Umphlets are produced on a machine. Previous production records, time studies, or standards show the following:

    Widgets: Average 50 a day with 10 employees

$$\frac{1000}{50} = 20 \text{ days}$$

20 days × 10 employees × 8 hours = 1600 worker-hours

Gadgets: Average 10 a day with 2 employees

$$\frac{250}{10} = 25 \text{ days}$$

25 days × 2 employees × 8 hours = 400 worker-hours
Umphlets: Average 3 a day, allowing for downtime; require 1 operator

$$\frac{60}{3} = 20 \text{ days}$$

20 days × 1 operator × 8 hours = 160 worker-hours
Total worker-hours for all three units:

1600 worker-hours (widgets) + 400 worker-hours (gadgets) + 160 worker-hours (umphlets) = 2160 worker-hours

3. Convert to worker-days:

$$\frac{2160 \text{ worker-hours}}{8 \text{ hours a day}} = 270 \text{ worker-days a month}$$

4. Average number of employees needed for the month:

$$\frac{270 \text{ worker-days}}{20 \text{ days a month}} = 13\frac{1}{2} \text{ employees for the month}$$

5. Add number of indirect employees. Three materials handlers take care of the gadget and umphlet operation. A combination setup person and packer handles the widget line. That's four employees each day all month.

6. Average number of employees needed in July:

$$13\frac{1}{2} \text{ direct}$$
$$\underline{4 \text{ indirect}}$$
$$17\frac{1}{2} \text{ employees}$$

7. Allowance for absences. Record for department shows your employees lose on the average a half-day each month:

$$17\frac{1}{2} \text{ employees} \times 4 \text{ hours a month absent} = 70 \text{ hours absent a month}$$

70 hours is about one-half of one employee for a month. So

$$17\frac{1}{2} \text{ employees needed}$$
$$\underline{\frac{1}{2} \text{ employee for absences}}$$
$$18 \text{ employees needed for the month of July}$$

You should be cautioned that this is a simplified example. In some cases the number of employees needed cannot be averaged by estimating gross worker-hours. Transfers of employees between operations can become impractical or can even be prohibited. The supervisor in the example, for instance, might not be able to use the umphlet operator on the widget line, or the widget operator on the umphlet line. In addition, you cannot presume that in practice you will have unlimited machines for assignment. Accordingly, you will encounter scheduling bottlenecks because of machine or space limitations and may have to plan second or third shifts.

Should you overstaff or understaff?

That depends. If you plan for too many employees, department costs will go up unless your schedule and machine availability will permit you to assign them to productive jobs. It's bad, too, to have idle people in the shop or to use them on make-work jobs. Overstaffing, however, does allow you to handle production emergencies and to cover peak loads.

Understaffing can be just as bad. It can get you behind in schedule and in trouble on deliveries. It can also give employees the feeling of being overworked. And it doesn't give you much flexibility.

Your company can minimize both overstaffing and understaffing by pooling the work force estimates of each supervisor and maintaining an optimum-size labor pool as a cushion against unpredictables—such as unusual absences or a sharp upward adjustment in schedules.

What is meant by balancing the work force?

Making sure that the number of employees on hand just matches the work load. Most departments have peaks and valleys that last an hour or a day. Mismatches that extend over a week, however, are costly and should be avoided. One way to balance your employee work load more consistently is to prepare a look-ahead work force trial balance, using a work sheet like the one illustrated in Table 8-1. This example looks 12 months ahead. If your work load is changeable, you could make such a sheet month by month.

What is the table of organization?

The expression *table of organization* (TO) is derived from military staffing practices. It implies that, for each department or unit, (1) staffing is limited to certain specified positions and (2) a specified number of people are prescribed for each position. When a department is "not up to its TO," either (1) vacancies exist as positions with no incumbents or (2) the number of incumbents in one or more position classes is less than that prescribed—or some combination of the two exists. The TO principle can beneficially be applied to business if the specific TO ca-

Table 8-1   WORK FORCE TRIAL BALANCE PLANNING WORKSHEET*

Dept: _____ Period: from _____ to _____ .

1. Number of workers needed to meet present work load:
   Direct
   Indirect   _____
      Subtotal   _____   _____

2. Number of additional workers to allow for:
   a. Scheduled workday losses
         Holidays
         Vacations   _____
           Subtotal   _____   _____
   b. Unscheduled workday losses
         Sickness and other excused absences
         Unexcused absences   _____
           Subtotal   _____   _____

3. Total number of workers needed to staff department at beginning of period (subtotal line 1 + subtotal 2a + subtotal 2b):   ════════

4. Number of workers to be added during the period to:
   a. Replace anticipated work force losses
         Retirements   _____
         Promotions and transfers   _____
         Discharges   _____
         Leave of absence   _____
           Subtotal   _____   _____
   b. Replace unanticipated work force losses†
         Resignations and quits   _____
         Disabilities   _____
         Deaths   _____
           Subtotal   _____   _____

5. Total number of employees needed to replace losses during the period (subtotal 4a + subtotal 4b):   ════════

6. Number of employees needed to meet anticipated change in department work load during the period:
   a. Additions to meet increase in work load
   b. Less: Removals to allow for decrease in work load   (−)_____

7. Total number of workers needed at end of period
         Number on line 3   _____
         Number on line 5   _____
         Number on line 6a or b (+ or −)   _____
           Total   _____

*All entries are in number of workers.
†If no past records are available, use 5% of the total on line 1.

pacity (or productivity) is carefully related to the organization's responsibilities and goals.

🔳 INTERVIEWING JOB CANDIDATES

CONCEPT   Interview questions should be strictly job-related and must be free from any implication of bias.

What should you talk about to job candidates?

Preview the job for the applicant. It's a great time-saver to tell the applicant what the fixed requirements of the job are. Mention such things as job title, relationships to other jobs, and the main activities involved in the job, such as walking, standing, sitting, or performing heavy work. Tell the applicant what kind of materials and machines are used and describe the working conditions.

It's especially wise to forewarn an applicant about any undesirable conditions, such as fumes, dampness, and night work. Don't scare the applicant, but be sure the facts are known ahead of time. Better that the applicant turn down the job than walk off it after three days.

You can also describe the good aspects of the job—what kind of advancement there is, the company's benefit programs, and so forth. This is the time to do some sound, factual selling, but don't make promises about raises or promotions. These can come back to haunt you later on.

What kind of questions should you ask the applicant?

Don't turn the interview into a "third degree" by asking too many point-blank questions—especially those that can be answered with a simple yes or no. The job seeker is likely to be on guard during the interview, anyway. For example, the answer will ordinarily be "yes" to a question like, "Did you get along well with your boss in the last place you worked?"

Ask "open-ended" questions that begin with *what, where, why, when,* or *who.* This gives the applicant a chance to talk and, while talking, to show you the kind of person he or she really is. If the applicant does most of the talking and you do most of the listening, you'll have lots of time to form an opinion. And that's the purpose of the interview.

Ask open-ended questions such as:

- What about your education? How do you feel that it would help you do the kind of work we do here?

- Where did you get your most valuable experience? Suppose you tell me about your working experience, starting with your first job.
- Whom did you report to in your last job? Can you describe that supervisor?
- When did you first decide you liked to do this sort of work? What have you found most difficult about it? Most pleasant?
- How would you describe your health? What kind of attendance record have you maintained during the last year?
- Why did you leave the job at the XYZ Company?

What kind of questions are you forbidden to ask a job applicant?

Be careful. Listen to whatever your personnel department advises. Otherwise, you as well as your company may get into trouble over some unintended equal employment opportunity infringement. The following is just a partial list of prohibitions:

- **Race or color.** Don't ask. Don't comment.
- **Religion.** Don't ask. Don't say, "This is a (Catholic, Protestant, Jewish, or other) organization."
- **National origin.** Don't ask. Don't comment.
- **Sex.** Don't ask. Don't comment. Don't indicate prejudgment about physical capabilities.
- **Age.** Don't ask, "How old are you?" Don't ask for a birth date. You *may* ask if the applicant is over the age of 18.
- **Marital status.** Don't ask for this, or for ages of children, or where a spouse works.
- **Disability.** You may ask if the person has a present disability that will interfere with the job to be performed, but you may *not* ask about past disabilities or illnesses.
- **Address.** You may ask for this and how long the person has lived there. You may ask if the applicant is an American citizen and, if not, whether the person has the legal right to remain permanently in the United States. It is generally unlawful to press for answers beyond this point.
- **Criminal record.** You may ask if the person has ever been convicted of a crime and when and where it took place. You may *not* ask if a person has ever been arrested, nor can you deny employment on this basis unless it can be proved it would damage the employer's business.
- **Physical capabilities.** Don't ask how tall or how strong an applicant is. This may indicate a sexist prejudice. You may explain physical aspects of the job, such as lifting, pulling, and so forth, and show how it must be performed. And you may require a physical exami-

nation. The hope is that if the applicant has a clear chance to estimate the job's physical requirements, the application will be withdrawn if the job appears too demanding or beyond the person's capabilities. Legally, however, you may not make that decision during an interview.

Questions about *education* and *experience* are pretty much unrestricted. The main point to be sure about in any interviewing area is that the question's relevance to the job for which the individual is applying can undeniably be shown. This legal requirement is called a bona fide occupational qualification (BFOQ).

What do you look for while interviewing an applicant?

Besides the factual things you obviously need to know about an applicant's skills and know-how, you'll want to be alert to what the interview tells you about:

Suitable background. Do the applicant's education and experience, and even residence and off-the-job associates, indicate that the person will be happy working with the people in your company? If education isn't a strong point and hobbies are bowling and baseball, the applicant won't find many friends among employees who take their education seriously and spend their spare time discussing opera and stamp collecting.

Desirable characteristics. Are the applicant's achievements outstanding? Did the person work five years at the XYZ Company without missing a day?

How about personal interests? If the jobs liked best in the past have been outdoor ones, such as truck driving, why is the applicant looking now for a confining job on an assembly line?

Try to spot attitude. Does the person act mature or sound as if given to childish boasting? Does the person listen to what you say? An example of an attitude you'll want to steer clear of is one where an individual goes out of the way to criticize the last company worked for, the people worked with, or the quality of the product. You'll probably be making no mistake in concluding that this individual is the kind of person who'd find everything wrong at your company too.

You can tell a lot about physical condition, too, from the interview. The person applying for a job who appears slow-moving and lethargic may put no energy into the job either. Remember, most people looking for work are trying to put their best foot forward. If an interviewee can't show you a very good side during the interview, there's a chance that you won't see anything better on the job.

What should you avoid in conducting a job interview?

James Menzies Black, an old friend of ours who used to be a director of personnel for a major railroad, cautioned:

1. **Don't be overly formal.** The more you do to help the applicant relax, the more effective the interview will be.
2. **Don't take notes.** A busy pencil writes off a productive interview. Train your memory so that you can make your notes after the interview is completed.
3. **Don't high-pressure applicants.** If you paint a glowing picture to job seekers that quickly fades after they are on the payroll, you will have disappointed employees on your hands. Worst of all, you will have employees who don't trust your word.
4. **Don't hire a chief when you really need a worker.** If an applicant is too intelligent or experienced to be happy in the job and there is little opportunity for quick promotion, say so. You want employee and job to match. That's why you conduct an interview.
5. **Don't tell applicants you are rejecting them for personality reasons.** If you think the experience or the knowledge to hold a job is lacking, be frank and say so. If you are refusing to hire for intangible reasons such as a poor personality, uncertainty about reliability, or a dislike of general attitude, keep your reasons to yourself. Frankness may offend applicants and will certainly discourage them for no good reason.
6. **Don't make moral judgments or give advice.** The applicant's personal life is no concern of yours.
7. **Don't ask trick questions that may embarrass.** If you see that there is conflict in the applicant's statements, you should certainly explore the matter, but do so discreetly. Your job is not to "catch" the prospect. It is to find out what you can about the individual.
8. **Don't let your facial expression, tone of voice, or gestures reveal your feelings.** You give applicants confidence by showing interest and sympathy. If they think you disapprove of what they are telling you, they will become silent or try to shift ideas around so that they will please you.
9. **Don't be impatient.** Try not to let the applicant know you're in a hurry, even if you are. A look at a watch has killed many an interview.

10. **Don't be misled by your prejudices.** Keep an open mind. Good interviews never allow their biases to cloud their judgment.

▣ SELECTING THE BEST PROSPECTS

CONCEPT   Selection should be based upon finding the persons whose qualifications best match the requirements of the jobs to be filled.

What can a supervisor do to improve the selection process?

Whenever a supervisor is given a chance to interview a prospective job candidate, that's a golden opportunity to help make sure the department gets a first-rate employee. Interviewing points that apply most directly to selecting employees are reviewed here.

Know What Kind of Employee You Want   Don't describe the person vaguely as a good worker who will stay on the job. That doesn't tell you much about the qualities you are looking for to suit the job that is open. Try making a checklist of necessary or desirable qualifications, such as:

- **Experience.** The applicant should have worked a couple of years on multiple-spindle drill presses, for example, even though they weren't exactly like yours.
- **Blueprint reading.** The person has to be able to work directly from prints.
- **Speed.** This job doesn't require a quick worker as much as it requires a steady, consistent worker.
- **Initiative.** Does the applicant's previous experience show work without close supervision?
- **Attendance.** Has the applicant a good record of attendance (because this job needs someone who's going to be here every day)?

See Enough Candidates   Your personnel department will probably screen out the obvious misfits before an applicant is sent to you for approval. But if you do the hiring directly, make a point of interviewing at least three candidates before making up your mind. That way you get a chance to make comparisons and to get the feel of the prevailing labor market. For some hard-to-fill jobs requiring special skills, you may have to see as many as 20 or 30 persons.

Will tests help to select better employees?

Over 50,000 firms think so. Properly selected, administered, and evaluated, so-called performance tests can be a big help in picking better workers. Tests may be simple and direct, such as those that show whether an applicant can read and write or perform the simple arithmetic that recordkeeping on the job may demand. Other, highly specific tests may enable an applicant to demonstrate the ability to perform the special skills your job demands. For instance, any person looking for a job can claim competence in operating a multiple-spindle automatic or a calculator. A ten-minute tryout will prove whether the claim is valid. These "can do?" tests, called *performance* (or *skill*) *tests,* are widely used.

Which tests are most sensitive to restrictions of the equal employment opportunity laws?

Psychological tests that attempt to find out whether a person has the ability to learn a particular kind of job (aptitude tests) can also be fairly reliable, but under present U.S. laws these are often open to challenge by the applicant. For that reason your company may or may not choose to use them.

Personality, intelligence, and job or career *interest* tests are widely used for applicants seeking higher-level management positions. But these, too, must be fully validated and their reliability proved before they can pass the civil rights hurdle. *Validity* simply means that the test really measures what it is supposed to measure. *Reliability* means that if an applicant were to take a test several times, the score would always be the same.

Underlying the challenges of validity and reliability is the requirement that any test given to applicants (1) should be directly related to the job's content and (2) should not discriminate unfairly against the person taking them. In other words, it would not be right to require that an applicant for a typist's job pass a test designed for an administrative secretary. Nor should the test be worded in such a way that it favors a person with a particular background over another who does not have it—unless it can be shown that the job requires that background.

Whom should you hire?

Deciding which applicant to hire isn't easy. But you can make a better decision if you separate facts from hunches—not that you should ignore your intuition or inferences. It's a good idea to take five minutes after you've interviewed an applicant to jot down what you think are the significant facts, and list your hunches too.

Facts may show that the job seeker has had ten years of experience on a milling machine, has good health, and can read blueprints. But your conversation may have brought out the feeling that the individual is stubborn and boastful and might be hard to supervise. Only you can tell which items you'll give most weight to. Some supervisors don't mind having a prima donna on their staff as long as that individual can produce. Others fear that a prima donna is likely to upset teamwork. And, of course, your hunches can be wrong.

You can be sure, however, that your choice will be better than flipping a coin if you've gone about your interview in a systematic way and if you've kept personal prejudices pertaining to race, religion, age, sex, or nationality out of your figuring.

How do you pick the best from the list of qualified applicants?

First, be sure that you have dropped no one from the list of possibilities because of discrimination or prejudice; in other words, be sure that all things are equal according to the law. Then, pick the applicant who fits your sense of what kind of person will do the job best. This is where your experience and intuition can help. For example, Bobby Knight, the highly successful Indiana University basketball coach, lists three things he looks for when recruiting basketball players:

(1) *Strength.* Wiry strength to hold onto the ball, to maintain a position on the boards or a defensive stance. (2) *Quickness.* The slow, plodding team will have trouble over the long season. (3) *Concentration.* There isn't a right way to play the game, but there are a lot of poor ways. You have to play in a way that utilizes the abilities of your team. Concentrate, and you will be successful.

Your department won't be playing basketball. But you can look for such things as (1) *perseverance,* as demonstrated by a work record that shows the applicant can stay with a difficult situation; (2) *alertness,* as indicated by the applicant's ability to follow your description of the work to be done—since many jobs require a person who can sense when a deviation from rigid procedures is desirable; (3) *cooperation,* as illustrated by the applicant's willingness to go through the red tape of employment interviewing and processing without quibbling about it. Other jobs, of course, may need another set of personal qualities. Initiative in a salesclerk, for example, may be more important than cooperation. Single-mindedness may be more valuable than alertness in a chemical processing plant that requires rigid conformance to prescribed sequence.

What good are physical examinations?

As a supervisor, you'll want to know whether a person assigned to your department has any physical limitations. There's no way of actually finding out about poor eyesight, a hernia, or a heart condition, for instance, without a complete physical examination. A physical defect doesn't necessarily rule out an applicant, but knowledge of it does ensure that person's being put on a job where the best work can be done and where the disability is not aggravated.

Should you check employee references?

Absolutely yes! It's foolhardy to hire anyone without checking with the last employer to find out the actual job the applicant held and to verify dates of employment. Most former employers will not tell you much more for fear of illegally prejudicing the applicant's chances. For this reason, it's wise also to tell the job candidate that you will be checking his or her education and employment statements. One good way to obtain the applicant's own views about his or her employment record is to ask, "What do you think your last employer would say about your performance, work habits, and attendance?"

Personal references, on the other hand, are usually not of much value. Few people will supply you with names of others who will say something bad about them.

5 MINIMIZING THE POTENTIAL FOR ABSENCES AND TURNOVER

CONCEPT   The selection process should seek to minimize the employment of people whose unsuitability will result in excessive absences and/or turnover.

What's the connection between the staffing process and high turnover and absenteeism among employees?

A high incidence of turnover and absenteeism among employees is a major indicator of an ineffective staffing and selection process. Other signs of ineffective staffing include excessive tardiness, poor quality of work, low productivity, and missed deadlines. Experts also identify low creativity and poor teamwork as other symptoms.

It costs upwards of $5000 to add an unskilled person to the payroll and as much as $15,000 to add an engineer or a computer programmer. A conservative estimate of the cost of keeping a semiskilled factory or office worker on the payroll for a year is $20,000. Figure it this way: Wages for a good employee run more than $12,000 a year. It costs an average of $2000 a year to train a new employee or keep an experienced employee up to production standards. Add another $3500 in fringe benefits that don't show up in salary. And cap this off with another $2500—the cost of depreciation on the capital investment that makes the job possible. Consequently, each employee who works for you must return about $20,000 or more in productive efforts before his or her employment can break even.

When the cost of hiring employees to replace those who quit or are discharged (turnover) is added to the losses of their costly services due to absenteeism, you can readily see why it is so important to hire people most suitable for the work in the first place.

How do you measure employee turnover?

Turnover is the name given to the measure of how many people come to work for you and don't stay for one reason or another. Turnover includes employees who are hired or rehired and employees who are laid off, who quit, or who are discharged. It also includes those who either retire or die.

For consistency's sake the U.S. Department of Labor suggests that the rate of turnover compare only the total number of separations (quits, fires, deaths, and so on) with the average number of employees on your payroll during a particular period. The *rate of turnover* is calculated as follows:

$$\frac{\text{Number of separations} \times 100}{\text{Average size of work force}} = \text{turnover percentage}$$

For instance, if you had an average of 50 employees during the month, but you laid off 3, the turnover would be 3. Your turnover rate would be $(3 \times 100)/50 = 6$ percent a month. If that rate persisted, your turnover rate for the year would be 72 percent (6×12).

Turnover rates vary from department to department, from company to company, and from industry to industry. The national average for all business in the United States is about 7 percent a month, or 82 percent a year!

Decisions as to what kind of separations and hires to include in turnover computations vary from organization to organization. Obviously, if certain kinds of separations or hires are excluded, the turnover rates will be lower. So it's good to know exactly what the specifications are when comparing turnover rates.

What causes high turnover?

Employee turnover is generally considered to be the best single measure of morale: good morale—low turnover; poor morale—high turnover.

Poor morale can result from many things, of course. Two of the most important causes are poor supervision and the wrong person on the wrong job. The latter situation points to a poor staffing procedure. Something has broken down, especially during the interviewing and selection stages—or during the placement process if a potentially good employee is assigned to the wrong job. Accordingly, high turnover rates can be greatly prevented by careful hiring and placement. It is far easier to provide effective supervision for employees who are well matched to their jobs.

What's so bad about absenteeism?

Absences (like turnover) are costly—to the organization as well as to the employee. If it costs about $20,000 a year to keep a person on the payroll, then each day that person is absent can cost your department something like $80 (based on 240 working days a year) in lost effort. Don't be misled, either, by the hourly worker who says, "I don't get paid when I'm not here, so what do you lose?" Absences frequently create a need for hiring temporary employees or for overtime caused by delays in getting an operation started or a machine running. And every supervisor can testify to the aggravation absence and lateness cause. Absenteeism is the biggest obstacle you have in your work force planning—from day to day or from month to month.

There are two popular ways to compute absenteeism rates:

1. $\text{Absenteeism rate} = \dfrac{\text{total days absent}}{\text{average size of work force}}$

   $= \text{average days absent per employee}$

2. $\text{Absenteeism rate} = \dfrac{\text{total days absent} \times 100}{\text{worker-days worked plus worker-days lost}}$

   $= \text{percentage of scheduled worker-days lost}$

For example, suppose that at the end of 6 months a supervisor found that the schedule showed a crew of 25 employees working for 120 days. Examining the record, the supervisor found that 10 employees had worked every day (10 × 120) for 1200 worker-days; 10 employees worked 116 days (10 × 116) for 1160 worker-days; 3 employees worked only 110 days (3 × 110) for 330 worker-days; and 2 employees worked only 100 days (2 × 100) for 200 worker-days. The total of worker-days worked is 2890. If all 25 employees had worked every day for 120 days, the total worker-days would have amounted to 3000. Therefore,

110 worker-days were lost (3000 − 2890). The department's absenteeism rate would be:

$$\frac{110 \text{ days absent}}{25 \text{ employees}} =$$

4.4 days lost per employee in 6 months, or 8.8 days a year

The percentage of scheduled worker-days lost each year would be calculated as follows:

$$\frac{110 \text{ days absent} \times 100}{2890 + 110} = \frac{110 \times 100}{3000}$$

$$= 3.7 \text{ percent of scheduled worker-days lost}$$

National averages for days lost per employee range from 9 days a year to as high as 3 days a month (36 days a year). Absence and lateness, like turnover, can be controlled by good supervision. But it's better to avoid this demand on your supervisory time and skill if you can. And you can, by screening out applicants who have displayed these undesirable characteristics in the past or are likely to develop them on the job in your company—simply because they are unsuited for the work they were hired to do.

How can better hiring reduce turnover and absences?

Selecting the proper person to fit first the company and then the available job opening hits the turnover and absenteeism problem at its source. There are hundreds of thousands of people looking for work who would be misfits almost anywhere. But there are millions who would probably be out of place in your company. Sue doesn't like close work. Pete can't stand heavy work. Joe wants a job with lots of room for initiative. Alma wants a job where she doesn't have to think. And so on. Turnover and absences show that Sue, Pete, Joe, and Alma didn't find work to suit them in your company.

To complicate the matter further, Joe may want a job that allows for initiative, but maybe he doesn't have the native ability to produce without close supervision. Alma wants a job where she doesn't have to think, but maybe all those jobs call for someone who can work rapidly and Alma is slow as can be.

A third complication, and perhaps the most serious, is that the ability to handle the human side of the job varies widely with different people. And, of course, the human relations requirements of jobs vary too. If you put employees who like to be one of the gang back in the corner working alone, they won't be happy no matter how much they like the work or how skillfully they can perform it. Similarly, a person who has never been able to get along well with superiors won't be much of a help on a job where there has to be a lot of close supervision.

Keep in mind that employees, too, are continually assessing the suitability of their employment after being hired. They ask themselves: "Is this the right job for me? Is this an organization I want to continue working for?" An effective staffing procedure is more likely to find these employees answering "yes" to these questions.

REVIEW

KEY CONCEPTS TO REMEMBER

1. Staffing of an organization is accomplished through a five-step procedure: (a) specifying the kinds of jobs and workers needed to attain an organization's objectives, (b) forecasting the numbers of employees needed to complete given work schedules, (c) recruiting candidates for unfilled job openings, (d) interviewing job candidates, and (e) selecting the most suitable prospects from among the applicants. Human resources personnel coordinate the staffing process, recruit, provide application forms, and perform the initial interviewing and screening of candidates. Supervisors have their greatest responsibility in Steps a, b, d, and e of the process. They should be prepared to exert a major influence in the selection of the right kind of people by participating fully in describing jobs, specifying criteria for applicants, and interviewing applicants.

2. Supervisors, better than anyone else, should know what kind of individuals the work in a department demands—that is, what skills, aptitudes, and interests are required—and the number of such individuals needed to get the work done economically, on time, and well. Forecasts of the numbers of employees needed to staff a department are determined by work loads, work schedules, vacations, and anticipated absence rates. A proper balance should be struck in the size of the work force so that a department is neither overstaffed nor understaffed. A work force trial balance helps to make this determination reliable.

3. Supervisors should begin an employment interview by describing the job, its environment, and its unattractive as well as its favor-

able features. Questions should be open-ended and focus on education, experience, skills, and job-related attitudes. Care should be taken during the interview to avoid bias or any implication of it. Questions that might be related to race, color, religion, national origin, sex, age, and marital status are to be avoided. In any event, all questions must be undeniably shown to relate to a job requirement, legally called a bona fide occupational qualification (BFOQ).

4. Effective selection is based upon matching an individual's knowledge, skills, and aptitudes with those required by the job. Selection judgment is improved when a number of candidates are interviewed. In addition to checking demonstrable skills, look also for evidence of perseverance, alertness, and cooperation. Employment tests—especially performance tests—help the selection process, but only when the tests meet the legal requirements of validity and reliability.

5. Careful selection of employees helps to prevent a high incidence of absences and turnover later on. Employees whose capabilities and interests match those of the job tend to be better satisfied with their work and reflect this in better attendance and greater staying power. It is costly to replace experienced employees with new ones. Absences are costly, too, both in lost productive efforts and in disruptions to efficient work scheduling.

SUPERVISORY WORD POWER

Application blank. A form used by an organization to legally and systematically gather and record information from a job applicant about his or her qualifications, education, and work experience.

Attrition. The gradual reduction of a work force by means of natural events and causes, such as retirements, deaths, and resignations, as opposed to reductions planned by management, such as discharges, layoffs, and early retirements.

Bona fide occupational qualification (BFOQ). A specified capability of a job applicant that can be undeniably related to a normal requirement of the job to be filled.

Employee turnover. A measure of how many people come to work for an organization and do not remain employed by that organization, for whatever reason.

Employment interview. A face-to-face exchange of information between a job applicant and an employer's representative in order to develop qualitative information about the applicant's suitability for employment.

Performance test. An employment test that enables job applicants to demonstrate that they can actually perform the kind of work required by the job in question.

Psychological test. A written examination, conducted by trained professionals, of a person's qualifications, interests, and aptitudes in order to judge objectively the individual's suitability for a particular job or kind of work.

Test reliability. A proven ability of a test to yield the same score for a candidate if the test were repeated.

Test validity. A proven ability of a test to measure what it purports to measure.

READING COMPREHENSION

1. In which aspect of the staffing process are supervisors *not* likely to play a major part? Which organizational unit usually handles that aspect?
2. What factors affect the determination of the size of a department's work force?
3. Gerry expects that his sales order department will have to handle peak loads during the spring and fall seasons. Should he plan to staff a year-round work force large enough to handle these peak loads when they occur? Why, or why not?
4. What role does employee turnover play in planning a work force trial balance? *Hint:* See item 4 in Table 8-1.
5. What is meant by an "open-ended" question, as used during an employment interview? Provide some examples.
6. What kinds of information can generally be obtained from a job candidate without infringing upon rights guaranteed by equal employment opportunity legislation?
7. Would it be wise to hire a college graduate for a job that requires only a high school education, as long as the applicant was willing to take the job at the prevailing wage rate? Why, or why not?
8. Explain the difference between an aptitude test and a performance test.
9. Which two factors are generally considered to be the two main causes of excessive employee turnover?
10. What are the main differences between the two ways of computing absence rates?

SELF-APPRAISAL

How would you rate Tricia as a staffer?

Tricia is the dispatching supervisor at a midwestern distribution "hub" of a national overnight-express delivery service. While staffing her department during the past year, Tricia has engaged in the various activities described below. Your assignment is to determine whether each of Tricia's activities represents a good, bad, or doubtful staffing practice and then to rate Tricia's performance as a staffer. On a separate piece of paper, copy the column headings shown below. In the column "Tricia's Staffing Activities" write the numbers 1 to 10 down the page to correspond to each of the ten activities. For each activity, place a check mark in the column that best matches your opinion of Tricia's action. After completing this activity, rate Tricia's overall performance as a staffer by using the scoring procedure described on page 187. Then compare your judgment with that of the experts.

Column headings:

Tricia's Staffing Activities	Good Practice	Bad Practice	Doubtful Practice

1. At the start of the year, Tricia carefully specified the types of jobs to be filled in her department and the kinds of people who might best fill them.
2. When it comes to recruiting job candidates, Tricia leaves it up to the company's human resources department.
3. Because of the press of other duties, Tricia was unable to interview the last batch of dispatching clerks who were hired.
4. When planning the size of her work force, Tricia adds in the need for indirect, as well as direct, labor.
5. Even though absences are fairly few among her 20 employees, Tricia includes an allowance for absences when planning work force size.
6. The company's distribution process cannot tolerate delays in dispatching; accordingly, Tricia tends to overstaff slightly.
7. Since it is difficult to find good dispatchers, Tricia doesn't tell job applicants about such unpleasant things as regular night hours and weekend work.
8. When interviewing job candidates, Tricia likes to ask blunt "yes or

no" questions that don't give the candidate a chance to offer qualifying explanations.

9. Tricia assumes that many men do not like the intense attention to detail required by dispatching, so she suggests to male candidates that they would not find this kind of work attractive.

10. It has been shown without a doubt that arithmetic skills are a prime requirement of dispatching, so Tricia does not hire anyone who does not pass a reliable, validated computational examination.

Scoring Give Tricia 1 point for each item that you marked as a *good* staffing practice. Give Tricia no points for items that you marked as either *bad* or *doubtful*.

Interpretation Human resources professionals gave Tricia 6 points. Here's the way they scored it: *good* for items 1, 2, 4, 5, 6, and 10; *bad* or *doubtful* for all other items. If you disagreed with their assessment, can you support your judgment?

CASE STUDIES

CASE 22 The Biased Interview

"Nancy, the carpenter's position you're applying for is very demanding physically. We work outdoors in some of the coldest, wettest, windiest weather. And building forms with heavy, rough-cut lumber is a totally different ball game from trimming a few windows with clean, dried pine." That's Jake Barnes talking, site supervisor for the Jarvis Construction Company.

Nancy sat straight up in her chair and answered with pursed lips: "I'm strong, healthy, and an experienced backpacker. I haven't had a serious illness for years."

"I'm glad to hear that," said Jake. "Your application says that you have only worked indoors doing remodeling and trim work. I don't know whether you can stand this hard work."

"Mr. Barnes, I wouldn't have answered your ad if I wasn't sure of my physical capabilities," replied Nancy.

"We've had a lot of turnover here; I only want to hire carpenters who will stick with us. I see that you are married; do you plan to have children soon?"

Nancy crossed her arms. "I don't plan to, but I don't see how that would make a difference. During my last pregnancy I never missed a day of work until right before the baby was born. I was back to work six weeks later."

Jake went on: "Another thing, Nancy. You would be the only woman in the crew. Can you handle hearing 'man talk'?"

"Mr. Barnes, I'm only interested in doing good work and getting more experience. I've often worked with men; it's never been a problem. Wouldn't you like to know something about my work experience, about my training?"

"Oh, I already know you're a good carpenter. I called your last boss. It's just that this job is really demanding, and I don't know whether you can handle it."

That did it for Nancy. She said, "You're not giving me a fair chance at this job, Mr. Barnes, and I'd like to speak to the owner." Jake agreed to call in Mr. Jarvis. Nancy spoke to him with considerable heat. "This isn't fair. Mr. Barnes has assumed from the start that I can't handle this job. He implies that I'm not strong enough, that I might be unreliable if I had another baby, and that I am unqualified because I'm a woman and the other carpenters are men. Won't someone listen to my qualifications? I'm a good carpenter, and I can do a good job for you."

If you were Mr. Jarvis, how would you proceed? Of the following five alternatives, which do you think might be most effective? Rank the alternatives on a scale from 1 (most preferable) to 5 (least preferable). You may add another alternative if you wish. In any event, be prepared to justify your ranking.

a. Finish the interview with Nancy, but choose not to hire her. The issues Jake was raising, although delicate matters, are legitimate concerns for this position.
b. Finish the interview and hire Nancy. It has been established that she has the carpentry and work skills that qualify her for the job. Plan a number of coaching sessions for Jake to improve his job-interviewing skills.
c. Finish the interview and hire Nancy. Fire Jake Barnes because of the serious possibility of his involving the company in crippling legal action because of his illegal job-interview questions.
d. Tell Nancy that it was improper for her to insist on seeing you. Jake is an authorized management representative of the company. It is not always possible to bypass the organization's chain of command just because one fails to succeed at a lower level. Send the hiring decision back to Jake, with whom it legitimately rests.
e. Finish the interview and hire Nancy. Sit down with Jake and Nancy in an effort to improve their personal attitudes toward each other.

CASE 23 Pumping the Work Force Forecast

The scheduling for a pump manufacturer calls for the following production during the next 4 months (approximately 80 working days):

Fabricate 6000 pump housings.
Produce 240,000 fittings on an automatic screw machine.
Assemble 5000 pumps.

A study of production records shows that three employees can turn out 30 pump housings a day, one screw machine operator can produce 3000 fittings a day, and five employees can assemble 50 pumps each day. Absences for the present work crew have averaged 1 day a month per employee.

How many employees must this plant retain in order to make sure that the schedule will be met?

CASE 24 The Superior Job Candidate

"At last," said Eduardo, "I've found the perfect stock clerk. Marcia has a wealth of experience. She has taken advanced courses in inventory planning and computerized controls. Compared to our other clerks, Marcia is far superior."

That was how Eduardo felt when he hired Marcia. Within a month, he felt less enthusiastic about her. Marcia *could* handle just about any assignment—perfectly. Trouble began, however, when it became apparent that the work of a stock clerk at Eduardo's company was mostly routine. In fact, Marcia found most of her work boring, and she let the other clerks know about it. In many ways, Marcia's superior attitude was disruptive, especially when she was asked to work along with others on group projects. Matters came to a head when Marcia confronted Eduardo on Friday afternoon of her fourth week. "I'm extremely dissatisfied with my job," she said. "I've been here a month and there hasn't been a challenge in anything I've done. Can't you find more important assignments for me? Otherwise, I don't see much of a future in working here."

1. What is the basic problem here?
2. How might it have been avoided?
3. Should Eduardo accommodate Marcia's request? Why?

3 The appraisal interview is a developmental exchange.

1 Employees have the right to know how well they are doing.

4 Employee appraisals often raise sensitive issues.

2 Appraisals evaluate employee behavior and job performance.

5 Appraisals require bias-free reasoning and documentation.

CHAPTER **9**

Appraisal of Employee Performance

LEARNING OBJECTIVES

After studying this chapter, you should be able to

1. Explain the main purposes and benefits of an employee performance appraisal.

2. Describe the kinds of factors that are evaluated and the formats used, suggest ways of reducing bias, and recognize the influence of the halo effect.

3. List the main steps in an appraisal interview and discuss techniques for making it more effective.

4. Discuss ways of handling sensitive problems that may arise during, or as a result of, the appraisal interview.

5. Explain the legal implications of a performance appraisal, recognize its limited relationship to financial rewards, and identify a number of extenuating circumstances that may cause poor performance.

PURPOSE OF APPRAISAL

CONCEPT   Employees have a right to know, and wish to know, how well they are performing on their jobs.

At its root, what is the true purpose of an appraisal?

There are three basic reasons for making an appraisal of employee performance:

1. **To encourage good behavior or to correct and discourage below-standard performance.**   Good performers expect a reward, even if it is only praise. Poor performers should recognize that continued substandard behavior will at the very least stand in the way of advancement. At the most drastic, it may lead to termination.
2. **To satisfy employees' curiosity about how well they are doing.**   It is a fundamental drive in human nature for each of us to want to know how well we fit into the organization for which we work. An employee may dislike being judged, but the urge to know is very strong.
3. **To provide a firm foundation for later judgments that concern an employee's career.** Such matters as pay raises, promotions, transfers, or separation can be handled more smoothly if the employee is aware of the possibilities beforehand.

Won't employees resent being evaluated?

The biggest fear in most supervisors' minds is that an employee will dislike being judged. Surprisingly, this fear is unfounded—if the appraisal is based on facts rather than opinion only and you display a willingness to change ratings if an employee can show you you're wrong. People want to know where they stand—even if it isn't good. But don't interpret this to mean that appraisal interviews are free from stress or that employees will make it easy for you. Chances are they won't.

Furthermore, do not let your discussion with the employee being rated take on the nature of an end-of-term school report. Mature adults resist this. Subordinates can easily regard the performance appraisal as just another way for the company to increase its control over them if this attitude prevails.

How often should you evaluate an employee?

Twice a year for a formal appraisal is a happy medium. If you rate too often, you're likely to be too impressed by day-to-day occurrences. If you wait too long, you're likely to forget many of the incidents that ought to influence your appraisal. Even if your company has a plan that calls for rating only once a year, it's good practice to make appraisals of your own—informally, perhaps—more often. This does not mean that you should not observe employee performance routinely—and compliment or criticize it, as the case may be. You should do this, of course, regardless of formal appraisal sessions.

What is the relation of performance appraisals to job evaluation, compensation rates, merit rating, and merit raises?

This is a sensitive question, often asked by employees. You should approach this issue carefully, since much depends upon your company's policies toward it. **Job evaluation** is a systematic method for appraising the worth of a particular job, *not* the individual who performs it. The **compensation** set for a particular job is the result of a job-pricing decision based upon the job's evaluation, which should have little or nothing to do with the person who ultimately performs the job. **Merit rating** is a term that is now obsolete. It once was synonymous with performance appraisal, and many employees still believe it is. The problem arises from its implication of **merit raises**—salary increases based upon merit. Most organizations strive to separate the performance appraisal session from decisions regarding issuance of merit raises. The purpose is to keep the focus of the appraisal on performance, not salary. This distinction is not always clear to employees.

It is a cardinal mistake, then, for a supervisor to stress the relationship of pay raises during the appraisal interview. It is only human for persons who have been told that their work is good to expect an increase in pay to follow. If your company's compensation plan doesn't work that way, you may suffer a very red face when an employee tells you later on, "You told me my good work would bring a raise or a promotion."

2 FACTORS AND FORMAT

CONCEPT   Appraisals evaluate, in a systematic way, an individual's job-related traits and behavior as they affect performance.

How formal will the performance rating procedure be?

Because of legal implications, most organizations now carefully specify and monitor their performance appraisal programs. Most appraisal formats incorporate some form of "graphic weighting scale." A simple version is shown in Table 9-1. Typically, these formats provide a choice of ratings for each factor, ranging from "superior" or "outstanding" to "expected level" and on down to "unsatisfactory." Numerical weights are often attached to each rating so that a total score for the overall appraisal can be obtained.

A variation of the above is the "forced-choice" format. This provides a series of paired descriptive statements for each factor being rated. One statement is always more positive or less negative than its opposing member. Thus, in making judgments, a supervisor is forced to choose very carefully between two somewhat similar evaluations.

What factors should you consider when appraising an employee?

These can vary from plan to plan. What you are trying to answer about an employee's performance, however, are these questions:

- What has the individual done since last appraised? How well has it been done? How much better could it be?
- In what ways have strengths and weaknesses in the individual's job approach affected this performance? Are these factors ones that could be improved?
- What is the individual's potential? How well could the employee do if really given a chance?

Table 9-1   EXAMPLE OF A GRAPHIC WEIGHTING SCALE

Factor	Rating*					Score
	A	B	C	D	E	
1. Quality of work	20	16	12	8	4	_____
2. Quantity of work	20	16	12	8	4	_____
3. Dependability	20	16	12	8	4	_____
4. Attitude	10	8	6	4	2	_____
5. Initiative	5	4	3	2	1	_____
6. Housekeeping	10	8	6	4	2	_____
7. Attendance	10	8	6	4	2	_____
8. Potential for advancement	5	4	3	2	1	_____
Total rating score						_____

* A: superior; B: very good; C: at expected level; D: below expected level, but shows improvement; E: unsatisfactory.

Factors that are judged in appraisal also tend to fall into two categories: objective judgments and subjective judgments. ***Objective factors*** focus on hard facts and measurable results—quantities, quality, attendance. ***Subjective factors*** tend to represent opinions, such as those about attitude, personality, and adaptability. Distinguish between the two. Be firmer about appraisal of objective factors than about those involving opinion only. But even subjective factors can be rated with confidence if they are supported by documented incidents. The sample performance rating form shown in Table 9-1 includes both objective and subjective factors. See Figure 9-1 for a rating scale that includes descriptions for each factor.

How can you make sure your ratings are consistent from employee to employee?

Before we answer this question, it should be stressed that each employee's rating is never measured against another's. Performance is always compared with the stated responsibilities and standards established for a particular job. If there is a variety of skills and experience among your employees, however, you may find it helpful to double-check your ratings to make sure that you are not favoring one employee or making an unsupported judgment about another. Accordingly, try this objective approach:

1. List the name of each employee down one side of a sheet of paper and the factors to be rated across the top.
2. Look only at one factor at a time. Take quality, for instance. If you have rated Tom only "fair" and Pete and Vera "good," ask yourself if you are using the same standards for each. Perhaps upon reconsidering, you'll want to drop Pete's rating to "fair" because Pete and Tom produce the same quality of work, whereas Vera's quality is demonstrably better than either Pete's or Tom's.

You may also want to consider whether or not you're rating all employees either too high or too low. In most work forces there is some sort of variation in performance levels. The performance of some employees will be exceptionally high and of some others exceptionally low, with that of the remainder somewhere in between. Keep in mind, however, that every employee can rate near or at the top if he or she performs well against the stipulated responsibilities and standards.

Doesn't an employee's rating represent only the supervisor's opinion?

A good performance rating includes more than just a supervisor's opinion. It should be based on facts. In the consideration of quality of performance, what is the employee's error record? As to quantity, what do the production records show? And as for dependability, what's the absence and lateness record? Can you cite actual incidents in which you may have had to discipline the employee or speak about the quality or quantity of output? Answering these questions makes your rating less opinionated and, consequently, more valid and worthwhile.

Such documented incidents become critical examples (often called **critical incidents**) of an employee's performance. These incidents should undeniably represent the quality—good or bad—of an employee's work. It is a good practice to make notes of such occurrences and place them in the employee's file. At appraisal time they serve to illustrate what you consider good or subpar performance and to support the ratings you make.

What's the halo effect? How can you avoid it?

Nearly all of us have a tendency to let one favorable or unfavorable incident or trait color our judgment of an individual as a whole. This is called the **halo effect.** There are a wide range of biases that can be introduced this way. Among the most insidious are these:

- **Recency.** Remembering only what has happened last week or last month.
- **Overemphasis.** Placing too much weight on one outstanding good or poor factor.
- **Unforgivingness.** Not allowing an employee's improved performance to outshine a poor record in the past.
- **Prejudice.** Allowing an individual's contrary personality to overshadow his or her good works.
- **Favoritism.** Being influenced by a person's likableness, despite a poor performance.
- **Grouping.** Tarring all employees in a substandard work group with the same brush.
- **Indiscrimination.** Being either too critical or too generous; no one obtains a good rating, or everyone does.
- **Stereotyping.** Basing judgments upon preconceived notions about such things as race, sex, color, religion, age, or national origin.

One of the best ways to minimize the halo effect is to rate all your employees on a single factor before proceeding to ratings for the next factor. This approach helps to focus your attention on each individual's qualities one at a time, rather than lumping them together into one generalization.

No. A popular format is shown in Figure 9-1. It is an example of a **behaviorally anchored rating scale** (BARS). Its various items, or standards, are described or illustrated in the form of the behavior expected of an employee. These descriptions are usually based upon critical incidents judged to be characteristic of the various levels of performance. This helps to provide greater objectivity in rating. The BARS's weakness is that it tends to focus on activity rather than results. Nevertheless, the BARS is generally considered the best and the most effective means of appraisal.

Many of the older formats emphasize an individual's traits, such as "initiative," "dependability," and "cooperation." The weakness with the **trait format,** however, is that the evaluation becomes almost unavoidably subjective. As such, trait evaluations are difficult to defend, especially in the courts.

Management by objectives (see page 102 in Chapter 5, and Table 4-1 on page 70) provides a unique form of **results-oriented appraisal.** This approach is sometimes used for supervisors and other highly motivated employees. It requires that specific objectives, in the form of measurable results, be agreed upon beforehand by both superior and subordinate. These objectives become the appraisal factors to be evaluated. The MBO approach is not particularly suitable for employees who rely heavily upon their supervisors to plan and control their work.

At the core of all successful appraisal formats, however, are clearly defined—and explicitly communicated—standards (or expectations) of employee performance on the job. Without these standards, appraisals become vague or contentious, are difficult to support, and lose their value as developmental tools.

3 THE APPRAISAL INTERVIEW

CONCEPT The appraisal interview is a developmental exchange between supervisor and employee, aimed at reinforcing appropriate—or correcting unsatisfactory—performance.

What is the best way to handle the appraisal interview itself?

Whereas there are any number of approaches you might use, there are seven steps that form a pretty good path toward understanding and acceptance of the appraisal.

Step 1. Prepare the employee, as well as yourself, to come to the

EXAMPLE OF BEHAVIORALLY ANCHORED RATING SCALE (BARS)

Superior

Performance Factors		Superior
1. Quality of work Evaluate accuracy, thoroughness, and neatness of completed work. Disregard the quantity of work		Rarely commits an error. Defect or reject rate is less than 0.003%. Quality of work is consistently exceptional 20
2. Quantity of work Evaluate amount of work performed and/or number of assignments completed, sales calls made, and so on. Disregard quality of work.		Regularly exceeds specified output, volume of work, or number of assignments by more than 15%. Consistently completes an extraordinary amount of work. 20
3. Dependability Evaluate ability to meet commitments and dead-lines and the extent of required supervision.		Consistently meets commitments and deadlines. Needs no supervision on routine tasks. 20
4. Attitude Evaluate general demeanor toward job, co-workers, supervisor and company.		Displays enthusiasm about the work and the company. Cooperates freely with associates. Always accepts suggestions and criticism in a constructive manner. 10
5. Initiative Evaluate ability to recognize problems and take correc-tive action, make suggestions for improvements, and accept responsibility for accomplishing unassigned tasks.		Regularly recognizes job-related problems and initiates corrective action. Has made at least three well-thought-out suggestions for work improve-ment (formally or informally) during the past evaluation period. 5
6. Housekeeping Evaluate cleanliness and orderliness of workplace and in-process storage areas and close-of-shift cleanup.		Maintains an exceptionally neat and orderly workplace, file drawers, and storage areas. Work surfaces are clean and uncluttered. Tools are always arranged neatly and/or put away at close of shift. 10
7. Attendance Evaluate attendance and tardiness.		No days lost. No times late. 10
8. Potential for growth and advancement Evaluate potential for increas-ing job knowledge and for ad-vancing to other jobs in the department and other jobs in the organization.		Given an opportunity, can assimilate more knowledge of company operations. Has demonstrated great potential for advancement in the entire organiza-tion. 5

Figure 9-1 Example of the behaviorally anchored rating scale.

Very good	At expected level	Below expected level	Unsatisfactory
Makes only an occasional error. Defect or reject rate is consistently less than 0.010%. Quality of work is high grade, but not exceptional. **16**	Errors are only occasionally troublesome. Defect or reject rate rarely exceeds standard of 0.010%. Quality of work is average. **12**	Errors are frequently troublesome. Defect or reject rate often exceeds standard of 0.010%. Quality of work is below average. **8**	Errors are frequently troublesome. Defect or reject rate regularly exceeds standard of 0.010%. Quality of work is unsatisfactory. **4**
Regularly exceeds specified output, volume of work, or number of assignments. Consistently turns out a good volume of work. **16**	Usually meets the specified output, volume of work, or number of assignments. Amount of work completed is about average for this job. **12**	Often fails to meet specified output, volume of work, or number of assignments. Amount of work completed is about 10% less than average for this job. **8**	Regularly fails to meet specified output, volume of work, or number of assignments. Amount of work is almost always greater than 11% less than average for this job. **4**
Meets commitments and deadlines 95% or more of the time. Needs minimum supervision on routine tasks. **16**	Meets commitments and deadlines 90% or more of the time. Needs occasional supervision on routine tasks. **12**	Meets commitments and deadlines less than 85 to 90% of the time. Needs constant checking, even on routine tasks. **8**	Meets commitments and deadlines less than 85% of the time. Work and progress must be checked all the time. **4**
Appears to be happy at his or her work. Cooperates freely with associates. Usually accepts suggestions or criticism in a constructive manner. **8**	Accepts most assignments without complaint. Cooperates with associates when requested to do so. Follows instructions. **12**	Frequently questions suitability of assignments. Complains regularly about the nature of the work. Cooperates with associates when requested to do so. Often rejects suggestions or criticism. **4**	Constantly complains about the work and the company. Regularly voices objection to assignments. Does not cooperate with co-workers. Is always negative toward suggestions and criticism. **2**
Usually recognizes job-related problems and initiates corrective action. Has made at least one well-thought-out suggestion for work improvement during the past evaluation period. **4**	Occasionally recognizes and acts upon job-related problems. Occasionally makes well-thought-out suggestions for work improvement. **3**	Fails to recognize job-related problems or to initiate action to correct them. Usually waits to be told what to do. **2**	Fails to recognize job-related problems or to initiate action to correct them. Always needs to be told what to do. Never displays any kind of initiative. **1**
Maintains a neat and orderly workplace, file drawers, and storage areas. Work surfaces are usually clean and uncluttered. Tools are put away at close of shift. **8**	Maintains a reasonably neat and clean workplace. Work surfaces are acceptably free from soil or debris that would interfere with work. Only occasionally does not put tools away. **6**	Often fails to maintain a reasonably neat and clean workplace. Work surfaces are often cluttered and not conducive to quality craft. Often fails to put tools away. **4**	Consistently fails to maintain a neat and clean workplace or work surface. More often than not, fails to clean up or put tools away at close of shift. **1**
1 to 2 days out sick, or 1 day absent of own accord, or 1 time late. **8**	2 to 3 days out sick, or 2 days absent of own accord, or 2 times late. **6**	3 to 5 days out sick, or 3 days absent of own accord, or 3 times late. **4**	More than 5 days out sick, or more than 3 days absent of own accord, or more than 3 times late. **2**
Given an opportunity, can assimilate more knowledge of company operations. Has demonstrated good potential for advancement in the department. **4**	Has pretty much acquired as much knowledge here as he or she can assimilate. Has demonstrated some potential for advancement in the department. **3**	Has difficulty in acquiring knowledge and skills here. Has demonstrated only limited potential for advancement. **2**	Has great difficulty in acquiring knowledge and skills here. Has demonstrated no potential for advancement here. **1**

meeting expecting to compare notes. That way, you have your facts at hand and the employee has the same opportunity to recollect about performance during the previous period.

Step 2. Compare accomplishments with specific targets. Don't be vague or resort to generalizations. Be specific about what was expected and how close the employee has come to meeting these expectations.

Step 3. Be sure to give adequate credit for what *has* been accomplished. It is a temptation to take for granted those things that have been done well and to concentrate on the deficiencies.

Step 4. Review those things that have *not* been accomplished. Emphasize where improvement is needed. And explore together with the employee how this can be done and why it is necessary for the employee to improve.

Step 5. Avoid the impression of your sitting in judgment. If there is blame to be shared, acknowledge it. Don't talk in terms of mistakes, faults, or weaknesses. Never compare the employee with a third person. Stick to a mutual explanation of the facts and what they imply to both of you.

Step 6. Agree on targets to be met during the period ahead. Be specific about them. Relate them to what has not been accomplished during the current period. This sets the stage for a more objective appraisal discussion next time around.

Step 7. Review what *you* can do to be of greater help. Improvement is almost always a mutually dependent activity. An employee who knows that you share responsibility for it will approach the task with greater confidence and enthusiasm.

Where should you conduct performance rating or appraisal interviews?

Do it privately, in your own office or in a private room. You'll want to be able to give the interview your undivided attention. And you won't want to be in earshot of other employees, either. Allow yourself enough time—at the very least a half hour. Otherwise, the whole procedure will be too abrupt.

What's the "sandwich" technique for telling employees about unfavorable aspects of their work?

The sandwich technique means simply to sandwich unfavorable comments between favorable comments, as shown in Figure 9-2. For example, say: "I've been pleased with the way you've stepped up your output. You've made real improvement there. I am a little disappointed,

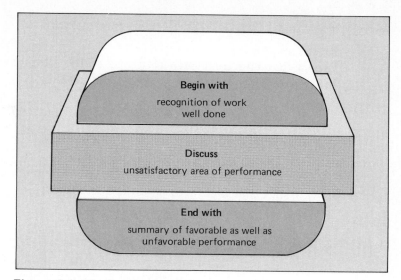

Figure 9-2 The "sandwich" technique.

however, by the quality of what you produce. The records show that you're always near the bottom of the group on errors. So I hope you'll work as well to improve quality as you did quantity. I feel sure you will, since your attitude toward your work has been just fine."

The same technique is a helpful guide to the entire appraisal/review discussion. Use it by starting the talk off with a compliment. Then discuss the work that must be improved. Finish by finding something else good to say about the employee's work. While some criticize the technique as "obvious," it is still an effective technique when constructive guidance is provided.

Should you leave room for employees to save face?

Call it what you want, but give employees every chance to tell you what obstacles stand in the way of their making good. Don't interrupt or say, "That's just an excuse." Instead, take your time. Let the person talk. Often the first reason given isn't the real one. Only if you listen carefully will you discover underlying causes for poor attitude or effort.

Confidence in you as a supervisor and in the performance rating system is important. So don't be too anxious to prove that the employee is wrong. Above all, don't show anger, regardless of what kind of remark the employee makes. That advice goes even if the employee becomes angry.

Should you discuss one employee's rating with another employee?

Never! Always avoid comparisons. And be sure that each employee knows that you treat each rating as confidential. Try to establish the entire procedure on the basis of confidentiality.

🔲 4 SPECIAL CONSIDERATIONS

CONCEPT   Supervisors must be prepared to handle a variety of sensitive issues that may arise from the appraisal.

How do you handle charges of bias or favoritism?

Unfavorable criticism stings an occasional employee so hard that it's not unusual for the person to react by charging bias or favoritism. Don't try to argue the employee out of it. Your direct denial probably won't be accepted anyway. Instead, try acknowledging that possibly you have erred in making your rating. But be prepared to document your reasoning.

For instance, say: "Tony, why do you think I might be favoring Sam? If I've given you that impression, perhaps you can help me see where I've been wrong." So Tony says, "Well, you give Sam all the easy jobs, and I get all the junk that no one else wants."

Your reply ought to be along these lines: "I don't agree that I give Sam the easy jobs, but I do find that I ask him to do lots of jobs that need first-rate attention. He seems easier to get along with when I need something done in a hurry. On the other hand, I've been hesitating to ask you to do anything out of the ordinary. That's because you act as if I'm taking unfair advantage of you. Don't you agree that it's just human nature on my part to lean on people who show they want to cooperate? Maybe it's been my fault that you feel I've favored Sam. I'll watch that in the future. But how about your pitching in and taking your share of the load? Will you try it that way with me, Tony?"

Isn't it dangerous to give employees a high rating? Won't they expect to get an immediate raise or a promotion out of it?

Knowledge of where an individual stands with the boss is every bit as important to a top-notch performer as it is to a mediocre employee—maybe even more so. If you fail to show your recognition of a good job, an employee is likely to feel, "What's the use of doing a good job? No one appreciates it."

Good workers are hard to come by. They should know how you feel, even when you can't show them an immediate reward. Remember, people work for lots more than what they get in the paycheck.

How can you tell employees their work is way below par?

Don't be too harsh on poor performers. Be especially sure that your treatment has encouraged the best kind of performance. Otherwise, they may feel that their poor showing is more your fault than their own.

Your guides should be these: Be firm. Nothing is to be gained by being soft. If work has been bad, say so.

Be specific. For example: "We've been over this before. During the last six months I've made a point of showing you exactly where you have fallen down on the job. Remember the rejects we had on the X-56 job? And the complaints on the motor shafts? Only last week you put the whole shop in a bad light by the way you mishandled the shaft job again. It looks to me as if you just aren't cut out for machine shop work. So I'm recommending that you be transferred out of this department. If there's no other suitable work available, I guess you'll have to look for work elsewhere."

Don't rub it in, though. Leave the employee's self-respect. End the discussion by summarizing what you have found satisfactory as well as the things that are unsatisfactory.

Isn't it true that no matter how well some employees do their job, there's little chance of their getting a better job?

Yes. It's especially hard on a good worker who is bucking a seniority sequence and who knows that until the person ahead gets promoted or drops dead, there is little chance to move up. Suppose a number-two laboratory analyst said to you: "Each time I get reviewed, you tell me I'm doing a good job. But this hasn't done me any good. I'm getting top dollar for the job I'm on, and until the number-one analyst changes jobs, I'm stuck. All the performance review does to me is to rub salt in the wound!"

A good way for you to handle this complaint is to admit the situation exists, but don't oversympathize. Try saying something like this: "Sure, I agree that it's hard waiting for your chance. But some workers make the mistake of depending entirely on seniority for their advancement. I don't want you to fall into that trap. When the next better job opens, I hope both of us can say that you're fully qualified. That's one of the good things about performance ratings. You can find out where your weak spots may be and correct them. For a person who has your ability and does as well on the job as you do, there's no reason why you have to limit your ambitions to the number-one specialist's job here. Maybe you'll be able to jump from a number-two job here to a choice job in another department in the company."

How soon should you appraise a new employee?

Don't wait for the formal appraisal time. Constructively criticize new employees as soon as a problem arises. Identify the cause of poor performance. Ask whether the unsatisfactory performance was due to forgetfulness, carelessness, lack of skill, or failure to understand the standards expected. Offer whatever assistance is needed. With new employees, you should document the conversation right away by sending them a memo and placing a copy in their personnel files. If the problem occurs a second time, immediately confront the employee and repeat the documentation. Otherwise, a poor start may deteriorate into an unsatisfactory, but permanent, employee.

5 LEGAL AND FINANCIAL ASPECTS

CONCEPT   The appraisal represents a critical, legal communication to an employee and should be supported by objective reasoning and documentable evidence.

What are the legal implications of a performance appraisal?

There are several. Most of them are related to the following legal doctrines:

- Equal pay for equal work.
- Absence of discrimination on the basis of age, sex, religion, color, or national origin.
- Accommodation of the physical and mental needs of the handicapped and of veterans of the Vietnam era.
- Equal employment opportunity.

To minimize accusations of noncompliance with these legal requirements, try to do the following:

1. Make certain that your appraisals are based on what the job actually requires employees to do, not on a comparison with other employees and not on what you'd like them to be able to do. That's the value of job analysis and a detailed job description.

2. Be especially cautious in making subjective judgments. Ask yourself, "Could I back them up if challenged?"
3. Stick to facts that can be documented. When in doubt, keep a record of an occurrence that might be disputed.
4. Never say anything, even in the spirit of "leveling" with an employee, that could possibly be interpreted as meaning that your appraisal was based on a favorable or unfavorable reaction to the individual's race, color, religion, age, sex, national origin, or veteran's status. It is difficult, of course, to be so neutral in your judgments, but you must do everything possible to avoid even the appearance of prejudice or discrimination. To do otherwise might bring you and your employer into court.

Should a supervisor keep a written record of what transpires during an appraisal interview?

First ask your employer or personnel department for advice on this one. Then listen to our answers. We'll give you two:

No. If you have developed a rapport during the interview that promises that the two of you will go forward with mutual confidence, you may destroy this valued atmosphere by putting a summary of your interview in writing.

Yes. If your appraisal has been negative and you expect that improvement may not be forthcoming, it's wise to make a written record that summarizes the interview, especially what you expect from the employee in terms of improved performance in the future. If you do make such a record and place it in the employee's official file, you will be expected by law to give a copy to the employee. That's the problem. You'll have documentation if you need it later on, but you may make an enemy of the employee (or at least make him or her wary).

It is also a good idea to collect in an employee's official file some sort of documentation of critical incidents. These might include regularly kept reports that show the level of and/or quality of output, written complaints or compliments from customers or internal staff members, and examples of very good or very poor work, such as a report filled with arithmetic or typing errors.

How do you convert employee performance ratings to money?

This is strictly a matter of your company's policy. About the only generality that can be drawn is that employees whose ratings are less than satisfactory should not be recommended for pay increases. Where a company has a rate range (maximum and minimum wage rates) for each job, many people believe that only workers who are rated "very good" or "exceptional" should advance to the maximum rate for the job.

If you can't give an employee a raise, why rate the employee at all?

Performance rating is so often associated with money that supervisors and employees alike lose sight of the other important benefits. Periodic performance reviews help a supervisor to:

- Point out strengths and weaknesses to employees so that they can cultivate the former and correct the latter.
- Provide a fair and unbiased method for determining qualifications for promotions, transfers, and special assignments.
- Recognize those employees who have exceptional ability and deserve training for higher positions and responsibilities.
- Weed out those who aren't qualified for the work they are now doing and to help assign them to more suitable work or, if they are wholly unqualified, to separate them from the company's payroll.

Where does comparable worth fit into this picture?

Only peripherally. *Comparable worth* refers to a concept used for evaluating the worth of widely dissimilar jobs. As a job-evaluation technique, it is concerned with job worth rather than the performance of a particular individual.

The Equal Pay Act charges discrimination if women aren't given pay equal to men's pay for equal work. In a great many instances, however, women perform work that is radically different from the work performed by men in the same organization. Nevertheless, these women often feel, with justification, that their pay is still not equal, all things considered. The concept of comparable worth is an effort to rectify this kind of situation. It makes it possible for the work—and the pay—of a toll collector, for example, to be compared with that of a nurse. Typically, this approach involves examination and comparison of four factors: level of know-how required, problem-solving entailed, accountability, and working conditions. The applicability of the comparable worth concept is challenged by some labor unions and women's organizations on the grounds that it emphasizes subjective judgments (often with a sexist bias) to a greater degree than do most traditional job-evaluation systems. Some employers also contend that it is the supply and demand of labor that really determines pay. Many people also say that they have little faith in an evaluation system that compares apples with oranges, as in equating a clerk's worth with that of a craftsperson.

Some employees try very hard, but their performance remains below par. What is the reason for this? What can be done about it?

If there is a weakness in performance appraisal programs, it is that management assumes employees have only to try harder in order to measure up to standards. This is often not the case. Many factors can contribute to employee performance. For example:

1. **Individuals may be assigned to work that does not match their capabilities.** It may be too easy or too difficult. One solution is a transfer to a more suitable job. Or the job might be redesigned to give the employee a better fit. An employee may not be able to handle the paperwork required. Perhaps it can be done by someone else. Or the job may require too little judgment for a highly intelligent person. Perhaps it can be rearranged to provide options that use this person's analytic ability.

2. **Employees may not have received proper training.** In any case of continued poor performance, the supervisor should first reexamine the training program and find a way to review the job procedure with the employee from start to finish. A key operating point may have been missed.

3. **Individuals may be victims of pressures from the work group.** An employee may be trying to conform to your job standards, but co-workers may be giving him or her a hard time. To correct this situation, you may need to approach it from the group's point of view to change or modify the co-workers' position.

4. **Workers may not be up to the job requirements, physically or emotionally.** A checkup by the company nurse or doctor may be in order. If there are persistent family problems—divorce, death, severe illness—you may try gentle counseling. Your objective should be to show that you are sympathetic but that there is a limit as to how long the related poor performance can be accepted.

5. **Your own supervision may be at fault.** It takes two to tango, and poor performance may be related to a supervisor's failure to provide clear-cut standards, to train employees effectively, or to help with problems and changes as they arise.

6. **Mechanical or procedural problems may exist.** Possibly there is some hitch in the operating process—improper tools, materials, or equipment—or a conflict in prescribed paperwork procedures. You may want to review these problems with your own boss or with the appropriate staff departments.

⬚ REVIEW

KEY CONCEPTS TO REMEMBER

1. The objective of performance appraisal is to help an employee improve the caliber of his or her job performance. When made aware of those areas in which he or she is already doing a good job and of those in which there is room for improvement, an employee can be encouraged to develop strengths and to overcome weaknesses. Generally speaking, employees welcome the opportunity to speak candidly with their supervisors about how well they are doing their jobs now and what they can do to improve their performance in the future.

2. The careful and fair application of both objective and subjective factors in appraisals will help assure employees that their ratings are based upon facts and not opinions. It is important to minimize the halo effect in making judgments, and it is essential that standards be clearly established for all factors that are evaluated.

3. An appraisal interview should be carefully prepared so that it progresses systematically. The interview should first accentuate the positive by giving credit where credit is due. It may then shift to a discussion of areas where performance is not up to standard. The interview should conclude with an agreement concerning concrete action for improvement or further development. The interview should always be regarded as a two-way street highlighted by a mutual examination of job requirements, a mutual review of how adequately they are being fulfilled, a mutual agreement on new targets, and a mutual responsibility for improvement.

4. Supervisors must be prepared to deal with sensitive issues, such as accusations of bias, negative employee reactions to criticism, and the inability to assure good performers of immediate or tangible rewards.

5. The appraisal of employee performance is an activity that is regulated by the Equal Employment Opportunity Commission (EEOC). The EEOC advises that appraisals must be based upon "critical work behaviors as revealed by a careful job analysis." Not only must evaluations be supportable by facts, but they must also be absolutely free from discrimination. Furthermore, carelessness or lack of effort are not the only causes of inadequate performance. Mismatches be-

tween jobs and workers, physical or emotional stress, poor supervision, and indefinite procedures may all bring about poor performance in spite of an employee's best efforts. Supervisors must be alert to these causes, make allowances for them, and remedy them when possible.

SUPERVISORY WORD POWER

Appraisal interview. A meeting held between a supervisor and an employee to review the performance rating and, using that evaluation as a basis, to discuss the overall quality of the employee's work and methods for improving it, if necessary.

Behaviorally anchored rating scale (BARS). A performance appraisal format that describes, and provides examples of, behavior that can be rated along a scale from outstanding to unsatisfactory behavior.

Comparable worth. A technique for evaluating the value of widely dissimilar jobs.

Critical incident. An actual and specific occurrence—either favorable or unfavorable—that serves to illustrate the general nature of an employee's performance.

Halo effect. A generalization whereby one aspect of performance, or a single quality of an individual's nature, is allowed to overshadow everything else about that person.

Job evaluation. A systematic technique for determining the worth of a job, compared with other jobs in an organization.

Performance appraisal. A formal and systematic evaluation of how well a person is performing his or her work and fills the appropriate role in the organization.

READING COMPREHENSION

1. What is it that employees expect to gain from a performance appraisal?
2. Distinguish between a job evaluation and a performance rating.
3. Explain the difference between an objective rating factor and a subjective one.
4. Erma complains that her supervisor keeps bringing up a mistake she made months ago, something that rarely occurs anymore. What

is the distortion that her supervisor is imposing on the performance appraisal? How might he lessen the tendency to make such distortions?

5. Should an employee accept all the responsibility for his or her future improvement as a result of a performance interview? Why?

6. Should performance ratings be treated confidentially, or is it all right for a supervisor to discuss one employee's rating with another? Why?

7. Why isn't it a good idea to wait until a formal appraisal session to correct the poor performance of an employee?

8. Would it be better for Mira to go easy on Tom during his appraisal interview rather than risk hurting his feelings in such a way that Tom can't save face? Why?

9. What is meant by the fact that the performance appraisal is a legally protected activity? Who protects it?

10. What are some possible causes of poor employee performance other than carelessness or lack of effort?

APPLICATION

SELF-APPRAISAL

How do you rate as a performance appraiser?

The following statements pertain to appraising performance and conducting an appraisal interview. Your assignment is to determine which of the statements are true, or represent sound practice, and which are false, or represent unsound practice. On a separate piece of paper, copy the column headings shown below. Write the numbers 1 to 15 down the page to correspond to each of the statements. Then place a check mark in the column that matches your opinion about each statement. After completing this activity, check your answers by using the scoring procedure described on page 211.

Column headings:

True, or Sound Practice	False, or Unsound Practice

1. The main purpose of a performance appraisal is to build a case for removing unsatisfactory employees.

2. Most employees welcome an opportunity to know how well their bosses think they are doing on their jobs.
3. It is a good idea to separate a consideration of pay for a job from an evaluation of an individual's performance on that job.
4. Evaluations are more defendable when they are based upon objective factors.
5. There is a danger that a critical incident may make such a strong impression that it will create a halo effect.
6. A danger with a behaviorally anchored rating scale is that it reduces objectivity in performance appraisal.
7. During an appraisal interview, supervisors should emphasize the infallibility of their judgments.
8. By beginning and ending the appraisal interview on a positive note, a supervisor is using the sandwich technique.
9. It is a good idea for a supervisor to discuss one employee's performance evaluation with another employee so that a second opinion can be obtained.
10. If Joe challenges your appraisal of him, you should be prepared to discuss the reasons for your judgment and to support it with documentation or examples.
11. If Mary warrants a high rating during your appraisal, you should assure her that her performance will result in either a pay raise or a promotion.
12. Supervisors should be careful not to point out unsatisfactory performance to new employees until they have been on the job for a few months.
13. It is probably a wise thing for a supervisor to prepare a written record of a negative appraisal.
14. Performance appraisals may be subject to review and examination by the EEOC.
15. Poor performance is almost always due to carelessness or lack of effort on the part of an employee.

Scoring   Give yourself 1 point for each of the following statements that you checked as *true,* or representing sound practice: 2, 3, 4, 5, 8, 10, 13, 14. Give yourself 1 point for each of the following statements that you checked as *false,* or representing unsound practice: 1, 6, 7, 9, 11, 12, 15.

Interpretation   Rate your performance as a performance appraiser according to the following scale: 14 or 15 points—excellent; 12 or 13 points—very good; between 10 and 12 points—satisfactory; less than 10 points—unsatisfactory.

Norma Jean has worked for three years as a buyer in the purchasing department of the Barnwell Company. Her supervisor, Mr. Morgan, consistently rated her performance as "very good," with a point total of 85 out of a possible 100. Typically, Norma Jean got top rating for her knowledge of the job and the quality and dependability of her work. The only reason that her aggregate score did not move her into the "excellent" range was that her rating for "Quantity of Work Produced" was never better than "fair." Six months ago, Mr. Morgan left the company and was replaced by dynamic young Ms. Conti. When the semiannual evaluations were filed, Ms. Conti judged Norma Jean's overall performance as only "fair," with a score of 70 points. Yesterday, Ms. Conti called Norma Jean into her office for the appraisal interview.

The news that her present rating was only "fair" upset Norma Jean. "How can that be?" she asked. "I'm working as hard as I always have. My previous supervisor was always more than satisfied with my work."

"I'm sorry, Norma," said Ms. Conti. "That's the way I see it. The amount of work you turn out is deplorably low. If you can't pick up speed, I'm going to have to put you on notice. As it is, I certainly won't be recommending you for a raise when that time comes around."

"That's not fair," said Norma Jean. "I work on purchases that need very precise specifications and quotations. You can look at my record and see that I make hardly any mistakes. No one else in the department is as reliable as I am."

"You're placing emphasis on the wrong thing," said Ms. Conti. "You slow everything down with your nit-picking on every requisition. There is no need for precision on 90 percent of what you do, yet you triple-check every 5-cent item as if it were golden. Either you learn to pick up speed, or you'll be looking for work elsewhere."

Obviously, there is something wrong with the past and present evaluations of Norma Jean's performance. Of the following five possibilities, which seems most likely to you? Rank them on a scale from 1 (most likely) to 5 (least likely). You may add another alternative, if you wish. In any event, be prepared to justify your ranking.

a. Ms. Conti dislikes Norma Jean and is "out to get her."
b. Mr. Morgan's standards for Norma's job emphasized quality and

dependability rather than output, although even Mr. Morgan had reservations about the quantity of work that Norma Jean produced.

c. As an entrenched employee, Norma Jean is resisting any change in performance standards applied to her job.

d. Ms. Conti and Norma Jean will have to have a meeting of minds about the job's demands before Norma Jean's performance will change and her evaluation improve.

e. Ms. Conti's threats will shift Norma Jean's concept of her job so that she emphasizes quantity rather than quality in the future.

How might Ms. Conti have improved this interview?

CASE 26   The Precision Appraisal Plan

The Precision Space Corporation wishes to establish a simple performance evaluation plan. Accordingly, its department supervisors have described the following conditions as relating to desirable employee performance:

"Precision is our watchword. Products shipped from this plant enter the space program and must be absolutely reliable."

"Cleanliness of work areas is essential in order to prevent product contamination."

"Each product we make is a new ball game. Employees must understand the whole process fully before tackling a new order."

"Our plant usually works on a 'cost-plus' contract."

"Most of our processes involve light handiwork, with few dangerous materials or machines."

A consultant proposes a standard rating format with five factors: quantity, quality, safety, housekeeping, and job knowledge. The consultant asks your help with the following.

On the basis of the information gathered from the supervisors, arrange the five factors according to their importance; enter them in the table on page 214, with the most important at the top and the least important at the bottom. Assuming that the total number of points that can be scored by an exceptional employee is 100, assign what you feel should be the maximum number of points for each factor. Enter these in the "Factor Weighting" column in the table.

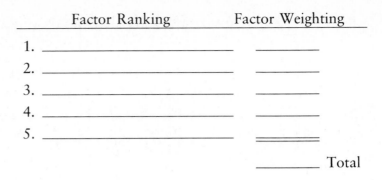

Factor Ranking	Factor Weighting
1. _____	_____
2. _____	_____
3. _____	_____
4. _____	_____
5. _____	_____

_____ Total

CASE 27 The Accomplished Department Head

Evelyn VanDyck, academic dean, thinks that Mr. Noland is the best chairperson of the English department that Apple Valley Community College has ever had. She invariably gives him the highest-possible ratings during their formal appraisal periods. Noland has a Ph.D. from a prestigious university and, it is generally agreed, is handsome and charming. The clincher in Ms. VanDyck's eyes, however, is that Noland is a prize-winning, published poet. There is no questioning Noland's modest, but notable, standing in the literary world.

Noland's duties as department chairperson are to supervise the other teachers, to coordinate their efforts to produce an integrated program of English study, and to review and help revise the detailed curriculum each year. He also has the prime responsibility for directing and motivating the teaching staff in his department.

Turnover in the English department has been strikingly high. Of the staff of six instructors, one to three have left the college every year of the last five, despite high pay scales at Apple Valley.

The teaching staff members do not share Ms. VanDyck's enthusiasm for Mr. Noland. They complain that he frequently defers department meetings, ignores requests or problems presented by his staff, is negative toward program development, and often asks at the last minute that others fill in for him at classes he must miss because of poetry readings.

a. Why do you think the academic dean continues to give Mr. Noland a good performance rating? What type of an appraisal error is she making?

b. What can the dean do to correct the problems raised by members of the English department staff?

CASE 28 The Dissatisfied Mechanic

Shawn was very unhappy. He had just discovered that raises had been handed out to several other mechanics in the maintenance shop of the

Flyaway Aviation Co., a regional commuter airline. As soon as his shift ended, he stormed into the office of his boss, Myra Maxwell, the shop supervisor.

"What happed to my annual raise?" Shawn demanded.

"Let's get one thing straight," said Myra. "There is no such thing as an annual pay raise at Flyaway."

"That's the first I've heard about it," said Shawn. "I got one last year when everyone got theirs. Now I find that everyone else just got a raise this year, and I didn't. Why was I passed over?"

"Everyone *did not* get a raise," said Myra. "Raises were only given to those mechanics whom I considered were doing outstanding work in the shop."

"Since when has my work not been outstanding?" asked Shawn.

"For a long time," said Myra. "I did speak to you about it at your last performance appraisal interview. I suggested then that your work warranted improvement."

"But I didn't think that it had anything to do with my annual merit increase," said Shawn. "I work as hard as anyone else out in the shop."

"I don't think you do," said Myra. "Several times I've noticed you taking a break when the shop was jammed up. And when things are slow, I never see you pitch in with some of the standby, shop cleanup work I've set aside for off-peak times."

"You never made that clear to me," said Shawn. "I have always thought that shop cleanup work was voluntary around here. And I don't see anything wrong in taking a break from time to time."

"Then that makes two things you don't seem to know much about," said Myra. "Both affect your performance, and that's enough to keep your work from being considered outstanding."

"That's downright unfair!" said Shawn. "I think that you have discriminated against me in not giving me my annual raise, and these are only excuses you're giving me now."

a. Do you agree or disagree with Shawn? Why?
b. What do you think has been wrong with the way Myra has conducted Shawn's appraisal interviews in the past?
c. What would you suggest Myra do in the future to avoid confrontations like these?

1 Employees need guided training related to job requirements.

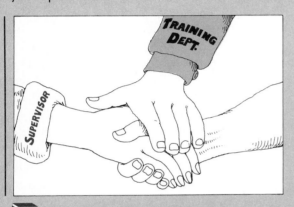

2 Supervisors are the primary source of employee training.

3 New employees benefit from an orientation to their jobs.

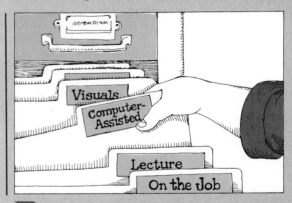

4 Training should be based upon proven ideas about learning.

5 Effective training uses a variety of training methods.

6 Training is useful only if it is transferred to the job.

CHAPTER 10

Training and Developing Employees

LEARNING OBJECTIVES

After studying this chapter, you should be able to

1. Explain why employees need to be trained and how to identify their needs.

2. Discuss the training roles of supervisors and their relationships with the training department.

3. Identify when employees should be trained, beginning with orientation programs.

4. Understand how employees learn best and how these learning principles can be used in the four-step method of training.

5. Choose appropriate training methods and aids to assist the learning process.

6. Define transfer of training and explain the actions a supervisor can take to ensure that a payoff is received from training.

TRAINING NEEDS

CONCEPT   Employees need systematic, guided training that begins with identification of job-related needs.

Will employees learn without being trained?

Yes. That's the danger. Whether employees are trained systematically or not, they will learn. What they learn may be good, or, more likely, it will be only partially correct. In some instances, what is learned may be downright wrong. A good illustration is the case of an assembler of tiny parts in an electronics plant. Her work was regularly judged to be of poor quality. Her supervisor wanted to get her off the job. The assembler insisted that she was doing her work exactly like the others on the production line. On close investigation it was found that the assembler, who did her work with the aid of a binocular microscope, was looking through the microscope with only one eye at a time. No one had ever told her that to get the right depth of vision she had to use both eyes. As soon as she was instructed in this technique, which took only about three minutes, her work was as good as that of her colleagues.

The point is that there are four ways to provide training: hit-or-miss, sink-or-swim, trial-and-error, and structured and systematic. The only dependable way is the last one: structured and systematic. It is based on a careful study of what the job requires in terms of knowledge and skills. Then it involves an orderly period of instruction provided by an individual who is familiar with the job, well versed in training techniques, and aware of the learning process.

Can you depend on an employee to learn a job by reading an equipment manufacturer's instruction manual?

Absolutely not. It's a very exceptional person who can learn how to operate equipment solely on the basis of an instruction manual. Instruction manuals are valuable reference sources, however, and they will help you prepare your training plan. But they are no substitute for personal instruction.

How much training can be accomplished through outside reading and by correspondence instruction?

If employees have the ambition to learn and to improve themselves—and if they are the rare persons who can absorb knowledge and develop skills through reading and self-help—they can learn much background material through reading or through correspondence courses. But make no mistake about it, this is the hard way! Few employees are up to it. Despite the claims of many advocates of correspondence courses, the percentage of workers who have learned their jobs this way is very small.

This is not to say, however, that outside reading combined with personalized instruction by the supervisor is not effective. It is, but the two must go hand in hand.

How will you know that training is needed?

There are two major ways to identify *training needs,* which are gaps between expected and actual performance. Both ways—informal and formal—are potentially useful. Informally, you should be on the alert for any of these conditions: too much scrap or rework, subpar production rates, out-of-line operating costs, a high accident rate, excessive overtime, and even a general state of poor morale. Although these symptoms may indicate the need for training, they may also result from poor employee selection, motivational problems, or job-related conditions. As a result, interpretation of these symptoms is best supplemented by some formal analysis of needs.

Formal approaches to assessing training needs are more structured. They attempt to identify the people who need training and the type of training they need and even to determine whether or not training is a viable solution to performance problems. Common methods of assessing needs include the use of surveys, interviews, and skills tests and the observation of employees while at work. If these methods are employed regularly, they can be especially useful for identifying trends or for making comparisons with other employees or departments.

How can you keep track of an individual's training needs and achievements?

The overriding idea is to be systematic, both in recording prior skills that have been acquired and in planning future training on the basis of needs that have been identified. The recordkeeping process can be a very simple one, like that shown in Figure 10-1, or it can be as detailed as you like. The important thing is to use it to (1) record what each worker can already do, (2) indicate what each worker doesn't need to be able to do, (3) plan ahead for what each worker has to learn, and (4) set definite dates for completing training in each part of the job.

An analysis such as that illustrated in Figure 10-1 is sometimes called a *skills inventory.* It tells you what skills each worker has acquired as well as the total skills capability and training needs of your department.

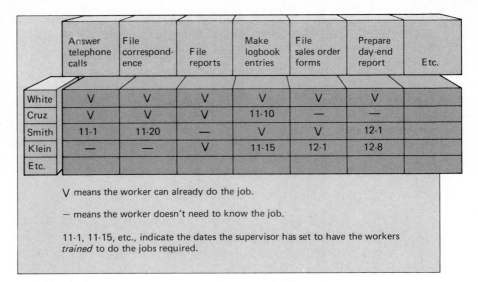

	Answer telephone calls	File correspondence	File reports	Make logbook entries	File sales order forms	Prepare day-end report	Etc.
White	V	V	V	V	V	V	
Cruz	V	V	V	11-10	—	—	
Smith	11-1	11-20	—	V	V	12-1	
Klein	—	—	V	11-15	12-1	12-8	
Etc.							

V means the worker can already do the job.

— means the worker doesn't need to know the job.

11-1, 11-15, etc., indicate the dates the supervisor has set to have the workers *trained* to do the jobs required.

Figure 10-1 Sample job instruction timetable or skills inventory.

2 A TRAINING PARTNERSHIP

CONCEPT   Supervisors are the primary source of employee training, but the training department and the worker are also key partners.

Why is a supervisor responsible for training employees?

Make up your mind that training is your concern and one of the most important ones. It is a key part of the job description of many supervisors. Training needs to be done day in and day out, for training is the only surefire way to build a work force that returns full value for every dollar invested. And with the rapid changes in technology, it is a valuable tool for achieving the retraining of many employees who would otherwise be unemployed. As a supervisor, you are judged by your ability to get the people who work for you to create a product or perform a service accurately and at low costs. Employee training is your most powerful tool in accomplishing that end.

Must supervisors do all the training themselves?

No. Instruction is a job that can be delegated—provided the employee who is to conduct the training is a skilled worker and a qualified trainer and has been given a systematic description of the key points to be covered. Just as you must know the ins and outs of teaching a job, any employees you appoint as instructors must also know how to train others. This means that they should have completed a course in effective training or have been thoroughly briefed, by you or someone else, on how to train. Few things are worse than bringing a new employee over to an older employee and just turning the latter person loose. If the older worker doesn't know how to train (or is not interested in doing so), the odds are 1000 to 1 that the new employee will never learn the job correctly. And the training process itself will be slow and costly. So don't depend on an older employee to show a new one the ropes, at least not without providing some guidance.

Caution: Even if you have qualified job instructors in your department, you can never completely delegate your training responsibilities. It's also important to be aware of, and show a personal interest in, every employee's progress. This will stimulate employees to want to learn and become equal partners in the training process. In other words, you must continue to supervise the training and the trainees, just as you supervise any other of your responsibilities, to be sure that they are meeting your expectations.

If supervisors are responsible for training, what's the purpose of a company's training department?

The function of a company training (or human resources development) department is to identify training needs, specify and/or provide training programs and methods, and assist or supplement supervisors and other managers in discharging their training responsibilities.

Generally, the training department people are experts in teaching methods. For example, training specialists can be of real help in determining specific training needs. They can help you recognize and interpret the training symptoms mentioned previously. You'll want their help, too, in learning how to be a good instructor and in training some of your key employees to be trainers. And the training department is invaluable in getting you started in making job breakdowns, lesson plans, and training timetables.

Certain employee training is best done by a central training group. Such general subjects as company history and products, economics, and human relations are naturals for them. Other classroom-type instruction (for instance, in basic literacy skills or statistical quality control) lends itself to centralized training too. But when the training department does these jobs for you, you must still assume the responsibility for requesting this training for your employees and for making sure they apply what they learn to their work.

3 *ORIENTATION TRAINING*

CONCEPT   New employees need an orientation to their jobs, co-workers, and work environment.

When does a good supervisor begin training an employee?

When a new employee is hired. There are two reasons for this. First, new workers who get off on the right foot by knowing what to do and how to do it are like a baseball team that builds a ten-run lead in the first inning. With a head start like that, there's a good chance of eventual success. The second reason revolves around the idea of the **teachable moment.** This is the time when new employees are most receptive to instruction, because they want to learn and succeed. Good supervisors respond to this need and begin training almost immediately.

Training recently hired workers, which is called **induction training** or **orientation training,** is a little like introducing friends at a club meeting where they are strangers. You'd want to introduce them to others and try to make them feel at home. You'd show them where to hang their hats and coats and where the rest rooms are. If you wanted to have them think well of your club, you might tell them something about its history and the good people who belong to it. If you had to leave them for a time to attend to some duty or other, you would come back occasionally to see how they were getting along. It's the same way with new employees who report to you. You want them to think well of you and to feel at home in your department from the beginning, so treat them accordingly.

What should be included in orientation training for new employees?

Orientation sessions should cover the major topics of probable interest to employees, as well as the items that you feel are important to their success. These include:

- Pay rates, pay periods, when pay is first received, deductions from pay, and how pay increases may be earned.
- Hours of work, such as reporting and quitting time, lunch periods, breaks, and cleanup time.
- Availability of overtime and overtime pay, and premium pay for working shift schedules.
- Time reporting systems, including location of time cards and how to punch in and out.
- Employee options under the company's benefit plans, such as group life, health, and dental insurance.

- Procedure to follow when sick.
- Procedure to follow when late.
- Basic safety rules, the procedure for reporting accidents, and the joint employee-company responsibility for identifying hazards under the Occupational Safety and Health Administration (OSHA) law.

Induction activities should also include:

- Tour of the department and other areas of the company.
- Introduction to co-workers.
- Assignment to a work area and identification of necessary resources.
- Location of cafeteria, lockers, and rest rooms.
- Location of first-aid facilities.

This basic information is a lot for new employees to swallow at once. So don't be afraid to ask questions to gauge their understanding or to repeat what you tell them several times. Better still, give them some of the more detailed information in small doses. Give them some today, a little tomorrow, and as much as they can take a week from now.

Note that in many companies new employees receive an orientation talk from the personnel or training department. As valuable as this talk may be, it won't help new employees half as much as an informal, one-on-one chat with their supervisor. You are an important person in their eyes, and you also want to begin developing a healthy work relationship with them. Grab the opportunity to do so!

4 FACTORS IN LEARNING

CONCEPT   Much is known about how employees learn best, and these ideas should be built into any training program.

What's the difference between acquiring knowledge and learning a skill?

Knowledge is information that can be learned from reading, from listening to an expert, or from keen observation. *Skill,* the capability to perform a job-related action, is a combination of relevant knowledge and physical or perceptual abilities. It is acquired through guided practice. For example, in operating a four-speed (manually shifted) sports car, you may be told that it is vitally important to reach certain minimum speeds before shifting from one gear to another. To apply this information, you will need to acquire a very special skill, a "motor" skill. Smooth shifting of gears will take place only after hours of practice learning the "feel" of pushing in the clutch and coordinating that with a sense of how fast the auto is moving. And all of this must tie in with a special movement of the gear stick by hand.

Almost all jobs in which an individual must place his or her hands, feet, or eyes on the material or equipment at the workplace require a unique combination of information and motor skills. In simple terms, then, the trainee on a job must not only acquire knowledge (knowing what to do and understanding why) but also learn a skill (being able to perform properly).

What can you do to make the job easier to learn and to teach?

Jobs that seem simple to you because you're familiar with them may appear almost impossible to a person who has never performed them before. You may have heard the advice given to the diner faced with the overwhelming task of eating an elephant: "Just take one bite at a time!" Similarly, experience has shown that the trick to making jobs easier to learn is to break them down into simple (bite-size) steps. That way, employees need to learn only one step at a time, adding steps systematically, rather than trying to grasp the whole job in a single piece. At an early stage, however, it is useful to portray the entire task to the trainees so that they can see how each step fits into the larger picture.

Breaking a job down for training purposes (a *job breakdown*) involves two elements:

1. You must observe the job as it is done and divide it into its logical steps. For instance, if the job is to provide written responses to customer complaints, the first step would be to read the letter. The next two steps would be to identify all issues raised and to select the specific nature of the problem to be solved. The fourth step would be to consult a company policy manual, and the fifth would be to determine the acceptable type of response. The sixth step would be to select appropriate standard paragraphs from a computer-based inventory of prepared statements. And so on until the job is finished. (See Figure 10-2.)

2. For each step in a job breakdown, you must now consider the second element—called the *key point.* A key point is anything at a particular step that might make or break a job or injure the worker. Essentially, it's the knack or special know-how of experienced workers that makes the job go easier or faster for them. The key point for the third step in the customer relations representative's job in the previous paragraph would be to know the knack of sorting out the real complaint from a variety of frustrations expressed by the customer. For the seventh step it would be the capacity to personalize a standard solution to fit the unique problem and individual.

JOB BREAKDOWN SHEET FOR TRAINING	
Task: Responding to customer complaints	Operation: Preparing written letter using word processor
Important Steps in the Operation	**Key Points**
Step: A logical segment of the operation during which something happens to advance the work.	Key point: Anything in a step that might Make or break the job Injure the worker Make the work easier to do (i.e., knack, trick, special timing, bit of special information)
1. Read the customer's letter.	Knack—avoid defensive reactions.
2. Identify all issues raised.	Take notes using only key words.
3. Select a specific problem to be solved.	Identify the real complaint from a variety of frustrations expressed.
4. Consult the company policy manual.	Use table of contents or index to find relevant material.
5. Determine acceptable response.	Knack—ask yourself how you would feel if you received that reply.
6. Pick appropriate standard paragraphs from computer files.	Refer to list of key words, and match with those in file paragraphs.
7. Tailor the letter to fit the individual.	Personalize letter by frequent use of customer's name and specific problem.
8. Proofread the product for errors.	Review letter once now; set it aside a while; return to it when you are "fresh."

Figure 10-2 Sample job instruction breakdown.

Figure 10-2 shows how this customer relations job might be broken down into several steps with their appropriate key points for training purposes. Table 10-1 lists a number of factors, and sample questions for each, that will help you identify key points in product- and machine-oriented jobs for training purposes. In professional and service-related jobs, key points often will revolve around factors such as logic, courtesy, timeliness, and accuracy.

Where will the key points for a job be found?

They may be found in a number of places: in an operating or maintenance manual prepared by the manufacturer of equipment; in a record of "bugs" or peculiarities that has been gathered on a particular operation, procedure, or piece of equipment; or in the mind and/or know-how of an experienced operator. One of the reasons that training results are often poor when an experienced employee has been asked to break

Table 10-1 KEY-POINT CHECKLIST

Key points are those things that should happen, or could happen, at each step of a job which make it either go right or go wrong. Key points include any of the following:

1. Feel. Is there a special smoothness or roughness? Absence of vibration?
2. Alignment. Should the part be up or down? Which face forward? Label in which position?
3. Fit. Should it be loose or tight? How loose? How tight? Can you show the trainee? When can you tell that a part is jammed?
4. Safety. What can happen to injure a worker? How are the safety guards operated? What special glasses, gloves, switches, shoes are needed?
5. Speed. How fast must the operation proceed? Is speed critical? How can you tell if it's going too fast or too slow?
6. Timing. What must be synchronized with something else? How long must an operation remain idle—as with waiting for an adhesive to set?
7. Smell. Is there a right or wrong smell about anything—the material, the cooking or curing during the process, the overheating of a machine?
8. Temperature. Is temperature critical? How can you tell whether it is too hot or too cold? What can you do to change the temperature, if necessary?
9. Sequence. Is the specified order critical? Must one operation be performed before another, or doesn't it make any difference? How can the worker tell if he or she has gotten something out of order?
10. Appearance. Should surfaces be glossy or dull? Should the part be straight or bent? How can you correct an unsatisfactory condition?
11. Heft. Is weight important? Can you demonstrate how heavy or light a part or package should be?
12. Noise. Are certain noises expected (purring of a motor)? Unacceptable (grinding of gears)?
13. Materials. What is critical about their condition? How can the worker recognize that? When should the material be rejected? What should be done with rejected material?
14. Tools. What is critical about their condition? Sharpness? Absence of nicks or burrs? Positioning? Handling?
15. Machinery. What is critical about its operation? How is it shut down in emergencies? What will damage it? How can this be avoided?
16. Trouble. What should be done in the case of injury to persons or damage to materials, parts, products, tools, or machinery? How can damage be recognized?

in a new one is that the older employee may "conveniently" forget or, more likely, not be aware of key points that she or he has come to take for granted through years of experience. Since experienced employees have "internalized" these key points, they may no longer be conscious of what they are doing. Their descriptions of the job may be either incomplete (missing key points such as "Speed up the engine if you feel that the auto is about to stall while shifting gears") or altogether wrong (such as "Depress the clutch pedal after you have moved the gearshift").

As you (or a trained observer) break down a job for training purposes, you'll want to check all three sources of key points—manuals, records, and current employees. Table 10-1 also lists a number of questions that help to identify key points for training purposes.

In what sequence must the parts of a job be taught?

The best way to teach a job is to present its elements in a logical order, or start with the easiest part and proceed to the most difficult. This isn't always possible, of course. But if you can arrange your employee training in a systematic sequence, learning will go more smoothly and teaching will also be easier. Figure 10-3 shows how you can arrange your training sequence so that the learner works up to the difficult parts gradually from sequence 1 to 4.

How do you train employees to do a job the way you want them to?

Training can be either a very simple and highly satisfying task or a very difficult and frustrating one. If you can grasp and apply just four fundamentals, you can be a superior trainer. If you don't use this approach, you'll spend the rest of your life placing blame where it doesn't belong, arguing that employees are unreceptive, untrainable, or unmotivated; however, the problem will lie within you.

The foundation of systematic, structured job training (commonly called *job instruction training,* or JIT) has four cornerstones:

Step 1: Get the workers ready to learn. People who want to learn are the easiest to teach. So let trainees know why the job is important, why it must be done right. Find out something about the employees as individuals. Not only does this make them have more confidence in you, but it reveals to you the extent of their present knowledge about the job, the amount and quality of their experience, and their attitude toward learning. This familiarization period helps the trainees to get the feel of the job you want them to do.

Step 2: Demonstrate how the job should be done. Don't just tell the

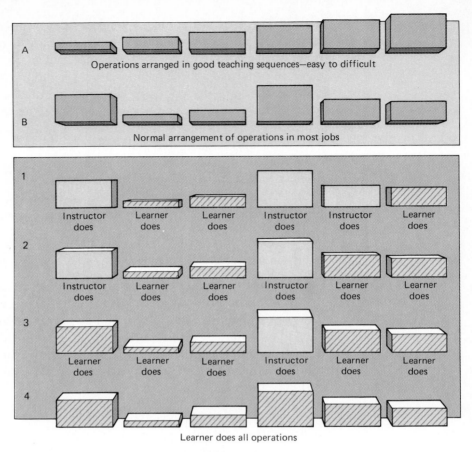

A — Operations arranged in good teaching sequences—easy to difficult

B — Normal arrangement of operations in most jobs

1 Instructor does | Learner does | Learner does | Instructor does | Instructor does | Learner does

2 Instructor does | Learner does | Learner does | Instructor does | Learner does | Learner does

3 Learner does | Learner does | Learner does | Instructor does | Learner does | Learner does

4 Learner does all operations

Figure 10-3 Arranging a preferable learning sequence.

trainees how to go about it or say, "Watch how I do it." Do both—tell *and* show them the correct procedure. Do this a little at a time, step by step. There's no point in going on to something new until the trainees have grasped the preceding step.

This is basically a reverse "show-and-tell" routine, with your role then repeated by a trainee. You would begin by telling the employee how to perform the first step (and why) and then demonstrating the procedure by doing it yourself. Next, you would ask the trainee to tell you how and why it is done (to check for comprehension) and then to demonstrate it to you (to check for proper procedure). In effect, this is a double process—tell and show (by you), followed by another tell and show (by the trainee).

Step 3: Try the workers out by letting them do the job. Let the employees try the job—under your guidance. Stay with the trainees at first to observe them so that you will know how they are doing.

Then praise them when they are doing well and provide constructive feedback when they are wrong. The mistakes they make while you're watching are invaluable to both you and the trainees. Errors will have a vivid impact on the trainees (who will try harder not to repeat them), and their mistakes will be useful to you as indicators of the things the trainees have not fully learned.

Step 4: Put the trainees on their own gradually.   Persons doing a new job have to fly alone sooner or later. So after they have shown you that they can do the work reasonably well while you're standing by, turn them loose for a while. Don't abandon them completely, though. Make a point of checking on their progress and workmanship regularly: perhaps three or four times the first day they are on their own, then once or twice a day for a week or two. But never think they are completely trained. There's always something an employee can learn to do—or learn to do better.

How skillful should you expect a trainee to become?

At one time, a supervisor expected employees to learn every facet of the job. A pipe fitter could measure, cut, thread, and join galvanized, lead, copper, and plastic pipe and make every kind of joint. Later, in many industrial situations, specialization became popular, and a pipe fitter was expected to develop a few skills well for a particular job in a specific plant. Now another trend is emerging—the idea of knowledge-based or skill-based pay. As employees acquire and demonstrate progressively higher levels of competencies, they can earn more. For this and other reasons, supervisors in many companies need to consider the concept of progressive levels of skills (or competencies) for training purposes. A supervisor should decide (1) what knowledge or skill is absolutely basic to the job at a minimum level of competency, (2) what knowledge and skill will bring the trainee up to an intermediate stage of competency (which may take from one to several months, according to the job), and (3) what knowledge and skill will be needed to bring the employee up to a mastery level (and this may take years of instruction and experience).

How do you get employees to want to learn?

Employees must see how training will pay off for them before they pitch into training with a will. So show the younger employees how training has helped others to get ahead and how it has built job security for them and increased their incomes. For older workers, stress the prestige that skill gives them with other workers. Show them how learning new jobs or better methods makes the work more interesting.

Telling workers why a job is done a certain way is often the key to securing their interest. To see the necessity for training, an employee needs to know not only *what* to do and *how* to do it but *why* it needs to be done.

How much should you teach at one time?

This depends on (1) how quickly a trainee can learn and (2) how difficult the job is. Each learner is different. Some catch on quickly; others are slow. It's better, therefore, to gauge your training speed to each situation. If an employee has trouble learning, try to find out why. With new employees, for example, it may simply be that they are nervous and trying so hard that they don't concentrate. So be patient. Help them relax. Make it easy for them to succeed. And when they complete even a small part of the new task successfully, be sure to praise them.

How smoothly should the training process proceed?

The learning process doesn't go smoothly for most people. We all have our ups and downs, depending on the material to be learned and even the time of day. Expect progress to be slow at first as the trainees struggle to set aside old ways of doing things. They may learn quickly for a while and then taper off to a plateau temporarily. They may even backslide a little. If this happens, reassure the trainees that their halt in progress is normal. Don't let them become discouraged. If necessary, go through the demonstration again so that they can get a fresh start. And pile on the encouragement.

How quickly do people forget what they have learned?

Rapidly. Research indicates that our learning disappears quickly unless we keep working at it. So for employees to become expert at the job you're teaching, you must keep repeating the important things you want them to retain. And they must practice new skills regularly under your supervision. It's not enough for them to qualify at a minimum level; they must overlearn a skill so that it becomes almost automatic. This is one reason why follow-up (Step 4 in the JIT approach) is so vital.

Can you teach old dogs new tricks?

Yes. Older workers can and do learn new methods and new jobs. And although they may learn at a slower rate than younger workers, this is mainly because older workers frequently have to unlearn what was taught to them in the past. Older workers often don't have the same incentive to learn that younger ones do. They tend to feel more secure in their jobs and have less interest in advancement. For these reasons, Step 1—getting the worker ready to learn—is of prime importance when you are teaching older workers.

5 TRAINING METHODS AND AIDS

CONCEPT   Effective training uses a variety of training methods and aids to facilitate employee learning.

What training methods should be used for instructing employees?

The key is to be aware of the many options available, recognize their unique strengths and weaknesses, and use the most appropriate one or ones. Training methods can be divided into those which primarily occur on the job (such as coaching or job rotation) and those which take an employee off the job (classroom lectures, for example). Other methods, such as vestibule and apprentice training, combine elements of both settings. The key questions to ask in making a good decision about methods to use are these: What is my objective (knowledge acquisition or skill development)? How much time, space, materials, or special preparation is required? Will the method make trainees be active or passive? How many employees must be trained at one time? If new job skills are the desired product, supervisors will often use one-on-one methods, since they provide personalized attention and have high impact on the trainees.

What's vestibule training?

When employees are trained by the company in the kind of work they are hired to perform but are separated from the actual job site and the related pressures of performance, the training is called **vestibule training.** It gets its name from the fact that such training is often done away from the noise, activity, and peer pressure associated with the trainees' future workstation—as if it were performed in the vestibule of the company before actual entry into the working area. Then, when the trainees gain competence and self-confidence in their new skills, they can be moved into the regular job site.

How valuable is apprentice training?

Traditionally, the top-notch, all-around skilled artisans were schooled through an *apprenticeship* program. This is a long, thorough, and costly training process that blends classroom instruction with hands-on skill practice under the guidance of experienced coaches. Apprenticeships may last from one to four years. They have two disadvantages, however. They prepare trainees for a wide variety of job skills, even though new employees may use only a small number of them in their first job. Also, the programs may fail to be tailored to your organization, requiring you to retrain apprentices immediately. The use of apprenticeship programs has declined somewhat, with more emphasis today placed on providing employees with just enough competency to perform a single job that the company needs done. As a result, the training is more focused, is done faster, and costs less.

How good are off-the-job training methods?

Although individualized training is effective for developing job skills, it can still be expensive and time-consuming for the supervisor. Some training can be conducted in small groups at less cost per person with equal success. This is particularly true when new policies or procedures need to be explained to all workers or when employees need to know the theory and background behind an operation. Value is also gained from the comments that experienced employees make to others in support of the ideas being presented.

Another alternative that relieves the supervisor of direct training responsibility is the use of self-paced instructional methods. *Programmed learning,* for example, exposes a trainee to a small block of information and then tests the trainee immediately to see if the material has been grasped. If the trainee answers the questions correctly, another block is provided. If the trainee cannot respond correctly, the block is repeated or rephrased and then the trainee is questioned again. This is a "small-bite" approach that allows trainees to move ahead at their own pace as they master the material. It also uses regular feedback to reinforce learning.

Many such training programs today are presented by mechanical and visual devices that add further stimulation and efficiency to the learning process. When programmed-learning materials are linked to a computer and a television screen, they are called **computer-assisted instruction** (CAI). Newer technologies involve the use of interactive videodiscs, which use exciting graphic displays, realistic experiences, and even touch-screen responses. They are expensive to produce but highly appealing to trainees, who suddenly become active participants. As a result, the chances of learning and retention are sharply improved.

What's the purpose of visual aids?

The classic Chinese proverb still tells the story best: One picture is worth 1000 words. Any device that helps trainees visualize what you're telling them speeds up the learning process. After all, most of us use our eyes to pick up 80 percent of what we know. So it's only natural for training that utilizes the visual sense to be more effective.

Visual aids may include a variety of devices, such as transparencies, slides and filmstrips, and motion pictures. Visual aids may also be simple and obvious, such as writing on a blackboard or demonstrating a point on a machine. Practically nothing beats making the demonstration right on the equipment a worker will use.

In the last few years, audiovisual instruction has increasingly invaded the training field. Tape cassettes linked to programmed texts, audio-TV cassettes with capsulated instructions, and closed-circuit television demonstrations and lectures—live or on tape—have demonstrated their ability to ensure consistent instruction. In the main, however, such methods are prohibitively expensive and are used only selectively where their cost can be justified.

6 OBTAINING RESULTS FROM TRAINING

CONCEPT   Training is useful only if it is transferred to the job and has a demonstrable payoff.

What are the direct and indirect costs of training?

All training, structured or catch-as-catch-can, is costly. There are direct costs of training materials, visual aids, and outside instructors. Indirect costs include the time of both supervisor and trainees, the effects of errors made, and the lost productivity during training. But the alternative—not training—may be the most expensive of all. The key is to plan carefully for systematic training in order to avoid the need to repeat it later. And there are many ways to hold down costs, like having a new employee learn while working alongside an experienced one.

What benefits can a supervisor expect from training?

In addition to making a better showing for your department in terms of improved quality and quantity of output or service, training puts you in a favorable light in other ways. Effective employee instruction:

- Smooths the way for intradepartmental transfers.
- Allows you more time for other supervisory tasks, such as scheduling work.
- Provides a reserve of trained personnel in your department for emergencies.
- Wins the confidence and the cooperation of your workers.

Perhaps most important of all, training your employees makes you a prime candidate for promotion. To achieve this result, you should try to assess, and improve, the payoffs from training. Measure the productivity of an employee before training and again after it is over. Compare the performance of trained workers to that of untrained ones, and project the improvements for the whole year. This analysis will convince you to continue your training efforts, and it will justify the time and costs of training.

How can a supervisor increase the probability that training will transfer to the job?

Many supervisors are effective trainers. Many employees want to learn new skills. Yet evidence suggests that much training (especially the classroom varieties) doesn't result in improved job performance. Training has failed if it has not been transferred to the job. The reasons are diverse—lack of supervisory reinforcement, impractical training, or even peer-group norms that create barriers to its use.

What can you do to aid the transfer of training? Discuss the objectives of training in advance with your new employees so that they will know what to expect. Point out effective workers to them so that they can have successful role models. Visibly monitor trainee performance; this lets the trainees know what you think is important. Praise successful behaviors regularly so that your new workers will feel good about their developing skills. Above all, consider training an important supervisory function and give it the attention it deserves.

KEY CONCEPTS TO REMEMBER

1. In the absence of sound training, employees learn their jobs haphazardly, inaccurately, or not at all. Only through careful assessment of needs, systematic instruction, and responsible follow-up can a supervisor be confident that employees will learn how to perform their work in the most effective manner. Recordkeeping is easier when a skills inventory is prepared for each employee.

2. Training is an important supervisory role, as well as a powerful tool for achieving bottom-line results. Although supervisors are ultimately responsible for the success of training, they can delegate some assignments to skilled employees. They should also call upon the training department for help in planning and designing good training programs.

3. New employees require special attention, and they are often receptive to any help received. Orientation training is a valuable tool for sharing important information regarding pay, benefits, and safe work practices with workers and for developing a relationship with them. They should also be introduced to their co-workers and shown relevant areas of the department and company.

4. Learning—the acquisition of knowledge and development of skills—can be accelerated in many ways. Identifying the key points through a job breakdown, sequencing them logically, showing as well as telling, repeating major ideas, and adapting to individual needs will all help the trainee. The four-step method of job instruction training (JIT) will also ensure that the process is systematic.

5. The process of instruction should use a variety of methods and aids, all carefully chosen to support the objectives of training. Both vestibule and apprentice training actively involve employees in the learning process while focusing on job-related skills. Programmed learning and computer-assisted instruction relieve the supervisor from direct instructional tasks while providing instant feedback to trainees on their performance.

6. Training can be costly, both directly and indirectly. Fortunately, it can also produce tremendous benefits if it is planned and conducted well. To facilitate the transfer of training from classroom to work site, supervisors can use a number of methods, such as discussing objectives, providing role models, monitoring performance, and praising successful behavior.

Job aids. Materials (charts, checklists, or visual displays) placed on or near the work area that help employees remember key points (what to do and when and how to do it) and perform effectively.

Job breakdown analysis. The segmentation of a particular job into those important elements, or steps, during which the employee must perform, induce, or supervise an action that advances the work toward its completion.

Job instruction training (JIT). A systematic four-step approach to training employees in a basic job skill: (1) prepare the workers to learn, (2) demonstrate how the job is done, (3) try them out by letting them do the job, and (4) gradually put them on their own.

Key point. The unique insight, knack, trick, timing, or special information that enables a worker to advance the work or task through a particular step in skillful and accident-free fashion; literally, the essential elements that make or break the job.

Knowledge. Information that can be learned from reading, listening to an expert, or keenly observing a situation. It is often a prerequisite to skill development.

Modeling. The process in which a skilled co-worker or supervisor demonstrates the performance of a key job skill and simultaneously explains the steps involved and the reasons for doing them.

Orientation training. The process in which new employees are introduced to their jobs, co-workers, and work environment through tours, personal introductions, and explanations; also known as *induction training*.

Programmed instruction. A self-administered teaching technique (using a specially prepared text or computer terminal) which presents information in very small, readily absorbed bits. These bits are followed immediately by related questions that test the trainee's comprehension by requiring correct responses before the trainee proceeds with the lesson.

Skill. The capability to perform a job-related action by blending relevant knowledge and physical or perceptual abilities.

Teachable moments. The specific times when employees are most receptive to receiving feedback and instructions from their supervisor and are therefore most likely to learn.

Transfer of training. The process in which trainees effectively apply to their jobs knowledge and skills gained in off-the-job training.

READING COMPREHENSION

1. Why is training an important supervisory function?
2. In what ways can a training specialist supplement the efforts made by supervisors to train their employees?
3. Mark's department is finally receiving the new computer terminals that other departments have had for several months. Would it be a good idea for Mark to let his employees learn all about the operation of the new terminals by reading the manufacturer's instruction manual? Why, or why not?
4. What information can you gain from a skills inventory?
5. What are the major questions in the mind of a new employee that should be addressed during orientation training?
6. Betty Jo, a checkout clerk in a discount store, has been told by her supervisor that she apparently understands how the cash register works but is too slow in operating it. Why does Betty Jo's acquisition of knowledge about her work differ from her skill development? How are these two factors related?
7. In a job breakdown, how do key points differ from important steps?
8. Why wouldn't a supervisor want to rigidly teach a job's sequence of steps in the same order as they are performed?
9. Derek, a new supervisor, is worried that his employees will not be excited about the training he plans to conduct for them. What can he do to stimulate them to want to learn?
10. What guidelines can a supervisor follow to make training more successful?

APPLICATION

SELF-APPRAISAL

What will help Greg learn?

Roxanna is the supervisor in a fast-food restaurant. Although the hours of work for her part-time employees are flexible, she has difficulty recruiting new workers, largely because they are paid the minimum wage. As a result, she has had continual difficulty attracting experienced employees. Most new workers are like Greg, who just began work today and will require extensive training and close supervision during the first several weeks. So Roxanna called the franchise's training director for help in directing Greg's training. A few days later, she received a list of trainee characteristics (see below) which the training director had indicated would provide her with helpful background information. Roxanna agreed with most of the items, but she felt they didn't provide enough direction on what she should *do* about them. She therefore developed an alphabetized list (see below) of possible implications and actions that might be undertaken to deal with each of the characteristics.

Your assignment is to put yourself in Roxanna's shoes, consider the implications of each trainee characteristic that Greg might manifest, and determine what should be done to capitalize on, or respond to, each of the trainee characteristics. On a separate piece of paper, write the numbers 1 to 8 down the page to correspond to each of the trainee characteristics. After each number on your list, write the letter of the supervisory implication and action that you regard as most appropriate for Roxanna to take. After completing this activity, check your answers by using the scoring procedure described on page 239.

Trainee Characteristics

1. Trainees are anxious about their performance.
2. Trainees can become overwhelmed with too many facts and too much knowledge.
3. Trainees wonder how all the pieces fit together.
4. Trainees don't know whether to concentrate on speed or quality of performance.
5. Trainees want to know about their progress.
6. Trainees have varied backgrounds and experiences.
7. Trainees learn differently—at different speeds and in different patterns.
8. Trainees want to know why they are being trained and what's going to happen.

Supervisory Implications and Actions

a. Teach skills and quality performance first; seek speed later.
b. Provide periodic performance feedback and constructive criticism.
c. Share facts and procedures in small bits; spread out training sessions.
d. Identify the needs and strengths of each trainee; adapt your approach to each one.
e. Provide a look at the "big picture"—tell the trainees how everything fits together.
f. Tell the trainees what your objectives are and what they will experience.

g. Ask the trainees questions to get them to relate training to their backgrounds.

h. Put the trainees at ease, for tension inhibits learning.

Scoring   According to a panel of experts, the following matches would be the most appropriate in helping Greg learn: 1–h, 2–c, 3–e, 4–a, 5–b, 6–g, 7–d, 8–f. Give yourself 1 point for each match you agreed with. (If you disagreed with any of the panel's decisions, can you justify your matches?)

Interpretation   A score of 7 or 8 points reflects *near-perfect* understanding of training principles and the training process. A score of 5 or 6 points indicates a *fuzziness* in your understanding of training principles and the training process. Review the text to clear up areas in which you disagreed with the panel's choices. A score of less than 5 points implies an *unsatisfactory* grasp of training principles and the training process. Review the entire chapter.

CASE STUDIES

CASE 29   The New Reservations Agent

When Malcolm finished his preassignment training as a reservations agent at Border to Border Airlines, his supervisor immediately rushed him into action. That was on Monday morning. The next few days were hectic, with several minor problems creating difficulties for Malcolm. For one thing, the computer had been down for two hours one day, and the backlog of requests was enormous. For another, soon after completing a reservation for one customer, Malcolm discovered that he had overlooked a notation on his computer screen indicating the flight was not scheduled daily, but only on Tuesdays and Fridays. When he tried to call the customer back, he was told that she had left for the airport already. When he questioned Sandy, a nearby colleague, he was told that the explanation for the notation was "in the instruction manual."

To make matters worse, Malcolm's supervisor stopped by with two pieces of feedback for him. The supervisor said he was dismayed to have received a call from an irate customer whom Malcolm had tried to help on a complex routing. Apparently, after Malcolm made several false starts, he had directed the customer to "call again later when the terminals weren't so busy." "Never do that again!" said his supervisor.

In addition, the supervisor reported that from monitoring Malcolm's calls he found that Malcolm had been averaging only about ten an hour. "Even for a new agent, that's a pretty dismal record. You ought to be handling at least 15 already, and the experienced agents are in trouble if they don't average 20."

"But what about our obligation to be courteous to each customer?" asked Malcolm. "After all, we were told in preassignment school to be pleasant and to stress total customer service and satisfaction."

If you were the supervisor, how would you approach this problem? Of the five alternatives provided below, which do you think might be most effective? Rank the alternatives on a scale from 1 (most preferable) to 5 (least preferable). You may add another alternative if you wish. In any event, be prepared to justify your ranking.

a. Formally assign Sandy as Malcolm's on-the-job trainer, and inform Malcolm to ask Sandy a lot of questions whenever a problem arises.
b. Send Malcolm back to preassignment school, suggesting that this time he ought to pay attention or he will be terminated before the end of his probationary period.
c. Give Malcolm the day off, and insist that he read the instruction manual thoroughly before returning to work the next day.
d. Tell Malcolm: "Hang in there, and things will get better. It just takes a long time to learn all the ins and outs of being a good reservations agent."
e. Pull Malcolm off the reservation lines temporarily, give him a thorough orientation, and then tell him and show him how to handle incoming calls.

CASE 30 The New Telephone Procedure

The supervisor of a rural office of a large electrical utility received a terse memo. It indicated that executives at headquarters were unhappy with the way some employees in the company were greeting customers when answering the phone. To avoid the possibility of problems in the rural office, the supervisor made a list of unacceptable practices and distributed the list to all employees during the next staff meeting. He explained that "pressure from the home office" was the major reason for his preparation of the list. During the next several days, the supervisor made a point of listening in on at least two phone conversations of each employee to make sure that the workers were not violating the preferred practices. In the table on page 241, put a check mark in the first column for each guideline for effective training that the supervisor apparently ignored or even violated; put a check mark in the second column for each guideline that the supervisor appears to have practiced or respected.

Guidelines for Effective Training	Ignored Guideline	Respected Guideline
1. Demonstrate how the job should be done.	_____	_____
2. Let the workers perform the job while being guided.	_____	_____
3. Periodically check on employee progress.	_____	_____
4. Explain why the procedure is to be used.	_____	_____
5. Break the job down into important steps and key points.	_____	_____
6. Present the parts of a job in a systematic sequence.	_____	_____
7. Provide a familiarization period for learning about the employee.	_____	_____
8. Assess whether or not the employee had a need for the training.	_____	_____

CASE 31 **It sounds good, but will they use it?**

The director of training and development for your company recently announced that she had contracted with a consultant to design and present a workshop entitled "Effective Time Management" for all employees. As a member of the Advisory Committee on Training, you have examined some of the materials the consultant prepared and also attended the pilot session. At this point you are convinced that the day-long program contains some good ideas and is skillfully presented. However, you are somewhat concerned about whether or not the major time management ideas will be actually *used* on the job by each of your workers. If they are not, dozens of hours of worker productivity will be lost, and it will be hard to convince employees to attend other training sessions in the future.

Before suggesting ideas for improvement, you decide to assess the relative importance of the barriers that operate to inhibit transfer of the training. Of the following six alternatives, which do you think is most likely to impede transfer? Rank the items on a scale from 1 (most likely) to 6 (least likely).

a. Trainees are often uncomfortable with any change and naturally resist it.

b. Trainees want to change, but a lack of resources on the job prevents them from doing so.

c. Trainees are discouraged from changing because of negative peer pressure.

d. Supervisors don't provide positive reinforcement for the new behaviors acquired in the workshop.

e. Trainees are excited about changing while they are attending a well-run workshop, but lose their enthusiasm once they are separated from the trainer.

f. The overall organizational climate doesn't support the need to change.

PART

4

Activating the Work Force

1 People behave differently because of their unique backgrounds.

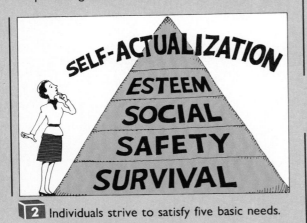

2 Individuals strive to satisfy five basic needs.

3 Supervisors are key forces in employee job satisfaction.

4 Attitudes and expectations also influence job satisfaction.

5 The work itself can provide motivation for better performance.

Motivating People at Work

LEARNING OBJECTIVES

After studying this chapter, you should be able to

1. Recognize some of the factors that influence the development of each person's unique personality.

2. Describe the five factors that make up Maslow's hierarchy of needs and explain how they influence an individual's motivation and behavior.

3. Explain the differences between satisfaction and dissatisfaction, according to Herzberg, and discuss how they affect a supervisor's ability to motivate employees.

4. Understand the concepts of expectancy theory, achievement and affiliation needs, and workplace harmony as they affect employee motivation, morale, and conflict.

5. Identify the elements found in a people-centered approach to job design and explain how, when incorporated into the work itself, they provide motivation and improve the quality of work life.

⬛ THE PERSISTENCE OF INDIVIDUALITY

CONCEPT   People behave differently because of their uniquely different backgrounds and personalities.

Why do people act the way they do?

If you mean, "Why don't employees act the way you wish they would?" the answer will take a long time. But if you are really asking, "Why do people act in such unpredictable ways?" the answer is simple: People do as they must. Their actions, which may look irrational to someone who doesn't understand them, are in reality very logical. If you could peer into people's backgrounds and into their emotional makeup, you'd be able to predict with startling accuracy how one person would react to criticism or how another person would act when told to change over to the second shift.

The dog who's been scratched by a cat steers clear of all cats. Workers who have learned from one boss that the only time they are treated as human beings is when the work load is going to be increased will go on the defensive when a new boss tries to be friendly. To the new boss such employee actions look absurd. But to the workers it's the only logical thing to do.

So it goes—each person is the product of parents, home, education, social life, and work experience. Consequently, when supervisors deal with employees, they are dealing with persons who have brought all their previous experiences to the job.

Then are all people different?

Each person *is* a distinct individual. In detail his or her reactions will be different from anyone else's. But to understand human relations, you must first know *why* people do things before you can predict *what* they will do. If you know that Bill dislikes his job because it requires concentration, you can make a good guess that Bill will make it hard for you to change the job by increasing its complexity. If Mary works at your company because of the socializing she has with her associates, you can predict that Mary will be hard to get along with if she's assigned to a spot in an isolated area.

The important tool in dealing with people is the recognition that although what they do is likely to differ, the underlying reasons for their doing anything are very similar. These reasons, incidentally, are called **motives,** or **needs.**

What determines an individual's personality?

Just about everything. An individual's personality cannot be neatly pigeonholed (as we so often try to do) as pleasant or outgoing or friendly or ill-tempered or unpleasant or suspicious or defensive. An individual's personality is the sum total of what the person is today: the clothing worn, the food preferred, the conversation enjoyed or avoided, the manners and gestures used, the methods of thought practiced, the way situations are handled. Each person's personality is uniquely different from anyone else's. It results from heredity and upbringing, schooling or lack of it, neighborhoods, work and play experiences, parents' influence, religion—all the social forces around us. From all these influences people learn to shape their individuality in a way that enables them to cope with life's encounters, with work, with living together, with age, with success and failure. As a result, personality is the total expression of the unique way in which each individual deals with life.

2 A POWERFUL PATTERN OF MOTIVATION

CONCEPT   Individuals strive to satisfy a hierarchy of five basic needs.

What do employees want from life—and their work?

Most of us, including employees, seek satisfaction from life in relation to what a very famous psychologist, A. H. Maslow, called the "five basic needs." (See Figure 11-1.) And we seek a good part of this satisfaction at our work. Dr. Maslow outlined the basic needs as explained below and conceived of them as a sort of hierarchy, with the most compelling ones coming first and the more sophisticated ones last.

We Need to Be Alive and to Stay Alive   We need to breathe, eat, sleep, reproduce, see, hear, and feel. But in today's world these needs rarely dominate us. Real hunger, for example, is rare. All in all, our first-level needs are satisfied. Only an occasional experience—a couple of days without sleep, a day on a diet without food, a frantic 30 seconds under water—reminds us that these basic needs are still with us.

We Need to Feel Safe   We like to feel that we are safe from accident or pain, from competitors or criminals, from an uncertain future or a changing today. Not one of us ever feels completely safe. Yet most of us feel reasonably safe. After all, we have laws, police, insurance, social security, union contracts, and the like, to protect us.

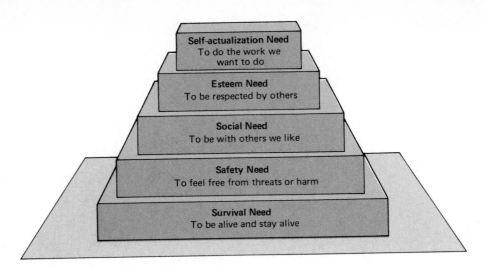

Figure 11-1 Maslow's hierarchy of needs.

We Need to Be Social From the beginning of time we have lived together in tribes and family groups. Today these group ties are stronger than ever. We marry, join lodges, and even do our praying in groups. Social need varies widely from person to person—just as other needs do. Few of us want to be hermits. Not everyone, of course, is capable of frank and deep relationships—even with a wife or husband and close friends. But, to a greater or lesser degree, this social need operates in all of us.

We Need to Feel Worthy and Respected When we talk about our self-respect or our dignity, this is the need we are expressing. When a person isn't completely adjusted to life, this need may show itself as undue pride in achievements, self-importance, boastfulness—a bloated ego.

But so many of our other needs are so easily satisfied in the modern world that this need often becomes one of the most demanding. Look what we go through to satisfy the need to think well of ourselves—and have others do likewise. When a wife insists her husband wear a jacket to a party, she's expressing this need. When we buy a new car even though the old one is in good shape, we're giving way to our desire to show ourselves off.

We even modify our personalities to get the esteem of others. No doubt you've put on your company manners when out visiting. It's natural, we say, to act more refined in public than at home—or to cover up our less acceptable traits.

We Need to Do the Work We Like This is why many people who don't like their jobs turn to hobbies for expression, and why so many people get wrapped up in their work. We all know men and women who enjoy the hard burden of laboring work, or machinists who hurry home from work to run their own lathes, or bored terminal operators who stay up late in their own homes playing with their own microcomputers. This need rarely is the be-all and end-all of our lives. But there are very few of us who aren't influenced by it.

In the 1960s and early 1970s many young people dropped out of society or set out to "do their own thing." This was largely an expression of the desire to fulfill oneself—what Maslow called "self-actualization."

Which of these needs is the most powerful?

The one or ones that have not yet been satisfied. Maslow's greatest insight was the realization that once a need is satisfied, it will no longer motivate a person to greater effort. If a person has what is required in the way of job security, for example, offering more of it—such as guaranteeing employment for the next five years—will normally not cause a person to work any harder. The supervisor who wishes to see greater effort generated will have to move to an unsatisfied need, such as the desire to be with other people on the job, if this employee is to be expected to work harder as a result.

It should also be noted that people tend to move up and down the hierarchy as one of their needs is threatened. For example, rumors of layoff can shift attention quickly back to "safety and security."

3 SATISFACTION AND DISSATISFACTION

CONCEPT Supervisors are key forces in providing employees with job satisfaction.

In what way can a job satisfy a person's needs?

It's a fact: Many people are happier at work than at home! Why? Because a satisfying job with a good supervisor goes such a long way toward making life worth living. Whereas all of us may complain about our jobs (or our bosses) from time to time, most of us respond favorably to the stability of the work situation. At home Jane may have a nagging husband, sick children, and a stack of bills to greet her at the end of the month. At work Jane can have an appreciative supervisor, a neat job with a quota she can meet each day, and assurance of a paycheck (and other benefits) at the week's end. No wonder Jane enjoys herself more at work than at home.

Or look at it this way. A rewarding job with a decent company and a straight-shooting boss easily provides the first two basic needs: (1) a livelihood that keeps the wolf away from the door and (2) a sense of safety from the fears of layoff, old age, or accidents. Satisfaction from the other three basic needs—to be social, to be respected, and to do the work we like—is often more a function of a person's supervisor than of the job itself.

A good supervisor can see that a person's job satisfies the *social need* by demonstrating to the rest of the work group the desirability of taking in a new worker. For instance: "This is Paula Brown, our new computer clerk. We're glad to have her with the agency. I've told her what a great gang of people you all are. So how about taking Paula along to the vending area during the rest break and showing her where she can get a cup of coffee."

To satisfy the *esteem need,* a good supervisor will make sure workers know when their work is appreciated. For example: "Paula, here's your locker. I think you'll agree that this is a pretty clean washroom. We feel that when we hire a first-rate person, we should provide first-rate conditions so that you can do the best possible work."

To satisfy the *desire to do worthwhile work,* a good supervisor gives thought to placing employees on jobs for which they have the most aptitude and training. The supervisor might say to Paula: "Since you've worked at this type of terminal before, suppose you start here. When you've got the hang of things, we'll give you a chance to broaden your experience on some more challenging assignments."

In what important ways does dissatisfaction differ from satisfaction?

One noted behavioral scientist, Frederick Herzberg, made these distinctions between them:

> **Satisfaction** for an employee comes from truly motivating factors such as interesting and challenging work, utilization of one's capabilities, opportunity to do something meaningful, recognition of achievement, and responsibility for one's own work.

> **Dissatisfaction** occurs when the following factors are *not* present on the job: good pay, adequate holidays, long-enough vacations, paid insurance and pensions, good working conditions, and congenial people to work with.

Herzberg bases these definitions on his *two-factor theory*. He says that every human being has two motivational tracks: (1) a lower-level one, animal in nature and bent only on surviving, and (2) a higher-level one, uniquely human and directed toward adjusting to oneself. Herzberg labels the first set of motivations "hygiene," or "maintenance," factors. We need to satisfy them, he reasons, to keep alive. People try to avoid pain and unpleasantness in life; they do the same on the job. Satisfaction of these needs provides only hygiene for people. These factors physically maintain the status quo, but they do not motivate. If they are not present in the workplace, an employee will be dissatisfied and may look for a job elsewhere that provides these factors. But the employee will not work harder just because these factors are given to him or her. Said another way, a general pay increase may keep employees from quitting, but it will rarely motivate an employee to work harder. (See Figure 11-2.)

How can supervisors provide the kind of satisfaction that motivates employees?

Herzberg feels that those job factors that provide genuine and positive motivations should be called *satisfiers*. (See the upper portion of Figure 11-2 for some typical satisfiers.)

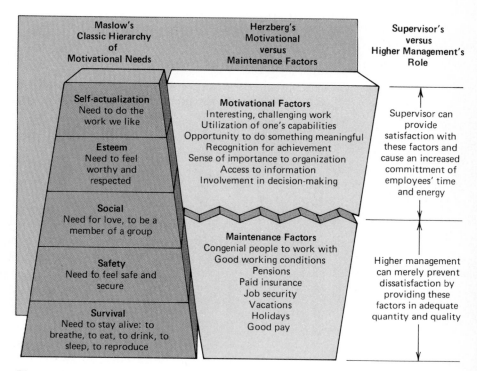

Figure 11-2 Employee needs that supervisors can satisfy.

Without splitting hairs, we can see that generally the company must provide the factors that prevent dissatisfaction. The supervisor tends to provide the factors that satisfy. Few supervisors can establish the basic pay rates for the organization. Almost all supervisors can motivate. For example, the supervisor can provide an employee with a specific, challenging goal: "Not many people can pack more than 200 cartons an hour. If you can pack 220 today, you'll be a great asset to this department."

Similarly, a supervisor can let an employee know that the work he or she is doing is appreciated: "The boss asked me today who it was that prepared these especially neat reports. I was pleased to tell her that you did!"

A supervisor can also help to make work more interesting by making suggestions, such as "Why don't we take fifteen minutes soon to see whether, together, we can find a way to break the monotony in your job?"

And a supervisor can always extend responsibility by saying to an employee: "Beginning today, will you make the decision as to whether off-grade products should be reworked or thrown away? If you make an occasional mistake, don't worry about it. In that area, your judgment is every bit as good as mine."

What happens when employees don't get satisfaction from their jobs?

Their morale drops, absences and lateness increase, and it becomes increasingly difficult to obtain their cooperation or to introduce necessary changes.

Shouldn't job satisfaction be primarily the company's responsibility—not the supervisor's?

The company's stake in good human relations is, of course, just as big as a supervisor's. And when a company helps a supervisor to establish the right climate for employee job satisfaction, a supervisor's work with people is a lot easier. But a supervisor's relationship with his or her employees is—ultimately—a very personal one. No amount of policies and procedures, fancy cafeterias, generous fringe benefits, or sparkling rest rooms can take the place of a concerned supervisor who treats his or her employees wisely and well. From your point of view, responsibility for employees' job satisfaction is one you must share with the company or parent organization.

4 EXPECTANCY, ACHIEVEMENT, AND HARMONY

CONCEPT   Employee performance is greatly influenced by the workers' expectancy of what the job will provide, their attitudes toward personal achievement, and their wish for harmony in the workplace.

If people all have the same fundamental needs, how much can a supervisor rely upon "push-button" motivation?

Not very much at all. There is a great danger in oversimplifying the analysis of human needs, especially at work. It is a mistake to assume too much about another person's motivations. It is an even bigger mistake to attempt to manipulate an employee's behavior by holding out false promises or by behaving insincerely and/or inconsistently.

One explanation of human behavior, for example, is that it depends on each employee's **expectancy** (or estimate) of what his or her actions may or may not bring. In effect, the employee makes three estimates: (1) Can I do what management is asking me to do? (2) If I can do it, will management be satisfied and reward me? (3) Will the reward given me be worth the effort? As you can see, a person's effort will be greatly influenced by the answers to these questions. According to Maslow, the supervisor may go through the right motions and still find that the employee doesn't perform as anticipated.

How important is achievement to today's employee?

It is probably more important to supervisors than to employees. One noted observer, David McClelland, believes that the need for achievement is especially strong among most people who enter the management ranks. Nevertheless, a great many other people feel its strong pull.

You can recognize the achiever, according to McClelland, if the person:

1. Likes to be able to control the situations in which he or she is involved.
2. Takes moderate risks but not long chances.
3. Likes to get immediate feedback as to how well he or she has done.
4. Has a tendency to be preoccupied with a task orientation toward the job to be done.

This last quality is one that supervisors must guard against, lest it distract them from the need to relate well to their subordinates.

McClelland believes that most people learn their motivation patterns from life's experiences rather than by feeling them instinctively, as Maslow suggests. In fact, McClelland believes that in addition to achievement, the needs for power and affiliation are the most common motivators.

Individuals who are *power*-motivated may see every situation in your department as one in which they must seize control or otherwise submit to your domination. The power seekers tend to be abrasive, insisting on doing the job their own way rather than going along with your instructions.

Employees who are motivated by *affiliation* are usually friendly and like to socialize. The affiliation seekers are often hard to motivate toward production for production's sake but may respond to the appeal for cooperation.

Achievement seekers will rise to challenges and seek freedom of choice in deciding how to do the job. But they may be inclined to take off in an independent direction and balk at working with other employees.

Is the object of good human relations to have one big happy family?

Have you ever known a family in which there wasn't some discontent? Where one child didn't feel that another one was favored by a parent? Or where there wasn't an occasional spat between husband and wife? Or where there wasn't a disreputable relative hidden somewhere? We can't believe you have. It's the same way in business. As a responsible supervisor you strive for harmonious relationships with your employees and with the others with whom you associate. But it would be foolish to expect that everything is going to be as smooth as cream all the time—or even most of the time. It's only natural for people to have differences of opinion and arguments.

What you should aim for in your area is to have the arguments settled in a peaceful and reasonable manner. Keep emotions and epithets out of it. Sure, you can expect occasional name calling—and loud voices and red necks. But the *general* level of human relations in your area should be friendly, with an attitude like this: "Okay, let's pull this issue apart. Tell me exactly what's eating you about this assignment. When I've seen your point, I won't promise you I'll agree with you. But I'll be a lot better able to give you a straight answer then." And after your decision: "Don't apologize for making an issue about it, Bill. That's your prerogative. And I'm glad you exercised it to get this matter cleared up. But how about in the future coming to me first before you get so hot and bothered about it?

5 MOTIVATION IN THE WORK ITSELF

CONCEPT   Employees can be greatly motivated by the quality of the work itself.

How can work be tailored to provide the greatest motivation for the persons who perform it?

By redesigning jobs according to *people-centered* considerations. Most work is first designed according to process-centered constraints. That is, emphasis is given to the dictates of (1) product specifications, (2) tool and machine requirements, (3) process-flow sequences, (4) computer-assisted controls, and (5) work-space layout. Only by a subsequent redesign will most work be made more satisfying and convenient to human beings.

Frank and Lillian Gilbreth pioneered the people-centered approach to job design in the early 1900s, describing human motions with *therbligs*. Later, this technique was systematized through the techniques of human factors engineering, or *biomechanics*. In today's office environment, with its increased automation and computer usage, **ergonomics** —the study of how workers react to their environment—is a major force in protecting the health of workers and in ensuring optimal efficiency.

Most present-day efforts at job redesign stress an accommodation of the psychological, as well as the physiological, needs of workers. And that is where supervisors enter the picture most actively.

How does the people-centered approach to job design differ from the process-centered approach?

It strives for maximum employee involvement in the design of each individual's job. It does not ignore process considerations. Instead, it encourages employees to view demands and restrictions as problems they are invited to help solve. The way in which this involvement takes place has led to its having many names: job enlargement, job enrichment, and work design or, sometimes, work redesign. The big difference is that the people-centered approach stresses genuine participation by employees, singly or in groups, in making their work effective and their jobs more attractive.

The boon to supervisors in the people approach is that it focuses everyone's attention on the "work itself" (another term sometimes used, defined in a later section). Supervisors aren't expected to be part-time psychologists or extraordinary leaders in seeking cooperation from their employees. It is the work that is examined, criticized, and restructured rather than human beings. The responsibility for these changes is no longer the sole burden of the supervisor; it is shared by all those employees who are able to, and wish to, get involved.

What factors of job design are most likely to increase the motivational aspects of work?

Two authorities from AT&T (where more than 30,000 employees have been involved in work design), H. Weston Clarke Jr. and Richard O. Peterson, advise that there are six critical factors. When added to the job, these factors—or dimensions—help to meet organizational needs and thus to promote productive performance in support of departmental or organizational goals. These dimensions include:

A whole job from beginning to end.   This functional completeness enables an employee to start his or her part of the work from scratch and see a definable product or service when the job is completed. Obviously, a worker in an auto factory cannot build a whole car. But it would be better if a wheel, for example, could be followed from the time it is uncrated until it is mounted on the car's hub.

Regular contact with users or clients.   The provision for an employee to have direct, consistent relationships with the person (department, regional office, or customer) who uses what is made or processed greatly enhances the individual's sense of being a person rather than an unknown cog in the machinery. Example: The person recording a sales order can call the salesperson for clarification if need be.

Use of a variety of tasks and skills.   The need to employ more than one skill and accomplish more than one task in getting the job done helps to relieve the sense of confinement and monotony. Example: An assembly worker uses a soldering iron as well as a wrench to join parts and to adjust critical mechanical tensions.

Freedom for self-direction.   This is the reality as well as the feeling of autonomy—that the employee can run the show as far as the job is concerned. In particular, it provides the opportunity to make choices about how the work will be done. Example: At a food processing plant in Kansas, autonomous work groups of from 7 to 14 members decide for themselves how to divide the work, screen and select new members, and counsel members who do not meet team standards.

Direct feedback from the work itself.   The employee can tell immediately by looking at the finished product or service whether it has been done rightly or wrongly. The worker does not have to wait for the supervisor, an inspector, or an accounting report to get this information. Example: In one AT&T department, keypunch operators decided to schedule their own work, verify their own output, and keep track of their own errors. In work that had previously been judged dead-end and boring, turnover was cut 27 percent, and 24 clerks found they could do what 46 had previously done.

A chance for self-development. Work that requires employees to stretch their minds and sharpen their skills makes these employees more valuable to themselves as well as to the company. It demonstrates that the benefits from work need not be one-sided, that both an employee's goals and a company's goals can be satisfied.

Should distinctions be made among the various kinds of people-centered job design?

Not necessarily, but it helps to add perspective to the ways that job design can be accomplished.

Job enlargement, for example, extends the boundaries of a job by adding differing tasks at the same level of expertise. First tried at IBM, the concept is to let manufacturing employees be responsible for the production step just before and just after the one they currently are doing. Thus punch press operators might fill their own tote boxes and carry the punched parts to the next operation. It provides an opportunity to get away from a fixed place all day and a chance to converse for a minute or two with adjoining operators and to feel that the job isn't limited to the second or two it takes to load the press and wait for the die to stamp out a part.

Job enrichment is an outgrowth of the job-enlargement concept. It expands a job vertically by adding higher-skill activities and by delegating greater authority. For example, the punch press operators might set up their presses with the die required for each new job, inspect their own work with gauges typically used by roving inspectors, and maintain their own output tallies.

Goal-oriented management is the approach developed by M. Scott Myers while at Texas Instruments Company in Dallas. Like "work itself," it emphasizes the need for supervisors to shift their thinking from "I am the boss who must think of everything" to "These are the goals we must reach together." Under the Myers system the supervisor leads (by "facilitating") and controls when necessary; employees are responsible for planning tasks and accomplishing them. Conversely, authority-oriented supervisors typically plan, lead, and control the doers, who have little say in planning how their work is to be accomplished. (See Figure 11-3.)

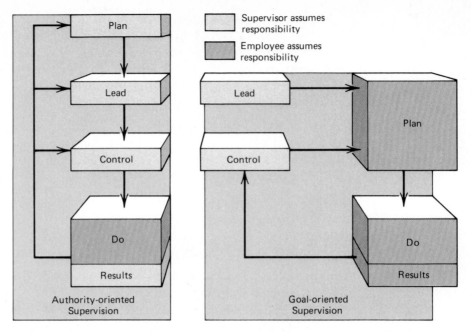

Figure 11-3 Job design differences using authority-oriented and goal-oriented supervision. (Adapted from a concept by M. Scott Myers, *Every Employee a Manager,* McGraw-Hill, New York, 1970, p. 99.)

Work itself was the term initially used by AT&T for the program it now labels *work design.* It typifies the people-centered job design approach featured in this chapter because it looks for a balance among process demands, organizational goals and restrictions, and employee abilities and interests.

Where does the biggest payoff come from in job design?

For the company or organization it comes in greater output per employee; improved quality of product or service; and—often most important—fewer absences, lower turnover rates, and greater cooperation from employees.

For employees there can be little doubt that job design adds a number of attractive ingredients to their work. Experts say that it improves the *quality of work life* itself. It offers greater freedom and flexibility and at the same time makes the work more challenging. Job design utilizes more of an employee's skills and does this more effectively than traditionally frozen methods.

◼ REVIEW

KEY CONCEPTS TO REMEMBER

1. Individual behavior is dependent upon a vast heritage of genealogical characteristics and is shaped by the forces of home environment, education, and work experience. This individuality causes people to behave as they do, even though such behavior often appears illogical to others.

2. Most people are motivated to satisfy five basic needs, arranged in a hierarchy. The physiological needs of survival and safety are at the bottom. The psychological needs of being social, winning the respect of others, and performing the work we want to do (self-actualization) are at the top. Each individual places different priorities on these needs, and these priorities differ from time to time. Once a need has been satisfied, it no longer serves to motivate behavior and the next lower unsatisfied needs must be appealed to.

3. The two-factor theory says that the three lower-level needs—the survival, safety, and social needs—do not provide motivation: they are "hygiene," or "maintenance," factors that incur only dissatisfaction if they are not satisfied. Only the two higher-level needs—the need for esteem and for self-actualization—are genuine satisfiers, says the theory. Accordingly, these are the true motivators. Since supervisors have little control over the dissatisfiers, their main motivational routes are through appeals to the satisfiers.

4. Employee motivation is also influenced by (a) the expectancy of rewards and the value placed upon them and (b) the degree to which an individual seeks achievement, affiliation, or power from the work. A contented work force and above-normal productivity do not necessarily go hand in hand. Permissiveness and indulgence, for example, induce carelessness and indifferent work habits. By setting high work standards and motivating employees to attain them, a supervisor must expect occasionally to cause tensions and outspoken disagreements. These exchanges, when resolved without delay, are healthy and tend to sustain high morale—along with the low absence rates and greater cooperation that are characteristic of a satisfied work force.

5. When jobs are redesigned through a people-centered, participative approach, employees center their attention on the work itself. As a consequence, the work becomes more nearly the kind of work em-

ployees want to do. It provides greater challenges and satisfaction—and becomes its own motivation force.

SUPERVISORY WORD POWER

Behavior. The actions people take, or the things they say, while coping with other people, with problems, with opportunities, and with situations.

Dissatisfaction. The state that exists when "maintenance," or "hygiene," factors such as good pay, job security, fringe benefits, and desirable working conditions are lacking.

Expectancy. An individual's judgment about the attractiveness of an assignment. It is based upon (1) whether or not he or she can actually do what is requested, (2) whether there will be a reward for this performance, and (3) how highly the person values the promised benefit in view of the effort required.

Job redesign. The process of carefully restructuring a job to foster productivity and to appeal to the interests of the employees who carry it out.

Motivation. The process that impels a person to behave in a certain manner in order to satisfy highly individual needs for survival, security, companionship, respect, achievement, power, growth, and a sense of personal worth.

Personality. An individual's unique way of behaving and of seeing and interpreting the actions of other people and events. Personality is shaped by heredity, parents' beliefs, upbringing, work experiences, and many other factors.

Quality of work life. The extent to which the work itself provides motivation and satisfaction because of the existence in the job design of functional completeness, contact with users, varied tasks and skills, autonomy, direct feedback from the work, and chance for personal growth.

Satisfaction. The state that exists when truly motivating factors—such as interesting and challenging work, full use of one's capabilities, and recognition for achievement—are provided.

Work itself. The concept that the nature and design of the jobs that employees hold will influence employee performance and satisfaction as much as or more than the interpersonal motivation provided by supervisors and management.

READING COMPREHENSION

1. What sort of things affect the development of an individual's personality?
2. Why is it possible for two employees to have entirely different reactions to the same boss?
3. If an employee's survival, social, and esteem needs were satisfied, which of Maslow's five needs should a supervisor appeal to next?
4. How might an individual's priorities of needs change with his or her growing maturity?
5. When worker motivation is still low despite good pay, fringe benefits, and desirable working conditions, what can a supervisor do to increase motivation?
6. How does Herzberg distinguish between satisfiers and dissatisfiers?
7. Explain the three estimates an employee makes about a work assignment in deciding whether or not he or she will try harder.
8. How would you draw the line between (a) a supervisor who is well liked and whose department is effective and (b) a supervisor who is well liked but whose department is not particularly effective?
9. Name at least five factors that, if built into jobs, add to the potential of the work itself to motivate employees.
10. After some changes had been made in the job, an employee complained to the supervisor: "This is job enlargement, all right, but it sure isn't job enrichment." What did the employee mean?

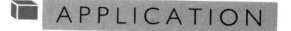

APPLICATION

SELF-APPRAISAL

How's your motivational IQ?

Although a supervisor's motivational skills are, like the needs of his or her subordinates, highly individualistic, there are a number of generally accepted concepts that prevail. Here is your chance to see how well you recall and understand these concepts. Listed on page 262 are a number of actions and attitudes a supervisor might take toward subordinates. Your assignment is to indicate which items are motivationally sound and which are not. On a separate piece of paper, copy the following column headings. In the column "Actions and Attitudes," write the numbers 1 to 15 down the page to correspond to each of the items. For each action or attitude, place a check mark in the column that matches your opinion. After completing this activity, check your answers by using the scoring procedure described on page 263.

Column headings:

Actions and Attitudes	True, or Sound Practice	False, or Unsound Practice

1. If you understand why a person acts as she or he does, you may be better able to predict what that person may do under a given set of circumstances.

2. You may better understand a person's motivations if you know more about that person's family, education, past and present living conditions, and work experiences.

3. The most fundamental of all motivational drives is the need for self-actualization.

4. In general, motivational needs appear in a random pattern, with no rationale to explain their priorities.

5. According to Maslow, once a motivational need has been satisfied, only an appeal to the next lower need will provide motivation.

6. Maslow's higher-level needs are more psychological than physiological.

7. Herzberg believes that motivation at work comes from a person's drive to satisfy Maslow's two highest-level needs.

8. Herzberg believes that when Maslow's lower-level needs are not met, employees will be dissatisfied; satisfaction of these needs will not motivate.

9. Herzberg believes that supervisors have their greatest motivational opportunities by improving conditions that improve the quality of their subordinates' work.

10. If an employee does not expect that a supervisor can deliver on his promises of rewards, that employee is not likely to try much harder.

11. Employees who are motivated by achievement may have problems working effectively with people whose primary need is for affiliation.

12. Supervisors who maintain a good state of morale and motivation in their departments will not encounter disagreements or conflict among their employees.

13. The introduction of therbligs, biomechanics, and ergonomics represents movement toward the people-centered approach to designing jobs.

14. One of the hallmarks of the people-centered approach is to isolate workers from criticism of their work by people who use their products or services.

15. The people-centered approach to job design tends to stress greater participation and involvement by employees in the structuring of their own work.

Scoring Give yourself 1 point for each of the following statements that you checked as *true*, or representing sound practice: 1, 2, 5, 6, 7, 8, 9, 10, 11, 13, 15. Give yourself 1 point for each of the following statements that you checked as *false*, or representing unsound practice: 3, 4, 12, 14.

Interpretation If you scored 13 points or more, you've got a high motivational IQ. You appear to be prepared to handle motivational problems intelligently. If you scored between 10 and 12 points, your motivational IQ needs some sharpening. Otherwise, you'll be making unnecessary mistakes in handling people. Review the items you missed. If you scored less than 10 points, your motivational IQ is likely to prevent you from becoming an effective supervisor. Review the entire chapter.

CASE STUDIES

CASE 32   The Conflicting Coffee Breaks

Two employees, Janet and Martha, work side by side as bank tellers. For several months, they relieved one another for their coffee breaks. Janet took the first break, from 9:45 to 10 a.m., and Martha took the second one, from 10 to 10:15 a.m. However, a new supermarket opened in the shopping center, and there was suddenly a large influx of shoppers coming in to cash checks right after 10 a.m. Accordingly, Jack Smith, their boss, asked Martha to postpone her coffee break until after 10:30 a.m. but told Janet she could continue on the same break as before. Martha thought this request over, and when she came in the next day, she told Mr. Smith that the new arrangement was unfair. If anyone should postpone her break, it should be Janet, because she had had the early one for a long time. When Mr. Smith asked Janet her opinion, Janet said that she had been handling the peak load alone from 10 to 10:15 a.m. for a long while. Now she ought to get the choice because she is still going to be on duty during the extended peak period.

If you were Mr. Smith, what would you do? Rank the following five alternatives on a scale from 1 to 5 in the order in which they appeal to you (1, most preferable; 5, least preferable). You may add another alternative if you wish. In any event, be prepared to justify your ranking.

a. Tell Martha that she is selfish for not going along with a simple adjustment and insist that she comply with your request.

b. Agree to Martha's suggestion instead, and tell Janet you expect her to cooperate.

c. Point out that the morning hours are busy for only a very short time, so this shouldn't be a factor.

d. Ask Martha and Janet to resolve this problem between themselves, as long as there is double coverage from 10 to 10:30 a.m.

e. Set up a rotating schedule.

CASE 33   Putting Maslow Into Practice

Hollie, who supervises the cassette reproduction room for a large audio manufacturer, made the statements below when talking to employees. Hollie is very aware of the five basic motivational needs described by A. H. Maslow: survival, safety or security, social, esteem or respect, and self-actualization. You can help Hollie by (1) identifying the need she is appealing to and (2) suggesting a way in which that need can be satisfied at work. On a separate piece of paper, write the letters "a" to "e" to correspond to each of the following statements. After each letter on your list, write the number 1, followed by the need Hollie is appealing to, and then write the number 2, followed by your suggestion for satisfying this particular need at work. Use the example as a guide.

"John, I know you're struggling on your present wages to meet family expenses, but your work is good and you can expect regular pay increments."

1. Survival needs
2. Merit pay programs

a. "If the boss approves, Marcie, I'm going to see that you get some free time to develop those product specification changes you suggested."

b. "I know that some of the organization changes around here have bothered you, Bob, but you can be sure of having a good job here for as long as you want."

c. "Debbie, the boss asked me why the stripping bottleneck suddenly disappeared, and I told him it was mainly the result of your good work."

d. "Felix, you don't have to stop talking with the others whenever I come into the room. I don't mind if you talk, as long as it doesn't interfere with your work."

e. "You can relax about that rent payment now, Harry. Your job has been reevaluated, and you'll be getting a nice increase in salary."

The Smithtown Dollhouse Company manufactures wooden dollhouses that are replicas of old homes. The dollhouses are expensive because of the materials used and the fact that all the work is done by hand. There are 20 workers, each performing a separate operation.

One worker cuts the house out with a band saw, another sands the pieces, another paints them, another worker assembles the houses, and so on. Everyone works in one large room behind the office. Most of the houses are sold through catalogs, but an occasional customer comes to Smithtown to make purchases at the office.

Morale among production employees is low, absences and turnover are high, and many of the finished houses require rework and touchups because of faulty craftwork.

1. What's wrong with the design of the production jobs?
2. How might you redesign these jobs to make the work more motivating?

1 Most supervisors can acquire and develop leadership skills.

2 Leadership provides direction that satisfies employee needs.

3 Leadership styles range from task- to people-centered.

4 Leadership styles should be chosen based upon the situation.

5 Leadership should be consistent with subordinates' expectations and values.

CHAPTER 12

The Art and Science of Leadership

LEARNING OBJECTIVES

After studying this chapter, you should be able to

1. Describe the essential skills of leadership.

2. Explain the relationship between leadership and motivation and differentiate between the assumptions of Theory X and Theory Y.

3. Recognize the various leadership styles, explain the contingency model of leadership, and identify the two concerns of the Managerial Grid©.

4. Discuss the factors a leader should consider when selecting a leadership style and explain the concept of the continuum of leadership styles.

5. Discuss the influence of employee personalities and expectations upon a leader's effectiveness and popularity.

 *LEADERSHIP DEFINED*

CONCEPT   Given fidelity of character, a supervisor may acquire and develop the skills required for effective leadership.

What is leadership?

Everyone will give you a different answer to this one. Our definition is this: **Leadership** *is the knack of getting other people to follow you and to do willingly the things that you want them to do.* It should go without saying that these things should be legitimate. They should represent actions that will advance your department toward its goals of higher productivity, improved quality of product or service, and conservation of its resources.

What personal skills does leadership require?

Here again, answers will differ. Most people will agree, however, that good leaders have mastered the following skills:

Persuasion. Some would call this sales ability. It is the ability to assemble and present to others a good case for what you think should be done. Persuasive talent alone will not make you a leader.

Influence. This is the ability to exert power over others. Many people possess or are given power, but few learn how to use it. Supervisors, for example, have the power and authority of their position. They have the power of greater knowledge of departmental and company operations than is possessed by their employees. They also have the power that comes from the prestige that is commonly associated with their work. None of this, however, will make you a leader until you learn to use this power to move others.

Rapport. In this sense, rapport is the art of creating among others a willingness to cooperate. It has a great deal to do with what behavioral scientists call "interpersonal skills." It requires a deep understanding of motivation and the ability to perceive the needs of others. Leaders first establish rapport; then they use their powers of influence and persuasion to activate individuals and groups in the pursuit of worthwhile goals.

Are good leaders born or made?

Very few are born leaders. Most leaders learn their skills. They do so mainly through hard work and careful study of their employees and the situations in which they do their jobs.

⟨12⟩ LEADERSHIP AND MOTIVATION

CONCEPT   Leadership relies upon providing direction that satisfies the motivational needs of others, and the direction chosen reflects a supervisor's assumptions about these needs.

How are motivation and leadership related?

Motivation is a power that arises within an individual to satisfy a need. As you've seen earlier in discussions about Maslow's and McClelland's views of motivation, needs cover a broad span, from the need for survival and safety to the need for self-esteem and fulfillment, and from the need for achievement to the need for affiliation and power. Leaders, as shown in Figure 12-1, act to provide satisfaction—or to offer a means of satisfaction—for the needs of others. Leaders don't really motivate. A leader succeeds by first understanding the needs of others and then applying persuasion and influence to show others that they will get the most satisfaction from following the leader's views.

A person can have motivation without another person's leadership. Leadership, however, cannot succeed without motivation on the follower's part. Take Mary, for example. She has a powerful need to show that she can perform a higher-level job. This may be a strong-enough motivation for her to attend night courses to acquire the necessary knowledge and skills. She will do this with or without the encouragement of her supervisor. On the other hand, there is Peter. He has the same aptitudes as Mary. With additional training, he, too, could perform a higher-level job. Peter's supervisor sees this aptitude and offers Peter all sorts of encouragement and assistance in acquiring the necessary skills.

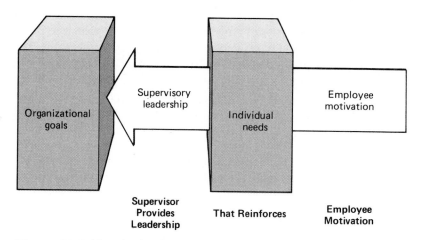

Figure 12-1 How leadership and motivation are related.

Peter, however, is content to stay where he is. His social needs are very strong. He wants to enjoy working with the people he's become friendly with. Enrolled in a night course at the supervisor's suggestion, he soon drops out. The leadership failed, despite the supervisor's influence and persuasion, because the supervisor was not properly tuned to Peter's motivational needs.

Turn Peter's situation around a little bit and look at it again. Suppose Peter is such a fun-lover that his work suffers. His boss tells him that if his performance doesn't improve, he'll lose his job. Peter's reaction is: "So what! I can get another job." At this point the supervisor uses the knowledge of Peter's social needs to persuade him that he'll enjoy working with his friends at his current job more than he might enjoy working with strangers at some other job. Peter accepts this advice and gets his act together so that he can hold his present job. The leadership provided by Peter's supervisor has succeeded. The supervisor established rapport and was tuned to Peter's motivational needs. She used the power of her position to influence Peter's judgment about the consequences of his performance. And then she persuaded Peter that it was in his best interests to improve the quality of his work.

Theory X, Theory Y. What's this all about?

To get along with people effectively, you must make a couple of fundamental decisions. First you must recognize your responsibility for managing human affairs at work. But you must always weigh this concern of yours against the practical urgencies of technical and administrative matters.

Douglas McGregor, late professor of industrial management at the Massachusetts Institute of Technology, had much to offer supervisors in his thoughtful work *The Human Side of Enterprise*. Most of today's management thinking was forged to meet the needs of a feudal society, reasoned McGregor. The world has changed, and new thinking is needed for top efficiency today. That's the core of this unique philosophy of pitting Theory X against Theory Y.

Theory X, the traditional framework for management thinking, is based on the following set of assumptions about human nature and human behavior:

1. The average human being has an inherent dislike of work and will avoid it if possible.
2. Because of this human characteristic of dislike of work, most people must be coerced, controlled, directed, or threatened with punishment to get them to put forth adequate effort toward the achievement of organizational objectives.

3. The average human being prefers to be directed, wishes to avoid responsibility, has relatively little ambition, and wants security above all.

Do these assumptions make up a straw person for purposes of scientific demolition? Unfortunately, they do not. Although they are rarely stated so directly, the principles that constitute the bulk of traditional management action could have been derived only from assumptions such as those of Theory X.

Theory Y finds its roots in recently accumulated knowledge about human behavior. It is based on the following set of assumptions:

1. The expenditure of physical and mental effort in work is as natural as play or rest.
2. External control and the threat of punishment are not the only means for bringing about effort toward organizational objectives. Individuals will exercise self-control in the service of objectives to which they are committed.
3. Commitment to objectives depends on the rewards associated with their achievement. The most important rewards are those that satisfy needs for self-respect and personal improvement.
4. The average human being learns, under proper conditions, not only to accept but also to seek responsibility.
5. The capacity to exercise a relatively high degree of imagination, ingenuity, and creativity in the solution of organizational problems is widely, not narrowly, distributed in the population among both men and women.
6. Under the conditions of modern industrial life, the intellectual potentialities of the average human being are only partially realized.

What makes Theory Y so applicable today?

Under the assumptions of Theory Y, the work of the supervisor is to integrate the needs of employees with the needs of the department. Hard-nosed control rarely works out today. Here are McGregor's words:

> [Supervisors] are dealing with adults who are only partially dependent. They can—and will—exercise remarkable ingenuity in defeating the purpose of external controls that they resent. However, they can—and do—learn to exercise self-direction and self-control under appropriate conditions....[The supervisor's] task is to help them discover objectives consistent both with organizational requirements and with their own personal goals.

In McGregor's mind, the ability to help employees to discover goals consistent with those of the organization is the essence of leadership. When a genuine commitment to these objectives is secured, said

McGregor, "supervision consists of helping employees achieve these objectives: to act as teacher, consultant, colleague, and only rarely as authoritative boss."

You can see that Theory Y—along with the style of leadership that it implies—is far more in tune with today's employees than is Theory X—and the autocratic style of leadership it implies. For you, the important variable will be your own assumptions about the motivation of the people you will supervise. If your assumptions are along the lines of Theory X, you will lean toward styles of leadership that differ from those you would use if your beliefs followed Theory Y. If your assumptions are correct about the motivations of others, then your leadership problems should be minor. But if your assumptions are wrong, your leadership is likely to be weak and ineffective.

3 LEADERSHIP STYLES AND CONCEPTS

CONCEPT   Leadership styles range widely from a job-, or task-, centered orientation to a people-, or relationship-, centered one, with many combinations in between.

What is meant by "styles" of leadership, and which are the most basic?

A *style of leadership* refers to the kind of approach a supervisor uses in trying to direct, activate, stimulate, or otherwise provide a motivational atmosphere for employees. The most traditional styles of leadership are these:

Autocratic, or directive, leadership.   Many people think that this style is old-fashioned, but it often works. The leader makes the decisions and demands obedience from the people supervised. The trouble with this "tell-and-sell" approach is that the supervisor better be right in what is demanded. This style reflects, of course, the assumptions of Theory X.

Democratic, or consultative, leadership.   This style continues to be a popular approach. The leader discusses options with, consults with, and draws ideas from the people supervised before making decisions. This promotes involvement and strong teamwork. Some critics, however, say that it leads to less than optimum compromises. In many ways, the consultative style is similar to what the Japanese call "consensus" management.

Free-rein, or participative, leadership.   This style is the most difficult approach for a supervisor. The leader acts as information center and exercises minimum control, depending upon the employee's sense of responsibility and good judgment to get things done. Advocates of this approach describe it as "integrative" leadership. Obviously, this style is in harmony with the assumptions of Theory Y. There are serious dangers, however, in using participative leadership: only mature individuals respond to it well, and there is always the risk that you will lose control of your operations.

Are the traditional styles the only way to lead?

Not at all. Two somewhat related approaches have become popular in recent years.

Results-centered leadership is akin to the "work itself" approach to motivation described on pages 255 to 258 in Chapter 11 or to what you have read about management by objectives on page 102 in Chapter 5. Using this technique, the supervisor tries to focus on the job to be done and to minimize the personalities involved. In effect, the supervisor says to the employee: "This is the goal the organization expects you to reach each day. Now let's work together to see how your job can be set up so that you can make your quota."

Contingency, or *situational, leadership* maintains that leaders will be successful in a particular situation only if three factors are in balance. This approach, advanced by Professor Fred Fiedler and documented in many studies, asks the leader to examine (1) the extent of rapport or good feelings between the supervisor and those supervised, (2) the nature of the job to be done, in terms of how carefully procedures and specifications must be followed, and (3) the amount of real power invested in the supervisor by his or her superiors.

What is the particular significance of the contingency approach?

It adds an important consideration when a supervisor is choosing a leadership style. As the term *contingency* implies, the style chosen depends upon the conditions of the three factors in any given situation. (See Figure 12-2.) Surprisingly, the autocratic, or authoritative, approach, which uses forceful directing and controlling, is most effective in either very favorable or very unfavorable circumstances. That is, it works best when relationships are either very good or very poor, job methods are either precisely defined or not defined at all, and the leader's true authority is either very strong or very weak. In the less clearly defined, or middle, situations, the participative approach is more likely to be successful.

In other words, an *authoritative style* works out best (1) in situations where the supervisor has lots of real power, the process requires strong

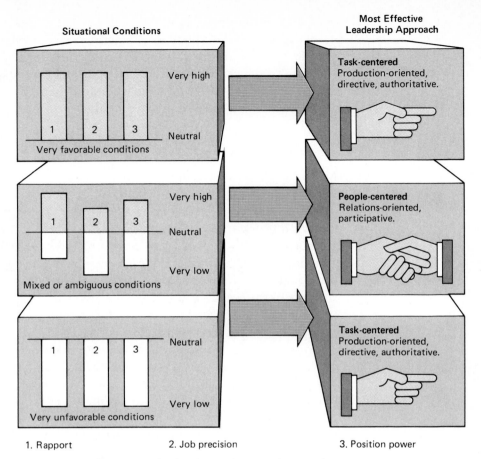

Most Effective
Leadership Approach

Very high

1   2   3

Neutral

Very favorable conditions

Task-centered
Production-oriented,
directive, authoritative.

Very high

1   2   3

Neutral

Very low

Mixed or ambiguous conditions

People-centered
Relations-oriented,
participative.

Neutral

1   2   3

Very low

Very unfavorable conditions

Task-centered
Production-oriented,
directive, authoritative.

1. Rapport   2. Job precision   3. Position power

Figure 12-2 Choosing a leadership style according to the situation.

control, and rapport with employees is good and (2) in situations where exactly the opposite conditions prevail.

A *participative style* is best where the supervisor's authority hasn't been clearly spelled out by top management or acknowledged by the employees, where the process and procedures are somewhat flexible, and where the rapport between supervisor and employees is only middling good.

The contingency approach tends to explain why dictatorial supervisors can be effective in some situations and not in others. Similarly, it helps to show where participative leadership may work best and to suggest where it might fail. An authoritative approach looks good for assembly-line workers or for labor crews cleaning up the area. A participative approach seems favorable on jobs for which exact procedures are hard to set or for jobs that require creativity or initiative. These conclusions are contingent on the authoritative leader's having either high or low position power and high or low rapport and on the participative leader's having moderate rapport and only so-so authority.

The terminology is getting a little confusing. Where do task-centered and people-centered leadership styles fit in?

Followers of the contingency theory are more likely to use the term *task-centered* for authoritative leadership and the term *people-centered* for anything from democratic to participative. In the answer to the next question, you'll find that a couple of famous researchers characterize the task-centered type as having a "concern for production" and the other as having a "concern for people." The terms aren't as important as grasping the idea that the two approaches differ in the focus of their attention. Some leaders are overly preoccupied with the job to be done. Others may worry only about the people who perform the work. Generally, you'll see that the experts believe that good leaders balance their attention between both factors.

Where does the Managerial Grid© fit in?

The **Managerial Grid**© helps supervisors assess their leadership approach. The Grid, devised by industrial psychologists Robert R. Blake and Jane S. Mouton, makes two measurements of a leader's approach: concern for production and concern for people. As shown in Figure 12-3, these two factors are typically plotted on a grid chart. The least concern for each factor is rated 1, the highest 9. To judge your own approach, first rate yourself according to your concern for people; say you think it is fairly high—a 6 score. Next rate your emphasis on production or job results; say you rate that as medium—a score of 5. You then find your place on the Managerial Grid© by putting a mark on the chart six squares up and five squares across.

Blake, Mouton, and others have given nicknames to various places on the grid. The lower left-hand corner (1,1) could be called the cream puff, a supervisor who doesn't push for anything. The upper left-hand corner (1 for production, 9 for people) can be called the do-gooder, a person who watches out for people at the cost of overlooking production needs entirely. The lower right-hand corner (9 for production, 1 for people) is the hard-nose, a supervisor for whom production is all that counts. The supervisor near the middle of the chart (5 for both production and people) is the middle-of-the-roader, a person who makes a reasonable push for both concerns. In the eyes of many, all supervisors should strive to make their leadership performance score 9,9 (highest for both production and people) so that they might be called professionals.

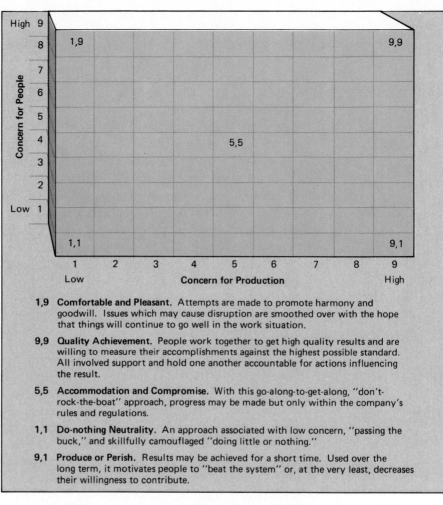

1,9 Comfortable and Pleasant. Attempts are made to promote harmony and goodwill. Issues which may cause disruption are smoothed over with the hope that things will continue to go well in the work situation.

9,9 Quality Achievement. People work together to get high quality results and are willing to measure their accomplishments against the highest possible standard. All involved support and hold one another accountable for actions influencing the result.

5,5 Accommodation and Compromise. With this go-along-to-get-along, "don't-rock-the-boat" approach, progress may be made but only within the company's rules and regulations.

1,1 Do-nothing Neutrality. An approach associated with low concern, "passing the buck," and skillfully camouflaged "doing little or nothing."

9,1 Produce or Perish. Results may be achieved for a short time. Used over the long term, it motivates people to "beat the system" or, at the very least, decreases their willingness to contribute.

Figure 12-3 The supervisory grid. (From Robert R. Blake and Jane S. Mouton, *The Grid for Supervisory Effectiveness*, Scientific Methods, Inc., Austin, Texas, 1975, p. 5. With permission of the copyright holders.)

The Grid implies the need for leadership that is fully balanced between all-out concerns for both people and production. This is somewhat at odds with the contingency approach, which suggests that certain situations respond best to a task- (or production-) centered leader and other situations to a people- (or relations-) centered leader.

4 SELECTING AN APPROPRIATE STYLE

CONCEPT Leadership styles should be selected with a keen sensitivity to the individuals and circumstances involved.

Surely the most difficult aspect of leadership involves the decision of when to lead and when to stand back. That is the value in employing the concept of situational leadership. Regardless of whether or not you accept the rather narrow prescriptions of Dr. Fiedler, the situational concept opens your mind to the wisdom of selecting a style that is most suitable for the individuals and circumstances involved.

Many successful managers will tell you that democratic leadership is the best method to use. The fact is, however, that whereas the democratic way may involve the least risk, you'll hamper your leadership role if you stick only to that method. You can play a round of golf with a driver, but you'll get a much better score if you use a wedge in a sand trap and a putter on the greens.

Suppose you have a problem with cutting down scrap in your department. You may find it wise to consult with all your workers in a group meeting to let them decide how they'll approach the problem (democratic leadership). Then let the inspector, when informed of the plan, adjust inspection techniques accordingly (free-rein). Then tell the scrap collector how you want the waste sorted (autocratic). You see, this way you'll be using all three styles of leadership to deal with the same problem.

A good way to consider such choices is to think of leadership as ranging along a *continuum* of styles, as shown in Figure 12-4. At one extreme, a supervisor relies upon complete authority; at the other, subordinates are allowed a great deal of freedom. Between the extremes are an infinite number of shadings of leadership styles to choose from.

Should your leadership approach be varied according to an employee's age?

One school of thought believes it should—provided that you are talking about a person's emotional maturity, not a chronological age. The *life-cycle theory of leadership* presumes that individuals—and newly formed groups of employees—move through progressive stages of emotional maturity. These stages can be likened to chronological ages. For example, children usually need firm, autocratic leadership. As children mature and start to "grow up" emotionally, they generally respond most favorably to democratic leadership. A mature person, however, is most likely to appreciate the opportunities for achievement that participative leadership offers. So it is with employee groups. A newly formed department will probably require tight, autocratic leadership. As time passes and people in the group get to know each other's capabilities and quirks, as well as the boss's, a democratic, consultative form of leadership will probably get the best results. A fully mature group, one that really knows

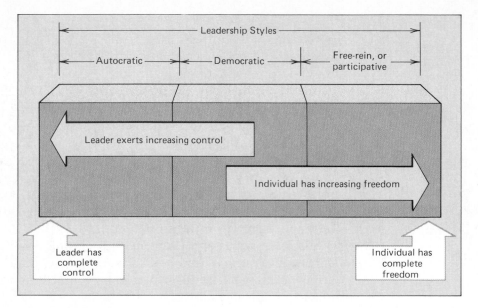

Figure 12-4 Continuum of leadership styles. (Adapted from Robert Tannenbaum and Warren H. Schmidt, "How to Choose a Leadership Pattern," *Harvard Business Review,* March–April 1958, pp. 95–101.)

its strengths and weaknesses, can be trusted to respond most effectively to participative leadership. You should be warned, of course, that many children are old beyond their years, and that many adults never do grow up. The same is true of employee groups. Individual or group, what counts here is emotional maturity.

What kind of leadership works best in an emergency?

Autocratic leadership is fast. When an emergency arises—say a live-steam hose breaks loose and whips about, endangering lives—you wouldn't want to pussyfoot around consulting employees as to what to do. You'd probably shout, "Hey, Smitty, cut the steam valve! Carl, watch the safety!"

Must a people-centered leader always get participation?

No. If you plan your big targets by first asking for and considering the opinions of your employees, they'll understand that there isn't time to handle every decision that way. Participation is a long-range affair. If you show that you want and respect employees' opinions—and that your decisions are affected by these opinions—you'll have achieved the goal of making employees feel they are part of a team. An occasional oversight or an infrequent decision made without their counsel won't destroy the feeling that generates cooperation.

By sowing the seeds of participation generously, you'll also find that you won't have to take over many of the minor decisions that occupy your attention otherwise. Employees who know from experience that their opinions are desired know in advance how the team (their team and yours) would act if it had a chance to go into a huddle. They'll act accordingly.

5 LEADERS AND FOLLOWERS

CONCEPT Supervisors can attract and hold valued followers when their leadership is consistent with the personalities and expectations of their subordinates.

How much does a supervisor's personality have to do with leadership?

A good personality helps. Employees may react more easily to a supervisor who has a ready smile and who is warm and outgoing. But personality must be more than skin-deep to be effective. Much more important is your real desire to understand and sympathize with the people who work for you. Fair play, interest in others, good decisions, and character will help make you a stronger leader than you would be if you relied solely on personality.

Likewise, one kind of leadership may fit your personality better than the other two do. And you may rely more on this kind of leadership than on the others. But work hard to keep from depending on just one approach.

What do employee personalities have to do with the kind of leadership you exercise?

Noted author Auren Uris advises that you'll find the following connections between leadership methods and types of personality:

- Aggressive, hostile persons do better under autocratic leaders. Their latent hostility must be firmly channeled to confine their work to constructive ends.
- Aggressive, cooperative persons work better under democratic or free-rein leadership. Their self-assertiveness takes constructive paths, and they will head in the right direction when on their own.
- Insecure persons, who tend to depend on their superiors, do better under the firmer hand of the autocratic leader.

- Individualists, or solo players, are usually most productive under free-rein leadership—if they know the job well.

Uris calls this point of view "followership." It is based on the well-established fact that certain kinds of persons naturally follow certain kinds of leaders better than others. The trick is to match them when you can.

What are some of the personal qualities employees like to see in their leaders?

Although our leaders don't always measure up to our expectations, there are a number of characteristics that most of us respond to. The following qualities not only are desirable but also tend to provide the foundation for leadership effectiveness:

Sense of mission. This is a belief in your own ability to lead, a love for the work of leadership itself, and a devotion to the people and the organization you serve.

Self-denial. This essential of leadership is too often played down. It means a willingness to forgo self-indulgences (such as losing your temper) and the ability to bear the headaches the job entails.

High character. Few persons become successful leaders who aren't honest with themselves and with others, who can't face hard facts and unpleasant situations with courage, or who fear criticism or their own mistakes, or who are insincere or undependable.

Job competence. There's been too much talk about the insignificance of technical job skill for the supervisor. A person who knows the job that is being supervised has one of the best foundations for building good leadership.

Good judgment. Common sense, the ability to separate the important from the unimportant, tact, and the wisdom to look into the future and plan for it are all ingredients that tend to make the best leaders.

Energy. Leadership at any level means rising early and working late. It leaves little time for relaxation or escape from problems. Good health, good nerves, and boundless energy make this tough job easier.

Meg Greenfield, a columnist writing in the *Washington Post,* has this to say about our expectations of a president's leadership:

We expect a human being who, to be successful, must combine in the right way many seemingly contradictory qualities: worldliness and idealism, toughness and charity, skepticism and belief, humility and self-confidence, enthusiasm and restraint.

That's a tall order, even for a president. It may not be much different, however, from what many employees expect of their supervisors.

Can leaders always be popular with the people they supervise?

Probably not. The very best leaders seem to combine the knack of leading with the knack of winning friends. But most supervisors are not that successful. Instead, they must be satisfied with respect and with followers. Why? Because many of the decisions that you must make as a supervisor will not favor everybody. Sometimes you will please nobody. The result is that you must often be satisfied with the knowledge that your leadership has been responsible, considerate, and equitable—regardless of how unfairly others may judge you.

REVIEW

KEY CONCEPTS TO REMEMBER

1. Leadership requires the ability to develop rapport with others and to apply appropriate persuasion and influence to obtain their willing cooperation in pursuing legitimate organizational goals. Given sound character in the supervisor, the skills of leadership can be acquired and developed.

2. Leadership is not a form of manipulation. Instead, it relies upon gaining a firm understanding of another's motives and providing conditions in the workplace that enable that person to satisfy his or her needs while also helping the organization to attain its goals. It is important that the assumptions concerning an employee's needs are, in fact, correct. The two opposing sets of assumptions about employee motivation are characterized by Theory X (the desire to avoid work) and Theory Y (the desire to perform work that is challenging and worthwhile).

3. Styles of leadership range from the autocratic approach (which is forceful and demanding) to the democratic, or consultative, approach to the free-rein, or participative, approach (which is loose and encourages employee responsibility and initiative).

    The results-centered approach is exemplified in management by objectives and in the "work itself" concept.

    The contingency, or situational, approach depends upon an analysis of the state of three factors present in a situation: (a) leader-member relationships, (b) task structure, and (c) position power of the leader. When the states of all three factors are either very favorable or very unfavorable, an authoritative approach is recommended.

When the states of the factors are not clearly defined, or are somewhere between favorable and unfavorable, a participative approach is recommended.

The Managerial Grid© classifies a supervisor's approach to leadership by rating it on two factors: a concern for people and a concern for production.

4. A leadership approach can be selected from a continuum of styles that range from strictly autocratic to purely participative. The best choice of style is one that most nearly matches the personality of the individuals involved and the circumstances of the situation. The emotional maturity of the subordinate is also a factor to be considered—the more mature the individual, the more likely that the participative style will be appropriate.

5. The success of leadership depends less upon technique than upon the creation of an enthusiastic attachment and deep-seated trust between supervisor and subordinate. While the expectations of some subordinates are often unreasonably high, a fair and considerate leadership will satisfy most employees.

SUPERVISORY WORD POWER

Contingency model of leadership. The belief that the leadership style that will be most effective in a given situation can be predicted by examining the intensity of three interacting factors: (1) the rapport between the leader and subordinates, (2) the precision with which the prescribed job methods must be followed, and (3) the amount of real power the organization has invested in the leader.

Continuum of leadership. A range of leadership approaches that progresses, with no clear-cut distinctions, from the extremes of autocratic control by the supervisor to complete freedom for subordinates.

Managerial Grid©. A method of evaluating a supervisor's approach to leadership by comparing the extent of his or her (1) concern for production and (2) concern for people.

Theory X. An essentially negative approach to human relations in which a supervisor presumes that most people don't like to work and, accordingly, must be pushed, threatened, and disciplined and that they wish to avoid responsibility and prefer job security above all. Employees must therefore be pushed constantly and threatened with loss of security and other punishments when they don't produce.

Theory Y. An essentially positive approach to human relations in which a supervisor presumes that, given meaningful work, most people will try hard to achieve, especially when there is an opportunity to improve their regard for themselves. Given these opportunities, most people will provide their own initiative and objectives and exert self-control to attain them.

READING COMPREHENSION

1. Which are the three skills most likely to be required of leaders? Can they be learned, or must a leader be born with them?
2. Give an example of how an individual's motivational needs offer an opportunity for effective action on the part of a supervisor.
3. As supervisor of the catalog section of a direct-mail house, Mary has come to believe that without her close supervision, employees in her department would never get their work done. Which of McGregor's assumptions about employees at work does Mary's view represent?
4. Describe what McGregor believed to be the essence of leadership.
5. Compare democratic leadership with participative leadership.
6. According to Fiedler's contingency model of leadership, what is likely to be the best approach in a situation where the supervisor has been newly appointed, relationships with the new group are standoffish, and the task to be performed requires great accuracy? Why?
7. In what ways is the Managerial Grid© related to Theory X and Theory Y?
8. Provide examples of the use of leadership styles at three different points along the continuum of leadership styles.
9. Which kind of leadership style—autocratic or participative—is least likely to be effective with an emotionally immature individual? Why?
10. Which kind of leadership style best fits an insecure employee? An aggressive, hostile person? A highly creative individualist? Why?

APPLICATION

SELF-APPRAISAL

How good a leader might you become?

Your success as a leader will depend not only upon innate qualities but also upon your knowledge of—and sensitivity toward—a number of established terms and concepts. The following statements pertain to various aspects of leadership. Your assignment is to see how well you might do in applying these aspects. On a separate piece of paper, copy the column headings shown below. Next write the numbers 1 to 15 down the page to correspond to each of the statements. Then, for each statement, place a check mark in the column that matches your opinion. When you have completed this activity, check your answers by using the scoring procedure described below.

Column headings:

Agree	Disagree

1. Leadership power is derived almost solely from the authority invested in the supervisor by the formal organization.
2. Most good leaders are born with a certain charisma.
3. Leadership should be confined to legitimate areas of influence.
4. Leadership includes the art of providing conditions that satisfy the motivational needs of others.
5. A believer in Theory X is likely to employ a participative leadership style.
6. An assumption of Theory Y is that people do not inherently dislike work, provided the work is challenging and worthwhile.
7. In the continuum of leadership, autocratic leadership and participative leadership are at opposite ends of the scale.
8. Fiedler's contingency model of leadership prescribes a choice of either a people-centered or a task-centered style of leadership, depending upon factors in the situation.
9. The Managerial Grid© considers the position power of the leader and the extent of the leader's concern for people.
10. The life-cycle theory of leadership suggests that the choice of style should reflect the chronological age of the employees involved.
11. It is vital that a modern supervisor offer employees an opportunity to participate in all decisions that affect them.
12. In case of fire, a supervisor should resort to the consultative leadership style.
13. Effective supervisors attempt to match their leadership style with the personalities and needs of their subordinates.
14. Leadership is enhanced when the leader displays the qualities of self-denial, good character, job competence, and sound judgment.
15. An effective leader will be a popular leader.

Scoring   Give yourself 1 point for each of the following statements that you agreed with: 3, 4, 6, 7, 8, 13, 14. Give yourself 1 point for each of the following statements that you disagreed with: 1, 2, 5, 9, 10, 11, 12, 15.

Interpretation   If you scored 13 points or more, your leadership knowledge is high. If you scored between 10 and 12 points, you may not have the knowledge needed to acquire all the followers you might. Review the items you missed. If you scored less than 10 points, your lack of knowledge is more likely to make you a follower than a leader. Review the entire chapter.

CASE STUDIES

CASE 35   The New Supervisor of Nurses

This action took place on the general surgery floor of a small hospital in western New York State. For several months the hospital trustees had debated the feasibility of building an addition that would have moved all critical-care facilities into a modern, fully equipped building. However, just last month, the decision was made not to expand but to modernize the present facilities. During the period of this decision making, the administrative organization of the hospital changed markedly. A new administrator from a large city hospital took over and brought in a new nursing head and several new nursing supervisors.

The general surgery floor on this particular shift (3 to 11 p.m.) is staffed by eight old-time registered nurses, three licensed practical nurses, and two nurses' aides. Molly P., the new nursing supervisor for this shift, reported for the first time on Saturday night. She observed during the shift that there were several infractions of sterile procedures, that on two occasions practical nurses administered injections (which, by law, must be handled by the registered nurses), and that there was a tendency for nurses to congregate at the nursing station for long periods of time. The first thing that Molly did when she went on shift Tuesday night was to call the entire staff together. She said that they should know that she expected all of them to adhere strictly to sterile procedures, that there must be no abrogation of R.N. responsibilities, and that "coffee klatching" at the nursing station must be kept to a minimum. To the best of Molly's knowledge, things improved on Wednesday and Thursday nights; but by the middle of the following week, she sensed a return to the general laxness that was evident when she first took over.

Molly waited until the next Monday. That night she met with each of her staff members individually in a quiet room. With each person, she reiterated her determination to "run a tight ship, medically," and then asked for cooperation. From most of the staff members, she got no meaningful replies. However, one of the older R.N.s looked her in the eye and said, "We've handled this floor in our own way for a number of years, and we've had no problems. Our record is as good as any in the hospital. We don't need your big-city ways here. And since the new addition won't be built, the chances are that you won't be here for long anyway."

If you were Molly, what would you do? Five approaches are listed below. Rank them on a scale from 1 to 5 in the order in which they appeal to you (1, most attractive; 5, least attractive). You may add another alternative if you wish. In any event, be prepared to justify your ranking.

a. Continue to insist on a high standard of performance while taking steps to weed out those staff members who don't or won't measure up.
b. Put off making changes until the staff is better unified under your leadership.
c. Relax the rule about "coffee klatching," but stick to the letter of the procedures for sterile practices and R.N. responsibilities.
d. Hold fast to your demands for a medically tight ship, but work along with each person to find a way to persuade him or her of the value of operating this way.
e. Get together with the other nursing supervisors to make certain that the procedures set down are uniform from floor to floor.

CASE 36   The Experienced Transferees

Due to the closing of several company plants, a number of employees have been transferred from various locations to your department. These are men and women reputed to have had good records elsewhere. Most of them have had extensive experience in other departments in the company. An examination of their employment records, however, shows that they have had little or no experience with the line of work performed in your department. Nevertheless, they do appear willing and cooperative. Which of the following approaches would you choose in order to make this group of transferees productive as quickly as possible? Why? Can you identify the leadership style of each alternate?

a. Hold a meeting with them to find out how they think the work should be handled; then proceed to make assignments.
b. Provide explicit directions for the time being, and accept no suggestions until the transferees have shown you they can do the work properly.

c. Allow the transferees to find out through experience on the job the best way to handle the work.

d. Interview each transferee so that you can better understand his or her preferences, and then make assignments accordingly.

CASE 37 The Flextime Option

You supervise a clerical section for a government agency in a congested downtown area. In a widely distributed memo, the agency has suggested that due to heavy traffic at opening and closing times, each department may stagger its hours according to a flextime schedule, if it wishes. Flextime does not appear to be suitable for the section that you supervise, since the work there requires considerable interchange between employees. Which of the following approaches to handling this problem do you prefer? Why? Can you identify the leadership style of each alternative?

a. Present the problem to your subordinates, and let them come up with a plan.

b. Issue a memo to your employees saying that the flextime option is not appropriate for their work and no changes in work schedules will be made.

c. Get your section people together and explain why no changes can be made in their work schedules.

d. Send a memo to your employees asking them for suggestions about how a flextime schedule might be implemented.

1 Communication is the process of sending and receiving messages.

2 Good communications are based upon analysis of the situation.

3 Body language and listening are vital communication skills.

4 Good communication creates positive working relationships.

5 Supervisors get work done by issuing orders and instructions.

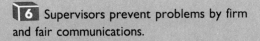

6 Supervisors prevent problems by firm and fair communications.

CHAPTER 13

Effective Employee Communication

LEARNING OBJECTIVES

After studying this chapter, you should be able to

1. Explain the process of communication, including the major steps essential for its success.

2. Choose appropriate spoken and written methods for communicating with individuals and groups of employees.

3. Assess the quality of your nonverbal communication skills and identify needed changes.

4. List the major communication guidelines that help create positive working relationships.

5. Use your knowledge of the communication process to make orders and instructions more acceptable to employees.

6. Describe several ways of avoiding trouble when orders and instructions are being issued.

◻ THE COMMUNICATION PROCESS

CONCEPT   Employee communication is a continuous process involving skillful sending and receiving of messages.

What is the meaning and significance of the term *communication* in supervision?

The term **communication** is defined as the process of passing information and understanding from one person to another. As a supervisory responsibility, the process is frequently called employee communication, although the communicating process is equally important between supervisors and between supervisor and manager.

The term *communications* is more narrowly used to describe the mechanical and electronic means of transmitting and receiving information, such as newspapers, bulletin-board announcements, computer printouts, radios, telephones, and video screens. Employee communication has many of the qualities—and limitations—of these means, but it is infinitely more subtle and complex. So employee communication needs to be managed carefully.

What can you do to help people understand what you mean?

To begin with, don't be afraid to occasionally repeat what you've stated. You can also ask an employee to repeat to you what you've just said. Another practice is to get the employee to ask questions; this will give you an indication of areas of weak understanding. But the best advice is to be specific and avoid the poor understanding that stems from the unclear meanings of words. Instead of saying, "Speed up the machine a little bit," simply tell the operator, "I want this machine run at 2100 rpm, not 1900 rpm." And rather than ordering: "Type this up as soon as possible," say, "I need this letter typed by 2 p.m. today." Similarly, specific expectations can be identified for most quality, quantity, and time standards.

How does communication activate the organization?

By providing the linking pin between plans and action. You may have a great set of plans and a fine staff, but until something begins to happen, you will have accomplished nothing. Neither motivation nor leadership can bring about action without communication. This is what starts and keeps the whole plan in motion.

Good supervisors keep learning about employee communication. They recognize that employee perceptions of their leadership are affected by how they pass information on to others through the process of communication. Unless employees know how you feel and what you want, the best management ideas in the world go to waste. Good communication is especially important when a supervisor is trying to build team spirit or when employees are insecure because of rapid organizational changes or threatened cutbacks.

What is meant by the communication process?

In a broad sense, it is the series of steps that enables an idea in one person's mind to be transmitted, understood, and acted on by another person. This process is illustrated in greater detail in Figure 13-1. Clearly, it is an essential ingredient in all human relationships. To be effective,

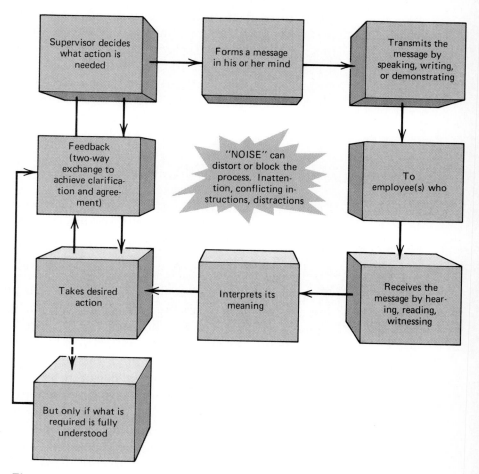

Figure 13-1 The communication process.

it requires that supervisors establish rapport with employees, be sensitive to how others perceive ideas and information, and minimize the noise that can detract from the process. It also requires that supervisors have better-than-average skill in using the spoken word, the written word, and the nonverbal signals that the face and body send out to others. Last, but far from least, it demands of supervisors that they be good at receiving communications from others. That is, they must be good listeners who are receptive to feedback and questions.

Some people talk about three-dimensional communication. What are they referring to?

Communication should not be a one-way street. For a complex, modern organization to function smoothly, communication must occur in three ways. First, not only must you furnish information downward to employees and upward to your manager, but employees must communicate their ideas and feelings upward to you. Second, since interdepartmental cooperation among supervisors is extremely important, there must be a horizontal flow of information too. Finally, there may also be a need to exchange information with "outside" sources, such as staff groups or external vendors, customers, and government agencies. In effect, this creates a challenging three-dimensional communication process—up/down, left/right, and in/out.

🔲 2 METHODS OF COMMUNICATION

CONCEPT   Effective supervisors select their communication methods on the basis of careful analysis of situational factors.

How can a supervisor choose which communication method to use?

This depends on the specific task as well as your objectives. If the task is a lengthy message, or one requiring a permanent record, you'll want to use a written form. On the other hand, if speed, informality, or personal impact is important, the spoken word is often preferred. Another supervisory choice revolves around whether to communicate with a single employee or the entire group. Person-to-person conversations allow the supervisor to control the flow of information and protect privacy. However, opening up communication among the entire department invites employee participation, develops commitment, and helps build team spirit. It demands that the supervisor become more of a facilitator, helping the group explore problems and make progress toward goals.

A maximum of "custom tailoring" to an individual employee is not only feasible but definitely in order. This becomes increasingly important as you develop a sound working relationship with each person. That's because an individual who is addressed singly but in the same way as everyone else usually resents such treatment in proportion to the degree of previously assumed familiarity. People are unique, and they like to be recognized for their differences. Supervisors can choose among a variety of spoken or written communication methods.

Spoken Communication In spoken communication the person addressed is immediately aware of the conditions under which the message is shared. Therefore, speed, tone, mood, gestures, and facial expressions may seriously affect the way the individual reacts.

1. **Informal talks.** These are still the most fundamental form of communication. They are suitable for day-to-day liaisons, directions, exchanges of information, progress reviews, and disciplinary sessions, as well as for maintaining effective personal relations. Even if the talks are brief, be sure they provide the opportunity for a two-way exchange. And if either party is likely to be emotionally involved in the subject, face-to-face communication should always be used (in preference to writing or using the telephone).

2. **Planned appointments.** These are appropriate for regular appraisal reviews, recurring joint work sessions, and so forth. The parties should be adequately prepared to make such meetings complete and effective by being up to date, by providing adequate data and information, and by limiting interruptions as much as possible. For extended projects or some employees (especially new ones, those with problems, or those who travel extensively), many supervisors have regular appointments on a daily (brief), weekly (longer), or monthly (extensive) basis.

3. **Telephone calls.** These are useful for quick checkups or for imparting or receiving information, instructions, or data. However, your telephone personality sometimes contradicts your real (face-to-face) self, so you should examine how you sound when talking on the telephone. Also, since the impersonality of routine calls is sometimes resented, you should occasionally follow up with personal notes to confirm the message.

Written Communication All messages that are intended to be formal, official, or long-term or that affect several persons in a related way should be written. Be sure that you use only a written communication to amend any previous written communication. Oral changes risk being forgotten, are recalled inaccurately, or are not passed along to co-workers.

1. **Interoffice memos.** Used for recording informal inquiries or replies, interoffice memos can also be of value if several people are to receive a message that is extensive or if data is numerous or complex. A memo can be a simple way of keeping your boss informed, and it can be read at his or her convenience. Memos should not be overused, or they will lose their impact and be ignored.

2. **Letters.** Usually addressed to individuals, letters are more formal in tone than memos. They are useful for official notices, formally recorded statements, and lengthy communications, even when the addressee is physically accessible. Letters are often valuable as a means of communicating involved thoughts and ideas for future discussion and development or as part of a continuing consideration of problems.

3. **Reports.** These are more impersonal than letters and often more formal. Reports are used to convey information, analyses, and recommendations to superiors and colleagues. They are most effective when based on the results of conferences, inspections, research, and careful thought. Reports should carefully distinguish objectively determined facts from more subjective guesses, opinions, impressions, and generalizations.

What can you do to communicate most effectively with groups of employees?

Plant or office groups that are uniform in status, age, sex, compensation level, occupation, and length of service provide a valid basis for highly pointed messages. This approach helps avoid the gradually numbing stream of form letters, memos, and announcements that are interesting to only a few of the recipients. Establishment of such groups on a continuing basis helps to build a sense of unity and group identity that fosters favorable group morale and group response. The appropriateness of different communication forms is summarized below.

Spoken Communication   Effective spoken communication with groups calls for special skills. However, the skills that are useful in a committee of equals may be inadequate in a mass meeting. Nor does your ability to conduct a conference attended by your own staff mean that you will have equal ability to contribute effectively as a staff member of a conference called by your superior. You may be skillful at resolving conflicts of interest among participants in a meeting, but it is much more difficult to remain objective when, as a member, you are emotionally involved in the discussion of the topic.

1. **Informal staff meetings.** These provide an opportunity for sharing useful information of common interest and for developing strong group cohesiveness. Properly supplemented with individual face-to-face contacts, they are an outstanding means of coordinating activities and building mutual understanding. Hold brief, informal staff meetings regularly or as the need arises—at the beginning or ending of the day or even during lunch or coffee breaks.

2. **Planned conferences.** These are relatively formal affairs. A common error is to create an agenda without consulting those who will attend. Most participants appreciate being asked for their input and having sufficient time to prepare any needed data, information, reports, and recommendations. Properly conducted, a planned conference can be extremely useful. If improperly managed, it can waste time, antagonize people, and discourage future participation.

3. **Mass meetings.** Meetings of large numbers of employees or managers can be valuable for celebrating occasions like the introduction of a new product, for making emergency plans when a crisis occurs, or for introducing new policies or key personnel. But because of the opportunity for emotions to flare and hostile questions to be asked, such meetings require that the presiding individual have great patience, skill, and a forceful personality.

Written Communication The effect of a single, isolated written communication to a group of employees is generally unpredictable. But a carefully planned program of written communications can develop a desirable cumulative effect.

1. **Bulletin-board notices.** For lengthy or formal announcements of new policies or promotions, bulletin-board notices are appropriate. They are most effective when they are accompanied by illustrations, when readers are constantly attracted to the area and interested in the topics, and when out-of-date material is promptly removed. Most bulletin-board announcements should be supplemented with other forms of written communications, because there is no certainty that they will be seen or read by all employees.

2. **Posters, exhibits, and displays.** These can serve a useful purpose by visually catching the attention of workers. They are typically expensive, require considerable space, and must be properly prepared. The most common subjects are introducing new company products, promoting quality production or service, increasing safety, cutting waste, and stimulating suggestions.

3. **Audio and visual aids.** Films, slides, flip charts, videocassettes, audiocassettes, and other visual materials have great potential value, but

only if they are used effectively. Many, such as films, require a thorough introduction and careful follow-up. Competent preparation and planning coupled with appropriate presentation skills should be applied to the use of all audio and visual materials.

Is any one method of communication better than another?

Each situation has its own best method or combination of methods. Some problems are urgent and demand an immediate response (an informal talk, telephone call, or handwritten memo). Some employees believe only what you put down on paper, so time spent communicating face to face with them is virtually wasted. If the same message must be conveyed to a large number of people, a memo or a mass meeting is best. So it seems that the most successful communicating is done by supervisors who (1) quickly analyze the situation they are encountering and (2) know and use many ways of getting their ideas, instructions, and feelings across to others.

Should a supervisor use the company grapevine as a means of communication?

Listen to it, for it's one way of getting clues about what's going on. But don't depend on it to provide totally accurate information. And don't make a deliberate practice of leaking information to the work group through the grapevine, for employees will then rely even less on your formal communication methods.

The grapevine gets its most active usage in the absence of good communication about company rules, employee benefits, opportunities for advancement, and performance feedback. If you don't tell employees—promptly—about the things that interest or affect them, the grapevine will quickly emerge. However, much of the grapevine information will be based on incomplete data, partial truths, and outright lies. And surveys show that even though employees receive a lot of information from the rumor mill and enjoy participating in it, they'd much rather get the real story from a responsible party—their supervisor. You can prevent a lot of emotional upsets among your employees, and build a lot of goodwill, by spiking rumors as soon as they appear. So show employees you welcome the chance to tell the truth.

⬛3 NONVERBAL COMMUNICATION

CONCEPT   Nonverbal behaviors—actions, body language, and active listening—are vitally important communication skills.

What kinds of communications are likely to speak louder than words?

The messages transmitted by your actions. Talking and writing are the communication methods most frequently used, of course. But regardless of what you say, employees will be most affected by what you communicate to them by your actions. What you do—how you treat them—is the proof of your real intentions. Going to bat for an employee who needs help provides concrete evidence of how highly you value that person's contributions on your team.

Even on simple matters, such as training an employee to do a new job, the act of showing how to do it (demonstration) is eloquent even when no words are spoken. Similarly, going to an employee's work site to chat rather than always requesting that the employee come to your office helps project a supportive image. The best communications are generally those that combine spoken or written words with compatible actions.

Body language. What's that?

Nonverbal body movements or facial expressions that may convey to others what is really on your mind are referred to as *body language.* These signals may be no more than a frown, a shrug of the shoulders, or a gesture with your hands. Unfortunately, they can be misinterpreted. For example:

- Nodding the head up and down can imply agreement with the speaker; shaking the head from side to side can be perceived as disagreement.
- Drumming the fingers or tapping the foot may mean "Hurry up. I'm impatient for you to get to the point."
- Raising the eyebrows may signal doubt, surprise, or skepticism.
- Rolling the eyes often expresses disbelief.
- Tight-lipped frowning may indicate displeasure or even disgust.

Many body movements such as these are unconscious and deeply ingrained, and they would be difficult for you to change. But try to assess whether people are reacting primarily to your words or to your body language. Observe the nonverbal signals from others; these can often provide you with solid clues to what is on another person's mind.

How important is listening? Can it be overdone?

Listening should make up at least a third of your communications. It is an active process that requires good eye contact, alert body posture, and the use of frequent verbal encouragement. It is a skill that must be continually practiced to be maintained. But it can provide great satisfaction both to you and to the speaker. Here are four basic suggestions that may improve your listening power:

Don't assume anything. Don't anticipate what someone will say. And don't let an employee think that you know what is going to be said, even if you do.

Don't interrupt. Let the individual have a full say. If you are busy, either set a time limit or schedule an appointment for a time when you can get the whole story.

Try to understand the need. Look for the real reason the employee wants your attention. Often this may be quite different from what first appears to be the purpose.

Don't react too quickly. Try not to jump to conclusions. Avoid becoming upset simply because a situation is explained poorly or an inappropriate word is used. Patience will produce a big payoff in understanding the other person's viewpoint.

However, active listening shouldn't take the place of definite actions and answers on your part. When you sense that an employee is rambling too far afield, return to the point with astute questioning. If an employee is wrong on a point of fact or company policy, make that clear. When group discussions turn into purposeless rap sessions, you have an obligation to set talk aside and take action. And when an employee comes to you with a problem and truly wants you to solve it with your knowledge and experience, give a straightforward reply. Only if you—and the employee—are more interested in helping the individual develop problem-solving skills than in immediately solving the problem should you shift your emphasis to helping the person arrive at his or her own solution. But this can be heavily time-consuming.

4 COMMUNICATION GUIDELINES

CONCEPT   Effective communication helps to develop positive working relationships with both a supervisor's boss and employees.

How can you get employees to believe what you tell them?

Be a straight shooter. Acting in good faith, building mutual confidence, welcoming employee ideas, and having a receptive attitude are all powerful foundations on which employees will learn to trust you. Being direct, open, and honest in all your conversations will help employees view you as a reliable source of information. Equally important, tell them the reasons for your actions so that they will not need to wonder, "Why did the supervisor say (or do) that?"

But what should you do when you don't have the answers to everything that is happening in the company?

If you don't know what's going on, you can't tell others or answer their questions. But you'll lose face if you have to say that you'll find out from someone else every time an employee asks about social security, the pension plan, or a leave-of-absence policy. If employees figure you're not as knowledgeable as you should be, they'll go to someone else—such as a shop steward or other employees—for information.

Two suggestions are in order. First, accept your responsibility to keep informed on matters of likely importance to employees. Read. Observe. Ask questions yourself. Anticipate what employees are interested in. Second, never bluff or pass the buck when you are caught unprepared. You may need to admit, "I don't know the answer to that one, but I'll certainly find out and let you know by tomorrow morning."

Where are the greatest dangers in communicating with employees?

There are many common hazards for supervisors. Some supervisors try too hard and wind up overcommunicating. They talk too much and listen too little, or they may be indiscreet and violate confidences. You must decide what employees are interested in hearing and what level of detail they need to know.

Other supervisors get into difficulty by expressing their views on intensely personal matters like politics, religion, and social values. And whatever you say, never make comments that have sexual overtones or use language that could create an offensive work environment. These can easily be interpreted by employees as a form of sexual harassment.

Another problem involves stepping on someone's ego. Many employees are quite sensitive and may feel threatened or hurt if you are tactless. Even a sharp tone of voice, being brusque, or using a poor choice of words may offend someone. Avoid putting people on the defensive, for it will defeat your purpose.

What kinds of things should I tell my boss?

Your success as a leader depends on how freely employees will talk to you and tell you what's bothering them. Your superior, too, needs similar information from you. Make a point of voluntarily keeping your boss informed on the following:

Progress toward performance goals and standards. This covers items such as deliveries, output, and quality. If possible, warn your boss in advance about foreseeable problems, while there is still time to obtain help.

Matters that may cause controversy. Arguments with other supervisors, a controversial interpretation of company policy, a discipline problem within your department—all are issues that should be brought to the attention of your superior. It's better to explain your side first and support it with the facts.

Attitudes and morale. Middle and top managers are relatively isolated from direct contact with the work group. This can not only frustrate them but deprive them of needed information about how employees feel. So make a point of telling your boss regularly about both the general level of morale and employee reactions to specific issues.

5 ORDERS AND INSTRUCTIONS

CONCEPT   Supervisors exercise their authority by issuing orders, instructions, directions, and commands.

How are orders and instructions linked to the communication process?

Orders and instructions are the most direct, authority-based kinds of communications. Although it is desirable for employees to agree with your rationale for an order, it is absolutely imperative that employees *understand* what must be done and do it. So as their supervisor, you have a double responsibility: (1) to make sure that employees know what to do and (2) to make sure that they do it properly. A sound understanding and application of the communication process will help you meet both these responsibilities.

How can you get the best results from the instructions and orders you issue?

By being sure that each instruction or order is the right one for the particular situation at hand and by being specific about what the employee is to do and what kind of results you expect.

Your orders are even more effective when you exercise care in selecting the person most likely to carry them out correctly. And you add power to your orders by expressing confidence as you deliver them. If necessary, repeat or rephrase an order for additional impact. Finally, your orders will be most effective if you regularly check to make sure they are carried out at the time and in the manner you prescribe.

When should you ask—rather than order—an employee to do something?

As often as possible. Many of today's employees resent being in positions where they must take orders. They want and deserve more consideration. Psychologists who study employee behavior report that most workers will rate a boss highly and will cooperate more willingly as a result if the boss phrases orders as requests. We know, too, that employees like to feel they have some say in decisions that affect them. Often they will work harder and be more committed when they have had a chance to participate.

So there's nothing wrong (and there's much good) in saying, "Will you try to get that machine cleaned up before quitting time?" Or "Won't you please hold your coffee break time down to fifteen minutes?" Such requests give workers the feeling that they have some freedom of action, and this autonomy is a source of job satisfaction for them. In addition, the use of requests instead of orders will make you seem less like a dictator.

6 AVOIDING PROBLEMS

CONCEPT   Supervisors can prevent many problems when they give orders by exploring situations, staying calm, and being fair.

What should you do when an employee willfully refuses to do what you ask?

The first piece of advice and the toughest to follow is don't fly off the handle. Review the order's fairness, the selection of the person to carry it out, and the probability that you were understood. If you think you've done your part, find out what the employee objects to. Ask for specifics: "What is it you object to? Why do you think it's unreasonable?" Chances are, a nonthreatening exploration of the situation will let both of you cool down and help you clarify the real problem. Perhaps you can even modify the order so that it will be accepted.

But if the employee continues to resist a reasonable request, you're faced with a disciplinary problem. Find a private place where you can talk calmly but firmly. Let it be known that you will take disciplinary steps if the problem isn't resolved. But try to avoid a showdown situation in which one (or both) of you will wind up losing.

Which guidelines may keep a supervisor out of trouble when directing, ordering, assigning, or instructing?

There are no assurances that employees won't get hung up when receiving a particular assignment, but here are 11 guidelines that should minimize trouble:

1. **Don't make it a struggle for power.** If you typically project an I'll-show-you-who's-boss image, you'll soon be fighting the whole department. Try to focus your attention—and the worker's—on the goal that must be met. The idea to project is that it is the *situation* that demands the order, not a personal whim of the supervisor.

2. **Avoid an offhand manner.** If you want employees to take instructions seriously, then deliver them that way. It's all right to have fun occasionally, but be clear and firm about those matters that are important.

3. **Watch out for your words.** Most employees accept the fact that the supervisor's job is to hand out orders and instructions. Their quarrel is more likely to be with the way these are given. Therefore, select words that will clearly convey your thoughts, and watch your tone of voice.

4. **Don't assume that the worker understands.** Encourage the employee to ask questions and to identify problems. Have the employee confirm understanding by repeating or demonstrating what you've said.

5. **Seek feedback right away.** Give the employee who wishes to complain about the assignment a chance to do so at the time. It's better to discover resistance and misunderstandings while there is still time to have them ironed out.

6. **Don't give too many orders.** Communication overload will be self-defeating, so be selective in issuing instructions. Keep them brief and to the point. If you can, wait until an employee has finished one job before assigning another one.

7. **Provide just enough detail.** Jobs differ on the complexity of information required to do them well, and workers differ on their needs for detail too. Old hands get bored listening to unneeded information; new employees may be hungry for supporting details. So think about, and adapt to, the information needs of the person you're addressing.

8. **Watch out for conflicting instructions.** Check to make sure you're not telling your employees one thing while supervisors in adjoining departments are telling their people another. Also, be consistent from day to day and employee to employee in the directions you provide.

9. **Don't choose only the willing worker.** Some people are naturally cooperative. Others make it difficult every time you ask them to do anything. Be sure you don't overwork the willing person and neglect the hard-to-handle people just to avoid confrontations.

10. **Try not to pick on anyone.** It is tempting to punish problem employees by handing them the unpleasant assignments. Resist this if you can. Employees have the right to expect the work to be distributed fairly, even if you have a grudge against one of them.

11. **Above all, don't play the big shot.** New supervisors are sometimes guilty of flaunting their newly gained authority. Older supervisors are more confident. They know that cracking the whip to gain employees' cooperation and respect may even backfire on them.

REVIEW

KEY CONCEPTS TO REMEMBER

1. Communication is the process of passing information and understanding from one person to another. Supervisors rely upon it daily to give orders and instructions, build team spirit, and receive feedback. Communication relationships must be maintained with employees and bosses, other supervisors, and important groups outside the organization.

2. Supervisors have a wide array of spoken and written methods to choose from when communicating with individuals or groups. Successful communication depends on analyzing each major situation and choosing the methods that best match the specific objectives the supervisor wishes to accomplish.

3. Although spoken and written words are generally the most visible element in communication, information exchange is greatly influenced by nonverbal factors. An employee's attitude, personality, tone of voice, and gestures are all important. Accurate receiving of messages is influenced by both observation and attentive listening.

4. There are many errors that supervisors can make when communicating with employees. Many of these can be prevented by staying informed, being sensitive to employee feelings, and anticipating what employees are interested in hearing. Similar guidelines apply to communication relationships with one's superior.

5. Giving orders and instructions is a fundamental part of most supervisors' jobs. Orders are more likely to be effective if they are clear, delivered confidently, repeated, and followed up to make sure action occurred. But much employee cooperation can be obtained by phrasing most orders as requests and providing explanations for them.

6. Sometimes employees may refuse to follow orders. The need for disciplinary action can often be prevented by following proven guidelines that help employees understand and accept orders and instructions. Avoiding power struggles and assumptions, keeping or-

ders simple, and using fairness in job assignments are good examples of effective supervisory guidelines.

SUPERVISORY WORD POWER

Active listening. The conscious process of securing information of all kinds (including feelings and emotions) through listening and observation. It involves giving the speaker full attention, listening intently and being alert to any clues of spoken or unspoken meaning or resistance, and actively seeking to keep the conversation open and satisfying to the speaker.

Body language. Nonverbal body movements, facial expressions, or gestures that may project and reveal underlying attitudes and sentiments. They may convey a message similar to, or different from, the words used.

Command. To give orders; to exercise authority forcefully with the expectation of obedience.

Communication method. The form or technique by which information is communicated, such as attitude, performance, appearance, speech, demonstration, or deed; conversation, discussion, dialogue, or book; telephone, recording, radio, public address system, or television.

Communication process. The giving and receiving of information and understanding as a result of thinking, doing, observing, talking, listening, writing, and reading. In supervision, it is the exchange (especially of accurate meaning) between supervisor and employee, leading to a desired action or attitude.

Feedback. Information provided by those engaged in the communication process that serves to clarify and/or verify understanding and to indicate either agreement or dissent.

Grapevine. The informal communication network that employees use to convey information of interest to them. It is fast, but lacks a high degree of accuracy and reliability.

Information. The knowledge (such as basic background data about a particular job), skills (such as a specific work procedure), and feelings (such as a display of confidence in an employee's ability to respond favorably) that are exchanged in the communication process.

Instruct. To furnish knowledge or information in a disciplined, systematic way with the expectation of compliance.

Noise. Any kind of distraction, physical or emotional, within an individual or the environment that distorts or obstructs the transmission of a message (such as an order or instruction) from one individual to another.

Request. To ask courteously; to make known your wishes with the implied expectation that they will be fulfilled.

READING COMPREHENSION

1. Why is it important for an organization to have effective communication?
2. Discuss the pros and cons of the grapevine.
3. How can supervisors develop high levels of credibility among their employees?
4. If you are unable to complete a project on schedule, is it preferable to inform your boss about it immediately or to wait until it is done and then provide a detailed explanation?
5. With all this emphasis on communication, isn't there a danger of overcommunicating? Or is it ever possible to overcommunicate?
6. Suggest a variety of techniques for helping supervisors listen more effectively.
7. What options does a supervisor have if an employee willfully disobeys an order?
8. Are there any conditions under which a supervisor should refrain from giving orders? If so, what are they?
9. Does listening have any role in the process of giving orders?
10. Supervisors are urged to be specific when they give orders and instructions. Give some examples of how objective terms and quantitative numbers can be used to provide greater specificity.

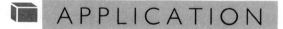 APPLICATION

SELF-APPRAISAL

How would you rate Karl as a listener?

Karl is the chief of police in a small midwestern city. At the request of a labor-management relations committee, he agreed to have a consultant interview the police officers to obtain their perceptions of his managerial actions. One set of questions focused on his communication practices, specifically his listening skills. The following statements reflect the officers' typical response to each question. Your assignment is to determine whether each of Karl's actions, as perceived by his officers, represents a good practice or a bad practice or needs some improvement. On a separate piece of paper, copy the column headings shown below. In the column "Karl's Listening Behaviors," write the numbers 1 to 10 down the page to correspond to each of the officers' observations. For each statement, put a check mark in the column that matches your opinion of Karl's action. After completing this activity, check your answers by using the scoring procedure described below.

Column headings:

Karl's Listening Behaviors	Good Practice	Bad Practice	Needs Some Improvement

1. If you have an appointment with Karl, he carefully sets his other work aside: if you interrupt him or talk to him on spontaneous occasions, he acts distracted.
2. He often jumps ahead to reach a personal conclusion regarding the case being discussed before the police officer can finish reporting the circumstances.
3. Karl occasionally plays with his tie while listening to others in meetings; he rolls it up tightly and then unrolls it, repeating this several times.
4. He asks a lot of questions during any conversation, many of which are penetrating and difficult to answer.
5. Karl stares intently at the police officer who is speaking.
6. He checks his watch frequently and visibly during a conversation; in meetings he sets his wristwatch's alarm to buzz at ten-minute intervals.
7. Frequently, Karl's conversations take sudden dramatic turns when he jumps to a different topic, often preceded by the transitional comment "That reminds me of another case I once worked on..."
8. While listening to a lengthy report on a case, Karl sometimes leans back in his chair and closes his eyes until the presentation is finished.
9. Karl's face is highly expressive when he is listening; some officers report, "You can read him like a book."
10. Whenever the phone rings, Karl answers it; if the mail is delivered, Karl opens it immediately; if other city department chiefs poke their heads into the office, Karl turns his attention to them.

Scoring Give Karl 2 points for each item that you marked as a *good* listening practice and 1 point for each item that you marked as *needs some improvement.* Give him no points for items that you marked as *bad* listening practices.

Interpretation   Applying principles of effective listening to Karl's behavior would give him a total of only 9 points. Here's how it should be scored: *good* for items 4 and 9; *needs some improvement* for items 1, 3, 5, 7, and 8; and *bad* for items 2, 6, and 10. If you interpreted the items differently, explain your opinion.

CASE STUDIES

CASE 38   The Man Who Wouldn't Move

Rachel Fields was at her wit's end. Office space was in heavy demand at the research laboratory where she was supervisor of the environmental monitoring section. Program funding had grown gradually over the past five years, but no new buildings were constructed to house the newly hired scientists. This had not been a problem until this year, when Rachel reached the absolute limit of her imagination in shuffling people around and even creating offices out of other work spaces. There was literally nothing left but an old work table in the space next to the noisy area where the coffeepot was located. And there was absolutely no construction money forthcoming.

But the problem would have been manageable even this year if it weren't for Dick Lansford. Dick had been with various units of the laboratory for 43 years and loved every minute of it. He never would have retired, except that his family had insisted on it. At first Rachel thought Dick's announcement of retirement was the answer to her dreams, as she could allocate Dick's office to the newest scientist the laboratory had just hired. Then the bombshell dropped when Dick walked into Rachel's office.

"Rachel, I've been down to the personnel office and the people there reviewed the policy on retirements for me," Dick said. "They discovered that I'm automatically eligible for status as a scientist emeritus."

"Yes, I believe that's true," Rachel replied cautiously.

"Furthermore," continued Dick, "the policy says that I may be granted office space to support the continuation of my work projects. So I just wanted to tell you how elated I am now that I won't have to move out of my office after all!" With that, Dick turned on his heel and went back to his office, whistling happily all the way.

Rachel called Personnel for additional details. She discovered that Dick was right, except he had left out one important detail—the granting of an office to a scientist emeritus was a privilege *subject to avail-*

ability of space. Now Rachel didn't know what to do. On the one hand, Dick had been a loyal and valuable employee for many years and would be heartbroken to be forcibly moved from his office. On the other hand, the laboratory desperately needed to assign Dick's space to the new scientist arriving in one week.

If you were Rachel, which of the following actions would you select to resolve this dilemma? Rank the alternatives on a scale from 1 (most preferable) to 5 (least preferable). You may add another alternative if you wish. In any event, be prepared to justify your ranking.

a. Write a memo to Dick, telling him that you're sorry but he simply must be out of the office within one week and that there is no other space available for him.

b. Hold your announcement of his eviction from the office until Wednesday, when you can make it at the weekly staff meeting, where there will be less likelihood of an argument's taking place (due to the presence of other scientists).

c. Place an announcement of the new office assignments on the department's bulletin board, which most employees check on a daily basis.

d. Don't bother with any formal announcement; simply have the building and grounds staff box up Dick's belongings over the weekend so that they will be all ready for him to pick up on Monday.

e. Go to see Dick in his office, explain the problem to him, and ask for his assistance in solving the dilemma you face; then follow up the decision with a short memo of confirmation.

CASE 39   Was That a Request, or a Command, or What?

During the course of a typical day, supervisors find themselves communicating in a variety of ways with their employees. Although there are many variations (even tone of voice and accompanying gestures make a difference), it is possible to classify communication efforts as:

a. Commands—forceful orders.
b. Instructions—directions explaining how to do something.
c. Requests—courteous invitations to engage in certain behaviors.
d. Suggestions—helpful ideas shared with others.
e. Information sharing—disclosure of relevant knowledge or feelings.

These are arrayed roughly in descending order according to their explicit or implicit use of authority. It is important for both supervisors and employees to recognize what form of communication is being used in a situation. Five communication examples are listed below. Your assignment is to match a lettered communication type from the list on page 308 with each of the numbered examples below. On a separate piece of paper, write the numbers 1 to 5 down the page to correspond to each of the examples. After each number on your list, write the letter of the appropriate communication type.

1. A supervisor of bank tellers asked Tom, "Are you willing to work three extra hours at the drive-up window on Thursday night?"
2. The programming manager at a radio station proposes to a new disc jockey. "If you would just lower your tone of voice slightly, it would make it more soothing for evening listeners."
3. "Did you know that we served an all-time record of 1782 meals during the evening shift yesterday?" Maria asked her employees.
4. "I'd advise you to throw the power switch first, disconnect the wires, replace the appliance, reconnect the wires, and only then turn the power back on," declared Katie.
5. "I know it's easier the old way," said Parker, "but company policy dictates that we always adopt the newest system, and that's precisely what we will do here."

CASE 40 Modifying the Method

In a classic case of overnight success. Ted's business has grown by leaps and bounds. Starting with a small camera shop, he has recently expanded to a complete line of photographic goods and related developing services in three locations in the city. He used to be able to communicate with his three employees by using a very informal "Hey, you!" approach—simply calling across the aisle to ask about a price, provide advice on the location of a display, or tell a clerk when to take a coffee break. Now, however, he has 26 employees working on two different shifts in the three retail outlet–service center establishments. The "Hey, you!" approach just doesn't work anymore. The following situations arose for Ted during the course of a recent week. What communication method or methods should he use to handle each of them?

a. Mary has been late for work twice this week. She is a new employee, still in her probationary period with the firm, and Ted decides to let her know that she will have only one more chance.
b. One of the developing machines broke down, and a backlog of work to be done on a short schedule has developed. Ted is anxious to discover whether either of the other two shops can handle the overload.
c. Ted is concerned about providing high-quality customer service.

Twelve employees come into face-to-face contact with customers, and Ted wants to tell these workers how to greet the customers, take their orders, and handle their problems.

d. Ted's accountant has announced that the firm set dramatic records last year for its level of profits. Ted would like to share his joy with his employees.

e. While attending a camera manufacturer's conference, Ted learned that one of last year's models has a defect in it which, if not corrected, will result in damage to each roll of film used. He feels obligated to tell both prior and future purchasers of that camera model about the defect.

5

Managing Problem Performance

1 Problem performance is often related to nonjob factors.

2 Supervisors should recognize early warning signs.

3 Counseling provides relief for many troubled individuals.

4 Absenteeism may also be reduced by employee counseling.

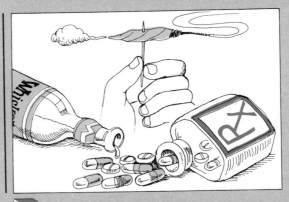

5 Some problem performance stems from substance abuse.

CHAPTER 14

Counseling Troubled Employees

LEARNING OBJECTIVES

After studying this chapter, you should be able to

1. Describe problem performance and distinguish between a neurotic person and a psychotic person.

2. Recognize the symptoms of an emotionally disturbed—or troubled—employee.

3. Explain the general approaches to employee counseling, discuss its limitations, and know when an emotionally disturbed employee should be referred to a professional counselor.

4. Identify the various kinds of absenteeism and know the recommended remedial approaches for each.

5. Recognize alcoholism and illegal substance abuse among employees and know the recommended remedial approaches for each.

PROBLEM PERFORMERS

CONCEPT   Problems with employee performance can often be attributed to troubling personal factors that arise from conditions not related to the job.

How would you define *problem performance?*

Problem performance encompasses (1) job performance that does not measure up to established standards of output or quality and (2) behavior that is distracting or disruptive to the normal conduct of operations. The former is routinely dealt with during performance appraisals. The latter problem is far more difficult to identify and to deal with. Yet it often leads to the former. It is problem performance of the latter kind that this chapter will focus on.

What kinds of employees become problem performers?

They are mainly people who have a difficult time in adjusting to life—work life as well as home life. Most people encounter periods in their lives when adjustment is difficult. At such times, their performance at work may suffer. This is usually a temporary condition, and their performance soon returns to normal.

There are many other people who are especially susceptible to stress, and their resulting performance lapses are deep and prolonged. The chances are that they are troubled by deeply rooted personal problems or by conditions in their personal lives that make adjustment especially difficult. These people can be described as "troubled." When this troubled state persists, there is a good chance that the troubled person is suffering from a problem with an emotional, rather than a physical, cause. For this reason, we speak of a person in this troubled state as emotionally disturbed.

Supervisors must learn to deal with employees whose difficulty in adjusting to emotional problems is only temporary and with those whose adjustment problems are chronic.

Where are these troubled people likely to be found at work?

Just about everywhere and in every form. They may appear as the chronic absentee, the willful rule breaker, the boss hater, or the troublemaker. They may also appear in more sympathetic form as the psychosomatic employee, the person who has lost self-confidence, the alcoholic, the pill popper, or even the work-obsessed individual. Symptoms of emotional problems may even emerge unexpectedly in the most normal and stable of individuals.

When do the personal problems of troubled employees become a concern of the supervisor?

When the *performance* of the troubled employee becomes unsatisfactory. (Note the emphasis upon performance.) Employees under stress often function far below their capabilities, or they may disturb the work of others. When either condition occurs, these employees become problems to themselves and to their supervisors. Ultimately, many of these troubled employees become the subject of grievances and discipline.

For many workers, the distinction between problems arising from their personal lives and those associated with their work becomes increasingly blurred. Sometimes, only the supervisor can sort these problems out. And, difficult as it may be, supervisors have a continuing responsibility to confront employee behavior that affects productivity.

Are these emotionally disturbed employees insane?

The overwhelming majority of troubled, or emotionally disturbed, employees are definitely not "crazy." Psychologists do, however, believe that one out of five workers is subject to emotional upsets that visibly disturb his or her work. The *behavior* of these employees is not normal. For example, when goaded by fear (instilled perhaps by a threat from a bill collector) or by anger (possibly the result of being refused a day off), they may act in a way that might be described as "crazy." But they are not (except for a very few) crazy, insane, or even abnormal.

What about psychotic and neurotic employees?

Both terms sound pretty ominous. But only the employee with a **psychosis** is seriously ill. The most common type of psychosis is schizophrenia, or split personality. Schizophrenics live partly in a world of imagination. When the world seems threatening to them, they withdraw. They may be able to adjust to life or even have a successful career, but when they lose their grip, their problem is beyond the scope of a layperson.

On the other hand, most people are neurotic to a degree. People who have exaggerated fears, who feel the need to prove themselves, or who are irritable, hostile, opinionated, timid, or aggressive (which somewhere along the line describes most of us) have the seeds of **neurosis** in them. It's when this condition becomes exaggerated that a neurotic employee becomes a problem to associates and to the supervisor.

Here are a just a few examples of neurotic employees: the lift-truck operator who boasts about drinking and sexual prowess; the supervisor who gets pleasure from reprimanding an employee in front of others; the mechanic who visits the nurse every other day with some minor ailment; the records clerk who meticulously arranges the workplace in the same manner every day and can't begin the job unless everything is exactly right.

Is an accident-prone employee likely to be emotionally disturbed?

That conclusion might be drawn, although it is dangerous ground to tread on. Studies at the Du Pont company, which has one of the best safety records in the world, point to some sort of underlying mental illness. Du Pont found that there was "a small group of individuals around whom occupational injuries seem to cluster in disproportionate numbers." Obviously, there is something more than hard luck plaguing a person whose career shows a long series of injuries. It would appear that a failure of the employee *as a whole person* is the core of the problem. He or she tends to evade rules, both at home and at work. The Du Pont researchers concluded that such employees "are victims of their own bottled-up emotions, which they turn against themselves" in the form of injury or accident.

In the opinion of most experts, the *fact* that a worker violates a safety rule is more important than *why* it was done. Pampering emotionally disturbed individuals in safety-related matters seems unwise. It may only serve to increase their demands and, at the same time, aggravate the severity of their injuries or the potential danger to others.

What makes some people overwork to the point of sickness?

A great many people (often called "workaholics") suffer from work addiction. To mask deep emotional problems, and sometimes very real difficulties in their economic or home lives, they burrow into their work. It is a form of retreat from reality. It helps them forget what seem like insurmountable problems. The difficulty from a supervisor's point of view is that the work of work addicts tends to be nonproductive. Paradoxically, as these work-obsessed individuals intensify their diligence, it impedes their output. Furthermore, they often stir up such waves in the office or plant that they cut down the output of their associates.

It is difficult for a supervisor to do much other than to recognize the work addict. These compulsive individuals are usually highly moral, ambitious, intelligent, honest, and intensely loyal to their employer. At higher levels, they are the persons who stuff the briefcase for what is often needless work in the evening or on weekends. They suffer from anxieties and depressions and generally will not respond to advice to take it easy. They need professional therapy that aims at improving self-understanding, flexibility, and creativity.

Why must so much attention be paid to troubled employees?

Mainly because there are so many of them. Hardly a week goes by in which a supervisor does not deal with problems created by a troubled employee. Happily, most of these problems are minor. If left unattended, however, they can begin to demand a major portion of a supervisor's time and attention.

There are also many sociological and humanitarian reasons for being concerned about problem workers. One big reason is that a problem employee is also probably a problem husband, son, daughter, or wife. But industry's concern, admittedly, is primarily an economic one. Problem employees are expensive to have on the payroll since their productivity suffers. They are characterized by excessive tardiness and absences. They are difficult to supervise. And they have a tendency to upset the morale of the work group. Consequently, a supervisor should be concerned about (1) hiring problem employees in the first place, (2) handling them on the job so that they reach an acceptable level of productivity with the least disruption of the company's overall performance, and (3) determining whether troubled employees have become so seriously maladjusted that they need professional attention.

▣ TROUBLED EMPLOYEES

CONCEPT   It is important that supervisors recognize the behavioral symptoms of troubled employees before the job performance of these workers is adversely affected.

How can you recognize an employee with an emotional problem?

Be careful here. There are a vast number of employees whose problems are minor or temporary. With a little help and patience, they are able to get themselves back on the track. Among this group, there are a few whose emotional problems are very deeply rooted. Their disturbances are very serious and are beyond the kind of relief a supervisor can be expected to offer. Unfortunately, it is very difficult, even for a trained observer, to tell when an employee has crossed over the line into the more serious category. Generally speaking, the symptoms of employees with emotional problems are similar. These people tend to run away from reality. They do this by going on sick leave or by making too-frequent visits to the dispensary; they may believe that their supervisors are against them, or blame their failures on other people and other things rather than accepting any blame themselves.

Many problem employees fall into these categories: They are perpetually dissatisfied, are given to baseless worries, tire easily, are suspicious, are sure that superiors withhold promotions, or believe their associates gossip maliciously about them. Some are characterized by drinking sprees, are given to drug abuse, are insubordinate, or have ungovernable tempers.

Among themselves, problem employees differ widely, just as more normal people do. But within the framework of their symptoms, they are surprisingly alike in their reactions.

What are the signs of a troubled worker—the employee who is about to become a problem?

Until now we've been discussing the general symptoms of problem performers. But you'll be more interested in pinning down the specific kinds of behavior that make employees a problem in your company. That way, you'll be better able to know what to do to aid them. Some specific signs of a troubled worker are as follows:

Sudden change of behavior. Pete used to whistle on the job. He hasn't lately. Wonder what's wrong?

Preoccupation. Judy doesn't hear you when you speak to her. She seems off in a fog. When you do get her attention, she says she must have been daydreaming. Is something serious bothering her?

Irritability. Albert is as cross as a bear these days. Even his old buddies are steering clear of him. He wasn't that way before.

Increased accidents. Bob knocked his knuckles on the job again today. This is unusual. Up until a couple of months ago, he hadn't had even a scratch in five years.

More absences. Sara is getting to be a headache. She wasn't in this morning again. She never was extra dependable, but now you'll have to do something to get her back on the ball.

Increased fatigue. Mary seems to live a clean life and keep good hours. But she complains about being tired all the time. Is it something physical, or is she worried about something?

Too much drinking. Ralph was so jittery at his machine this afternoon, you felt sorry for him. And he had a breath that would knock you over. You know he used to like going out on the town, but this is different.

Reduced production. Tanya has slowed down, and for no apparent reason.

Waste. Darnell's work often has to be done over again.

Difficulty in absorbing training. Pera can't seem to catch on to new assignments.

Substance abuse. Dan has that spaced-out look. He's having trouble finishing the last assignment you gave him. Either he's so hyped up with excitement that he can't concentrate or he's drowsing over his desk.

3 EMPLOYEE COUNSELING

CONCEPT   Counseling—within carefully prescribed limits—offered by a supervisor to a troubled employee may improve performance by providing a degree of relief from anxieties.

What can you do about your troubled workers?

Let's make this clear. We are not talking here about psychotic persons or the ones with serious neurotic disorders. *They need professional help.* Nor are we talking about routine performance appraisals, where it can be assumed that criticism will be received and suggestions for improvement will be discussed rationally and objectively. What follows here applies mainly to counseling efforts with mildly troubled employees.

You can help troubled employees toward better adjustment only after establishing an empathic atmosphere. You must first reassure them that you are trying to help them keep their jobs or enjoy their work more. You are *not* looking for ways to punish them or for an excuse to get rid of them. No approach will do more harm to an emotionally disturbed person than adopting an attitude that says "Better get yourself straightened out or you'll lose your job." Emotionally disturbed people are fearful or angry enough without feeling additional pressure from their supervisors. You must genuinely want to help them, and you must project this conviction to them. With such empathy as a foundation, you must then give the troubled employees every opportunity to help themselves.

Employee counseling is essentially a problem-solving technique. It is task-oriented; that is, it deals with a specific, job-related condition. The supervisor's role is a facilitating one. You do not direct or control the session; the employee does. The counselor listens rather than talks. You do not criticize or argue. Nor do you offer "evaluative" opinions. You do not "judge" an employee's personal problems. Instead, you aim to act as a "sounding board" to help release the pressures that are adversely affecting performance. If the counseling is successful, the employee—not the supervisor—solves the problem.

It cannot be overemphasized, however, that supervisors have great limitations in their counseling roles. *They are not psychologists or social workers,* and they can do more harm than good if they attempt rehabilitation beyond their training and experience. They cannot be "fix-it persons" for employees' personal problems. Supervisors should be, of course, experts at recognizing these problems and be sympathetic toward them. Beyond that, their counseling roles should be restricted to providing "emotional first aid."

How is employee counseling approached?

The researchers in this field suggest that a supervisor can best counsel employees if these six rules are followed for each interview:

1. Listen patiently to what the employee has to say before making any comment of your own.
2. Refrain from criticizing or offering hasty advice on the employee's problem.
3. Never argue with an employee while you are counseling.
4. Give your undivided attention to the employee who is talking.
5. Look beyond the mere words of what the employee says—listen to see if he or she is trying to tell you something deeper than what appears on the surface.
6. Allow the employee to control the direction of the session.

What results should you expect from counseling an employee?

Recognize what you are counseling an employee for, and don't look for immediate results. Never mix the counseling interview with some other action you may want to take—such as discipline.

Suppose Ruth has been late for the fourth time this month. The company rules say she must be suspended for three days. When talking to Ruth about the disciplinary penalty, try to keep the conversation impersonal. Your purpose at this point is to show her the connection between what she's done and what is happening to her.

Now in the long run you may wish to rehabilitate Ruth because she's potentially a good worker. This calls for a counseling interview. And it's better to hold the interview with Ruth at a separate time. (Of course, it would have been better to hold the interview before she had to be disciplined.)

A counseling interview is aimed at helping employees to unburden themselves—to get worries off their chest. Whether or not the conversation is related to the problem they create for you at work is not important. The payoff comes as they get confidence in you—and consequently don't vent their hostility and frustrations on the job. Experience seems to show that this will happen if you are patient. It won't work with every troubled employee, of course, but it will with most of them.

How do you start a counseling session?

Find a reasonably quiet place where you're sure you won't be interrupted and won't be overheard. Try to put the employee at ease. Don't jump into a cross-examination. Saying absolutely nothing is better than that. If Ralph has become a problem because of spotty work, you can lead into the discussion by saying something like this: "Ralph, have you noticed the increase in the orders we're getting on the new model? This is going to mean a lot of work for the company for a long while ahead. I guess it has meant some changes too. How is it affecting the operation of your machine? What sort of problems has it created?"

Note how the supervisor talks only of performance problems. Only the employee—never the supervisor—should introduce anything whatsoever about personal problems.

How many counseling interviews should you have with a problem employee? How long should a counseling interview last?

These are hard questions for clear-cut answers. For a less serious case, one interview might clear the air for a long time. With employees whose emotional problems are more serious, it may take five or ten 15- to 30-minute conversations just to gain confidence. And with still others, the counseling will have to become a regular part of your supervisory chores with them.

You can readily see that counseling can be time-consuming. That's why it's so important to spot worried workers early and take corrective action while you can help them with the minimum drag on your time.

As to how long an interview should last—you can't accomplish much in 15 minutes, but if that's all you can spare, it's a lot better than nothing. At the very least, it shows the employee you're interested in the problem. Ideally, an interview should last between three-quarters of an hour and an hour.

How can you recognize when an employee needs emotional first aid?

Dr. Harry Levinson, a nationally recognized authority and founder of the Levinson Institute, advises that the basic steps (Figure 14-1) for you to take in administering emotional first aid are to:

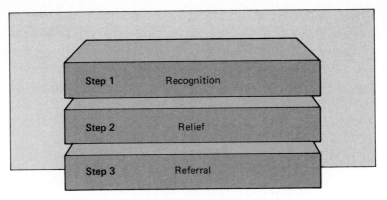

Figure 14-1 Levinson's three-phase guideline for supervisors to follow in counseling troubled employees.

1. Recognize the emotional disturbance.
2. Relieve acute distress by listening (counseling).
3. Refer cases beyond your limits to professional help.

To recognize the employee who needs counseling help, says Dr. Levinson, look for three major signs:

Extremes. The ordinarily shy person goes even deeper into a shell. The hail-fellow-well-met steps up social activities to a fever pitch.

Anxiety. If withdrawal or activity brings no relief, the employee may become panicky or jittery, show extreme tension, flush in the face, or perspire heavily.

Breakdown. If still unable to cope with the anxiety, the problem employee may break down altogether and be unable to control thoughts, feelings, or actions. Thinking becomes irrational. The person doesn't make sense to others. Emotions may become irrational. For instance, the tidy person may become slovenly, the quiet person noisy.

How can you provide relief for the emotionally troubled employee?

Dr. Levinson suggests you may be helpful simply by letting the emotionally disturbed employee know how much the current distress is affecting the job—and how much of this the company will tolerate. Above all, a person under stress may add to it materially with fears of what the company might do if and when it discovers the condition. If you can offer some rule of thumb, even if it's not entirely sympathetic, you at least provide something concrete to guide the employee's actions. (For example: "We appreciate the fact that you have something bothering you. And we're willing to go along with your present performance for a couple of weeks or so. But if it doesn't improve after that, we'll have to find a solution.")

If the employee voluntarily brings the problem to you, you can help most by listening, advises Dr. Levinson. This is more difficult than it appears, he cautions. Listening must mean truly *nonevaluative* listening—no interruptions, advice, prescriptions, solutions, pontifications, or preaching.

Nancy Hull, a former chemical-abuse counselor and an authority on the subject, also cautions about the legal aspects of counseling. In the film *The Troubled Employee*, produced by Dartnell Corporation of Chicago, Hull suggests a conservative approach to what an employee may consider a confrontation. Hull's nine dos and don'ts of counseling are shown in Table 14-1 on page 324.

When should you call for professional help?

Dr. Levinson offers this rule of thumb: *If after two listening sessions you seem to be making little headway in establishing confidence, you should report the case (in confidence, of course) to the company nurse or the company physician.*

Dr. Levinson also advises that your approach in referral should be that of opening another door for additional help. Don't ever suggest by action or word that the employee is "crazy," hopeless, or unworthy of attention.

What do the professionals do for troubled employees that supervisors can't do?

Two kinds of industrial professionals usually work with mentally disturbed employees whose adjustment is beyond the limits of the supervisor's help:

- The **psychiatrist** is a fully qualified physician who has practiced medicine before qualifying for this specialty. An **industrial psychiatrist,** because of specialized training and experience, can diagnose more closely what an individual's trouble is and prescribe the proper kind of treatment. No supervisor should try to do either.
- The **counselor,** or **industrial psychologist,** works with the great majority of emotionally disturbed employees who do not need full-scale psychiatric treatment. Because of specialized training, the counselor's biggest asset is the ability to listen understandingly to an employee's account of problems. The professional counselor has an advantage over the line supervisor, since the counselor doesn't have the authority to discipline, promote, or fire the employee and therefore has a greater chance of winning the employee's confidence.

Table 14-1 NINE DO'S AND DON'TS OF EMPLOYEE COUNSELING

1. *Do* let the employee know that the company is concerned with work performance only.

2. *Do* be aware that personal problems generally get worse, not better, without professional help.

3. *Do* emphasize confidentiality.

4. *Do* explain that going for help does not exclude the employee from standard disciplinary procedures and that it does not open the door to special privileges.

5. *Do* explain in very specific terms what the employee needs to do in order to perform up to the company's expectations.

6. *Don't* diagnose; you are not an expert.

7. *Don't* discuss personal problems during counseling unless they occur on the job.

8. *Don't* moralize; restrict the confrontation to job performance.

9. *Don't* be swayed or misled by emotional pleas, sympathy tactics, or "hard-luck" stories.

Adapted from "The Dos and Don'ts of Confrontation," by Nancy Hull, in *The Troubled Employee*, a film produced by Dartnell Corporation, Chicago. With permission of the copyright holder.

14 REDUCING ABSENTEEISM

CONCEPT   Certain forms of absenteeism can be materially reduced by employee counseling.

Absentees are a special kind of problem people. How lenient should you be with them?

It depends on the reasons for absence. Professor P. J. Taylor of London University, who was formerly medical director of Shell (U.K.) Ltd., observes that 60 percent of all absentees have serious or chronic illnesses and 20 percent have acute, short-term illnesses such as the flu; 10 percent feel unwell because of minor illnesses such as colds, and they do or don't report to work according to their attitude about their jobs; and the final 10 percent are completely well but feign illness to enjoy a day off.

It is the group of absentees who make up the bottom 20 percent who are suspect. Industrial psychologists call their virus **voluntary absence.** In many, this is deeply rooted. The Puritan ethic of work does not apply to them. There is an inevitable conflict between the desire for more leisure and more work. This tug is especially evident among younger workers. They often reflect an attitude of "entitlement." They feel that, somehow, the job is owed to them and that they have no responsibility for delivering a fair day's work in return.

Many authorities, however, still contend that employees who are chronically absent from work are mentally ill. They reason that the reality of work must be so unbearable to these emotionally disturbed employees that they literally escape from reality be staying away from work. Regardless of the reason, you can help reduce absenteeism by:

- Firming up your rules about it.
- Being consistent in applying penalties.
- Trying to get at the reasons why an employee is frequently absent.

The last method requires the counseling technique. It is important that each individual case be followed up promptly. In your discussion of the problem with employees, be sure to permit them to explain their reactions to the job itself, the people they work with, the working conditions, their tools and equipment, the kind of training they receive. You thereby avoid their feeling that you are placing all the blame on them. And if they are specific in their reactions, you then have specific complaints, rather than vague dissatisfactions to deal with.

Don't overlook, however, the power of job satisfaction in luring absence-prone workers back to the job. Surprisingly, however, physical working conditions seem to have little effect. In company after company, attendance figures show little variation between the dirty, unpleasant areas and those that are clean and well lighted. Even most incentive schemes aimed at reducing absences are relatively ineffective. Closeness of the work team, its homogeneity, and the state of its morale seem to have the greatest effect.

How effective is counseling in reducing absenteeism?

Success depends on the root cause of individual absences. See how the patterns and the motivations differ:

Chronic absentees. The people who have little capacity for pressure, either on the job or off, may be prime candidates for counseling. But first they must be made fully aware of the consequences of poor attendance. Theirs is a habit, usually of long standing, and correction requires pressure to attend as well as hand holding.

Vacationing absentees. The people who work only so long as they need the cash and those who then treat themselves to a day or two off are difficult cases. These employees are often extremely capable on the job, but they feel no deep responsibility for it. Vacationers make a conscious choice to be absent and are rarely helped by counseling.

Directionless absentees. The younger employees who have as yet found no real purpose in work may simply follow the lead of the vacationer, who appears to lead a footloose, exciting life. A Dutch-uncle talk with the directionless absentee may be more effective than counseling.

Aggressive absentees. The persons who willfully stay away from work in the hope that their absence will cause an inconvenience for you are probably emotionally disturbed. This kind of behavior, however, requires professional counseling to correct it, not the kind of ordinary counseling that a supervisor can provide.

Moonlighters. The persons who hold more than one job are often either too tired to come to work or faced with conflicting schedules. Straight talk, rather than counseling, is prescribed. When attendance is affected, the moonlighter must be forced to make a choice between jobs.

Occasional absentees. The persons who seem to have slightly more absences than the rest of your staff are probably prime candidates for counseling. Their absences are legitimate. Their illnesses are real. Their problems are often temporarily insurmountable. These people deserve a mixture of sympathy, understanding, and sometimes outright advice. This might also be the time for you to take a look in the mirror. For example, are you contributing to the absenteeism by lack of support and training?

In summary, you can probably help people who are absent for the following reasons:

1. Getting to work is a problem, real or imagined.
2. Off-job pressures are so strong that they weaken the employee's resolve to get to work.
3. The employee is imitative, easily led or misled.
4. The work appears boring, disagreeable, or unattractive.
5. Working relationships are unpleasant.
6. There are in fact off-job problems—child care, serious illness, court appearances—that need immediate attention.
7. Absence or lateness has become a habit.

You will have difficulty, however, helping people who are absent because of these reasons:

1. The work or the pay associated with it holds no strong attraction.
2. Off-job pleasures have a greater appeal than work.
3. The employee is willfully absent in order to disrupt or inconvenience the organization.

🔲5 THE PROBLEMS OF SUBSTANCE ABUSE

CONCEPT   Increasingly, supervisors must deal with problem performance that stems from substance abuse.

How much distinction should be made between alcohol abuse and drug abuse?

In principle, there may be very little difference. In practice, there are significant differences, especially legal ones. Many of the counseling approaches, however, are the same for both problems.

What can you do for alcoholic employees?

Whatever you attempt, proceed slowly and cautiously. Not all heavy drinkers are alcoholics. And the more they drink, the less likely they are to admit to anyone (even themselves) that their ability to handle liquor has gotten out of their control.

An alcoholic employee is really just another kind of problem employee—only the case is an aggravated one and may need the help of a professional. Nevertheless, many alcoholic workers have rescued themselves with the aid of Alcoholics Anonymous (AA), an association of ex-alcoholics who, because they don't preach and because they emphasize the individual's need to face weaknesses, have perfected the art of listening without being either sympathetic or critical.

Your best bet, however, is to recognize an alcoholic in the early stages. Then you can apply the same techniques to gain the person's confidence that you would with any other problem employee. Your objective is to provide security at work and to help with talking out problems. If these employees can be helped to recognize that excessive drinking is a problem they aren't handling, then you can refer them to the company doctor or nurse, who in turn may be able to persuade them to look into Alcoholics Anonymous or to visit a psychiatrist or a special clinic for alcoholics.

How can you tell whether or not you've got an alcoholic employee on your hands?

To guide you in recognizing alcoholic employees, Professor Harrison M. Trice of Cornell University advises that you look first to the employee's absence record. A sharp rise in the overall rate of absences almost always accompanies the development of drinking problems, he says. In a study of 200 cases of alcoholism in industry, Professor Trice also noted five differences from the normal conception of absences among problem drinkers:

Absences are spread out through the week. Neither Monday nor Friday absences predominate (probably because the alcoholic is trying to be careful not to draw attention to the condition).

Partial absenteeism is frequent. A worker often reports in the morning but leaves before the day is over.

There may be frequent short absences from the workplace during the workday. Changes in behavior, especially a deterioration in performance, also may take place as the day progresses.

Tardiness is not a marked feature of alcoholism in industry. The widespread notion that a problem drinker comes late to work was not substantiated.

How should you approach counseling an employee you believe to be an alcoholic?

Alcoholism requires a special form of counseling, say those who have coped most effectively with it. For example, the U.S. Department of Health, Education, and Welfare (HEW) in its *Supervisors' Guide on Alcohol Abuse* offers these hints to supervisors who are faced with this problem among their employees:

1. Don't apologize for confronting the troubled employee about the situation. Your responsibility is to maintain acceptable performance for all your employees.
2. Do encourage the employee to explain why work performance, behavior, or attendance is deteriorating. This can provide an opportunity to question the use of alcohol.
3. Don't discuss a person's right to drink. It is best not to make a moral issue of it; HEW views alcoholism as a progressive and debilitating illness, which, if untreated, can eventually lead to insanity, custodial care, or death.
4. Don't suggest that the employee use moderation or change his or her drinking habits. A person who is an alcoholic cannot, at the start, voluntarily control drinking habits.
5. Don't be distracted by the individual's excuses for drinking—a difficult spouse, problem children, financial troubles. The problem as far as you are concerned is the employee's drinking and how it affects work, behavior, and attendance on the job.

6. Don't be put off by the drinker's assertion that a physician or a psychologist is already being seen. The employee may claim that the physician or the psychologist doesn't consider the drinking a problem or thinks the use of alcohol will subside once the "problems" are worked out. Therapists probably wouldn't say that if they knew an employee's job was in jeopardy because of alcohol abuse; they would attach a new importance to the drinking habits.
7. Do remember that the alcoholic, like any other sick person, should be given the opportunity for treatment and rehabilitation.
8. Do emphasize that your major concern as a supervisor is the employee's poor work performance or behavior. You can firmly state that if there is no improvement, administrative action—such as suspension or discharge—will be taken.
9. Do state that the decision to accept rehabilitative assistance is the employee's responsibility.

Ann St. Louis, personnel counselor for Canada's Department of National Revenue, whose program maintains a 90 percent recovery rate among alcoholic government workers, adds this thought:

> An employer—far better than wife, mother, minister or social agency—can lead an alcoholic to treatment by "constructive coercion." Give an employee every chance to take treatment, but make it clear that he must cooperate or lose his job. This has proven to be more effective than loss of friends or family.

How widespread is drug abuse among employees?

It is not so pervasive as you might think. Because regular drug use is incompatible with regular attendance, drug users tend not to select most regular or demanding kinds of employment. Attempts on a company's part to screen out hard-drug users before employment have not been particularly successful. Dismissal afterward can be difficult because drug users are good at hiding the tools of their habit even if they cannot conceal its symptoms.

Symptoms of drug use are well known. At work they manifest themselves objectively in terms of poor or erratic performance, tardiness, absenteeism, requests to leave early, forgetfulness, indifference to deadlines and safety, and in many instances theft of company property.

Treatment and rehabilitation for drug users are as difficult and complicated as for alcoholics, and the treatments are somewhat similar. Company policies against drug addiction, however, tend to be firmer than those against drinking and alcoholism. For one thing, the addict is different from the alcoholic because many addicts try to involve other people in drugs. The danger of an alcoholic's inducing another employee to begin alcoholism is slight. Then, too, drug use is illegal; in most instances, use of alcohol is not.

Here again, a supervisor's responsibility should be limited to the detection of drug addiction, prevention of the use or sale of drugs on company property, and counseling of drug users, including referral—if indicated—to the appropriate company authority.

What sort of responsibility do supervisors have for counseling employees with terminal illnesses?

Much has to do with your own sense of compassion, as tempered by your company's policies. Increasingly, supervisors must cope with employees who are suffering from terminal illnesses, such as cancer and AIDS. The presence of these employees can be demoralizing to others on your staff as well. In general, the advice seems to run this way:

- Allow the affected employee to choose whether or not, and how, to tell other employees of his or her condition.
- Develop some sort of transitional role for the employee. It should be one that matches the individual's capacity for work and still reflects his or her value to the company.
- Within these limits, avoid special treatment and expect the employee to follow established rules, regulations, and standards of performance. That's what most terminally ill people who choose to keep working prefer. This enhances their sense of worth as adults who are still 100 percent alive and not 85 percent dead.

REVIEW

KEY CONCEPTS TO REMEMBER

1. Supervisors have a legitimate interest in employee performance that either (a) does not measure up to established standards or (b) is disruptive to the normal conduct of operations. Such problem performance is often a reflection of problems in an employee's personal life. Troubled employees are not "crazy" or insane. Mostly, they suffer from temporary emotional problems stemming from an inability to adjust to the stress of life or work. This failure to cope

sometimes causes them to behave unproductively or erratically on the job and to interrupt the regular harmony of the workplace. Accident-prone behavior, extreme preoccupation with work, excessive absenteeism, and substance abuse are common manifestations of the troubled worker.

2. Troubled employees can be recognized by such disharmonious conduct as sudden changes in behavior, preoccupation, irritability, increased accidents or absences, unusual fatigue, irrational anger or hostility, heavy drinking, or symptoms of drug abuse.

3. Constructive counseling by a supervisor can help a great many troubled employees improve their performance or control their behavior, provided the degree of their maladjustment is slight and the underlying causes are not intense. The objectives of the counseling process are to (a) recognize the symptoms of a troubled employee, (b) provide relief if the symptoms and causes are minor (to ease the employee's return to satisfactory performance), and (c) refer the employee to a professional counselor if the conditions are anything but minor.

   It can't be overstated that in all forms of counseling absolute privacy and confidentiality must be maintained. Even a slight breach will destroy credibility with the problem employee, and it may also damage confidence with other employees.

4. Constructive counseling can also reduce absenteeism among chronic and occasional absentees. Other forms of absenteeism respond better to a three-part program involving (a) clear-cut rules, (b) consistent penalties, and (c) counseling to determine—and confront—the reasons for the absences.

5. Alcoholism and drug abuse are found among special kinds of problem employees. Counseling by the supervisor, combined with an insistence that performance standards be met, may be helpful. In anything but minor cases, professional assistance or advice from groups such as Alcoholics Anonymous should be sought.

SUPERVISORY WORD POWER

Adjustment. The process whereby healthy as well as disturbed individuals find a way to fit themselves to difficult situations by yielding to a degree and by modifying their feelings and their behavior to accommodate the stresses of life and work.

Employee counseling. A task-oriented, problem-solving technique that features an empathic, interactive discussion—emphasizing listening—aimed at helping an employee cope with some specific aspect of his or her work life.

Hostility. A feeling of enmity or antagonism; an aggressive expression of anger displayed by problem employees as an unconscious, unwitting relief from fears about their security or other feelings of inadequacy.

Neurosis. An emotional disorder, relatively mild in nature, in which employees have feelings of anxiety, fear, or anger that drive them unknowingly or unwillingly to say and do things they would not normally choose to say and do and which often act against their own interests.

Psychosis. A severe mental disorder or disease in which employee feelings of hostility or persecution are gravely magnified and actions are irrational and unmanageable to the extreme.

Withdrawal. A passive way for emotionally disturbed employees to cope with their anxieties, in which they retreat from confrontations, appear unduly preoccupied, discourage social overtures, and keep very much to themselves.

READING COMPREHENSION

1. Why is it so important for supervisors to identify and attempt to help troubled employees in their workforce?
2. When a supervisor is thinking of counseling an employee, should the emphasis be placed on behavior, performance, or attitude? Why?
3. Differentiate between a neurotic employee and a psychotic employee. Which of these should be referred to a professional counselor?
4. List at least five symptoms of an employee with a possible emotional problem.
5. Describe the characteristics of the counseling approach.
6. List the three phases of Dr. Levinson's approach to employee counseling.
7. What symptoms characterize an extremely disturbed employee who ought to receive professional help without delay?
8. Discuss the difference between valid absences that result from bona fide illness and absences that psychologists describe as voluntary absences. What is a supervisor's role in minimizing the latter?
9. What should a supervisor stress when counseling an employee who has shown signs of alcoholism?
10. Why might a company have policies for confronting drug abuse that are different from those for dealing with alcohol abuse?

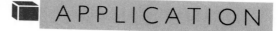

APPLICATION

SELF-APPRAISAL

What's your employee-counseling IQ?

The following statements pertain to employee counseling. Your assignment is to determine which statements are true, or represent sound practice, and which are false, or represent unsound practice. On a separate piece of paper, copy the column headings shown below. In the column "Counseling Statements," write the numbers 1 to 15 down the page to correspond to each of the statements. Then place a check mark in the column that most nearly matches your opinion about each statement. After completing this activity, check your answers by using the scoring procedure described on page 334.

Column headings:

Counseling	True, or Sound Practice	False, or Unsound Practice

1. Problem performance may occur among employees who are normally your best and most reliable workers.
2. When a symptom of an employee's emotional disturbance emerges, it is best to ignore it until the behavior becomes unmanageable.
3. Supervisors should not attempt extended counseling with psychotic employees or those who have severe neuroses.
4. Employees with emotional disturbances have difficulty in adjusting to the requirements of a particular situation—in life or on the job.
5. Probably one of the most reliable signs of a troubled employee is a sudden change in a person's normal behavior.
6. Employee counseling is essentially a technique by which a supervisor solves an employee's personal problems.
7. If, during a counseling session, the employee makes some inaccurate statements about job conditions, the supervisor should set the record straight before the counseling proceeds further.
8. A supervisor should expect that after a counseling session an employee's performance and behavior will return immediately to normal.
9. You have counseled Pamela three times about her unsatisfactory performance, but her behavior continues to be erratic and irrational. You should conduct at least one more counseling session before referring her to a professional counselor.

10. A good starting point for controlling absenteeism is a firm set of rules regarding it.

11. Bob stays home from work during critical work periods in order to create an inconvenience for his boss. This aggressive form of absenteeism may require professional counseling.

12. Individuals who have only slightly more absences than others are the best candidates for counseling.

13. The surest sign of an alcoholic worker is an increase of Monday and Friday absences.

14. When a supervisor is dealing with employees whose abuse of alcohol or illegal substances affects their work, a direct confrontation is recommended.

15. Supervisors should make every exception possible for terminally ill employees who do not keep their agreed-upon commitments for satisfactory performance while they remain working.

Scoring   Give yourself 1 point for each of the following statements that you checked as *true*, or representing sound practice: 1, 3, 4, 5, 10, 11, 12, 14. Give yourself 1 point for each of the following statements that you checked as *false*, or representing unsound practice: 2, 6, 7, 8, 9, 13, 15.

Interpretation   If you scored 13 points or more, you have acquired enough basic knowledge of employee counseling to make a good beginning. If you scored between 10 and 12 points, your employee counseling will begin on shaky grounds. Review the items you missed. If you scored less than 10 points, your employee-counseling attempts are likely to do more harm than good. Review the entire chapter.

CASE STUDIES

CASE 41   The Irrational Documents Clerk

Benny was not exactly a knockout as a documents clerk for the Northern Empire Power and Light Company, but he was reasonably dependable. He got most of his work done on time, and his error rate on document coding was no worse than the average clerk's rate. His manner was generally pleasant, although he was considered somewhat of a loner by his associates.

That has all changed during the past three months. Benny's output has deteriorated markedly. He no longer meets his deadlines. And his boss, Aretha Ford, keeps discovering costly miscodings in the documents Benny prepares. Benny appears to be working hard, but his results are no longer satisfactory. When approached by other clerks to make corrections in the documents he sends them, Benny flares up. On some occasions, he has been downright insulting.

Yesterday, Aretha asked Benny to come to her office to talk about this problem. She opened the discussion by saying: "Your error rate on document preparation has become entirely unacceptable lately. So has your output. This can't keep on. What can you do to bring your work back into line?"

Benny was silent for a few minutes, so Aretha repeated her question. Then, without warning, Benny slammed his fist down on the desk. He shouted obscenities and heaped abuse upon Aretha: she was unfair, played favorites, expected too much of him, didn't understand his situation; if she wanted him to quit, why didn't she say so; and so on.

If you were Aretha, what would you do now? Of the following five alternatives, which do you think would be most appropriate? Rank the alternatives on a scale from 1 (most preferable) to 5 (least preferable). You may add another alternative if you wish. In any event, be prepared to justify your ranking.

a. Don't say anything for the time being; allow Benny to keep on talking.

b. Advise Benny that he isn't making sense; tell him that when he is ready to talk rationally, you'll resume the discussion.

c. Carefully show Benny why his accusations are not justified by the records.

d. Wait a while; then tell Benny that you want to help him if he's suffering from some sort of emotional problem.

e. Tell Benny that you understand how he feels, but say that it would be better if he faces up to his problem now.

CASE 42 The Tippling Night Porter

Frank is a veteran porter in a very large hotel in Washington, D.C. He works the 11 p.m. to 7 a.m. shift. He shows up for work on time and regularly, but two or three nights a week he arrives after having spent a couple of hours in a bar down the street from the hotel. The maintenance supervisor has cautioned Frank about this in a joking manner. Lately, though, Frank's first few hours on the job are almost completely nonproductive as he wanders from place to place with his vacuum cleaning kit without putting it to use. At this point, Frank's supervisor should

a. Stop joking with Frank about his drinking and insist that he not come to work with liquor on his breath or he will be fired.

b. Tell Frank that she doesn't care about his drinking as long as he does his job properly. If he can't do that, he'll get the axe.
c. Let Frank know that his poor performance can't continue and that if it means joining AA, he should do that.
d. Take the position that Frank has been a good employee in the past and that he'll straighten himself out soon.

What other suggestions can you make for Frank's supervisor?

CASE 43 The Downer Dealer

Newspaper offices are often hectic places. Reporters and copy editors work long and often irregular hours. News assignments are made in, what to many appear, haphazard fashion. These assignments, along with whatever disciplinary control that is exerted over reporters, are the responsibility of the managing editor, the assistant managing editors, and the copy chiefs. In addition to the reporters, there are a number of other professional employees, such as feature writers, researchers, and librarians. There are also many nonprofessional and unskilled employees, whose work takes them in and out of the newsroom. These people include the maintenance and housekeeping crews, as well as messengers from various express services, who are not directly employed by the newspaper. In any event, there is a general atmosphere of informality throughout. Other than a recognition that they must meet the newspaper's deadlines, most of the professional staff think of themselves as individuals with a great deal of independence in how they go about their assignments and what they do when not on them.

The following incident, however, presented a dilemma to the assistant managing editor who was supervising the second shift of a Midwestern newspaper. She walked into the employee's lounge at about 10:30 p.m. There, she quite clearly observed one reporter selling another a couple of dozen "downers." Since she knew both reporters on a personal as well as a professional basis, she was puzzled for the moment about how to handle the situation. A number of possible alterates came to her mind, including the following:

1. Look the other way and forget that she saw anything.
2. Tell the "dealer" to report to the newspaper's personnel department first thing in the morning.
3. Give both employees a lecture on the dangers of drug abuse.
4. Ask both employees to come to her office before they leave so that she can discuss the situation with them before taking action.

a. If you were the assistant managing editor, which of those courses of action would you take? Why?

b. If none of these approaches seems particularly appropriate, what other courses of action would you advise the assistant managing editor to consider?

c. Would you suggest a different approach if these were nonprofessional employees? Why or why not?

CASE 44   She's a Charmer, But...

Julie Garvo is 23 years old and serves as a paralegal clerk in a large law firm. She's been employed there for six months. Julie is charming and energetic and is very popular with the office staff and with the lawyers.

Julie, however, is frequently late for work. She takes long lunch hours and has been absent from work an average of two days a month for the past three months. She apologizes when she saunters in late, but seems unconcerned about this or her absences. To her co-workers, Julie readily admits that she doesn't have a great deal of interest in her work. The best thing about the job, she says, is that it pays well enough for her to do some of the other things she likes to do in her off-hours.

Julie's supervisor, the office manager, observes, "She's a charmer, but she's become a problem here." If you were this supervisor, what would you do?

a. Encourage Julie to improve. Sympathize with her lack of interest and try to make the job less boring for her.

b. Have a shoulder-to-shoulder talk with Julie, pointing out the importance of her creating a good work record.

c. Suggest that Julie seek professional counseling to "get her head on straight."

d. Come to the point with Julie: either the lateness and absences stop, or she will be fired.

Are there any other suggestions that you can make to Julie's boss?

1 Supervisors must anticipate and resolve grievances.

2 Supervisors require skills in handling group relationships.

3 Participation can enhance a supervisor's effectiveness.

4 Limited conflict within and between groups must be expected.

5 Cooperation protects and advances mutual interests.

CHAPTER 15

Converting Complaints and Conflict Into Cooperation

LEARNING OBJECTIVES

After studying this chapter, you should be able to

1. Describe effective methods for handling and preventing grievances.

2. Explain the formation, roles, and influence of informal groups in an organization.

3. Discuss the use of participatory management with groups of employees.

4. Identify the most common sources of conflict in an organization and describe some effective ways to resolve conflict.

5. Discuss ways in which cooperation can be obtained from associates, staff people, individuals, and groups.

COMPLAINTS AND GRIEVANCES

CONCEPT   Supervisors must anticipate and resolve complaints and grievances before these can interfere with employee performance.

How much attention should supervisors pay to employee complaints?

Just as much as is necessary to remove the employee complaints as obstacles to their doing a willing, productive job. That's the main reason supervisors should act as soon as they even sense a complaint or grievance. A gripe, imagined or real, spoken or held in, blocks an employee's will to cooperate. Until you've examined the grievance and its underlying causes, an employee isn't likely to put out very much for you. And if the complaint has merit, the only way for you to get the employee back on your team 100 percent is to correct the situation.

Can you settle every grievance to an employee's satisfaction?

No. It's natural for people sometimes to want more than they deserve. When an employee complains about a condition and the facts don't back him or her up, the best you can do is to demonstrate that the settlement is just—even if it isn't exactly what the employee would like.

What's the most important thing you can do when handling grievances?

It can't be said too often: Above all, be objective, be fair. Get the employees' point of view clear in your mind. If they have an opportunity to make themselves understood, their grievances may turn out to be something different from what appears on the surface.

To be really fair, you must be prepared to accept the logical conclusion that flows from the facts you uncover. (See Figure 15-1.) This may mean making concessions. But if the facts warrant it, you often have to change your mind or your way of doing things if you are to gain a reputation for fair dealing.

If you find you've made a mistake, admit it. A supervisor isn't expected to always be right. But your employees expect you to be honest in every instance—even if it means your eating crow on occasion.

When you give your decision on a grievance, how specific should you be? Should you leave yourself a loophole?

A supervisor is paid to make decisions. When the grievance has been fully investigated and you've talked it over with the parties involved, make your decision as promptly as possible. Be definite in your answer. State your decision so that there's no mistake about what you mean. If

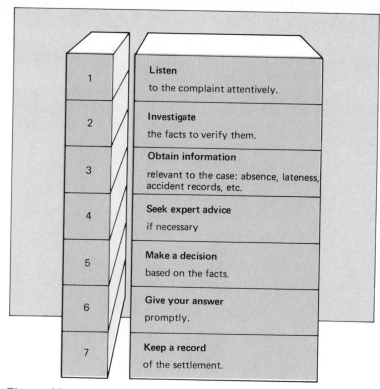

Figure 15-1 Grievance handling process.

1	**Listen** to the complaint attentively.
2	**Investigate** the facts to verify them.
3	**Obtain information** relevant to the case: absence, lateness, accident records, etc.
4	**Seek expert advice** if necessary
5	**Make a decision** based on the facts.
6	**Give your answer** promptly.
7	**Keep a record** of the settlement.

it involves a warning rather than a more serious penalty—for breaking a safety rule, for instance—don't give this kind of reply: "I'll withhold the warning this time, but next time it won't be so easy for you." Instead, use this clear-cut approach: "There appears to be a good reason to believe that you misunderstood what I expected of you. So I'll tear up the warning and throw it away. Next time, you'll get a written warning. And if it happens a second time, it will cost you a week off without pay."

Must you give your decision right away?

No. But don't sit on it forever. Nothing breaks down the grievance procedure like procrastination. If you can't make up your mind on the spot, or need to check even further than you did originally, tell the employee and the steward that you'll give a definite answer this afternoon or tomorrow. Stick to this promise. If you run into an unexpected delay, let them know about it. For instance: "Sorry I can't let you know this afternoon as I'd hoped, but the paymaster has been tied up all morning. I won't be able to check the time sheets until late this afternoon. But I will let you know first thing in the morning."

How important is the grievance procedure as such? Wouldn't it be simpler if employee grievances were all handled informally?

Where a union is involved, the grievance procedure becomes a very important matter. The procedure may vary from company to company (see Chapter 22), but in any case your guide should be this: Know the authorized grievance procedure in your organization and stick to it. It's up to you, too, to see that the steward also observes the provisions of the grievance clause.

Take special notice of what may appear to be tiny technicalities, and be sure you observe them. For instance, some contracts call for the supervisor to give an answer within 24 hours after the complaint has been presented in writing. Be sure you do so that you can't be accused of stalling or even lose the grievance entirely on such a technicality.

Of course, it would be desirable if grievances could all be settled in a casual, informal manner. But where a union is concerned, experience shows that it's best to be businesslike and to stick to the letter of the contract procedure. On the other hand, don't get so engrossed with the process itself that you overlook the original purpose of the grievance procedure—to settle grievances fairly and promptly.

What happens to grievances that go unsettled?

They continue to fester. Frequently a supervisor feels that he or she has taken care of a complaint just by soft-soaping the aggrieved employee. This is a mistake. The grievance will continue to simmer in the employee's mind, even if nothing more is said about it to the supervisor. And dissatisfaction is contagious.

An unsettled grievance is like one rotten apple in a basket. It spoils the good ones—the good ones don't make a good apple of the rotten one. An offended or angry employee tends to make other employees lose confidence in the supervisor. The co-workers may encourage the dissatisfied employee to pursue the matter if it appears that you have been evasive.

It's easy to see that it would be better to prevent grievances in the first place. What can you do to keep from having to wait until one occurs?

The trick lies in detecting situations that breed grievances and then correcting these situations. Don't make the mistake of planting seeds of trouble where trouble doesn't exist, though. A perfectly happy worker may be able to find something to complain about if you ask directly,

"What is there about your job that you don't like?" Leave that type of open-ended prospecting to company-directed attitude surveys.

A rule of thumb, however, is that you can reduce the number of grievances by applying common sense to your relationships with your staff. For example:

1. Give employees prompt and regular feedback about how well they are doing their jobs. Uncertainty in this area is a major source of employee dissatisfaction.
2. Remove, or try to ease, minor irritations as they arise. The presence of unnecessary aggravations tends to magnify the more serious complaints when they occur.
3. Listen to and encourage constructive suggestions. Take action whenever it is reasonable and nondisruptive.
4. Make certain of your authority before making a commitment to an employee. Then be sure to keep your promises.
5. Render your decisions as soon as possible when responding to employee requests. A prompt no is often more welcome than a long-delayed yes.
6. If you must take disciplinary action, do not make a public display of it. Keep it a private matter between you and the employee.

2 GROUP DYNAMICS

CONCEPT   Many of a supervisor's daily encounters are with groups of employees or with employees within groups.

Why are group relations more important today than they were in years past?

Business, industrial, service, and government enterprises are larger and more complex. As a result, they depend more on the effectiveness of group effort. At the turn of the nineteenth into the twentieth century, employees worked more by themselves, and their productivity often depended on their efforts alone. Then, too, many of the jobs were unskilled. People were hired to do routine work or to perform a specific task that a machine performs today. Automation, computers, and modern technology made those jobs scarce. Instead, modern jobs involve great interdependence among individuals and among departments and demand close cooperation among all parties.

As Casey Stengel, the eccentric but immensely successful manager of baseball's Dodgers, Yankees, and Mets, observed: "It's easy to get the players. Gettin' 'em to play together, that's the hard part."

Which groups take priority: the formal or the informal ones?

Formal groups do, such as your own department or assigned work teams within your department. They have been set up routinely to carry out the work in the best fashion. But informal groups require your attention and consideration too. A supervisor must be realistic about formation of informal groups within the department:

1. **Informal groups are inevitable.** They'll form at the water fountain and and in the locker room. They will be made up of carpoolers and those with common interests in sports or politics. You will find them everywhere. There is no way to blot them out.
2. **Informal groups can be very powerful.** They influence your employees strongly. To enforce compliance among group members, such groups often establish sanctions that run counter to a supervisor's formal authority. Most informal groups, however, can be assumed to work either for you or against you, depending upon your relationships with them.
3. **Informal leaders tend to emerge within these groups and to guide opinion within them.** Supervisors should be aware of such leaders and be prepared to contend with their influence.

What causes employees to create their own informal groups?

There are a number of causes. Most powerful is a common specialty or skill. For example, the keyboard operators in a data processing office are naturally going to find things in common to talk about. Other common experiences, backgrounds, or interests will also serve to pull parts of a formal grouping of employees into "cliques." Proximity plays a role, too. Workers who are physically close together tend to form close relationships to the exclusion of others in the department who are in more remote locations.

Membership in informal groups is developed gradually. Over a period of time, an individual begins to feel that he or she is accepted by the others. In return, the individual begins to accept—and carry out— the interests and behavior of the group. The bonds are tighter when the attraction is fostered by a desire for protection or support (often with regard to the company or management). Groups are less cohesive when the common bond is more casual, as with hobbies and sports.

A supervisor must be careful in his or her relationships with informal groups. They can't be ignored; more often they can be helpful. On the other hand, giving these groups too much attention, especially to the exclusion of those outside the groups, will surely bring about dissension and lack of cooperation.

How does a group of employees differ from any single employee in the group?

Take a group of ten employees who work in a small can-filling line in a food-packing plant. This group is respected and feared by its supervisor as one of the most productive, most-likely-to-strike groups in the plant. Yet in the group are three people who, polled separately, are strongly against a walkout. And there are another three who, when working with other groups, are low producers. This is typical. Each person in a group may be a fairly strong individualist when working alone. But when people work in a group, the personality of the group becomes stronger than that of any single individual in the group. The group's personality will reflect the outlook and work habits of the various individuals, but it will bring out the best (or worst) in some and will submerge many individual tendencies the group does not approve of.

Furthermore, each group sets the standards of conduct—or **norms**—for its members. Norms are accepted ways of doing things, an accepted way of life within the group. The group's ways may not be the best ways. Often, group norms stand in the way of doing things the way the company and the supervisor want them done. But the group will support the group standards. Individuals who don't conform will be cut off from the group's gossip sessions and social activities. It's not uncommon for the group to ridicule those who don't "play ball" or to purposely make it difficult for outsiders to get their own work done.

What are work groups likely to do best?

Solve work problems. Groups, formal or informal, seem to have an uncanny knack for unsnarling complex work situations. In a few minutes they can straighten out crossover procedures between employees. They often know causes of difficulty hidden from the supervisor. Typically, they are acutely aware of personality conflicts between their members. Thus a group's ability to put together jointly held know-how in a constructive manner is one that experienced supervisors like to tap. The technique of securing group aid this way in solving departmental problems is called **participation.**

In what ways are groups most likely to cause problems?

By ganging up to present mass resistance (spoken or silent) and by pressuring individual members to conform to the group's standards. Strong work groups stick together. They will protect one of their loyal members, and they will force a nonconformist to go along with the majority. The pressure can be so strong that even an eager beaver or a loner can be made to fall in line—or to quit. Groups are powerful. Their support is to be cherished. Their enmity can be awesome. For these reasons prudent supervisors seek a group's help in establishing attainable work goals.

Which comes first, the individual or the group?

It's almost impossible to say. We do know that the group is not just the sum of the individuals in it. Individually each of your employees may be loyal and honest. But as a group each person may be more loyal to the group's interest than to you. As a result, the individual may cheat a little on output or quality, if that's the standard the group respects.

It seems unavoidable that you must place your bets on the group's being collectively stronger than any of its individuals. Hardly any one person can stand up to group pressures for long. The person who does so may keep on working in your area but is no longer a member of the group. Such persons become oddballs, difficult for you to deal with fairly and intelligently because you're never sure what standards of performance to impose on them—theirs or the department's. For that reason don't press individuals to support you in favor of the work group. Accept the fact that they will be loyal to you when this loyalty doesn't put them at odds with their peers.

By and large the supervisor's charge is to treat each person as individually as possible without challenging the prerogatives of the group the individual works in. The work group is an organization for which you are expected to provide direction and inspiration, not moral judgments.

3 GROUP PARTICIPATION

CONCEPT   A participative approach tends to enhance a supervisor's effectiveness with employee groups.

How can a supervisor set goals with the work group without sacrificing authority?

Unless the people you supervise believe that what you want them to do is to their advantage as well as to yours, you'll have little success as a supervisor. The solution lies in permitting the members of the work group to set their goals along with you and in showing them that these goals are attained through group action—teamwork.

It may be only natural for you to feel that to permit the group to get into the decision-making act will be hazardous to your authority. It needn't be. First of all, make it clear that you'll always retain a veto power over a group decision (but don't exercise it unless absolutely necessary). Second, establish ground rules for the group's participation beforehand. Explain what's negotiable and what's not. Make these limitations clear. Finally, provide enough information for the group so that its members can see situations as you do. It's when people don't have enough facts that they rebel against authority.

In dealing with work groups, try to make your role that of a coach. Help employees to see why cost cutting, for instance, is desirable and necessary to prevent layoffs. Encourage them to discuss ways to cut costs. Welcome their suggestions. Try to find ways of putting even relatively insignificant ideas to work. And report the team's achievements frequently. Emphasize that good records are the result of the team's united effort, not your own bright ideas.

Of course, it goes without saying that certain decisions—such as those concerning work standards or quality specifications—may be beyond the group's control or even yours. (See Figure 15-2.) Consequently, you should make it clear at the start what work conditions are off limits as far as group participation is concerned.

What makes group participation so effective?

You'll hear a lot about the wonders of participation in one form or another, such as "consensus management" or "Quality Circles." Most

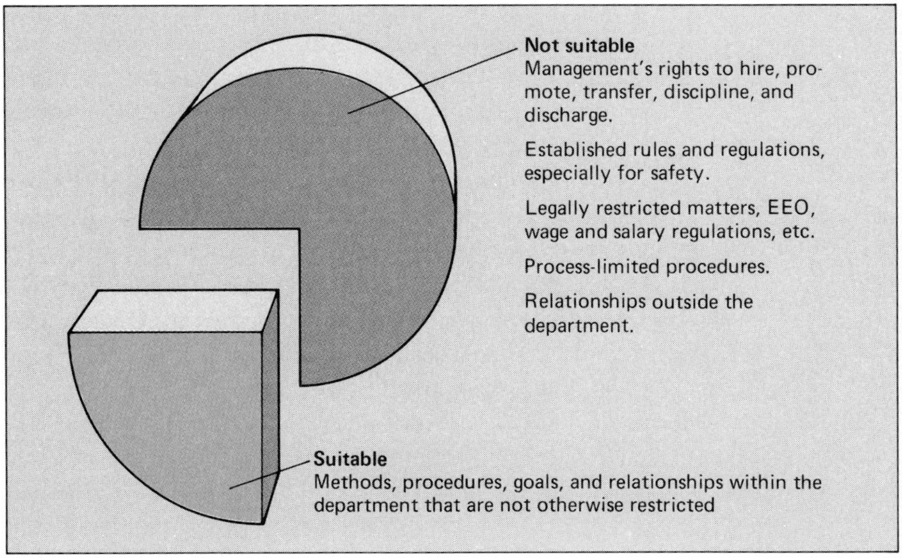

Not suitable
Management's rights to hire, promote, transfer, discipline, and discharge.

Established rules and regulations, especially for safety.

Legally restricted matters, EEO, wage and salary regulations, etc.

Process-limited procedures.

Relationships outside the department.

Suitable
Methods, procedures, goals, and relationships within the department that are not otherwise restricted

Figure 15-2 Areas suitable for and areas usually not suitable for participatory management methods.

of what you'll hear is true. In today's employer-employee relations, few techniques have been as successful in developing harmony and attaining common goals as has the development of participation by management and supervision.

Participation is an amazingly simple way to inspire people. And its simplicity lies in the definition of that word: "to share in common with others."

Sharing, then, is the secret. You must share knowledge and information with others in order to gain their cooperation. You must share your own experience so that employees will benefit from it. You must share the decision-making process itself so that employees can do some things the way they'd like to. And you must share credit for achievement.

How often can group participation be expected to work in your behalf?

Only as often as the group's perception of a situation leads the members logically or emotionally, or both, to the conclusion that what you wish is good for them. Keep in mind that merely permitting participation will not manipulate the group to your point of view. And the larger the group, the more forces are at work in it with which your ideas must cope.

If the majority can be expected to agree with your inclinations when given your view of the facts, then the majority may sway group attitudes in your direction. But even this won't always be the case. If, for example, Carlos is cantankerous, but because of seniority or outspokenness has the respect or fear of the rest of the people in the word processing pool, the group may never buy an idea of yours that discredits him. Conversely, the group may (for reasons that are hard to determine) rebel against Carlos and accept your new idea.

There are two rules of thumb to guide you: (1) Without group support your chance of achievement is slim, and (2) your best chance for winning group support is to let the forces within the group itself struggle toward a decision with minimum interference from you. This isn't to say you must stand by helplessly while the group strikes off in the wrong direction. You can supply sound direction by providing facts that might be overlooked and by asking the group to weigh pros and cons of various alternatives.

🔳4 *RESOLVING CONFLICT*

CONCEPT   A limited amount of conflict within or between groups is to be expected; intense or disruptive conflict, however, should be resolved without delay.

Is the presence of bickering and disputes a sign of poor supervision?

Not necessarily. It is human to quarrel and complain. When many people must work together, conflict is inevitable. Accordingly, a small amount of conflict can be a good thing. It is when there is no end of quarreling and confrontation that supervisors should begin to worry about how good a job they are doing.

What are the main sources of conflict in an organization?

There are many. People with different ideas about what should be done and how to do it are a common source. Departments that are sometimes at cross-purposes—such as production and maintenance, production control and sales, sales and credit, accounting and retailing, purchasing and engineering—cause intergroup difficulties. But most of the causes of conflict in a supervisor's department are closely related to the work itself: how it is laid out and the way in which the supervisor manages the employees. In particular, a supervisor should be on guard against:

1. **An appearance of an unfair allocation of tools, materials, supplies, and other resources.** There are few shops where there is always enough of everything to go around equally. The supervisor must often make the hard decisions about who will have what, how much, and when. When these decisions are made openly and fairly, employees are more likely to accept them without quarreling with one another. If allocations are made slyly or on the basis of favoritism, trouble will brew.

2. **Expressed disagreements about what's important and what is not.** If these are the result of lack of information or misinformation, they should be cleared up right away. If the disagreements arise because individuals see things differently, the supervisor must try to get to the root of the problem. For example, a press operator may constantly push his benchmate for work to be processed, whereas the benchmate may insist that her work can't be released because its quality isn't good enough. The first individual sets priority on output, the other on quality. The supervisor must find an answer to this question: Are these priorities (or goals) merely a reflection of each individual's values—or are they related to the department's established goals and standards?

3. **Changes in work flow or conditions that imply a change in status.** If in the past Anita handled incoming orders first before passing them on to Jack for posting, Anita may regard her work as more valued than Jack's. A change in the order of flow so that Jack handles the orders first may disturb Anita's sense of status. And she may begin

finding fault with everything that Jack does. Experienced workers tend to develop "territorial rights." Hence, they feel that they should resist outside forces such as a new supervisor, new employees, or any changes in which they have not participated.

4. **A growing sense of mistrust among employees.** This is liable to occur when things in the department are generally going wrong. If business is bad, or if the department has been criticized for mistakes or low productivity, employees may look around for others on whom to place the blame. The production department, for example, will blame off-grade products on the maintenance people—the equipment was faulty. The floor salesperson may blame the cashier for a lost sale. The nurse may blame the nurse's aide for upset patients.

5. **Lack of stability in departmental operations.** Change is so threatening to many people that they will naturally take out their fears and anxieties in quibbling and complaints. Many times, change is something beyond the supervisor's control. But the supervisor can pour oil on troubled waters simply by maintaining an air of calm. He or she can, for example, talk with employees about the reasons for the change, how long it will last, and how it will affect—or not affect—normal operating conditions.

How does competition differ from conflict?

The former is usually productive; the latter is often counterproductive. The right kind of **competition** can stimulate a healthy, controlled battle between two individuals. Informal contests allow employees to try to excel at meeting departmental goals that are mutually beneficial. Carried too far, however, the contestants may lose sight of the common good and become antagonistic. **Conflict** tends to pit individuals and groups against one another in trying to control the department's resources in pursuit of their own goals. A lathe operator, for example, may insist on taking the only available tool in order to finish his or her *own* quota on time. He or she may not worry about whether or not this slows up another operator or the department in meeting its goals. Or a salesperson may demand the major portion of the section's travel expenses because his or her *own* customers are most important.

What's a good way to handle conflict in your department?

First, be alert to its presence. Next, seek out its causes. Then meet it head-on. A basic approach involves five steps:

---

1. **Decide what it is that you want to have accomplished.** Do you want peace and quiet at any price? Or do you want better quality? Greater productivity? A project finished on time? Fewer mistakes in transcribing? An end to delays caused by quarrels between the maintenance person and your production operator? Nothing will be resolved unless you first make up your mind what the desired outcome should be.

2. **Call together the people who can best settle the issue.** If the conflict is strictly between you and an individual, limit the confrontation to the two of you. If others are involved, invite them into the discussion. If a disinterested party, such as the quality-control department, can shed light on the subject, ask for its participation. If a referee or someone who can speak authoritatively about the company's viewpoint is needed, then get your boss into the act.

3. **Be ready to bargain; don't hand out edicts.** Conflicts are truly settled by negotiation. A short answer tends only to put off the problem, and it will keep recurring. If you keep your eye on the objective you have set, there are usually many ways to attain it. Remember that each individual has an objective too. If the maintenance department, for example, can provide the necessary repairs while still keeping its costs in line—and dependable repairs are your objective—then let the maintenance people do it their way.

4. **Don't be distracted by the red herring of personalities.** Whereas many people do rub one another the wrong way, most conflicts have a much more tangible basis. That's the value of keeping the eyes of all concerned on the main objective. It tends to push personality conflicts into the background. Finally, try not to get emotionally involved yourself. Most importantly, don't choose sides.

5. **Focus attention on mutually beneficial outcomes.** Above all, don't make performance comparisons between individuals. This will only heighten competition and stress. Instead, hold up total organizational results as the criterion for success. If Kevin insists that Sharon takes up more than her share of the keyboard time, for example, try to reach a solution that makes the most effective use of the keyboard. That way, both Sharon and Kevin can contribute to departmental effectiveness, even though both may have to give in a little while doing so.

How can "I'm okay, you're okay" help to resolve personality conflicts?

This kind of analysis, often called *transactional analysis* (TA), helps to provide insights because it simplifies some of the apparently complex interactions that take place between people. This analysis maintains that there are four possible views of a relationship that can be held by the employee, the supervisor, or both:

1. **I'm not okay. You're not okay.** This is a negative view that implies an employee's dissatisfaction with her or his own behavior but also, in effect, says that the supervisor's actions are just as bad. It is somewhat like the attitude of a rebellious child quarreling with a parent. At work it might arise when an employee accused of pilfering materials says that the boss does the same thing.
2. **I'm not okay. You're okay.** This is often the mark of the person who has lost self-respect or of a person who places all the responsibility on the boss's shoulders. This person often feels unable to do the job without continual assistance from the supervisor. Supervisors should strive to get out from under this kind of dependence.
3. **I'm okay. You're not okay.** This is the parental kind of role supervisors often assume. Essentially it means treating the employee like a child. Such an attitude invites rebellion or loss of any hope the employee may have that the job can be done to the supervisor's satisfaction.
4. **I'm okay. You're okay.** This is the mature, or adult, way to handle conflicts. It assumes that each individual respects the other. Starting from a point of mutual respect, each person tries to understand— although not necessarily agree with—the other's point of view. The supervisor says to the employee: "I understand why you may think I'm taking advantage of your good nature, but listen to me long enough so that you understand my point of view. Once we're sure we understand one another, maybe we can come to some sort of agreement that gives you some satisfaction while making sure that the job gets done."

When transactional analysis is used, any of the first three approaches tends to keep the conflict going, even to heat it up. The fourth approach, which encourages positive stroking, can be very effective if carried on honestly. It helps provide a solid basis for cooperation and compromise.

5 SECURING COOPERATION

CONCEPT   Cooperation from employees and associates can be encouraged by showing how cooperation protects or advances their interests.

Why don't some people cooperate?

For a very natural reason: they see no personal advantage in doing so. A terrible attitude? Not at all.

Not one of us does anything for nothing. We do some things for money, others for lots of other reasons. Joe works well because he likes the feeling of being with a gang of people. Jane works hard because she gets a sense of accomplishment from what she is doing. Louise puts in top effort because her job makes her feel important.

Hardly anyone works for money alone. We all expect different satisfactions in different proportions from our work. So don't be annoyed when a worker's attitude when asked to cooperate seems to say, "What's in it for me?" That's your signal to get busy and to find some way of providing satisfaction for that person on the job.

How do you go about getting cooperation from your associates?

The secret of getting along well with other supervisors is much the same as that of winning cooperation from your employees: find out what they want most from their work, then satisfy these desires. With your associates, though, it's not so much a problem of providing satisfaction as it is of not blocking their goals and ambitions.

Face up to the fact that, to a degree, you and your associates are competing—for raises, promotions, praise, popularity, and a host of other things. If you compete too hard, or compete unfairly, you won't win much cooperation from the other supervisors. And your chances of getting ahead depend on your ability to run your department in smooth harmony with those departments that interlock with yours.

Winning friends among other supervisors means intelligent sacrifice. Occasionally you'll have to put aside your wish to make your department look good so that you don't put the supervisor of the next department behind the eight ball. Willingness to lend a hand when another supervisor falls behind and avoiding hairsplitting when allocating interdepartmental charges and responsibilities will also help.

Above all, let other supervisors run their own shows. Don't try to give orders in their departments or encourage disputes between your workers and theirs.

As in the case of an individual employee who doesn't play ball with the others, if you don't conform to a reasonable degree, you'll have the supervisory group down on you—and cooperation will be long in coming. To turn this group solidarity to your advantage, aim at giving the supervisory organization the advantage of your own positive leadership. Help other supervisors set worthwhile goals, and the chances of all of you working together will be improved.

How can you get along best with staff people?

Generally speaking, staff people in your organization are almost entirely dependent on the cooperation of you and other supervisors. And in this case cooperation will breed cooperation. When you cooperate with staff people, their jobs are made infinitely easier. Their superiors judge them by their success in getting your assistance and by the degree to which you accept and act on their advice. So when you cooperate with staff people, you're actually helping them get more satisfaction from their work. And you can be pretty sure that they'll go a long way toward helping you make a good showing on *your* job.

Wouldn't you like to have a data processing specialist report to your boss: "It's a pleasure to work with a supervisor like Jill. She never seems to hide things or get her back up when I offer suggestions. She is quick to see how what we're doing will improve operations in the long run. Not that Jill buys everything I say. She doesn't. She has her ideas too. But together, I think Jill and I are really accomplishing things out there."

Individual or group of individuals—what's the best way to avoid misunderstanding and to gain willing cooperation?

The starting place is respect for others' points of view, no matter how much they vary from your own. For the manager this implies an appreciation of subordinates for what they really are. It's wishful thinking—and downright harmful—to measure someone against a mythical ideal such as the perfect person for the job.

Try to remind yourself that by definition you, as a supervisor, deal in other people's lives. An order to take any action in the company is interpreted all down the line in terms of personal effects on people. And the effectiveness of the implementation of any order is a matter of approval or disapproval on the part of your subordinates and your associates.

Many managers never learn that their subordinates are constantly evaluating the manager's actions and varying their efforts accordingly. It's certainly the rare subordinate who will risk telling the boss when he or she is making mistakes, particularly if the boss isn't one who takes criticism willingly. Thus many supervisors never get any critical feedback about themselves. Fortunately, if you can make the first step, you'll find yourself a new and better kind of supervisor. You'll gain a new awareness that there are more consequences to any action involving people than those on the surface. And the consequences often interfere with productivity, because people who are working on their own frustrations have less energy to devote to the job.

Of course, it isn't always possible to solve the human problems that can result from a necessary and unpleasant management action. But sensitive supervisors enjoy two distinct advantages over their less sensitive counterparts:

1. An awareness of others' needs aids in avoiding unnecessary human problems that ordinarily seem to be cropping up each day.
2. A pattern of awareness of others' needs in itself tends to blunt the edge of problems and conflicts that cannot be avoided, because subordinates and associates know that the supervisor has tried.

REVIEW

KEY CONCEPTS TO REMEMBER

1. A vigilance toward those conditions which induce employee grievances, combined with (a) an attitude that invites employees to air their grievances and (b) a cheerful readiness to deal with complaints justly and harmoniously, has an inestimable value in creating and maintaining good morale.

   A supervisor's handling of grievances should be characterized by objectivity, consistency, and absolute fairness. Thus a careful examination of the conditions, events, and attitudes relevant to the grievance should precede its resolution. Grievance discussions should be conducted in a businesslike manner, the settlement concluded without undue delay, and corrective action discharged promptly without future prejudice toward the complainant.

2. Since supervision is involved with organized human effort, group dynamics—group relationships—are present in every situation. Work groups may be either formal, established by management, or informal, spontaneously created by their members because of mutual interest.

   Because groups can exert such tremendous influence in work situations, supervisors must weigh the characteristics of a group's norms and behavior just as carefully as those of an individual.

3. With groups especially, the principle of participation presents an effective approach. By recognizing a group's ability to attain (or block) goals, a supervisor who invites participation encourages the group to direct its influence in a productive manner. While respecting the power and legitimate interests of work groups, supervisors should not abandon the management's responsibility to the group or relinquish their essential authority.

4. Conflicts are natural in any organization. The supervisor's responsibilities are to try to understand the causes of these conflicts and to resolve them in a way that will contribute to meeting the objectives of the work group and the organization. Conflict is best resolved by focusing on mutually beneficial goals, by seeking areas of compromise, by examining facts, and by keeping personality differences out of the discussion. Transactional analysis (TA) can be helpful in dealing with personality differences.

5. An awareness of an employee's point of view and the reasons for it—especially when this awareness is projected to the employee by attentive listening—can be one of the most effective ways for a supervisor to induce cooperation.

SUPERVISORY WORD POWER

Competition. A relatively healthy struggle among individuals or groups within an organization to excel in striving to meet mutually beneficial, rather than individual, goals.

Conflict. A disruptive clash of interests, objectives, or personalities between individuals, between individuals and groups, or between groups within an organization.

Formal work group. A group or team of employees who are assigned by management to similar activities or locations with the intent that they work together in a prescribed way toward goals established by management.

Grievance. A job-related complaint stemming from an injury or injustice, real or imaginary, suffered by an employee for which relief or redress from management is sought.

Group dynamics. The interaction among members of a work group and concurrent changes in their attitudes, behavior, and relationships; similarly, the interaction—in changing attitudes, behavior, and relationships—between a work group and others outside the group.

Group norms. Beliefs held by a group about what is right and what is wrong as far as performance at work is concerned.

Informal work group. A group that forms spontaneously among employees who work near one another, who have common personal interests, or who work toward common job goals, whether or not these goals are the ones set down by management.

Morale. A measure of the extent (either high or low) of voluntary cooperation demonstrated by an individual or a work group and of the intensity of the desire to meet common work goals.

Participation. The technique in which a supervisor or manager shares work-related information, responsibilities, decisions, or all three with the work group. Participation may be used to determine the way a job should be performed, how a group should divide up the work, and what the work goals should be.

Transactional analysis (TA). A way of improving relationships between people that emphasizes communication and is based upon an understanding of each individual's parental, childish, or adult (mature) attitudes toward one another.

READING COMPREHENSION

1. Why should every complaint be treated as if it were important?
2. How specific and conclusive should a supervisor's settlement of a grievance be? How quickly should it be delivered?
3. To what extent are grievances handled differently when there is a formal grievance procedure prescribed by a labor contract?
4. Describe a situation in which you might be a part of both a formal group and an informal group at the same time.
5. Give an example of how a group's norms might differ from the standards of performance set by the company.
6. Why would an experienced supervisor encourage group participation in solving a work problem?
7. What areas of supervision are not usually appropriate for participatory management?
8. Distinguish between competition and conflict in an organization.
9. John and Mary are quarreling over who should have the use of a lift truck first while loading cartons into a truck for shipment. What steps would you take to settle this dispute?
10. Can cooperation be forced on others? Why, or why not?

▪ APPLICATION

SELF-APPRAISAL

How well can you handle complaints and conflicts?

The following statements pertain to complaints and grievances, group dynamics, participation, conflict, and cooperation. Your assignment is to determine which statements are true, or represent sound practice, and which are false, or represent unsound practice. On a separate piece of paper, copy the column headings shown below. In the "Statements" column, write the numbers 1 to 15 down the page to correspond to each of the statements. Then place a check mark in the column that most nearly matches your opinion about each statement. After completing this activity, check your answers by using the scoring procedure described on page 359.

Column headings:

Statements	True, or Sound practice	False, or Unsound practice

1. For a supervisor, a good starting point in handling grievances is to be objective and fair.
2. If a grievance is handled well, the employee will be satisfied with the settlement.
3. Decisions on grievances should be made promptly, even if there isn't time to gather the relevant facts.
4. Jane has established a sound working organization for her employees; she can now be sure that no informal groups will form.
5. Although the practice is not sanctioned by management, employees who stock shelves at the Shop-Now Supermarket make a practice of washing up ten minutes before quitting time. This is an example of a group norm.
6. Informal work groups emerge within formal organizations to satisfy the special interests of their members.
7. Supervisors who invite participation from their employees sacrifice their authority.
8. Sharing—of information, responsibility, and decision making—is at the center of successful participation.
9. Legally regulated matters, such as equal employment opportunity issues, are not usually suitable for participatory management.
10. Bickering and conflict are sure signs of poor morale in an organization.
11. There is only one telephone in Mary's department, and there are five employees who must share it. This is an example of a scarce resource that may cause conflicts among employees.
12. Many conflicts are solved by bargaining and compromise.
13. Transactional analysis is most effective when people are persuaded to discuss their differences from a parental point of view.
14. When employees are paid well for their work, you can be certain that they will cooperate freely.
15. A sensitivity toward the interests and needs of others often opens the door to their cooperation.

Scoring   Give yourself 1 point for each of the following statements that you checked as *true*, or representing sound practice: 1, 5, 6, 8, 9, 11, 12, 15. Give yourself 1 point for each of the following statements that you checked as *false*, or representing unsound practice: 2, 3, 4, 7, 10, 13, 14.

Interpretation   If you scored 13 points or more, you appear to be a pretty good peacemaker. If you scored between 10 and 12 points, you may spend more time than you like settling disputes. Review the items you missed. If you scored less than 10 points, your department may be in a constant state of complaint and conflict. Review the entire chapter.

CASE STUDIES

CASE 45   The Invalid Grievance

Tony Fiori works on the loading dock for the Astro Chemical Company in Greenbelt, New Jersey. When Tony's mother died in Brownsville, Texas, he was granted a three-day emergency leave, in keeping with the company's policy. Tony ended up missing four days because of last-minute changes in the funeral arrangements. He was docked pay for the extra day he missed.

Tony lodged a grievance with his supervisor, Gail Stafford. Tony claimed that events beyond his control led to his missing his fourth day of work. "You may have a point," said Gail. "I'll go to bat for you." Gail then went to the personnel director to discuss the matter. The personnel director showed Gail that the company policy clearly did not allow for an exception. Accordingly, Tony's grievance wasn't valid, and he would have to lose the pay for the extra day missed.

Gail disagreed with that decision, especially since she knew that it would be unpopular with Tony. Nevertheless, the personnel director insisted that the grievance must be denied.

If you were Gail Stafford, how would you proceed next in handling this grievance? Of the five alternatives provided below, which would you prefer most? Rank the alternatives on a scale from 1 (most preferable) to 5 (least preferable). You may add another alternative if you wish. In any event, be prepared to justify your ranking.

a. Put off telling Tony in the hopes that the matter will become less important to him.

b. Tell Tony immediately, letting him know that you disagreed with the decision but that it was based on company policy.

c. Advise Tony that the grievance is still under consideration and that it will be a while before a decision is reached.

d. Convey the decision to Tony right away, explaining why the grievance had to be denied.

e. Since it was his decision, ask the personnel director to convey the settlement to Tony.

CASE 46   Tell Them to Lay Off Me!

Deep in the Ozarks is a knitting mill that moved there from New England during the Great Depression of the mid-1930s. The mill has grown during the last decade, however. From what had been essentially a subcontracting facility, manufacturing its goods for large eastern apparel firms, the mill now operates independently. It produces its own line of sportswear under its own, well-known brand name. Its sales representatives call directly on major department stores and retail chains throughout the country. In many ways, the mill, now known nationally as Linda Kay Fashions, could be considered a major success story.

Inside the home office at Linda Kay Fashions, however, there is a small drama unfolding. In many ways, it has the aspects of a soap opera. Nevertheless, it is a very real situation to its participants.

Here is what is happening. In a group of seven Linda Kay employees who work as a team to receive, record, and process sales orders, Stella is the least productive. Typically, she takes the most time at coffee breaks and spends more time in the lounge than any of the other employees. Yesterday, she complained to the group's supervisor that others in the group were "petty and impossible."

"What makes you say that?" asked the supervisor.

"Because they continually harass me and pressure me for more production."

"Perhaps they are right about your production," said the supervisor.

"Right or wrong," said Stella, "tell them to lay off me. Who is running this department, anyway? You or them?"

a. What do you think of Stella's complaint?

b. What is the problem here?

c. How should the supervisor handle it?

CASE 47   Inviting Participation

Oprah is the newly appointed supervisor of the clients' records department of a large commercial service firm in California. She is to supervise 17 workers; nearly all of these employees have been with the company for some time and have established lasting friendships and informal groups. Oprah wants to invite the employees to participate in decision making at regular meetings she plans to hold. She wants to be sure to use good practice in conducting these meetings.

Your assignment is to prepare a checklist of important ideas for Oprah to review before each meeting. These should help Oprah achieve her goals of productive participation. Use the guidelines given on pages 346 to 348 of the text.

Factors That Encourage Participation

a. Extent of authority: _____

b. Information available: _____

c. Topic areas to cover: _____

d. Suggestions to make: _____

e. Teamwork to stress: _____

f. Credit to be given: _____

g. Other factors: _____

h. Other factors: _____

i. Other factors: _____

1 Good discipline corrects as well as punishes.

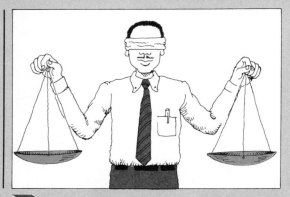

2 Employees accept fair, equitable, and consistent discipline.

3 Positive, progressive, "hot stove" approaches work best.

4 Disciplinary measures must fall within prescribed policies.

5 Discipline must also conform to legal requirements.

CHAPTER 16

How and When to Discipline

LEARNING OBJECTIVES

After studying this chapter, you should be able to

1. Explain the purposes of employee discipline and identify the most common types of offenses that require action.

2. Discuss the range of employee responses to disciplinary action and describe those employees most likely to warrant such action.

3. Differentiate between positive and negative discipline, explain progressive discipline, and know the four elements of the "hot-stove" rule.

4. Discuss the emphasis placed upon behavior rather than personality, list the prescribed steps in the behavior modification approach, and know the limitations placed upon supervisory authority in disciplinary matters.

5. Explain the two criteria for just cause, recognize common pitfalls in administering discipline, and discuss the importance of keeping proper support records.

PURPOSE

CONCEPT   Properly administered discipline corrects as well as punishes, and it helps to develop self-control among employees.

What is the real purpose of discipline?

The real purpose of discipline is quite simple. It is to encourage employees to meet established standards of job performance and to behave sensibly and safely at work. Supervisors should think of discipline as a form of training. Those employees who observe the rules and standards are rewarded by praise, by security, and often by advancement. Those who cannot stay in line or measure up to performance standards are penalized in such a way that they can clearly learn what acceptable performance and behavior are. Most employees recognize this system as a legitimate way to preserve order and safety and to keep everyone working toward the same organizational goals and standards. For most employees, self-discipline is the best discipline. As often as not, the need to impose penalties is a fault of management as well as of the individual worker. For that reason alone, a supervisor should resort to disciplinary action only after all else fails. Discipline should never be used as a show of authority or power on the supervisor's part.

What sort of infractions most typically trigger the need for disciplinary action?

They vary all over the lot. It isn't so much the nature of the infraction, but its degree. A small infraction of some standard or rule may often be tolerated. When the breech becomes large or persistent, however, the need for discipline becomes urgent and obvious.

In addition to poor performance—either of output or quality—infractions that most commonly result in disciplinary action include absenteeism, insubordination, carelessness or negligence, horseplay or fighting, dishonesty or falsification of company records, slowdowns, abusive or obscene language, alcoholism, and drug use or possession.

EMPLOYEE EXPECTATIONS

CONCEPT   Employees will accept discipline when it seems fair and just and when it is applied consistently and equally to all.

When do employees resent discipline?

Employees don't object to the idea of rules and regulations, but they frequently object to the way a supervisor metes out discipline. In civil life, if a person breaks the law, the police officer only makes the arrest. The person is tried before a jury of peers who are guided by the rulings of an impartial judge, who in turn determines the punishment.

Now compare the civil procedure for handling lawbreakers with what happens in the company. As supervisor, you're often called on not only to put the finger on the wrongdoer but also to hear the case and decide the penalty. To many employees this seems unfair because you've acted as police officer, judge, and jury.

So don't take your job as disciplinarian lightly. It's a great responsibility and requires impartiality, good judgment, and courage.

Incidentally, when rules are thought by the work group to be reasonable, the group itself will impose a discipline to keep its members in line.

Why do employees break rules?

As in most personnel problems, only a small percentage of workers cause disciplinary problems. People who break rules do so for a number of reasons—most of them because they are not well adjusted. Contributing personal characteristics include carelessness, lack of cooperation, laziness, dishonesty, lack of initiative, chronic lateness, and lack of effort. The supervisor's job, as a result, is to help employees be better adjusted.

People break rules less often when the supervisor is a good leader, when a sincere interest is shown in employees, when employees get more enjoyment from their work. After all, if an employee finds the work uninteresting and the boss unpleasant, is it surprising that the employee will find reasons for being late or for staying away from work altogether?

Sometimes the real reason an employee breaks rules or seems lazy on the job has nothing at all to do with working conditions. The employee may be having worries at home—money problems or a nagging spouse— or may be physically sick. You might ask, "What concern is that of the supervisor?" It isn't—unless the supervisor wants that employee to be more cooperative and productive at work. If you're smart enough to see the connection, then you can do much to improve this worker's performance. Don't snoop in personal affairs, but do offer a willing and uncritical ear. Let the employee get to know that you're an understanding person, that the boss is someone to talk to without getting a short answer or a lot of phony advice.

So when an employee breaks a rule, make discipline your last resort. Search hard for the reason the employee acts that way. Then try to see what you can do to remove the reason.

What kind of handling do employees expect from a supervisor in the way of discipline?

Justice and equal treatment. Being soft, overlooking nonstandard performance, and giving chance after chance to wrongdoers does not win popularity among most employees. In fact, it works the other way and destroys morale. That's because the majority of people who work hard and stay in line are frustrated and disappointed when they see others get away with things. Of course, no one likes to be punished. But everyone likes to be assured that the punishment received is in line with the error. ("Let the punishment fit the crime" is the advice given in Gilbert and Sullivan's *Mikado*.) No one likes to be treated better or worse than anyone else for the same fault.

3 ADMINISTRATIVE GUIDELINES

CONCEPT   Discipline is most effective when applied positively, progressively, and in accord with the "hot-stove" rule.

Some people talk about negative discipline and say positive discipline is better. What does this mean?

When you have to penalize someone, that's negative. If you can get an employee to do what you wish through constructive criticism or discussion, that's positive.

Supervisors, more than employees, understand that disciplining is an unpleasant task. All a supervisor wants is to run the department in peace and harmony, to see that things get done right, and to ensure that no one gets hurt. The supervisor who can establish discipline through good leadership won't have to exercise negative discipline through scoldings, suspensions, or discharges.

What is meant by progressive discipline?

This means that the penalties for substandard performance or broken rules get increasingly harsh as the condition continues or the infraction is repeated. (See Figure 16-1.) Typically, a first offense may be excused (but not overlooked!) or the worker may be given an oral warning. A second offense elicits a written warning. A third infraction may bring a temporary layoff or a suspension. The final step occurs when an employee is discharged for the fourth (or a very serious) infraction.

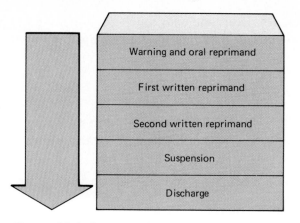

Warning and oral reprimand

First written reprimand

Second written reprimand

Suspension

Discharge

Figure 16-1 Example of steps in progressive discipline.

What is the "hot-stove" rule of discipline?

It is an allegory used to illustrate the four essentials of a good disciplinary policy. (See Figure 16-2.) If the stove is red-hot, you ought to be able to see it and to know that if you touch it, you will be burned; that is the principle of **advance warning.** If you touch the hot stove, you get burned (penalized) right away; that is the principle of **immediacy.** Every time you touch a hot stove, you will get burned; that is the principle of

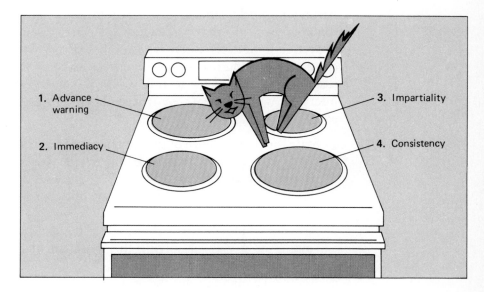

1. Advance warning

2. Immediacy

3. Impartiality

4. Consistency

Figure 16-2 "Hot-stove" rule for discipline.

consistency. Everyone who touches a hot stove will get burned because it plays no favorites; that is the principle of *impartiality.*

[4] SUPERVISORY APPROACHES

CONCEPT   Supervisors must learn to administer discipline firmly, but sensitively, and within prescribed organizational policies.

Can a supervisor administer discipline and still remain on friendly terms with employees?

Yes, but only by focusing on performance, or behavior, not by focusing on personalities or attitudes. Make no mistake: disciplinary action can be an unpleasant experience for supervisor and employee alike. You cannot overlook poor performance or misconduct. Such problems rarely solve themselves. A supervisor must face up to them. Nevertheless, as with grievance handling, a supervisor must listen to an employee's explanation with the intent of understanding before evaluating that point of view. If criticism or action is indicated, make it clear that this is a response to unacceptable practice or conduct. It is not a condemnation of the employee as a person. Your objective is to instill self-control, not to embarrass an individual or to penalize for the sake of punishing.

People speak of a behavior modification approach to discipline. What does that mean?

Behavior modification (BM) prescribes a step-by-step procedure forsupervisors to follow in practicing positive discipline. It is based upon proven assumptions about what makes people most likely to respond constructively to criticism and requests for improvement. The six steps a supervisor should try to follow—in sequence—during a disciplinary interview with an employee are listed below, along with an example of each:

1. **State the performance or disciplinary problem:**   "Lester, you've damaged a lot of merchandise in the warehouse lately by driving the prongs of your lift truck into it."
2. **Ask the employee for his or her view of the problem:**   "Can you tell me why this is happening?"
3. **Ask the employee for a solution to the problem:**   "What can you suggest as a way of solving this problem of damage to merchandise?"
4. **Agree on a plan to solve the problem:**   "Okay, we'll check the brakes on the lift truck, and you'll cut down on your speed and exercise

special care so that damage to merchandise from that cause will be eliminated."

5. **Give the employee an oral or written warning:** "This time, I'll let this problem go with an oral warning. If the problem continues, however, I'll have to place a written warning in your personnel file."

6. **Set up a date for a review:** "Let's hope that the problem has been solved. We'll meet three weeks from now to see what kind of progress has been made."

Note the emphasis upon performance as the problem, not attitude or personality. Note, too, the involvement of the employee in analyzing the problem and offering suggestions—including an improvement in his own behavior—for its solution.

Should the damage continue, this will be reviewed at the next meeting. Step 5 will then include, at the least, a written warning and possibly a more severe penalty, such as notice of suspension or discharge if the condition does not improve.

How far can a supervisor go in handling discipline?

That depends on your company's management policy—and on the labor agreement, if your company has a union.

Legally, a supervisor can hire and fire. But firing is a costly action. Breaking in a new employee can cost anywhere from $500 for an unskilled laborer to several thousand dollars for a skilled mechanic. So most companies have tried to approach discipline from a positive direction. And since discipline puts a supervisor in such a responsible position, many companies have carefully spelled out just how far a supervisor can go before having to check with the boss.

Labor unions, in their desire to provide the maximum protection from injustice or unfair treatment, maintain that discipline shouldn't be handled by management alone. Unions contend that they, too, should help decide on an employee's punishment. How much say a particular union will have depends on how successful the union has been in writing this privilege into the contract or in establishing precedents for its participation.

So tread carefully in disciplinary matters. Find out from your company's policy-level management (your immediate superior or the personnel manager) just how far the company wants you to go—and how much involvement you must allow the union.

What determines the action you should take?

Facts rather than feelings. No one can make a decision without all the facts, or at least all that can be reasonably gathered. If a situation arises that looks as if you've got to take disciplinary action, look hard before you leap. Take time to investigate. Let the employee tell the full story—without interruptions. Check with witnesses for their observations. Look in the company records to see what other supervisors have done in the past. Speak to your boss or the personnel manager to get advice.

For instance, someone tips you off that Will Jones is going to take home a baby Stillson wrench in his lunch box tonight. You stop Will at the time clock. Sure enough—there's the wrench tucked underneath a wad of sandwich wrappers. Your first reaction is to fire Will on the spot for stealing. But should you?

Suppose, on checking, you found any of these circumstances:

- Will had asked the toolroom supervisor for the wrench and received permission to borrow it overnight for a home-repair job.
- Will had told two of his co-workers that he was just borrowing the wrench overnight and planned to return it in the morning.
- Will could prove that the wrench was one he actually had bought himself to use on his job.
- According to the personnel department, the company had agreed with the union not to fire any ten-year employee for petty thefts; the most Will's penalty could be for a first offense would be one day off without pay.

Wouldn't any of these facts change your decision?

How effective are warnings?

Warnings can do a lot of good—if you make them more than idle threats. Your warnings put employees on notice that their performance isn't up to standard. It gives you a chance to explain a rule that they may have taken only lightly before—and to make the penalty clear to them. When you warn employees, that's the perfect time for you to be constructive, to offer help, to practice positive discipline.

To make a warning a valuable piece of evidence in a union grievance, you should always make a written record of it. You'd be surprised how much weight arbitrators and the Equal Employment Opportunity Commission (EEOC) give to notations that you have written in your pocket notebook or the department logbook or have inserted in the employee's personnel file.

Some companies make this written notation a formal practice by requiring that supervisors fill out a form to be filed by the personnel department. These notations are called **written reprimands,** and copies of the reprimand are sent to the employee and the union.

Under what circumstances can you fire an employee?

As mentioned previously, the supervisor's authority is limited by the company's policy and by its agreements with the labor union, if one exists.

Speaking generally, however, some employee offenses are worse than others. Drinking or sleeping on the job, smoking in restricted areas, willfully destroying property, and falsifying time cards are often charges that result in discharge. It is also easier to generalize about offenses such as fighting on company property and gross insubordination. All these wrongdoings have one thing in common—they are single incidents rather than an accumulation of minor offenses, and many of these single acts require immediate action by the supervisor.

To handle any of these serious offenses and still leave yourself free from reversal later on, there's an effective action you can take. It's short of discharge, but it certainly gets the culprit out of the company quickly and legally. This action is called **suspension.** It follows the advice arbitrators give employees: "Obey first—argue later."

To suspend an employee, you merely say something like this: "You've come to work with a load on. I think you're under the influence of liquor right now and are unfit to do your job. You could be subject for dismissal for being in this shape. I haven't made up my mind yet whether that's what I'll do. But in the meantime, you're suspended. Punch out your time card and don't come back to work until I call you. I'll try to let you know definitely tomorrow."

By suspending, you have demonstrated your willingness to enforce your authority when needed. And you have protected both yourself and the company from looking weak, foolish, or indecisive. If tomorrow, in the opinion of your boss, the personnel manager, or the company's lawyer, you can't make the discharge stick, you and the company are still in an effective position. It's when you cast the die—fire an employee and then have to take him or her back—that you have to eat crow.

What consideration should be given to an employee's good work record?

There's danger in carrying the rule book too far. Treating each offender equally does not mean that you should not weigh personal factors too. For instance, what was the worker's attitude when the rule was broken? Was it done deliberately or accidentally? Was the worker emotionally upset by a circumstance beyond control (such as worrying about a sick child at home)? How long has the person worked for the company? What kind of work record has there been? Remember, it costs money to fire a good employee. Even civil courts put on probation a guilty person who has been considered a good citizen in the past.

In many instances, it is also good to wipe an employee's slate clean now and then. For example, if an employee who had a poor absence record two years ago has been near perfect since then, the employee should not have the past record brought up if at a later date there is another absence problem.

5 LEGAL RAMIFICATIONS

CONCEPT   Discipline must conform to various legal requirements and be supported by documentation for just cause.

What are the underlying legal requirements needed to demonstrate just cause for disciplinary action?

There are two requirements, and they apply to almost all situations. There must be

1. **Prior notification of the types of performance or behavior that can lead to disciplinary action.**   The notifications can be either oral or written. It is much better when they have been published and prominently displayed. Company rules and regulations do not cover everything, however. Neither do published standards. That's why it is so important for supervisors to communicate expressly to their employees exactly what the standards of performance and conduct are in their particular work area.
2. **Prior notification of the penalties for unacceptable performance or behavior.** As with the first requirement, notifications of penalties are best when published and prominently displayed. Here again, supervisors should regularly make it clear to employees exactly what these penalties are and when they may be imposed. Where a progressive disciplinary policy is in effect, the steps in the progression should be communicated—in advance—to employees.

When can't you make disciplinary action stick?

When the action has not been carefully planned and documentation gathered to support it. Actions must be based upon genuine evidence, free from bias and discrimination. Impulsive, spiteful actions will backfire. Arbitrators, called in by labor unions to judge poorly conceived charges, are quick to spot weak cases and reject them. So are representatives of the EEOC. Dead beyond recall are the days when supervisors, or any other managers, could resort to discipline without being able to support their charges beyond a doubt.

As difficult as the disciplinary problem has become, however, most penalties and discharges can be made to stick—provided the supervisor makes none of the following mistakes:

No clear-cut breach of rule. In one company a supervisor fired an employee for sleeping, only to see the decision reversed by the arbitrator. The union brought out the fact that the supervisor had made the observation from 60 feet away. The arbitrator ruled that at this distance the supervisor was "likely to see what he wanted to see."

Inadequate warning. Arbitrators frequently feel that workers are entitled to sufficient warning that their conduct won't be tolerated—even though the rules and penalties are in an employee manual. Typical is the case of an employee who has had a record of poor attendance for months without having been disciplined; suddenly the supervisor cracks down without warning and fires the employee.

Lack of positive evidence. Take this case of loafing—always a difficult charge to make stick: The company went along with the supervisor and fired a worker caught loafing. The arbitrator reversed the company's decision because (1) the supervisor had not been in the department continually but had popped in and out during one afternoon and (2) the person's job entailed occasional waits for material. Furthermore, the company could produce no time sheets that showed reduced output in black and white. The arbitrator ruled that the supervisor might have come into the department at the times the employee had been legitimately waiting for materials.

Prejudice. Real or imagined discrimination or favoritism weakens a disciplinary ruling. If a supervisor has shown that she had it in for a worker and just waited for an opportunity to enforce a penalty, an arbitration case may bring this out. If the supervisor has let some workers get away with the same offense for which she punishes another, she'll have a hard time justifying such unequal treatment.

Inadequate records. The value of written records of warnings and reprimands can't be overemphasized. It's especially valuable for documenting action taken to correct an accumulation of minor offenses. You may not want to discharge a person who's been late the first time—or even the fifth. But when it gets to be a frequent and costly habit, you'll want to take action. Unless you've built up a record of warnings and kept a file of them that can be shown to the union and an arbitrator if necessary, your case will be hard to prove.

Too-severe punishment. Many arbitrators recommend progressive punishment and look unfavorably on too-severe discipline—especially for first offenses. For instance, a supervisor in a can company noticed a worker away from his workstation ten minutes before the end of the shift. A look at the employee's time card showed that he had punched out a half minute early. The man was fired because not long before that he had received a written reprimand for doing the same thing. He had been warned that the next time he'd be fired. An arbitrator ruled that a penalty was called for—but not such a severe one. Do it progressively, the arbitrator said—just a little tougher each time. A lighter penalty would keep an old (seven years' service) and valuable employee on the payroll.

Violation of policy or labor contract. Care should always be taken to ensure that infractions and discipline accurately reflect a company's established policies and/or, if a union is present, provisions of the labor contract.

How can you make sure that your records will support a disciplinary action?

By taking care to make the proper records at each step of a progressive disciplinary action. Follow carefully your company's policies and procedures in this matter. The legal concept of **due process** is gradually taking hold in all areas of employment, especially those involving job security. This means that all employees, regardless of union representation, are entitled to a fair and just hearing under adequate legal protection. Under such circumstances, a supervisor's opinions and recollections will not carry much weight. They will have to be supported by specific documentation. Records that help to provide this documentation include:

- **Regularly kept records,** such as time cards showing absences and latenesses, visits to the dispensary, production and quality-control tallies, and the like.
- **Written complaints** from customers or other contacts that can be identified without qualification with the individual who is to be disciplined.
- **Examples of unsatisfactory or careless work,** including mistyped letters, incorrect tabulations on reports, damaged goods—all tagged or marked in such a way as to identify the culpable individual.
- **Written summaries of appraisal and/or disciplinary conferences,** which should contain specific rather than general statements, including dates, figures, and clearly described incidents. The hard part here is that the law seems to say that copies of these reports (which are retained in personnel records) must be given to the individual at the time they are written.

- Dr. George Sutcliffe of Piedmont Community College, Virginia, urges every supervisor to maintain a daily diary of infractions: whenever an incident occurs, the supervisor should make a "personal critical incident" notation regarding the employee involved. Since the incidents are recorded while fresh in the supervisor's mind, they help not only in conducting performance appraisal interviews but also in justifying and supporting later disciplinary action.

REVIEW

KEY CONCEPTS TO REMEMBER

1. Most employees exert the necessary self-control to keep themselves out of trouble. Only a few employees find it difficult either (a) to meet work standards or (b) to conform to the rules and regulations imposed by an organized activity. Accordingly, effective discipline is aimed not so much at punishing bad performance as at encouraging good performance. As such, discipline should be looked upon as a form of training. Its objective is to help wayward employees develop their own self-control so that they are not drawn over the line that separates acceptable from unacceptable behavior.

2. When exerting discipline, supervisors are placed in the unenviable role of acting as police officer, judge, and jury. Employees will accept discipline from their supervisors, however, when it appears to be fair and just and consistently applied.

3. Effective discipline should be an essentially positive effort. Its three hallmarks are (a) punishment that is suitable to the importance of the offense, (b) penalties that become progressively severe as offenses are repeated, and (c) discipline that follows the "hot-stove" rule (that is, discipline should be given only if there has been adequate warning, and it should be immediate, consistent, and impartial).

4. The supervisor's role in maintaining discipline requires unusual self-control, objectivity, and integrity. Not only must the supervisor identify and apprehend transgressors, but he or she must also determine the nature and the extent of the guilt and impose the penalties. Such judgments involve (a) full examination of mitigating circumstances, (b) sensitivity to each individual's characteristic response to correction or encouragement, and (c) consideration of past and improved performance.

5. Disciplinary actions are increasingly subject to legal scrutiny for implications of prejudice or discrimination. For such actions to measure up to the test of just cause, two criteria must be met: (a) prior notification of what constitutes unacceptable behavior and (b) prior notification of what the penalties for this behavior will be. Accordingly, care should be taken to see that there has been a clear-cut breach of a rule or standard, adequate warning, positive evidence, absence of prejudice, written records, and a penalty in line with the infraction. Employees are entitled to, and expect, due process; they are represented in this regard by labor unions and by the EEOC and other federal, state, and local agencies.

SUPERVISORY WORD POWER

Discipline. The imposition of a penalty by management on an employee for the infraction of a company rule, regulation, or standard in such a manner as to encourage more constructive behavior and to discourage a similar infraction in the future.

Due process. An employee's legal entitlement to a fair hearing, usually before an impartial party and with appropriate representation, before discipline can be meted out.

Just cause. A reason for disciplinary action that is accurate, appropriate, well founded, deserved, and meets the test of prior notification of unacceptable behavior and its penalty.

Penalty. A punishment or forfeiture imposed by management on an employee in order to impose discipline. Typically, such penalties include suspensions, loss of time and/or pay, demotion, or loss of job—that is, discharge.

Reprimand. A severe expression of disapproval or censure by management of an employee, usually written as well as oral, and retained in an employee's personal file.

Suspension. The temporary removal by management of a privilege (particularly the right to report to work and receive pay for it) from an employee until the proper penalty for a rule infraction has been determined and imposed.

Warning. A reprimand so worded as to give formal notice to an employee that repetition of a particular form of unacceptable behavior, such as infraction of a rule, will draw a penalty.

READING COMPREHENSION

1. Why might a well-behaved employee appreciate the presence of disciplinary regulations in the workplace?
2. Discuss the similarities between rules and regulations at work and in civil life.
3. In what way does the enforcement of discipline at work differ from that in civil life?
4. Distinguish between negative discipline and positive discipline.
5. When Carlos saw Jane sneaking out early again, he fired her on the spot, even though he hadn't given her any prior warning. The discharge didn't stick, and Carlos was advised to use progressive discipline in future cases. How might he do that?
6. The "hot-stove" rule is meant to help supervisors remember four important points about discipline. Briefly describe each.
7. What kinds of restraints may be placed upon a supervisor's authority to handle discipline independently?
8. Explain the difference between suspension and firing, or discharge, of an employee.
9. In order for disciplinary action to be supported by just cause, what two basic requirements must be met?
10. Why are written notations regarding warnings of possible, or actual, disciplinary action so important?

APPLICATION

SELF-APPRAISAL

How effective is Rita's disciplinary action likely to be?

Toby, a checkout clerk in a convenience store, has repeatedly made costly errors in ringing up sales. His boss, Rita Kahn, has approached the problem in various ways, as her statements on page 378 indicate. Your assignment is to determine whether Rita's disciplinary actions are likely or unlikely to be effective in correcting Toby's performance. On a separate piece of paper, copy the following column headings. In the column "What Rita Said to Toby," write the numbers 1 to 10 down the page to correspond to each of Rita's statements. Then place a check mark in the column that most nearly matches your opinion of each of Rita's approaches, as reflected in the statement. After completing this activity, check your answers by using the scoring procedure described below.

Column headings:

What Rita Said to Toby	Likely to Be Effective	Unlikely to Be Effective

1. "Clerks who avoid mistakes at the checkout counter get the more attractive shift assignments."
2. "An occasional mistake of 5 or 10 cents is reasonable on this job, not sizable ones of a dollar or more, especially if they are frequent."
3. "I'll show you what to be careful about so that you can avoid being penalized for ringing up the wrong sales."
4. "The rules about misrings are considered to be fair by the other clerks. You can check this out."
5. "We may overlook these misrings with some clerks, but not with those who don't show a real interest in the company."
6. "As far as I'm concerned, Toby, only careless people like yourself make misrings."
7. "I've noticed several times in the last month that you've been underringing sales on our dairy items, but I just haven't found the time to speak to you about it until now."
8. "What suggestions can you make, Toby, to avoid your making misrings on products that have fluctuating prices?"
9. "I'll make a notation in my files that you have received a warning that continued misrings of over a dollar will be considered justification for suspension."
10. "Now that I've spoken to you about this matter, we can forget about it unless it comes up again in the future."

Scoring   Give Rita 1 point for each item that you marked as *likely to be effective*. Give her no points for items that you marked as *unlikely to be effective*.

Interpretation   The experts' judgment is that Rita's discipline will be only somewhat effective. She has stumbled in four vital areas. Here's the way they scored it: *likely to be effective* for items 1, 2, 3, 4, 8, and 9; *unlikely to be effective* for all other items. If you marked nine or more items correctly, you are likely to make a good start in administering effective discipline. If you marked seven or eight items correctly, you may encounter some problems in establishing effective discipline. Review the items you missed. If you marked less than seven items correctly, discipline is unlikely to be effective under your supervision. Review the entire chapter.

CASE STUDIES

CASE 48　The Dozing Delivery Person

Bobbie Barra is a recent community-college graduate who works as a jack-of-all-help for a small auto parts distributor in Colorado. His job calls for him to do a little of everything, from stocking shelves and analyzing inventory reports to driving the delivery van. The work is not particularly challenging, but it was the best job that Bobbie could find in this ski area, which is especially attractive to him. Bobbie admits that he'd rather ski than work, and this has begun to show in his work. When the opportunity presents itself, Bobbie leaves work early or reports in late. During the day, he roams through the warehouse talking about downhill runs with the shipping clerks. When Bobbie's job calls for making small deliveries around town, he takes more time than seems reasonable. His usual excuse is, "Traffic was terrible today!"

Bobbie's supervisor, Stanley Kovacs, is usually forgiving, but last week, Bobbie really ticked him off. A dealer, to whom Bobbie had made a delivery, called Stanley and asked if he knew that his driver had been sleeping for the last two hours in the company van, which was parked in the dealer's lot. When Stanley confronted Bobbie with this upon his return, Bobbie pleaded: "Don't get mad at me. I was only dozing for a minute or so. I was up late last night on the slopes and I just couldn't keep my eyes open. You wouldn't want me to drive the company van when I'm half asleep, would you?"

If you were Bobbie's boss, what would you do? Of the five alternatives provided below, which would you choose? Rank the alternatives on a scale from 1 (most preferable) to 5 (least preferable). You may add another alternative if you wish. In any event, be prepared to justify your ranking.

a. Ask your boss to speak to Bobbie so that Bobbie can see just how important it is to improve his behavior.

b. Tell Bobbie that sleeping on the job is carrying a good thing too far. Explain that taking more time than is reasonable on deliveries is occasionally all right, but tell him that if he's caught sleeping again, you'll recommend his discharge.

c. Tell Bobbie he's suspended as of now. Explain that another employee will be assigned to his work until a final decision is reached.

d. Tell him that from now on you won't tolerate any goofing off of any kind. Warn him that the next time he roams around the shop or takes too long with deliveries, you'll initiate disciplinary action.

e. Advise Bobbie that his performance is making you lose respect for him: he is showing himself to be thoughtless and inconsiderate.

Sissy Spotswood, a records clerk in a large federal agency, has been found guilty of gross negligence. Her errors on processing insurance claims have totaled several thousand dollars. The union representing Sissy agrees that this is the case. Sissy's supervisor wants to fire her. In similar cases in the past, that is what has been done. Higher management, however, now suggests a different form of discipline. It recommends that Sissy be demoted to a lower-paying job where she will have practically no chance of making damaging errors in the future. When Sissy reacted negatively to this offer, management said, "Take it or leave it!"

a. What do you think of this alternative?
b. Will the supervisor's authority suffer as a result?
c. How do you think the union will respond?

CASE 50   The Safety Reprimand

Juan Carli had been given an oral warning once before to keep the safety gates up surrounding a giant bar-cutting machine in the special-order metal department. Other workers passing on the walkway near the cutter could be injured if the cut bar kicked out even a foot. Yet once again, Ellen Eaves, Juan's supervisor, started down the walkway and saw that the gates were down. Ellen said: "Juan, I've warned you about the safety gates before. This time I'm going to give you a formal reprimand." When Ellen got back to her office a few minutes later, she began filling out the form shown in Figure 16-3. Your assignment is to complete (on a separate piece of paper) the form as if you were Juan's supervisor.

> **Notice of Reprimand**
>
> Department: _____
> Name of employee reprimanded: _____
> Supervisor: _____
> Date of offense: _____
> Date of reprimand: _____
>
> Nature of violation:
> ☐ Production delay   ☐ Safety violation
> ☐ Material wastage   ☐ Administrative violation
> Description of violation: _____
> _____
>
> Comments: _____
> _____

Figure 16-3 Notice-of-reprimand form.

Improving Departmental Productivity

1 Productivity measures compare output with input.

2 Technical and/or human factors can improve productivity.

3 Improved productivity begins with time measurements.

4 Systematic improvement comes from improved work methods.

5 Creative employees are good sources for better work methods.

CHAPTER 17

Improving Productivity and Innovation

LEARNING OBJECTIVES

After studying this chapter, you should be able to

1. Calculate productivity ratios and percentages and understand the relationships of outputs and inputs to rising or falling productivity rates.

2. Recognize the differing potentials of human factors and technological factors for productivity improvement.

3. Describe the principle of work measurement and the principle of, and procedure for, work sampling.

4. Understand and describe various approaches to methods improvement, including motion economy and value analysis.

5. Explain various approaches to creative thinking and innovation, including free association of ideas, brainstorming, and intrapreneurship.

▣ UNDERSTANDING PRODUCTIVITY

CONCEPT   Productivity measures how much output is being created by a given set of inputs.

What is productivity?

There are many definitions and most of them are complex. Yet productivity is a very simple and vital concept. Dr. C. Jackson Grayson, chair of the American Productivity Center, says it best of all: "Productivity is the process of getting more out of what you put in. It's doing better with what you have."

How is it measured?

Technically, **productivity** is a measure of how efficient a person or an operation is; it is determined by comparing (1) the value of the output result with (2) the cost of the input resource. It is usually expressed as a ratio (or rate):

$$\text{Productivity} = \frac{\text{output}}{\text{input}}$$

For example, productivity of a hand-assembly department in a furniture factory might be stated as five chairs per labor hour. The number of chairs is the output; the labor expended is the input. If the furniture factory wished, it could convert both figures to dollars. If so, the value added to the chairs by the assembly operation might be estimated at $3 each, or a total of $15. If an assembler is paid $5 an hour, then the productivity of the assembly operation would be $15 divided by $5, or 3:1.

Ratios can also be converted to percentages, and some companies state productivity that way. For instance, the 3:1 ratio is 300 percent and the 2:1 ratio is 200 percent. Very often you will hear productivity compared to what it was previously. This is usually expressed as a percentage increase or decrease. For example, if your department's productivity ratio was 2:1 last year and improved to 2.2:1 this year, it would be correct to say that your productivity had improved by 10 percent:

$$(2.2 - 2.0) \div 2.0 = 0.10 = 10\%$$

How can supervisors tell how good their departmental productivity is?

Few people can say for sure what is good or bad. But you can easily tell whether your productivity is improving or falling off. There are four basic possibilities, as shown in Figure 17-1:

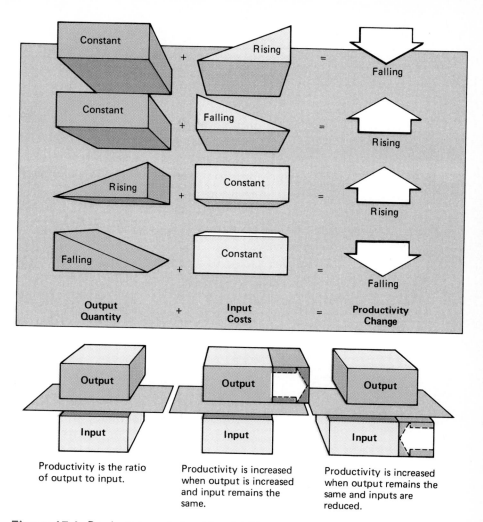

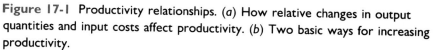

| Output Quantity | + | Input Costs | = | Productivity Change |

Productivity is the ratio of output to input.

Productivity is increased when output is increased and input remains the same.

Productivity is increased when output remains the same and inputs are reduced.

Figure 17-1 Productivity relationships. (*a*) How relative changes in output quantities and input costs affect productivity. (*b*) Two basic ways for increasing productivity.

- If output remains the same but costs go up, productivity is *falling*.
- If output remains the same but costs go down, productivity is *rising*.
- If output goes up and costs remain the same, productivity is *rising*.
- If output goes down and costs remain the same, productivity is *falling*.

If output and productivity both change, you will have to use this formula: Productivity equals output value divided by input costs.

Are productivity considerations limited to manufacturing operations?

No. The same principle applies everywhere. In many clerical and service operations, productivity measures are made exactly as in manufacturing. A typist's productivity, for example, would be the number of letters or lines typed per hour worked. A supermarket checkout counter clerk's output would be the number of items checked (or dollars taken in) a day. A bank teller's productivity would be the number of transactions handled an hour, day, week, or month.

The only limit to the application of productivity is the need to obtain a reliable measurement of output. It is difficult, for example, to measure the value of a nurse's output, although many hospitals talk about the number of patients tended by one nurse per shift as a measure of productivity.

Another factor to watch is the impact that quality demands have on productivity. If quality requirements are raised, output may drop accordingly. Or, if product specifications are loosened, output may rise solely because of this change and not represent a real improvement in productivity.

2 HUMAN FACTORS

CONCEPT   Productivity can be made to increase as a direct result of improving technological or human contributions, or both.

What factors can contribute to productivity improvement?

There are two basic ingredients that supervisors can work on to improve productivity.

Technological Factors   These include:

- **Product or service design.**   Some things are easier to make or deliver than others.
- **Plant and equipment.**   Up-to-date and well-maintained facilities and equipment make a big difference in productivity.
- **Mechanization.** The introduction of automation, computer controls, robots, and the like, increases speed, precision, and efficiency.
- **Process layout and methods.**   Congestion and backtracking hinder productivity; order and unimpeded flow accelerate it.
- **Condition of materials.**   Presorted and stacked parts speed machine loading. Carbonless forms with preprinted routing instructions improve typing efficiency.

- **Extent of power used.** Electricity, steam, compressed air, fuel—these all apply leverage to human effort.

Human Factors   The obvious ones are ability, knowledge, and motivation. What is not so clear is the extent to which dozens of other people-oriented factors are important. Among those that deserve attention are individual education, experience, levels of aspiration, work schedules, training, organizational groupings, personnel policies, leadership, and—very important—pay practices.

What may not be so important as was once thought is the physical environment, but it cannot be ignored.

See Figure 17-2 for an indication of the relative input of human factors in operations with varying degrees of technology.

What role does employee job satisfaction play in improving productivity?

It is the most important factor not yet fully exploited. In high-technology industries—such as petroleum refining—job satisfaction may be a smaller, though still vital, factor than technology. In most work, however, there is an increasing need to place major emphasis on the role of job satisfaction. In the long run, people control the work pace. They can be devilishly clever in thwarting machines.

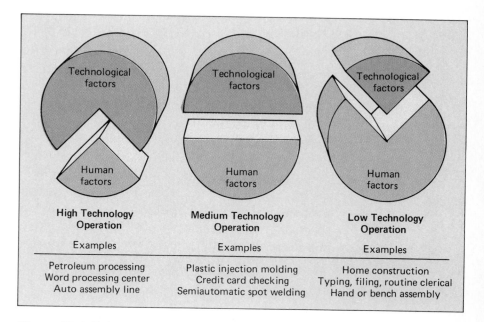

Figure 17-2 Relative impact of human factors on productivity as compared with impact of technology factors.

Supervisors must try to match jobs with each person's own kind of job satisfaction. Productivity gets its strongest boost from the human side when supervisors support employees in their individual search for job satisfaction. The trick, of course, is to balance employees' needs for satisfaction with the organization's need for productivity and cost control.

In what ways is the Quality-Circle movement related to the human element in productivity improvement?

It is at the heart of it. As you'll see in the detailed discussion of Quality Circles that appears in Chapter 18, that movement, which began as a way to improve quality by involving concerned employees, quickly showed that its benefits spilled over into productivity improvements as well. In fact, in many organizations, quality circles are aimed as much at productivity as they are at quality.

3 WORK MEASUREMENT

CONCEPT   The foundation stone of productivity improvement is a knowledge of how much time it takes to get a particular job done.

What has work measurement got to do with productivity improvement?

It is the foundation stone of productivity improvement. Work—human effort—is the basic input in a great many processes. Unless you have a good idea of how much work is entailed, it is almost impossible to know where to look for productivity improvements or to tell whether or not you've accomplished anything when you're through. **Work measurement** is the term generally applied to any method of determining how long it takes to do a job. Work measurement usually refers to how long it would take an individual (or group of individuals) to perform a specific task. However, when a worker is assisted by, or paced by, a machine, this may also be considered. Since human accomplishment is affected by how much physical effort and skill go into a job, work measurement usually takes those factors into account too.

What are the main ways in which work is measured?

Making *time studies* of the actual job as it is performed (using some sort of stopwatch) is by far the most common way. Other methods range from rough-and-ready measures to ultrasophisticated techniques.

The crudest measures involve simply looking at historical records that show how much an employee has produced in a day, week, or month.

The most elaborate approach uses tiny building blocks of time units based on *motion studies.* Experts add the time for every motion required on a job (lifting, pulling, straightening, and so forth) to find the total time needed. The measuring units are called *predetermined elemental time standards.* These are referred to with a variety of proprietary names, such as MTM, Work Factor, and ZIP Standard Data.

Still another very useful method for work measurement is work sampling, which will be described below and on pages 390 to 391. This method is especially suitable for supervisory use, although many work improvement analysts rely on it almost exclusively.

Whatever the work measurement technique—precise or rough-and-ready—the times that are found become time standards, or simply *standards.* These standards for various jobs are accumulated in a company's record files or are often available (for jobs commonly performed in commerce and industry) for purchase from consulting firms.

How is work measurement data used?

Time data is widely used for a number of practical purposes. It enables managers and supervisors to:

1. Estimate accurately how long future jobs will take.
2. Establish reliable work schedules.
3. Provide employees with specific work standards in terms of either (a) time allowed to get a job done or (b) number of output units that must be produced in a certain time period.
4. Estimate the labor costs for products to be made or services to be performed.
5. Provide a basis for employee wages, especially those that include extra pay (wage incentives) for work that exceeds the time standard.
6. Provide fundamental measures for productivity.

What is work sampling? How good is it?

Work sampling is a rough-and-ready approach to work measurement. It is relatively easy to do. It has some shortcomings, but it is especially suitable for supervisors who wish to get a quick idea of the productivity of their departments.

Work sampling (also called *ratio delay*) is accomplished by making random observations of various activities in the work area. It enables a supervisor to find the proportion of delays and interruptions that occur as related to the total time required to do a job. For instance, if you wanted to find out how much of the time a lift truck was actually out of operation, you'd visit the truck a predetermined number of times a day, say, ten. These visits would not be at regular intervals; they would be at random. If in ten days you made 100 observations, and if during 23 of them the truck was idle, it would be statistically safe to conclude that the truck was idle 23 percent of the time. You could make the same sort of study on any number of items—as long as you make enough observations and the observations are made at random. If one were to make observations every hour on the hour, this would introduce a pattern that might bias the results.

How is a work sampling study conducted?

The observer records what each employee is doing at the instant the employee is observed. The record is made by checking a box under each of a set of previously determined categories. Different categories are used by different companies, but a fairly typical list might be

Working. This means actually performing work—running a machine, using a tool, entering records, and so forth.

Preparing to work. Under this heading would come such things as observing a job to determine how to proceed, listening to instructions, and asking questions relative to the job.

Travel. This would include getting tools or supplies and walking or riding to the job in the case of, say, a maintenance worker who is sent out from a central location or a clerk going to and from a copying machine.

Delay. This category is usually for delays for which the employee is not responsible—waiting for materials or waiting for some other worker to finish part of the job.

Idle. This is time for which the worker is responsible—time spent talking (not about the job), "roaming," or simply looking off into space. Table 17-1 illustrates a fairly detailed work sampling study of typical clerical operations.

Do employees object to work sampling?

Not usually, if it is properly explained to them beforehand. They should be told that the purpose is not to check up on individual employees but to determine what management can do to make it possible for them to work more steadily and effectively. Excessive travel, for example, may show the need for more convenient location of tools and supplies; waiting for other employees may indicate a need for better scheduling. If

Table 17-1   EXAMPLE OF WORK SAMPLING STUDY OF CLERICAL EMPLOYEES

Observation Sheet

	9:09	9:57	11:18	1:15	2:43	3:11	3:52	4:21	4:39
Chavez	7	8	1	1	3	5	6	3	1
Yost	2	1	6	4	1	3	7	6	2
Albers	7	4	5	1	8	1	1	3	8
Dowdy	7	8	7	4	1	1	2	1	8
Rozetti	4	1	2	5	7	5	1	4	1

Random Observation Times

Activity Category Code Numbers

1. Keyboarding
2. Taking dictation
3. Transcribing from machine
4. Clerical activity at desk
5. Away from desk, but in office
6. Talking, telephoning
7. Personal
8. Not in office

Date: _____7/21_____   Supervisor (Observer): _____F. Diehl_____

Summary of 990 Observations

Category	Number of Observations	Percentage of Observations
1. Keyboarding	487	49.2
2. Taking dictation	23	2.3
3. Transcribing from machine	86	8.7
4. Clerical activity at desk	71	7.2
5. Away from desk, but in office	36	3.6
6. Talking, telephoning	68	6.9
7. Personal	113	11.4
8. Not in office	106	10.7

there is excessive idle time because employees are loafing on the job, the supervisor will realize that control must be tightened. Generally, however, sampling shows that the delays for which the employee is *not* responsible account for the greatest amount of wasted time.

14 METHODS IMPROVEMENT

CONCEPT   The systematic way for increasing productivity is to improve the methods used for performing work.

What is implied by the term *methods improvement?*

Any change in the way a task is performed so that it lowers the cost, shortens the time, or improves the quality of the product or service provided by the task is called a **methods improvement.** The *process* of methods improvement is simply the organized use of common sense to find better ways of doing work.

Methods improvement has many names, and it takes many forms. It may be known as work simplification, time-and-motion study, operations analysis, methods engineering, systems engineering, methods and systems analysis (especially for clerical and service work), waste reduction, motion economy, or even quality circles.

Methods improvement has been applied by expert and novice alike to such diverse fields as construction, supermarkets, and endless paperwork systems in offices. Lillian Gilbreth, a noted pioneer in work simplification, made great improvements in hospital care by rearranging nurses' stations and by simplifying food service, housekeeping, and patient care activities.

The methods improvement process has many variations. It is usually effected, however, by observing each minute segment of a job and then examining these segments for ways to do the job better as a whole. That's the kind of "up-close, small-scale" methods improvement we'll talk about here. There are, of course, many other approaches (involving large-scale application of automation and computers) that are used effectively by methods engineers and other analysts. For your part, however, you'll need no stopwatch, video camera, or computer—only pencil and paper, some guidelines we'll provide you with, good judgment, patience, and ingenuity.

What kinds of questions can lead you to find opportunities to improve productivity or cut costs?

Ask challenging questions—questions that probe into every detail. You are probably familiar with Rudyard Kipling's famous poem:

> I keep six honest serving men
> They taught me all I knew;
> Their names are What and Why and When
> And How and Where and Who.

This often-quoted poem is your personal key to work simplification. Use it to remind yourself to ask:

- **Why** is the job done in the first place? Perhaps the job can be cut out altogether. Why is each of the details necessary? Give the third degree to each step. Is it really a must, or is it done "because we've always done it that way"?
- **What** is done? Have you recorded each detail so that you actually know? When operators pick up a part, for instance, they may not only be picking it up, they may be aligning it for insertion into the machine or feeling the surface for burrs.
- **Where** is the work done? Why is it done at that place? Where could it be done better, faster, more cheaply, more easily?
- **When** is it done? Why is it done then? When should it be done to do it better, faster, more cheaply, more easily?
- **Who** does it? Why does this person do it? Who might be better equipped, be better trained, have more available time to do it more cheaply?
- **How** is it done? Why do we do it this way? How could the method be improved by doing two or more operations at once, by mechanizing it, by using a fixture?

In what phase of a job does the greatest room for improvement lie?

In the operations that actually do something to the product or service—shape it, change it, add to it in any way that makes it worth more. These operations are called the value-added operations because they add to the value of the product or service. Look at each job as if it were divided into three steps:

Makeready. This includes the effort and the time that go into setting up the equipment or the machine or placing the parts in the machine. A painter makes ready to paint a house by mixing the paint, raising the ladder, spreading the drop cloths, and so forth.

Do. This is the actual work that adds value to the product. A painter adds value to the house by putting a coat of paint on it. A worker adds value to a piece of $\frac{1}{8}$-inch iron rod by cutting it into 2-inch lengths for bolts. Value is added by heading it. And value is added again when threads are cut on the other end.

Put-away. This phase covers anything that's done after the "do" is finished. It includes unloading, disposing, storage, transfer, cleanup. The painter puts away by taking down the ladder, removing the drop cloth, cleaning up any spots on the floor, washing the brushes, and storing the materials and equipment.

The reason you're advised to concentrate on a "do" operation is that if you eliminate it, you automatically eliminate the makeready and the put-away associated with it.

How can you develop new and better methods?

Uncovering delays and finding out what's wrong are valuable accomplishments, and their worth shouldn't be minimized. But this effort doesn't pay off until you've devised a better way to do the job. There are many approaches from which to choose:

Eliminate. First look for the chance of dropping out a part of or the entire operation. There's no point in wasting time improving methods if the job doesn't have to be done at all.

Combine. Doing two or more things at once saves time. Often it saves additional time by eliminating the transportation, storage, and inspection that previously took place between operations.

Change sequence. Frequently you can do things more easily or cheaply by changing the order in which they are done. For example, it is best to finish a part only after the shaping operations have been completed.

Simplify. After you've searched the first three approaches in this list, look for ways of doing the job in a simpler manner. Here's where you try to cut down on wasted motions, replace hand operations with mechanical ones, and provide fixtures for positioning and chutes for feeding. But remember, don't try to simplify until you've first tried to eliminate, combine, or change sequence.

In what ways does motion economy help improve productivity?

Motion economy is the use of the human body to produce results with the least physical and mental effort. It's been given long study by methods engineers and physiologists. Here are some of the principles of motion economy that are generally agreed on as aids to getting a job done with the least labor:

- **Motions should be productive.** Every motion a person makes should be concentrated on "do" operations that bring the job closer to a finish. Hands, for instance, should not be wasted in holding the work; they should be released for more value-added operations.

- **Motions should be simple.** The fewer parts of the body used, the better. Use a finger and a thumb rather than the whole hand. Grasp an object by reaching with the forearm rather than with the whole arm. Motions should be along curved paths rather than straight lines, because most of the body members swing from joints in a circular motion.

- **Motions should be rhythmic.**   Arrange the work so that it's easy to work with smooth motions. It's easier, too, for hands to move in opposite directions and in similar motion paths.

- **Make workers comfortable.**   The workbench, the keyboard, the chair should all be arranged so that the operator feels comfortable whether the work requires sitting or standing or walking.

- **Combine two or more tools.**   Picking up and laying down tools takes time. It's quicker to reverse a tool with a working edge on either end than to pick up and lay down two separate tools.

- **Pre-position tools and materials.**   Having things arranged so that they are already aligned before the operator picks them up speeds the job. If a form needs to be turned over or around, the job needs positioning.

- **Limit activity.** A person works comfortably within the swing of the arms forward and up and down. If the person has to reach or stretch beyond that normal work area, turn around, bend, or stoop, it takes time and is fatiguing.

- **Use gravity when possible.**   Materials can be fed by gravity through bins and chutes. The part then comes out the bottom of the chute right at the worker's hand each time.

Who takes care of automation?

The highly engineered and/or large-scale approaches to improving productivity are usually the responsibility of engineering specialists and computer systems people. *Automation*—once thought of as simply a form of stepped-up mechanization with a degree of self-control in the process—has exploded in some industries. In fact, hundreds of thousands of fully automatic devices called *robots* are already in place in hundreds of manufacturing plants. But it is the computer that has made the big difference. It has enabled engineers to look at an entire process—department-sized or even plant-sized—and to tie the scheduling and operation of dozens of separate machines and subprocesses into a whole. When this happens, the term applied is *computer-assisted manufacturing, computer-integrated manufacturing,* or, sometimes, *data-integrated manufacturing.* Productivity gains of better than 50 percent are commonplace as a result of using such automated systems.

Similarly, *office automation* links together by means of computers any number of previously independent clerical and administrative activities. Methods improved this way have triggered large gains in the productivity of offices and of paperwork operations.

Supervisors may or may not have an opportunity to make significant inputs into automation decisions. One thing is sure, however: supervisors are the ones who will be charged with making automation work. As a consequence, supervisors will be expected to ease the problems associated with shop-floor changes, to counsel employees about relocations and displacements, and to train them to handle the new system.

Where does value analysis fit into this picture?

To our way of thinking, *value analysis* (also called **value engineering**) is simply productivity improvement focused on a product rather than on a process. However, Lawrence D. Miles, who conceived of value analysis while at the General Electric Company in 1947, defined it this way: "Value analysis is an arrangement of techniques which makes clear the functions the user wants; establishes the appropriate costs for each; then causes the required knowledge, creativity, initiative to be used to provide each function at that cost."

Miles's "functions" are of two classes: use and esteem. The use function provides the action that customers want from the product or service. An esteem function pleases them and causes them to buy it. Take an automobile. Use function: transportation. Esteem function: chromium trim.

The objective of value analysis is to keep the use and the esteem functions that customers want—but at a lower cost. Value analysts do not directly lower cost. They only provide criteria for decision makers (including supervisors) whose actions will lower cost. A value analysis study usually consists of five phases:

1. Gathering information to identify functions
2. Creating ideas to serve functions at less cost
3. Evaluating ideas for practicality
4. Investigating sources of supply and improvement
5. Reporting findings to decision makers

5 INNOVATION AND CREATIVITY

CONCEPT   Creative supervisors and employees are valuable sources of innovative ideas for improving work methods.

Where do work improvement ideas come from?

From supervisors, their employees, and methods improvement specialists. The best and most practical ideas for small scale work improvements are most likely to come from first-line management. One authority has estimated that one work improvement idea from a supervisor is worth ten from another employee. That's because the supervisor has a better overview of the job than a worker does. An astute supervisor can see the forest as well as the trees.

In many companies a methods department is staffed by methods engineers whose job is to simplify and improve work procedures. They help supervisors do a better job of lowering costs. They need your cooperation in spotting cost-cutting targets and in making the improved methods work after they are installed. You should form a habit of working hand in hand with the people in the methods department. You can do a lot for them, and they can do much for you.

Do you have to be a special sort of genius to think up good ideas?

No. Although it used to be supposed that creative imagination was a gift that a few lucky individuals possessed, research seems to prove otherwise. All of us are born with an ability to be innovative or creative to some degree. The trouble is that we have not made enough use of it—or have been discouraged from using it.

Exactly what is creative thinking?

It is simply the ability to put your mind to a problem that hasn't been solved by a routine method and to come up with a brand-new solution or batch of solutions. Many experts think that the secret of creativity lies in *free association of ideas,* that is, the mind's ability to make a connection between two vastly different objects or ideas. Take this example: A factory was spray-painting bedsprings automatically. Drips and "teardrops" were a big problem. The engineer tried all the obvious ideas. He speeded up the spraying and then slowed it down; he changed paint consistency, surface preparation, drying heat, and airflow. No luck. Then the supervisor of the operation came up with the bright idea of whacking the painted springs automatically with a rubber hose. It worked! Paint flew off like the dust from a rug she had seen her grandmother beat with a rug beater. Not only was the drip problem solved, but also enough paint was collected in gutters beneath the springs to paint twice as many springs as before.

The free association of ideas was linking the painting problem with getting dust out of a rug.

What isn't creative thinking?

Critical, negative thinking tends to discourage the flow of ideas. Alex Osborn, the founder of brainstorming, always advised innovators to think the "green-light" way. When the green light is on, you don't stop to judge the merit of the ideas that emerge. The time to apply "red-light" thinking is after you've created a batch of ideas and want to evaluate their potential for improving the methods under review.

What is the best way to generate innovative ideas on your own?

There is no one best way, but successful innovators follow a systematic approach something like this:

1. **Narrow down the problem or the target.** It's easier to think of ideas for changing the way day-old reports are filed, for example, than to redesign the entire filing system.
2. **Learn to concentrate.** Try writing the problem on a sheet of paper and keeping it in front of you to focus your attention.
3. **Persevere.** Good ideas don't always come quickly. So if you can't produce a workable solution today, try again tomorrow.
4. **Preserve.** When you come across good ideas, write them down before they're forgotten. Put these in a special file (an "idea bank"), and search it occasionally for possible applications.
5. **Build your confidence.** Look for early breakthroughs on small matters; then raise your sights to more difficult challenges.
6. **Use your unconscious mind.** Remove blockages by sleeping on a problem, letting your mind wander, taking a break.
7. **Keep ideas flowing.** When you have a hot hand, don't stop generating ideas just because it's quitting time.
8. **Take action.** Ideas may strike you in a sudden burst of inspiration. Nothing much will come of them, however, unless you convert them to practical usage.

What's the difference between brainstorming and creative thinking?

Brainstorming is the group approach to idea generation. The term was invented by Alex Osborn, an advertising executive, and he set four rules for a successful brainstorming session:

- **Don't criticize ideas.** There's a time for judicial thinking, but not while brainstorming.
- **Welcome ideas freely.** That is, the wilder the idea, the better. A "can you top this?" attitude is encouraged. Participants use others' ideas as jumping-off places for their own.
- **Strive for quantity.** Experience shows that the more ideas there are,

the better they are likely to be. A seemingly remote idea from one person may trigger a more valuable idea from another.

- **Combine and improve.** Ideas are like building blocks. Brainstorming participants are encouraged to suggest how an idea can be expanded upon or how two ideas can be combined into a single idea that is better than either idea alone. (Note the use here of work-simplification techniques.)

How good are employee suggestion plans for getting ideas from your employees?

It depends on the company, the way the plan is carried out, and the manner in which the supervisor supports the plan. Some companies have had phenomenal success with plans. Others have been unsuccessful. The National Association of Suggestion Systems reports that on the average you can expect 238 suggestions a year for every 1000 eligible employees; of these suggestions, about 25 percent will be worth accepting.

To make your company's plan a success, get interested in it. If you adopt a negative attitude, employees will also be cool toward the plan. Find out what part you play in the plan's administration, and recognize that the degree to which your employees participate will be a measure of how well you stimulate cooperation.

Intrapreneurship? What's that all about?

It is an increasingly popular way of stimulating innovation and creativity within an established organization. Unhappily, in some companies there is little opportunity for entrepreneurial vision. Highly creative people become discouraged under these conditions and leave to implement their ideas elsewhere. Many progressive organizations, however, are now making it both convenient and rewarding for these individuals to stay and become *intrapreneurs* right where they are. Under various administrative arrangements, they are encouraged to extend their creativity beyond routine methods improvements. They may run their own independent operations within a larger department. Or they may be turned loose on a particular research project they have conceived of. Or they may be given seed money to start a small business under the protective umbrella of the parent corporation.

Whether or not formal intrapreneurship is available, the concept of becoming the creative director of one's own business is an idea that supervisors can readily apply to their everyday responsibilities.

▢ R E V I E W

KEY CONCEPTS TO REMEMBER

1. Productivity is akin to efficiency. It compares (a) the output value of the product or service produced with (b) the costs of the input resources (labor, materials, equipment) that are used to make the product or provide the service. Productivity is the "bottom line" for supervisory performance evaluation. Productivity increases whenever the output rises faster or falls slower than the input; it decreases when the opposite occurs.

2. Productivity improvement is affected by the contributions of two factors: technological and human. Responsibility for the former is shared by all members of management, whereas the latter is primarily the concern of first-line supervisors.

3. Work measurement determines the times needed to perform tasks or jobs; these times are typically converted into time or work standards. In turn, these standards form the basis of work schedules, job assignments, wage incentives, budgets, product or service costs, and ultimately a company's pricing structure. The technique of work sampling provides a valuable shortcut to work measurement: by making random observations of workers' activities, the supervisor is able to find the proportion of delays and interruptions as related to the total time spent on a job.

4. The time needed to perform a task is directly proportional to the way in which the job is performed. The time needed can almost always be reduced through the application of various techniques for methods improvement and motion economy that simplify work procedures and utilize work-assisting devices, tools, and machinery. Large-scale productivity gains are mostly achieved through the introduction of automation, robots, and computers. Value analysis is a form of productivity improvement that focuses on the product rather than on the process by which it is made.

5. Supervisors and their employees, because of their nearness to the work, can be especially creative in suggesting new ways for improving productivity. Such innovation is related to an individual's ability to obtain a free association of seemingly unrelated ideas. When this process is carried out in group sessions, it is called brainstorming. Intrapreneurship is a popular way of encouraging the entrepreneurial spirit within the structure of an established organization.

SUPERVISORY WORD POWER

Brainstorming. A group approach to idea generation that encourages free association of ideas among participants, while forbidding negative judgments, in order to generate a maximum number of ideas in a short period of time.

Ergonomics. The study of how workers react to their physical environment. It is useful in designing more comfortable and productive workstations.

Free association of ideas. The ability of the mind to unconsciously visualize relationships between seemingly different objects and ideas.

Intrapreneurship. A concept of stimulating creativity in which individuals act in an innovative and entrepreneurial way with the support of, and within the structure of, an established organization.

Motion economy. The selection and use of the human movements that are the quickest, most comfortable, and least fatiguing in performing a particular task.

Productivity. The measure of efficiency that compares the value of outputs from an operation with the cost of the resources used.

Standard. The normal or expected time required to perform an operation or process or make a product, computed on the basis of past performance, estimates, or work measurement.

Work improvement. Any of many systematic methods of work analysis (especially methods improvement) aimed at finding simpler, faster, less physically demanding ways of accomplishing a given task while at the same time increasing productivity and reducing costs.

Work measurement. The determination, by systematic and (ideally) precise methods, of the time dimension of a particular task. How much work is there to be done? How long will it take a particular machine or a trained person to do it properly?

Work sampling. A technique for finding out what proportion of employees' time is used productively on job assignments, compared with the proportion that is not.

READING COMPREHENSION

1. What two factors determine the productivity measurements of an operation? Why is higher productivity so greatly valued by an organization?
2. A bank estimated that each transaction handled by a teller contributed 20 cents to the total value of the bank's services. The average

teller receives $7.50 an hour and can handle 75 transactions an hour when fully occupied. What is the productivity of the average teller, expressed as a ratio? As a percentage?

3. Which factor—technology or human effort—is most likely to contribute the largest share toward productivity improvement in a highly automated chemical plant? In a window-washing operation?

4. Why is work measurement sometimes called the foundation stone of productivity improvement?

5. What factors that detract from productivity are likely to be uncovered by a work sampling study?

6. What are the six key words of Rudyard Kipling's "six honest serving men"?

7. Why can it be said that the elimination of a "do" operation is like "killing three birds with one stone"?

8. Compare, for the sake of value analysis, the use function and the esteem function.

9. Why do brainstorming sessions strive for large quantities of ideas? Wouldn't it be better to stress the quality of the ideas?

10. Differentiate intrapreneurship from entrepreneurship. Why is the former so valuable to established organizations?

 APPLICATION

SELF-APPRAISAL

How good will you be at making productivity improvements?

Imagine that you are supervising a department with presumed low productivity. Your assignment is to determine which of the ideas presented on page 403 would be effective in trying to improve productivity and which would not. On a separate piece of paper, copy the column headings shown below. In the column "Ideas for Improving Productivity," write the numbers 1 to 10 down the page to correspond to each of the ideas. Then place a check mark in the column that most nearly matches your opinion of each idea. After completing this activity, check your answers by using the scoring procedure described on page 403.

Column headings:

Ideas for Improving Productivity	Effective	Ineffective

1. Look for corrective ideas right away; it will be a waste of time to make your own productivity calculations.
2. If the records show constant output and falling input, do nothing, since this indicates rising productivity.
3. If your operations are heavily influenced by technological factors, don't search for ideas that affect human productivity.
4. Disregard considering the establishment of a quality circle, since you know that most of your problems affect output only.
5. Set up a system for measuring the work inputs and outputs of your operations on a continuing basis.
6. Results of a work sampling study show delays because of material shortages. Report this to the purchasing and inventory-control departments.
7. Ignore an employee's suggestion for reducing "makeready" time, since the big savings will come from eliminating the more important "do" operations.
8. Accept an employee's suggestion for using ergonomic chairs and positioning devices for work at computers.
9. Rely exclusively on logic and sound reasoning to create ideas that will be worthwhile.
10. After pinpointing problem areas, hold a brainstorming session to get ideas from your staff.

Scoring Give yourself 1 point for each of the following ideas that you checked as *effective:* 2, 5, 6, 8, 10. Give yourself 1 point for each of the following ideas that you checked as *ineffective:* 1, 3, 4, 7, 9.

Interpretation If you scored 9 or 10 points, you're likely to have success as a productivity improver. If you scored 7 or 8 points, you're likely to find yourself struggling to keep your operations productive. Review the items you missed. If you scored less than 7 points, your operations are likely to be under constant pressure for productivity improvement. Review the entire chapter.

CASE STUDIES

CASE 51   The Clerical Bottleneck

It looked like a simple operation, but it wasn't. "Cents-off" coupons received from supermarkets were shipped to the Coupon Clearinghouse Center in Iowa for sorting, tabulation, and processing. On the basis of the figures prepared in Iowa, the various manufacturers would make refund payments directly to the supermarkets.

Mona F. was in charge of the tabulation section of the clearinghouse. She had a dozen regular employees reporting to her, and during peak promotion periods she could hire an additional ten workers on a part-time basis. The need for the extra help was dictated by the flow of coupons through the tabulation section. This became a major bottleneck, since coupons that were not marked by a universal product code had to be counted by hand.

A month or so ago, Mona came up with a brilliant, but simple, idea for improving the counting operation. Her idea was to have the employees weigh the nonstandard coupons, instead of counting them. She had found out that a pound of one type of coupon, for example, contained 500 coupons, plus or minus 15 coupons. In effect, 500 coupons could be "weigh-counted" in 15 seconds, whereas it might take 5 minutes to count them by hand. The new method would result in a savings of up to 90 percent on labor time.

Even allowing for possible miscounts, Mona estimated that she could reduce the number of permanent counters from 12 to 8. Mona presented the idea to her boss, who liked it very much. His query, however, was: "How will your staff react to the reduction in force due to this methods improvement? Do you think you can make the change without destroying morale?"

If you were Mona, how would you approach this problem? Of the five alternatives provided below, which do you think might be most effective? Rank the alternatives on a scale from 1 (most preferable) to 5 (least preferable.) You may add another alternative, if you wish. In any event, be prepared to justify your ranking.

a. Bring the staff together to discuss which people should be laid off as a result of the change.
b. Explain the plan and declare that it will become effective at the beginning of the month; tell the workers that staff reductions will be handled according to seniority.
c. Introduce the change gradually, hiring no new or part-time staff and allowing natural attrition to take care of staff reductions.
d. Present the plan to the staff and explain its possible disruptions; then hold a brainstorming session to deal with the problems associated with the plan.
e. Decide to drop the idea completely, since it would be too disruptive.

CASE 52 The Dwindling Packaging Rate

Hector was puzzled. The output for his crew of five packers in the shipping room of the Astral VCR Company had dwindled steadily over the past several months, yet the crew seemed to be as busy and hardworking as ever. Accordingly, Hector checked the standards for his operations to make sure they were fair. They appeared to be. They showed that, given the proper, preformed packaging materials and the appropriate packaging machinery, one packer could package 100 VCRs a day. That would come to 500 packages a day for his crew of five. Yet the daily tallies showed only 450 VCRs being packed. Yesterday, Hector was told by his boss, "Find out what's happening to productivity in your department—and why!"

a. What is the current productivity of an average packer at Astral, stated in terms of VCRs a day and an hour?
b. What sort of things may possibly be affecting productivity that are not reflected in the work measurement standard?
c. How might Hector now identify the causes of the dwindling productivity?

CASE 53 The Wheels-Are-Us

The Topsy's-It Toy Company makes thousands of miniature wooden autos. The costliest part of its operation is attaching the wheels to the axles. This work is speeded up by the use of special assembly devices. The trouble is, however, that each time an auto with a different wheel size is assembled, it takes an inordinate amount of time to put away one device and make ready the one for the new size. A methods improvement team studied this assembly operation and came up with two alternate recommendations for the supervisor to choose from:

a. Design new assembly *devices* that would yield the following times: makeready time per change, 2.5 hours; put-away time per change, 1.5 hours; time to assemble 1000 units, 16 hours.
b. Retain the present assembly devices, but modify assembly *techniques* for faster times, such as these: makeready time per change, 3.6 hours; put-away time per change, 2.0 hours; time to assemble 1000 units, 14.4 hours.

The average number of auto assemblies made per run is 500, and the company makes 200 changeovers a year. That is, it makes 200 runs of 500 units each.

1. Which recommendation would you accept?
2. Why? Show your calculations.
3. What might you try to improve next in the recommendation you've chosen?

1 Quality involves inspection, correction, and prevention.

2 Supervisors have a major responsibility for quality.

3 Employees can make or break a quality assurance program.

4 Statistical quality control makes use of mathematical tools.

5 Quality depends upon commitment by the entire organization.

CHAPTER 18

Building a Higher Quality of Performance

LEARNING OBJECTIVES

After studying this chapter, you should be able to

1. Explain the meaning of quality and differentiate between corrective and preventive costs of quality assurance.

2. Discuss the breadth of a supervisor's responsibility for quality and list a number of ways this responsibility can be carried out.

3. Describe the six principal reasons for errors and defects in employee performance and discuss the need for instilling a respect for quality among employees.

4. Understand the concepts and purpose of statistical quality control, make use of frequency-distribution and quality control charts, and explain a reliability measure.

5. Describe the main features of Zero Defects and Quality Circle programs and explain the value of participative approaches for solving quality problems.

QUALITY ASSURANCE

CONCEPT Assurance of the quality of goods or services produced can be a costly process involving programs of inspection, correction, and prevention.

To begin with, what—exactly—is meant by *quality*?

Quality is a measure of the degree to which a process, product, or service conforms to the requirements that have been established for it. This means that quality is not merely a descriptive term; to have meaning, quality must be defined in highly specific terms. For example:

- "This process (operating an air-driven nut runner) must conform to the requirement that the machine's pressure be held to 90 pounds per square inch (psi), plus or minus 5 psi."
- "This product (a box of cereal) must conform to the requirement that it weigh no more than 16¼ ounces and no less than 16 ounces."
- "This service (recording of telephone sales orders) must conform to the requirement that *all* prices be exactly as they appear in the published catalog."

How do you differentiate among the many other terms associated with quality?

Unfortunately, many quality-related terms have evolved without precise definition. To clarify the generally accepted usage of some important terms, make a note of these:

Quality assurance encompasses all the efforts taken by an organization to ensure that its processes, products, and services conform to the requirements set for them.

Quality control (QC) is much like quality assurance, except that its use projects a negative connotation, rather than the more positive and preventive nature implied by quality assurance.

Acceptable quality level (AQL) is another term for quality, although many purists do not like the term because it implies an acceptance of less-than-perfect performance.

Inspection is the process of examining a process, product, or service to determine whether or not it conforms to the established requirements and, if not, the extent of the deviation. Inspections can be made before, during, or after a process or product is completed.

Nondestructive testing is an inspection that does not break, distort, or otherwise damage the product being made. A farmer who candles an egg is applying nondestructive testing. Industry techniques include x rays, sound waves, temperature flow patterns, magnetic fields, and ultraviolet rays.

Are quality problems limited to the manufacture of products?

Far from it. Poor workmanship causes costly quality problems in just about every line of work, including clerical. For example, a close watch should be kept on any of the following that apply to your organization:

- **Accounting.** Billing errors, payroll errors, accounts payable deductions missed, percentage of late reports, incorrect computer inputs, errors in special reports as audited.
- **Data processing.** Keypunch cards thrown out for error, deductions missed, computer downtime due to error, rerun time.
- **Engineering.** Change orders due to error, drafting errors found by checkers, late releases.
- **Hotel operation.** Guests taken to unmade or occupied rooms, reservations not honored, inaccurate or missed billing.
- **Marketing and sales.**   Orders or prices written up incorrectly, errors in contract specifications, wrong copy or prices in advertisements and catalogs.
- **Maintenance.** Callbacks on repairs, wrong parts installed, downtime due to faulty maintenance.
- **Retailing.** Wrong product on shelves, incorrect pricing, merchandise damage in handling, storage, or shipping.

How much does poor quality cost?

It costs industry billions of dollars each year. It is most obvious in the form of product liability suits (a million claims for a total of $50 billion in damages in a year is not unusual) and manufacturers' recalls to repair defective goods. Billions of dollars are lost to poor quality, however, in two other ways:

Corrective costs. These costs include money down the drain for any of the following: (1) damaged parts and materials that must be scrapped or, at best, reworked; (2) the time and effort of redoing poor work; (3) the cost of warranties that presume errors will be made that must be corrected later; and (4) the cost of handling customer complaints. Corrective quality is by far the most costly approach to quality problems, accounting for 2 to 10 percent of sales revenue.

Preventive costs. These are the costs of trying to prevent poor workmanship or defective goods in the first place. They include routine (1) inspection, (2) testing, and (3) quality-control procedures, including education and motivation programs. It is a rare organization where the costs of preventive quality, however, exceed 3 percent of total sales revenue.

🄰 QUALITY AND THE SUPERVISOR

CONCEPT   Supervisors have a major responsibility for making an organization's quality-assurance effort successful.

How great is a supervisor's responsibility for quality assurance?

It is a very large, but shared, responsibility. First of all, it should be made clear that the attainment of quality does not reside in a single person or even a single department. Every activity of an organization contributes to, or detracts from, the quality of its products or services. These include, especially, such functional departments as product design, methods engineering, purchasing, and maintenance and repair. The functions that receive the greatest amount of heat, however, are (1) the inspection and quality-control departments and (2) the supervisor's own operations. Inspection and QC are expected to catch errors and defective work before it leaves the department. Supervisors are expected to make certain that the errors and defects do not occur in the first place.

In many organizations there is an unending battle between inspection and supervision. The reasons are clear: supervision is continually pressured from above for output; inspection is pressured to make sure that output conforms to requirements. To keep jurisdictional disputes to a minimum, many companies deliberately separate the two departments.

Few supervisors, however, deny their responsibility for quality as well as output. The disputes arise mainly over who is the best judge of quality—and who has the authority to stop production when quality falls below specifications. This is something that you should have your boss make crystal clear for you. Otherwise, chaos will prevail.

There is a long-standing guideline, however, that should govern any supervisor's approach to a responsibility for quality: *Quality must be built into the product. No one can inspect it in.*

Additionally, the person most respected for quality assurance in Japan, an American—W. Edwards Deming—prescribes seven more guidelines for supervisors, as listed in Table 18-1.

Table 18-1	SEVEN POINTS FOR THE SUPERVISION OF QUALITY

1. Refuse to allow commonly accepted levels of delay or of mistakes, defective material, or defective workmanship.
2. Search continually for problems in the system and seek ways to improve it.
3. Focus supervision on helping people to do a better job.
4. Provide the tools and techniques that will enable people to have pride in their workmanship.
5. Eliminate fear. Encourage two-way communication.
6. Break down barriers between departments. Encourage problem solving through teamwork.
7. Institute a vigorous program of education and training to keep people abreast of new developments in materials, methods, and machinery.

Source: Adapted from the works of W. Edwards Deming.

What should you do if there is no inspection or quality-control department at your location?

If you make a product, the chances are that there will be an official inspection department somewhere in your organization—even if it doesn't carry on its activity in your department. If such is the case, you might first ask the central inspection department for advice in setting up your own quality checks. If you must go it alone or if yours is a service operation, however, try this analysis of your quality problem:

- What is my inspection problem? What do I have to do to maintain quality?
- Shall I assign the inspection to someone as a part-time or a full-time job?
- Shall I do the inspecting myself? If so, how much time can I devote to it?
- Should I try to inspect all the work produced or only a sample of it? Or should I confine myself to the first piece on a new setup only?

Once you have considered these questions and decided on your approach, you can proceed to the next question.

How can you make your own checks of quality?

Keep in mind these ten points:

1. Set up some specific quality standards, such as dimensions and appearance. Keeping examples of acceptable and nonacceptable work on exhibit helps.

2. Put specifications in writing. See that your employees get a copy to guide them.
3. Allocate some of your own time for inspection. The total amount isn't so important as doing a certain amount each day.
4. Pick the spots where quality can best be made or lost. There is no point in spending your time checking operations where nothing much can go wrong.
5. Make inspection rounds from time to time. Change the order of your trips frequently.
6. Select at random 5 or 10 percent of the pieces produced (for example, letters typed) at a particular station. Inspect each one carefully.
7. Correct operating conditions immediately where your inspection shows material to be off grade or equipment to be faulty.
8. Consult with employees to determine the reason for poor workmanship or unacceptable products. Seek their cooperation in correcting conditions and improving quality.
9. Check the first piece on a new setup or a new assignment. Don't permit production until you are satisfied with the quality.
10. Post quality records, scrap percentages, and so forth, to keep employees informed of the department's performance.

3 EMPLOYEE CONTRIBUTIONS

CONCEPT Employees can make or break a quality program, but they must first be given the proper information, training, and equipment.

How can you get employees more interested in quality?

It's been popular to complain about the "I don't care" attitude of some employees. Your viewpoint should be that if employees don't care about quality, it's because you have failed to sell them on its importance.

To get a worker to become quality-conscious, start right from the first day by stressing quality as well as output. Emphasize that the two must go hand in hand in your department. Whenever you show an employee how to do a job—especially a new one—be specific as to what kind of work is acceptable and what kind will not meet specifications. Explain the reason behind product or service quality limitations, and try to give your employees the little tricks of the trade that help to make quality easy to attain.

Why do employees make errors?

Generally speaking, there are six reasons why employees make mistakes—and most of them begin with management inadequacies rather than with employee shortcomings. The experience of companies that have improved their quality shows these potential causes of errors:

- Lack of training
- Poor communication
- Inadequate tools and equipment
- Insufficient planning
- Incomplete specifications and procedures
- Lack of attention or concern

Poor communication, for example, can be overcome by taking the extra time to make sure each person fully understands the instructions. In written orders, don't leave loopholes that can lead to misinterpretation. One small company with a large staff of Spanish-speaking people had the workers repeat the orders that were given to them. It took a few minutes, but it actually saved time. Rejects and rework tumbled to a fraction of 1 percent.

Lack of concern, however, is completely different from the other potential causes of error and is perhaps the most serious. This is very personal and stems from employees' attitudes. You must reaffirm that management is interested in employees and will help them do their jobs to perfection. You, as a supervisor, must re-create the old-fashioned pride in one's craft. You must motivate employees so that they have a personal attachment to their jobs and will be proud of the quality of the work they do..

What can you do to help employees understand that the customer is the real quality boss?

Try to provide employees with a customer's-eye view of your product. Workers who handle the same product every day tend to lose their objectivity. They begin to take minor defects for granted. To help them see the product as the customer does, get samples of customer complaints (about specific defects) and circulate them in your department. Explain how the customer uses your product or service—how it will be compared with that of a competitor and how its quality may affect a purchase decision.

4 STATISTICAL QUALITY CONTROL

CONCEPT Statistical quality control makes valuable use of mathematical techniques for monitoring and controlling the quality of processes, products, and services.

What is meant by statistical quality control?

Statistical quality control (SQC) simply means that numbers—statistics—are used as a part of the overall approach to controlling quality. Statistics are tools and in no way relieve supervisors or employees from a concern with quality. Used properly, however, statistics can be of considerable aid.

In many industries, it is only the techniques of SQC that make rigid specifications economically attainable. For example, JC Penney Co., Inc., orders millions of knitted garments each year. It uses various inspection and statistical methods to screen the thousands of samples submitted to the company for purchase. As a consequence, the company rejects 30 percent of the submissions, thus preventing subsequent disasters at the sales counters.

In Japan, the practice of SQC is so widespread that a great many employees, including truck drivers and workers of all kinds, prepare and maintain their own quality-control charts.

What are some of the tools of statistical quality control, and how do they affect the supervisor's job?

Greatly increased demands for precision parts have stepped up the need for better methods to measure and record the accuracy with which manufacturing people meet product specifications. Statistical methods speed up this measuring process, and more and more companies use them in some form or other. Don't let any fear you may have of mathematics prevent your using statistical methods.

Three statistical quality-control tools are encountered most commonly:

1. **Frequency-distribution chart.** Hold on. It isn't as bad as it sounds. Probably you'll recognize it by its more popular name—a tally card. If you were asked to place an "X" in the appropriate space for every shaft diameter you gauged in a given lot, chances are that you'd come up with a tally that looks something like Figure 18-1.

   In this case the nominal shaft diameter was 0.730 inch with a tolerance of ± 0.002. This tally gives you a picture of just what and where the shaft variations are instead of merely recording whether a shaft is good or bad. This frequency-distribution chart (or **histogram**) helps tell you the causes of the variation. The wide distribution in this case indicates tool wobble. A picture that showed parts bunched around a point below or above the nominal 0.730 inch (say, at 0.728) might mean that the setup must be adjusted.

2. **Quality-control chart.** This is an hour-by-hour, day-by-day graphic comparison of actual product quality characteristics. On the chart

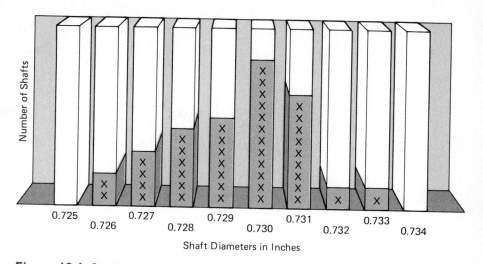

Figure 18-1 Simple frequency-distribution chart (or histogram) used in statistical quality control.

are limits that reflect the person's or the machine's ability to produce, as shown by past experience. Statisticians make use of the knowledge of shop tolerances and analysis of previous frequency-distribution tallies to establish these limits. Whenever the inspections plotted on the control chart show that the product is getting outside the predicted control limits, that's a signal for the supervisor or the operator to correct what is being done so that the product comes back into specification.

In Figure 18-2, the part being made is supposed to measure 0.730 inch. The tolerance specs are ±0.002, or from 0.728 to 0.732 inch. The quality-control statistician has predicted in advance from a frequency-distribution diagram that most production will vary within these control limits—the 0.7285 and 0.7315 lines. When quality stays within these limits, it is said to be on the highway. It is to be expected that a few products will fall outside the limits into the shoulder. But when the trend of measurements indicates that product quality is drifting progressively into the shoulder area, it's time to check the process. Any product that goes beyond the upper or lower specification limits (goes into the ditch) is rejected.

The value of the chart lies in its ability to tell the supervisor and the operator whether they are within bounds or whether they are losing control of the process, before the process goes completely haywire.

3. **Sampling tables.** The trend today has been away from 100 percent inspection, which is costly and often misleading. (In a 100 percent

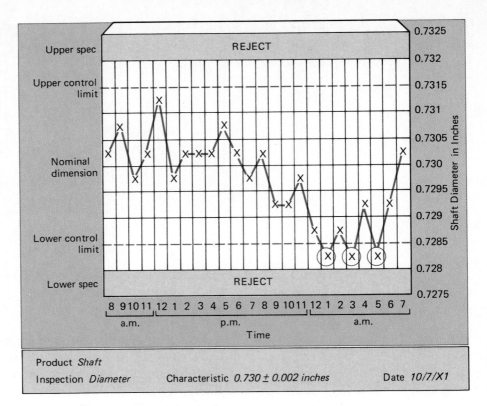

Figure 18-2 Quality-control chart.

check of a load of oranges, does this mean that each orange has been inspected for color, ripeness, thickness of skin, appearance? Or does it mean that each orange was inspected for appearance only?) The first solution to less than 100 percent checking was spot-checking, but this proved unreliable. Today most sampling is done according to the size of the lot of goods produced and according to tables designed by statisticians for this purpose. These sampling tables guide the quality-control manager in the determination of how large a sample to take and how often to take it.

Is there a connection between reliability and statistical quality control?

Yes, indirectly, and it often has a direct relationship to product liability claims. *Reliability* is defined as the probability of a product's performing a specific function, under given conditions, for a specified time without failure. It must measure up specifically, therefore, to (1) what it's supposed to do (such as, for a bolt, hold 500 pounds of direct pull); (2) the circumstances under which it will be used (such as temperatures up to 185°C in an acid atmosphere); and (3) the length of time it should perform before it breaks or stops working (such as 25,000 fastenings or 39 months). Reliability can be determined either by direct test (using the product until it fails) or by statistical computation (based on assumptions about the design and work characteristic of the product). Reliability is usually expressed as the (mean) time expected between failures—as, say, 1/0.002 or 500 hours. Because the assumptions made vary in the degree of confidence the estimator has in them, reliability figures are often qualified as having, say, 85 percent confidence (or being 85 percent sure to last as long as predicted but having a 15 percent risk of not lasting that long).

Reliability enters statistical quality-control considerations when you are deciding on the limits of variation, on how far from standard the product can be without being rejected. Obviously, the tighter the variable limits, the greater the reliability of the product. However, this does not mean that a perfect part will be reliable forever. It will be reliable only as long as it was designed to be under the specified operating conditions.

5 ZERO DEFECTS AND QUALITY CIRCLES

CONCEPT   The ultimate in quality achievement depends upon complete commitment and maximum participation by the entire organization.

What is Zero Defects?

It's the approach to quality that put an American on the moon. It was conceived by Philip Crosby at about the time that everything that could go wrong with the U.S. space program did go wrong. What Crosby did was to remove the emphasis on statistical quality control and expert quality monitors and place the responsibility for quality in the hands of the employees. *Zero Defects* (ZD) stressed personal motivation. It attempted to instill in each individual a pride in his or her work. It was the first quality program to put quality on a personal basis. ZD techniques were aimed at stimulating everyone involved to care about accuracy and completeness, to pay attention to detail, and to improve work habits. In this manner everyone worked toward reducing his or her own errors to zero.

Most other quality programs at that time attempted control by rejecting work that didn't measure up to minimum standards. ZD reversed this philosophy. It aimed for products of consistently high quality by eliminating all errors made by all the people designing, producing, selling, and servicing the items.

What made ZD work so well?

It got great results for three good reasons:

1. **The quality standard was very explicit: Do it the right way from the start.** As Philip Crosby said, "What standard would you set on how many babies nurses are allowed to drop?"
2. **There was complete commitment by everyone.** From sweeper to top executive, from production worker to clerical employee, everyone was encouraged to spot problems, detect errors, and prescribe ways and means for their removal.
3. **Action was taken immediately to change behavior and to remove conditions that cause errors.** Crosby maintained that 90 percent of all error causes could be acted upon and fully removed by first-line supervisors. In other words, top management had to do its part to improve conditions, but supervisors and employees could handle most problems right at the operating level.

If ZD was so good, what's all the excitement now about Quality Circles?

If you agree with the participative aspect of ZD, then you'll probably agree that the Quality-Circle movement is the next logical step forward. Both programs are based on the belief that quality cannot be produced or controlled by a single individual or department. Both programs conceive of quality as the result of dozens, perhaps hundreds, of interactions. These take place between the designer and the manufacturing department, between manufacturing and purchasing, between sales and production, between the keypunch operator and the computer programmer, and so on and on. In technical terms, quality is the end result of a complex system. The Quality-Circle concept accepts quality as a starting point (as with ZD) and *then* concludes that only by bringing together the people who are directly involved in the system will the obstacles that block good quality and error-free performance be removed.

Quality Circles were conceived of by an American statistician, W. Edwards Deming (abetted by Joseph M. Juran, a noted quality consultant) and introduced in Japan in the 1950s. Gradually, firms in the United States, such as General Motors and Westinghouse Electric Corp., got wind of the idea. These companies formed small groups of 10 to 15 employees to meet regularly to examine and suggest solutions to common problems of quality. By 1990, the number of U.S. firms using these circles had grown into the thousands. Circles are found just about any-where, in small companies as well as large, in hospitals as well as banks, in government agencies, and in offices as well as factories.

How does a Quality Circle operate?

Since the Quality-Circle concept is based on maximum—and voluntary—involvement of employees from top to bottom of an organization, Quality-Circle programs are almost always initiated at the executive level. If the program doesn't get all-out support at that level, it proba-bly won't work at any level. Next, the Quality-Circle idea is fanned out into the total organization. It is typically spearheaded by a "facilitator" or "coordinator." That person helps to organize the departmental and interdepartmental circles. He or she also provides the necessary training in problem and opportunity identification and in methods improvement and problem solving.

Each circle is made up exclusively of volunteers, who meet on com-pany time. They place personnel and labor relations problems off lim-its. Also prohibited are discussions about the performance or lack of performance of specific individuals. Typically, a new quality circle will focus on simple workplace problems. Early achievements build confi-dence and experience. Later on, the circle will tackle more ambitious problems, ones that extend beyond its own control and involve other departments and other circles. As its expertise grows, the circle will shift gears from problem solving to problem preventing.

Is quality the only focus of a Quality Circle?

It started that way, but most circles have found that quality is inevita-bly tangled up with every imaginable kind of operating problem. As a consequence, most circles will turn their attention to any troublesome problem. And most organizations with a Quality-Circle program cite example after example of productivity improvement.

You may have observed by now that all quality improvement ap-proaches have much in common with productivity and cost improve-ment programs. There is a great deal of desirable overlap. Many of the techniques of quality improvement have been borrowed from work sim-plification, for example. The reason for these similarities is that at the heart of all improvement programs are the problem-solving and decision-making techniques described in Chapter 6. The Quality-Circle move-ment makes special use of all the approaches associated with problem solving and methods improvement, as shown in Figure 18-3. There is one extremely important factor, however, that is vital to the

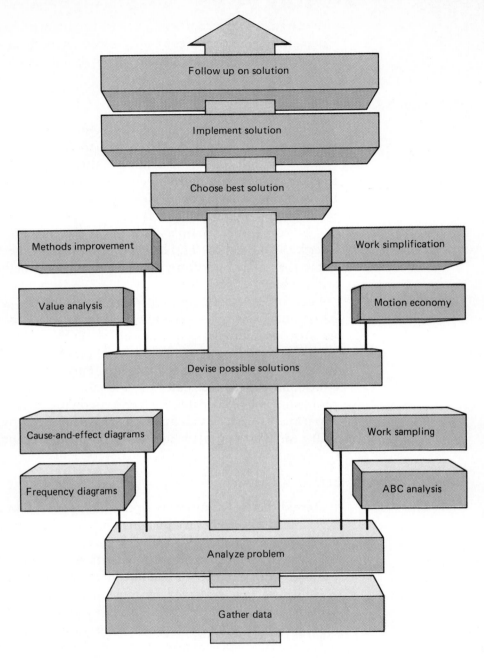

Figure 18-3 Problem-solving process in Quality Circles.

success of Quality Circles. Circles utilize what appear to be the common truths of motivation, group dynamics, Theory Y, and participation that can lead an employee or group of employees to try harder.

Employees make this extra effort because the work itself becomes more challenging and fulfilling. Quality Circles not only improve quality and productivity, but they can also improve the quality of an employee's work life.

REVIEW

KEY CONCEPTS TO REMEMBER

1. Quality is a measure of the degree to which a process, product, or service conforms to the requirements that have been established for it. The cost of correcting defects and errors is high compared with the cost of preventing poor quality in the first place. Concerns for quality extend far beyond the manufacture of products into every kind of service that is provided internally, as well as externally to customers.

2. Whereas quality must represent a total effort of all functions combined—design, materials, purchasing, manufacturing or operations, and inspection—it is the first-line supervisor who is in a key position to see that quality is built into the product or service as it is produced. In the absence of, or as a supplement to, a formal inspection or quality-control department, supervisors may provide these functions themselves for their operations.

3. Employees will work at higher levels of craftsmanship if they are properly trained; are equipped with the right tools, specifications, and instructions; and have become motivated toward achievement of high levels of performance.

4. Statistical quality control (SQC) provides a valuable method for monitoring and controlling quality performance. The three principal tools of SQC are frequency-distribution charts, quality control charts, and sampling tables. Reliability is a special concept that establishes the probability of a product's performing a specific function, under given conditions, for a specified number of times (or period of time) without failure.

5. The concepts of Zero Defects and Quality Circles have been especially effective in quality-assurance programs. They both illustrate that most errors of workmanship can be eliminated if each individual is properly motivated and supported throughout the entire organization. The success of Quality Circles is highly dependent upon

group participation techniques applied to solving problems of quality and productivity.

SUPERVISORY WORD POWER

Acceptable quality levels (AQL). A general form of specification that tells a supervisor the kind of tolerance (in terms of percentage of rejects, extent of rework, number of defects, number of customer complaints, frequency of stockouts, extent of delays in service) limiting what will be judged as acceptable performance.

Defect. Any variation (in the product or service) from specifications that falls outside the prescribed tolerances and thus causes (1) the product to be rejected, discarded, or reworked or (2) a service to be interrupted, declined, or delayed.

Quality. The measure of the degree to which a process, product, or service conforms to the requirements that have been established for it.

Rework. To remanufacture, do over, adjust, modify, or otherwise repair a product or a service that has been rejected because of an observed or reported defect.

Specification. The definitions (preferably written) of expected performance of a product (or quality of a service), usually stated in finite measurements of size, shape, finish, durability, and so forth.

Tolerance. Essentially a statement of precision that establishes limits within which the product or the service must meet the specification; for example, a machined part specified to be 1 inch in diameter with a tolerance of ± 0.005 inch.

READING COMPREHENSION

1. What is wrong with defining a product or service as one of "high quality"?
2. Suggest the kinds of errors or defects that might occur in the work of computer keyboarders, supermarket checkout clerks, bricklayers, waitresses, bank tellers, and file clerks.
3. Why might there be occasional jurisdictional disputes between supervisors and inspectors?
4. What are some of the things supervisors should do for themselves in seeking to ensure quality performance in their departments?
5. Besides poor workmanship, what are some of the things that can contribute to defects and errors?

6. What is meant by the statement "The customer is really the quality boss"?
7. How does statistical quality control differ from inspection?
8. In what way does statistical quality control depend upon a reliability determination?
9. In what way are Zero-Defects programs and Quality-Circle programs alike?
10. What is it about the Quality-Circle approach that enables employees to contribute to the quality of their own work lives?

APPLICATION

SELF-APPRAISAL

How do you rate on quality know-how?

If you, as a supervisor, were to go all out for the highest quality you could attain for your department, what approaches would you use? Ten approaches to quality are presented in the following statements. Your assignment is to determine which ones represent good practice and which represent poor practice. On a separate piece of paper, copy the column headings shown below. In the column "Approaches to Quality," write the numbers 1 to 10 down the page to correspond to each of the approaches. Then place a check mark in the column that most nearly matches your opinion of each statement. After completing this activity check your answers by using the scoring procedure described on page 424.

Column headings:

Approaches to Quality	Good Practice	Poor Practice

1. Find out far in advance exactly what requirements the process, product, or service is expected to conform to.
2. Place primary emphasis upon corrective measures for ensuring quality in your department.
3. Try to build quality into the product, rather than depending upon inspection to find the defects after they have been made.
4. Leave inspections entirely to the inspection department.

5. Before placing the blame for a defect or an error on an employee, make certain that the employee had adequate equipment, materials, tooling, supplies, and instruction.
6. Explain to employees that it is you, and only you, whom they must satisfy with the quality of their work.
7. Rely upon 100 percent inspection of large batches of incoming raw materials, forms, supplies, and so forth.
8. When mass-producing any product or service, consider tracking quality trends with statistical quality control.
9. Ignore the Zero-Defects concept because it has been outdated by Quality Circles.
10. Make a special effort to secure employee participation in identifying and solving quality-related problems.

Scoring   Give yourself 1 point for each of the following statements that you checked as *good practice:* 1, 3, 5, 8, 10. Give yourself 1 point for each of the following statements that you checked as *poor practice:* 2, 4, 6, 7, 9.

Interpretation   If you scored 9 or 10 points, you rate high on quality know-how. Your department can be almost defect- and error-free. If you scored 7 or 8 points, work in your department is not very likely to be defect-, or error-, free. Review the items you missed. If you scored less than 7 points, you rate low on quality, and workmanship in the department you supervise is likely to be under fire constantly. Review the entire chapter.

CASE STUDIES

CASE 54   The No-Fault Quality Problem

"No way that it happened in my area!" That's the response Sally Parker is hearing from all the employees in her department. Sally is the supervisor of ceramic-parts finishing for the Fast-Fire Spark Plug Company. Last month, despite a seemingly infallible program of statistical quality control, an entire shipment of spark plugs was rejected by a major distributor of auto parts. The problem was traced to a high percentage of defects in the ceramic parts made in Sally's department.

The molding operators claimed that their work had been flawless. They suggested that perhaps the furnace operators were at fault.

The furnace operators were certain their work had been right on target, but they thought that maybe the finish-grinding had not been up to standard.

The finish-grinders reported that they had been especially careful.

They said that perhaps the machine maintenance crew had let the grinding machines get "out of spec."

The machine maintenance workers insisted that they had been on top of that out-of-spec problem. Maybe, they suggested, the purchasing department has been allowing some substandard raw materials to slip through.

So it went. No one seemed to be able to pinpoint where the fault lay.

If you were Sally, how would you go about solving this problem so that it would not happen again? Of the five alternatives provided below, which do you think might be most effective? Rank the alternatives on a scale from 1 (most preferable) to 5 (least preferable). You may add another alternative if you wish. In any event, be prepared to justify your ranking.

a. Consider this a once-in-a-lifetime mystery and forget about it. It is not likely to happen again.

b. Assume that a recurrence can be avoided only by persuading employees in all areas to regard this as a problem for which they all have responsibility and to understand that you will look to them collectively for a solution.

c. Focus on an investigation of the "out-of-spec" problem that the finish-grinders mentioned and the maintenance crew acknowledged.

d. Assume that this is really a problem for which the inspection and QC departments should be held responsible. Ask them to come up with a plan to forestall its recurrence.

e. Confront the employees in each operating area. Advise them that they will be held solely responsible for defects in their areas and that a repetition of this problem will not be tolerated.

CASE 55   The Dried-Out Burger

"I can't eat this hamburger," declared the irate customer. "It's completely dried out!"

"I'm sorry," said the assistant manager of the fast-food restaurant, "we'll make you a fresh one."

"I don't have time to wait," said the customer. "This will be the last time I eat here."

When Gilda, the assistant manager, spoke to the counter person, he said that he had served the customer a wrapped hamburger that the fry cook had placed on the serving rack. "I assumed that it was okay," he said. "That customer seemed like an old crab. Nothing would have satisfied her. The hamburger wasn't that bad. She must have just gotten tired of waiting 'till we could get around to her."

The fry cook, when asked for her explanation of the dry hamburger, said, "We had been very busy earlier, and I made up an extra large batch so that I could stay ahead."

"You know," said Gilda, "that our standard says that you should never put more than ten hamburgers up at a time. From the look of things, you must have had a couple of dozen in the serving rack. When they dry out, we can't serve them; they must be thrown into scrap."

"Maybe I did," said the fry cook, "but I can't see what difference an occasional dry hamburger is going to make."

a. What do you think of the counter person's view of the situation?
b. How valid was the fry cook's explanation?
c. If you were Gilda, what would you do to prevent the serving of cold hamburgers in the future?

CASE 56 The Best and the Worst of It

On the quality control chart for the production of a high-priced facial lotion, the pH specification is 7.0, with tolerance limits of $\pm$ 0.02. The control of pH is very important, since it measures acidity, with 7.0 being neutral. The manufacturer wishes to maintain this reading to avoid potential skin irritation, which could mean possible product liability suits from customers. Operators make check readings of the pH meter on the lotion flow line once each hour and record them on a chart, like the one provided on page 427. Here are the readings made by operators on the first, second, and third shifts:

8 a.m. to 4 p.m.:   7.00, 6.99, 6.98, 7.00, 7.01, 7.02, 7.01, 7.00
4 p.m. to 12 a.m.: 6.98, 7.00, 7.02, 6.99, 7.02, 7.03, 6.99, 6.98
12 a.m. to 8 a.m.: 6.99, 7.00, 6.98, 6.97, 6.98, 6.96, 6.97, 6.95

a. Using the information supplied, complete the quality control chart in Figure 18-4. (Refer to Figure 18-2 for guidance.)
b. Which shift operator has the best control of the operation?
c. Which shift operator appears to have lost control of the operation?
d. Which operator appears to have more consistent control, the one on the first shift or the one on the second?

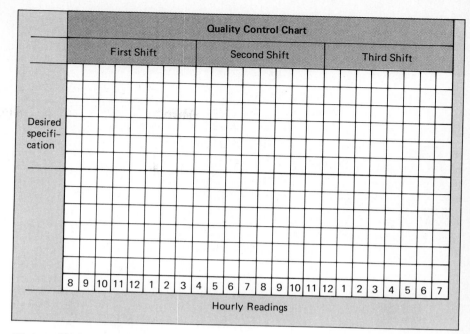

Figure 18-4

1 Cost control requires accurate cost records and awareness.

2 Budgets establish departmental cost standards.

3 Cost reduction depends upon carefully planned priorities.

4 Cost-improvement ideas come from a variety of sources.

5 Employee resistance to cost reduction can be substantial.

CHAPTER 19

Controlling Costs and Budgets

LEARNING OBJECTIVES

After studying this chapter, you should be able to

1. Discuss the importance of recordkeeping and differentiate among unit costs, standard costs, and budgeted costs.

2. Explain the purpose of budgets in cost control, describe the cost variance report, calculate unit costs, and explain the way in which flexible budgets are designed.

3. Understand how to select cost targets and assign priorities to them and recognize a belt-tightening program.

4. Identify and evaluate the principal sources of cost improvement ideas, list some positive approaches, and explain why some cost improvement suggestions might be rejected.

5. Discuss the reasons for employee resistance to cost reduction programs and describe several ways for securing workers' support and cooperation.

ACCOUNTING RECORDS

CONCEPT Effective cost control begins with accurate records of costs as they occur and an understanding of the accounting reports that document them.

Which comes first: cost control or cost reduction?

Pressure to keep costs in line with established cost standards *(cost control)* comes first in the life of a supervisor. This is closely followed by calls to reduce (or "improve") existing costs. Note that the term *cost improvement* is often used to soften the implication of the real objective: **cost reduction.**

How important is recordkeeping to cost control?

Unless you have furnished to you—or keep—accurate and up-to-date records, controlling costs is next to impossible. When you say "control," it's the same as saying "keep within limits." If you don't know what the limits are—or how well you're holding costs within those limits—you can't very well take any meaningful action.

What must you know about accounting?

You don't have to know double-entry bookkeeping in order to understand cost figures. But you should make a point of understanding the accounting terms your company uses. Don't be afraid of appearing dense: you're a supervisor, not an auditor. Ask questions, if need be, until meanings are clear.

There are three basic measures of cost, however, that accountants use for their own cost control. You are very likely to encounter all three:

1. **Unit costs.** These are the costs, partial or total, which a department (or the company as a whole) accumulates per unit of product or service processed or produced. Unit costs can be expressed in so many dollars and cents per unit, per pound, per gallon, per ton, per sales call, per order, per dollar of billing, per insurance policy issued, and so on.
2. **Standard costs.** These are unit costs that have been set down as "allowable" costs—for materials, for direct and indirect labor, for manufacturing, for marketing, for administration, and the like. As such, these costs become the standards toward which a supervisor is ex-

pected to strive and against which cost performance is judged as either good or bad.

3. **Budgeted costs.** These are the cost guidelines (or targets) issued to supervisors and managers by accountants at the beginning of an accounting period. The budget provides a supervisor with a figure for each item of expense that can be charged to the operation during that period. A supervisor may be able to control some of these figures, while others may be apportioned to him. The budgeted figures may cover only a few items, or they may be presented in considerable detail. In either case, the expectation is that the supervisor will live within or not exceed the budget. Budgeted costs are often called a budget, an expense budget, or an operating budget.

2 BUDGETED COSTS

CONCEPT   Budgets establish departmental cost standards and targets and are used to monitor cost performance.

How do budgets fit into the cost control picture?

Budgetary controls are very similar to cost controls and standards. Typically, the accounting or financial department provides a supervisor with a list of allowable expenses for the month. These are based on the expectation of a certain output, say, 4000 units of production. These allowable expenses become the department's cost standards to be met for the month. At the end of the month the accounting department may issue the supervisor a *cost variance report* (Table 19-1). This tells whether the department has met its standards, exceeded them, or fallen below them. Note that in Table 19-1 the department has exceeded its overall budget by $800. It has, however, met a number of its standards while spending more for material handling, overtime, operating supplies, and maintenance. The supervisor will be expected to do something to bring these cost overruns back into line next month. On the other hand, the department used less than was budgeted for gas, water, and steam. If this keeps up, the accounting department may develop a new standard for those expenses and allow the supervisor less money for them in the future.

Supervisors and others in management use the cost variance report to guide cost control actions. In effect, the report says to a supervisor: "When your costs are under or equal to budget, they are in control. When your costs are over budget, you must exert control to bring them back into line."

Table 19-1   COST VARIANCE REPORT

Department *Assembly*   Dept. no. *707*   Month *July*
No. of units scheduled for production *4000*
No. of units actually produced *4020*
Production variance *+20 units*

Account Title	Actual	Budget	Variance*
Direct labor	$ 8,000	$ 8,000	$ 0
Indirect labor:			
Material handling	900	600	+300
Shop clerical	500	500	0
Supervision	1,200	1,200	0
Overtime	100	0	+100
Shift premium	0	0	0
Operating supplies	500	400	+100
Maintenance and repairs	1,900	1,400	+500
Gas, water, steam, air	1,600	1,800	−200
Electrical power	800	800	0
Total controllable budget	$15,500	$14,700	+$ 800

* + means over; − means under.

Aren't unit costs likely to vary in relation to how much work a department is doing?

Yes. Total costs, studied alone, may be misleading. Suppose labor charges were $20,000 in May and then dropped to $15,000 in June. Did you cut costs by 25 percent? The total cost figures would lead you to believe so. You can't really tell, however, until you compare the units produced (the "throughput") for each month. If the throughput was 20,000 units in May, for example, and only 12,000 in June, then unit labor costs actually went up. How is that figured?

You will usually find your costs expressed in "rates"—so many dollars per unit, per ton, per gallon, per meal served, per insurance claim processed, or per dollar of value of the product or service. In the case described in the last paragraph, the rate of labor costs per unit was calculated in the following way.

For May:

$$\$20,000 \div 20,000 \text{ units} = \$1.00 \text{ per unit}$$

For June:

$$\$15,000 \div 12,000 \text{ units} = \$1.25 \text{ per unit}$$

Cost per unit, then, went *up* by 25 percent in June.

Is that where flexible budgets come in?

More or less. Many expense budgets are presented as a set of budgets in order to anticipate the impact of possible changes in output levels. Such a *flexible budget* may offer several budget options to make allowances for variations in justifiable expenses for varying levels of output. If, for example, a department is scheduled to produce 2000 tons of materials during the budget period, the allowance for direct labor may be pegged at $10,000. If the production schedule is to be raised to 2500 tons, the budget may allow $12,500 for direct labor.

This flexibility is not necessarily absolutely proportional to the changes in output level. The concept, however, is that when output rises, expense allowances will also rise, and when output falls, expenses will also drop.

Furthermore, many expenses—like rent, heat, light, and indirect labor, for example—tend to remain the same regardless of output levels. Even on a flexible budget, these so-called *fixed costs* may be the same for each output level.

An example of a flexible budget is shown in Table 19-2.

3 COST IMPROVEMENT STRATEGIES

CONCEPT   Cost reduction strategies can be either broadly focused or specific in nature, but their success depends upon carefully planned priorities.

How sweeping are cost reduction programs likely to be?

It depends. A strategy for cost reduction can be either applied to the entire organization or confined to the operations of a single department. If it is organizationwide, the program is likely to be sweeping in nature and administered from the top down. If it is a departmental effort, the chances are that the strategy will be a piecemeal one. It will nibble away at costs under a plan conceived of, and implemented by, the department's supervisor.

Supervisors will be expected to accept the disruptions and to clear the path for changes dictated by large-scale, long-term cost improvement programs. Usually, however, supervisors are concerned with modest, ongoing plans for cost reduction. When these are initiated by supervisors, their success will depend upon how well they are thought through and how stubbornly they are pursued. As the hare and tortoise fable pointed out, "Slow and steady wins the race"—even the cost race.

Table 19-2 FLEXIBLE BUDGET

Account Title	Monthly Allowances*			
	3500 tons	4000 tons	4500 tons	5000 tons
Direct labor	$ 7,000	$ 8,000	$ 9,000	$10,000
Indirect labor:				
Material handling	600	600	900	1,200
Shop clerical	500	500	500	500
Supervision	1,200	1,200	1,200	1,200
Overtime premium	0	0	450	450
Shift premiums (2d and 3d)	0	0	0	100
Operating supplies	350	400	450	500
Maintenance and repairs	1,200	1,400	2,000	2,800
Gas, water, steam, compressed air	1,500	1,800	2,100	2,400
Electrical power	700	800	900	1,000
Total controllable costs	$13,050	$14,700	$17,500	$20,150
Insurance	$ 120	$ 120	$ 120	$ 120
Taxes	80	80	80	80
Depreciation of equipment	400	400	400	400
Building occupancy	800	850	900	950
Total allocated costs	$ 1,400	$ 1,450	$ 1,500	$ 1,550
Total allowable costs	$14,450	$16,150	$19,000	$21,700

*Based upon four operating levels in terms of tons produced.

Where are the most promising cost targets to be found?

These usually emerge from a systematic search of the most obvious sources of expense, such as:

Product or service costs. Both the total and unit costs.

Process, or operations, costs. All, or any part, of the department's operating procedures.

People costs. Both direct and indirect. The latter refers to labor costs that support the central operations of a line department—such functions as maintenance, material handling, inspection, housekeeping, and other service functions.

Equipment and tools costs. Either in general or for a particular machine or device.

Materials costs. The materials that go into a product and, often just as important, the operating supplies consumed during the process or while providing the service.

Utilities costs. Power, fuels, water, steam, compressed air, and other utilities used by the department.

Communications costs. Telephone, facsimile, copying, mail, and so forth.

Information costs. Data collection, processing, retrieval, reporting, and analysis.

How should you set your cost-target priorities?

Approaches vary here. Short-term priorities are usually assigned to obvious "action-now" projects. Those projects that take time to carry out, however, are usually held back for an assessment of what they might entail as compared with their returns. On the basis of such an evaluation, targets can be picked and their priorities assigned according to ratings something like these:

1. **Most obvious.** Sometimes the cost element that is most out of line is so obvious that no further search need be made. Occasionally, this choice can be misleading; the true cause of the high cost may lie elsewhere, and the obvious element is only a result.
2. **Easiest.** The course of least resistance is also often the best path to follow to cost savings. A small savings that is quickly reaped with little effort cannot be ignored. Starting with a sure thing can be a good way to build momentum in a cost reduction campaign.
3. **Worst first.** Sometimes a cost situation is so critical that it begs for immediate attention. If such is the case, it is probably wise to attack that cost target first. Otherwise, it may interfere with a more orderly progression toward long-term goals.
4. **Fastest payback.** Sometimes a company's financial policy dictates that those projects that pay back their investment fastest be given highest priority. Certainly, for those cost reduction projects that do require significant investment, this is a sensible choice.

What is meant by a "belt-tightening" program?

This usually refers to a short-term plan—often dictated from above—to cut costs just as fast as you can. Such an approach is negative in nature, in that it allows little room for creative cost "improvements." Instead, belt-tightening will emphasize any of the following approaches:

Stop spending. Costs are cut through the simple expedient of restricting spending to necessities only. Spending for frills, conveniences, and luxuries is stopped. Sometimes the halt is only temporary, for a few weeks or so. Sometimes it can become a permanent way of life. In that case, a supervisor and staff must learn to operate frugally, always.

Do without. This is much like stopping, except that the implication here is that the belt-tightening will be of short duration. The expenses not incurred during this period, however, represent a real contribution to savings. Money not spent for wiping rags today, for example, may never have to be spent later on.

Postpone spending. With this approach, spending is postponed, or deferred, until a later time when the pressure to cut costs is not so severe. Unlike stopping or doing without, postponing implies that the money will be spent, but at a later date. Deferred maintenance work is the most common of these postponed costs. Many times the money that must be spent to do the job later on is greater than what might be needed in the first place. A machine that is not lubricated today may need a new bearing tomorrow. A building that needs only one coat of paint this year may need two coats next year.

Plug leaks. Since the savings strategy is obviously more of a negative philosophy than a positive one, a supervisor is encouraged to find out where expenses are leaking through the controls—and to plug them up. A supervisor might observe, for instance, that over a period of several months overtime has been resorted to far more often than necessary in order to solve delivery problems. The supervisor might now try to plug that leak by developing better schedules as a means of ensuring that orders are filled on time.

4 *COST IMPROVEMENT SOURCES*

CONCEPT Cost improvement ideas may be gathered from a variety of sources, using a number of proven techniques.

Who can provide the necessary cost-cutting ideas?

There are three good sources, all very close to home:

Yourself. Build up a backlog of ideas the year round. Whenever you see or read about something that might work in your department, jot it down in a notebook or place it in a folder. Call these files your "idea banks." Later, when your attention is drawn to costs for any reason, check over your files to see what might be useful. (See, especially, Chapters 17 and 18 for ideas on improving productivity—and quality-related costs.

Your employees. Employees probably know more about the ins and outs of the job than you do. If you encourage employees properly, they are likely to have ideas for cutting production corners or for reducing waste. (See Section 5 of this chapter for ways to stimulate the flow of employee ideas.)

Staff departments. Once you have pinpointed a cost target, staff specialists like industrial engineers and methods and systems people can provide expert help. They can call upon vast reservoirs of examples of how costs were reduced in similar target areas in other departments or other companies.

How helpful are cost reduction committees?

Cost reduction committees were the forerunners of Quality Circles. Many still survive. Many companies obtain impressive results by using a committee to initiate and oversee a cost reduction campaign. Other organizations use a committee to sustain ongoing cost improvement activities. Such committees (and they go by any number of names) provide lots of chances for participation, and they tap a large reservoir of people in the organization for ideas.

What about positive ways to improve costs?

As compared with belt-tightening, the following six approaches to cost improvement tend to accentuate the positive. Each technique provides a different tool for cutting at the roots of cost problems. If one technique doesn't work, try another—or a combination of two or three.

Reduce waste. Where can you find waste in raw materials and operating supplies? How about people? Are you wasting their efforts? Are you getting the most from utilities, or are you wasting water, steam, electricity?

Save time. Can you speed up or double up your equipment? Will time studies show you where time itself can be saved? Are you doing everything you can to get full use of your employees' time?

Increase output. You can cut cost rates—and improve productivity—by stepping up the amount of work put through your department. Sometimes there's a rhythm that goes with high production that's lost with lower production. Sometimes when you cut back, you need the part-time services of several different people, whereas if you increased output, these same people would be working 100 percent of the time. With the higher output base, unit cost rates would actually be lower.

Spend wisely. Cutting costs doesn't always mean that you stop spending. In fact, it's a popular and true expression that you have to spend money to make money. Often top management is more alerted to the need for wise spending during a cost-cutting campaign than at other times. So look for ways to spend money that will ultimately save money, such as on mechanization or on replacement of slow machines with newer, faster ones.

Use space more intelligently. Space—for storage, manufacturing, and shipping—costs money. This cost goes on whether output is high or low. If you can figure out how to get more use out of the same space, you cut costs. Double or triple stacking of pallet loads, for instance, cuts charges for storage space by a half or two-thirds.

Watch your inventories. It may make supervisors feel comfortable to know they have a big backlog of materials and supplies to use or to be shipped, but this is a very costly feeling. Generally, it's a good idea to stock as little as you can safely get away with, especially if supplies can be purchased and delivered quickly. When using up materials in storage, it's also a good idea to use the oldest stock first, before it gets soiled or damaged or becomes obsolete.

Why might an apparent money-saving idea sometimes be turned down by top management?

Mainly because the idea doesn't pay off quickly enough. It is exasperating, of course, for a supervisor to come up with an idea for saving $500, for example, only to have it rejected. Here's the way upper management may have evaluated the idea: Your plan will clearly save $500 a year, but its implementation (hooking up a new keyboard network) will cost the company $3000. This means that it will take six years for your idea to pay off. The cost of financing investments is so great that many companies have adopted the policy that a new machine or piece of equipment must pay for itself in five years or less. In fact, some companies insist on a payoff period of only one year!

Another factor is that your idea is often in competition for investment money with ideas suggested by other supervisors. Obviously, higher management will choose the ideas with the best and fastest payoffs.

▣ *EMPLOYEE REACTIONS*

CONCEPT Employee resistance to cost-cutting changes is likely to be high, so employees require special motivational efforts on the part of their supervisors.

Why do employees fear cost reduction?

Unless you can sell cost reduction to employees, they are likely to be indifferent at best, rebellious at worst. After all, to employees cost cutting may mean loss of work, overtime, their jobs. They feel that cost cutting threatens their security.

What are some chief criticisms employees have toward cost-cutting or productivity improvement campaigns?

Employees often think that management itself throws away money through poor planning and downright misjudgment as to what's really important—and that applies to supervisors too.

Here are some typical worker opinions:

- "One employee saved the company about $2000 one day and the next day almost got laid off for turning in 20 minutes overtime."
- "We put in a new machine, then ripped it apart and sent it away. It probably cost the company $500 to do it. They waste lots of money by not planning the big things."
- "They changed construction of this particular item four or five times, got just short of production, and then the whole thing was called off. What that cost I couldn't even guess!"

Sitting as you do on the management side of the fence, you can understand the reason behind many moves that look wasteful to employees. But the tip-off for you is that the employees frequently don't see the situation the way you do because no one has taken time to make it clear.

Your cue to selling cost reduction is to give employees the facts and help them see that cost cutting (or productivity improvement) helps them; it does not work to their disadvantage.

What is the union's attitude likely to be?

Not much different from that of a rank-and-file employee, except that the union's official opinion may be more contentious. Here are five reactions often heard from labor union leaders when asked to cooperate in cost reduction activities:

- "Layoffs are a prenegotiation strategy of the company to scare us."
- "These layoffs (related to cost reduction) are aimed at weakening the union."
- "This industry is trying to speed up operations in order to produce the same amount of goods and services with more profit and fewer jobs."
- "Management isn't doing a good job of managing. Why should it tell our workers to do a better job before it mends its own fences?"

- "Management keeps 'crying wolf' about international competition, and then it tries to switch our jobs overseas."

Make no mistake about it, much of what the labor leaders say may be true in particular instances. Consequently, if you have a union that actively supports your cost-cutting efforts, you—and your company—have made a convincing case for the need for cost improvement.

Over the long haul, what is the best way to cut through employee resistance and build support for cost improvement?

It will take a long-range effort on your part and must be reinforced by sound planning and a genuine concern for employee welfare. The seven suggestions that follow will provide a firm foundation for your efforts:

1. **Talk to employees about cost reduction in terms of their interests.** You must see their point of view, or they'll never be able to get yours. In face-to-face conversations, show them how the company's interest in profits relates directly to a worker's interest in higher wages and job security. Show that one can't be achieved without the other.

2. **Bring the cost picture down to earth.** Don't talk in global terms of standard costs, of productivity ratios, or even about hard times. If company sales have fallen off, talk in terms of its impact upon the services produced in your department: "We processed 10,000 forms the first quarter, but our schedule calls for only half as many to be handled this quarter." If rising materials charges are a factor, pick up a product your employees make and tell them: "Last year, fabric for this item cost 50 cents, now it costs 60 cents—a rise of 20 percent."

3. **Set specific goals.** Don't say, "We've got to cut costs to the bone." Instead, suggest a specific program: "Our records show that keyboarding costs must be lowered by 10 percent. We'll have to figure a way to improve our methods to do this." Or, "Defective production that had to be scrapped cost us $1200 last month. This month, let's get it down below $1000."

4. **Invite participation.** Let employees know that you need their help in solving cost problems—and that help means more than cooperation. Tell them you need their ideas, too, and will welcome any suggestions.

5. **Explain why and how.** The reasons for each specific change should be spelled out. And employees need your help, too, in deciding how to attain the cost-cutting goals you set.

6. **Train for cost improvement.** One of the key elements in quality-circle programs is the training provided to employees in the tech-

niques of problem solving and methods improvement. Try to incorporate these self-developmental elements into your cost improvement training activities.

7. **Report cost progress.** Score keeping appeals to the achievement needs in many employees. Reports of progress toward cost goals (posted on bulletin boards, for example) stimulate competitiveness and self-motivation.

REVIEW

KEY CONCEPTS TO REMEMBER

1. Effective cost control and cost improvement both depend upon the availability of accurate records. Costs may be measured and reported as total costs, unit costs, or standard costs or in the form of budgeted costs (or expenses).

2. Budgets establish departmental cost standards, or targets. They are essentially tables of allowable expenses for a given period, like a month or a year. Unit costs are especially useful, since they translate total costs into comparable measures. Flexible budgets are used to provide a number of optional tables of expenses in order to anticipate variations in output levels during the period.

3. Cost improvement efforts can be large-scale and long-term or piecemeal and short-range. Supervisors usually initiate the latter. The most promising cost targets are close at hand, including the costs of products or services, processing, people, equipment and tools, materials and supplies, utilities, communications, and information. Many cost reduction programs are negative in nature, featuring several belt-tightening approaches including stopping or postponing spending and doing without.

4. Ideas for cost improvement come from supervisors, their employees, staff departments, and cost reduction committees, including quality circles. Positive programs for cost improvement include reducing waste, saving time, increasing output, spending wisely, conserving space, and controlling inventories. Cost improvement ideas that require expenditures for their implementation are often in competition with other ideas that require financing.

5. Employees are often fearful that cost reduction programs will bring about unpleasant changes and/or threaten their job security.

Labor unions tend to have similar reactions, and they support the resistance that these attitudes induce. Supervisors must struggle to modify these fears in order to obtain employee cooperation and support for cost and productivity improvements. This is accomplished by—among other things—honest, candid, factual communication and by inviting employee participation in solving cost-related problems.

SUPERVISORY WORD POWER

Budget. A plan, or forecast, especially of expenses that are allowable in the operation of a department.

Cost variance report. A listing of allowable expenses compared with the actual expenses incurred.

Direct costs. Variable costs that can be clearly identified as adding value directly to the goods produced or services rendered.

Fixed costs. Costs which tend to be constant, at least on an annual basis, and which are not related to the rate of production, services rendered, or amount of sales.

Flexible budget. A budget that presents several options based upon possible variations in output levels.

Indirect costs. Variable costs which are essential to the production of goods or rendering of services but which do not clearly add value to them or do not do so in an easily measurable way.

Standard costs. The normal, or expected, costs of an operation, product, or service (usually including labor, materials, and overhead charges) computed on the basis of past performance, estimates, or work measurement.

Unit cost. The cost of producing a single product or unit—measure of output of a product or service.

Variable costs. Costs that tend to vary (directly or indirectly) according to the volume of goods produced, services rendered, and/or sales generated.

READING COMPREHENSION

1. Jane has been told that cost control in her department is all right but that she must now make some cost improvements. What is the distinction?
2. Distinguish between total costs and unit costs.

3. "You are over budget this month," the plant manager told the department supervisor. What report would have given the manager that information?

4. Bud's total cost for computer paper was $1000 in January and $750 in February. His department serviced 80 accounts in January and 50 in February. Did his unit cost for paper go up or down in February? Show your calculations.

5. Marty supervises a manufacturing department. His payroll for assembly workers has varied with his department's output, but the payroll for clerical help has stayed constant. How can this be?

6. Compare a belt-tightening cost program with a cost improvement program.

7. How are cost reduction committees and Quality Circles alike? How are they different?

8. Why can better use of space be considered a cost improvement method?

9. How might a labor union's attitude differ from an employee's attitude toward cost reduction programs?

10. Which approach—(a) or (b)—is more likely to stimulate employee cooperation in cost reduction? Why? (a) "Your jobs are threatened now by price-cutting competitors." (b) "You can help protect your jobs from price-cutting competitors if we can find a way to reduce our department's scrap percentage from 5 to 2 percent a month."

APPLICATION

SELF-APPRAISAL

How good a handle do you have on costs?

The following statements pertain to conceiving and implementing cost control and improvement programs. Your assignment is to determine which statements are true, or represent sound practice, and which are false, or represent unsound practice. On a separate piece of paper, copy the column headings shown on page 444. In the column "Cost Control Statements," write the numbers 1 to 10 down the page to correspond to each of the statements. Then place a check mark in the column that most nearly matches your opinion about each statement. After completing this activity, check your answers by using the scoring procedure described below.

Column headings:

Cost Control Statements	True, or Sound Practice	False, or Unsound Practice

1. Good cost controls require good cost records.
2. Unit costs are usually more helpful in tracking cost progress than are total costs.
3. When a department's costs are equal to or below budget, they are under control.
4. A flexible budget allows for variations in output levels.
5. Supervisors are concerned only with short-range, piecemeal cost reduction plans.
6. An edict that all spending must stop or be postponed is the starting point for all cost improvement programs.
7. Cost reduction committees and Quality Circles are essentially the same thing.
8. You sometimes have to spend money to save money.
9. Employees tend to accept cost reduction programs, while labor unions resist them.
10. A cost improvement program can be made more effective by including plans for employee involvement.

Scoring   Give yourself 1 point for each of the following statements that you checked as *true,* or representing sound practice: 1, 2, 3, 4, 8, 10. Give yourself 1 point for each of the following items that you checked as *false,* or representing unsound practice: 5, 6, 7, 9.

Interpretation   If you scored 9 or 10 points, you've got a good handle on cost improvement concepts and methods. If you scored 7 or 8 points, you may let some costs slip through your fingers. Review the items you missed. If you scored less than 7 points, your containment of costs may be more like a sieve. Restudy the entire chapter.

CASE STUDIES

CASE 57   The Unwilling Workers

They were a sullen bunch, thought Andrés Gonzales, the supervisor of the housekeeping crew for the Monarch Hotel chain's four-star resort hotel in Florida. The chain had just announced a companywide belt-tightening cost reduction program. A lid has been placed upon all wage increases until January, which is three months away. All departmental requests for new equipment, even for replacement parts, are to be postponed until January too. When Andrés complained to his boss that half the vacuum cleaners needed major repairs or replacement, his boss told him that he'd just have to "make do."

The housekeeping employees were none too happy about any of this, but one thing in particular really upset them. The belt-tightening program dictated that all overtime would have to stop until the spring season began. Wages were low enough anyway, many employees thought. It was the possibility of working overtime at time-and-a-half pay that made the wages halfway bearable. Now, that was out too.

Within a week after the announcement of the program, Andrés became aware that he had a serious problem on his hands. Employee resistance took the form of a slowdown. Jobs that normally took a half hour were now taking an hour or more. Jobs that one crew member could ordinarily handle alone were now requiring an additional worker. There was a rash of minor disruptions too—water valves left open, damaging flooring and carpets; bundles of bed linens inexplicably soiled; and a flood of complaints from guests about poorly serviced rooms, requiring callbacks.

If you were Andrés, what would you do to gain acceptance for the company's belt-tightening program? Of the five alternatives provided below, which do you think might be the most effective? Rank the alternatives on a scale from 1 (most preferable) to 5 (least preferable). You may add another alternative, if you wish. In any event, be prepared to justify your ranking.

a. Call a meeting; make it known that the slowdowns and disruptions must stop or there will be mass firings.
b. Call a meeting; appeal to the better nature of your employees and ask for their cooperation "for the duration."
c. Call a meeting; listen to complaints and ask for ideas for softening the impact of the program, but tell the employees they must get back into line until you can petition for relief.
d. Go to your boss; show her that the belt-tightening program is backfiring, since it's costing more money than it saves.
e. Try to live with the situation until January; there's little you can do about these conditions.

CASE 58   Kindly Make Every Effort...

Leopold G., the supervisor of the weaving department, received this note from the controller of the textile plant: "Kindly make every effort to reduce your operating costs this month by 5 percent. Our schedules call for a throughput the same as last month." The supervisor looked at last month's total charges, which came to $20,000. Of that total, $10,000 was a direct labor charge; he decided that since these men and women were on piece rates, this figure could not be cut. However, he felt that the $2500 he had incurred in indirect labor might be reduced drastically, since he had "borrowed" much of it from the labor pool to do a cleanup job. Operating supplies had come to $1500, and that surprised him. But, on thinking about it, he recalled that $500 had come from a requisition for wiping rags, and he would not have to reorder them this month. Maintenance was still running heavy, he felt, and the charges of $3000 were sure to be repeated this month. His prorated share of electricity came to $1200, and he felt that there was nothing he could do about that. Water, too, at $1800 a month, was a steady charge that he could not avoid.

a. How many dollars must Leopold save this month to meet the 5 percent reduction "requested" of him?
b. From which two of his budget items will he be able to make these savings?
c. How much will he save from each?

CASE 59   The Creeping Cost of Operating Supplies

Last year, the cost of operating supplies in the copying department of a real estate agency came to a total of $1600. During that year the agency published 1000 listings. This year, copying costs have been inching up at the rate of an additional 10 percent every three months. Listings, however, will remain the same at 1000.

a. What was the unit cost of copying per listing last year?
b. If the increases in copying costs continue, what will be the total cost of copying this year?
c. What will that make the unit cost per listing this year?

1 A strong body of law protects employee rights and privileges.

2 Disadvantaged employees need special support from supervisors.

3 Rights of women, too, need enhancement by their supervisors.

4 Younger and older workers benefit from special consideration.

5 Supervisors must be alert to issues such as employee privacy.

CHAPTER 20

Equal Opportunity Under the Law

LEARNING OBJECTIVES

After studying this chapter, you should be able to

1. Identify and interpret the major equal employment opportunity legislation, explain the intent of affirmative action plans, and describe the role of the Equal Employment Opportunity Commission.

2. Discuss the special problems of disadvantaged workers and suggest ways for integrating these employees successfully into the workplace.

3. Discuss the importance of women in the workplace and their difficulties in advancing from their traditional roles, including related subjects such as job evaluation, comparable worth, and sexual harassment.

4. Suggest ways for motivating younger and older employees and discuss the unique assets and drawbacks of aging workers.

5. Explain the legal and social aspects of an employee's right to privacy and the impact this has on a supervisor's right to manage.

THE LEGAL BASIS

CONCEPT   A strong body of law establishes the rights and privileges of all job applicants and employees, regardless of race, color, national origin, sex, handicap, or age.

In the eyes of the law, who is a minority employee?

Just about everyone who is not a middle-aged white male of European heritage and the beneficiary of a fairly adequate primary education. The generally more useful term applied to minorities today is **protected groups.** A protected group consists of people who, historically, have encountered discrimination in the American workplace. Most of the relevant laws specifically identify these people as ethnic and racial minorities (blacks, Hispanics, Asians, and Native Americans, in particular), women (white as well as black), disadvantaged young persons, handicapped workers, veterans of the Vietnam war era, and persons over 40 years of age.

The basic equal employment opportunity laws say that an employer cannot discriminate because of race, color, religion, sex, national origin, or age. In trying to make these laws work, various agencies of the U.S. government have interpreted them to apply to all victims of prejudice and discrimination. There has also been a special concern for those who are uneducated and have grown up in extreme poverty such as occurs in many urban ghettos and some rural areas.

What has caused this intensified concern for minorities?

Great social forces at work in the past 40 years have altered the values of many people. What were once acceptable stereotypes of blacks and women, for example, are no longer tolerated—either by law or by society in general. Family life-styles and marriage patterns have radically changed. And with them, our notions of what are appropriate occupations and behavior for women—or men—have changed too. A great many people enjoy relatively affluent and privileged livings. This makes for harsh comparisons with those who do not have jobs or who are relegated to second-class work and often second-class pay. The power of television and instant communications intensifies the awareness of these differences. People—especially those who believe that their second-class status is the result of discrimination (as it often is)—are impatient for improvement. The newer laws are a direct expression of the public's general dissatisfaction with these conditions and its wish to provide equal employment opportunities for all.

There is a great body of federal, state, and local laws. These have been reinforced by a number of significant rulings in the courts. The laws are further supported by guidelines laid down by the **Equal Employment Opportunity Commission** (EEOC), the federal agency charged with enforcing the law.

There is no need for you to be bogged down with the details, which are extensive. A synopsis of the major federal laws, popularly referred to as the **equal employment opportunity (EEO) laws,** is provided for your review in Table 20-1. Most importantly, these laws specify that the great majority of business firms and public institutions cannot:

- Make any distinctions based on race, sex, or national origin in any condition of employment, including hiring, setting wages ("equal pay for equal work"), classifying, assigning or promoting, and allocating the use of facilities, and in training, retraining, and apprenticeship programs.
- Distinguish between married and single people of one sex and not of the other.
- Deny employment to women with young children unless the same policies apply to men with young children.
- Penalize women because they require time away from work for childbearing.
- Maintain seniority lists based solely on sex or race.
- Establish jobs as either men's or women's. The only exceptions allowed are jobs for which the employer can prove that there is a bona fide occupational qualification (BFOQ).
- Discriminate against workers 40 years of age or over in hiring, firing, promoting, classifying, paying, assigning, advertising, or eligibility for union membership.
- Similarly discriminate against qualified handicapped persons. The law defines handicapped, or disabled, persons as individuals who (1) have a physical or mental impairment (the term *impaired* is preferred by many) which substantially limits one or more major life activities, (2) have a record of such impairments, or (3) are regarded as having such impairment. You can see that the definition covers almost everything.

Obviously, EEO legislation was designed to protect minority groups of all definition from discrimination. Its principal intent, however, has been to encourage more rapid utilization of blacks and women in the work force. Note that the law is *not* a labor-management law: it is directed at employers, and they must comply without obstruction from labor unions.

Table 20-1	SYNOPSIS OF MAJOR FEDERAL LAWS ENACTED SINCE 1960 THAT AFFECT EQUAL EMPLOYMENT OPPORTUNITY

Law	Provision
Equal Pay Act (1963)	Amended the long-standing Fair Labor Standards Act of 1938 to require the same pay for men and women doing the same work.
Titles VI and VII, Civil Rights Act of 1964 as amended by Equal Employment Act of 1972	Prohibits job discrimination in all employment practices on the basis of race, color, sex, religion, or national origin. This includes recruiting, selecting, compensating, classifying, assigning, promoting, disciplining, and terminating, as well as eligibility for union membership. The EEOC administers these laws and monitors related affirmative action programs.
Executive Order 11246 of 1965 as amended by Executive Order 11375 of 1967	Prohibits discrimination in employment in organizations having contracts of $10,000 or more with the federal government. The orders require that these organizations institute affirmative action programs and recruit and promote women and minorities where necessary.
Age Discrimination in Employment Act (1967) as amended in 1975	Prohibits discrimination in hiring and employment of workers over 40 years of age unless BFOQ can be established.
Rehabilitation Act of 1973 and Executive Order 11914 of 1974	Prohibits discrimination of physically and mentally handicapped applicants and employees by federal contractors.
Vietnam Era Veteran's Readjustment Assistance Act of 1974	Prohibits discrimination—by federal contractors—in employment of disabled veterans and veterans of the Vietnam war; also specifies certain affirmative actions in the employment of veterans.

Where does affirmative action apply?

In enforcing the provisions of the equal employment opportunity laws, the EEOC has encouraged firms to engage in **affirmative action programs.** An affirmative action program consists of positive action taken to ensure nondiscriminatory treatment of all groups that are protected by legislation that forbids discrimination in employment because of race, religion, sex, age, handicap, Vietnam era war service, or national origin. The EEOC emphasizes that results count, not good intentions. If company statistics on pay and promotion, for example, show that the current status of minority groups is inferior to that of most other employees in that company or geographic area, the company may be directed to set up an affirmative action program. Companies with federal contracts over $50,000 and with more than 50 employees have no choice. They must have a written program in working order.

In investigating EEO discrimination charges, what areas are most sensitive?

The EEOC will look for three possibilities:

Differential treatment. This occurs when a member of a protected group is treated differently from a nonmember in the same situation.

Disparate effect. When a job requirement acts to exclude a protected group, it creates a disparate effect. The employer must demonstrate that the requirement is a "business necessity" and thus a BFOQ.

Evil intent. This is present, for instance, when an employer or supervisor is "out to get" a member of a protected group.

These infractions are most likely to occur in recruiting, interviewing, selecting, assigning, appraising, training, promoting, and disciplining employees. Supervisors are intimately involved in all these areas. Accordingly, they bear a great deal of the responsibility for carrying out the spirit, as well as the requirements, of the law.

What is meant by reverse discrimination?

This is what many persons believe happens to men and also to members of the white race when preference in employment is shown to women, minorities, or both. In the *Bakke* case of 1978, the Supreme Court said in effect that it was wrong to use quotas designed to accommodate women and blacks in such a manner as to withhold employment from eligible men and whites. At the same time, however, the Supreme Court upheld the principle of affirmative action programs.

As you can infer, supervisors must tread a very unbiased line in this matter. They must be sure to support the principle of equal employment opportunity and affirmative action; yet they must also be careful not to use these guidelines unfairly to discriminate against nonminorities.

2 DISADVANTAGED MINORITIES

CONCEPT A significant part of the population has traditionally been "disadvantaged" and requires especially supportive treatment from their supervisors.

You hear of unemployed persons and of the hard-core unemployed. What's the difference?

The majority of unemployed persons are people who move in and out of the work force temporarily as they lose or quit one job and seek another. There are millions of other unemployed persons, however, who are out of work more of the time than they are employed. These are the especially disadvantaged. Typically, they have the following characteristics that make them a challenge to their supervisors when they finally find what they hope will be good jobs:

- They are school dropouts, usually with only a sixth- or seventh-grade education. Many do not speak or write English. As many as 30 percent have less than fifth-grade reading and arithmetic skills.
- They are single heads of households, men and women with large family responsibilities that tend to overwhelm them with problems.
- They have poor work histories. Few have worked at anything but day labor or in casual service as dishwashers or porters, for example. They have not been prepared for work by their families, their communities, or their schools.
- They are plagued by personal problems. They have little experience in managing a regular income and may need help in handling credit, balancing a budget, or even learning how to cash a paycheck.

Recently employed hard-core or disadvantaged persons are troubled by job and business conditions that others accept as routine. They often have difficulty in getting along with the boss or with their co-workers. For example, one 24-year-old ghetto youth said that he reacted at first to orders from his supervisor the way he'd react to being pushed around by a street-gang leader: "I had to learn not to take orders personally. When someone told me to get this or do that, I'd get mad. Finally, I learned that the boss was reacting to the pressure of his job and had nothing against me." In like fashion, many of the disadvantaged view rules and regulations as something devised to harass them, not as reasonable guidelines for organized behavior that everyone has to follow.

Is it true that many disadvantaged people get "tested" out of jobs?

It was true to a great extent until 1971, when the United States Supreme Court (*Griggs v. Duke Power*) handed down a decision barring "discriminatory" job testing. Few tests, however, are intentionally discriminatory; it is just that most tests have been built around cultural models of white, middle-class people. As you can see by definition, privileged people are not typical of the hard-core unemployed, and tests—when used indiscriminately—screened out the latter. Nevertheless, as a result of the Supreme Court decision, testing for selection, placement, or training in industry has been modified to identify aptitudes and skills of disadvantaged persons rather than unwittingly separating out from the labor force people with untapped potential.

Federal guidelines for employment testing require that tests be validated (if adverse impact is present) so that a test really measures what it says it measures and does not exclude minorities or women in a discriminatory fashion. Tests must be validated on two counts:

Content validity. This means that the test content is truly related to the job requirements. It would be unfair to give a complex typing test requiring 100 words a minute when the job requires only the simplest sort of typing at 60 words a minute.

Construct validity. This means that the test is put together in such a way that it does not screen out applicants who could pass the content part if only they could understand the test questions themselves. For example, applicants might be able to demonstrate mechanical aptitude if they could read the questions. Perhaps the test should be administered orally rather than in writing.

What works and what doesn't work in training hard-core employees?

Training fundamentals do not vary from situation to situation or from person to person. It is more a matter of intensifying the fundamental techniques. Companies like Chrysler, Western Electric, Lockheed, and the Equitable Life Assurance Society have found that the following guidelines need special emphasis:

1. **Make the training specific.** Avoid generalizations and abstractions. Talk about concrete things such as pounds, inches, steel, and paper. Show how each new subject relates to a job or to a product.
2. **Rely on demonstrations.** Actions and illustrations, plus live demonstrations, communicate far more effectively than do words alone with an audience for whom speaking, reading, and other verbal skills are underdeveloped. Repeat and repeat the demonstration until you are sure the trainee has understood what you are doing.
3. **Overtrain rather than undertrain.** Err on the side of providing more information and more skills than are needed for the work to be done. That way, trainees will be less likely to underperform on the job, and they'll have more confidence in their ability to do it well.
4. **Offer personal aid.** It may not seem germane to a training effort for a supervisor to help a trainee get a ride to work, have a garnishment reduced, or even provide jail bail, but it helps to keep the

trainee's mind on what is being learned and, of course, it builds confidence in the boss.

5. **Provide lots of follow-up.** In some cases, the most meaningful training takes place when a supervisor shows a trainee again on the job what may have already been shown in training. That's because it is on the job that learning becomes most relevant and least academic.

6. **Reassure and recognize frequently.** It may seem like pampering to assure a person repeatedly that progress is good or to tell that person (and others) constantly how well the work is going; but with people who have been on the receiving end of put-downs most of their lives, it takes an overabundance of encouragement to reinforce their confidence in themselves.

7. **Use the buddy system.** Appoint a co-worker, preferably a disadvantaged person, from whom the trainee can get private counseling. The first days on a new job are often full of hazing and mistakes. At one St. Louis plant, for instance, a trainee inadvertently was doused with oil on his first day in the shop. He would not have returned to the job after lunch, he said, if his buddy hadn't shown him that it was an accident and that it wouldn't happen again.

3 WOMEN IN THE WORKPLACE

CONCEPT   Women, too, have traditionally been denied equal opportunities in the workplace, and these rights must now be protected and enhanced.

How important are women to national productivity?

They are absolutely essential. Out of every five persons working in the United States, two or more are women. And they perform work of increasing importance. Consider these two facts: Women now occupy more than 40 percent of all managerial and professional positions; nearly two-thirds of all technical, sales, and administrative support jobs are filled by women.

It is instructive to look at the turnaround in the nature of women earning money since the beginning of this century. U.S. Department of Labor figures reported that in 1900 only one out of twenty married women was at work and two out of every three women in the labor force were single. By 1971, four out of every ten married women were at work, and only one out of every four women in the work force was single. In 1985, 59 percent of the women in the work force were married and 16 percent were widowed or divorced. Regardless of marital status, the increase in the number of women working has been nothing less than spectacular, as illustrated in Figure 20-1.

But what about compensation for women?

Unfortunately, that's another story, and it is one that makes many women justifiably unhappy. Estimates vary, but it would appear that—on average—women receive only about two-thirds to three-quarters of the pay that men do in the labor market. How can that happen? Mainly because women have traditionally been shunted toward lower-paying, lower-status jobs and blocked from advancement into higher ones.

Why doesn't job evaluation put an end to this discrimination in pay?

It does, but only for work that is performed and compensated for under a job-evaluation plan. Even then, it does not close all the possible loopholes. And of course it can do nothing to remedy the lack of opportunities, which is the role of the EEO legislation.

The relevant law of the land (the Fair Labor Standards Act as amended by the Equal Pay Act of 1963 and again by Public Law 92-318 in 1972) stipulates that all employees, regardless of sex or other discriminatory identification, should receive the same pay for the same kind and amount of work. *Job evaluation* is the basic means for making sure that this

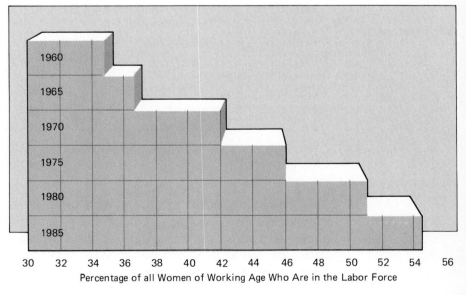

Source: U.S. Department of Labor

Figure 20-1 Growth in the percentage of women who work.

occurs. The "equal pay for equal work" standard, like job evaluation, requires scrutiny of the job as a whole. Its intention is that job titles be ignored and attention focused on actual job requirements and performance. The law examines four factors in particular: equal skill, equal effort, equal responsibility, and similarity of working conditions. Whereas the law does acknowledge some exceptions, it will not permit the concepts of "women's jobs," "men's jobs," "job lists for nonwhites," and the like. On the other hand, the law does permit the use of merit pay plans that recognize a difference, within a job pay range, of different levels of performance among individuals or as reflected by seniority.

What is meant by comparable worth?

This is a concept used for evaluating widely dissimilar jobs. The Equal Pay Act of 1963 charges discrimination if women aren't given pay equal to men's pay for equal work. In a great many instances, however, women perform work that is radically different from the work performed by men in the same organization. Nevertheless, these women often feel, with justification, that their pay is still not equal, all things considered. The concept of **comparable worth** is an effort to rectify this kind of situation. It makes it possible for the work—and the pay—of a toll collector, for example, to be compared with that of a nurse. Typically, this approach involves examination and comparison of four factors: level of know-how required, problem solving entailed, accountability, and working conditions. The applicability of the comparable worth concept is challenged by some labor unions and women's organizations on the grounds that it emphasizes subjective judgments (often with a sexist bias) to a greater degree than do most traditional job-evaluation systems. Some employers also contend that it is the supply and demand of labor that really determines pay. Many people also say that they have little faith in an evaluation system that compares apples with oranges, as in equating a clerk's worth with that of a craftsperson.

For most women, what appears to be the main ingredient missing in the labor market in general and in their jobs in particular?

An opportunity equal to that of men for securing intellectually challenging employment and a chance for advancement in proportion to their performance and capabilities. Too often in the past, the traditional or stereotypical attitude of management and supervision was essentially protective. The question asked was "Is the work fitting for a woman?" not "What is she capable of?" Accordingly, women generally found themselves restricted to secretarial and clerical routines in the office and to benchwork or nonthink jobs in the plant.

Worse still has been the tendency for a supervisor to grow dependent on the know-how and can-do of a particular woman worker while at the same time concealing the true extent of her capabilities from others in management; thus her advancement and development are stymied, to say nothing of limitations that are put on her income. And of course there are endless instances where the capabilities of an individual are freely acknowledged in an organization as long as it is confined to activities considered suitable for women.

The time has come—in fact, is long overdue—for supervisors and managers to open, rather than to block, the way outward (in terms of job scope) and upward (in terms of training, status, and financial opportunity) for the women who work for them. The supervisor who is progressive and liberated in the management of women will find that *all* employees are more highly motivated and have a greater loyalty and devotion to the company's objectives.

How differently from men should you treat women at work?

There should be no basic difference in how you supervise women and men. The principles of sound, equitable, and considerate management should apply just as fully to the supervision of women as to the supervision of men. It probably can't be repeated often enough that a person is a person is a person. Regardless of sex—and color and national origin and religious preference—the starting point in good human relations is the recognition of each person's unique individuality and the conviction that he or she will respond most favorably when treated with respect and thoughtfulness.

Can a woman do every job a man can do?

For every job a man now does, there is a woman, somewhere, who can do it as well or better. But, in general, there is no good reason to demand that women do every job that men do. In a great number of jobs requiring heavy physical effort, women—compared with men—have limited capabilities.

In spite of such limiting factors, to say nothing of stereotyped thinking in making job assignments, the latest U.S. Census reported one or more women in every one of the 479 occupational classifications. In fact, there were thousands working as welders, drafters, and painters and at maintenance crafts. Certainly, the employment of so many women in nontraditional jobs is an object lesson on the speciousness of withholding from any woman the opportunity to perform the kind of work for which she may be qualified.

But what about charges of sexual harassment?

The statistics often cited are shameful. Apparently, there are a great many men who purposely or inadvertently mix sexually oriented behavior or overtures with their work. Supervisors are the persons most notably (if not justifiably) charged with such harassment. Obviously, they are also the ones who must guard against any actions that give substance to the charge.

In a study of federal office workers, for example, a majority of women listed these types of occurrences that they found sexually oriented and particularly distasteful:

1. Confrontation with letters, phone calls, or materials of a sexual nature.
2. Pressure for sexual favors in return for preferred job assignments or job security.
3. Touching, leaning over, cornering, or pinching—regardless of how nonsexually oriented the intentions might be.
4. Pressure for dates off the job, for whatever reason.
5. Sexually suggestive looks or gestures.
6. Teasing, joking, remarks, or questions that have sexual overtones.

The message seems clear. Men, and women, who want to play games or seek favors with sexual implications must not do so at work. Supervisors have the responsibility for maintaining the proper levels of sexual decorum, even to the point of appearing stuffy and straight as a consequence.

4 YOUNGER AND OLDER WORKERS

CONCEPT   Younger, as well as older, workers require a special kind of nurturing from their supervisors.

What characterizes the younger work force?

First of all, it is within this group that the highest levels of unemployment occur, especially among black teenagers. As a consequence, the typical younger worker under 25 enters the labor force with a jaundiced eye toward business—toward what is called "the establishment." The disadvantaged younger worker, especially, enters the labor market keenly distrustful of the establishment's intent.

Younger workers may come from backgrounds that are rich or poor. Their education may be complete, or they may be dropouts from the school—or straight—scene. They may have ambition in the traditional sense—to achieve—or they may wish only to collect enough paychecks to underwrite their next adventures. They may be white Caucasians or black, Puerto Rican, or Chicano. Their politics may be radically left or head-knocking, hard-hat right, or younger workers may have no social concerns at all. Their distinguishing characteristics are (1) a deep preoccupation with themselves as individuals with unique prerogatives and (2) an almost universal suspicion of everything traditional.

The disadvantaged younger workers begin the battle for survival, let alone work, with several handicaps—most of which are neither of their own choosing nor of their own making. They suffer from all the usual wounds of the poor—poor background at home, poor education, poor diet, poor health, poor legal protection. They may be white, but the chances are that their skin is brown, yellow, or black. The probability is that they have never worked at a decent job with fair pay or in an enlightened environment. They may never have enjoyed any of the social comforts that the vast majority experience. Their politics may be militant, but it is more likely to be nonexistent. Their distinguishing characteristics are (1) an outlook that recognizes no values beyond those of today, (2) a disbelief in the possibility that business will ever provide an honest opportunity to succeed, and (3) a hopeless feeling that the cards are stacked against them.

Deep down, the typical younger worker asks, "What's in it for me now?"

Deep down, the disadvantaged younger worker asks, "What's the use of trying?"

How serious does this make the generation gap in business?

It is at its most critical in the realm of what any older person will accept without complaint and what a younger person will refuse to do, regardless of pay. Whereas an old-timer will brag about the scars from welding sparks, a 22-year-old packs up and quits. A veteran grimly clenches his nostrils as he seals up a coke-oven door in a steel mill; the recent high school graduate balks at that and asks his union steward to get him off that job. A woman who has worked for years as a blotter clerk in a stockbroker's cage swallows her boredom; a young woman says that life is too short for that.

What is the root of this difference? The answers vary. Some say it is the permissiveness and the relative affluence in which most young people have grown up. Others say it is simply the difference between a compelling reason to earn a full-scale livelihood (as most older, married persons must) and the wish only to make enough cash for walking around. Then, too, younger people are better educated, have higher levels of expectation, are more mobile, and are more aware of attractive conditions elsewhere. For whatever reason, younger persons are not docile. Either the job will be made more tolerable for them—or they will walk away from it.

What can a supervisor do to better motivate and manage young workers?

Supervisors should take their cues from younger workers' complaints. Specifically, a supervisor must:

1. **Exert authority only from reason.** Dependence on power invites rebellion. A supervisor's authority ought to make sense in terms of its conservation of effort and resources, its recognition of the humanness of employees, and its understanding of the value in change as well as in conformance.

2. **Learn to move faster in making changes.** This century moves ever faster in its development of knowledge and technology. Tradition has lost much of its value and meaning. It should be tested constantly against current needs. Letting go of the old must be achieved with dispatch. Neither progress nor capable young workers will wait very long for you to embrace the new.

3. **Convey the meaning of each assignment.** There is nothing unique about the younger worker's cry for relevance. Men and women have wished to gain this from their work since time began. In order to apply oneself, one needs to know why a job must be done a certain way, why it must be done at all, and how it relates to what is going on around one.

4. **Make sure the younger workers know what results are expected of them.** Vague admonitions rather than specific goals and targets will weaken a younger person's resolve. Make certain, too, that the wage system is clearly understood—exactly how pay will be related to accomplishment.

5. **Provide support and assistance.** Especially in job training, a supervisor's desire to help employees become proficient is welcomed as an expression of respect and confidence.

6. **Praise freely when it is deserved.** Younger people are less confident of their performance and need constant feedback as to its quality. Conversely, when you criticize, it is important to be tactful. Similarly, discipline must appear to be reasonable rather than arbitrary.

7. **Enrich the nature of the work.** Monotony stems from repetition that allows no room for improvisation and ingenuity. By stretching the limits of each job and by incorporating into it elements of depth, employees will have the freedom, should they choose it, to provide their own variety while they are still committed to a specific, demanding goal.

When does a worker become considered as older?

The Age Discrimination in Employment Act categorizes people over 40 years of age as older. Most authorities, however, observe that by age 45, employees have become older. They are mature, settled, experienced, and usually well trained. But they already have family responsibilities, often heavy ones; and signs of both physical aging and emotional wear are becoming evident.

What is important to keep in mind is that age affects each person differently. Its effect depends on a large number of factors: heredity, durability, physical condition, exposure to weather, extreme living or working conditions, climate, indulgence in food or drink, drug abuse, and emotional and psychological strains. Nevertheless, it is a good rule of thumb for a supervisor to look for signs of change due to age in any employee over 50 years old. Changes may be physical or mental, slight or marked. Changes may affect the older worker's performance for better or for worse. But change there is.

What are the chief assets of older workers?

Older workers have many. According to Dr. William A. Sawyer, formerly medical director of the Eastman Kodak Company and later medical consultant to the International Association of Machinists, AFL, these are the assets older workers take to work:

Safety. They have far fewer accidents.

Attendance. They have a better absence record. They are sick less often, although their illnesses tend to last longer than those of younger people.

Judgment. The variety of their work and social experiences tends to improve older workers' judgment and to familiarize them with a variety of work situations.

Loyalty. Broad experience has helped older workers to recognize good supervision when they get it—and to reward that supervision with the loyalty it deserves.

Skill. Once acquired, job skills rarely start to fade before a person reaches 60, often not until much later.

What are the chief drawbacks of older workers?

Older workers have many liabilities. But their experience and skills often permit them to compensate for the liabilities. On the whole, older workers tend to be:

Slower. Age slows athletes and workers. But whereas older people work more slowly, they may make fewer mistakes.

Weaker. Their strength fades, too, although by now they may have learned to work more intelligently, not harder.

Less resilient. Older workers haven't the endurance they once had. Fatigue—mental and physical—sets in faster. And illnesses and accidents keep them off the job longer than they would a younger person. But remember, older workers are less likely to have either happen.

Suffer from poor eyesight. Near vision may suffer—they may need bifocals to correct it. But if vision also includes the ability to understand what we see, then older workers aren't much worse off than their sharp-eyed children.

Is it true that older workers learn less readily than younger ones?

This is a tricky question because the learning process is so complicated. It's best answered by saying that older persons, with their greater experience, could learn just as quickly as younger persons—if the older persons were as well motivated. Younger people learn faster because they want to learn, because they see learning as a key to their futures. Older persons may see no benefit from learning. They have done their bit, they may think, so why try to learn something new?

Older workers are likely to learn best when they are kept apprised of how well they are doing. Experience has made them especially sensitive to this form of motivation. It satisfies both their achievement need and their need for respect. The value that older workers place on their pride is so high in a learning situation that an error is less acceptable to them than to younger persons.

Under what conditions do older workers have the most difficulty in learning a new job?

Older adults have the most trouble learning a new skill when that skill conflicts with one they have already learned. Experience grows strong roots. When learning a new skill means cutting off those roots, the older workers may not be psychologically ready to learn something new.

To make a difficult learning task easier, it's wise to demonstrate to older workers the similarities between what they have been doing and what you're asking them to do now. For instance, in the case of the older typist, the supervisor could show that the procedures for handling word processing equipment are basically the same and that the differences are mainly a matter of degree. It's always easier for anybody to learn if the move is gradual from the familiar to the unfamiliar.

How can you best motivate older workers?

By understanding them and helping them to understand themselves. As all of us grow older, the gap widens between what we are and what we'd like to be. It's only natural for us to adopt an "I am what I am" attitude—especially when someone asks us to improve or to change our ways. In fact, the very stability that makes older workers an asset also makes it harder for them to learn, since this stability is based on their having found contentment with their present lot. So the problem of getting them to want to change, or to do better, resolves itself in your ability to get them to try.

To get older persons to try, you must help them to be less critical and less self-conscious. Show them what other older workers are doing—in your company, if possible. Urge them to talk to others who have changed.

A word of caution: Keep performance standards high—for both output and quality—for older workers. There should be no rewards for age in terms of relaxed requirements. It is precisely these qualities that make older workers valuable to the organization.

5 SPECIAL PROBLEMS IN A CHANGING ENVIRONMENT

CONCEPT   Changes in both the social and legal environments create special problems of supervision in handling sensitive issues of privacy and other employee rights.

How strong are the laws protecting an employee's right to privacy?

The law regarding the crucial right to privacy at work is not as clear as it might be. It varies from state to state too. In general, however, the law works two ways: (1) employees are entitled to know what information is on file about them, and (2) supervisors are restricted in their efforts to find out confidential information about their employees or to pass on to others outside the company information that has been gathered about an employee. Here are some examples of practices that are illegal or generally thought to be an invasion of employee privacy:

- Monitoring or recording telephone conversations without the employee's knowledge and consent.
- Using extraordinary means—such as calling a neighbor—to check on an employee's absences or off-job behavior.
- Random searches or "fishing expeditions" through an employee's locker or personal space at work. A search is acceptable only when a person in authority needs specific information for operations.

- Releasing information about an employee's performance to others outside the organization without the employee's permission.

What about lie detectors and drug tests?

The use of lie detectors is severely restricted to specified occupations (such as security guard) or for particular situations. They can no longer be randomly used. In general, such tests (including testing for drug usage) are acceptable only if it can be clearly demonstrated that they are needed (1) to protect the business itself or its customers from damage or theft or (2) to protect employees from interference or harm. Most organizations adopt and publish a policy on these matters. It is the supervisor's responsibility to assist in the dissemination and enforcement of this policy.

Does privacy extend to sensitive issues, like AIDS?

The legal view on this is also uncertain. In most instances, supervisors must rely upon policies adopted by their employers and comply with them. This must be done regardless of how other employees may view the matter. As with many issues that are, or were, controversial, a good guideline for supervisors is this: *Guard against being overzealous in taking positions whenever issues are still under debate. Support the letter of whatever law applies and your company's policy for implementing it.*

To what extent does this concern for protected employees and for employee rights affect a supervisor's right to manage?

It complicates a supervisor's life, for sure. But it can be handled if you follow these priorities:

1. First things should come first. It's a supervisor's job to deal promptly and firmly with subordinates whose performance is unsatisfactory, who act in an unsafe manner, or who are uncooperative or abusive. This is consistent with laws about management and labor relations. Furthermore, it matches what most employees expect of a boss.
2. Thereafter, full respect and attention should be given to equal employment opportunity laws and other legislation intended to protect the rights and welfare of people while at work. This should include an attitude of accommodation toward social concerns that are increasingly reflected in workplace practices, such as pregnancy leaves and child-care or parental-assistance programs.

REVIEW

KEY CONCEPTS TO REMEMBER

1. A large body of equal employment opportunity (EEO) legislation has been enacted to protect and enhance the rights of minority groups, including blacks, women, Hispanics, Orientals, handicapped workers, older workers, and Vietnam era veterans. This places great responsibility upon supervisors to make sure that these laws are effective in the workplace.

   The federal agency charged with enforcing EEO laws is the Equal Employment Opportunity Commission (EEOC). The EEOC encourages, and often requires, the formation of affirmative action programs to ensure a more equal representation of minorities in a company's work force. The EEOC looks, especially, for evidence of differential treatment, disparate effect, or evil intent.

2. Minority and disadvantaged workers represent a special kind of supervisory problem in that they often enter the work force poorly prepared in terms of education, environmental conditioning, and job skills. For this reason, it is essential that employment and advancement tests demonstrate their content and construct validity.

3. Women are increasingly a major and valued portion of the work force. Nevertheless, the quality of their participation continues to need protection and enhancement. This is evident in the difference between women's compensation and that of men, despite the efforts of job-evaluation programs to equalize pay. Most women ask only that their worth be judged on their merits and that they be given opportunities equal to those given to men for higher-paying and higher-status jobs. Sexual harassment in the workplace also continues as a threat to a woman's dignity, welfare, and opportunities. Supervisors share a direct responsibility with higher management to prevent such harassment.

4. Younger workers represent a special kind of supervision problem in that they bring to work very high expectations but very little self-discipline. On the other hand, most older workers suffer limitations caused by deterioration in pace, strength, eyesight, and resilience. These are more than counterbalanced, however, by older workers' experience, skills retention, superior attendance, steadiness, safe working habits, and loyalties to their company and supervisors.

5. Increasingly, the law—and society in general—believes an employee's right to privacy should be protected. This view has many ramifications in the areas of drug testing, lie detectors, and workplace monitoring and in policies toward employees with terminal illnesses, such as AIDS. Nothing in any of the laws designed to protect the rights, or enhance the opportunities, of employees deprives supervisors of their fundamental right—and responsibility—to manage.

SUPERVISORY WORD POWER

Affirmative action. An in-company program designed to remedy current and future inequities in employment.

Differential treatment. The act of treating a member of a minority, or protected group, differently from other applicants or employees in a similar situation.

Discrimination. Any managerial action or decision based upon favoring or disfavoring one person or member of a group over another on the basis of race, color, ethnic or national origin, sex, age, handicap, or Vietnam era war service, or union membership.

Disparate effect. The enforcement of job requirements that have the effect of excluding a member of a protected group.

Equal employment opportunity (EEO). A system of organizational justice, stipulated by law, that applies to all aspects of employment and is intended to provide equal opportunity for all members of the labor force.

Protected groups. Certain minority and/or disadvantaged groups in the population, which are stipulated by the equal opportunity legislation as warranting special protection in employment matters.

Reverse discrimination. The notion that the implementation of affirmative action programs deprives qualified members of nonprotected groups from their rightful opportunities.

Sexual harassment. Repeated or unwarranted verbal or physical advances or sexually explicit remarks that are offensive or objectionable to the recipient.

Stereotype. The characterization of an individual on the basis of a standardized, oversimplified view of the characteristics believed (often wrongly) to be held in common by the group to which the individual is assumed to belong.

READING COMPREHENSION

1. What is meant by affirmative action, and how does it tie in with EEO legislation?
2. In seeking to ensure conformance to EEO laws, what evidence of discrimination does the EEOC look for? In which areas of management are these most likely to occur?
3. Distinguish between the content validity and the construct validity of employment tests.
4. Which approach do you think would motivate the company's "hard-core" van driver most: offering the driver membership in the company's recreational club or allowing the driver to take the keys of the van home at night? Why?
5. What is wrong with classifying a job as either a man's or a woman's, from both a legal standpoint and a practical one?
6. The men in Jane's work group repeatedly—but jokingly and admiringly—address her as "Marilyn," an obvious reference to her physical resemblance to Marilyn Monroe. Jane doesn't particularly like this and complains to her supervisor. What should the supervisor do?
7. If 19-year-old Pete is dissatisfied with his job and blames his unrest on the meaninglessness of his work, what is the possibility of this charge being justified? What might Pete's supervisor do about this situation?
8. Why do you suppose that older workers have fewer accidents than younger ones do?
9. Why might an employee who works at a computer keyboard object to the number of her keystrokes being counted electronically as a measure of her performance? Do you believe that her employer has a right to make these measurements?
10. If, as a supervisor, you suspected an employee of drug dealing, would it be all right to inspect that employee's locker? Why?

APPLICATION

SELF-APPRAISAL

What kind of EEO rating would you give Pearl?

Pearl B. is the supervisor of a small group of employees who perform a variety of operations. During the course of last year, Pearl had to make a number of decisions and took the actions described on page 470. Your assignment is to decide whether or not Pearl's actions would ensure that her employees receive the equal employment opportunities the law requires.

To carry out this assignment, on a separate piece of paper draw three columns as shown below. Under the column headed "Actions/Decisions" write the numbers 1 to 15 to correspond to each of the actions or decisions described below. Then place a checkmark in the column that best represents *your* opinion as to whether Pearl's decisions would or would not ensure EEO protection under the law. After you complete the assignment, self check your answers by using the scoring procedure described on page 471.

Column headings:

Actions/Decisions	Would Ensure EEO Protection	Might Not Ensure EEO Protection

1. Turned down a leave for a married man to take care of his child but approved a similar one for an unmarried mother.
2. Offered training in computer operations to all employees in her department who wished to take it.
3. Established a policy of moving only women into telephone sales, since that particular job had always been better performed by women.
4. Told Mannie, a Hispanic employee from the Barrio in Los Angeles, that she would make no exception for his difficulty with English when issuing him his operating instructions.
5. Asked job applicants to take tests that met the conditions of content and construct validity, even though some could not pass the tests.
6. Made certain that all jobs in her department were classified under the company's approved job-evaluation plan.
7. Was especially considerate of Mimi Brown's lack of strength when she asked Mimi's group to pitch in on the weekly chore of stacking heavy goods in the warehouse.
8. Invited each employee to present his or her credentials as a candidate whenever a new job opening occurred in the department.
9. Explained the reason behind what appeared to be an unreasonable assignment to young Angela Pickens.
10. Showed old Jake Samchick the similarity between the computer keyboard and his typewriter when he had difficulty learning the computer-based tallying system.
11. Turned down a handicapped job applicant whom Pearl thought would be unsuited for much of the work performed in her department.
12. Set up a "vestibule" training area to help prepare workers recently hired from the city's ghetto area.

13. Rejected a male job applicant as "not occupationally qualified" for the job of modeling women's lingerie for retail clothing buyers in the company's showroom.

14. Advised Alice, when conducting Alice's performance appraisal, that there was no point in her thinking about being promoted to shipping clerk because that kind of work was too heavy for a woman.

15. During the first few weeks after hiring Andrew, a young man from a poverty stricken rural area, went out of her way to help him adjust to the strict rules and regulations that characterized work in her department.

Scoring Give Pearl 1 point for each action that you felt *would ensure EEO protection*. Give her no points for actions that you felt *might not ensure EEO protection*.

Interpretation Management experts gave Pearl only 9 points on the issue of ensuring that employees get full protection under EEO legislation. Here's the way they scored it: *would ensure* for actions 2, 5, 6, 8, 9, 10, 12, 13, and 15; *might not ensure* for all other actions. If you agreed with the experts 13 to 15 times, the chances are that employees who work for you would get an equal employment opportunity. If you agreed only 12 times or less, your actions might tend to invite challenges or discrimination from the Equal Employment Opportunity Commission. In the event of any disagreements with the experts, however, can you support your judgment?

CASE STUDIES

CASE 60 Jack versus Jill

In the southwestern office of the Century Credit Company, Jill J. was the first woman ever promoted to the position of senior credit underwriter. Jill was neat, pleasant, and capable. Her work continued to improve, and she was given increasingly responsible assignments. Jack Y., however, a long-service credit clerk in the office was irritated by Jill's progress. As a consequence, he confronted Mr. Gallo, the office manager, one afternoon and said, "When are you going to show some spine around here and stop favoring Jill just because you're afraid of the EEOC? There are at least half a dozen men around here who can do the job she has—and do it better. It's got us so upset that we may just get together and give Jill a really hard time. Then you'll see whether she's as competent as you think she is!"

If you were Mr. Gallo, how would you respond to this confrontation? Of the five alternatives listed below, which do you think might be the most effective? Rank the alternatives on a scale from 1 (most preferable) to 5 (least preferable). You may add another alternative if you wish. In any event, be prepared to justify your ranking.

a. Ignore the incident entirely.
b. Call the male employees together and tell them that you won't be threatened.
c. Advise Jill that you may have to hold back on any advancement for a while until the men get more adjusted to working with women.
d. Tell Jack that Jill's advancements have been based entirely on merit; make it clear that you won't be coerced into treating her differently.
e. Call a meeting of all employees, including Jill, and explain why she has deserved her promotion.

CASE 61   Upward on Cannery Row

In a West Coast cannery, Luis Valdes, a 45-year-old ex-migratory worker, was hired into the steam-pack operation. For his first few weeks on the job, Luis performed general labor, helping the operator to load the vats and to mop up spills. He was eager and attentive; and, although his English was not particularly good, he seemed to get the idea of what was wanted from him. Accordingly, the steam-pack supervisor suggested that Luis might swing over to the second shift as a number 2 operator. In preparation for this move, the supervisor should:

a. Assemble a series of operating manuals for Luis to study.
b. Ask the day-shift operator to tell Luis exactly what will be expected of him.
c. Show, by demonstration, how each step of the steam-pack operation is performed, and have Luis repeat each step while the supervisor watches him.
d. Tell Luis that he should clear up any questions he has about the steam-pack operation now before he swings over to the second shift.

CASE 62   Banking Jobs for All Ages

If you were the branch manager of a bank in a booming industrial area where it was very difficult to attract and hold younger people, how might you suggest to your various supervisors that they adjust their job openings and work assignments to accommodate and make the most valuable use of the larger supply of older people in the local labor market? You know that business at the tellers' windows has a great deal of variety: some is routine, such as accepting deposits and cashing checks;

other transactions are more complex, such as making out certified checks, selling traveler's checks, and opening up new accounts. Then, too, at some hours of the day, business is hectic and fast-paced; at other times it is relatively slow. In the cashier's department, keypunching is generally a "high-production" job, whereas resolving and verifying balances is a more painstaking one.

What are your suggestions for making the most of the younger and older workers in the local labor market?

Think first about the characteristics of younger workers, their attitudes toward their work, what they expect and enjoy most and what they like least. Then think about what the text says about older workers, their strengths and their weaknesses. With this knowledge in mind, what might be done to modify and restructure work at the bank to make it more appealing and more effective for both younger and older workers? Consider, especially, changes that affect:

- Work schedules.
- Division of work.
- Employee training.
- Job progression.

1 Accidents and health hazards endanger many workplaces.

2 A government agency (OSHA) enforces strict work safety standards.

3 Supervisors play the key role in accident prevention.

4 Common accidents can be prevented in a number of ways.

5 Rigorous reporting and investigation reduce accidents.

CHAPTER 21

Employee Safety and Health Under OSHA

LEARNING OBJECTIVES

After studying this chapter, you should be able to

1. Discuss the extensive list of factors—in addition to human error—that contribute to occupational injuries and illnesses.

2. Explain various facets of the Occupational Safety and Health Act and its enforcement.

3. Evaluate several common approaches to accident prevention—including the three Es of engineering, education, and enforcement—and discuss the effectiveness of safety clothing, safety posters, and safety committees.

4. Identify the most common types of occupational accidents and the places where they occur and describe several ways for preventing each.

5. Compute occupational-accident incident and severity rates and understand the procedures for investigating and analyzing an accident.

SAFETY AT WORK

CONCEPT Accidents and hazards to health represent costly factors in the work environment and must be guarded against constantly.

What causes accidents?

People do, mostly. And for a variety of reasons. Sometimes employees are careless. Sometimes the boss hasn't given proper instructions. Sometimes employee attitudes are to blame. Sometimes the supervisor hasn't helped employees to understand the dangers involved in their work. Sometimes equipment fails. Sometimes machines are not properly guarded. But there is *always* a person who could have prevented the accident by taking proper protective or control action.

This is not to remove the responsibility from the company, institution, or agency involved. Ownership and management must be committed to the principle of accident and health protection. This often means a sizable investment in protective equipment and time-consuming safety and health measures.

How costly are work-related accidents?

Very costly, indeed. The annual bill to industry is close to $50 billion, and it is rising. The human costs, however, are even greater. Consider the physical pain and suffering that is caused by a disabling injury, the loss of self-esteem that can accompany becoming dependent upon others, or the disruption to a family that occurs when the breadwinner loses his or her normal source of income.

How much of the blame can be placed on accident-prone employees?

Some blame belongs there, but it would be wrong to overemphasize their presence. Examination of safety records often shows that just a few employees account for the bulk of the accidents—that the great majority of employees rarely have accidents. Those people who get injured frequently are spoken of as **accident-prone.** This means that for one reason or another they have an innate tendency to have accidents and hence are prone to injury. Psychologists have shown, however, that only a small percentage of so-called accident-prone employees are truly accident-prone. Most of these habitual sufferers can actually be made accident-free by proper job placement, training, and encouragement. If one or more of your workers appear accident-prone, don't dismiss them as not your responsibility. Instead, encourage the development of work habits that will protect these employees from themselves. (See Chapter 14, "Counseling Troubled Employees," for more specific advice on this problem.)

Where else, then, does the blame lie?

Finger pointing isn't the most effective way to prevent accidents. There are many commonly recognized causes of accidents besides those immediately attributable to employee carelessness or inattention. Among them are these:

- Absence of, or faulty, protective devices.
- Ineffective specifications for safety clothing.
- Inadequate ventilation or the presence of fumes.
- Presence of hazardous or unauthorized materials.
- Wrong tools, materials, or supplies issued for the job.
- Absence of a safety standard for the operation.
- Lack of safety training for a specific task.
- Inadequate or improper instructions.
- Safety rules or procedures not enforced.
- The wrong person placed on an unsuitable task.
- Poor housekeeping or sanitation at the workplace.
- Pressure from supervision to disregard safe procedures in the interest of faster movement or greater output.

Do not disregard the fact, of course, that each of these causes is directly or indirectly related to the faulty performance of an individual or group of individuals somewhere along the line.

2 OSHA'S MANDATED SAFETY STANDARDS

CONCEPT   The federal government establishes and monitors (through OSHA) strict standards for protection of safety and health at work.

What role does the federal government play in the prevention of accidents?

Since 1971, a major one. Until that time the safety of an employee at work was largely the result of efforts on behalf of state governments, insurance companies, independent safety organizations such as the National Safety Council, and the employer. Passage of the Williams-Steiger Occupational Safety and Health Act of 1970 (effective April 1971) and the creation of the *Occupational Safety and Health Administration* (OSHA) have put the federal government and the Department of Health, Education, and Welfare (HEW) squarely into the safety act in every significant plant and office in the United States. The purpose of OSHA is to establish safety and health standards with which every employer and every employee must comply. And to make sure that there is compliance, OSHA makes more than 100,000 inspections annually.

How much leeway for variances does OSHA permit?

Very little. The act minces no words. For example, the General Duty clause states that each employer:

1. Shall furnish to each employee employment and a place of employment that are free from recognized hazards causing or likely to cause death or serious harm to employees.
2. Shall comply with occupational safety and health standards promulgated by the act.

The poster that OSHA requires each employer to display in the area adds this:

> The act further requires that employers comply with specific safety and health standards issued by the Department of Labor.

The standards (called National Consensus Standards) are derived from the American National Standards Institute (ANSI) and the National Fire Protection Association (NFPA) and are supplemented by the Established Federal Standards, which were derived from previous acts. Set down in a tightly packed, 250-page volume called "Occupational Safety and Health Standards; National Consensus Standards and Established Federal Standards," published by the *Federal Register* (vol. 36, no. 105, part II), May 29, 1971, the standards specify just about everything imaginable. They include specifications for guarding walks and walking surfaces, means of egress, powered platforms, environmental controls, noise, radiation, hazardous materials, sanitation, first-aid services, fire protection, compressed gases, material handling, machine guards, portable tools, welding, and electrical installations and pay particular attention to paper, textile, laundry, sawmill, and bakery operations.

The OSHA standards are regularly revised and updated and published in the *Federal Register*.

What happens to a company when it doesn't meet the OSHA standards?

It is given a citation. A severe penalty and fine will follow if the problem is not corrected. More specifically, the citation is issued to the manager in charge of the facility. It may even be issued, for example, to a supervisor who refused to make certain that a prescribed machine guard was in place. A company and an individual may seek a temporary variance from the standard, but in most instances the only recourse is to take corrective action as soon as possible. In many cases, heavy fines and even jail sentences have been imposed on companies and managers who failed to comply promptly with the citation.

How far beyond safety does OSHA extend?

The Occupational Safety and Health Administration looks deep into the areas of employee health that may be affected by substances in, or conditions of, the process or working environment and into *general sanitation* on the premises. The sanitation standards are spelled out under the section "General Environmental Controls." An important area is housekeeping. For example, containers for waste disposal must be available and should be the kinds that don't leak and can be sanitized. Extermination programs must be in effect for vermin control. Food and beverage consumption on the premises is regulated.

Washrooms, toilet facilities, and water supplies are considered. Provision must be made for clearly labeling potable and nonpotable water. Toilet facilities are specified according to the number and sex of employees. Showers, change rooms, and clothes-drying facilities must be provided under certain circumstances.

OSHA pays notable attention, of course, to the presence of, and impact of, *hazardous materials.* Probably the most publicized material has been asbestos. Other particularly dangerous materials or conditions include vinyl chloride, which produces liver cancer; fumes from lead; coal dust; airborne textile fibers; and radiation. Even high noise levels can be injurious and must be guarded against.

How has OSHA affected safety training?

It has made it mandatory. Supervisors are expected to make certain that safe procedures are taught not only to new employees but also as an ongoing program.

General safety training applies to the proper observance of safety regulations, routing for emergency egress in case of fire or other common danger, accident and injury treatment and reporting, and fire and explosion emergency activities.

Specific employee training required by OSHA applies to occupational health and environmental controls, hazardous materials, personal protective equipment, medical and first aid, fire protection, material handling and storage, machine guarding, and—for welding—cutting and brazing.

Where do employees fit into the OSHA picture?

The law insists that they, too, act safely within established standards—provided that employers live up to their responsibilities. In other words, an employee who refused to wear the safety glasses provided by the employer in prescribed areas could be cited. A bearded employee might be required to shave to make his respirator fit. Specifically, OSHA states:

> The Williams-Steiger Act also requires that each employee comply with safety and health standards, rules, and orders issued under the Act and applicable to his conduct.

Employees have several important rights under OSHA, however. For example, they may:

1. Request an inspection if they believe an imminent danger exists or a violation of a standard exists that threatens physical harm.
2. Have a representative (such as a union steward) accompany an OSHA compliance officer during the inspection of a workplace.
3. Advise an OSHA compliance officer of any violation of the act that they believe exists in the workplace, and question, and be questioned privately by, the compliance officer.
4. Have regulations posted to inform them of protection afforded by the act.
5. Have locations monitored in order to measure exposure to toxic or radioactive materials, have access to the records of such monitoring or measuring, and have a record of their own personal exposure.
6. Have medical examinations or other tests to determine whether their health is being affected by an exposure, and have the results of such tests furnished to their physicians.
7. Have posted on the premises any citations made to the employer by OSHA.

▣ ACCIDENT PREVENTION: THE BASICS

CONCEPT Supervisors play the key role in accident prevention by emphasizing safety awareness, education, and enforcement.

With whom does accident prevention begin?

Good supervision is the starting place for an effective accident-prevention program. No amount of machine guards or safety rules will stop accidents from happening if supervisors aren't absolutely sold on the fact that it can be done—and that it's their responsibility.

Take the slogan "Safety first." What does it mean to you? Does it mean "Safety measures come ahead of everything else in my department," or is it just another slogan? Keep asking yourself that question every time you urge a worker toward higher production. Be sure that you don't ever give quantity or cost priority over safety. If you do, you'll find that your accident record suffers—and someone may get hurt.

Shouldn't employees have a responsibility for safety?

By all means! People failure is at the heart of all accidents. Supervisors cannot be everywhere at once, and they shouldn't want to be. So in the long run, it will be your employees who cause—or prevent—accidents in your department. But you've got to take the lead in showing them how prevention is achieved.

1. **Instill in employees the belief that they are the most influential source of accident prevention.** Do this with the aid of your safety engineer, if you have one. Discuss the particulars of the accidents that have occurred in your organization. Seize every opportunity to let employees see cause and effect for themselves.
2. **Show employees how to develop safe working habits.** People have to be trained to work safely just as they must be trained to work accurately. Few persons are naturally cautious—or know instinctively where danger lies. The first day on the job in a foundry, for example, a worker may be worried about burns from the hot metal and hardly realize that eye injuries, dermatitis, and crushed toes are just as likely to happen.
3. **Be specific about prevention techniques.** Don't preach about them. Instead, when an accident occurs close to home, talk it over with one—or many—of your employees. Get their ideas on how it could have been prevented. Ask them if similar situations could arise in their areas. Continually bring the conversation around to the role of the human element.
4. **Set a good example.** Supervisors should go out of their way to observe the letter of every safety rule themselves. Never—never—yield on safety in favor of your own convenience.
5. **Firmly enforce job safety standards.** Don't be surprised that many employees think of safety as a matter of "Don't do this or that"—or as just so many rules and regulations. Let employees know immediately the danger to themselves—and your dissatisfaction—when they don't follow the safety guidelines you've outlined for them. Reason and encourage first, but penalize if you don't get the necessary conformance.

What is the basis for accident prevention?

Accident prevention requires a balanced, three-pronged attack. For years, the National Safety Council has stressed the three Es—engineering, education, and enforcement. (See Figure 21-1.) Think, for example, of the way the use of safety belts has evolved as a preventive measure for reducing the severity of auto accidents. First, the belts were designed to protect drivers and passengers; that's *engineering*, but it wasn't enough. Next, various agencies and insurance companies mounted campaigns showing consumers the protection offered by proper use of the belts; that's *education*, but it wasn't enough either. Finally, a great many states passed legislation—*enforcement*—requiring that drivers and passengers use the belts under penalty of law. It took the three elements of the program, combined, to make the use of auto seat belts effective as a safety measure.

You can observe the three elements of accident protection in the workplace too. For instance:

- To *engineer* a job for safety is to design the equipment, lay out the work, plan the job, and protect the individual—all with accident prevention as a first ingredient. Placing safety guards on machines is one example of engineering. Another is arranging a job so that employees do not work in a room where toxic fumes are generated by the process. Still another is providing protective eye shields, gloves, or safety shoes.
- To *educate* for safety is to show employees where, why, and how accidents can happen and to develop in them safe work habits and the desire to avoid injury. Helping workers to analyze the danger spots in

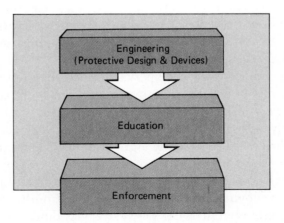

Figure 21-1 The three Es of safety and accident prevention.

their jobs and training them to build a defense against each is an example of education for safety.

- To *enforce* safety is to make an actuality of the slogan "Safety first." Employees work most safely when they want to be safe, but they need guidance in the form of regulations and discipline to protect safe workers from those who would cause accidents through unsafe acts.

But isn't accident prevention really the safety specialist's job?

Safety engineers do an excellent job of carrying out the three Es of safety. But they would be the first to admit that without the supervisor's help, safety programs would flop. The supervisor is the key safety person, especially in education and enforcement.

How much good is safety clothing if employees won't wear it?

It's generally been proved that employees will wear safety goggles and other protective clothing *if* they have been trained to do their work in such clothing, *if* they understand how it protects them, and *if* everybody—co-workers as well as the supervisor—expects them to wear it.

To make safety clothing more acceptable to employees, there are many things you can do:

1. **Let employees help decide which kind of protection suits the situation best.** Discuss the hazardous situation with them first. If working near a degreaser requires wearing a respirator, talk over with them the various kinds of respirators available. Give them a chance to make suggestions as to what they think is best.

2. **Offer a selection.** If employees say that such and such a safety goggle makes them uncomfortable, it helps if you can offer a choice of three or four kinds. "Surely," you can say, "you ought to be able to find one that you like."

3. **Set an example yourself.** If the job calls for hard hats, wear the heaviest, brightest one yourself. Then you can say, "I know that the hard hat looks uncomfortable, but I hardly even know I'm wearing it anymore."

4. **Get help from the informal leaders in the work group.** If you can get an older, respected employee to set the style in safety gear, other workers are likely to follow suit.

5. **Show that you mean business.** If employees can't be cajoled, encouraged, or led to wear their safety clothing, then take disciplinary action. If you're consistent and if the protective equipment is suit-

able, OSHA and even most labor unions will back you up strongly on this point.

How effective are safety posters?

This is a debatable subject. Most authorities feel that "scare" posters on highways have done little to reduce accidents. Posters in the company can be more effective when they are keyed to your area's condition and your own safety program. For instance, if your emphasis is on safety goggles this month, posters that reinforce or repeat this emphasis will help. The mistake is to expect a series of posters to do your safety job for you. They'll help a little. But the big job is up to you.

Posters, like other forms of communication, need to be changed frequently in order to attract fresh attention. It's better to have none than to have a dust-covered one that's been on a bulletin board for two or three months.

What can be done to make safety committees more useful?

If you or your company has organized departmental safety committees, see that the committee has a real job to do. Don't let meetings turn into coffee klatches. And don't use them solely as a sounding board for your inspirational appeals for safety. Treat the safety committee as a business organization:

Assign specific problems. If your medical department or first-aid room tells you there's been a rash of small cuts on hands and arms, get the committee to investigate this condition to find out what the facts are, where they occur, and to whom. Then ask for a specific recommendation on how to correct the situation.

Expect results. Make it clear that being on a safety committee entails more than sitting in on a meeting. Assign area safety responsibilities to the members. Let them assist with inspections. Ask for a report on the minor accidents in each area. Have the members tell what improvements have been made and what more can be done.

Have members participate on investigations. Talking about safety isn't as effective as getting out on the floor to see what's being done about it. Use this opportunity to demonstrate the company's efforts and expenditures for safe working conditions. Emphasize that unsafe practices are just as important to watch out for.

Delegate duties. If the committee plans a safety competition, let it handle the publicity, the method of making awards, and the establishment of rules. Committee members know their co-workers better than anyone else does—and can guess what will work best.

⃞4 ACCIDENT PREVENTION: THE SPECIFICS

CONCEPT   There are a number of good ways to prevent the most common accidents, such as those involving lifting, falling, machinery, hand tools, electricity, and fires.

Where do most industrial accidents occur?

They have their greatest frequency and severity in the manufacturing, mining, food processing, construction, transportation, and hotel industries, as shown in Figure 21-2. They occur least frequently in banks and insurance companies. However, in all industries most on-the-job accidents occur in these places:

- Around hand lift trucks, wheelbarrows, warehouses, cranes, and shipping departments. More industrial accidents (nearly one-third) are caused by handling and lifting materials than by any other activity.
- Near metal- and woodworking machines, saws, lathes, and transmission machinery such as gears, pulleys, couplings, belts, and flywheels.
- On stairs, ladders, walkways, and scaffolds. That's because falls are the third most common source of industrial injury.
- Anywhere hand tools are used. Chisels, screwdrivers, hammers, and the like, account for 7 percent of industrial disability.
- Everywhere electricity is used, especially near extension cords, portable hand tools, electric droplights, wiring, switchboards, and welding apparatus.

Where are most office accidents likely to occur?

Offices may be safer than factories or construction sites, but 1 out of every 27 office workers is injured each year. These accidents tend to happen in the normal work areas or in stockrooms, where makeshift ladders or stools are often used to enable an employee to reach overhead storage space. In the offices themselves, the culprits are the most innocent of booby traps: a small plastic wastebasket left in an open aisle, desk or file drawers left open, and electrical extension cords. These are easy to trip over or walk into. Then there are swivel chairs that tip over, spilled coffee on a polished floor, letter openers that accidently stab, unanchored filing cabinets that tip, loaded file boxes that strain the backs of those who carry them, and even paper edges that cut the fingers and gummed envelopes that cut the tongue.

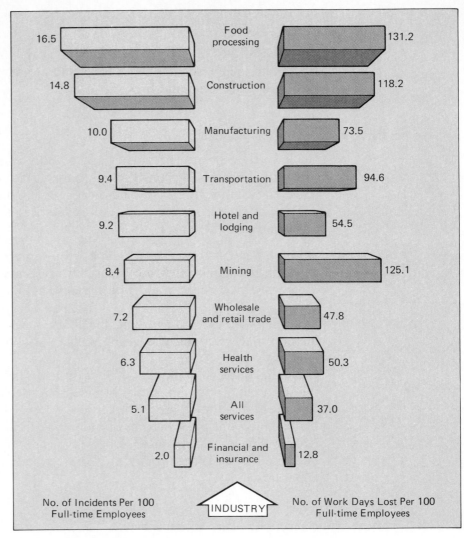

Source: Bureau of Labor Statistics

Figure 21-2 Selected accident rates for various industries.

How do you prevent lifting and material-handling accidents?

Heavy loads are only one reason for lifting accidents. Most lifting accidents happen because an employee doesn't have the knack of lifting with the legs, rather than the back. If you try to pick something up by bending over it and pulling backward and upward with your arms, it tends to strain the muscles and ligaments in the back. Instead, get as close to the object as possible. Crouch down beside it; if it's a case or carton, get the inside of your thighs as close to it as possible. Get a firm grip with your hands and arms. Keep your back straight as you pull the object toward you. Then simply stand up.

Try this knee-lift method yourself until you get the feel of it. Whenever a new employee enters your department, show how it's done. Let the person practice the lift a few times while you watch.

Of course, it goes without saying that when loads get too heavy—over, say, 50 to 100 pounds—you should instruct employees to get help. This may be another pair of hands or a lift truck, jack, crowbar, block and tackle, crane, or any handling device that suits the purpose.

Accidents often happen when a worker trips while carrying materials. That's one reason clean floors and aisles are so important.

Accidents that happen while workers are using mechanical lifting devices are frequently the result of overloading or improper usage. Make it a point to check load ratings on slings, cables, and cranes. Don't permit an inexperienced employee to operate any mechanical equipment without first showing the person the right way.

How do you prevent accidents on machinery, machine tools, and power-transmission equipment?

Not only is machinery the number two cause of accidents in manufacturing and construction, but it also causes the most severe injuries. Since the turn of the century, both employers and machine builders have done much to protect machine operators through the judicious use of safety guards and devices. But don't take this action for granted. Whenever a new machine is installed in your department, inspect it before it goes into action. Try to be certain in your own mind that a worker will be adequately protected.

Many machine tools cannot be fully protected. So it's a good practice to caution employees about wearing loose clothing, long-sleeved shirts, string neckties, and so forth, around moving machinery. Stay with new and old employees alike until you're sure that each is aware of the danger a machine holds and is able to steer clear of trouble. Of particular importance is knowledge of how to shut machinery down in a hurry. You should drill machine operators until they know so much about "off" and "on" control locations that they can turn their machines off blindfolded.

How do you prevent falls?

In theory, falls can be prevented 100 percent. In practice, it's not quite that easy. One big obstacle to perfection is that employees tend to take falls for granted. It's the mark of a timid person, workers often say, to worry much about them.

To minimize falling injuries in your department, keep an eye out for these causes:

Unsafe floors and work surfaces. See that employees keep floors and workplaces swept clean. Don't permit spillages to remain unguarded or uncleaned for even a minute. Your keen interest in this matter helps dramatize its importance.

Unsafe ladders, stairways, and scaffolds. Ladders should never be used if there is any doubt about their condition or suitable length. Stairways should have railings and be well lit. Scaffolding should be checked by a qualified mechanic or an engineer.

Improper footwear. There's a lot of stress on the use of safety shoes to protect the feet. But sensible, low-heeled shoes, with soles in good shape and uppers laced to support the foot, are an excellent guard against falls too.

Unsafe practices. Employees may think you're nagging if you insist they hold on to a railing when going up or down stairs. But if you insist that they observe safe practices when walking and climbing, or especially when working overhead, they will respect you for your interest in their welfare. That's the point to stress—how safe practices protect them and not just the shop's accident record.

Inadequate lighting. This often contributes to unsafe footing on stairs and walkways and in storage areas.

How do you prevent hand-tool accidents?

Squashed thumbs and scraped knuckles by the hundreds of thousands bear painful tribute to the misuse of hand tools. Tools in bad shape, such as a chisel whose head looks like a mushroom, should be taken out of service and repaired or thrown away. Proper tools for the job should be available, and employees should be instructed about the danger of using the wrong tool for a job—as in using a knife as a screwdriver or a file as a driftpin to remove a drill from a chuck.

Some employees, especially those who have not come up through the apprentice ranks, won't know how to handle tools properly unless you show them how. In securing employee cooperation in this, appeal to their sense of professional skill. No one likes to look like an amateur. So see that a file is used with a handle and never hit with a hammer (it might shatter), thumbs are out of the way of handsaws, and open jaws of monkey wrenches are facing the user when he or she pulls on the handle.

Portable hand tools all have their own peculiarities too. Check with the manufacturer's instruction manual to be certain you know, and your employees follow, the maker's guide for safe use.

How do you prevent low-voltage electric shocks?

The term *low voltage* covers anything under 600 volts. Since deaths due to contact with 110 volts (ordinary house-lighting circuits) are common, it's absolutely foolhardy to take any chances with electrical hazards. Injuries from electrical sources happen from touching live parts, short circuits, accidental grounds, overloads on the system, and broken connections.

Advise your employees to report to you any evidence of hot wires, tingling shocks from machines or equipment, abnormal sparking, frayed insulations, loose connections, or any other electrical fault. Don't investigate the cause yourself. Get the plant electrician—and quickly.

Portable electric power tools should always be grounded before being connected to an electric outlet. This is done by connecting a separate wire between the frame of the tool and a good ground—such as a pipeline or I beam. Today many companies have grounded, three-prong outlets to accept three-prong plugs, but the existence of a three-prong plug doesn't guarantee that the circuit is grounded. Check with the building electrician on this.

Electricity's safety valves are fuses, fused switches, and circuit breakers. These protect equipment and circuits from overloads. Disconnect switches are dangerous. Do not permit production operators to touch them. That's a job for an electrician.

If one of your employees is knocked out by an electric shock, see that he or she is removed from the electrical source first (be careful, or others may also be shocked) and then given artificial respiration.

What sort of fire prevention measures should you enforce?

Good housekeeping is one of the best. Where floors, benches, desks, corners, and machines are kept clean and neat, fire has a hard time getting a foothold. Watch out for material piled too close to overhead sprinklers, fire extinguishers, and hoses. Material too close to the sprinklers cuts down on their effectiveness. Blocked fire extinguishers may mean the difference between a fire that is put out in a few seconds and one that gets a toehold in a minute. And never permit a fire extinguisher or a fire bucket to be used for any purpose other than to fight fires. Also check regularly to see that they're full.

Check with your safety engineer, personnel manager, or superior to determine the best practices for handling flammable liquids, such as solvents of any kind. Some of the precautions will seem overdone, but in the long run no safety measure with flammable materials can be too extreme.

Don't be lenient with employees who smoke in unauthorized areas. It may seem like a little thing, but it's the carelessly flipped butt where people don't expect it that can cause the big trouble.

Set this rule for yourself and your employees: Regard every open light, every flame, every match and cigarette, and every bit of oily waste or thimbleful of flammable liquid as potentially dangerous. Discipline taken to enforce safety measures is the least difficult to gain support for from labor unions. So sell each employee on the personal stake held in fire prevention in the plant or office.

In case of fire, what should you do?

Experts disagree as to which one of these things you should do first. But they all agree that these three things should be done immediately:

- Report the fire by telephone, or see that the message is carried to the company or local fire department. Many building-wrecking fires have gotten away from persons who were sure they could put them out themselves.
- See that employees are evacuated. Safety to persons comes before property. See that all employees in the department know about the fire and are evacuated from the building or out of the area—except those officially designated to fight the fire.
- Fight the fire with hand extinguisher or hose. Speed is absolutely essential—thus the need for keeping fire extinguishers in good condition, keeping them unblocked, and knowing how to use them.

5 ACCIDENT REPORTING AND INVESTIGATION

CONCEPT   Accident prevention also depends upon rigorous measurement, reporting, investigation, and analysis of the causes of accidents.

To what extent does OSHA specify accident recordkeeping?

It insists that every company or separate establishment maintain a log of illnesses and accidents as they occur. Beyond that, the forms already used by your organization to monitor these matters and to investigate accidents are probably satisfactory.

The OSHA log (Form 200) is used to record each occupational injury or illness and identify whether it has caused a fatality, a lost workday, a permanent transfer to another job, or a termination of employment. In the area of *illness identification* OSHA has expanded typical coverage; OSHA requires a report on occupational skin diseases or disorders, dust diseases of the lungs (pneumoconioses), respiratory conditions and poisoning due to workplace exposure to toxic materials, disorders due to other physical agents, and traumas (emotional shocks).

In addition, OSHA standards require that additional specialized records be maintained on such items as scaffolding, platforms, man lifts, fire extinguishers, cranes, derricks, and power presses. These records should include maintenance and inspection dates. Still other records are required for radiation exposure, flammable and combustible liquids inventories, and the monitoring of toxic and hazardous substances.

Whereas your company will probably specify what records must be kept and who will maintain them, the supervisor—as in so many other areas—is a pivotal person in collecting the data.

How are accident rates classified and measured?

OSHA and the U.S. Bureau of Labor Statistics have worked together to establish (1) what constitutes an incident (or accident case) and (2) how to measure the incident rate (frequency rate) and severity rate.

A *recordable incident* (or *accident case*) is one which involves occupational injury or illness, including death. Not recordable are (1) first-time ailments that involve one-time treatment or (2) minor cuts, scratches, or burns that do not ordinarily require medical care, even if such treatment is provided by a physician or registered nurse.

Accident rates are measured by two very similar formulas. The first formula measures an *incident rate* by comparing the number of accident cases that have occurred with the total number of hours worked by all employees during the same period. The second formula measures a *severity rate* by comparing the number of lost workdays that have occurred with the total number of hours worked by all employees during the period. For consistency's sake, all rates are computed using a standard based upon the expectations of 100 employees working 2000 hours a year, or 200,000 hours.

To illustrate the use of these formulas, we'll apply the following data. Suppose that plant XYZ has 200 employees each averaging 40 hours a week for 50 weeks (or 2000 hours a year each). During the year, 12 accident cases are recorded, and a total of 88 workdays are lost as a result.

$$
\begin{aligned}
\text{Incident rate} \\
\text{(Frequency rate)} &= \frac{\text{number of recordable cases} \times 200{,}000 \text{ hours}}{\text{total hours worked by all employees during the year}} \\
&= \frac{12 \text{ cases} \times 200{,}000 \text{ hours}}{200 \text{ workers} \times 40 \text{ hours/week} \times 50 \text{ weeks/year}} \\
&= \frac{2{,}400{,}000}{400{,}000} \\
&= 6 \text{ incidents per 100 full-time employees}
\end{aligned}
$$

Using the data provided, the severity of these accidents—as gauged by the total lost workdays they caused—is measured in the following way.

$$\text{Severity rate} = \frac{\text{number of workdays lost} \times 200,000 \text{ hours}}{\text{total hours worked by all employees during the year}}$$

$$= \frac{88 \text{ workdays lost} \times 200,000 \text{ hours}}{200 \text{ workers} \times 40 \text{ hours/week} \times 50 \text{ weeks/year}}$$

$$= \frac{17,600,000}{400,000}$$

$$= 44 \text{ workdays lost per 100 full-time employees}$$

Similar incident and severity rates can be calculated for disabling injuries only or for illnesses only.

It should be noted that some organizations compute these rates according to 1,000,000 hours worked a year rather than the 200,000 hours used by the Bureau of Labor Statistics. If so, the rates would be five times greater.

How do you investigate an accident?

If an accident should happen in your department or to an employee under your supervision, one of the best ways to prevent its happening again is to investigate the accident to find out exactly why it happened. Once you have determined this, you can establish safeguards to protect individuals from any unnecessary dangers. This is an important point to understand, since there is a little risk in everything we do—even staying at home in bed. But many of the chances employees take are unnecessary. Accident investigation will uncover these and enable you to do something about minimizing them. When you are checking on accidents, your primary goal is to find causes, not to fix the blame. Look for answers to such questions as these:

- **What happened?** Who got hurt? How badly? What material was spoiled? Was any equipment damaged? Does it need repair before being put into operation again? Who, besides the injured individual, was involved?
- **Why did it happen?** Was it solely human error? If so, was it due to a lack of skill? Of knowledge about key points? Was it mainly carelessness? What part did the process play? Was it functioning properly or erratically at the time? How about the equipment involved? Was it in good working order? Did the individuals involved know how to operate it properly?
- **What needs to be done to prevent this from happening again?** Does it require special training? A specific new rule or regulation? A change

in process procedure? Different kinds of equipment? Additional safe-guards on the equipment?

- **What steps have you taken to prevent recurrence?** How much of the above have you put into practice with improved training and instruction? Have you worked out a prevention plan with process engineers, systems designers, or housekeeping and maintenance staffs?
- **What still needs to be done?** Do you need further assistance from your boss or from the appropriate staff departments? Should you enlist the help of the safety committee? Have you set up a follow-up procedure that won't be dropped until the entire prevention plan is implemented?

Doesn't insurance or workers' compensation take care of accident costs?

Not by a long shot. A company's liability insurance usually pays only the cost of a worker's compensation for an injury received at work. The cost of liability insurance to a company depends on how good a safety record the company has. The difference between a good and a bad record isn't peanuts. It means real money in insurance rates. **Workers' compensation** refers to the amount of money an employer must pay to an injured employee as determined by a schedule of awards established by a state's legislature. These specified payments are based upon the assumption that the injury (or illness) has permanently restricted an employee's earning capacity. In a great many instances, employees do not agree to accept these stipulated payments, and they go to court to attempt to obtain a larger settlement from the employer. Many companies carry insurance to bear the cost of workers' compensation payments and any other compensation settlements that may arise from job-related injuries or illnesses. Compensation payments such as these, however, do not tell the whole story of the cost of accidents.

It's been estimated that for an accident that comes to $1000 in compensation, a company pays another $5000 for related expenses. Examples of related expenses are cost of time lost by employees who stop to watch the accident or assist; time lost by supervisors helping during the accident and later investigating the accident, making changes in production schedules, and assigning and breaking in new workers; cost of medical care; loss of material, damage to equipment, productive time lost on machines, and—not to be overlooked—cost of the insurance that pays for the compensation.

Should a supervisor give an injured employee first aid?

That depends on the practice in your company and on your own qualifications. There should be no question, however, about your responsibility to see that an injured employee gets first aid—quickly and properly. Permit only trained people (such as graduates of the Red Cross first-aid course) to attend the patient. Know who these people are ahead of time and how to summon them without delay.

If your plant has a nurse or a physician who has been called, stay until you are sure that the injured employee is under medical care.

What conditions should a supervisor look for when making safety and sanitation inspections?

Conditions and OSHA requirements vary, but you'll find a good starting set in Table 21-1 (on pages 495 and 496). For each item listed, it is a good idea to check with your superior to see what the specific OSHA standard is so that you can know exactly what to look for.

How prevalent are wellness programs?

Increasingly, prevention programs extend beyond safety to health and wellness. For example, in 1988 the U.S. Department of Health and Human Services reported that the following wellness programs were most common in industry: smoking control, health risk appraisals, back care, stress management, exercise and physical fitness, off-the-job accident prevention, nutrition education, blood-pressure control, and weight control.

The effectiveness of such programs is debated. And, surprisingly, they are not as popular with employees as was once expected. Nevertheless, they indicate how broad an employer's concern for safety and health enhancement can grow.

REVIEW

KEY CONCEPTS TO REMEMBER

1. An accident is evidence of something wrong in the workplace—with an employee, a machine, methods, materials, or a supervisor. While there is evidence that some people are accident-prone, the great majority of accidents are attributable to human error by ordinary people somewhere along the line. Only aware and responsible people can recognize these wrongs—and correct, guard against, and avoid them.

Table 21-1 SAFETY AND HOUSEKEEPING CHECKLIST

	Condition Okay	Needs Correction
Buildings:		
Windows clean and not broken	‾‾‾	‾‾‾
Painting and upkeep satisfactory	‾‾‾	‾‾‾
Door jambs clean	‾‾‾	‾‾‾
Fire doors unblocked	‾‾‾	‾‾‾
Unsafe practices:		
Employees operating without authority	‾‾‾	‾‾‾
Employees working at unsafe speeds	‾‾‾	‾‾‾
Employees making safety devices inoperative	‾‾‾	‾‾‾
Employees using unsafe equipment	‾‾‾	‾‾‾
Employees lifting improperly	‾‾‾	‾‾‾
Employees assuming unsafe positions	‾‾‾	‾‾‾
Bulletin boards and safety signs:		
Clean	‾‾‾	‾‾‾
Readable	‾‾‾	‾‾‾
Material changed frequently	‾‾‾	‾‾‾
Material removed when obsolete	‾‾‾	‾‾‾
Protective equipment and clothing:		
Equipment and clothing in good condition	‾‾‾	‾‾‾
Equipment and clothing used when needed	‾‾‾	‾‾‾
Additional equipment or clothing needed	‾‾‾	‾‾‾
Sufficient storage space for equipment	‾‾‾	‾‾‾
Floors:		
Loose material	‾‾‾	‾‾‾
Slippery, wet, or oily	‾‾‾	‾‾‾
Badly worn or rutted	‾‾‾	‾‾‾
Garbage, dirt, or debris	‾‾‾	‾‾‾
Stairways and aisles:		
Passageways, aisles, stairs unblocked	‾‾‾	‾‾‾
Stairways well lighted	‾‾‾	‾‾‾
Aisles marked and markings visible	‾‾‾	‾‾‾
Lighting:		
Lamp reflectors clean	‾‾‾	‾‾‾
Bulbs missing	‾‾‾	‾‾‾
Any dark areas	‾‾‾	‾‾‾
Material storage:		
Neatly and safely piled	‾‾‾	‾‾‾
Passageways and work areas not blocked	‾‾‾	‾‾‾
Fire extinguishers and sprinklers clear	‾‾‾	‾‾‾
Machinery:		
Machines and equipment clean	‾‾‾	‾‾‾
Sufficient containers for waste materials	‾‾‾	‾‾‾
Guards on and operating	‾‾‾	‾‾‾
No drips or oil leaks	‾‾‾	‾‾‾
Cutoff switches accessible	‾‾‾	‾‾‾

Table 21-1   SAFETY AND HOUSEKEEPING CHECKLIST
(Continued)

	Condition Okay	Needs Correction
Employee facilities:		
Drinking fountains clean	_____	_____
Locker rooms and toilets clean	_____	_____
Soap and towel supply satisfactory	_____	_____
Tools:		
Right tools for the job	_____	_____
Tools used correctly	_____	_____
Tools stored properly	_____	_____
Tools in safe condition	_____	_____
Electrical hand tools grounded, used properly	_____	_____
Ladders in good condition, used properly	_____	_____
Electrical:		
Motors clean	_____	_____
No exposed wiring	_____	_____
Temporary wiring removed	_____	_____
Switch boxes closed	_____	_____
Proper fusing	_____	_____
Pressure:		
Gauges working properly	_____	_____
Cylinders secured from falling	_____	_____
Pressure vessels inspected regularly	_____	_____
Steam:		
Steam or water leaks	_____	_____
Insulation condition	_____	_____
Gases, vapors, dust, and fumes:		
Ventilation all right	_____	_____
Masks and breathing apparatus available where needed	_____	_____
Dust-collection system satisfactory	_____	_____
Material-handling equipment:		
(Check for cleanliness, safe condition, and operation)		
Cranes, platforms, cabs, walkways	_____	_____
Chains, cables, ropes, block and tackle	_____	_____
Industrial trucks	_____	_____
Railroad equipment—rolling stock, tracks, signals, roadbed	_____	_____
Conveyors—drives, belt condition, guards	_____	_____
Elevators, hoists	_____	_____
Hand trucks and wheelbarrows	_____	_____
Fire protection:		
Hoses and extinguishers well marked	_____	_____
Hoses and extinguishers not blocked	_____	_____
Extinguishers inspected regularly	_____	_____

2. The Occupational Safety and Health Act of 1970 created a large body of standards for safe working conditions, sanitation, and the handling of hazardous materials. The law is enforced by the Occupational Safety and Health Administration (OSHA), which places a great deal of responsibility for its implementation upon supervisors. Employees, too, are expected to participate actively and are given certain rights in that regard.

3. Accident prevention is a major supervisor responsibility which is shared with employees, often under the guidance of a company safety specialist. Most accidents can be prevented by a unified program that encompasses (a) engineering—proper job and equipment design; (b) education—effective employee communication and training; and (c) enforcement—consistent adherence to, and enforcement of, the prescribed safe practices.

4. The most common accidents involve lifting, slipping or falling, machinery, hand tools, and electricity. Fires, too, cause a great deal of damage to property and personnel. These common accidents and fires can be prevented by following a number of established safety precautions.

5. OSHA specifies that a great many accident records be maintained in a prescribed fashion. Calculation of accident incident (frequency) and severity rates is a helpful way to measure the effectiveness of safety programs. Supervisors are directly involved in the investigation and analysis of accidents and their causes. Regular safety and housekeeping inspections are useful for monitoring the implementation of safety and health standards and conditions.

SUPERVISORY WORD POWER

Accident. An unplanned or uncontrolled event in which action or reaction of an object, material, or person results in personal injury.

Hazard. A potentially dangerous object, material, condition, or practice that is present in the workplace, to which employees must be alert and from which they must be protected.

Occupational Safety and Health Act. Comprehensive legislation that establishes standards and calls for the inspection of safety and health conditions and the investigation of all serious accidents and alleged safety or health hazards.

Spontaneous combustion. Ignition of a substance with the heat generated by the rapid oxidation of its own constituents when exposed to air and with no other heat supplied.

Workers' compensation. Financial reparations or awards granted by an employer (often in accord with rate tables prescribed by a state's legislature) to an employee who has suffered an on-the-job injury or illness that is judged to have permanently restricted the employee's earning capacity.

READING COMPREHENSION

1. Many accidents are caused by the ever-present human factor. Name at least six other possible causes of accidents.
2. Distinguish between the Occupational Safety and Health Act and the Occupational Safety and Health Administration.
3. Vivian, housekeeping supervisor in a state mental institution, devotes time each day to safety training for her employees. This activity fits into which phase of the three Es of accident prevention? What are the other two phases?
4. Can an employee refuse to conform to an OSHA safety standard? Why, or why not? What are an employee's rights under the act?
5. What can a supervisor do to instill safety consciousness in employees?
6. What limits the effectiveness of safety posters, safety campaigns, and the like?
7. Would it be a good idea to make the wearing of safety clothing optional? Why, or why not?
8. In what places do accidents most commonly happen?
9. Distinguish between an accident incident (or frequency) rate and an accident severity rate.
10. Why should a supervisor want to investigate an accident?

APPLICATION

SELF-APPRAISAL

How's your OSHA quotient?

Listed on page 499 are a number of statements about OSHA and about accident prevention. Your assignment is to determine which statements are true, or represent sound practice, and which are false, or represent unsound practice. On a separate piece of paper, copy the column headings shown. In the column "OSHA and Accident-Prevention Statements," write the numbers 1 to 15 down the page to correspond to each of the statements. Then place a check mark in the column that most nearly matches your opinion about each statement. After completing this activity, check your answers by using the scoring procedure described below.

Column headings:

OSHA and Accident-Prevention Statements	True, or Sound Practice	False, or Unsound Practice

1. The main costs of industrial accidents can be measured in dollars and cents.
2. There is nothing that can be done to improve the safety performance of accident-prone employees.
3. Accidents are entirely a matter of a human error made by each person who has an accident.
4. OSHA declares that an employer shall furnish to each employee a place of employment that is free from recognized hazards.
5. OSHA standards have little basis in previously developed standards; most of them were new when the law was passed.
6. Sanitation in the workplace is a particular concern of OSHA.
7. Under OSHA, employees have rights but not responsibilities.
8. The three Es of accident prevention are engineering, education, and evaluation.
9. Safety specialists and safety engineers make or break an accident-prevention program.
10. Supervisor Myrna insists that employees wear the prescribed safety clothing, but she invites them to participate in the choice of styles.
11. Safety committees should act mainly as sounding boards for ideas generated by the safety engineer and/or the department supervisor.
12. The most important thing to do in case of an industrial fire is to try to put it out as quickly as possible.
13. Accident rates measure the frequency and severity of the incidents of occupational injuries and illnesses.
14. Under OSHA, a recordable accident case is only one that involves lost workdays.
15. Workers' compensation is an award made to employees for making safety suggestions.

Scoring   Give yourself 1 point for each of the following statements that you checked as *true*, or representing sound practice: 4, 6, 10, 13. Give yourself 1 point for each of the following statements that you checked as *false*, or representing unsound practice: 1, 2, 3, 5, 7, 8, 9, 11, 12, 14, 15.

Interpretation   If you scored 13 points or more, your OSHA quotient is *excellent*. Nevertheless, check out the items you missed so that you don't stub your toe. If you scored between 10 and 12 points, your OSHA quotient is *marginal*. You may mash your finger if you're not careful. Review the items you missed. If you scored less than 10 points, your OSHA quotient is *unsafe*. You and those who work for you are in danger. Carefully review the entire chapter.

CASE STUDIES

CASE 63   The Safety-Switch Cutout

Ned was employed as a labeling machine operator in the packaging department of a detergent manufacturer. In order to make his daily quota, Ned would frequently cut out the safety switch that prevented him from loading new rolls of labels while the machine was operating. He figured he gained at least five minutes of production on every changeover that way. It was against company rules to do so, however. When the company's safety engineer made a visit to inspect the plant, he saw what Ned was doing and advised Ned's boss that he must put an end to that practice right away. As soon as the engineer left, Ned's boss warned Ned that he must not cut out the "safety" anymore. Two weeks later, Ned's supervisor again caught Ned with the switch cut out. "Pack up your gear and get out," he told Ned. "You're through around here. The one thing we cannot tolerate is a violation of an important safety rule." Ned left his machine, but instead of packing his gear, he went to the plant superintendent to plead his case. The following day, Ned was back on the job, and the superintendent sent for Ned's boss. "We won't fire Ned this time," he said. "I don't think he realized that we were so serious about the ruling. But you better get that situation straightened out so that he never cuts out that switch again."

If you were Ned's supervisor, what would you do? Of the five alternatives listed below, which do you think might be the most effective? Rank them on a scale from 1 (most preferable) to 5 (least preferable). You may add another alternative, if you wish. In any event, be prepared to justify your ranking.

a. Accept Ned's reinstatement as a lesson learned about safety rule enforcement.
b. Post a notice on the bulletin board informing all department employees that any infraction of a safety rule will lead to immediate dismissal.
c. First, review Ned's daily quota to be sure that there is an adequate

allowance for changeover; then advise him that he will be severely
disciplined for any other violation of a safety rule.

d. Institute a practice of showing each employee once a week how he
or she can work more safely; also advise the workers of the firmness of the rules and their penalties.

e. Insist that Ned was in the wrong, that he knew what he was doing, and that he be fired.

CASE 64 Mary's Pinched Ring Finger

While filing computer reports in a steel filing cabinet, Mary McDonald
pinched the knuckle of her ring finger. It happened when the sleeve of
her jacket caught in the steel drawer as she slammed it shut. Her supervisor examined the operation of the drawer and declared that the
accident should not have happened. Other file clerks, however, observed
that the opening and closing of the file drawers was a constant hazard.
In fact, many of the clerks declared that they had torn a blouse or had
a finger pinched.

a. To what extent do you think that these accidents were caused by the
file clerks rather than by the design and operation of the drawers in
the file cabinets?

b. Using the three Es of accident prevention, what sort of a safety program would you recommend for this particular hazard?

CASE 65 The Changing Safety Record

Last year, the Fruitwood Furniture Company had an accident incident
rate of 25 per 100 full-time employees and an accident severity rate of
50 workdays lost per 100 full-time employees. The company employs
300 people full-time, each of whom works an average of 2000 hours a
year. This year, Fruitwood had 60 recordable incidents resulting in a
total of 180 lost workdays.

a. What are the incident (or frequency) and severity rates for this year?

b. Has Fruitwood's accident record improved or gotten worse since last
year?

1 Supervisors are legal agents of management in labor matters.

2 A large body of law governs labor-management relations.

3 Supervisory actions greatly influence labor agreements.

4 Supervisors are pivotal implementers of labor contracts.

5 Grievance procedures provide systematic means for settlement.

22

The Supervisor's Role in Labor Relations

LEARNING OBJECTIVES

After studying this chapter, you should be able to

1. Discuss the supervisor's legal and practical responsibilities in labor-management relations.

2. Identify the main features of the labor-management relations laws as outlined in the text.

3. Explain the collective bargaining process, its participants, and its objectives.

4. Discuss supervisors' roles in implementing a labor contract and their relationships with union representatives.

5. Describe a typical grievance procedure and discuss how a supervisor can contribute to its effectiveness.

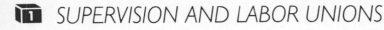

SUPERVISION AND LABOR UNIONS

CONCEPT   Supervisors are considered legal representatives of management in matters affecting labor union recognition and in the implementation of labor contracts that may result from it.

What role does the first-line supervisor play in labor matters?

In the eyes of the law, supervisors are the responsible agents of their companies. Your employers are held responsible for any action you take in dealing with employees or with labor unions, just as if they had taken the action themselves. For this reason, if for no other, it is essential that a supervisor be familiar with labor law on two particular points: (1) the way in which your actions affect labor unions in their attempts to gain or retain bargaining rights for employees and (2) the labor contract that your company may have signed with a union and the impact this has on policies, practices, and procedures that make for amicable labor relations.

Why do employees join labor unions?

Employees join labor unions for at least three reasons:

1. **The union offers services and security in collective activity that many individuals cannot, or do not wish to, provide by acting alone** That's the underlying purpose of labor (or trade) unions: to promote, protect, and improve—through joint action—the job-related economic interests of their members.
2. **Membership is often compulsory.**   In three-quarters of the labor agreements, an individual must join or at least pay dues if she or he wants to keep a job. The idea behind compulsory membership is that everyone should pay his or her fair share of the cost of the benefits derived from unionism and that no one should get a free ride.
3. **Membership provides a sense of independence from management's power to hire, promote, or fire at will.**   No matter how fair-minded a management may try to be, many individuals feel "pushed about" or helpless in today's increasingly large and complex organizations. For many such individuals, union membership provides a feeling of strength that is otherwise lacking.

What should be your attitude toward an existing union?

Don't be antiunion. Adopt the attitude that once your company has made an agreement with a union, your best bet is to work as hard as you can to get along with that union. Don't waste your energy trying to undermine the union. Instead, put your efforts into making your department a better place in which to work.

It would also be a big mistake, however, to turn over to the union your interests in, and your responsibilities to, your employees. It's more important than ever, when your company has a union, to show employees that you still consider them your department's greatest asset. If you abandon their interests, you're likely to find employees looking to their union representatives rather than to you for leadership.

Should you feel hurt when your employees display strong loyalties to their union?

No. An extensive study of employees' loyalties showed rather conclusively that it's natural for workers to have dual loyalty—to their supervisors and to their union leaders. Employees look to their boss for sound business judgments and for the satisfactions that come from doing a purposeful job under good working conditions. Employees look to their union for the social prestige of belonging to an influential group and as a protector of their economic interests and job security. An employee who works for a good company and a considerate boss and who also is represented by an honest, active union enjoys this relationship. Asking an employee to choose between the boss and the union would be a little like asking a child to choose between mother and father.

What kind of a union is an ESOP?

It isn't a union at all. An ESOP is an **employee stock ownership plan.** It is something akin to profit sharing, in that employees may purchase shares of common stock in a company and—thus—become part owners. Some ESOPs are of great advantage to employees, giving them genuine opportunities to share in the management of their companies. Other ESOPs often provide employees with very little say in the management of the business; workers are given only a chance to share in profits, if there are any, through dividends on common stock, or in losses, if the stock's market price declines. In any event, ESOPs are not really a direct concern for traditional labor-management relations.

🗂️2 LABOR-MANAGEMENT LAW

CONCEPT Labor-management relations are governed by a large body of law: the most basic is the National Labor Relations Act, which is administered by the National Labor Relations Board.

Wasn't everything much simpler before the Wagner Act?

There's no denying that supervisors had a much freer hand in dealing with employee matters before the Wagner Act. But there is also considerable evidence that, unions or not, supervision has actually become more intelligent and more effective since the right of employees to organize has been protected by law.

The *Wagner Act* (correctly called the *National Labor Relations Act*) describes the conditions under which workers can bargain collectively through their authorized representatives. The act did not create any new rights. It was intended to safeguard and enforce existing rights.

The Wagner Act does not set up any specific working conditions (as so many people erroneously believe) that employers must give to their employees. It does not concern itself with the terms of the union agreement. All it does is guarantee that employees may act in a group together—rather than as individuals—if they so desire, in bargaining for their wages, hours, and working conditions.

The supervisory job has been made tougher where unions exist, simply because whenever a supervisor deals with an individual employee's problem, he or she must always take into account the whole employee group's position as set forth in the labor contract.

How did the Taft-Hartley Act change the Wagner Act?

The labor law of the land is the National Labor Relations Act (the Wagner Act) as amended by the *Taft-Hartley Act (Labor-Management Relations Act)* in 1947. The Taft-Hartley Act clarified and added to the list of unfair practices that could be charged against management. But more significantly, the act imposed on unions certain controls over their organizing activities, their internal union organization, and their collective bargaining methods.

Under the law, unions and their agents are forbidden to

- Attempt to force an employer to discharge or discriminate against former members of the union who have been expelled for reasons other than nonpayment of regular union dues or initiation fees.
- Attempt to force an employer to pay or deliver any money or other things of value for services that are not performed. This outlaws featherbedding and other make-work practices.
- Restrain or coerce other employees into joining or not joining a union.
- Require excessive or discriminatory fees of employees who wish to become union members.

In addition, individual employees are protected in their desire to bargain or not to bargain collectively:

- They may take up a grievance directly with management—provided that the settlement is in line with the union contract and a union representative is given an opportunity to be present.
- If they are professional employees, they have a right to vote with a company's other professional employees on whether they want a collective bargaining unit of their own.

Other significant changes enacted by the Taft-Hartley Act are

The 60-day notice of contract termination. If either the company or the union wants to end the contract, it must give the other party 60 days' notice—even though the contract has a definite termination date. During the 60-day period no employee can strike or slow down; management cannot alter, in a manner contrary to the contract requirements, the employment status or working conditions of any employee.

The 80-day injunction. Should a labor dispute, in the opinion of the President of the United States, imperil the health and safety of the nation, procedures are set up so that after proper investigation the President may petition the federal district court for an injunction to stop the strike or lockout. During this 80-day cooling-off period, certain other procedures must be followed. Toward the end of the cooling-off period, if the dispute remains unsettled, the National Labor Relations Board (NLRB) must take a secret ballot of employees to ascertain whether they wish to accept the terms of the employer's last offer. If still unsettled after 80 days, the strike or lockout may resume.

Right to sue for damages. Both companies and unions may sue in federal court for damages caused by breach of contract. Employers may also sue for damages arising out of illegal strikes and boycotts.

Plant guards' units. Plant guards are permitted to form their own bargaining group but may not bargain collectively through a union associated with other employees.

Freedom of speech. Employers and unions are given equal rights to speak their minds freely about each other—except when they actually utter a "threat of reprisal, or force, or promise of benefit." (Note that "promise of benefit" is not considered to restrict a union from describing the potential benefits to be derived from union membership.)

Union shop, closed shop—what's this all about?

The *closed shop* was outlawed by the Taft-Hartley Act. In a closed shop, a man or woman had to belong to the bargaining union before he or she could be hired. The *union shop* is somewhat similar. The difference lies in the fact that a person need not be a union member at the time of hiring. But an employee must (usually after a 30- or 60-day trial period) become a member of the union in order to stay on the payroll.

Under the Taft-Hartley Act, the only reason for which a union may force a company to fire a worker is that he or she does not pay union dues. This protects the individual from being discriminated against by the union. In the union shop agreement, it's common for a company also to sign a checkoff agreement with the union. This means that the company will collect employees' union initiation fees and dues and turn them over to the union. The employee must first sign an authorization card that gives the company permission to do so.

What is a right-to-work law?

When the Taft-Hartley Act outlawed the closed shop, it also permitted the individual states to pass laws making the union shop illegal. Such laws, enacted in 21 states, are called *right-to-work laws.* In these states, forced membership in a labor union is discouraged or is plainly illegal. Where unions do gain recognition, either an open or an agency shop prevails. In an *agency shop,* all employees must pay union dues (ostensibly for bargaining and other services), but they are not required to become union members. Thus, it is possible for 51 percent of a company's employees to be union members and 49 percent to be nonmembers, even though 100 percent contribute to the union's administrative expenses.

Are there any other labor laws that a supervisor should know about?

Two important laws are the Walsh-Healey Public Contracts Act and the Fair Labor Standards Act. Generally, your company will watch for compliance, but since the laws influence decisions that affect you, here's a fast rundown.

Walsh-Healey Public Contracts Act   Walsh-Healey sets the rules for any company that works on a government contract in excess of $10,000. The act forbids hiring boys under 16 and girls under 18. It limits the basic hours of work to 8 a day and 40 a week. The employer must pay time and a half for overtime. The act sets up strict standards for safety, health, and working conditions and also may establish a minimum wage for a particular industry.

Fair Labor Standards Act   Also known as the *Wages and Hours Law,* this act regulates methods of wage payment and hours of work for any industry engaged in commerce between two or more states. The law restricts the employment of children over 14 and under 16 to nonmanufacturing and nonmining positions and prohibits the employment of children between 16 and 18 in hazardous jobs, including driving or helping a driver of a motor vehicle. The law sets the minimum wage ($3.35 an hour since 1981) and prescribes that time and a half must be paid for all hours worked over 40 in a week. It also establishes what is "work" and what is not—such as waiting in line to receive paychecks, changing clothes, washing up or bathing, and checking in or out. (All this may be considered work in a union agreement if the parties so agree.)

The Fair Labor Standards Act also sets up guidelines for determining which supervisors must be paid overtime and which need not. In order to be classed as an *exempt* executive, a supervisor must:

- Have as a primary duty the management of a recognized department or subdivision.
- Customarily and regularly direct the work of two or more other employees, exercise discretionary powers, and have the power to hire or fire or make suggestions and recommendations which will be given particular weight in the hiring, firing, advancement, and promotion of subordinates.
- Not perform nonexempt (clerical, nonadministrative) work more than 20 percent of the time (40 percent in retail trade).
- Receive a salary of at least $155 per week.

If an employee's salary is over $250 (as in the case of a highly paid staff specialist) there are fewer restrictions on what he or she can do and still be exempt from overtime.

Nonexempt employees include almost all wage-roll and clerical people; overtime provisions of the law apply to them. Professional employees who require advanced knowledge, customarily acquired through prolonged instruction and study of a specialized field, are usually considered exempt. However, apprenticeship, a college degree, and routine training will not necessarily qualify an employee as a professional.

What is the purpose of the Disclosure Act of 1959?

Officially designated as the **Labor Management Reporting and Disclosure Act** of 1959, Public Law 86-257 (also known as the **Landrum-Griffith Act**) compels employers to report:

- Payments to labor union officials, agents, or shop stewards (for purposes other than pay for work).

- Payments to employees (other than regular wage payments) or to groups or committees of employees for purposes of persuading other employees regarding choice of a union or other union matters.
- Payments to a consultant on labor union matters.

Payments that must be reported also include reimbursed expenses. More important, the law also compels a labor union to make a more complete disclosure regarding the sources and disbursement of its funds.

The law is aimed primarily at (1) preventing unethical collusion between a company and a union or other interference with the due process of collective bargaining, (2) preventing the misuse of a union's funds by its leaders, and (3) otherwise minimizing the possibility of labor "racketeering."

What's the purpose of the NLRB?

The National Labor Relations Board is a government agency made up of five members appointed by the President of the United States. Its duty is to:

- Administer the National Labor Relations Act and, in so doing, determine proper collective bargaining units.
- Direct and supervise recognition elections.
- Prevent employers, employees, and unions from violating the act through unfair labor practices, as defined in the statutes.

The NLRB is not a federal court with power to settle disputes, but it makes the major decisions about how the National Labor Relations Act should be interpreted. Since it is not a court, you may occasionally read of a company or a union petitioning a federal district court or the United States Supreme Court to set aside a ruling made by the NLRB. The federal court or the Supreme Court, in such a case, would have the final say—not the NLRB.

▣ COLLECTIVE BARGAINING

CONCEPT   Supervisors are rarely involved directly in the bargaining process, but their actions deeply affect the resulting labor contracts.

How does a labor union get the right to bargain for your employees in the first place?

Within certain limits, labor unions have the legal right to try to persuade a company's employees to allow the union to represent them in the employees' dealings with management. Management also has the right to try to persuade its employees that they might be better off without union representation. When 30 percent of the employees show interest, the union is entitled to ask for a **representation election** among the company's employees. This election is supervised by the NLRB. If the union wins the election, management must then bargain collectively with employees through the union. If the union does not win a majority in the election, the union has no further say in labor relations matters at that company. It may, however, petition for another election after one year.

During a contest for representation by a labor union, what should the company's supervisors do?

You've pretty much got to take your instructions from the company, even if your personal inclination is to remain neutral or even to support the union's membership drive. Under these circumstances, most companies will expect supervisors to support the company's position. In that case you may be asked to:

- Represent the company to your employees in a positive way: "This is the company's record for fair treatment. I don't think you really need a union to get a good deal here."
- Raise questions about employees' relationships under union representation. "Have you been told what your strike benefits will be? Is it clear to you what the union will ask for in the way of dues?"

On the other hand, there are a number of things that your company cannot ask you to do, nor should you do them on your own. For example:

- Don't promise rewards for not joining the union.
- Don't make threats about what will happen if the union wins, such as saying that the plant will be closed or the union will call a strike.
- Don't pressure employees to commit themselves to the company. You can't, for example, ask what employees' attitudes are toward the union, whether or not they have signed a representation card, or whether they went to a union rally.
- Don't try to spy on employees' union activities. Don't stand near the door at a union meeting to see who is attending or even to count noses.
- Don't invite employees into your office to discuss the union. This, like most of the points already mentioned, is considered by the law to be intimidating and to imply an ultimate discrimination against employees who show an interest in union membership. When in doubt about what to do or say, ask your boss before doing or saying anything. Labor law is both expansive and complex; it takes an expert to interpret it properly.

What does collective bargaining include?

Collective bargaining takes place only after a labor union has won a representation election. When authorized representatives of the employer and authorized representatives of the employees bargain together to establish wages, hours, and working conditions, this process is called *collective bargaining.* Various labor laws have determined what are fit matters for collective bargaining and what are not. Generally speaking, however, the term *working conditions* is so broad that almost anything that affects employees at work or the manner in which they carry out their jobs can be included.

The mere fact that a matter, such as the establishment of wage rates, is a fit subject for collective bargaining doesn't necessarily mean that the union can control the way it is handled. The union can bargain for its position, and management has to bargain in good faith over the issue. But the company does not have to accept the union's position. Several considerations will determine the issue's final disposition: the reasonableness of the union demand; the desirability of the demand to employees, management, and stockholders; the ability of the company to pay for its cost; the judgment of management as to its worth; and, finally, the bargaining strength or weakness of the union or the company.

Does collective bargaining end with the signing of the contract negotiations?

Collective bargaining usually starts with the negotiation of the union agreement and the signing of the labor contract. But it doesn't end there. Supervisors, managers, employees, and union stewards must live with the agreement for the next 365 days or longer. Applying the contract and interpreting its meanings from day to day are what make collective bargaining effective. The contract, like any other contract, is rarely changed during its life. But there are dozens, sometimes hundreds, of occurrences between supervisor and employee that require astute judgment on how the situation should be handled to best carry out the meaning of the contract. It is such interpretation and differences of opinion between management and unions that make labor relations a key supervisory headache and responsibility.

Why don't supervisors sit in with the management bargaining team at a union contract negotiation?

Bargaining is a delicate matter of strategy and power. It's a little like playing poker. If there are too many kibitzers, a good hand can be spoiled by unwanted expressions and remarks.

If your company does not invite you to sit in on negotiations, don't feel slighted. In most companies, the bargaining team is handpicked from the top plant management group.

How does the supervisor's day-to-day administration of the contract influence contract negotiations?

In many ways. If day by day a supervisor neglects or ignores grievances, assigns jobs unfairly, or neglects safety and other working conditions, collective bargaining will be made more difficult. Each time during the year that you throw your weight around thoughtlessly or take advantage of letter-of-the-law loopholes in the contract, you add to the store of incidents that the union representatives will bring to bear in order to win their demands at contract time.

Take seniority as an example. Suppose you stand on your management right (and the absence of a specific contract clause to the contrary) to assign overtime only to the workers you favor, regardless of their seniority. Once or twice you defend your position by saying that the overtime required the special skills of the two class A operators you held over. But the union observes that several times you've held over class A operators just as a convenience: the bulk of the work could have been done by laborers. When contract time rolls around, you can bet that the union negotiators will be in there pitching for a definite clause to spell out exactly how overtime will be distributed.

It's far better to handle your decisions reasonably and equitably during the year so that at contract time the union will accept more general provisions. This leaves the details to be worked out during the year on a mutual basis as the occasion arises. Experience seems to show that the more general type of contract is easier for all members of management to administer.

🔢 *CONTRACT ADMINISTRATION*

CONCEPT Supervisors are the pivotal implementers of labor contracts; they must deal productively with union representatives without yielding their authority to manage.

Why does a supervisor's authority in labor relations vary according to the employing organization?

Your primary responsibility to your company in labor matters is to protect the interests and the rights of management. How far supervisors can exercise authority in carrying out this responsibility will depend on the extent to which the front office feels that supervisors can act without first checking to see if their decisions are in line with company policy.

In most companies supervisors have no authority to adjust wage rates directly; they are limited merely to reporting a wage-rate request and analyzing the job conditions. On the other hand, in most companies supervisors are expected to take direct and immediate action in the case of willful damage to equipment, unsafe actions, or refusal to follow a work assignment.

But regardless of administrative differences from company to company, the first-line supervisor is usually the first contact between employees and management and between union representatives and management. Since what you do and say in labor matters has such vital consequences to your company's overall relationship with employees and their representatives, you must be alert to your company's labor practices. Your actions are not confined only to yourself and a single employee. They could very well have companywide impact. Under certain circumstances, your actions could cause your employer to be charged by the union with breaking the contract or even with breaking the law.

Supervisors in the past have been charged with unfair labor practices of interference and discrimination. What's this all about?

Supervisors are most directly affected by the section of the Wagner Act that prohibits unfair labor practices. Actually, there are five unfair labor practices, but the following two most frequently involve supervisors.

Interference   This would most likely take place during a union's organizing drive or an NLRB representation election. Supervisors should be especially careful at that time to avoid (1) any actions that affect an employee's job or pay, (2) arguments that lead to a dispute over a union question, (3) threats to a union member through a third party, or (4) interactions without advice from top management with any of the organizing union's officers.

Discrimination   This term applies to any action (such as discharge of an employee, layoff, demotion, or assignment to more difficult or disagreeable work) taken by any member of management on account of the employee's union membership or activity. To be on safe ground, once a union has won recognition it's wise not to discuss union matters as such with employees or to express an opinion for or against a union or unionism. This is good practice off duty as well as on.

The simplest way to avoid charges of discrimination is to disregard completely an employee's union membership when you make decisions regarding job assignments, discipline, and promotions. Before you act, make sure in your own mind that you have separated ability, performance, and attitude toward the job from the employee's stand on unionism or zeal in supporting it.

How far does a union shop steward's authority go?

A *steward* is to the union what you are to the company. It's a union steward's job to protect the rights of union members just as it's yours to protect the rights of management. But in protecting these rights, a union shop steward has no authority to run your department or to tell you or any employee what to do.

You may get the impression that a steward is telling you what to do. A new steward may even feel that it is his or her job to do so. All the steward has authority to do, however, is to advise you or employees of his or her understanding of how the contract limits your actions and decisions. It goes without saying that you are the department executive, and you are not obligated to share your responsibility with anyone.

It is good practice, however, to keep stewards informed of what you are doing—so that they can make their position known. It also shows that you are not trying to take unfair advantage of the stewards.

How friendly should a supervisor be with a shop steward?

Be as cordial as you can without giving up your right to run your department. You may personally resent a steward who is a continual thorn in your side. But remember, the steward is an elected representative of the group. Stewards speak not only as individuals but also for the employees they represent.

You can gain confidence, if not cooperation, from shop stewards if you let them know what's going on. They have status to protect, just as you do. If you try to keep them in the dark or treat them as if they are insignificant, they may react by showing you just how important they are. So don't keep a steward at arm's length. Get to know him or her as you would any other employee. You will have many mutual problems. There's nothing wrong with enlisting a steward's help in solving some of them.

Suppose you are planning to start up a second shift on one of the machines in your department. You intend to post a bidding sheet for a new operator. You lose nothing by telling the steward of the new job opportunity in advance. And it gives you a chance to enlist the steward's help when you say: "We're going to be needing a good operator to run the number 6 machine on the second shift. We agree with the union that the job should go to the worker with the most seniority who is really qualified to do a good job. But let's see that we get some good people bidding."

Some stewards just won't cooperate. How do you handle them?

You can help aggressive stewards blow off steam if you maintain a constructive approach and show them you understand their problems. After all, their jobs can be thankless ones. Check yourself, too, to be sure that it's not your own aggressive actions that make a steward hard to get along with. Try to approach each problem not as a battle between the two of you but as a problem that you are both trying to solve in accordance with the labor agreement. Don't say only, "Let's see what the contract says." Show that you, too, are interested in justice for your employees: "Let's see how we can do the most we can for this employee without making a decision that is out of line with the contract."

Always keep in mind, however, that it is cooperation you are seeking, not co-management.

🔲 5 *GRIEVANCE PROCEDURES*

CONCEPT   The grievance procedure provides a systematic, objective way of dealing with employee grievances.

Why is there a grievance procedure? Wouldn't it be better to settle gripes informally without all the red tape?

Most union contracts establish a step-by-step grievance procedure. Experience has shown both management and labor that it's best to have a systematic method of handling complaints. Without a formalized procedure, management (in dealing with unionized employees) would find it difficult to coordinate labor and personnel practices from department to department.

The formal procedure provides an easy and open channel of communication for employees to bring complaints to the attention of supervision. And it guarantees that these complaints won't be sidetracked or allowed to ferment without corrective action being taken. Good supervisors and wise managements know that an unsettled grievance, real or imaginary, expressed or hidden, is always a potential source of trouble. The grievance machinery helps uncover the causes and get the grievance out into the open. (See Chapter 15.)

Is there a standard grievance procedure set down by law?

No. The actual grievance procedure will vary from company to company. It will depend on what the company and the union have agreed on and have written into the labor contract.

A typical grievance procedure has from three to five steps, as shown in Figure 22-1, and usually originates after an employee is dissatisfied with a supervisor's response.

Step 1. Supervisor discusses complaint with employee and union steward.

Step 2. Superintendent and labor relations manager discuss complaint with union grievance committee.

Step 3. Site manager and labor relations manager discuss complaint with union grievance committee.

Step 4. General company management discusses complaint with national union representative and union grievance committee.

Step 5. Dispute is referred to impartial umpire or arbitrator for decision.

It should be emphasized that a serious and prolonged effort should be made by both parties to settle the grievance at each step—including the first. Prompt action by supervisors has been shown to be effective in solving as many as 75 percent of all grievances at the first step.

Why do supervisors sometimes get overruled?

If supervisors have made every effort beforehand to be sure their decisions and actions are in line with the company's interpretation of the contract, there can be only three reasons why they should be overruled. The supervisor may have acted on insufficient or incorrect facts. This is probably the most common reason. The supervisor may occasionally be made the sacrificial lamb when the company realizes at the third or fourth step of the procedure that its interpretation of the contract won't stand up to the union's position. Or both the supervisor and the company may be overruled by the arbitrator at the last step.

Why don't grievances go right to the arbitrator in the first place?

Unions and managements seem to agree on this point: they'd both rather settle their household quarrels between themselves than invite a stranger in to settle disputes. Both parties reason, and rightly, that they know more than anyone else about their affairs. In the long run, union and management must learn how to settle their differences themselves with-

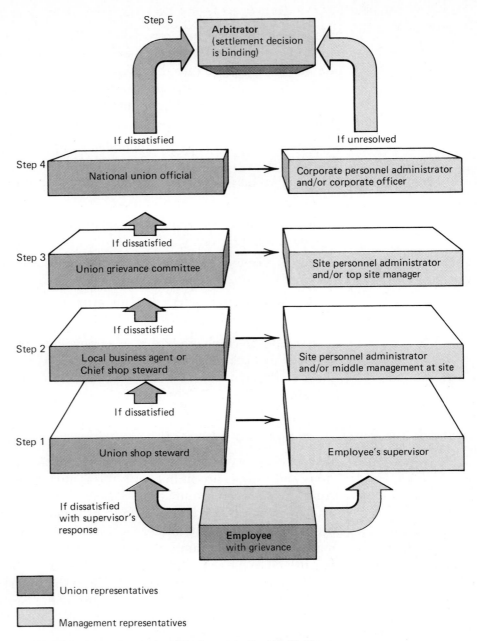

Step 5

Arbitrator
(settlement decision
is binding)

If dissatisfied   If unresolved

Step 4   National union official → Corporate personnel administrator and/or corporate officer

If dissatisfied

Step 3   Union grievance committee → Site personnel administrator and/or top site manager

If dissatisfied

Step 2   Local business agent or Chief shop steward → Site personnel administrator and/or middle management at site

If dissatisfied

Step 1   Union shop steward → Employee's supervisor

If dissatisfied with supervisor's response

Employee with grievance

Union representatives

Management representatives

Figure 22-1 Example of a formal grievance procedure.

out continually depending on a third party. It's been said by both union and management that nobody wins an arbitration. But when it's needed, peaceful arbitration is far better than strikes or lockouts.

REVIEW

KEY CONCEPTS TO REMEMBER

1. In dealing with employees and labor unions, the laws of the land view supervisors as responsible agents of the companies they work for. Workers join labor unions because unions provide security through collective representation, because membership is often compulsory, or because unions provide a sense of independence from management's power. Regardless of a supervisor's attitude toward organized labor, he or she is bound to behave in accordance with labor laws and to abide by the agreements that may be derived from collective bargaining.

2. The basic labor-management law is the National Labor Relations Act, or Wagner Act (which protects the rights of employees to bargain collectively for wages, hours, and working conditions) as amended by the Taft-Hartley Act. Other related legislation includes the Labor Management Reporting and Disclosure Act, Walsh-Healey Public Contracts Act, and Fair Labor Standards Act. Most of these are under the supervision or administration of the National Labor Relations Board (NLRB).

3. Collective bargaining between management and a labor union takes place after a union has won a representation election. The end result of a collective bargaining negotiation is a labor contract. Supervisors are not ordinarily included directly in the bargaining process, but their actions during the preceding years greatly influence the terms of the contract.

4. Supervisors play vital roles in administering the labor contract. Accordingly, it is important that supervisors (a) maintain their own interest in, and responsibility toward, the well-being of their employees and (b) protect their own authority and rights as managers to direct, motivate, and control their staffs—modified only by the contractual limitations. It is also important that supervisors refrain from interference during union representation elections and from discrimination at all times, but especially during contract administration.

5. Employees' grievances are primarily in the domain of the supervisor. It is in the supervisor's interest to listen to, understand, and resolve them at the first level of management rather than to have them move beyond his or her control into the formal channels of referral specified by the grievance procedure.

SUPERVISORY WORD POWER

Arbitration. The settlement of a labor dispute or employee grievance by an impartial umpire selected by mutual agreement of the company and the union.

Collective bargaining. The process of give-and-take engaged in by the management of a company and authorized representatives of its collective employees (a labor union) to reach a formal, written agreement about wages, hours, and working conditions.

Grievance procedure. A formalized, systematic channel for employees to follow in bringing their complaints to the attention of management. Typically, it prescribes a progression of appeals from lowest to highest authority within the company and the employees' organization.

Labor contract. The written agreement that binds a company's management and its employees' organization (labor union) for a stipulated period of time to certain conditions of pay, hours, and work and any other matter the parties deem appropriate.

Unfair labor practices. Those practices engaged in by either management or labor unions that are judged by the federal labor law (National Labor Relations Act) to be improper, especially in that they (1) interfere with the rights of employees to organize or (2) discriminate against employees for labor union activities.

READING COMPREHENSION

1. Suggest two good reasons why a supervisor should know about labor-management relations laws.
2. Why might a well-paid employee who enjoys his or her job still want to join a labor union?
3. Compare the objectives of the Wagner Act with those of the Taft-Hartley Act.
4. How do the closed shop, union shop, and agency shop differ? Which is most closely associated with right-to-work laws?
5. Distinguish between a representation election and a collective bargaining session.
6. What three principal matters are always fit subjects for collective bargaining discussions?
7. What is the difference between unfair labor practices involving interference and those involving discrimination?

8. Contrast a shop steward's responsibility with that of an employee's supervisor.
9. Describe a typical grievance procedure. At what point does a supervisor usually bow out?
10. Contrast the role of an arbitrator and that of the NLRB in settling labor disputes.

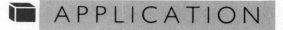

APPLICATION

SELF-APPRAISAL

How good is your supervisory discretion in labor contract administration?

Listed are twenty topics that are typically included in a labor contract. Your assignment is to determine which topics are most likely to involve supervisory discretion during the course of a contract period and which are least likely to involve a supervisor. On a separate piece of paper, copy the column headings shown below. In the column "Labor Contract Topics," write the numbers 1 to 20 down the page to correspond to each of the labor topics. Then place a check mark in the column that most nearly matches your opinion about each topic. After completing this activity, check your answers by using the scoring procedure described on page 522.

Column headings:

Labor Contract Topics	Most Likely to Involve Supervisors	Least Likely to Involve Supervisors

1. Defining the union bargaining unit.
2. Specifying the kind of shop: union, open, agency, and so forth.
3. Withholding union dues by the company.
4. Evaluating and selecting employees for promotions.
5. Implementing the grievance procedure.
6. Selecting the method of arbitration.
7. Considering seniority in transfers and layoffs.
8. Establishing wage scales.
9. Administering call-in pay.
10. Establishing pay periods and method of payment.
11. Making decisions regarding severance or dismissal pay.

12. Establishing shift differentials.
13. Establishing overtime pay.
14. Deciding when to pay for hazardous or severely disagreeable work.
15. Establishing when work clothing will be supplied by the company.
16. Making up shift-schedule assignments.
17. Deciding on the number of paid holidays.
18. Deciding on the policy for sick-leave pay.
19. Handling seniority rights and benefits for persons returning from maternity leave.
20. Deciding on company-paid life and medical insurance.

Scoring Here's how a panel of experts evaluated the list: topics 4, 5, 7, 9, 14, and 16 were *most likely to involve supervisors;* topics 1, 2, 3, 6, 8, 10, 11, 12, 13, 15, 17, 18, 19, and 20 were *least likely to involve supervisors.* Give yourself 1 point for each answer you agreed with.

Interpretation If you scored 16 or more points, your judgment on labor contract matters is *very good.* Do check with your instructor, however, about the items on which you disagreed with the experts to see if your reasons are justified. If you scored less than 15 points, your judgment on labor contract matters is *not too good.* Review your choices with your instructor to see if you can justify the differences between your opinions and those of the experts.

CASE STUDIES

CASE 66 The Unwilling Word Processing Operator

Olga is a word processing operator in a state agency whose employees are represented by a union of government workers. Olga works in a word processing pool made up of employees with low seniority. They have no regularly assigned jobs. Each morning they report to the pool's supervisor, Daryl Dowd, to find out where they will work that day. Sometimes Daryl holds an operator over on the same job he or she worked on the day before. Sometimes, in order to place the best operators on a particularly demanding assignment, Daryl pulls an operator off a continuing assignment. When the work load in the pool is relatively light, Daryl lets the operators pick the jobs they'll work on. When the calls for operators from various departments are frequent, however, Daryl makes all the assignments and listens to no arguments.

Lately, Olga has begun to feel that Daryl is taking advantage of her good work and her good nature. She rarely gets to stay on the same assignment (which is desirable because it means a chance to get the feel of the work and the people in a particular department) more than one day at a time. Besides, many of the jobs that Daryl gives her are unattractive ones. The work is especially painstaking, for example, or it has to be done under pressure, or the people in the department are unfriendly.

Olga brooded about this situation over a long weekend. On Monday morning, when Daryl wanted to send her up to the tenth floor to work in the budget-review department, Olga boiled over. "Send someone else up there to do their kind of picky work today," she told Daryl. "I won't take another assignment like that until every other operator in the pool has been rotated to as many rotten jobs as I've had!"

"You're going to have to work on any assignment that's legitimate for the word processing pool, regardless of whether you like it or not," said Daryl. "So get going!"

Olga just stared at Daryl. "There's no way you can make me take this one. I'm sure that my shop steward will back me up in this," said Olga. And with that, she stormed off to the lounge.

If you were Daryl, what would you do? Five alternatives are provided below. Rank them on a scale from 1 (most preferable) to 5 (least preferable). You may add another alternative if you wish. In any event, be prepared to justify your ranking.

a. Insist that Olga either report to the assignment on the tenth floor or sign out her time card and be put on suspension.

b. Get the shop steward to talk to Olga to persuade her to go back to work on the budget-review assignment.

c. Tell Olga that just this once she won't have to accept the assignment.

d. Carefully review with Olga her assignments for the last few weeks so that you can both agree upon whether they were particularly difficult or not.

e. Acknowledge that Olga may have a reasonable complaint; say that you'll try to equalize assignments in the future, but tell her she must take the one she's been handed for the day.

CASE 67 The Striking Longshoremen

The International Longshoremen's Association has been increasingly unhappy about its pay scale. The national contract has terminated. Now, members of the union along the Gulf Coast have decided to strike if their demands are not met. Workers will stop working and go on strike in two weeks if an agreement is not reached by then.

What can be done on a federal basis to prevent the impending strike?

Describe the process and name the legislation or executive order that would be placed in effect.

CASE 68   Nine Who Did Wrong

Each of the following nine labor actions is a violation of one of the principal labor and employment laws. On a separate piece of paper, write the name of the law that is violated by each action. (Consult Chapters 20, 21, and 22, if necessary.)

a. The Jasper Company refuses to talk about its wage scale to a union agent duly selected by employees.

b. A labor union insists that the Axe Construction Company discharge Tony, one of its employees, because he was expelled from the union for disagreeing with its policies.

c. The supervisor of the receiving department insists that a worker uncap a tank car of chemicals even though a needed safety respirator is not available.

d. A company refuses to hire Audrey Hill solely because she is married and her future supervisor thinks that she will quit soon to have a baby.

e. Torger Branson, who works for National Distributors, did not receive time-and-a-half pay for the hours over 40 that he worked last week.

f. Astro Metals Manufacturers hires 17-year-old George Cone to work on a job connected with a large government contract it has recently acquired.

g. A union prohibits one of its employees from speaking up on a complaint she has against the company's management.

h. Stan's supervisor assigns Stan to a very unpleasant task in order to discourage him from asking other employees to sign union membership cards.

i. The Texto Company fails to report to the government its arrangement for reimbursing shop stewards for their expenses while attending union conventions.

Personal Development Portfolio:

TOWARD MASTERY OF YOUR JOB

525

What skills will you need
to succeed and survive
as a supervisor?

HOW CAN YOU GET THE MOST FROM THIS PORTFOLIO?

APPLY YOURSELF TO EACH OF THE FOUR PORTFOLIO FILES THIS WAY:

Complete the self-assessment exercise that appears on the second page of each file. It will help show you where you stand before you review the material that follows.

Study the advice presented in each file. It is arranged in the question-and-answer format that was used in the previous chapters of the text.

Where indicated, prepare your own career paths, objectives, timetables, and developmental programs as illustrated in the file.

Make notations of the material that seems especially appropriate to you. Use these notations as a guide to searching for, and collecting, information elsewhere that will enhance and personalize your own file.

Study the Key Concepts to Remember, which appear on pages 553 to 554. They provide a summary of the high points in the Personal Development Portfolio.

Review the vocabulary in Supervisory Word Power, which appears on pages 554 to 555. These words will extend your conversational facility in the critical areas of self-development.

Complete the final four Case Studies, which appear on pages 555 to 557. These will provide you with experience in analyzing and solving problems that can occur while you are following a self-development program.

Career planning begins with a candid self-assessment. Before doing anything else, complete the Personal Effectiveness Inventory (Table PDP-1) on the facing page. This is for your guidance in planning a self-improvement program, so do be realistic. Get a second opinion too. Ask a friend—or even your boss—to make a similar assessment of your effectiveness for comparison purposes. The inventory consists of criteria that many authorities believe are needed for success in supervisory and management positions. Accordingly, the purpose of the assessment is not only to affirm your strong points but, especially, to identify areas that need further development.

To complete the table, place a check mark in the column to the right of each numbered skill that best matches your assessment of your proficiency. If you believe that you are *less than strong* in a skill that stands in the way of your career advancement, place a check mark in the "Needs Improvement" column too.

On what is a career development program based?

It has four vital components:

- **A candid self-assessment.** You have already begun your self-development if you have completed the Personal Effectiveness Inventory in Table PDP-1.
- **Firm and realistic job goals.**   These should be based upon what you want to accomplish in your career specifically and in your life generally. They will be limited, of course, by the unimproved weaknesses that stand out in your Personal Effectiveness Inventory.
- **A concrete program for development.**   Every weakness points toward a corrective course of action. These actions should be spelled out in detail—a course to take, a book to read, a seminar to attend, an on-job practice to engage in. Action plans should also pin down the time to begin and complete each phase. A modest but concrete development program is better than an ambitious but vague one.
- **Motivation and commitment.**   Career growth has its pluses and minuses. Upward movement usually means greater status and a more affluent life-style. It also means very hard work, sacrifice of leisure time, removal from the easy friendship with people in the department, and an occasional unpleasant decision to make. That is the trade-off. To go ahead, supervisors have to value the benefits above

Table PDP-1 PERSONAL EFFECTIVENESS INVENTORY

Skills	Proficiency			
	Weak	Adequate	Needs Improvement	Strong
1. *Oral communication:* Ability to express ideas effectively in individual or group situations.	_____	_____	_____	_____
2. *Written communication:* Ability to write clearly, concisely, and correctly.	_____	_____	_____	_____
3. *Leadership:* Ability to get ideas accepted and acted upon by an individual or a group.	_____	_____	_____	_____
4. *Interpersonal sensitivity:* Ability to be perceptive about the concerns and needs of others and the impact of your own behavior on others.	_____	_____	_____	_____
5. *Planning and organizing:* Ability to plan a course of action for self and others and to get results.	_____	_____	_____	_____
6. *Problem solving:* Ability to identify causes, analyze problems, and propose workable solutions.	_____	_____	_____	_____
7. *Decisiveness:* Ability to make sound decisions and a willingness to take action.	_____	_____	_____	_____
8. *Time management:* Ability to make effective use of job-related time to meet schedules, deadlines, and other commitments.	_____	_____	_____	_____
9. *Stress tolerance:* Ability to perform under pressure.	_____	_____	_____	_____
10. *Creativity and innovation:* Ability to conceive, recognize, and accept or implement new and/or imaginative ideas.	_____	_____	_____	_____
11. *Flexibility:* Ability to recognize changing conditions and to implement necessary changes.	_____	_____	_____	_____

the new obligations. Without personal drive and commitment to the goals you have chosen, a self-development program becomes an exercise in self-deception.

What is a career path? How is it found?

A *career path* maps out the most logical and practical roadway to a position, or series of positions, that an individual believes holds the most attractive occupational and personal rewards. As stated earlier, you may decide that your career lies in your present job. If so, you'll be mainly concerned with the improved performance, broader scope of responsibilities, larger salary, and heightened personal satisfaction.

If, however, your sights are on a career beyond your present position, you'll need to develop a more complex plan. Your target can be the next higher position in your organization, or it can be one at the same level but with a different range of responsibilities, or it can be a job much further up the management hierarchy. An example of a career path is illustrated in Figure PDP-1. This individual—let's call her Patty—has picked a long-range target of becoming the general manager of a profit center. To get there, Patty has plotted a path that will move her from a staff-supervisory position in quality control (1) to being a production-line supervisor (2), then upward to production manager in a different division (3), across to an entirely different functional area as a marketing manager (4), and, it is hoped, after a number of years, to general manager of her original division (5).

To make her career path workable, Patty should include target dates for each move, say "in two or three years" or "in five years." And, most important, Patty's plan must identify (1) any personal weaknesses in her present performance and (2) the knowledge, skills, or experience needed to move her from one step to another along her career path. For example, Patty's performance on her present job may be marred by a poor employee safety record. She'll have to plan to do something to get that straightened out before she can realistically expect to get a crack at the line production job. Looking ahead to what it will take for her to move from the line job (2) to the divisional production manager's job (3), Patty may decide that she has to acquire a broader technical knowledge of the process. To do so, she may enroll in the appropriate technical course at a local university. The point is that each new job will have its own particular set of requirements. Patty will need to anticipate them and acquire the necessary credentials before she can seriously think about moving ahead to the next position in her career plan.

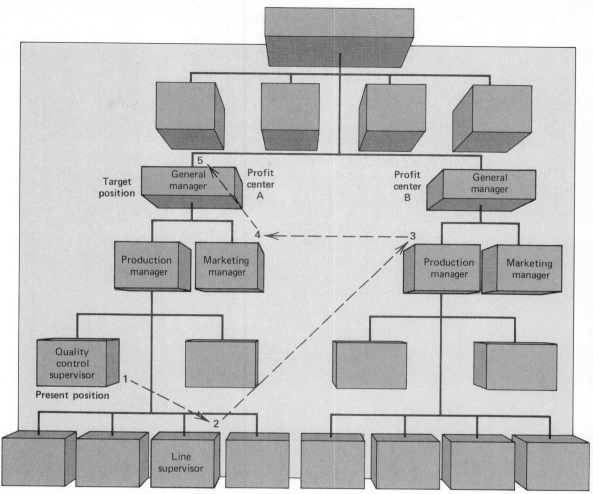

Figure PDP-1 Example of a career path.

How can you make sure that your plan for self-improvement or for career advancement becomes reality?

Self-delusion is paved with good intentions. To avoid shortfalls in your improvement plans, don't try to do too much too soon. Plan ahead for one step at a time. Do this planning in detail and do it realistically. Set targets that can be reached and place some kind of deadline for them, as shown in Figure PDP-2. Put both your goals and your plans into writing. Tack them up in a place where they will constantly remind you of your commitment to them. Check your progress regularly.

SELF-DEVELOPMENT SCHEDULE

Supervisor: _____ Joanne Carleo _____

Weak Spots	Plan for Corrective Action	When to Do It	Action Complete
Telling employees where they stand	Prepare calendar with a different worker to be talked to each week	At once	✓
Poor department safety record	Hold monthly meetings with work group	Begin June	✓
Keeping up with job technology	Subscribe to *Personal Computing*	At once	✓
No activities out-side of work	Join Data Processing Association	Next year	
Speaking in front of groups	Enroll in Dale Carnegie course in public speaking	Next winter	
Cost estimating	Take correspondence course in accounting	Not scheduled	

☐ This year's plan   ☐ Next year's plan   ☐ Future

Figure PDP-2 Self-development schedule.

What about networking and mentors?

You'll help your career along with either or both. **Networking** is what used to be called "connections." Today's differences are that networks are built by, or tapped by, an individual along lines of knowing what's going on and what's opening up in an organization rather than on formal lines of authority and status. Networks are very informal, and the individuals in them often have little or no direct influence. But, by working the network, you can do a better job of planning your career moves and selecting the best preparation for them.

A **mentor,** on the other hand, is someone in a position of influence or authority who is interested in you and your career. A mentor is best utilized as an adviser. He or she will have a good idea of the best path to travel and the kind of training and skills you'll need to pursue it. It is not a good idea to expect a mentor to do much more than point the way. It is unfair to ask him or her to risk personal security and reputation on your behalf. If, however, a mentor goes out on a limb for you, don't let him or her down.

How can you attain the formal education needed for your career?

Face it, the person with the better education has an advantage over the person without it. But this doesn't mean you can't do anything about it. There's plenty you can do to improve your knowledge.

First, examine your own attitude toward further education. Is it strictly negative? If so, you'd better change in a hurry. Convince yourself that you, too, can learn new techniques and accept new ideas. If you want to learn, learning is made easier.

Next, pick out the soft spots in your educational armor. Is it reading and writing? Is it a weakness with figures? These can be improved quickly through correspondence and home-study courses or in an evening course at a local university. Adult education courses at your local high school also offer help in these areas.

If your weakness is in a technical line—say, your company is processing chemicals or constructing complicated electronic equipment or your job involves simple metallurgy—you can find courses at technical institutes and universities that will help you understand such processes better even if you don't become an expert.

Caution: You may not be able to take a course in physical chemistry, for instance, if you haven't had a previous course in basic chemistry. So your plan for improvement may often have to be a long-range one. Here's a suggestion: You may be able to enroll in an advanced course just as a listener. You can thus get a feel for the subject and its terminology, with only a little prior preparation.

In your programming, don't scatter your efforts indiscriminately. Pinpoint your educational efforts to strengthen your weak spots. Later on, if you like, you can add frills.

How can you take best advantage of your company's training and development program?

Show that you're interested. In most progressive companies today, the personnel manager or the training director is eager to help supervisors who want to help themselves. Don't be ashamed to ask for help, and don't think you'll be revealing a secret weakness. One of the necessary qualities of an executive is the ability for self-analysis and the determination to improve.

Stay alert, too, to management development opportunities. **Management development** (it may also be called executive or supervisory development) is the term applied to the systematic inventory, appraisal, and training of management people. Programs vary according to an individual company's policies. Sometimes they include only top management people and often are not extended to the first-line supervisory level.

If there's a program in your company that applies to you, you'll probably hear about it from your boss. But don't expect your company to take care of your self-development program. It's really up to you.

Where can you go for outside help and guidance?

For educational guidance outside your company, try your local centers for adult education or vocational guidance, a nearby community college, or a university extension service. Or write either of the nationwide management clubs mentioned in Chapter 1. Another source to try is any nearby chapter of the American Society for Training and Development.

For information about specific correspondence or technical courses, write to:

American Society for Training and Development
1630 Duke Street
Alexandria, Virginia 22313

American Society for Engineering Education
1 DuPont Circle, N.W.
Washington, D.C. 20036

National Home Study Council
1601 18th Street, N.W.
Washington, D.C. 20009

American Personnel and Guidance Association
5999 Stevenson Avenue
Alexandria, Virginia 22313

What will outside reading do for you?

Some people can learn a lot just by reading. Others find it difficult to get much from the printed page. But if you're one of the former, try to set up a planned reading program. Include in it at least one good newspaper (such as *USA Today* or *The Wall Street Journal*), one good news magazine (such as *Time* or *Newsweek*), one good management magazine (such as *Business Week* or *Industry Week*), and one good technical magazine or journal that serves your field (such as *Modern Office Technology* or *Popular Computing*). Don't just subscribe to them or have your name put on the routing list. Read them—and try to apply what you find in them. In addition, you ought to set up a library of business and professional reference books for yourself.

To what extent will career goals conflict with other aspirations in life?

They can be compatible, but the higher you move in a career, the more likely it is that other life values will suffer. This need not be, if you also build into your career plans a place for the other things you hold dear—family, friends, leisure, health, service, faith. You will be able to make such plans only if you have developed maturity, however. *Maturity* means the ability to stand outside yourself and make an honest judgment of your thoughts and behavior. It usually means—among other things—exercising a great deal of self-control, being able to hold your temper when others are losing theirs, accepting an occasional failure as well as success, and evaluating the talents and the intent of others fairly, regardless of your personal views.

How *purposefully* busy are you? The Time Management Survey (Table PDP-2) below is designed to help you answer that question. Your responses should lead you to the major challenge of **time management.** It involves dividing your time into two compartments: (1) the time that you *can* control and (2) the time that you *can't* control. When

Table PDP-2	TIME MANAGEMENT SURVEY		
Time Management Practices and Styles	Least Like Me	Neither Least nor Most Like Me	Most Like Me
1. It is difficult for me to meet delivery or project deadlines without working overtime or letting other work slip.	3	2	1
2. I usually can be depended upon to meet my time commitments.	1	2	3
3. My estimates about how quickly something can be done are usually correct; they rarely take longer than I expected.	1	2	3
4. I carefully examine schedules that I am given beforehand, rather than waiting until the work is behind schedule to complain.	1	2	3
5. When making promises about getting a new job done, I take into account how long it takes to get started on something new.	1	2	3
6. I base my time decisions on concrete knowledge of how long it has taken me to do a similar job in the past.	1	2	3
7. I regularly use some sort of systematic plan for the use of my time.	1	2	3
8. I often find myself caught up in disruptive, time-consuming telephone calls.	3	2	1
9. I rarely find the opportunity to let someone else do a job that I can do better.	3	2	1
10. I like to get a head start on work that I know will be time-consuming.	1	2	3

Scoring: 24 to 30, *outstanding!*

17 to 23, *satisfactory,* but there is room for improvement in some areas, notably those you circled as "1."

10 to 16, *poor.* Time gets away from you. Go to work on the items you circled as "1."

your boss wants you at a meeting, for example, that's time you can't control. So is the time you have to spend on an unexpected breakdown or an emergency. In your own situation, there are probably a number of other demands placed on your time, not at your convenience but at that of someone else. It's a good idea to make a list of these potentially uncontrollable occurrences right now. This is important because you'll want to think about them differently from the way you think about time demands that you can control. As a consequence, your approach to time management can be guided by two general rules:

1. Systemize and prioritize the management of your controllable time.
2. Minimize the amount of your uncontrollable time. This has to be done in bits and pieces, and probably over a long period of time. And, since this time is often controlled by others, you'll have to work out ways to gain some concessions from them in the interests of your own flexibility while still accommodating their needs.

What can you do to manage your time better?

Here are seven good guidelines to follow:

1. **Make up your mind fast.**   This is not to advocate snap judgments, but it's a fact that 85 percent of the problems that face you aren't worth more than a few minutes of your time. So learn to say "yes" or "no," "we will" or "we won't." Employees and associates like working with decisive people—even when they aren't right all the time. And few things save time like a decisive answer—time saved for you and your employees.

2. **Be specific about dates.**   You promise to get out an order "sometime next week." What happens? You're likely to find several deadlines coming due at the same time. If you're specific—Wednesday for Triangle and Thursday for Superior—you've started to systematize your thinking.

   Or let's say Pete calls you on the phone. Can he drop by to see you? Any time, you say. So Pete drops by just when you're up to your ears in a line changeover. Pete doesn't get much attention, your changeover gets the "one-eye-only" treatment, and your time budget suffers.

3. **Control the telephone.**   It's a monster to supervisors in some shops. But it needn't be (if your boss will cooperate). If you can get someone else to answer it for you, do. Then call back when you have the time. Avoid using the telephone for routine messages that can be forwarded through the interoffice mails. And watch your-

self so that you don't develop telephonitis and bother others with it unnecessarily.

4. **Write down reminders.**   Don't trust yourself to remember things to do. Use a surefire reminder system, such as jotting down important jobs to be done on your desk calendar or in a pocket notebook. One supervisor we know jots down anything she feels she should remember or act upon on a little sheet of paper. Then she tosses it into a desk drawer. Each morning she shuffles the notes to see what she must do out of the ordinary for that day. When it's done, she simply tears up the slip.

5. **Limit chitchat.** Conversation—with employees and other supervisors—is vitally important to your role as supervisor. But you've got to keep it under control or it will eat up all your spare time. So limit casual conversation to a few pleasantries when you can. Nothing ruins your day quite so well as a couple of 20-minute conversations with your associates about the fish they didn't catch or the status of a do-it-yourself project.

6. **Set up a time budget.**   Try something like that shown in Figure PDP-3. Place your time allotments into four categories:
    a. *Routine work*, such as checking time sheets, answering mail, and handling normal paperwork.
    b. *Regular job duties*, such as the important ones of supervising, training, controlling, and appraising.
    c. *Special assignments*, such as serving on committees or assisting on special projects.
    d. *Creative work*, such as developing new methods to improve your department's quality or productivity.

7. **Begin each workday with a plan.**   Each day will present a new set of problems, so take five minutes to tailor your plans before the workday begins. Use your desk calendar to list the things you want to do that day.

How can you use ABC analysis to control time?

ABC analysis is a concept that predicts that 80 percent of your time will be spent on only 20 percent of your problems. (See pages 121 to 122 and Figure 6-4.) To make this idea pay off for you, the 20 percent of the problems that you work on should be rated as class A—the vital ones. The president of a major appliance firm, for example, begins his day by labeling each task ahead as A, B, or C. Class B items aren't quite

8	MONDAY	TUESDAY	WEDNESDAY	THURSDAY	FRIDAY
	ROUTINE	ROUTINE	ROUTINE	ROUTINE	ROUTINE
9	Inspection and supervision of operations REGULAR	Individual work with staff REGULAR	Inspection and supervision of operations REGULAR	Individual work with staff REGULAR	SPECIAL WORK
10					Inspection and supervision of operations REGULAR
11		Inspection and supervision of operations REGULAR		Control studies and reports	
12			Division staff meeting REGULAR	REGULAR	Our staff meeting REGULAR
1	L	U	N	C	H
2	Interviews and contacts REGULAR	Interviews and contacts REGULAR	Interviews and contacts REGULAR	Interviews and contacts REGULAR	CREATIVE WORK
3	Planning and organizing REGULAR	Inspection and supervision of operations REGULAR	SPECIAL WORK	Inspection and supervision of operations REGULAR	
4					
5	ROUTINE	ROUTINE	ROUTINE	ROUTINE	ROUTINE

Figure PDP-3 Example of a time budget.

so important as A items. And class C problems are very small fish, even though there are lots of them. The president goes after A items first and then tries to get to the Bs. Invariably, says the president, a surprising thing happens. When he gets to the Cs, he can "wipe out a lot of them in one sweep." These are the tasks, of course, that can be disposed of quickly with a telephone call, a jotted note, or a brief instruction to employees as you walk through the shop.

In planning to concentrate your time on the "vital few" problems and let the "trivial many" await their turn, how do you recognize the vital few?

Experience will provide a good basis. You may waste a couple of hours the first time around on what turns out to be an inconsequential problem. The next time it comes up, however, either you will know how to dispose of it quickly or you will know that you should put it far down on your priority list.

There are other ways, too, of judging a problem's importance. For example, ask yourself any of these questions:

Where did it come from? If the problem arose as a directive from your boss or a request from the sales department, it may need top priority. If it came from a lesser source, perhaps you can delay it. In organizational matters, you must be realistic and hardheaded politically.

What is its potential for trouble? Some unsolved problems can cause other problems to pile up elsewhere. Suppose there is a machine that needs a minor repair. You put it off. But that machine is in the main line of flow in your operation. It is in a position to cause quality problems, and if it breaks down altogether, it will hold up production. The repair problem is minor, but its potential for trouble is great. Get to it sooner rather than later.

Is it aimed at results rather than activity? Dr. George Odiorne, who popularized MBO, warns that supervisors and managers devote too much time going through motions that are essentially trivial. On paper, their efforts may look good; they write reports, keep their files up to date, and attend all the meetings. But they don't get results in terms of greater output, better quality, or lower costs. Odiorne says that these managers have wasted their time by falling into the "activity trap."

How quickly can it be disposed of? Watch your answer on this one. It is what R. Alec Mackenzie calls the "time trap." Many problems look as if they can be handled quickly. It is a temptation to jump into them without thinking. But what was supposed to be done with a three-minute phone call turns into several phone calls. What should have taken only a minute or two of discussion grows into a major hassle. Tasks that can truly be handled quickly should be grouped together and finished in one block of time. Problems that need a major effort should be budgeted for your undivided attention, with enough time allotted for their solution.

If you delegate a big share of your work to your subordinates to save time, won't you be charged with passing the buck?

Not necessarily. Subordinates expect that they'll have to carry the ball along with you. After all, that's the name of the game. Furthermore, most people want to feel important enough to the operation to be asked to do some of the boss's work. But even if this weren't so, it's imperative for other urgent reasons that you learn to delegate a good portion of your personal work load.

Delegation is an essential ingredient of good management. And, to be painfully frank, it's often the only way you'll be able to keep your head above water. The average managerial job is so fraught with responsibilities that you could worry yourself into an 80-hour, jam-packed week just checking up on every detail yourself. If you allow yourself to fall into that trap, you're on your way out as a supervisor.

Delegation means, of course, that you've got to trust others on your staff to do the job nearly as effectively as you'd do it yourself. And if you can steel yourself to leave them alone, they usually will. With a big difference, however. Others won't do the job exactly the way you'd do it yourself. They'll also regard some factors as more important than you think they are. Worse still, they'll overlook or ignore other factors that you think demand top priority. That's the way of delegation. So learn to accept the fact of less-than-perfect results and to delegate just the same. Without delegation, you won't be able to make the grade as a supervisor and still maintain your cool.

In delegating to make better use of your time, there are two good rules of thumb to follow:

1. Try not to spend time working on tasks that are below your capabilities. These are the things that you *can* do, of course, but that others should be doing for you.
2. Don't give your priorities to a series of trivial jobs while putting the big job on "hold." It's important that you take on the big job first. If the trivial jobs are urgent, then you should delegate them right away to the most qualified subordinates.

FILE 3 Coping With Stress

Poor time management often leads to stress. The supervisory job is the kind of position in which, by its nature, you are asked—or expected—to do more than most people can in a normal workday. When you find that you are not accomplishing what you believe you should be, you may become frustrated. Frustrations exert pressure on your mind and eventually on your nerves and body. Such pressure is popularly known as *stress.* In its exaggerated state, it is often called "burnout." As a matter of practical fact, almost everybody suffers from stress. It is when stress places a load on the body or mind beyond a point that can be tolerated that stress becomes a medical problem.

To get some indication of whether or not you are buckling under stress at this time, complete the Stress Indicator Barometer (Table PDP-3) on the facing page.

Twenty stress indicators are listed in the table. For each condition, circle the number of the answer at the right that best describes the frequency with which that condition occurs in you. Add the numbers you have circled. Then use the scoring key at the end of the table to assess your ability to manage stress.

Why do some individuals thrive on pressure, whereas others seem to be crumpled by it?

Probably because those who don't show signs of wear and tear (1) have learned their stress limits and (2) have kept their stress load within them. Your mind and body flexes freely under tolerable stress, somewhat like a steel beam flexes under a heavy load. If the load is within its stress limits, the beam will snap back into line when the load is removed. If, however, the beam is overloaded, it will be bent out of shape. Loads that are too heavy for *you* to carry will bend your mind or body out of shape too. There is always a limit beyond which the mind or body will flex no longer. At that point, you show some of the signs indicated in Table PDP-3. Accordingly, you "manage" this stress by finding ways of relieving it, by re-distributing it, or by removing it.

For example, you shift some stress to others by delegating. You remove some of it by obtaining additional resources (people, tools, information, and the like) to help out in your department. You can also make sure that stress doesn't all come at once by planning and controlling your personal time more effectively. The steel beam, for exam-

Table PDP-3 STRESS INDICATOR BAROMETER

Conditions	Frequency		
	Never	Sometimes, or Mild	Frequently, or Severe
1. General irritability.	1	2	5
2. Difficulty in getting along with others.	1	2	5
3. Feelings of guilt.	1	2	5
4. Worry about seemingly small matters.	1	2	5
5. Depression, or lack of enthusiasm.	1	2	5
6. Concern that nothing gets done on time.	1	2	5
7. Overeating.	1	2	5
8. Insomnia.	1	3	10
9. Substance abuse, excessive use of alcohol, or use of illegal drugs.	1	5	10
10. Use of prescribed sleeping pills, pain killers, or pep pills.	1	3	10
11. Increased use of tobacco.	1	3	10
12. Feelings of weakness or dizziness.	1	5	10
13. Difficulty in concentrating.	1	2	5
14. Loss of appetite.	1	2	5
15. Increased occurrence of cuts, bruises, falls, or minor accidents.	1	3	10
16. Stomach cramps, upsets, diarrhea.	1	3	10
17. Temper tantrums.	1	5	10
18. Impatience with delays.	1	2	5
19. Changes in bodily functions, missed menstrual period, unusual premenstrual tensions.	1	3	10
20. Unusual spate of lost personal objects like keys, glasses, and notebooks.	1	3	10

Scoring: 20 to 50, *normal.* Indicates good tolerance of, or management of, stress.
51 to 99, *marginal.* Indicates greater-than-average difficulty in coping with stress.
100 or above, *watch out!* Indicates very low tolerance and/or severe difficulty in managing stress.

ple, can carry a load of 100 tons in 24 hours, *provided* that no more than 5 tons are placed on it at a time. That's why so many bridges bear signs that read "Maximum load is 10 tons." You can't go around wearing such a sign; employees and associates often have little sympathy for one's limits, anyway. Instead, you must learn exactly how much stress you can bear before you suffer a strain, and then you must develop a plan for managing stress so that it never exceeds that limit.

Where is stress likely to come from?

Career counselors tell us that stress at work originates from three sources:

1. **The work environment.**   This includes just about everything, from malfunctioning machinery, faulty materials, tight schedules, pinching budgets, and pressure-cooker deadlines to your hardheaded boss, your uncooperative associates, and your disinterested employees.
2. **Your inner self.** This is pretty deep stuff, but it includes such things as a loss of self-confidence, sensitivity to criticism about your performance, fear of failure, and doubts about your ability to cope with stress, wherever it originates.
3. **Interpersonal relationships.**   This combines the worst elements of the first two. Most work situations involve some sort of interpersonal transaction. For example, you may want a machine repaired in a hurry so that a critical order can be shipped. You've got to persuade the maintenance supervisor that this job should get his top priority. The degree of stress generated by this situation may depend entirely on your interpersonal skills. If you handle this transaction well, the machine will be back on line without delay. On the other hand, if you end up quarreling with the other supervisor, the stress of the machine breakdown will be compounded by the stress of the quarrel.

In regard to the stress coming from the supervisory job itself, which conditions are likely to need a fundamental improvement?

Harry Truman was partly right when he said, "If you can't stand the heat, stay out of the kitchen." The supervisory job is, by its nature, stressful. That's what makes it so invigorating and challenging. As another wise person once said, "If there were no stress, you might as well be dead." But there is a great difference between an invigorating amount of stress and too much stress. A basic goal in stress management, therefore, is to try to eliminate persistent but unnecessary stress. There's enough of the other kind already to make many of your days hectic. Among the basic sources of stress that should be corrected are the following:

- **Ambiguity about the results for which you are held responsible.**   If your organization provides a job description for your position, make sure that it is specific about vital results such as output expected per shift, the acceptable percentage of rejects or errors, allowable expenses, and tolerance for employee absences, tardiness, and accidents. Be wary about performance expectations in these and any other areas that are described with such loose terms as *good, better, soon,* and *improved.* Ask, politely but firmly: "How good?" "How much better?" "How soon?" "How big an improvement?" These are reasonable questions, and they will do much to take the vagueness—and stress—out of the measurements by which you will be judged.

- **Inadequate resources for the job at hand.** Few things are more frustrating than being pressed to get results without having been given the resources to get the job done properly. You'll want to try to make certain that the performance demands that are made of you are matched from the start with adequate labor, equipment, materials, and supplies. Supervisors often make their biggest mistake by saying "yes" to a request before carefully sizing up the situation. This doesn't mean that you should say "no" all the time, either. It may mean that you'll need to say: "Yes, it can be done, *but only* by postponing job 2"—or by allowing the staff to work overtime, or by subcontracting a part of the project, or by purchasing partially finished components, or by making any other necessary increase or adjustment in your resources, methods, and deadlines.

- **Conflicting demands and instructions.** These often stem from having two bosses. This situation shouldn't happen, of course, but it does. And, as matrix organizations increase in number, it will happen more often. When faced with the stress of conflict in orders or instructions, don't let it pass by simply blowing off steam. Instead, make the results of such a conflict clear to both parties as soon as you can. Show them how it affects productivity, costs, or customer relations. Here, again, situations are most likely to be corrected for reasons that bring benefits to those who cause the situation.

There are sources of stress outside work, aren't there?

Of course. Not only that, but the sources of stress outside business are probably more powerful and less manageable. So far, we've talked about how to avoid or minimize stress at work, especially stress arising from time pressures. You should not overlook the very important matter of stress sources outside work. These are often just as hard to avoid or reduce. The same principles prevail, however. You must:

1. Alter or change the conditions of your personal environment to reduce stress if you can.
2. Be realistic about your personal ambitions and capabilities, but don't undersell yourself to yourself.
3. Identify those necessary interpersonal transactions where your performance is unsatisfactory, and do something to improve your skills in those areas. Admittedly, none of this is easy to do. Accordingly, if the strain you feel—from stress at work or elsewhere—is great, you'll need professional counseling. This might be obtained from a variety

of professionals, including doctors, lawyers, and accountants; marriage counselors, psychologists, and clinical social workers; and religious or spiritual advisers.

Besides trying to control stress at the source, what else can you do personally to lessen its impact?

The three fundamental approaches to management of stress, no matter what its origin, were outlined in the last section. In a more specific context, however, there are several other constructive things you can do to lessen the impact of stress on your system:

1. **Understand your limitations and live within them.** Acknowledge such truisms as "Everybody can't be president" and "Rome wasn't built in a day." This calls for you to (a) be realistic about your true capabilities, (b) exploit them only as far as they'll carry you, (c) try not to move too far too fast, and (d) accept the fact that it's usually more satisfying to do well at a lesser job than to feel relentlessly pressured at one slightly above your capacity.
2. **Break away, if necessary, before you break yourself.** Don't run away from every crisis, but if you find yourself crumbling, do make time to remove yourself physically from the stressful situation. Take fifteen minutes or more to think, meditate, pray, relax—so you can get a fresh perspective.
3. **Get more genuine exercise.** It's a fact that tensions are reduced when the blood circulation rises. Even if you're not athletically inclined, find a half hour each day to loosen up your body in some relaxing form of exercise. Such activity need not be too vigorous—walking, bike riding, bowling, or lawn mowing may do you as much good for relaxation purposes as jogging, tennis, or swimming.
4. **Select and pursue at least one diversion.** Most important, this should be something you truly enjoy doing, not something that you feel is a matter of obligation. Let it be stamp collecting, woodworking, or machine-shop work, local politics, gardening, gourmet cooking, card playing, or needlepoint. If it's a true diversion, you will find that you are totally absorbed in it, that time flies and cares are forgotten during your involvement. The purpose of the diversion is to give your mind a rest from stress so that it can recharge its psychological energy cells.
5. **Take time to look at the world around you.** Most people who are troubled by stress tend to turn their vision inward. This is like trying to climb out of a pit by digging downward. The escape from pressure usually lies in the other direction, outside oneself. The world is a very big place, and simply taking five minutes to look at the morn-

ing or evening sky helps to place personal matters in perspective. Similarly, the act of getting concerned about other people's problems has a tension-relaxing effect. To test the degree to which you are inwardly turned, observe how well you can listen to others without interruption. Ask yourself how often you try to top another person's miseries with a story about one of your own. Does only the work that you do seem important? Many of us who would never think of ourselves as egotists are concerned only with ourselves. It's a malady brought on by stress. And one of the best proven cures for it is to immerse yourself in trying to come to the aid of others.

You will succeed as a supervisor not only because of the extent of your basic competencies but also to the degree that you learn to fit into and master the organization you serve. Call it politics, organizational sensitivity, or just plain practicality, you must learn to go with the flow most of the time rather than swimming upstream. Your relationship with your boss is probably the best barometer of your organizational fit. By completing the Organizational Acceptance Rating Sheet in Table PDP-4 below, you can get an indication of how you stand with your current organization and with your boss, in particular.

Table PDP-4	ORGANIZATIONAL ACCEPTANCE RATING SHEET		
Conditions	Not True	Partly True	Mostly True
1. You receive raises as frequently as your associates.	1	2	3
2. Your boss gives you a free hand with your employees.	1	2	3
3. Your boss knows very little about your life away from work.	3	2	1
4. Others in your organization are always encroaching on your turf.	3	2	1
5. When you've made a mistake, your boss will stand up for you.	1	2	3
6. You are among the last to learn about impending changes in the organization.	3	2	1
7. You don't like the way your company does a lot of things.	3	2	1
8. You have found a number of supportive associates within your organization.	1	2	3
9. The other people in your organization seem to carry grudges forever.	3	2	1
10. Your boss gives weight to your opinions before making decisions that affect you.	1	2	3

Scoring: 24 to 30, *insider*. You're part of the team! However, review the items you circled as "1" or "2" to see how you can strengthen your position even more.

17 to 23, *"fringesider."* You are not fully accepted yet. Check the items you circled as "1" to see why you haven't yet been welcomed onto the team.

10 to 16, *outsider*. You are definitely not one of the team. Examine the items you circled as "1" to plan a comprehensive program for gaining the support of your boss and your colleagues.

To complete the table, circle the number to the right of each item that most nearly describes the condition in your organization. Add the numbers you have circled. Then use the scoring key at the end of the table to assess your standing in the organization.

How can you put your best foot forward in an organization?

There are many ways to gain personal acceptance in an organization, but here are some that have been particularly effective.

1. **Demonstrate your job competence.** Few things gain respect like an individual's ability to do a job well. Your job is supervision. So show that you can run your operation like a clock, that companywide problems never have their origin in your department, and that you've got your employees well motivated and under control.

2. **Become an integral part of the information network.** Almost all organizations, public and private, derive a great deal of their power from the information they assemble and control. By becoming a part of the information network of an organization, you become an integral part of the organization. Accordingly, make an early effort to know (a) the extent of unique information the organization possesses, (b) how to gain access to it, (c) how to contribute to it, and (d) how to use it in your operation. This does not imply that you should try to tap secret documents. It does mean, however, that you should know how to obtain and exchange the data you need to improve productivity and smooth out operations in your department.

3. **Go with the flow of the organization.** That is, try to find a way to go along with the organization's standards and its general style of management. A maverick has a hard time proving his or her worth. It's better to give up a little of your independence in return for the support you'll eventually need if you are to be fully effective in any organization. After all, that's what an organization is—a cooperative effort. Loyalty, too, plays a part here. If you disagree with some of the things that are going on, don't stand aside and criticize; try constructively to improve them.

4. **Build a personal support system.** It can be awfully lonely in an organization without friends, especially without influential friends. Accordingly, it is wise to be somewhat selective about the people in the organization with whom you develop special rapport. Be cordial and courteous to everyone, of course. These qualities provide the lubrication that enables interpersonal contacts to revolve. But it is important that you go beyond that by making friends (business friends, not necessarily personal friends) with those people who are—

or whose positions make them—influential in the organization. A first step is to develop a good relationship with the key person in the department that precedes or follows yours in the product or service flow. If you make things reasonably comfortable for them, they may be expected to come to your aid when you need help. A next step is to establish contacts in key staff departments (if you're a line supervisor, or in line departments if you're a staff supervisor). You'll want to be able to get confidential advice, and perhaps a little extra cooperation, from those in a position to do you good in payroll, accounting, sales order, field service, inventory, and production control, for example. In a great many instances, you will be able to develop this network only by first demonstrating that you will discharge your own responsibilities in a way that, at the very least, does not create problems for these key people. People for whom you do favors do you favors. People about whom you say good things speak well of you. That's politics, of course, but it's also the fact of organizational survival and success. Make no mistake: your personal support network depends on such trade-offs.

What sort of attitudes and actions should you avoid?

Always keep in mind that an organization is a group of people working together toward common goals. Large organizations are made of many smaller, overlapping organizations. These are groups within groups. As a consequence, at any one time at work you'll be a member of many organizations. What you say and do to make you a hero in one organization may make you an outcast in another. If you're strong enough and right enough often enough, you can say and do just about anything you please and few people will take sides openly against you. Most of us, however, are not like the 8-foot bear who can "sleep anywhere he pleases." We've got to be more politic. This means that it's not too wise to take extreme positions. You needn't always be at the middle of the road, but you don't want to get so far away from the consensus that you can't make a compromise when good judgment dictates one. Here are some additional points to remember:

- It's important that you show others that you are willing to pull your weight in the total organization. There are always a number of dirty assignments; make sure that you take your share.
- You can't go far—or for long, either—with a win-lose attitude toward your peers. Resource allocations can spark battles between departments. Each wants the new clerk, the extra lift truck, first access to the computer terminal, and the like. If you insist on getting the

most or the best every time, you'll inevitably make enemies. Organizations create mutual dependencies. You'll need to learn when to fight for a particular resource and when you will contribute more to the organization's goals if you let another department have the resource without a quarrel.

- It's also wise to avoid being characterized as a "negative," a person who resists every change. Try to check yourself before you think or say: "We've tried that before and it didn't work." "It isn't practical in the shop." "We're too busy with more important matters to be bothered right now."

- Finally, don't hog all the credit. Most of your accomplishments depend on the contributions of others. When reporting progress, give others the credit they deserve, and then some. Go out of the way to tip your hat (in your reports to your superiors) to anyone who can reasonably be said to have been a party to a success. It costs very little to be generous and it goes a long way toward defusing any potential undercutting of your organizational ambitions.

How can you draw favorable attention to your capabilities without appearing offensive or objectionable?

The larger the organization, the more difficult it is for you to gain broad visibility. Doing a superb job in your own niche usually isn't enough. Your good works will go unrecognized elsewhere unless you make a conscious effort to display them. This does not mean that you should make a nuisance of yourself in this regard. However, to help you in both your present job and your career, you should practice the two techniques described below.

Find Ways to Exhibit Your Leadership and Initiative It may be more comfortable for you to sit back and let others start a project rolling. After all, the old army saying "Never volunteer!" has its merits; it keeps your extra burdens light. But if you really want to show your talents, this is one way of separating yourself from the pack. You'll want to pick your spots, of course. You don't want to become the company dray horse who can be counted on to carry all the heavy loads. Instead, try to be a part of the leading edge of those committees, projects, and operational changes that are being watched over or spurred on from above. Sometimes all that is needed is for you to speak up in favor of a project that is stalled on dead center.

There are always opportunities, too, to institute a new method or procedure in your own department without waiting for a companywide program. When you do so, be sure to go on record with a memorandum to your boss and to any of the staff departments to which it may have special interest. Suppose, for example, you institute a daily error-watch reporting system for your employees, and it makes an observable inroad into reducing errors. Send a copy of the form you use and the results obtained to your boss and to the quality-control department.

Look for, or Accept, Challenging Responsibilities This idea is an extension of gaining visibility for your leadership and initiative qualities. It will require an extra effort on your part, since these opportunities often will not come to you; you'll have to seek them out. They may be found, however, wherever a problem exists—within your own operations or anywhere in the total organization. You may many times encounter a condition that you know to be unsatisfactory. You may assume that either nothing can be done about it or it is the affair of someone else, usually one of the adjacent line or staff departments. Don't let the problem die there. Instead, try tackling a material shortages problem, a duplication-of-effort problem, or a communication problem, for example. These often occur at the interface between departments. They give you a chance to work with others in positions of responsibility outside your department. It will usually be up to you to be the spearhead, but if you can bring about a solution or an improvement, you'll have something to show, not only upstairs but next door.

How do you go about asking for a raise?

Assuming your timing is correct, you'll want to approach the raise problem in much the same manner you would if you were trying to sell your boss a new idea. Here are a few tactics to consider.

Come Right Out and Ask for It The direct approach will force a "yes" or "no" answer, so be certain your performance warrants more money before you try it. To be on firm ground, have some facts on hand that can show how your job has grown bigger or how your efforts have become more effective: "I know the company expects to get a return on all the money it spends—including my salary. So I've made a list of new duties I've picked up since last year. And the shop records show that absences in my department are down 3 percent over last year, scrap is down 4 percent, and direct labor cost per unit has been reduced 7 cents."

Pick a Salary Goal Instead of vaguely asking for "more money," it puts you in a better negotiating position if you can name the dollar figure you have in mind. Be certain that it is reasonable in light of (a) your performance and (b) the salaries of others in your organization. Don't set it too low, however. The chances are great that your boss will interpret your salary target as a top figure to consider and will work downward from there. The point of naming a salary goal is to establish the range of your request, with the thought that you may be willing to compromise between your goal and your current salary.

Stress the Value of Your Contribution   People who get ahead are those who can—and do—point to their efforts to help the organization attain its goals. Specifically, find ways to document your productivity, dependability, management-mindedness, and initiative. Show that you do more than the minimum required without having to be pushed. Guard against making the plea that you need the money, however. It's a poor business argument. Your personal finances are your own affair. You weaken yourself in the boss's eyes by asking for a raise because you can't manage at home.

Wait and See   In many companies, this is the only tack you can follow. But, generally speaking, it's wise for you to put a little pressure on from time to time. For instance, you might say, "I'm not asking for a raise at this particular moment, Ms. Jones, but I'd like to review my past six months' performance with you so that when raises are possible again, I'll be sure that my performance will warrant one."

REVIEW

KEY CONCEPTS TO REMEMBER

1. **Taking charge of your career.**   Personal growth and improvement are the direct result of self-development. Other people may offer valuable advice and guidance, but each individual must furnish his or her own initiative, application, and persistence.

   Plans for career development should be based upon an objective assessment of present performance as compared with job demands and future opportunities for growth and advancement.

   Self-development is essentially a form of adult education directed at improving personal knowledge, skills, and attitudes. This education can be accomplished through formal instruction, guided experience, and relevant reading.

   It is essential that plans for self-improvement be (a) practical, (b) specific in nature, and (c) firm in setting goals and timetables for attainment.

2. **Managing job-related time.** An awareness of time, its incredible value, and its fleeting elusiveness, together with an ability to utilize and conserve it, is what distinguishes an outstanding supervisor from an ordinary one.

   It takes self-discipline and conscious control to prevent personal time from being frittered away on nonessential, nonproductive activities. Inevitably, wasted time leads to job stress.

   Capable supervisors are tempted to consume too much of their own time by doing too much themselves, retaining too many responsibilities instead of delegating time-absorbing routines to their subordinates.

3. **Coping with stress.** An overload of stress can come from (a) the work environment, (b) your inner self, and (c) poorly handled interpersonal relationships. Job stress is often magnified by (a) ambiguity concerning responsibilities and results, (b) resources that do not match responsibilities, and (c) conflicting demands and instructions. Individuals manage stress by (a) understanding their limitations and living with them, (b) breaking away to regroup when pressures become extreme, (c) getting the proper exercise, and (d) developing outside interests that distract and relax.

4. **Moving up in your organization.** Few people rise far in management without having found a way to harmonize their personal goals and actions with those of their superiors and the organization as a whole. To do so requires tact and a degree of compromise, but it does not necessarily mean that you must sacrifice your independence or integrity.

   Your acceptance and support by the organization will depend in large measure upon (a) how well you demonstrate competence in your work, (b) the readiness with which you accommodate group goals and consensus, (c) your contribution to, and use of, the information network, and (d) the power and influence of the personal support system that you build.

   Raises and promotions are not the inevitable reward for good work. Your petitions for either should follow a well-conceived program that demonstrates the value of your contributions to the organization.

SUPERVISORY WORD POWER

Career path. A logical and reasonable series of occupational assignments that lead toward a career goal.

Management development. A systematic program for improving the knowledge, attitudes, and skills of supervisors and managers.

Mentor. A knowledgeable, often influential, individual who takes an interest in, and advises, another person concerning that person's career.

Networking. The informal process of getting to know, and to create confidence among, other persons who—through mutual exchange—help advance one's career.

Stress. On- or off-job pressures that place a burden on an individual's physical, mental, or nervous system.

Time budget. A charting technique for planning the systematic distribution of a supervisor's time.

Type A individual. A person, characterized by high standards of achievement and an urgency to attain them, who is especially susceptible to stress.

Vital few. In ABC analysis, the small portion of items or problems (about 20 percent) that account for a very large portion (about 80 percent) of the time and money spent to solve or control them. The remainder are dubbed the "trivial many."

APPLICATION

CASE STUDIES

CASE 69   **The Dead-End Job**

Myra couldn't believe it. This was the third time in a row that she had been passed over for a promotion. Two years ago, it had been because she "didn't have enough experience with the company." Last year, it was because she hadn't acquired the "necessary qualifications for upgrading." Yesterday, the reason given was that she "appeared to be satisfied" with her present job and was probably "best suited" to stay there. Myra fumed; then she stormed into the office of the director of human resources development. "I'm sick and tired of being passed over for the better jobs in this organization," she said. "I like my present job. But I don't want to stay there forever. What can I do to break out of this dead end?"

a. What do you think might be some of the causes for Myra's being passed over for promotion?
b. If you were the human resources development director, what advice would you give Myra?

CASE 70   "Get Your Priorities Straight!"

Tomas was deep into his review of the week's time sheets when the phone rang. It was a call from the plant manager's office advising him that there was a productivity committee meeting for all supervisors at 11 that morning. Tomas looked at his desk calendar. He was supposed to deliver his time sheets to the payroll office by noon, and it was 10 a.m. already. Just then, the chief inspector walked into Tomas's office. "There's a small problem developing out there on the assembly line right now. If you don't get it straightened out soon, it may end up with having to shut down the line." Tomas dropped everything and went out into the shop. The quality problem was a sticky one, and it was 11 a.m. before it was corrected.

When Tomas got back into his office, the phone was ringing. "Where are those time sheets?" queried the payroll supervisor. "I'll get them up to you in a few minutes," Tomas said. And he set to work on them again. At noon, the phone rang again. This call was from a very angry plant manager, who wanted to know why Tomas had not attended the productivity meeting. Tomas explained the quality control problem and the need to get the time sheets into payroll. The plant manager was not sympathetic. He said, "You better get your priorities straight in the future."

a. Should Tomas have gone to the meeting? Why?
b. How would you have advised Tomas to arrange his priorities for handling the problems he faced this morning?

CASE 71   The Unfaceable Day

"I can't face this day," said Vito to his wife as he drank his third cup of breakfast coffee. "What's wrong?" asked his wife. "Just about every-thing," said Vito. "We just got through laying off a third of the office staff to cut costs. That was bad enough. Telling people they'd be going on unemployment, with no hope of their being called back. Now, we've got a big surge of orders to process. And my boss says that we've got to make do with the help we have. No temporaries. No callbacks. How am I ever going to press the remaining help to do more than normal? As it is, they've all slowed down the pace to stretch out the work."

"You'll manage, somehow," soothed Vito's wife. "Maybe," said Vito as he chewed on a couple of antacid tablets before he lit up his first cigarette of the day. "I guess I'll have to just act like a monster man to get everyone back into line!"

a. What's wrong with Vito's approach to his staff?
b. How would you suggest he handle this situation?

c. What kind of advice can you give Vito, generally, to enable him to cope better with his stress?

CASE 72   The Deferred Raise

"Everyone wants a raise right now," said Rod's boss. "Cost of living is rising. Bills are piling up. People have payments to make on their cars. You're no different, Rod. I can't see any reason to give you special consideration. I won't say 'no,' but any thought of a raise for you will have to be deferred for six months." As supervisor of the reports distribution section of a large computer services firm, Rod felt that he had been working his tail off. Not only did he need the raise, he felt sure he deserved one. Right now. Not six months from now.

a. What seem to be the weaknesses of Rod's present petition for a raise?
b. If you were Rod, what kinds of arguments would you prepare to persuade your boss that a raise ought to be forthcoming now—not deferred for six months.?
c. If you still didn't get the raise, what would you do during the next six months to make your case ironclad when it comes up for consideration?

Bootstrapping Your Career in Supervision and Management: With 22 Action Planning Checklists

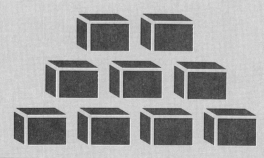

The success—or shortcomings—of your career will depend largely upon the skills you acquire and develop by yourself and the programs you devise to capitalize on them. Other people may offer advice and guidance—and even an occasional assist—but, in the main, advancement in supervisory and management careers is a bootstrapping operation.

Starting from scratch

If you are just now beginning to seek a career in supervision and management, it is important to find a starting point that best suits your aptitudes and potential. Your first place of employment will probably not be your last, but some places provide a better springboard than others. These are some of the more important aspects of employment to consider:

Blue-Collar or White-Collar?   Do you prefer activities associated with production or construction, working close to tools and machinery? Or is your preference for clerical, desk-related, and clean-hands operations?

Inside or Outside?   Do you like to be close to your support system along with the comfort of daily routines that are clearly set? Or does the independence and challenge of sales and other field-related activities exert a greater appeal?

People Relationships versus Technical Expertise?   Do you favor activities in which interpersonal relationships play a large part? Most supervisory and management positions place greater emphasis upon interpersonal skills than on technical expertise.

Line versus Staff?   Line jobs often carry with them the authority and visibility that lead to advancement. Work in line activities also tends to provide more action and a sense of being at the heart of an operation. Staff activities, on the other hand, may be less stressful and more rewarding from a creative and intellectual point of view.

Manufacturing or Services?   The downtrodden manufacturing industries are now experiencing a rebirth, with opportunities for advancement growing again. The major economic growth, however, continues to be in service-related industries such as banking and finance, food service, hotel and restaurant management, and in wholesaling and retailing.

Large or Small Company?   The job security, good working conditions, and opportunities for advancement without changing employers makes work in many large organizations attractive. There are drawbacks, of course, with the pressure to conform, reels of red tape to put up with, and responsibilities that are narrowly specialized. Work for smaller organizations, on the other hand, presents an opposing set of advantages and disadvantages. Pay and benefits are often less attractive, as are job security and chances for advancement. Responsibilities in small companies, however, are usually more varied and challenging, with a minimum of red tape and a great deal of informality.

Private or Public Employment? Risks of employment in private industry are generally considered to be greater, but with the possibilities of greater financial rewards. Public employment, while usually less remunerative, is more secure and may provide a greater sense of social contribution.

An Awareness of the Flames. The better positions in supervision and management are always challenging and demanding. Some jobs, however, are characterized by too much heat. These are the ones that cause "burnout"—since they often demand the impossible. This kind of pressure isn't always apparent at the start, so it pays to explore advancement opportunities carefully before pursuing them. You *should* expect a good job to demand much of you, but not so much that you can't do it well every day without feeling exhausted.

Planning a career search inside or outside your present organization

The competition for good jobs in supervision and management is now more intense than ever. This is especially true of the higher paying, more interesting positions. Curiously, neither the available positions nor the better ones necessarily go to the most qualified candidates. In a great many instances, these jobs are won by those people who plan and carry out the most appropriate search. So, whether you are exploring opportunities for advancement with your present employer or somewhere else, your career search should combine at least five essential elements: (1) a seek-and-search timetable, (2) a realistic list of job factors that you consider necessary to make a job attractive and appropriate for you, (3) a resume that clearly and concisely demonstrates your most valuable qualifications, (4) preinterview research and preparation, and (5) a strategy for handling interview questions so as to favorably differentiate you from other candidates.

Elements 4 and 5 will be discussed in detail below. Suffice it to say about elements 1, 2, and 3 that diligence is required in making out applications and seeking interviews. Resumes should be carefully prepared. Persistence is a strong tool for prying open the best positions in supervision and management. On the other hand, you should also be ready to accept something less than the perfect assignment in order to get a foothold in the area or field that is attractive to you. Most people have to perform work that has its menial, tedious, and unattractive facets so that they can show their potential. Good supervisory and management positions are obtained by building upon a record of sound performance in lesser assignments.

Preparing for a career-advancement interview

Many a good position is lost before the candidate walks in the door for an interview. A successful advancement-interview requires planning, research, and rehearsal—even for jobs within your own company. Days before your interview, you should:

1. **Find out more about your potential employer, department, or boss.** Consult the company's annual report, published reports about it found in a library, or someone who is working there now. You'll want to know something about the background of the company or department, its financial condition, its products, services, and personnel along with any problems it is seeking to solve. After all, your application will have told the interviewers something about you; it will give you an equal edge to know something about the company or department that is interviewing you.

2. **Review your strengths and weaknesses.** Plan to put your strongest qualities forward—as they relate to the job in question. Be prepared also to defend your weaknesses. You must be ready to acknowledge, for example, that you may have little experience in a particular line of work. If you are prepared, however, you can counter with a reply that this has not been a serious problem in the past since you are an attentive and diligent learner.

3. **Anticipate the kinds of questions that you might be asked.** Generally, speaking, interview questions fall into two categories:
   - **Substance questions.** These seek out concrete information about you, your education, and your work history. Reply to them in short, specific sentences. Be concise: you'll want to guard against rambling. Typical questions are: "Tell me about your background." "What are your major accomplishments?" "How does your education or experience qualify you for this this position?" "Why should we hire you (or promote you to) this position?"
   - **Poise questions.** These are asked by interviewers to judge your personality, your ability to reply under stress, and the extent to which you would fit in with the people at that company (or de-

partment) and its philosophy. There are usually no "right" or "wrong" answers to these questions, so try to answer directly and honestly. Often, the interviewer doesn't care so much about *what* you say as about *how* you answer. Obviously, don't get angry. Don't allow yourself to become too negative. Your objective is to project a pleasant, positive outlook. Typical questions here are: "What kind of people do you enjoy working with?" "What kind of situations have you found most unsatisfactory?" "How would you handle a disagreement between you and one of your employees?" "Tell me about your worst boss?"

4. **Rehearse your interview beforehand.** Like an actor before a play or a golfer practicing her swing, it helps to rehearse beforehand what your answers and behavior during the interview will be. Have a friend ask you the questions outlined above. Try out your answers by speaking aloud. Record them on tape to see how they sound and whether the tone of your voice reflects confidence. Think through what you want to say and revise your answers so that you can make the most concise and effective replies.

Your interview strategy

Some authorities describe the job interview as "the 60 most critical minutes of your life." That may be an exaggeration, but it points up the wisdom of having a preplanned strategy for making the most of brief period of time. You won't be able to control the interview; the interviewer will. Nevertheless, you can contribute greatly to its success by following a strategy that places you and your capabilities in the best best possible light. For example, a winning strategy can be based on the following nine points:

1. **Make a good appearance.** Neatness in dress and care in grooming are absolutely necessary. Generally speaking, your clothing choice ought to be conservative so as neither to distract from your person nor from what you are saying.

2. **Be on time.** It is even better if you arrive a few minutes early. This gives you a chance to catch your breath and to become comfortable in strange surroundings. If kept waiting for the interview, don't be impatient or demonstrate nervousness. It's not unusual for someone to observe, and to report on, your behavior while you're waiting.

3. **Take advantage of the "warm-up" period.** Most interviewers use the first few minutes to get a "feel" of your personality before they proceed to the substance questions. During this period, try to relax yourself and to tune your ear to the voice and manner of the interviewer.

4. **Be pleasant and cordial.** As in most human exchanges, a smile goes a long way in gaining acceptance. As a job candidate, you are a guest, even when applying for advancement in your own company. Your behavior should readily indicate appreciation for the opportunity to present yourself for consideration. Don't approach the interview as an imposition placed upon you or as an opportunity to debate.

5. **Project a positive image.** This is especially true when applying for a supervisory or managerial position, which implies that you would be representing the employer, both to employees and to the community. A positive image can be projected in a number of ways. Shake hands firmly. Look the viewer in the eye in a friendly fashion. Listen attentively. If you miss a question or don't understand it, ask that it be repeated: this demonstrates your interest. Don't be afraid to display enthusiasm. Take your time, if needed, to think through what you want to say before answering difficult questions. Try to keep your replies short. Don't smoke, even if a cigarette is offered you.

6. **Ask the interviewer questions.** If you have done your homework, you can ask questions that demonstrate the validity of your interest in the position. Don't dwell on pay or benefits. Do ask about the company's or department's product or service line, its plans for growth, and what the normal promotion paths might be for a person of your qualifications.

7. **Differentiate yourself from other candidates.** Your career-search preparation should help here. Try to focus on the two or three things that you do best. Such as: "I have a strong sense of commitment." "I meet my objectives." "I work well with people." "I can handle, and am ready to perform, a variety of assignments." Show how these can contribute to a solid performance as a supervisor. In replying to questions, don't be afraid to repeat these qualifications.

8. **Close the interview firmly.** Most employment interviewers will control the close of the interview. Nevertheless, it is appropriate and it makes a good impression if you also sum up forcefully your understanding of what has transpired and your concluding view of the job opening. Say something like this: "I understand that you will be interviewing several other candidates, but I do wish to emphasize how interested I am in filling this position. I believe that my qualifications, by reason of education, experience, and motivation, would enable me to perform this job very well. You would find me an excellent employee and supervisor." When the interview is concluded, thank the interviewer. Shake hands if possible. Leave in a business-like fashion.

9. **Follow up.** Regardless of the outcome of the interview, it makes a good business impression for you to write a brief note, thanking the company or department head for the interview and expressing your continued interest in the position. (If the job no longer appeals to you, write anyway, asking that your name be removed from the list of active candidates.) It is also appropriate to telephone the interviewer periodically to determine the status of the job opening and to ask that your application be kept active. Don't, however, persist to the point of becoming a nuisance, especially if you are told that the job has been filled. As an applicant, you will "lose" many interviews before you "win" one. Approach each as an opportunity for improving your job-advancement skills, and be appreciative of the company or department that gave you the chance. Persistence in your career search and maintaining a positive outlook will eventually pay off.

A strategy for survival and advancement

Once you have secured the particular position in supervision and management that you want, you'll have to work just as hard to succeed in it. Don't let this phase be accidental. It requires a plan and policies, too, for your personal guidance.

1. **Be a team player.** The big difference between academic pursuits and those of business or other real-life occupations is that you will be able to accomplish very little at work without the support of your co-workers, whether they are supervisors, managers, or other professionals. Almost everything productive that happens in organizations takes the combined, and coordinated efforts of many people with many different skills. Trouble lies ahead if you try to go it alone. It is far better to acknowledge your dependency upon others.

2. **Establish credibility.** Your previous achievements won't be mounted on a plaque and hung on a wall in your office. Your new boss will judge you, not by what you say or may have done before, but by what you accomplish now—and every day thereafter. It is performance that counts. Performance means discharging your responsibilities productively and with a minimum of complaints or callbacks. It also means being dependable, showing that you can meet your obligations by the designated times. Your reputation for performance will be established, or discredited, within your first few months on a new assignment. If it is good, you are on your way upward. If it isn't so good, you may be heading toward a dead end—or even on your way out.

3. **Do right by your boss.** Will Rogers, the cowboy philosopher once said, "I never met a man I didn't like." The reason for these almost unbelievably happy circumstances is that Rogers found a way of finding something in everybody to like. It may seem too much to ask for you to like *every* boss that you have. It is almost certain, however, that your bosses will always like you a little better if you try to perform your job so that that it helps them to meet their performance goals, too. Few bosses will exploit you. Most will want to do right by you. Many bosses may seem unreasonably demanding at times, but this is usually in response to the pressures imposed by the organization on them. It will be counterproductive to set yourself against your boss. Instead, try to cultivate a productive, friendly relationship. Put yourself on the boss's side, for example, by asking about the direction the company is moving in and what your department can do to help cope with upcoming changes.

4. **Dress appropriately.** Advising women or men about what to wear at work is a sensitive issue, but there do appear to be certain agreed-upon guidelines for business wear.

   For *women*, for most supervisory and management positions, one experienced counselor advises, "tailored clothing only. No frills, ruffles, straps, or plunging necklines. Don't affect a 'feminine' style of dress. Try suits and blazers in plain, neutral colors, or understated plaids. Choose dresses in dark colors, worn with or without blazers. Use scarves for accents. Wear dark pumps with medium or low heels. Stud earrings and modest necklaces are all right, but avoid dangling bracelets."

   For *men*, for most office, sales, or clerical supervisory and management positions, the same counselor suggests, "dark or gray suits, solid, pinstripe or shallow plaids. Navy blazers and gray trousers are popular. Wear dress shirts in solid colors, mostly white, pale blue, or yellow. Choose from a variety of ties in muted colors in contrast to the suit. Solids, stripes, or small patterns are preferred. Wear calf-length hose in dark colors to match the suit, and black or brown, 1-inch belts. Tassle loafers, wingtips, or lace-up shoes are fine. Avoid flashy cuff links, rings, or neck chains."

5. **Build a network.** Networking is now an accepted dynamic of business and organizational life. At its simplest, networking is just another name for making friends. Among these friends, however, should be people who are supportive to you career-wise as well as personally. Your work associates will provide an important part of this network. Most importantly, you should try to make business friends of people at higher levels of management in your own organization.

The main purpose of such a network, however, is *not* to use these friends in seeking advancement, but as a means of exchanging information, contacts, and resources. A good way to expand your network is to join a professional association related to your field and to volunteer your time to it. That way, you can establish credibility based upon your service and can exchange useful information as a result.

6. **Observe these guidelines.**   Management development experts generally agree on these ten fundamental guidelines to help keep your supervisory and management career on an upward path:
   - Know where your job fits into the organization.
   - Put your efforts into tasks that your boss values.
   - Don't be afraid to ask questions, and learn where to go for answers.
   - Learn to communicate—and to the right people.
   - Always share credit; never spread blame.
   - Let others know when you've done a good job. It's not enough to be good; influential people have to know about it.
   - Be sensitive to office politics.
   - Cultivate a career-support network.
   - Don't let emotions control your actions; try to stay cool and reasonable.
   - Learn how to manage stress *before* you need to.

*Review and upgrade
your career-advancement
potential with these
22 action planning checklists*

Advancement in supervision and management depends far more onaction than on words. The 22 checklists that follow are designed to help you plan to put effective action behind your supervisory performance. Each checklist contains 15 action points. Taken together, they summarize the key points presented in the text's first 22 chapters. In that way they provide a quick and comprehensive review of the book's highlights. They will also help you to assess the current state of your effectiveness and to prepare a program for bootstrapping your career in supervision and management.

By comparing each checkpoint with conditions on your present job, or with your present qualifications, you can decide whether or not corrective action is needed now. If your review assures you that a particular item is in good shape or has already been taken care of, then check "No" under the Action Needed heading. On the other hand, if you feel that conditions need improvement, check "Yes" for Action Needed. This means that you are not satisfied with conditions or with your present qualifications—and that you intend to take positive steps to improve them. Don't stop with the check mark. Also write down a date for when you intend to have the particular condition under control or your qualifications upgraded. When you have completed the corrective action, you can then mark that item off your Action Needed list.

Action Planning Checklist I

The Supervisor's Role in Management

<table>
<tr><td></td><td colspan="2">Action
Needed</td><td>Date
Completed</td></tr>
<tr><td></td><td>Yes</td><td>No</td><td></td></tr>
</table>

1. Made a commitment to no longer work with your "hands on" the job and to embrace the management viewpoint.

2. Resolved to maintain good health, work hard, set a good example for your employees, and continue to learn.

3. Identified those individuals and groups to whom you now owe a responsibility: higher management (especially your boss), staff departments, fellow supervisors, and your employee work group.

4. Checked out the resources which enable you to carry out your job responsibilities: facilities, equipment, tools, power, utilities, materials, supplies, and information (dollar value of all this).

5. Gotten the "personnel jacket" particulars about your work force: personal data on each employee—age, length of service, work history, present job title and description, and pay rate.

6. Found out about current and upcoming production schedules and other output requirements and project deadlines.

7. Found out exactly what the quality requirements or specifications of your product or service are.

8. Pinned down the cost and expense limitations under which you will be expected to operate.

9. Accepted the fact that pressures on you will be many and varied, with changing worker attitudes the most pressing of all.

10. Given thought to how well your present abilities measure up to the demands for technical, administrative, and human relations skills—and what you might do to improve them.

11. Prepared to balance your supervisory efforts between task-centered concerns and employee-centered ones.

12. Reviewed the managerial process so that you can anticipate problems and decisions requiring planning, organizing, staffing, activating, and controlling.

13. Accepted the fact that your supervisory role will often be ambiguous and will occasionally put you in the middle between higher management and your employees.

14. Guarded against pitfalls for new supervisors: poor relationships with others in the organization, failure to plan ahead, confusion about your managerial role, lack of initiative, discouragement, and the inability to successfully meet changing conditions.

15. Adopted an attitude of doing the best you can today with a plan for developing your knowledge and skills so that you can do even better tomorrow.

Action Planning Checklist 2

Coping with Your Unique Environment

	Action Needed		Date Completed
	Yes	No	

1. An awareness of the seven environmental factors with which supervisors must cope: technology, legal restrictions, pressures from above, organizational policies and procedures, competition for scarce resources, a burgeoning information load, and the rising expectations of employees.   ___ ___ _____

2. Allowances made for the impact of the time factor on departmental operations.   ___ ___ _____

3. A weather eye out for changes that will affect operations.   ___ ___ _____

4. An understanding of what work really is and how it applies to departmental operations.   ___ ___ _____

5. An understanding of why people work.   ___ ___ _____

6. An ability to differentiate work from other human activities.   ___ ___ _____

7. Consideration of the effect that job satisfaction may have upon employee effort.   ___ ___ _____

8. Recognition of the extent to which job challenges can influence employee performance.   ___ ___ _____

9. Provision of enough meaningful work to keep employees challenged and productive.   ___ ___ _____

10. An awareness of the differences with which individuals perceive their work and the reasons why.   ___ ___ _____

11. A plan for anticipating negative perceptions of work in your department and for presenting it in a more favorable light.   ___ ___ _____

12. A sensitivity to, and allowances made for, a good employee's occasional bad day.   ___ ___ _____

13. A determination to make accurate and sufficient information available to employees regarding their work.   ___ ___ _____

14. Recognition of the possible relationship between the lack of job satisfaction on an employee's part and poor management on the supervisor's part.   ___ ___ _____

15. Ways and means devised for improving the quality of work life in your department by (a) soliciting employee feedback, (b) facilitating rather than directing, (c) providing flexibility in assignments, and (d) conveying a sense of meaning to employees' work.   ___ ___ _____

Action Planning Checklist 3

Supervision and the Management Process

1. Determination to think—and act—like a manager, in a truly professional manner.

2. Recognition that there is an established body of management principles and practices to draw upon for guidance.

3. Identification of the five management process functions: planning, organizing, staffing, activating, and controlling.

4. An ability to relate the five managerial functions to operations at the supervisory level.

5. An understanding of the conversion process that transforms input resources into output results as it applies to your operations.

6. Identification of the resources available to you for the conversion operations in your department.

7. Identification of the results expected from the conversion process in your department, in terms of product or services created and their related quality and cost specifications.

8. An ability to relate management principles to the management process.

9. Adherence to Fayol's main principles of management:
   a. Division of work
   b. Responsibility matched by authority
   c. Discipline matched by loyalty   d. Unity of command
   e. Unity of direction
   f. Personal interest second to the organization
   g. Fair pay for employee contributions
   h. Chain of command   i. Persistence of order
   j. Equity   k. Initiative.

10. An understanding of, and proficiency in using, the systematic (or "scientific") management approach.

11. An understanding of, and proficiency in using, the human relations (or behavioral) management approach.

12. An understanding of, and proficiency in using, the quantitative management approach.

13. An understanding of, and an awareness of the prevalance of, systems in organizational relationships.

14. An understanding of the relationship of Japanese "consensus" management to the participation concept advocated under human relations management.

15. An awareness of the significance of, and application of, the contingency (or situational) management approach.

Action Planning Checklist 4

Making Plans and Carrying Out Policy

	Action Needed		Date Completed
	Yes	No	

1. Time set aside for planning: 5 to 10 minutes daily, 15 to 30 minutes weekly, 1 to 2 hours monthly. — — _____

2. Knowledge of organizational policies and procedures that affect departmental goals, plans, and operating practices. — — _____

3. Goals based on a realistic appraisal of departmental strengths and weaknesses and company-imposed limitations. — — _____

4. Departmental goals arranged in a hierarchy (in order of their priorities). — — _____

5. Goals clearly stated (a) as measurable output expected, (b) in explicit and quantified terms, and (c) in relation to a specific period of time. — — _____

6. Consideration of What, Where, When, How, and Who in making plans. — — _____

7. Plans, procedures, and regulations that fit into chosen goals. — — _____

8. Plans flexible enough to permit change if needed. — — _____

9. Control limits and procedures set for plans so that you can monitor progress toward attainment of goals. — — _____

10. Schedules set that neither underutilize nor overload departmental staff and equipment. — — _____

11. Care not to overcommit your staff or equipment or to make delivery promises that can't be met. — — _____

12. Ability to prepare and use, where appropriate, a Gantt-type production planning and/or progress control chart. — — _____

13. An understanding of how PERT or CPM works so that you can make valid contributions in the form of task sequences and time estimates to the specialists who prepare such plans. — — _____

14. Ability, for clerical work, to prepare and use a work distribution chart as a basis for making job assignments. — — _____

15. Prudence in checking company policy implications before taking trend-setting action at the departmental level. — — _____

Action Planning Checklist 5

Exercising Control of People and Processes

	Action Needed		Date Completed
	Yes	No	

1. Knowledge of your company's information system and how it affects controls in your area of responsibility. — — _____

2. Understanding of a supervisor's judgmental and problem-solving–decision-making roles in implementing controls. — — _____

3. Knowledge of how control standards and procedures are linked to plans and goals. — — _____

4. Ability to define and identify control standards and tolerances as they affect your operations. — — _____

5. Ability to use historical records and systematic analysis to establish standards for your department. — — _____

6. An understanding of the control process and a supervisor's role in it. — — _____

7. An ability to distinguish between preventive, concurrent, and corrective controls and identify the application of these in your area of responsibility. — — _____

8. Departmental standards and controls established to cover employee performance, machine operations, product or service quality, costs and expense, time-related factors, and materials usage. — — _____

9. Control standards that are clearly written, numerically expressed where possible, and based upon historical records or systematic analysis. — — _____

10. A periodic review to make sure that existing control standards are correct and relevant to the person or process being controlled. — — _____

11. An understanding of the intent and use of budgetary controls received and the extent to which you must conform to them. — — _____

12. Application of the management-by-exception principle to the control process as much as is possible. — — _____

13. Sensitivity to the people problem when exercising control. Emphasis on motivation rather than punishment. — — _____

14. Encouragement of employee self-control whenever feasible and appropriate. — — _____

15. An understanding of, and receptivity to, management by objectives (MBO) if applied to your area of responsibility. — — _____

Action Planning Checklist 6

Managing Information and Solving Problems

	Action Needed		Date Completed
	Yes	No	

1. Skills developed for detecting and describing existing and potential problems in your department. — — ————

2. An ability to distinguish between what actually is occurring and what should have occurred, in order to precisely define the problem gap. — — ————

3. An ability to pursue a systematic procedure in analyzing and solving problems. — — ————

4. Persistence in tracking down real causes of problems so as not to be misled into treating symptoms. — — ————

5. Not being satisfied with the first, seemingly easy, solution; searching always for alternatives to remove root causes. — — ————

6. A recognition of the point where problem solving ends and decision making begins. — — ————

7. An ability to assist a specialist in preparing a decision-tree analysis for problems affecting your areas of responsibility. — — ————

8. An understanding of cost-benefit judgments in evaluating proposed solutions to operational problems. — — ————

9. Balance maintained between intuitive judgments and those based upon systematic and logical analysis of a situation. — — ————

10. A willingness to seek opinions and advice from employees in problems that affect them, especially those problems that will require employee support for their solutions. — — ————

11. A knowledge of the nature and extent your company's management information system (MIS) and how it serves your operational area. — — ————

12. Specific knowledge of how your department feeds data into the company's MIS and the exact form in which this information should be provided. — — ————

13. Preparation of a diagram illustrating the information system within your own department (using Figure 6-5 in Chapter 6 as a model). — — ————

14. An awareness of how information and computer systems in your organization have changed, are changing, and will change the content of employees' jobs. — — ————

15. A sensitivity toward employees' fears of the impact of computerization and other technological changes on their jobs and their job security; a continuing effort to counteract these fears by your personal interest and intervention. — — ————

Action Planning Checklist 7

Organizing an Effective Department

	Action Needed		Date Completed
	Yes	No	

1. An understanding of the steps in the organizing process.

2. The work of your department organized in such a way as to focus on its objectives and responsibilities.

3. An awareness of, but not conflict with, the informal organization in your operational areas.

4. Identification of both line and staff responsibilities—in your department and with other company departments.

5. Identification of your company's organizational structure—divisional or product, geographic, customer, or matrix.

6. An estimate of the degree of centralization and decentralization in your company and in your department; satisfaction with the extent of your own span of control, neither too narrow nor too broad.

7. Construction of an organization chart for your areas of responsibility.

8. A clear understanding of your responsibilities and related authorities according to Class 1—complete, Class 2—limited, and Class 3—none.

9. Full development and utilization of your personal sources of authority.

10. Cooperation with, and utilization of, company staff departments.

11. Identification of operational areas in your department where a staff department may exert functional authority.

12. Regular use of delegation within your department to relieve yourself of unnecessary work and to develop the skills and confidence of subordinates.

13. Knowledge of the chain of command in your organization and a general conformity to it.

14. Regular review of your department's organization structure to minimize communications problems, avoid having an employee answer to two people, ensure clear designation of work duties, and retain flexibility for contingencies.

15. Periodic use of organization development (OD) techniques to uncover and clarify areas of conflict and blockage within your department's organizational structure.

Action Planning Checklist 8

Staffing with Human Resources

1. An understanding of the five-step staffing process and the supervisor's role in it.

2. An awareness of the supervisor's responsibility in having the right workers on the right jobs in sufficient numbers at the right time.

3. Alertness to symptoms of poor human resources staffing: high labor costs; excessive absenteeism, latenesses, and turnover; poor quality of work; lowered productivity.

4. Periodic review to make certain that employees are placed on jobs that best suit their capabilities.

5. Periodic forecasts of your department's work force needs.

6. Care taken to neither understaff nor overstaff.

7. As an aid in carrying out your forecast, preparation of a work-force trial balance sheet that anticipates (a) payroll separations and (b) changes in departmental workloads (using Table 8-1 in Chapter 8 as a model).

8. An ability to interview job candidates objectively, using open-ended questions, especially, to probe the suitability of education and experience for the open position.

9. Knowledge of legal (especially EEOC) guidelines that must be observed in conducting employment interviews and in selecting and placing employees.

10. Improvement of your interviewing skills such as question asking, listening, and evaluation.

11. An ability to describe a job accurately and to specify the qualifications of the person who might fill it.

12. Periodic review to assess the applicability of performance tests as aids in selection of applicants for jobs in your department.

13. Knowledge of, and an ability to calculate, your department's turnover rate.

14. Knowledge of, and an ability to calculate, your department's absenteeism rate.

15. A plan for keeping turnover and absenteeism rates within standards acceptable to the parent organization.

Appraisal of Employee Performance

	Action Needed		Date Completed
	Yes	No	

1. An attitude toward appraisals that focuses on the major goal of improvement of the individual's performance so as to match the job's requirements.   ___ ___ _____

2. Care in separating the discussion of an employee's appraisal rating from any talk, or consideration, of money.   ___ ___ _____

3. Knowledge of the distinctions between a graphic rating scale, a forced-choice appraisal format, and a behaviorally anchored rating scale (BARS).   ___ ___ _____

4. A conscious effort to apply the same standards to all, so that your ratings are consistent from employee to employee.   ___ ___ _____

5. Maintenance of a file of critical incidents, or specific and representative examples, of each employee's behavior so as to support the appraisal you make.   ___ ___ _____

6. Your guard up against the halo effect, which discriminates for or against a person, based upon a single incident or trait.   ___ ___ _____

7. Proper preparation for and conduct of the appraisal interview: privacy, enough time, emphasis on job standards, credit where it is due, mutual examination of the facts supported by critical incidents, focus on the future, and sharing by you of responsibility for the individual's performance.   ___ ___ _____

8. Establishment of a positive, constructive atmosphere during the appraisal interview so that employees do not feel that they sit in the judgment of a person who believes himself or herself to be infallible.   ___ ___ _____

9. Willingness to listen to an employee's rebuttal of your ratings and to change those ratings if the argument is sound.   ___ ___ _____

10. Treatment of an individual's appraisal as confidential, with respect to his or her associates or peers.   ___ ___ _____

11. Strict observance of legal (especially EEOC) regulations as they affect the performance appraisal and the interview.   ___ ___ _____

12. Maintenance of the proper records of the appraisal interview and discussions that take place during it.   ___ ___ _____

13. A continuing interest in, and appraisal of, the individual's performance, so that your judgment isn't a one-time thing.   ___ ___ _____

14. Your active assistance to the employee in helping to overcome specified weaknesses or to develop desirable skills.   ___ ___ _____

15. Thoughtful reexamination of conditions beyond an employee's control that may be contributing to substandard performance: a poor skills-job match, inadequate training, work group pressure, physical or emotional problems, insensitive supervision, and technical problems in the process or procedures.   ___ ___ _____

Training and Developing Employees

	Action Needed		Date Completed
	Yes	No	

1. A continuing alertness for symptoms of training needs—such as lowered output, off-standard quality, higher costs, accidents, or poor morale. — — ————

2. Use of a systematic, rather than hit-or-miss, approach to each and all training problems in your department. — — ————

3. Training in your department based upon (a) an analysis of skills needed and (b) a planned timetable for completion (modeled after Figure 10-1 in Chapter 10). — — ————

4. Formation of a working partnership with the professional training staff so that you may benefit from their advice and assistance. — — ————

5. Care in orienting each new employee to your department, using the list of items in the text as a guide. — — ————

6. Preparation of a simple job breakdown sheet, with key points identified, before beginning employee training on a particular job (see Figure 10-2 and Table 10-1 in Chapter 10.) — — ————

7. Knowledge and use of the four-step, job-instruction-training method (JIT). — — ————

8. Proper employee preparation and motivation provided before training begins. — — ————

9. Use of training demonstrations that combine telling and showing. — — ————

10. Training coverage broken into easily learned segments; not attempting too much during a single session. — — ————

11. The training sequence arranged so that the learner begins with the least difficult segments and progresses to the most difficult (as illustrated in Figure 10-3 in Chapter 10). — — ————

12. Encouragement of questions from the trainee throughout the entire training process. — — ————

13. Provision of feedback and follow-up to the trainee throughout, offering either encouragement or correction as the training progresses. — — ————

14. Use of programmed-learning and computer-assisted-training materials, as well as a variety of audio-visual aids, to supplement, stimulate, and reinforce the learning process. — — ————

15. Training efforts tailored to fit the needs and learning capabilities of each individual, rather than simply provided across-the-board without thought to need and relevance. — — ————

Action Planning Checklist 11

Motivating People At Work

	Action Needed		Date Completed
	Yes	No	

1. An acknowledgment that people act as they must, that their behavior is essentially rational in terms of their needs. ___ ___ _____

2. Identification of the inevitable differences among your employees as to motivation, goals, and personality and the influence of these factors on their performance. ___ ___ _____

3. Recognition of the impact of heredity, environment, and experience on an individual's personality. ___ ___ _____

4. Restraint in jumping to conclusions about the consequences of an individual's personality; an attitude of "live and let live" with respect to personal preferences. ___ ___ _____

5. An assessment of each employee's current level of need according to Maslow's hierarchy: survival, security, social, respect, and self-fulfillment. ___ ___ _____

6. In trying to provide motivation, always searching for conditions that can fill an unsatisfied need. ___ ___ _____

7. An attempt to create conditions at work that Herzberg characterizes as "satisfiers": recognition for achievement, interesting and meaningful work, opportunities for utilization of one's capabilities, responsibility for one's own work. ___ ___ _____

8. Feedback to higher management of the absence of "hygiene" factors that may become "dissatisfiers" to your employees. ___ ___ _____

9. Open praise for an employee's good work and opportunities for employees to provide their own self-discipline. ___ ___ _____

10. An understanding of the concept of "expectancy" that influences the degree to which an employee will undertake unpleasant or difficult work. ___ ___ _____

11. Wariness of your own inclination to overachieve to the extent that you become so task-oriented that you minimize human relationships. ___ ___ _____

12. Maintenance of a general atmosphere of courtesy and comradeship in your department, despite occasional flareups. ___ ___ _____

13. A readiness to modify (or redesign) existing jobs in your department so as to accomodate physical and psychological needs among your employees: ergonomic compatibility, provision of a whole job, contact with users and clients, variety of skills, freedom for self-direction, feedback from the work itself, and a chance for self-development. ___ ___ _____

14. Consideration given to enlarging or enhancing the narrower, more monotonous, and less demanding jobs in your department. ___ ___ _____

15. Emphasis placed upon ways employees can attain organizational goals without sacrificing the quality of their own work life. ___ ___ _____

Action Planning Checklist 12

The Art and Science of Leadership

	Action Needed		Date Completed
	Yes	No	

1. An awareness of the importance of leadership skills (persuasion, influence, rapport) as contrasted with so-called "inborn" leadership traits.

2. An acknowledgment that effective leadership depends upon providing motivation rather than upon manipulation.

3. A determination, through self-analysis, of whether your assumptions about employees represents a Theory X or Theory Y viewpoint.

4. An attempt to help employees to discover personal goals consistent with those of the organization.

5. Development of skills in applying all three kinds of traditional leadership approaches: autocratic, democratic, and participative.

6. Differentiation between results-centered and situational leadership approaches.

7. Balanced application of leadership techniques contingent upon the particulars of each situation.

8. A concern for people (people-centered leadership) equal to your concern for results (task-centered leadership).

9. Demonstrated personal progress toward point 9.9 on the Managerial Grid.

10. Recognition of the choices that can be made by a supervisor along the continuum of leadership styles.

11. Consideration of the maturity (not age!) of an individual when selecting an appropriate style of leadership.

12. An attempt to match your leadership style to the followership inclinations of each employee.

13. Consistency in the nature of your relationships with others: superiors, subordinates, and peers alike.

14. Maintainance of good examples of personal commitment and a willingness to make sacrifices to help your employees meet department objectives.

15. A conscious effort to treat employees equitably in similar situations, to neither play favorites nor pick on those you don't particularly like.

Action Planning Checklist 13
Effective Employee Communications

	Action Needed		Date Completed
	Yes	No	

1. Communications whose purpose is to link plans to action. — — _____

2. Repetition, feedback, and questioning regularly used as techniques to avoid misunderstandings and to reinforce understanding. — — _____

3. A minimum of "noise" in your communication system: employees ready to listen, absence of conflicting instructions, employees and supervisors talking about the same thing. — — _____

4. Expertise in, and reliance upon, many methods rather than a single method of communication. — — _____

5. Emphasis upon the free flow of information up, down, and across your department. — — _____

6. Development of your *person-to-person* communication skills: *spoken*—informal talks, planned appointments, telephone calls, etc.; *written*—interoffice memos, letters, reports. — — _____

7. Development of your *group* communications skills: *spoken*—informal staff meetings, planned conferences, mass meetings; *written*—bulletin board notices, posters, displays, audio and visual aids. — — _____

8. An awareness of body language; a realization that your actions often speak more convincingly than your words. — — _____

9. Knowledge of the grapevine, but its use avoided for supervisory communications: rumors spiked as soon as possible. — — _____

10. Development of your active listening skills, using your responses to establish empathy and rapport; a willingness to listen without interrupting or taking offense, with your emphasis upon face-to-face communications. — — _____

11. A willingness to track down and retrieve job-related information for employees who need it or request it. — — _____

12. Guarding against overcommunicating and talking on sensitive subjects. — — _____

13. Your boss kept regularly informed of accountable, controversial matters and employees' attitudes toward organization policy, but without betraying confidences. — — _____

14. Care in issuing orders and instructions so that they are clear in terms of quantity, quality, and time factors: an awareness that words mean different things to different people and that hard facts are better than vague generalities. — — _____

15. Avoidance of any semblance of a power struggle when issuing orders, using requests as often as possible and commands only in emergencies or when a high degree of coordination is needed. — — _____

Action Planning Checklist 14

Counseling Problem Employees

Action Needed   Date Completed
Yes   No

1. An awareness and sensitivity to employees who display emotional problems, without overreacting to them.

2. Recognition that all people have soft spots in their emotional armor, and this does not mean that they are crazy.

3. Tolerance for the work-addicted individual, with your guard up to prevent this from happening to you.

4. An ability to distinguish between evidence of neurotic behavior (which may be tolerated) and psychotic behavior (which is bizarre and may become threatening to the individual or to others in the workplace).

5. Recognition of the signs of poor emotional adjustment—sudden changes in behavior, preoccupation, irritability, increased absences, fatigue, accidents, waste, too much drinking, and substance abuse.

6. A desire to help employees to adjust to their emotional problems—rather than to ridicule them for these problems or to minimize their importance to the individual.

7. Time set aside in your schedule to counsel employees who need attention.

8. Conduct of your counseling sessions in a nonthreatening manner, with emphasis on nondirective interviewing.

9. Development of your listening skills so as to become a nonevaluative listener—a person who does not comment or pass judgment on what is said.

10. Readiness to refer an emotionally disturbed person to your company nurse, doctor, or psychologist for professional advice and treatment whenever your own efforts are not fruitful.

11. A combination of firmness and empathy when counseling employees with problems of absenteeism, alcoholism, or substance abuse.

12. Selective use of different counseling approaches for the willful absentee (vacationers, the directionless, moonlighters, and the aggressive) and the chronic and the occasional absentee.

13. An alertness for early-warning signs of alcoholism and substance abuse in an employee.

14. A willingness to confront an alcoholic employee—or a substance abuser—with the choice of abstinence or losing his or her job.

15. A sensitivity, along with an expectancy of useful performance, in dealing with employees who have terminal illnesses.

Converting Conflict into Cooperation

	Action Needed		Date Completed
	Yes	No	

1. Respect for and attention to all grievances, real or imagined. — — _____

2. A desire to resolve the issue or grievance clearly, whether or not the solution is one that fully satisfies the employee. — — _____

3. An unwavering standard of fairness when judging the merits of a complaint; decisions based on facts and rendered in clear-cut terms with full explanation of your reasoning and in strict conformance to whatever formal grievance procedure that may exist. — — _____

4. A sensitivity to the dynamics of group relationships in your department. — — _____

5. An awareness of, without prying into, the attitudes of informal work groups in your department. — — _____

6. Recognition that many individuals will look to you for protection from unreasonable group pressures so as to ensure personal freedom of performance. — — _____

7. A determination to integrate individual and group goals with those of the organization. — — _____

8. An opportunity offered for employees—collectively—to participate in solving work-related problems. — — _____

9. A firm stand to uphold goals, policies, procedures, and rules that are judged to be inflexible if work is to be coordinated in a safe and productive way, regardless of a group's attitudes toward them. — — _____

10. An acceptance of a limited amount of conflict or competition as normal so long as it is not intense or disruptive. — — _____

11. An awareness of common sources of conflict and competition: unequal distribution of resources, disagreements about what is important, changes in work flow, infringement on territorial rights, mutual mistrust, and constant change. — — _____

12. Prompt settlement of disputes in an objective and professional manner. — — _____

13. Maintenance of an "I'm okay, you're okay" attitude when dealing with stress situations, by stroking and by placing emphasis upon performance rather than attitudes. — — _____

14. Cooperating with, rather than resisting, advice and suggestions from staff personnel. — — _____

15. Encouraging cooperation from employees and peers by focusing on common objectives. — — _____

Action Planning Checklist 16

How and When to Discipline

	Action Needed		Date Completed
	Yes	No	

1. Discipline conceived of as an ongoing program to encourage desired performance and to discourage undesirable behavior. — — _____

2. Discipline used only for corrective purposes and never as a display of personal power or authority. — — _____

3. Establishment of rules that are reasonable and regarded by the work group as mutually beneficial to them and the company. — — _____

4. An understanding of how rules are broken: willfully by frustrated or disturbed employees and unthinkingly by untrained or misinformed workers or by employees distracted by personal problems. — — _____

5. Standards of performance and departmental rules enforced fairly, neither too leniently nor vindictively. — — _____

6. Discipline that stresses the positive rather than the negative; improvement rather than punishment. — — _____

7. An approach to meting out corrective discipline that is progressive, with penalties for successive infractions increasingly severe. — — _____

8. Advance warnings of possible disciplinary action communicated to employees through training sessions, bulletin boards, manuals, and face-to-face discussions. — — _____

9. Corrective discipline exercised without undue delay; the principle of immediacy. — — _____

10. Disciplinary action that is consistently applied in like situations and for similar failures to meet standards or to conform to established rules. — — _____

11. Use of behavior modification techniques when conducting disciplinary interviews so as to (a) emphasize performance and (b) involve the employee in the corrective solution. — — _____

12. Knowledge of your company's policies, procedures, and regulations (and the influence of the labor contract if there is a trade union present) as they affect enforcement of performance standards and organizational discipline. — — _____

13. Enforcing discipline that meets the legal requirements of prior notice of (a) what constitutes unacceptable performance or behavior and (b) the corresponding penalties. — — _____

14. Care in making notations in your own records of oral or written warnings; maintenance of production, quality, safety, and absence records so as to detect and correct off-standard performance before it gets out of control. — — _____

15. A double check of what it takes to make corrective discipline stick before taking action: clear-cut breach of a rule, adequate warning, undeniable evidence, impartiality, credible backup records, and appropriate penalties. — — _____

Improving Productivity and Innovation

	Action Needed		Date Completed
	Yes	No	

1. Knowledge of which input resources and output values can be used to measure productivity in your department.   — — _____

2. A record kept of the basic productivity trend in your department.   — — _____

3. Identification of the specific technological factors that can affect productivity for better or worse in your department.   — — _____

4. A knowledge of how much time it does and should take to perform the various tasks and work under your supervision, given the quality of workmanship expected.   — — _____

5. Periodic work-sampling check of your work force to observe the degree of travel, delay, or idleness that prevails.   — — _____

6. Periodic review of tasks under your supervision to identify those that most need a methods-improvement analysis.   — — _____

7. Routine thought given to improvement of each of the three task elements—"make ready," "do," and "put away"—of jobs in your department.   — — _____

8. A challenging attitude toward existing procedures in terms of what is being done, where, when, why, and how.   — — _____

9. Systematic application of (a) the *methods-improvement* checklist—eliminate, combine, change sequence, and simplify—and (b) the *motion-economy checklist*—productive, simple, and rhythmic motions; comfortable workplaces; combining of tools; pre-positioning of tools and materials; etc.   — — _____

10. Acceptance of high-technology innovations from automation, computer-assisted systems, and office automation or the introduction of people-oriented participative approaches, such as Quality Circles, to improve productivity.   — — _____

11. An alertness to value-analysis applications, especially by substituting less expensive, easier-to-work-with materials and parts in the product being made.   — — _____

12. Seeking, stimulating, and accepting creative ideas and suggestions from employees—either through formal suggestions systems, Quality Circles, or brainstorming sessions.   — — _____

13. When stimulating innovative thinking on the part of your employees, brainstorming principles are observed: no criticism, anything welcomed, quantity stressed, combining and improving on what already has been suggested—evaluating later on.   — — _____

14. Development of your own ability to create new ideas, using the list of suggestions in the text.   — — _____

15. An alertness to opportunities for practicing intrapreneurship in your department.   — — _____

Action Planning Checklist 18

Building a Higher Quality of Performance

1. An understanding of the proper way by which quality must be defined: specific standards that must be conformed to.   —   —   ———

2. A familiarity with the terminology associated with quality assurance: quality control, acceptable quality level, inspection, and nondestructive testing.   —   —   ———

3. Recognition that quality applies to services and to workmanship associated with service activities, as well as to products.   —   —   ———

4. Knowledge of what makes up both corrective and preventive quality costs in your company, and especially in your area.   —   —   ———

5. A clear-cut understanding of your specific responsibility in maintaining quality in your department, including your relations with (and authority relative to) an existing inspection or quality control department.   —   —   ———

6. Acceptance of your responsibility to maintain an ongoing surveillance of quality and workmanship in your department, following the ten points outlined in the text.   —   —   ———

7. Regular personal tours made of your department to inspect for quality and workmanship and to detect potential quality problems.   —   —   ———

8. Action taken to correct conditions that interfere with good workmanship: repair of machines and tooling; upgrading of raw materials and supplies; and provision of proper workplace arrangements, adequate lighting, and sufficient storage space.   —   —   ———

10. An awareness of causes contributing to employee mistakes: inadequate or faulty training, communications, tools and equipment, planning, specifications and procedures, and attention.   —   —   ———

11. An ongoing communications and training program to inform employees of quality standards, instruct them in the proper methods for attaining them, and alerting them to the impact of their work—favorably or unfavorably—upon customers or clients.   —   —   ———

12. An understanding of the principles and procedures of statistical quality control, including the frequency-distribution chart, quality-control chart, and sampling tables.   —   —   ———

13. An understanding of the relationship between reliability and statistical quality control.   Yes   —   ———

14. Conviction that the underlying principle of Zero Defects (*Do it the right way from the start*) can be an invaluable guide to better quality.   —   —   ———

15. Knowledge of how and why Quality Circles can help to improve, not only quality, but also productivity.   —   —   ———

Action Planning Checklist 19

Controling Costs and Budgets

	Action Needed		Date Completed
	Yes	No	

1. Knowledge of costs and expenses for your department and maintenance of appropriate records for your guidance and action.

2. An understanding of basic cost and accounting terms, such as unit costs, standard costs, and budgeted costs.

3. An ability to interpret a budget and take action based upon a cost-variance report, as illustrated in Table 19-1 of Chapter 19.

4. An ability to compute and compare unit costs.

5. An understanding of a flexible budget and how it is prepared, as illustrated in Table 19-2 of Chapter 19.

6. Acceptance of your responsibility in routine, recurring, organization-wide cost-reduction programs.

7. An ongoing search for cost-reduction targets: in processes, procedures, personnel, equipment, materials and supplies, utilities, communications, paperwork, and information.

8. An ability to plan and implement an intense, but temporary, "belt-tightening" program.

9. Use of participative approaches to seek cost-cutting ideas from employees and staff departments.

10. Development of a program for ongoing cost curtailment, such as: reducing waste, saving time, increasing output, spending wisely, using space more intelligently, and trimming your inventories.

11. An understanding of why some cost-saving ideas may be rejected (for good reason) by higher management.

12. A sensitivity to employee—and labor union—resistance to cost-reduction efforts, with a plan to minimize or overcome such resistance.

13. Establishment of specific, attainable cost-reduction goals with and for employees—for factors and conditions that they can affect or control themselves.

14. Encouragement of, and receptivity toward, employee ideas and suggestions for cost reduction.

15. A continuing communications program to inform employees of the genuine need for cost control, using concrete examples and specific figures; enhanced by training for cost improvement, and reports of progress toward cost goals.

Action Planning Checklist 20
Equal Opportunity under the Law

	Action Needed		Date Completed
	Yes	No	

1. An acceptance of a very broad definition of "minorities" as "protected groups" under the law: including blacks, women, ethnic minorities (such as Hispanics, Orientals, and Native Americans), disadvantaged, handicapped, Vietnam War veterans, and workers over 40 years of age. — — _____

2. Knowledge of, and respect for, the basic legal protections against discrimination in all aspects of employment because of race, religion, national origin, age, or sex. — — _____

4. Understanding of the legal and practical implications of an affirmative action program. — — _____

5. An understanding of EEOC's three culpable variations of discrimination: differential treatment, disparate effect, and evil intent. Recognition of the need to document a bonafide occupational qualification (BFOQ) exception to the EEO laws. — — _____

6. A determination to give all employees a fair chance to learn a job and to prove their ability to perform satisfactorily. — — _____

7. An expectation of satisfactory performance from all minorities once they have become an integral part of your work force. — — _____

8. Patience and understanding offered to employees from disadvantaged backgrounds. Intensified—and perhaps longer than usual—training for the hard-core unemployed. — — _____

9. Care in using and interpreting test results for employment, selection, placement, training, and promotion purposes. — — _____

10. Avoidance of stereotyped thinking about why women work—as well as their interest in, and capability to perform, various types of work. — — _____

11. Absolutely equal pay and treatment for women who perform the same work as men (and vice versa) with equal opportunities for training, development, and advancement. — — _____

12. A strict avoidance of any form or implication of sexual harassment, either by you or by any member of your staff. — — _____

13. A determination to bridge the generation gap between you and younger employees, by being supportive to their efforts, trying to make work more meaningful, and providing feedback. Yes No _____

14. An alertness to obsolescence among workers over 50, with job assignments that make the most of their skills—good attendance, judgment, and loyalty—while minimizing their slower pace, lessened physical strength, and often poorer eyesight. — — _____

15. An observance of an employee's right to privacy, the restrictions affecting drug and lie-detector tests, and the generally higher expectations of entitlement of today's more informed, better educated work force. — — _____

Action Planning Checklist 21

Employee Safety and Health and OSHA

	Action Needed		Date Completed
	Yes	No	

1. A recognition of the potential for immense financial costs and human damage due to work-related accidents and health hazards.

2. Knowledge of the prime causes of work-related accidents, as listed in the text.

3. Knowledge of OSHA standards as they apply to safety and health conditions in your areas of responsibility.

4. Careful safety training for new employees and an ongoing program for all employees.

5. Knowledge of and protection of employees' rights under OSHA.

6. A continuing search for better accident prevention and safety procedures—the engineering of safety.

7. An ongoing program to educate and motivate employees to work safely—with emphasis upon accident awareness and prevention.

8. Enforcement of safety and health rules and regulations—no matter how small—and without exception.

9. Insistence that employees wear the designated protective clothing and in the prescribed way.

10. Knowledge of accident potential and prescribed safe working conditions associated with: lifting and material handling, machinery, hand-tools, falls, low-voltage electricity, and even offices.

11. Relentless surveillance of potential fire conditions in your department, making sure that employees have foreknowledge of what to do if a fire occurs.

12. Prompt reporting of occupational injuries and illnesses that occur in your department so that they may be entered in the company's OSHA log.

13. An ability to make calculations of accident incident and severity rates.

14. Prompt investigation of accidents and occupational illnesses large and small, to identify and remove causes, not to fix blame.

15. Maintenance of approved conditions and procedures affecting environment and sanitation in your department: ventilation, waste disposal, food handling, washrooms, lighting, handling and storage of hazardous materials.

Action Planning Checklist 22

The Supervisor's Role in Labor Relations

1. Full recognition that in the eyes of the law a supervisor acts as a representative of the company in labor relations matters involving its employees.

2. Maintenance of a neutral attitude toward unions and union membership, unless your company explicitly directs otherwise.

3. An understanding of why employees might join a union; not asking that an employee give you undivided loyalty.

4. Care not to interfere or discriminate against union activity, as proscribed by the Wagner Act, especially during an organizing drive.

5. Protection of individual's employee's rights to take up grievances directly with management, under the provisions of the Taft-Hartley law.

6. Clear identification of those employees who report to you as being either exempt or nonexempt under the Fair Labor Standards Act (Wages and Hours law).

7. Firm observance of the proscriptions of the various equal employment opportunity laws which require: equitable assignments, pay, and opportunities for training and promotion regardless of race, religion, sex, age or national origin—all of which transcend any particular labor contract agreements.

8. Acceptance of the supervisor's limited, but sensitive, role during recognition elections and collective bargaining negotiations.

9. Diligence and precision in interpreting and applying labor contract matters during the life of the contract.

10. Care to avoid any implications of *interference* during union organizing drives or *discrimination* at any time.

11. Cordial, cooperative relationships with your department's shop steward but (a) no abdication of your rights to manage nor (b) any form of co-management.

12. Knowledge of and adherence to the prescribed steps in your organization's grievance procedure, where one exists.

13. A desire to resolve grievances in your department at your level, based upon a knowledge of facts and strict conformity to the labor contract and company precedents.

14. A willingness to check first with your human resources department, or someone in higher authority more broadly informed than you, before rendering decisions in labor matters that you suspect may be sensitive.

15. Your handling of grievances so thoroughly and fairly that, should an unresolved case go to arbitration, your case could be effectively presented.

10

Appendixes

A

Planning the Day's Work

1. Do before the shift begins (15–30 minutes)
    a. Check production schedule and/or work orders for the day.
    b. Check equipment to be used—its availability and condition.
    c. Check supply of materials for the day.
    d. Check tools needed for the day.
    e. Arrange equipment, materials, and tools for the day.
    f. Prepare a firm work schedule for the day.
2. Do at the beginning of the shift (15–30 minutes)
    a. Check attendance and assign employees to work stations.
    b. If necessary because of absences, balance the work force against the work load by rearranging assignments or by securing additional help from other departments.
    c. Assign production and/or work orders to employees.
    d. Stress critical quality areas to watch for.
    e. Specify when work should be completed.
3. Do during each work day (6–7 hours)
    a. Check quality of work with each employee. Approve, correct, instruct, or train as needed.
    b. Check work progress with each employee. Add help, allow more time, or assign additional work as appropriate.
    c. Check on housekeeping. See that it is satisfactory at all times. Good work cannot be done in an untidy place.

d. Stay on the floor most of the time—supervising and/or being available for questions, assistance, and instructions.
e. Be on the floor immediately before and after all breaks and for a full 15 minutes before quitting time.
f. Inspect critical quality points as work progresses. Correct problems as soon as they are detected.
g. Provide a final inspection of parts, subassemblies, reports, and paperwork before they move on to other departments or to customers.
h. Check periodically to see that tools and equipment are in proper operating condition.
i. Check periodically to see that materials and supplies are on hand.
j. Report and/or request maintenance, repair, or replacement of defective tools and equipment.
k. Check accident hazards. Be sure that employees are following safe practices and OSHA safety and health specifications, and that they are wearing proper protective clothing and equipment.
l. Prepare time cards, work distribution sheets, work orders, material distributions, and other routine reports.

4. Do once a day (15–30 minutes)
   a. Observe one employee or work station continuously for 15 minutes. Look for time wasted, dull or improper tools, need for work-positioning jigs and fixtures, interferences, delays and bottlenecks, and excess time getting materials orders or parts. Try to find ways to cut costs or to make improvements in any of these.
   b. Alternatively, select one employee or small group of employees with whom to interact. Ask about problems they are presently encountering and for suggestions they have for overcoming them.

5. Do before going home (15 minutes)
   a. Make a list of unsolved problems that came up during the day. Think about ways to handle them.
   b. Complete all paperwork. Avoid holding any paperwork for the following day.
   c. Make a notation of any critical problems or exceptional accomplishments of each employee for that day—for later use in personnel appraisals and actions.
   d. Make a list of jobs that must be done the following day. Take it home with you and read it before coming to work.

APPENDIX **B**

Supervisory Responsibility Survey

SUPERVISORY RESPONSIBILITY SURVEY			
	Yes	No	Don't Know

Do you feel it is your responsibility to...

	Yes	No	Don't Know
1. Request that additional employees be hired as needed?	___	___	___
2. Approve new employees assigned to you?	___	___	___
3. Explain benefit plans to employees?	___	___	___
4. Tell employees about upgrading and pay ranges?	___	___	___
5. Make sure employees know rules of conduct and safety regulations?	___	___	___
6. Train an understudy?	___	___	___
7. Hold regular safety meetings?	___	___	___
8. Prepare employee work schedules?	___	___	___
9. Assign specific duties to workers?	___	___	___
10. Assign responsibilities to assistants or group leaders?	___	___	___

...select and train your employees?

...make work assignments and maintain discipline?

	11. Delegate authority?	___ ___ ___
	12. Discipline employees?	___ ___ ___
	13. Discharge employees?	___ ___ ___
	14. Specify the kind and number of employees to do a job?	___ ___ ___
…make work assignments and maintain discipline?	15. Determine the amount of work to be done by each employee in your group?	___ ___ ___
	16. Authorize overtime?	___ ___ ___
	17. Enforce safety rules?	___ ___ ___
	18. Transfer employees within your department?	___ ___ ___
	19. Interpret the union contract?	___ ___ ___
	20. Process grievances with shop stewards?	___ ___ ___
…handle employee problems with the union?	21. Prepare vacation schedules?	___ ___ ___
	22. Recommend changes in the contract?	___ ___ ___
	23. Lay off employees for lack of work?	___ ___ ___
	24. Grant leaves of absence?	___ ___ ___
	25. Explain to employees how their pay is calculated?	___ ___ ___
	26. Determine allowances for faulty material or interruptions?	___ ___ ___
…know how pay and incentive systems work?	27. Approve piece rates or standards before they become effective?	___ ___ ___
	28. Answer employees' questions regarding time studies or allowances?	___ ___ ___
	29. Start jobs in process?	___ ___ ___
	30. Stop jobs in process?	___ ___ ___
	31. Authorize setup changes?	___ ___ ___
	32. Approve material substitutions?	___ ___ ___
	33. Requisition supplies to keep your department running?	___ ___ ___
…make these operating decisions?	34. Determine whether material should be scrapped or reworked?	___ ___ ___
	35. Replan schedules upset by breakdowns?	___ ___ ___
	36. Take unsafe tools out of service?	___ ___ ___
	37. Correct unsafe working conditions?	___ ___ ___

	38. Know how an order flows through the company from start to finish?	___ ___ ___
...tie in with other departments?	39. Understand what the staff departments do? Your relationship to them?	___ ___ ___
	40. Authorize maintenance and repair jobs?	___ ___ ___
	41. Requisition tools?	___ ___ ___
	42. Investigate accidents?	___ ___ ___
	43. Make suggestions for improvements in operating procedures in your department?	___ ___ ___
...be concerned with the way the job gets done?	44. Recommend changes in department layout?	___ ___ ___
	45. Suggest material handling methods to be used in your department?	___ ___ ___
	46. Discuss with staff members the operating problems caused by proposed design changes?	___ ___ ___
	47. Cut down on waste of materials and supplies?	___ ___ ___
	48. Keep adequate production records for checking output per machine and per worker-hour?	___ ___ ___
...think about how much things cost?	49. Participate in setting up your department budget?	___ ___ ___
	50. Investigate charges against your budget?	___ ___ ___

Checklist for Accepting the Assignment of a New Department

1. Operational information
   a. What is the basic function of this department?
   b. Is there a current set of departmental objectives?
   c. Is there a current departmental expense budget?
   d. Where are the current operating schedules? Is the department ahead, behind, or on schedule?
   e. What are, and where are, the various performance standards for output, quality, units costs, etc.?
   f. What historical, statistical data is available?
   g. When do the seasonal peaks or troughs occur?
   h. When do busy periods of the day, week, or month occur?
   i. What are the basic safety precautions, rules, and regulations that pertain to this department?
2. Organizational relationships
   a. How is the department organized? Is there an organization chart?
   b. What are the main working relationships with (i) other line departments, (ii) other staff departments, (iii) the central office or headquarters, (iv) vendors and suppliers, (v) customers or clients,

and (vi) regulatory agencies or bodies? Who are the contacts? Telephone numbers?

   c. What support services are available? Purchasing? Maintenance? Housekeeping? Personnel? Payroll? Reproduction? Transportation? Who are the contacts? Telephone numbers?

   d. What, if any, labor union is recognized in the department? Who is the local representative, or shop steward?

3. Departmental staff

   a. Is there an assistant supervisor or administrative assistant? Who is it? What are the normal duties of this person?

   b. Who could substitute for the supervisor in an emergency?

   c. Which employees have the longest service? How long have they been on their present assignments?

   d. What sort of turnover has the department experienced, generally and by position?

   e. Are the performance appraisal records available for all the staff? Do they include absence, sickness, and accident histories?

   f. Are any employees due soon for transfer or retirement?

   g. For each employee, how much leave or vacation time has been taken this year? How much remains?

   h. Which positions are most strongly staffed? Which need strengthening?

   i. What training programs are currently in progress?

4. Facilities and security

   a. What equipment, tools, machinery, utilities, and the like are assigned to this department? What are their capacities and/or operating rates? What is their downtime and repair history? Who are their qualified operators?

   b. Who, or what department, is responsible for repairs, window washing, floor polishing, etc.?

   c. Where are raw materials and operating supplies stored? How and when are they obtained? Who has authority to withdraw them?

   d. What keys to equipment, files, safes, stockrooms, warehouses, or premises are there? How many duplicates? Who holds them?

   e. Is there a schedule for opening and closing the premises? Who opens up and locks up?

   f. Where are the appropriate, nearby (i) fire station, (ii) first-aid facility, (iii) doctor, and (iv) police station? What are their telephone numbers?

Index